Strategic Level

Paper P6

Management Accounting Business Strategy

CIMA Study Text

KAPLAN

PUBLISHING

FOULKS LYNCH

British Library Cataloguing-in-Publication Data

A catalogue record for this book is available from the British Library.

Kaplan Publishing Foulks Lynch
Unit 2 The Business Centre
Molly Millars Lane
Wokingham
Berkshire
RG41 2QZ

ISBN 1 84390 910 3

    978 1 84390 910 1

© FTC Kaplan Limited, June 2006

Printed and bound in Great Britain.

Acknowledgements

We are grateful to the Chartered Institute of Management Accountants, the Association of Chartered Certified Accountants and the Institute of Chartered Accountants in England and Wales for permission to reproduce past examination questions. The answers have been prepared by Kaplan Publishing Foulks Lynch.

INTRODUCTION

This is the third edition of this Study Text. Our aim was to produce an even better, more syllabus-tailored, exam-focused and student-friendly range of publications. To achieve this we have worked closely with numerous CIMA tutors and experts, and we are confident that this Study Text forms the best resource for your exam preparation.

It covers all syllabus topics to the required depth, and contains a wealth of exam-style and practice questions. Throughout the text you will find plenty of relevant examples, activities, diagrams and charts. These will put the subject matter in context and help you absorb the material easily.

The following points explain some of the concepts we had in mind when developing the layout of this book.

DEFINITION

- **Definitions**. The text defines key words and concepts, placing them in the margin with a clear heading, as on the left. The purpose of including these definitions is to focus your attention on the point being covered.

KEY POINT

- **Key points**. Also in the margin, you will see key points at regular intervals. The purpose of these is to summarise concisely the key material being covered.

- **Activities**. The text involves you in the learning process with a series of activities designed to catch your attention and make you concentrate and respond. The feedback to activities is at the end of each chapter.

- **Self-test questions**. At the end of each chapter there is a series of self-test questions. The purpose of these is to help you revise some of the key elements of the chapter. All the answers to these questions can be found in the text.

- **End of chapter questions**. At the end of each chapter we include examination-type questions. These will give you a very good idea of the sort of thing the examiner will ask and will test your understanding of what has been covered.

Good luck with your studies!

CONTENTS

Syllabus and learning outcomes   vii

Helping you with your studies   xi

The examination   xii

Maths tables and formulae   xiv

Chapter 1   Business strategy   1

Chapter 2   The competitive environment   25

Chapter 3   Regulation in major markets   49

Chapter 4   Stakeholders   73

Chapter 5   Customers and suppliers   91

Chapter 6   IT and competitive position   123

Chapter 7   The internet and electronic commerce   147

Chapter 8   Strategic options   163

Chapter 9   Product portfolio evaluation   187

Chapter 10   Benchmarking and value chain analysis   213

Chapter 11   Acquisition and divestment strategies   235

Chapter 12   Process innovation and re-engineering   249

Chapter 13   The role and responsibilities of directors   269

Chapter 14   Measuring performance: financial measures   289

Chapter 15   Non-financial and multidimensional performance measures   311

Chapter 16   Business unit performance   341

Chapter 17   Lean systems, R&D, and product and process development   361

Chapter 18   Knowledge management   385

Chapter 19   Information strategy and implementation   407

Chapter 20   Change management   433

Chapter 21   Answers to practice questions   451

Index   505

SYLLABUS AND LEARNING OUTCOMES

Syllabus outline

The syllabus comprises:

Topic		Study Weighting
A	Assessing the competitive environment	20%
B	Interacting with the competitive environment	20%
C	Evaluation of options, planning and appraisal	30%
D	Implementation of strategic plans	30%

Learning aims

Students should be able to:

- identify and evaluate approaches to strategic management

- explain the place of the enterprise in the broader economic and social environment

- apply contemporary thinking on strategic management

- identify and utilise appropriate tools for strategic analysis

- evaluate appropriate strategic options and make recommendations

- evaluate the linkages between strategic planning and the implementation of those plans

- design and recommend appropriate performance measurement systems.

Learning outcomes and syllabus content

A – Assessing the competitive environment – 20%

Learning outcomes

On completion of their studies students should be able to:

- identify relevant stakeholders in respect of an organisation (4)

- evaluate the impact of regulatory regimes on strategic planning and implementation (3)

- evaluate the nature of competitive environments, distinguishing between simple and complicated competitive environments (2)

- distinguish the difference between static and dynamic competitive environments (2)

- evaluate strategies for response to competition. (2)

Syllabus content

- PEST analysis (2)

- SWOT analysis (2)

- Interacting with stakeholders and the use of stakeholder mapping (4)

- Regulation in major markets (WTO, EU, NAFTA, Asia-Pacific) (3)

- Country analysis and political risk (3)

- Porter's Diamond and its use for assessing the competitive advantage (2)

- Porter's Five Forces model and its use for assessing the external environment (2)

- Qualitative approaches to competitive analysis (2)

- Competitor analysis and competitive strategies (both qualitative and quantitative tools of competitor analysis will be used) (2)

- Sources, availability and quality of data for environmental analysis. (2)

B – Interacting with the competitive environment – 20%

Learning outcomes

On completion of their studies students should be able to:

- evaluate the impact and influence of the external environment on an organisation and its strategy (2, 3)

- recommend pro-active and reactive approaches to business/government relations and to relations with civil society (4)

- discuss how stakeholder groups work and how they affect the organisation (4)

- discuss how suppliers and customers influence the strategy process and recommend how to interact with them (5)

- evaluate the impact of electronic commerce on the way business is conducted and recommend an appropriate strategy (7)

- evaluate the strategic and competitive benefits of IS/IT and advise on the development of appropriate strategies. (6)

Syllabus content

- Derivatives of PEST such as STEEP (social, technological, environmental, economic and political factors) and PESTEL (political, economic, sociocultural, technological, environmental and legal factors) (2)

- Approaches to business-government relations and with civil society (Braithwaite and Drahos) (4)

- Stakeholder management (stakeholders to include government and regulatory agencies, non-governmental organisations and civil society, industry associations, customers and suppliers) (4)

- The customer portfolio: customer analysis and behaviour, including the marketing audit and customer profitability analysis as well as customer retention and loyalty (5)

- Negotiating with customers and suppliers and managing these relationships (5)

- The impact of IT (including electronic commerce) on an industry (utilising frameworks such as Porter's Five Forces, the Value Chain) and how organisations can use IT (including the Internet) to enhance competitive position (6, 7)

- Competing through exploiting information (rather than technology), e.g. use of databases to identify potential customers or market segments, and the management of data (warehousing and mining) (6)

- The relationship between current and predicted strategic importance of IS/IT (the applications portfolio) (6)

- Implications of these interactions for Chartered Management Accountants and the management accounting system (6)

C – Evaluation of options, planning and appraisal – 30%

Learning outcomes

On completion of their studies students should be able to:

- evaluate strategic options (8, 11)

- evaluate the product portfolio of an organisation and recommend appropriate changes to support the organisation's strategic goals (9)

- prepare a benchmarking exercise and evaluate the results (10)

- identify an organisation's value chain (10)

- evaluate the importance of process innovation and re-engineering (12)

- discuss and apply both qualitative and quantitative techniques in the support of the strategic decision making function (8, 9)

- discuss the role and responsibilities of directors in the strategy development process. (13)

Syllabus content

- Mission statements and their use in orientating the organisation's strategy (1)

- Forecasting and the various techniques used: trend analysis, system modelling, in-depth consultation with experts (Delphi method) (8)

- Scenario planning and long range planning as tools in strategic decision-making (including gap analysis) (8)

- Strategic options generation (e.g. using Ansoff's product/market matrix and Porter's generic strategies) (8)

- Audit of resources and the analysis of this for use in strategic decision-making (8)

- Management of the product portfolio (9)

- Benchmarking performance with the best organisations (10)

- Value chain analysis (10)

- Acquisition and divestment strategies and their place in the strategic plan (11)

- The role of IT in innovation and business process re-engineering (12)

- The role and responsibilities of directors in making strategic decisions (including issues of due diligence, fiduciary responsibilities) (13)

D – Implementation of strategic plans – 30%

Learning outcomes

On completion of their studies students should be able to:

- evaluate and recommend appropriate control measures (14–17)

- prepare and evaluate multidimensional models of performance measurement (15)

- identify problems in performance measurement and recommend solutions (14, 16, 17)

- evaluate and advise managers on the development of strategies for knowledge management, IM, IS and IT that support the organisation's strategic requirements (18, 19)

- identify and evaluate IS/IT systems appropriate to the organisation's strategic requirements, and recommend changes where necessary (18, 19)

- discuss the role of change management in a strategic context. (20)

Syllabus content

- Assessing strategic performance (i.e. the use and development of appropriate measures that are sensitive to industry characteristics and environmental factors) (14)

- Non-financial measures and their interaction with financial ones. (Note: candidates will be expected to use both qualitative and quantitative techniques) (15)

- Multidimensional models of performance (e.g. the balanced scorecard, the results and determinants framework, the performance pyramid) (15)

- Business unit performance and appraisal, including transfer pricing, reward systems and incentives, and agency theory. (Note: Details of agency theory will not be tested) (16)

- Project management: monitoring the implementation of plans (19)

- The implementation of lean systems across an organisation (17)

- Change management in a strategic context (20)

- Marketing in a strategic context (5)

- The purpose and contents of IM, IS and IT strategies, and the need for strategy complementary to the corporate and individual business strategies (19)

- The concept of knowledge management and its role as a key element in an organisation's success (18)

- Critical success factors: links to performance indicators and corporate strategy, and their use as a basis for defining an organisation's information needs (15)

- The role of research and development in an organisation, particularly the need to integrate product and process development (17)

HELPING YOU WITH YOUR STUDIES

Take control

Create favourable conditions and a positive attitude.

- Plan to study at specific times each week. Devise a schedule and set goals.

- Choose a location where you can concentrate.

- Ask questions to be an active learner and to generate interest.

- Continually challenge yourself.

Study

Develop good learning techniques

- Use the **SQR3** method – it works with reading accountancy and management subjects. **Survey** (get an overall picture before studying in detail), **Question** (important things to learn are usually answers to questions), **Read** actively (to answer your questions), **Recite** (recall what you have read and connect topics) and **Review** (what you have covered and accomplished).

- Use the **MURDER** method – **Mood** (set the right mood), **Understand** (issues covered and make note of any uncertain bits), **Recall** (stop and put what you have learned into your own words), **Digest** (go back and reconsider the information), **Expand** (read relevant articles and newspapers), **Review** (go over the material you covered to consolidate the knowledge).

- Use **repetition** to increase remembering.

- Create **associations** and analogies to relate new ideas to what you already know and to improve understanding.

Practise

Practise under exam conditions

- **Practise** as much as possible – go through exam style and standard questions under exam conditions.

Prepare for the exam

Develop exam technique

- Be familiar with the structure of your exam and know how to approach and answer the questions.

THE EXAMINATION

Format of the examination:

There will be a written examination paper of three hours, plus 20 minutes reading time, with the following sections:

	Marks
Section A: A maximum of four compulsory questions, all relating to a single scenario.	50
Section B: Two questions, from a choice of four, each worth 25 marks. Short scenarios will be given, to which some or all questions relate.	50
TOTAL	<u>100</u>

Note: The first twenty minutes of your exam is reading time. During reading time you can read, annotate and highlight the question paper, but you are not allowed to open the answer book, write in the answer book, add any loose sheets/supplements to your answer book or use a calculator. This change to the duration of the exams has been introduced by CIMA after we published our Exam Kits. Therefore you will notice that the exam length stated in this section will differ from the one stated in the Exam Kit. The length of the exam stated here is the correct one.

Before sitting the exam make sure that you are familiar with CIMA's *Exam Rules & Regulations*. You can find this document on the CIMA website (www.cimaglobal.com).

Examination tips

- Spend the first 20 minutes of the examination **reading the paper** and where you have a **choice of questions**, decide which ones you will do.

- **Divide the time** you spend on questions in proportion to the marks on offer. One suggestion is to allocate 1½ minutes to each mark available, so a 10-mark question should be completed in 15 minutes.

- Unless you know exactly how to answer the question, spend some time **planning** your answer. Stick to the question and **tailor your answer** to what you are asked.

- **Fully explain** all your points but be **concise**. Set out all workings **clearly and neatly**, and state briefly what you are doing. Don't write out the question.

- If you do not understand what a question is asking, **state your assumptions**.

- If you **get completely stuck** with a question, leave space in your answer book and **return to it later.**

- Towards the end of the examination spend the last **five minutes** reading through your answers and **making any additions or corrections**.

Answering the questions

- **Multiple-choice questions**: Read the questions carefully and work through any calculations required. If you don't know the answer, eliminate those options you know are incorrect and see if the answer becomes more obvious. Remember that only one answer to a multiple choice question can be right!

- **Objective test questions**: These might ask for numerical answers, but could also involve paragraphs of text which require you to fill in a number of missing blanks, or for you to write a definition of a word or phrase, or to enter a formula. Others may give a definition followed by a list of possible key words relating to that description.

- **Essay questions**: Make a quick plan in your answer book and under each main point list all the relevant facts you can think of. Then write out your answer developing each point fully. Your essay should have a clear structure; it should contain a brief introduction, a main section and a conclusion. Be concise. It is better to write a little about a lot of different points than a great deal about one or two points.

- **Computations**: It is essential to include all your workings in your answers. Many computational questions require the use of a standard format: company profit and loss account, balance sheet and cash flow statement for example. Be sure you know these formats thoroughly before the examination and use the layouts that you see in the answers given in this book. If you are asked to comment or make recommendations on a computation, you must do so. There are important marks to be gained here. Even if your computation contains mistakes, you may still gain marks if your reasoning is correct.

- **Reports, memos and other documents**: Some questions ask you to present your answer in the form of a report or a memo or other document. Use the correct format – there could be easy marks to gain here.

MATHS TABLES AND FORMULAE

Present value table

Present value of 1.00 unit of currency, that is $(1+r)^{-n}$ where r = interest rate; n = number of periods until payment or receipt.

Periods (n)	Interest rates (r)									
	1%	2%	3%	4%	5%	6%	7%	8%	9%	10%
1	0.990	0.980	0.971	0.962	0.952	0.943	0.935	0.926	0.917	0.909
2	0.980	0.961	0.943	0.925	0.907	0.890	0.873	0.857	0.842	0.826
3	0.971	0.942	0.915	0.889	0.864	0.840	0.816	0.794	0.772	0.751
4	0.961	0.924	0.888	0.855	0.823	0.792	0.763	0.735	0.708	0.683
5	0.951	0.906	0.863	0.822	0.784	0.747	0.713	0.681	0.650	0.621
6	0.942	0.888	0.837	0.790	0.746	0705	0.666	0.630	0.596	0.564
7	0.933	0.871	0.813	0.760	0.711	0.665	0.623	0.583	0.547	0.513
8	0.923	0.853	0.789	0.731	0.677	0.627	0.582	0.540	0.502	0.467
9	0.914	0.837	0.766	0.703	0.645	0.592	0.544	0.500	0.460	0.424
10	0.905	0.820	0.744	0.676	0.614	0.558	0.508	0.463	0.422	0.386
11	0.896	0.804	0.722	0.650	0.585	0.527	0.475	0.429	0.388	0.350
12	0.887	0.788	0.701	0.625	0.557	0.497	0.444	0.397	0.356	0.319
13	0.879	0.773	0.681	0.601	0.530	0.469	0.415	0.368	0.326	0.290
14	0.870	0.758	0.661	0.577	0.505	0.442	0.388	0.340	0.299	0.263
15	0.861	0.743	0.642	0.555	0.481	0.417	0.362	0.315	0.275	0.239
16	0.853	0.728	0.623	0.534	0.458	0.394	0.339	0.292	0.252	0.218
17	0.844	0.714	0.605	0.513	0.436	0.371	0.317	0.270	0.231	0.198
18	0.836	0.700	0.587	0.494	0.416	0.350	0.296	0.250	0.212	0.180
19	0.828	0.686	0.570	0.475	0.396	0.331	0.277	0.232	0.194	0.164
20	0.820	0.673	0.554	0.456	0.377	0.312	0.258	0.215	0.178	0.149

Periods (n)	Interest rates (r)									
	11%	12%	13%	14%	15%	16%	17%	18%	19%	20%
1	0.901	0.893	0.885	0.877	0.870	0.862	0.855	0.847	0.840	0.833
2	0.812	0.797	0.783	0.769	0.756	0.743	0.731	0.718	0.706	0.694
3	0.731	0.712	0.693	0.675	0.658	0.641	0.624	0.609	0.593	0.579
4	0.659	0.636	0.613	0.592	0.572	0.552	0.534	0.516	0.499	0.482
5	0.593	0.567	0.543	0.519	0.497	0.476	0.456	0.437	0.419	0.402
6	0.535	0.507	0.480	0.456	0.432	0.410	0.390	0.370	0.352	0.335
7	0.482	0.452	0.425	0.400	0.376	0.354	0.333	0.314	0.296	0.279
8	0.434	0.404	0.376	0.351	0.327	0.305	0.285	0.266	0.249	0.233
9	0.391	0.361	0.333	0.308	0.284	0.263	0.243	0.225	0.209	0.194
10	0.352	0.322	0.295	0.270	0.247	0.227	0.208	0.191	0.176	0.162
11	0.317	0.287	0.261	0.237	0.215	0.195	0.178	0.162	0.148	0.135
12	0.286	0.257	0.231	0.208	0.187	0.168	0.152	0.137	0.124	0.112
13	0.258	0.229	0.204	0.182	0.163	0.145	0.130	0.116	0.104	0.093
14	0.232	0.205	0.181	0.160	0.141	0.125	0.111	0.099	0.088	0.078
15	0.209	0.183	0.160	0.140	0.123	0.108	0.095	0.084	0.079	0.065
16	0.188	0.163	0.141	0.123	0.107	0.093	0.081	0.071	0.062	0.054
17	0.170	0.146	0.125	0.108	0.093	0.080	0.069	0.060	0.052	0.045
18	0.153	0.130	0.111	0.095	0.081	0.069	0.059	0.051	0.044	0.038
19	0.138	0.116	0.098	0.083	0.070	0.060	0.051	0.043	0.037	0.031
20	0.124	0.104	0.087	0.073	0.061	0.051	0.043	0.037	0.031	0.026

Cumulative present value of 1.00 unit of currency per annum, Receivable or Payable at the end of each year for n years $\dfrac{1-(1+r)^{-n}}{r}$

Periods (n)	Interest rates (r)									
	1%	2%	3%	4%	5%	6%	7%	8%	9%	10%
1	0.990	0.980	0.971	0.962	0.952	0.943	0.935	0.926	0.917	0.909
2	1.970	1.942	1.913	1.886	1.859	1.833	1.808	1.783	1.759	1.736
3	2.941	2.884	2.829	2.775	2.723	2.673	2.624	2.577	2.531	2.487
4	3.902	3.808	3.717	3.630	3.546	3.465	3.387	3.312	3.240	3.170
5	4.853	4.713	4.580	4.452	4.329	4.212	4.100	3.993	3.890	3.791
6	5.795	5.601	5.417	5.242	5.076	4.917	4.767	4.623	4.486	4.355
7	6.728	6.472	6.230	6.002	5.786	5.582	5.389	5.206	5.033	4.868
8	7.652	7.325	7.020	6.733	6.463	6.210	5.971	5.747	5.535	5.335
9	8.566	8.162	7.786	7.435	7.108	6.802	6.515	6.247	5.995	5.759
10	9.471	8.983	8.530	8.111	7.722	7.360	7.024	6.710	6.418	6.145
11	10.368	9.787	9.253	8.760	8.306	7.887	7.499	7.139	6.805	6.495
12	11.255	10.575	9.954	9.385	8.863	8.384	7.943	7.536	7.161	6.814
13	12.134	11.348	10.635	9.986	9.394	8.853	8.358	7.904	7.487	7.103
14	13.004	12.106	11.296	10.563	9.899	9.295	8.745	8.244	7.786	7.367
15	13.865	12.849	11.938	11.118	10.380	9.712	9.108	8.559	8.061	7.606
16	14.718	13.578	12.561	11.652	10.838	10.106	9.447	8.851	8.313	7.824
17	15.562	14.292	13.166	12.166	11.274	10.477	9.763	9.122	8.544	8.022
18	16.398	14.992	13.754	12.659	11.690	10.828	10.059	9.372	8.756	8.201
19	17.226	15.679	14.324	13.134	12.085	11.158	10.336	9.604	8.950	8.365
20	18.046	16.351	14.878	13.590	12.462	11.470	10.594	9.818	9.129	8.514

Periods (n)	Interest rates (r)									
	11%	12%	13%	14%	15%	16%	17%	18%	19%	20%
1	0.901	0.893	0.885	0.877	0.870	0.862	0.855	0.847	0.840	0.833
2	1.713	1.690	1.668	1.647	1.626	1.605	1.585	1.566	1.547	1.528
3	2.444	2.402	2.361	2.322	2.283	2.246	2.210	2.174	2.140	2.106
4	3.102	3.037	2.974	2.914	2.855	2.798	2.743	2.690	2.639	2.589
5	3.696	3.605	3.517	3.433	3.352	3.274	3.199	3.127	3.058	2.991
6	4.231	4.111	3.998	3.889	3.784	3.685	3.589	3.498	3.410	3.326
7	4.712	4.564	4.423	4.288	4.160	4.039	3.922	3.812	3.706	3.605
8	5.146	4.968	4.799	4.639	4.487	4.344	4.207	4.078	3.954	3.837
9	5.537	5.328	5.132	4.946	4.772	4.607	4.451	4.303	4.163	4.031
10	5.889	5.650	5.426	5.216	5.019	4.833	4.659	4.494	4.339	4.192
11	6.207	5.938	5.687	5.453	5.234	5.029	4.836	4.656	4.486	4.327
12	6.492	6.194	5.918	5.660	5.421	5.197	4.988	7.793	4.611	4.439
13	6.750	6.424	6.122	5.842	5.583	5.342	5.118	4.910	4.715	4.533
14	6.982	6.628	6.302	6.002	5.724	5.468	5.229	5.008	4.802	4.611
15	7.191	6.811	6.462	6.142	5.847	5.575	5.324	5.092	4.876	4.675
16	7.379	6.974	6.604	6.265	5.954	5.668	5.405	5.162	4.938	4.730
17	7.549	7.120	6.729	6.373	6.047	5.749	5.475	5.222	4.990	4.775
18	7.702	7.250	6.840	6.467	6.128	5.818	5.534	5.273	5.033	4.812
19	7.839	7.366	6.938	6.550	6.198	5.877	5.584	5.316	5.070	4.843
20	7.963	7.469	7.025	6.623	6.259	5.929	5.628	5.353	5.101	4.870

FORMULAE

Annuity

Present value of an annuity of $1 per annum, receivable or payable for n years, commencing in one year, discounted at r% per annum:

$$PV = \frac{1}{r}\left[1 - \frac{1}{[1+r]^n}\right]$$

Perpetuity

Present value of $1 per annum, payable or receivable in perpetuity, commencing in one year, discounted at r% per annum:

$$PV = \frac{1}{r}$$

Note on calculations

The examiners draw on knowledge of the P2 paper for relevant calculations. For example:

- May 2005 Question 1(a) NPV

- November 2005 Question 1(b) Equivalent annual value

- November 2005 Question 5(a) Expected values

Knowledge of management-level paper (especially Paper P2) is assumed by candidates studying for this paper. Candidates are advised to revise these and similar calculations as part of their preparation for this paper as they are not repeated in this Study Text.

Chapter 1

BUSINESS STRATEGY

Syllabus content

- Mission statements and their use in orientating the organisation's strategy

This chapter introduces many concepts that are relevant to the whole of the rest of the text – many of the terms and ideas that will be encountered, many of the ways of viewing business strategy, and many of the main writers and their interpretations of the meaning of strategy.

Contents

1   Strategy and mission

2   Definitions of strategy

3   Developing strategy

4   Strategic decisions

1 Strategy and mission

1.1 Organisations and their objectives

Organisations are created to carry out activities that cannot be achieved by individuals alone. Such activities can be technical, benefiting from economies of scale and specialisation, or they can be social and satisfy human need for companionship.

There are many definitions of an organisation. A useful one is given by Watson:

Organisation – Social and technical arrangements resulting from a number of people being brought together in various relationships in which the actions of some are planned, monitored and directed by others in the achievement of certain tasks.

Most definitions broadly follow what is known as the RUGS perspective, that is they assert an organisation is:

- **Rational** – consciously designed to employ efficiently various means of utilising human, financial and technical resources in order to **achieve the organisation's end** most effectively.

- **Unitary** – organisational members constitute a recognisable, unified and discrete body stemming from their mutual dependence in **achieving common tasks**.

- **Goal seeking** – exists to pursue particular **aims and objectives** that were given at the outset of its operations or subsequently agreed by the organisation's members.

Every organisation needs to be clear about its goals. As the environment changes and presents new challenges, organisations need to review and reassess their goals. Some organisations will discover that their goals are no longer relevant and they are drifting. Others will find that their goals are clear, relevant, and effective. Still others will discover that their goals are no longer even clear and that they have no firm direction. The purpose of developing a clear set of goals for an organisation is to prevent it from drifting into an uncertain future.

Considerable confusion exists over the use of the terms goals and objectives. The *Oxford English Dictionary* includes the following definitions:

- Goal – object of effort or ambition

- Objective – the point aimed at.

The similarity of these terms causes some writers to use them interchangeably whilst others refer to them as two specific concepts – one related to intermediate issues (**means**) and the other to ultimate purposes (**ends**). Unfortunately, there is no consistency as to which term refers to which concept. We will usually use the terms interchangeably, or else explain exactly what we mean by them.

DEFINITION

Organisation – Social and technical arrangements resulting from a number of people being brought together in various relationships in which the actions of some are planned, monitored and directed by others in the achievement of certain tasks.

KEY POINT

The purpose of developing a clear set of goals for an organisation is to prevent it from drifting into an uncertain future.

1.2 Hierarchy of objectives

Most writers agree with the idea that organisations have a hierarchy of objectives. At each higher level in the hierarchy the objectives are more relevant to a greater proportion of the organisation's activities so that the objectives at the top of the hierarchy are relevant to every aspect of the organisation. The following diagram illustrates the hierarchical relationship of mission, goals, objectives, strategy, tactics and operational plans.

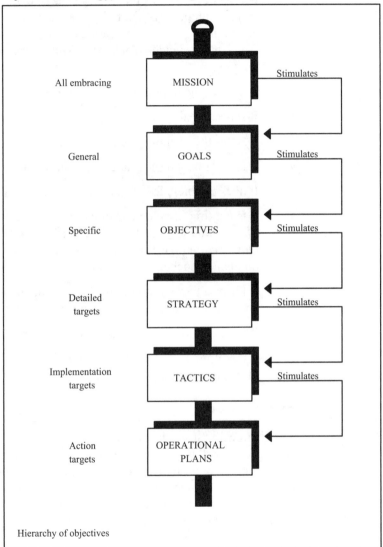

Diagram: Hierarchy of objectives in an organisation

DEFINITION

Mission statement – A statement in writing that describes the basic purpose of an organisation, that is what it is trying to accomplish.

The topmost statement of organisational objectives is usually termed 'the mission'. This is where we start.

1.3 The importance of the mission statement

A mission statement is a statement in writing that describes the basic purpose of an organisation, that is what it is trying to accomplish.

A mission is the raison d'être of an organisation, which is central and overriding. If it is subject to change there can be considerable disturbances within the organisation. It is normally very general and visionary. It should be viewed as where the organisation is conceived to be throughout time rather than where it currently is or where it wants to get to at any one moment in time.

1.4 Characteristics of a good mission statement

A mission statement can be viewed as a statement primarily directed towards the employees of an organisation that should assist in the attainment of the objectives of the organisation. In short, a mission statement will have some or all of the following characteristics:

- It is usually a brief statement of no more than a page in length. (Some companies have produced very effective mission statements comprising a single sentence, although there are also successful company credos that extend into several pages, for example the statement written by William Hewlett for Hewlett-Packard '*What is the HP Way?*', which is relatively lengthy.)

- It is a very general statement of entity culture.

- It states the aims (or purposes) of the organisation.

- It states the business areas in which the organisation intends to operate.

- It is open-ended (not stated in quantifiable terms).

- It does not include commercial terms, such as profit.

- It is not time-assigned. (For example, the credo of JC Penny Company *The Penny Idea* was formulated in 1913, that of Johnson and Johnson *Our Credo* in the 1940s, and some missions are carved on stone or etched on plaque, such as that found at Unilever House.)

- It forms a basis of communication to the people inside the organisation and to people outside the organisation.

- It is used to formulate goal statements, objectives and short-term targets.

- It therefore guides the direction of the entity's strategy and as such is part of management information.

Example: ICI plc

The chemical industry is a major force for the improvement of the quality of life across the world. ICI aims to be the world's leading chemical company, serving customers internationally through the innovative and responsible application of chemistry and related sciences. 'Through achievement of our aim, we will enhance the wealth and well-being of our shareholders, our employees, our customers and the communities which we serve and in which we operate.'

Activity 1

Consider the usefulness or otherwise, of the following mission statements:

1   Courses for careers, research for results

2   To be a pioneer in graphite communications

3   To be excellent in our chosen field, and provide the best in customer service and quality that resources permit

4   Kill Caterpillar

Feedback to this activity is at the end of the chapter.

1.5   Mission statements with an external orientation

A mission's goals do not have to be 'internal'. Some of the most effective are directed outside the company, on customers, or competitors. Federal Express Corporation's US operation developed a short but powerful mission statement: *Absolutely, Positively Overnight!* Everyone in the company knew what that statement means. Almost nothing more has to be said to ensure that every action of every person is aimed at total customer satisfaction. Another short credo that says it all belongs to PepsiCo. PepsiCo's mission has long been simply to *Beat Coke*, a mission it has yet to achieve. Honda, faced with the prospect of Yamaha dethroning it as the world's leading motorcycle maker, penned the memorable mission, *We will crush, squash, slaughter Yamaha!*. It did! But like that of Federal Express most mission statements place an emphasis on serving the customer. Here is another example:

> 'The mission of our company, as William Hesketh Lever saw it, is to make cleanliness commonplace, to lessen work for women, to foster health and to contribute to personal attractiveness so that life may be more enjoyable for the people who use our products.'
>
> *Plaque: Unilever House*

Mission statements like these will prompt people to think first about the customer, and will provide a gauge against which employees can judge their efforts to satisfy customers. It will equip employees with a strong inner compass for navigating their actions. It will stamp the culture of the organisation. Mission statements are like visions or dreams.

1.6   The search for a mission

According to Peter Drucker there are a number of fundamental questions that an organisation will need to address in its search for purpose. These are:

- What is our business?

- What is value to the customer?

- What will our business be?

- What should our business be?

Although seemingly simple these questions are among the most difficult the strategist will need to solve. Successful planners will raise these questions and seek to answer them correctly and thoroughly. The mission of an organisation is generally influenced by five key elements:

- the **history** of the organisation

- the **current preferences** of the organisation's management and owners

- the **environmental factors** influencing the organisation

- the organisation's **resources**

- the organisation's **distinctive competence**.

Producing a formal mission statement is not an easy task. It will relate to a lot of factors and people, including in many cases, shareholders, customers, employees and the public. The organisation's mission acts as an 'invisible hand' that guides widely dispersed management to work independently and yet collectively towards the achievement of the organisational goal.

To summarise these points, a mission statement for an organisation should incorporate a number of different factors. These include:

- the business domain in which the organisation will operate

- the organisation's raison d'être (or reason for existence)

- the stakeholder groups the organisation will serve.

The top level of management should be responsible for the preparation of a statement of corporate mission. Consequently, the mission statement should incorporate the broad aims of the executive management.

1.7 The relevance of a mission for strategic planning

A statement of corporate mission is inextricably linked with the organisation's goals and objectives, although a distinction can be drawn between these aspects of the strategic planning process. Whilst the organisational objectives comprise the specific targets of the company and the goals comprise its broad aims, the mission encapsulates the reason that the entity exists in terms of the service and utility provided to meet specific needs of society. Refer back to the diagram which illustrates the hierarchy of objectives in an organisation and you will see this relationship again.

Before setting about the preparation of a strategic plan the management should consider the mission of an organisation. Many commentators have suggested that consideration and determination of the mission and its articulation into a statement of corporate mission constitutes the first stage in the strategic planning process and that therefore it is central to the whole planning process.

Johnson and Scholes have suggested that 'the mission of an organisation is the most generalised type of objective and can be thought of as an expression of its raison d'être'. On the other hand, some commentators believe that the mission statement is the end product of the process of strategic planning and this illustrates the confusion that often exists between the organisation's mission and its goals and objectives.

Activity 2

Think about the organisation you are currently employed in, or one that you have been employed in, or one that you know of, and then draft a Mission Statement that would be appropriate for it.

There is no feedback to this activity.

2 Definitions of strategy

2.1 Concept

DEFINITION

Strategy: a course of action, including the specification of resources required, to achieve a specific objective (CIMA Official Terminology).

A strategy is 'A course of action, including the specification of resources required, to achieve a specific objective' (CIMA Official Terminology). This definition, although stated in a single sentence, provides a framework that can be expanded, shaped, applied and developed much further.

Because of the rapid technological and social changes affecting an organisation's environment, there is a need for strategies to achieve agreed goals and objectives, giving a sense of purpose and direction to the organisation.

In military terms, 'strategy' refers to the important plan. Where the objective is to defeat the enemy, the strategy will be to deploy the resources available in a manner that is likely to achieve the aim.

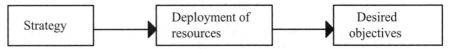

2.2 A wider view

We view strategy as the organised development of resources to achieve specific objectives against competition from rival organisations. It is the use of all the entity's resources – financial, manufacturing, marketing, technological, manpower, etc – in the pursuit of its objectives.

It is a set of policies adopted by senior management that guides the scope and direction of the entity. It takes into account the environment in which the company operates.

Scope used in this context relates to size and range, and direction describes product/market positioning. In simple terms, an entity's environment relates to the uncontrollable factors that influence it. All three terms will be discussed in more depth later.

2.3 The strategy is the organisation

The view that the organisation is the fundamental strategy is supported by both Henry Mintzberg and Igor Ansoff:

'The one goal all of the players may share is the need for a common playing field.'

H Mintzberg, *'Power in and around Organisations'*

'For over one hundred years, the firm has been the principal and successful instrument (strategy) of social progress. It is a breeder of wealth.'

I Ansoff, *'Implementing Strategic Management'*

The organisation is, therefore, seen as a creator and distributor of wealth and the wealth both sustains the organisation and provides satisfaction (by way of payment) to the people working within the organisation.

2.4 Adaptation to its environment – Hofer and Schendel

According to Hofer and Schendel a strategy is the mediating force or 'match' between the organisation and the environment. It is viewing the internal capabilities of the organisation and, in the light of these, identifying the opportunities or threats that exist externally.

By using the organisation as a strategy for the fulfilment of needs, it must continue to grow and devolve thereby creating more wealth from its environment. The organisation will only be efficient, however, if it controls its wealth and its interaction with the environment providing that wealth.

DEFINITION

The **corporate strategy** is the pattern of decisions in a company that determines and reveals its objectives, purpose or goals, and produces the principal policies and plans for achieving those goals.

2.5 The organisation viewed as a multi-decision-making system

According to Andrews, a successful organisation is achieved by a system of plans, decisions and actions. The corporate strategy is the pattern of decisions in a company that determines and reveals its objectives, purpose or goals, and produces the principal policies and plans for achieving those goals.

Andrews also argues that the strategy should define the range of business the company will pursue, the kind of economic and human organisation it is or intends to be, and the nature of economic and non-economic contributions it intends to make to its stakeholders.

The pattern of decisions means an interdependence of purposes, policies and action that is crucial to the strategy and the organisation's ability to identify competitive advantages.

KEY POINT

Mintzberg's five Ps are: plan, ploy, pattern, position and perspective.

2.6 Mintzberg's 5 Ps

Mintzberg also suggests various definitions of strategy, covering the five Ps:

- Strategy as a **plan** that can be defined and followed.

- Strategy as a **ploy** that can be seen as a move in a competitive business game.

- Strategy as a **pattern** of consistent behaviour, giving the impression of a logically thought out strategy.

- Strategy as a **position** is a means of identifying where an organisation places itself in an environment or market.

- Strategy as a **perspective** consists not just of a chosen position but also of a unique way of perceiving the world. In this respect Mintzberg is suggesting that the organisation's strategy is similar to the individual's personality.

Activity 3

Look at the five different descriptions of strategy given by Mintzberg, and identify which ones imply deliberate managerial actions, and which ones imply a more emergent approach.

Feedback to this activity is at the end of the chapter.

2.7 Levels of strategy (Johnson and Scholes)

Johnson and Scholes identify three levels of strategic activity.

- The **corporate or generic strategy** – what business or businesses the firm is in or should be in and how integrated these businesses should be with one another. It consists of the strategic planning at a corporate level and is not confined to one particular area – marketing, personnel, production/operational and financial implications are all taken into consideration. It covers a longer time period and has a wider scope than the other levels of corporate planning.

Johnson and Scholes claim that corporate strategy is concerned with the scope of an organisation's activities and the matching of these to the organisation's environment, its resource capabilities and the values and expectations of its various stakeholders.

Students often complain that the formulation of corporate strategy is too far removed from their likely level of activity, but an understanding is essential for all management in that the principles of corporate strategy are equally appropriate for the smaller organisation. Whatever the level on which a manager operates within an organisation, they can have some influence over that organisation's corporate strategy.

- The **business strategy** – how each business attempts to achieve its mission within its chosen area of activity. Here strategy is about which products or services should be developed and offered to which markets, and the extent to which the customer needs are met whilst achieving the objectives of the organisation. It includes corporate planning at the tactical level and consists of the allocation of resources for complete operations. It is means-oriented and is mainly administrative and persuasive in its endeavours.

- The **functional strategy** – how the different functions of the business support the corporate and business strategies. Such corporate planning at the operational level is means-oriented and most activities are concerned only with the ability to undertake directions.

The boundaries between the three categories are very indistinct and much depends upon the circumstances prevailing and the kind of organisation.

Overall, corporate planning is concerned with the scope of an organisation's activities and the matching of these to the organisation's environment, its resource capabilities and the values and expectations of its various stakeholders.

Activity 4

A traditional manufacturer of diaries opened a publishing subsidiary. While the core business, diaries, declined, the publishing business was astonishingly successful. Classify the following strategic issues according to their level of strategy:

(a)   Should the profits from the publishing company be used to rescue diaries, or grow the publishing company more quickly?

(b)   Should the diaries move up market?

(c)   How can the costs of the diaries be reduced, to improve the margin?

(d)   Should the publishing company move into publishing novels?

(e)   Should the diary business be sold to a rival, so that resources can be focused on the publishing company?

Feedback to this activity is at the end of the chapter.

2.8 Strategic planning, tactical planning, and operational strategy (Anthony)

Anthony defines three main levels of planning:

- strategic
- tactical
- operational

Strategic planning

Planning comprises long-term/strategic planning and short-term operation planning. The latter is usually for a year. A series of short-term plans should lead to the success of the long-term plan.

Strategic planning is primarily concerned with determining the organisation's future and is sometimes opportunistic rather than systematic (for example, exploiting the situation of a competitor's failure).

Tactical planning

Tactical planning is concerned with the contributions of the various functions and departments towards achieving the corporate objectives and strategies. Tactical planning is also concerned with resources allocation between the various departments.

At the tactical level the organisation is concerned about the evaluation of alternative courses of action. Decision processes may involve the estimation of the probabilities of different outcomes. Such decisions will also include the forecasting of the market and competitor responses. The objectives, criteria and

standards for performance evaluation will be laid down. This is in order that the effectiveness of strategic implication and operational efficiency can be properly monitored and measured.

The tactical level will also be responsible for laying down details of policies. These policies establish contingency decisions, which will state a response to reoccurring situations. Policies are necessary in order to guide and standardise the organisation's responses to particular situations, this then having the effect of achieving a consistent response.

Operational planning

Operational planning may include such things as close consultation with customers or clients, organisation and management development, staff training and development, financial and budgetary management.

With all planning it is important that some sort of assessment criteria are associated with the plan and this should be done as the plan is formulated. These assessment criteria will allow managers to ascertain whether or not the plan's strategies have been implemented or achieved and whether they have been achieved within the timescale laid down.

There are a number of elements to operational planning which include:

- Establishing programmes that specify a series of actions, procedures or rules that may be necessary in order to achieve a particular higher-level objective. Programmes are also used in order to allocate tasks and responsibilities to individuals and also to lay down timescales in which these tasks need to be completed.

- Laying down procedures which detail the way in which reoccurring issues or problems should be tackled. A procedure can be defined as a series of rules.

- Establishing a budgetary plan that involves planning, in detailed quantitative terms, the projected results for future periods. The projected results can be compared against the actual results. Budgetary planning is an important part at the operational level of the strategic plan, as it compiles a co-ordinated framework of estimated sales, output and productivity, etc. Budgetary planning is a detailed expression of the plans and proposals that were originated in much broader context at the corporate or tactical level.

It can be said, therefore, that operational planning is concerned with the detailed planning, quantification and implementation, at a departmental or functional level, of the specified strategies and courses of action necessary to achieve the overall plans and objectives of the organisation.

2.9 Examples

Examples of planning at the different hierarchies within an organisation may be as follows:

Strategic	*Tactical*	*Operational*
Choosing objectives	Formulating budgets	Implementing budgets
Organisational planning	Planning staff levels	Controlling hiring
Policy setting:	Formulating:	Implementing policy
– personnel	– personnel practices	Implementing policy
– financial	– working capital plans	Implementing policy
– marketing	– advertising programme	Implementing policy
– research	– research projects	Implementing policy
Factory acquisition	Plant rearrangement	Production schedules

3 Developing strategy

3.1 Modes of strategy-making – Mintzberg's view

There is no one best way of managing the strategy of an organisation. A flexible, reactive style may suit a small firm in a rapidly changing environment, whereas a large company may need to take a long-term view and plan accordingly. Strategies may evolve in different ways and Mintzberg has identified several modes of strategy-making.

Strategies may come about in opportunistic or **entrepreneurial** ways. An organisation may take advantage of changes in the environment or recognise new skills in an opportunistic manner or a firm may be set up by an entrepreneur because of an opportunity in the marketplace.

- In the entrepreneurial mode, strategy-making is dominated by the active search for new opportunities, and is characterised by dramatic leaps forward in the face of uncertainty. Strategy is developed by significant bold decisions being made. Growth is the dominant goal of the organisation, and in uncertain conditions, this type of mode can result in the organisation making significant gains.

- The organisation operating in this mode suggests by its actions that the environment is intractable, a force to be confronted and controlled. Power is centralised in the chief executive, with an unwillingness to 'submit' to authority.

Another mode of strategy-making is sometimes called **adaptive** because it fits the description that managers give of how strategies come about in their organisations. They see their role as strategists as being involved in a continual proactive pursuit of a strategic goal, countering competitive moves and adapting to their environment whilst not rocking the boat too much.

Four major characteristics distinguish the adaptive mode of strategy-making:

- Clear goals do not exist in the adaptive organisation; strategy-making reflects a division of power among members of a complex coalition. The adaptive organisation is caught in a web of political forces – unions, managers, owners, lobby groups, government agencies, and so on. There is no one central source of power, no one simple goal. The organisation cannot make decisions to 'maximise' any one goal such as profit or growth; rather it must seek solutions to its problems that satisfy the constraints.

- In this mode, the strategy-making process is characterised by the 'reactive' solution to the existing problems rather than the 'proactive' search for new opportunities. Adaptive organisations seek conditions of certainty wherever possible, otherwise they seek to reduce existing uncertainties by for example negotiating long-term purchasing arrangements to stabilise sources of supply, etc.

- In this mode, organisations make decisions in incremental, serial steps. Because its environment is complex, the adaptive organisation finds that feedback is a crucial ingredient in strategy-making. Strategy-making focuses on what is familiar, considering the convenient alternatives and the ones that differ only slightly from the status quo.

- Disjointed decisions are characteristic of the adaptive organisation. The demands on the organisation are diverse, and cannot be reconciled easily, therefore decisions are made in a piece-meal manner.

3.2 Planned strategies

Planned or **deliberate** strategies come about where there are precise intentions that are written down and imposed by a central leadership. There are a large number of controls to ensure surprise-free implementation in an environment that is controllable.

- There are three essential features of the planning mode.

- The analyst plays a major role in strategy-making.

- This mode focuses on systematic analysis, particularly in the assessment of the costs and benefits of competing proposals. Formal planning involves both the active search for new opportunities and the solution of existing problems.

- This mode integrates decisions and strategies. For example, planning can ensure that the decision to acquire a new company complements (or at least does not conflict with) the decision to expand the product line of an existing division.

3.3 Imposed strategies

A strategy may be **imposed** on the organisation. Government policies may have an impact on the strategy; this has been the case for those public utilities recently privatised. Recession and threat of a takeover may force a strategy of cost cutting and retrenchment. Technological developments may cause an organisation to develop new products to replace those that have become obsolete.

The conditions that drive an organisation to favour one mode of strategy-making over the others are outlined below.

- **Entrepreneurial mode** – requires the strategy-making authority to rest with one powerful individual. The environment must be flexible, and the organisation oriented toward growth. These conditions are most typical of organisations that are small and/or young.

- **Adaptive mode** – suggests the organisation faces a complex rapidly changing environment and a divided interest group. Unusually large established organisations that have invested significant resources in controlling the diverse interest groups fall into this mode – for example, hospitals and amenities.

- **Planning mode** – organisations must be large enough to afford the costs of formal analysis, must have goals that are operational, and must face an environment that is reasonably predictable and stable.

3.4 Emergent strategies

What can go wrong with a planned approach to strategy formulation?

- The obvious possibility is that an intended strategy is not implemented, perhaps because its underlying assumptions turn out to be invalid or because it is overtaken by the pace of developments.

KEY POINT

Emergent strategies are strategies that are not laid down in a formal planning process, but arise from existing patterns of behaviour.

- A more subtle point is that defined patterns of behaviour will already exist in an organisation, and superimposing a new strategy is not a straightforward task. Existing patterns of behaviour may themselves help to shape a planned strategy. Alternatively, if the planned strategy runs counter to existing patterns of behaviour this may lead to unintended modifications. The effect described here is that of emergent strategies – elements of strategy not laid down in a formal planning process but arising from existing patterns of behaviour.

3.5 Doubts about the deliberate approach

Here, we develop in greater detail the doubts about the deliberate approach that have exercised the emergent strategists.

Setting corporate objectives

A criticism frequently levelled at the practice of spelling out corporate objectives is that the exercise descends into the formulation of empty platitudes that offer no positive directional indicators for decision-making. It is too simplistic to suggest that the problem arises from poor planning. It is frequently the case that contradictory objectives are implied by the firm's long run strategy and the conflicting interests of key stakeholders – maximising profit for the shareholders may involve employee redundancy as a consequence of restructuring.

The difficulties of forecasting accurately

The development of a forecasting capability, and the development of models which relate environmental changes to corporate performance, are significant aspects of strategic planning. The general level of practice concerning environmental issues is still quite primitive (and some writers argue that more complex methods would not be very much more effective, since the environment is inherently unpredictable).

There are difficult problems associated with trying to accurately forecast for the long term:

- The fact that it is a long-term period.

- The complexity of the environment that needs to be forecast.

- The rapidity and novelty of environmental change.

- The interrelationships between the environmental variables involved.

- The limitations of the data available.

- The amount and complexity of the calculations involved.

Several studies have shown that assessing the likelihood of future events is one of the hardest things that executives are asked to do, and most are not particularly good at it. However, this is only half the problem; even if strategists guess what is going to happen, they still have to devise effective responses and implement them effectively.

Writers such as Hannan argue that this is virtually impossible in all but the most stable markets, and argue that good management at least gives a firm a chance to change as things develop, while a long-term strategy might develop the company in inappropriate ways.

Short-term pressures

The pressures on management are for short-term results and ostensibly strategy is concerned with the long term, e.g. 'What should we be doing now to help us reach the position we want to be in, in five years time?'. Often it is difficult to motivate managers by setting long-term expectations when short-term problems can consume the whole working day. This is particularly true if senior managers are prone to changing their long-term strategy frequently, which may sound contradictory but is in fact rather common.

Rigidity

Operational managers are frequently reluctant to specify their planning assumptions because the situations that their plans are designed to meet may change so rapidly that they can be made to look foolish. Even if a plan is reasonably accurate, the situation might change for reasons other than those forecast. Executives are often held prisoner by the rigidity of the planning process, because plans have to be set out in detail long before the period to which they apply.

The rigidity of the long-term plan, particularly in regard to the rationing and scheduling of resources, may also place the company in a position where it is unable to react to short-term unforeseen opportunities, or serious short-term crisis.

Stifling initiative

If adherence to the strategy becomes all-important, it discounts flair and creativity. Operational managers can generate enthusiasm or dampen down potential trouble spots, and quick action may be required to avert trouble or improve a situation by actions outside the strategy. If operational managers then have to defend their actions against criticisms of acting 'outside the plan', irrespective of the resultant benefits, they are likely to become apathetic and indifferent.

The cost

The strategic planning process can be costly, involving the use of specialists, sometimes a specialist department, and taking up management time. The process generates its own bureaucracy and associated paper or electronic data flow. Personal authorities are, to a greater or lesser extent, replaced by written guidelines.

A plan adds unwarranted comfort

Such writers as Ralph Stacey argue that the main reason that long range plans are popular is that they give security to executives, and allow the deployment of a range of instruments that managers feel comfortable about – budgeting, long term cash flows, investment appraisal and so on. Consequently, the firm is frequently surprised when the real world stubbornly refuses to behave in the way that planners have predicted, and the strategies developed by their techniques have become irrelevant. For Stacey, good management is about coping with things that are unexpected and poorly understood, and less about preparing for some anticipated but seldom-realised future.

Why start now?

A general attitude particularly shown by managers in small growing companies is that they have managed quite successfully in the past without formalised strategic planning systems. So why start now?

Management distrust of techniques

The strategic planning process involves the use of management accounting techniques, not least forecasting, modelling, cost analysis and operational research. This can produce adverse reactions for two reasons. Firstly, senior management may distrust 'laboratory techniques untested in their ambit of activity', and secondly, they might distrust the recommendations of younger specialist people who are, 'on balance heavy on academic learning but light on practical experience'. It is worth pointing out that it is not only managers in post that distrust many techniques used in long-range strategic management; there are many academics that greatly distrust these models.

The clash of personal and corporate loyalties

The adoption of corporate strategy requires a tacit acceptance by everyone that the interests of departments, activities and individuals are subordinate to the corporate interests. Department managers are required to consider the contribution to corporate profits or the reduction in corporate costs of any decision. They should not allow their decisions to be limited by departmental parameters. It is only natural that managers should seek personal advancement. As a company is the primary vehicle by which this can be achieved, a cleavage of loyalty may occur. A problem of strategic planning is identifying those areas where there may be a clash of interests and loyalties, and in assessing where an individual has allowed vested interests to dominate decisions.

Empirical evidence

If long range strategy really were as effective as its supporters claim, then it should be possible to produce evidence to demonstrate that companies that adopt a long range view and planning techniques consistently out perform those that do not. Unfortunately, the result of a large number of studies is inconclusive, with some studies finding some evidence, but many finding none at all. Scott Armstrong's exhaustive review of all the evidence suggested that planning might give a small advantage in some manufacturing environments only, but other writers, Henry Mintzberg in particular, have been extremely critical of the theory and practice on planning.

The problems that strategic planners try to solve are real – adaptation, positioning and resource use, etc are major problems that must be resolved in some way.

Thinking about these problems, and taking the most appropriate action, is the best that a firm can hope to achieve. Some firms may be able to do these things through a planning process better than they would have done without one. For other firms, the opposite will be the case.

3.6 Emergent strategy processes

In the section above, we considered the various objections that emergent strategists have raised against the deliberate approach. In this section, we look at some emergent strategy processes.

Incrementalism – muddling through?

Charles Lindblom suggested that managing strategies through logical, planning mechanisms was not realistic. Because of the complexity of organisations and the environments in which they operate, it would be difficult for managers to consider all the strategic options and measure them against preset, unambiguous objectives.

He argued that strategic choice takes place by comparing possible options against each other and considering which would give the best outcome. Lindblom called this strategy building through 'successive limited comparisons'.

For Lindblom, the key constraint on the development of effective strategy (or policy, since he was addressing his remarks to the public sector) was the influence of key **stakeholders**, that is the political pressures exerted by those with an interest in the identification and pursuit of strategic objectives. For a commercial company, these are not less important.

Logical incrementalism

This deprecation of incrementalism was challenged by Quinn, who argued that there were very good reasons why senior managers should take an incremental approach, but dismissed Lindblom's pejorative diagnosis.

Quinn argued that strategies emerged from the organisational periphery following political processes. The political strength behind each new idea is a signal to top management about the likely feasibility of implementing the idea, and whether or not it would be successful. If the new strategy is a success, it can be developed and become part of the core business of the firm. If unsuccessful, it can be dropped without endangering the key aspects of the firm's strategy and performance.

In this model, senior management sit above the political activity, but are able to make rational judgements about what should be tried and when. Further, they may become involved in coaching and developing the ideas that they see as likely winners.

Quinn goes further and identifies the political subsystems that are likely to develop and support strategic ventures. These include:

- **International posture subsystem** – looking at opportunities to extend the company's range of activities abroad.

- **Technology growth subsystem** – parts of the organisation looking to grow the company's activities by internal development.

- **Product-line-positioning subsystem** – those looking at the organisation in terms of its existing products and markets, and what can be done to enhance these.

- **Acquisition subsystem** – those parts of the organisation that can see potential synergies in a wider variety of products and markets than could be developed internally in the short term.

The political subsystems are informed about what they do themselves, and what they are capable of. In short, they are political alliances based around expertise. Therefore, it is not necessary for senior management to know everything and understand exactly what the strengths and limitations of each subsystem might be. Rather, they need only to make choices about which ventures to support now, which to support later and which to reject.

These political activities do not replace the environmental and internal scanning processes of strategic management described in the previous chapter, as it is vital that executives understand them as fully as possible. However, the source of new ideas, and the political will to implement them, is seen as a political process, rather than an intellectual one.

The advantages of the logical incrementalist approach include:

- better strategic selection

- wider involvement in the strategy-making process

- a greater sense of commitment to what gets decided upon

- the means to coordinate new activities across the organisation.

Roles for middle and senior managers

Quinn's theory of logical incrementalism sees middle management as political actors, jockeying for influence and a grip on strategic direction. The role of senior management is to preside above this activity, steering the organisation through a series of logical, connected steps that extend the scope of the firm's activities and build competitive advantage in the longer term. That is to say that the seniors direct the energy and invention of middle management by favouring and selecting some strategic ideas over others.

Quinn suggests four key roles for the senior managers in this process:

- improve the quality of information used in key decisions

- overcome personal and political pressures resisting change

- deal with the varying lead times and sequencing of events in the decisions

- build organisational awareness and support for the strategies.

Of course, there are difficulties that could be experienced by a firm relying on this method.

It tends to ignore problems at the centre of the business, by keeping strategic change to the periphery.

3.7 Intended and emergent strategies

We tend to visualise a strategy as being formulated, perhaps through some planning process, resulting in a clear expression of direction that then comes about or is actually realised. It is conceived of as a deliberate, systematic process of development and implementation. However, in many organisations that attempt to formulate strategies in systematic ways, the intended strategies do not become realised, or only a part of what was intended actually happens.

Mintzberg states that strategies are much more likely to emerge rather than be due to a deliberate planning process.

> 'One idea leads to another, until a new pattern forms. Action has driven thinking, and a new strategy has emerged... Out in the field, a salesman visits a customer. The product isn't right, and together they work out some modifications. The salesman returns to the company and puts the changes through; after two or three more rounds, they finally get it right. A new product emerges, which eventually opens up a new market. The company has changed strategic course.'

The figure below shows that the actual outcome, the organisation's realised strategy, can come about through a planned, deliberate formulation and implementation. The realised strategy can also come about from a pattern in a stream of decisions (emergent strategy).

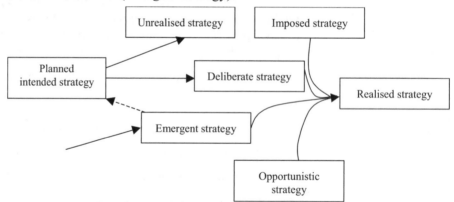

Crafting a strategy

Mintzberg likens the management of a strategy to a potter crafting clay. The clay is thrown and by shaping the clay on the wheel, the potter gives it shape through a gradual process.

> 'The crafting image captures the process by which effective strategies come to be. The planning image, long popular in the literature, distorts those processes and thereby misguides organisations that embrace it unreservedly.'

According to Mintzberg there are five activities involved in strategic management:

- **Manage stability** – managers should know when to change and not assume perpetual environmental change. A large proportion of managers' time should be spent effectively implementing the strategies, not planning them.

- **Detect discontinuity** – strategic managers must be able to recognise the changes that are significant to their organisation.

- **Know the business** – including an awareness and understanding of the operations in the organisation.

- **Manage patterns** – managers should have the ability to detect emerging patterns and help them take shape; knowing which emergent strategies to nurture.

- **Reconcile change and continuity** – requires a combination or bringing together of the future, present and past; understanding that an obsession with either change or continuity can be counterproductive.

A simple example of an emergent strategy would be one that arises from an external stimulus not envisaged in the planned strategy. This could happen if a supplier, pursuing modern ideas on supplier/customer relationships, encouraged a partnership approach to sourcing. It is easy to imagine that purchasing staff in the customer organisation might see benefits in this and could pursue the idea to the point where sourcing strategy took on an aspect not at all contemplated when planned strategic developments were laid down.

4 Strategic decisions

4.1 Drucker's analysis

Management strategy can also be categorised into attempts to help to provide particular sets of plans to meet the needs of particular types of problems. These plans would be in response to changes in the environment and would aim to promote better decision-making. Drucker, in his book *Managing for Results*, discusses business strategies and states that whatever a company's programme it must decide:

- what opportunities it wants to pursue and what risks it is willing and able to accept

- its scope and structure, and especially the right balance between specialisation, diversification and integration

- between time and money, between building its own or buying, i.e. using sale of a business, merger, acquisition and joint venture to attain its goals

- on an organisation structure appropriate to its economic realities, its opportunities and its programme for performance.

There are three kinds of opportunities.

- **Additive** – exploitation of existing resources.

- **Complementary** – involving structural changes in the company.

- **Breakthrough** – changing the fundamental economic characteristics of the business.

The right opportunities will not be selected unless the company attempts to maximise opportunities rather than minimise risk. Risks can be placed in four categories:

- those that must be accepted

- those that can be afforded

- those that cannot be afforded

- those the company cannot afford to miss.

Quantitative techniques can be used to evaluate the likely outcomes of different decisions.

4.2 Characteristics of strategic decisions (Johnson and Scholes)

In their book *Exploring Corporate Strategy*, Johnson and Scholes outline the characteristics of strategic decisions. They discuss the following areas:

- Strategic decisions are likely to be affected by the scope of an organisation's activities, because the scope concerns the way the management conceive the organisation's boundaries. It is to do with what they want the organisation to be like and be about.

- Strategy involves the matching of the activities of an organisation to its environment.

- Strategy must also match the activities of an organisation to its resource capability. It is not just about being aware of the environmental threats and opportunities but about matching the organisational resources to these threats and opportunities.

- Strategies need to be considered in terms of the extent to which resources can be obtained, allocated and controlled to develop a strategy for the future.

- Operational decisions will be affected by strategic decisions because they will set off waves of lesser decisions.

- As well as the environmental forces and the resource availability, the strategy of an organisation will be affected by the expectations and values of those who have power within and around the organisation.

- Strategic decisions are apt to affect the long-term direction of the organisation.

Johnson and Scholes argue that what distinguishes strategic management from other aspects of management in an organisation is the complexity. There are three reasons for this:

- it involves a high degree of uncertainty

- it is likely to require an integrated approach to management

- it may involve major change in the organisation.

Summary

Key points of this chapter are:

- The organisation's mission can be formal (say, in writing) or informal, and represents its basic purpose or raison d'être. That is what the organisation wants to be, or to accomplish. Defining the mission of the organisation is important because it affects everything else.

- We have seen that there are many different definitions of strategy ranging from the simple to the complex. However, most of these definitions interpret a strategy as being some sort of future plan of action.

KEY POINT

Strategy involves the matching of the activities of an organisation to its environment and resource capability.

KEY POINT

Strategic decisions affect the long-term direction of the organisation.

- The levels of strategy can be classified as corporate, business, and operational or functional. The corporate strategy is the most general level of strategy in an organisation. The business strategy relates to how an organisation approaches a particular market or activity. The operational and functional strategies are those made at operational levels, e.g. personnel policy, pricing strategies.

- The logical incrementalist view holds that different political forces lead to the incremental development of strategy, but the role of senior management makes this logical and focused on the long-term prosperity of the organisation.

- There are no specific learning outcomes from the study guide linked to this chapter as it provides an overall introduction to corporate strategy. However, some of the overall learning aims of the syllabus are relevant.

Having completed your study of this chapter you should have achieved the following learning outcomes:

- identify and evaluate approaches to strategic management

- apply contemporary thinking on strategic management

- evaluate the linkages between strategic planning and the implementation of those plans.

Self-test questions

1   Describe the 'RUGS' organisational perspective. (1.1)

2   Draw a diagram of the hierarchy of objectives. (1.2)

3   List eight characteristics of a good mission statement. (1.4)

4   Give a simple definition of strategy. (2.1)

5   What are the five Ps of strategy according to Mintzberg? (2.6)

6   List the three different levels of strategy identified by Johnson and Scholes. (2.7)

7   What are the three levels of planning according to Anthony? (2.8)

8   Distinguish between entrepreneurial and adaptive approaches to strategy formulation. (3.3)

9   What is an emergent strategy? (3.4)

10   What are the difficulties in forecasting accurately for the long term? (3.5)

11   What, according to Mintzberg, are the five activities involved in strategic management? (3.7)

12   Name Drucker's three kinds of opportunities. (4.1)

13   What, according to Johnson and Scholes, are the characteristics of strategic decisions? (4.2)

Exam-type question

Corporate mission and strategies

(a) The managing director of TDM plc has recently returned from a conference entitled 'Strategic planning beyond the 90s'. Whilst at the conference, she attended a session on 'corporate mission statements'. She found the session very interesting but it was rather short and she has asked the following questions:

- 'What does corporate mission mean? I don't see how it fits in with our strategic planning process.'

- 'Where does our mission come from and what areas of corporate life should it cover?'

- 'Even if we were to develop one of these mission statements, what benefits would the company get from it?'

Required:

Prepare a report that answers the managing director's questions. **(15 marks)**

(b) **Required:**

Distinguish between the following pairs of concepts.

(i) Intended strategy and realised strategy.

(ii) The rational model of strategy making and the concept of emergent strategies.

(iii) Strategic and non-strategic decisions. **(10 marks)**

(Total: 25 marks)

For the answer to this question, see the 'Answers' section at the end of the book.

Feedback to activities

Activity 1

The first is the mission statement of a British University. It identifies that the range of courses offered will be restricted to those that lead to an obvious career path, and research will be developed in partnership with those who have a commercial interest in discovery, rather than simply a sense of curiosity. As you might expect, this is a University with great ambition but relatively few resources, and therefore focuses its activity into areas where it may compete effectively against its more august rivals. Note that the mission statement here implicitly describes both the customers it seeks and the services it wishes to offer.

The second is the mission statement of a manufacturer of lead pencils. This is not a silly joke, something very much like it can be found. The important point is that it suggests innovation in a field more usually noted for cost based competition. Part of the company's business is providing jokey, amusing slogans on its pencils, and the mission statement was chosen to reflect this. Note that this mission is directed at the customers, any message for employees is rather too subtle to operate effectively.

Nigel Piercy has argued that any mission statement containing the word 'excellent' (such as the third example in the activity) should not be taken seriously . Excellence subject to resource constraints also appears rather qualified. However, this particular firm embarked on a rapacious programme of take-overs in a field where this was comparatively unknown. The resource base expanded, but very little of these extra resources found their way into product quality and customer service, leading to great cynicism from staff.

The final statement is a translation of the mission of Komatsu, who set their sight on taking Caterpillar's domination of the tracked vehicle market. They picked out the weaker points of their rival's operation, its softest markets and poorest products, and spent two decades building up the competencies and driving them out.

Activity 3

Strategy as plan: Clearly deliberate. A plan, and the actions necessary to carry it out must be consciously worked out. Should actual behaviour deviate from planned behaviour, various contingency plans and feedback mechanisms will route actions back to those intended.

Strategy as ploy: Clearly deliberate. It implies that customers, markets, rivals and the capabilities of the strategist's own company are understood sufficiently well that actions can be devised and implemented to gain an advantage over a rival.

Strategy as pattern: Emergent. The consistent behaviours that could be mistaken for logical decisions might have routes that are quite different. Entrepreneurial and innovative companies frequently argue that their strategies for the next few years will, in practice, be determined by things that they haven't yet thought of.

Strategy as position: Mostly deliberate. Writers such as Michael Porter, who have written much on the subject, generally argue that strategy is about achieving a desired position in the market place. However, some writers, such as Mintzberg, point out that often positioning happens by accident as well as design.

Strategy as perspective: Deliberate. Perspective implies that the environment is scanned, and the results pondered, in a systematic way. However, such writers as Gerry Johnson use the word paradigm to describe the more subjective and emergent factors that go into making up a perspective.

Activity 4

Most of the issues require some contribution from all levels. However, the principal decision-making levels are:

(a) **Corporate level**. Movement of resources between business can only be decided at the highest level.

(b) **Business level**. Only managers who understand the particular markets concerned can really work out the most effective strategy (technically called positioning). Senior managers will be interested in associated costs and benefits, while functions will need to know how they can produce a superior product that appeals to the new target market if this option is selected.

(c) **Functional level**. Good functional managers, in operations and cost accounting in particular, should be able to produce a range of alternative projects to reduce costs. Business level strategy will be concerned with the effect the changes may have on other functions. For example it is possible to reduce costs by lowering quality, but this may make the product harder to sell at the same price. Thus the functions would have achieved their cost reduction targets, but the strategic objective of improving the margin may fail if this quality-based option is selected.

    (d)   **Business level**. The publishers are best placed to know whether they have, or could gain, the skills necessary to diversify in this way. Naturally, the senior corporate levels will be concerned about costs and benefits of this move, compared with other possible projects.

    (e)   **Corporate level**. Acquisitions and disposals to strengthen the group of businesses can only be made at the highest level.

Chapter 2

THE COMPETITIVE ENVIRONMENT

Syllabus content

- PEST analysis.

- Derivatives of PEST such as STEEP (social, technological, environmental, economic and political factors) and PESTEL (political, economic, sociocultural, technological, environmental, and legal factors).

- SWOT analysis.

- Porter's Diamond and its use for assessing the competitive advantage of nations.

- Porter's Five Forces model and its use for assessing the external environment.

- Qualitative approaches to competitive analysis.

- Competitor analysis and competitive strategies (both qualitative and quantitative tools of competitor analysis will be used).

- Sources, availability and quality of data for environmental analysis.

Contents

1   Introduction

2   Competitive environments

3   PEST analysis

4   SWOT analysis

5   Porter's Diamond and the Five Forces model

6   Data for environmental analysis

1   Introduction

In this chapter and the next one we will consider some of the most basic forces that affect the structure, conduct, and performance of company strategic planning systems. These forces make up the business environment. They have a great impact on the company, while the reverse is seldom true. They are the 'uncontrollables', to which companies adapt through setting the 'controllable' factors, their strategies. We will look at PEST analysis as a means of appraising influences on organisations.

We also look at corporate appraisal or SWOT analysis. This stage of the strategic planning model draws on the data obtained about: objectives, current position, extrapolated position, gaps and environmental forecasts; and considers the significance and implications of the company's consequential strengths, weaknesses, opportunities and threats.

Porter's diamond tries to isolate the national attributes that further competitive advantage in an industry. Porter's five forces model helps to illustrate how profits may be divided up between competition, suppliers and buyers according to the strength of their bargaining position.

2   Competitive environments

2.1   Some basic definitions

Environment

Much of the relevant work in this area has been carried out by open systems and contingency theorists, and Burns and Stalker's and Lawrence and Lorsch's research is particularly relevant. Ruth Carter et al provide a useful definition of environment:

> 'The set of elements that affect the system, but are not controlled by it. Though clearly relevant to the system, they are regarded as falling outside its boundary.'

Obviously, there are some components within the system over which the management of an organisation have little control and some writers rather confusingly refer to these as forming part of the internal environment.

Different environments

An organisation's environment can be split into:

- **Macroenvironment** – Those components of the environment that may potentially affect the organisation but whose relevance is not specific at a particular time. They are the broad forces – demography, economics, law and politics, culture and technology – that exercise a profound influence on the organisation's microenvironment.

- **Microenvironment** – The part of the environment that is directly relevant to the organisation in achieving its goals. It varies depending on the domain the organisation has chosen for itself.

- **Domain** – What an organisation stakes out for itself with respect to the range of products or services offered and markets served. (In the UK, *The Sun* and *The Guardian* are both newspapers but they report news differently, carry different features and appeal to different segments of the newspaper market.)

KEY POINT

The macroenvironment comprises the broad forces that exercise a profound influence on the organisation's microenvironment.

KEY POINT

The microenvironment is that part of the environment that is directly relevant to an organisation in achieving its goals.

2.2 Environmental influences

The environment exerts three basic forms of influence upon the organisation:

- It offers threats (to the well-being of the organisation, such as Government legislation, or, say, national action by trade unions) and opportunities (for exploitation, such as growth in market demand, or new technological possibilities).

- It is the source of organisational resources (human resources come from outside the organisation, as do funds and supplies generally).

- It contains interest or 'pressure groups' that have some kind of direct interest in organisational activities (these range from the general public and Government bodies to 'action' groups such as Greenpeace and Animal Rights).

KEY POINT

An organisation can be thought of as an open system that is influenced by a complex political, economic, social and technological structure of variables that can change.

2.3 The environmental segments

The environment consists of those factors that can affect an organisation's operations, but which its management have little or no power to influence or control. An organisation can be thought of as an open system that is influenced by a complex political, economic, social and technological structure of variables that can change.

2.4 Types of business environment

Unless business planners are able to identify the actual and potential forces of change on their businesses, they will have no means of knowing what steps to take to minimise the danger or to cash in on the opportunities which the changes present. It is incumbent on strategic planners to take the steps necessary to collect, analyse and interpret relevant information on the key factors, or segments. It may be a case of closing the stable door after the horse has bolted if historic information only is produced, that is after the changes have taken, or are taking, place. Information must be made available which shows the magnitude and rates of change of significant events and activities.

Four types of business environment are:

KEY POINT

The four types of business environment are: simple, complex, static and dynamic.

- **Simple environment** – Some organisations are fortunate to operate in business environments in which they only have to cope with relatively few uncertainties or change agents. It could be said that these organisations are in simple environments.

- **Complex environment** – The more complex an organisation's environment is, in other words the more variables there are that can change, the more uncertainty it faces. Complexity usually relates to the diversity of the environmental segments, and the extent to which they are interrelated. For example, because of their size and the diversity of their product-market involvement, the Hanson group of companies are operating in a very complex business environment.

Example

The concept of the strategic business unit (SBU) was devised by General Electric (GE) of America. In the 1960s GE found that despite substantial growth in sales, its profits were not increasing proportionately. GE's top management came to realise that one of the major causes of the inadequate profits was the complexity and number of its product-markets and the lack of balance between them. Accordingly, therefore, in 1971, it restructured its 170 or so departments into just 50 strategic business units. Other large companies were later to imitate GE by applying the same concept.

- **Static environment** – An organisation operating in a static environment faces no change of significance or relatively little change in the variables that give rise to uncertainty. The organisation is thus able to place confidence in its forecasts and assumptions. The business managers will be guided by their experience of the business environment in which they operate. They will be influenced by past events and the impact they had on organisational performance. The forecasting methods will, in the main, be statistical by nature based on projecting from past trends. There is, however, still a danger of unanticipated or unpredicted change, which should not be ignored.

- **Dynamic environment** – The degree of environmental dynamism relates to the rate and frequency of change of the factors that give rise to uncertainty. An organisation that operates in an extremely dynamic environment is faced by rapid, and probably novel, change and thus plans its future facing a very uncertain business situation.

  The business planners operating in this type of environment will need to consider the novelty of future events and not be influenced solely by past events and results. They will need to be very sensitive to change, and forecasting will be based on a mix of statistical and intuitive techniques. There is a danger that the organisational structure, and culture, will be unable to cope with the change required. A dynamic environment is far more risky than a static environment.

We can see from this that different types of environment can be classified into two major groups: (a) by speed and nature of change (static or dynamic), and (b) by convolution (simple or complex). Four strategic scenarios can therefore be identified, as illustrated in the diagram below.

Convolution / Nature of change	Static	Dynamic
Simple	Simple/Static	Simple/Dynamic
Complex	Complex/Static	Complex/Dynamic

Diagram: Strategic scenario determination

These four scenarios represent extremes and a continuum of other situations range between them.

Activity 1

Describe two situations, the first where the environment is simple and dynamic and the second where the environment is complex and stable.

Feedback to this activity is at the end of the chapter

2.5 Strategic implications of different environments

The practical implications, then, are that each company faces a particular environmental outlook. Building on our previous overview we shall distinguish four such environmental vistas.

- **Stable and unchanging** – In this case the organisation can focus its attention on its past decisions and results, and on attempting to correct its past mistakes. Tactical planning is more important than strategic planning. (For example, British Telecom until recent years operated in a stable marketing environment and could safely invest large amounts of resources in the pursuit of achieving a maximally efficient telephone service.)

- **Stable with minor fluctuations** – This describes an environment characterised by cyclical and/or seasonal fluctuations within a fairly stable structure. (For example, a local government education service will adopt a set of procedures for educating children, only having to adjust its scale of activity to accommodate the changing numbers of children in education.)

- **Gradually changing in a predictable fashion** – This is where an organisation recognises that its environment is slowly being changed into something new and predictable. With this recognition it can begin to make the necessary adjustments to its goals, strategic direction, organisation structure, and systems so that it can proceed in a meaningful way for the future. (Thus with the predictable changing values of women the Girl Guide movement shifted its programmes toward developing the 'new woman' rather than the 'future wife and mother' though some evidence of reversion to the older ideals is evident in the movement's recent (April 2002) re-branding.)

- **Rapidly changing in an unpredictable fashion** – Within this environment an organisation operates in highly turbulent and unpredictable businesses. Strategic planning is much more important than tactical planning, and effectiveness (doing the right things) is just as essential as achieving efficiency (doing things the best way). (Thus National Health Service hospitals in recent years have endured a succession of shocks and surprises. Private medical care, rapidly changing medical technology, in-depth appraisal of their activities by the National Audit Office (and Audit Commission), new government policies and constraints, rising costs and consumerism have led to hospitals closing, 'opting out', and finding creative ways of adapting to their environment in order to survive.)

An organisation can react to its environmental situation (or opportunities and threats) in several ways. It may do nothing if it is convinced that the problem is insignificant or short-term. It may decide to monitor the environment carefully but not to respond just yet. It may increase its flexibility through contingency planning and product-market development. It may decide that the situation is important and urgent and want to plan major strategic change.

The term **incremental strategy** describes the situation where a company plans and implements changes gradually in a piecemeal way by using small fine-tuning strategies, which although relatively small and incremental in nature collectively represent a considerable change to the company's strategic position over a long time. Incremental strategy, by the nature of what it is, often takes the form of departmental planning.

The term **corporate strategy** is used to convey a much different planning philosophy. This is used when there are significant changes in the environment, or where over time the company has got 'out of fit' with its environment, and now requires major strategic change that affects all, or most, aspects of its activities.

3 PEST analysis

3.1 Introduction

The external environment consists of factors that cannot be directly influenced by the organisation itself. These include social, legal, economic, political and technological (SLEPT) changes that the firm must try to respond to, rather than control. An important aspect of strategy is the way the organisation adapts to its environment. PEST analysis divides the business environment into four systems – political, economic, social (and cultural), and technical.

Other variants on the acronym/mnemonic that you may encounter are STEEP (social, technological, environmental, economic and political factors) and PESTLE (political, economic, sociocultural, technological, environmental and legal factors). Don't let this worry you: it simply depends whether the writer groups certain factors together or includes them separately — 'legal' within 'political' for instance.

PEST analysis can also be used as part of an Industry Analysis. This analysis attempts to determine the factors that will affect the probability or other measures of success within an industry. The analysis therefore includes PEST as well as other similar theories such as Porter's Diamond and SWOT analysis.

3.2 The political environment

This also includes the legal environment. Relevant factors include:

- trading regulations

- price controls (e.g. EC Common Agricultural policy may result in a minimum price for a product)

- taxation (e.g. the level of corporation tax will affect the amount an enterprise can reinvest)

- employment legislation

- nationalisation/denationalisation.

The problem facing strategic planners is how to plan for changes in the political environment. As change is not predictable, the planner needs to approach the problem by considering what type of political change could affect the enterprise rather than trying to estimate all the political changes that might occur.

The main feature of the legal environment is its increasing complexity. This is typified by company legislation. From 1948 to 1967 there were no major changes to company law; since then there have been four major acts, plus the consolidating 1985 Act (the Companies Act 1989 amended certain provisions of the Companies Act 1985).

This pattern is repeated in almost all areas. Employee legislation, consumer protection, planning and building regulations are all areas directly affecting business activities in which the legislation has become much more complex.

The political and legal influences in the business environment will be discussed further in the next chapter.

3.3 The economic environment

The economic environment tends to be characterised by periods of rising incomes and economic activity, followed by slowdowns, and then recovery. This process is called the trade cycle.

The business cycle (or trade cycle)

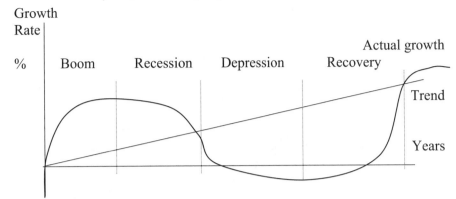

(a)   **Boom phase**

- excess aggregate demand

- inflationary pressures

- deepening balance of trade deficits (imports > exports)

- unemployment below normal levels.

(b)   **Recession phase**

- three successive quarters of falling growth

- aggregate demand weakening

- unemployment rate rising

- business confidence and investment falling.

(c)   **Depression phase**

- unemployment rate in excess of normal levels

- falling rate of inflation

- some real price and wage cuts

- consumer confidence and spending low.

(d)   **Recovery phase**

- upturn in economic growth rate

- unemployment rate declines

- cautious recovery of business confidence and investment.

The current position of an economy within its trade cycle is usually a matter of some speculation by economists, but in business terms the effect of each stage on particular markets must be understood by strategists working in that sector.

Economists believe that the trade cycle is caused by variations in the level of Aggregate Demand.

Governments use demand management *policies* to try to compensate for these variations.

Governments have three sets of macroeconomic policy goals:

(a) To maintain internal equilibrium

- appropriate level of unemployment

- appropriate level of inflation.

(b) To maintain external equilibrium and avoid Balance of Payments problems.

(c) To have a satisfactory level of economic growth.

The relationships involved can be summarised in a policy matrix as set out and discussed below.

Internal Equilibrium

	Inflation	**Unemployment**	
External Equilibrium	Excess demand	Poor International Competitiveness	**Deficits**
	Imported Inflation	Deficient Demand	**Surpluses**

Table: Macroeconomic policy analysis

Policy instruments available to governments in order to tackle each of the main macro-economic problems can then be summarised as below.

Excess Demand

- Reduce government expenditure.

- Raise taxation.

- Raise domestic interest rates.

Poor International Competitiveness

(a) Protectionist policies

- tariffs and quotas on imports

- export subsidies.

(b) Supply-side policies

- increase incentives to business (e.g. reduce taxes)

- improve training and labour skills

- remove trade union power to allow wage reductions

- restructure economy to produce higher value exports or replace imports.

(c)   Reduce exchange rate.

Imported Inflation

Here another large trading partner is sucking in extra exported products

- Raise exchange rate.

Deficient Demand

- Raise government expenditure.

- Reduce taxation.

- Cut domestic interest rate.

- Reduce exchange rate.

An analysis of economic factors should also include:

- growth in demand for goods and services

- availability of finance/level of interest rates

- availability of manpower/unemployment rates

- import controls

- exchange control.

The UK economy has been subject to considerable change. Several features characterise this change:

- steady, but relatively slow growth in output

- decline in employment

- a net oil exporter

- rates of inflation often above other Western economies.

These have resulted in major changes in the economic environment faced by most companies.

The emergence of the 'single market' of the European Community (EC) members in 1992/93 caused further considerable changes. In essence, the analysis of economic factors is still split between national and international, but the term 'national' now includes all EC member states. The 'domestic' market thus comprises not 60 million but 320 million people.

3.4   The social or sociocultural environment

Business operates within a social framework. Four aspects of this are relevant:

- **Power** – who has it, how effective is it, and how is it used?

- **Leadership** – who are the leaders, what are their qualities and weaknesses?

- **Culture** – the values and traditions within which the business must operate. One problem facing multinationals has often been a failure to cope with the different cultural values of the countries within which they operate.

- **Risk** – the attitudes towards risk and risk-taking.

KEY POINT

The social environment refers to the overall social framework within which a business operates.

The social environment also covers the study of population trends. The strategic planner will make use of such trends to determine the size, type and location of the marketplace for products or services.

- **Size** – The expected growth or decline in national and international population.

- **Type** – Changes in the age distribution.

- **Location** – The expected drift of population into different parts of the country, e.g. the south east of the UK.

Culture is the term given to the composite set of values, beliefs and prejudices, legal and political systems, attitudes, ideas and conventions which a society has adopted as a way of facilitating the way of life which has the greatest general appeal. It acts by persuasion and self-interest, not compulsion, and does not possess legal sanction. The members of its society conform to its cultural framework because the penalty is likely to be rejection.

The **sociocultural** environment therefore relates to a wide range of aspects such as:

- living patterns and styles

- society's attitudes and beliefs

- customs

- power – who has it, how effective it is, and how it is used.

3.5 The technological environment

The technological environment determines the type of products that are made or services that are sold. It also determines the way in which products are made or services are provided.

Examples of recently developed new products can be found in biotechnology, and pharmaceuticals and data storage devices. The rate of change in these industries, and the high costs of research and development have profound effects on the structure of the industry and the way that the industry competes.

Examples of changes in the way in which products are made include the use of robotics and computers. Their introduction either results in lower costs of production or better quality products or both, although the benefits of the application of computers is often over rated. Advances in material science include the use of ceramics and carbon-based material where once only metal would have been found.

An example of change in services would be the steady growth in the use of the internet for retailing and financial services.

Much has been made of the application of new technologies to communications and business, particularly the internet and other high technology, and 'third wave' technologies, based on information (the first wave was agriculture based and the second wave was industry based). However, it is worth noting that the effect of these, on productivity and so on, tends to be rather overrated. Professor John Kay recently observed that the new technologies rarely enable anyone to do anything new, and are not always any more efficient than existing techniques. Further, the late twentieth century has seen a return to the use of fossil fuels. Although scientific advance in genetics and biotechnology are impressive, these have yet to make significant differences to the consumers.

KEY POINT

The technological environment determines the type of products that are made or services sold. It also determines the way in which products are made or services provided.

3.6 Problems with using PEST

Creating and using a PEST analysis often has two particular problems.

- That of classifying PEST factors – it is not always clear which environment is the source of an important issue. For example, is a trade tariff against imports a political, economic or legal issue? Derivatives of PEST such as SLEPT, STEEP and PESTLE may sometimes help, but equally they may add to the confusion.

- The degree of uncertainty that will always be present when we are trying not only to identify the present environment but also to forecast possible changes in the environments. The extent of a threat from a possible change in an environment depends on two factors that are difficult to predict: the impact of the event on the entity; and the probability of the event occurring.

DEFINITION

SWOT analysis:

'A critical assessment of the Srengths and Weaknesses, Opportunities and Threats (SWOT analysis) in relation to the internal and environmental factors affecting an entity in order to establish its condition prior to the preparation of the long term plan.' *(CIMA: Management Accounts: Official Terminology).*

4 SWOT analysis

4.1 The concept

When developing strategy, the organisation's current strengths, weaknesses, opportunities and threats need to be ascertained. The work involved draws on the data obtained about objectives, current position, extrapolated position, gaps and environmental forecasts, and is sometimes called corporate appraisal.

Corporate appraisal is 'A critical assessment of the strengths and weaknesses, opportunities and threats (SWOT analysis) in relation to the internal and environmental factors affecting an entity in order to establish its condition prior to the preparation of the long term plan' (*CIMA: Management Accounts: Official Terminology*).

The factors involved in SWOT analysis are wide ranging and include decision variables which strengthen or constrain the operational powers of the company, such as the size of its markets, the competitive forces in the markets, opportunities for new products, availability of skilled labour, control of vital raw materials and access to additional capital.

4.2 Competence and competitive profile

The appraisal process will raise serious questions and may produce surprises. The findings need to be compiled into a presentation format which will take the form of what Ansoff refers to as a Competence and Competitive Profile. If correctly formatted and presented, the document will be a succinct summary of the appraisal and will concentrate management's attention on the main areas for resolution. The company profile provides details of current and projected corporate resources in terms of capacity, location, costs, operational flexibility, relevant details of past operational performances and trends, by activities, divisions and cost centres, as well as a survey of the major influences and pressure points impacting on the operational environment, such as target markets, market shares, competitive activities, product mix, technological factors, economic trends and assumptions.

4.3 SWOT analysis

KEY POINT

SWOT analysis is an important tool as it enables management to focus on the core competencies of the organisation.

The SWOT analysis is an essential tool in strategy formulation as it focuses the mind of management on the essential aspects of core competence. There is no hard and fast rule for the timing of the analysis. SWOT takes place at the start of the strategy formulation process. It therefore drives the formulation of strategy. SWOT takes place after a position audit and highlights the resources and weaknesses identified. It serves to summarise the key issues in an economical way.

John Argenti suggests that the SWOT analysis should be no larger than a flip chart and suggests the cruciform style shown below. The example shown illustrates the SWOT analysis for a shipping company.

STRENGTHS	WEAKNESSES
Ability to offer stockholding facilities Knowledge of Baltic market Self-reliant site management Low cost base Quality and flexibility Shipping of other products	Reliance on the Russian market Low profile in marketing The strong £ sterling Under-utilisation of the key Flixborough site
OPPORTUNITIES	THREATS
Expansion of ship management Emerging markets in Baltic States Steel, pulp and cement cargoes Captive customer syndrome through stock management schemes	German ship owners Competitors Spoiling tactics of overseas agencies Uncertainties in the value of euro Level of UK interest rates.

Table: Example of SWOT analysis for an organisation

The SWOT analysis traditionally focuses on internal and external factors.

Activity 2

Consider the SWOT analysis of a major company that had experienced an uninterrupted period of growth, profits and excellence of over twenty years in the information technology business. What do you see as the likely problems the company will face if it continues to compete in the way it has done in the past?

	Environmental opportunity	Environmental threat
Internal strength	• Rated number 1 in customer service • Highest reputation in user support • Product quality and reliability unparalleled	
Internal weakness	• Growing markets for innovative firms • Customers growing more sophisticated	• Price competition emerging • Product innovation very weak • Customers growing more sophisticated

Feedback to this activity is at the end of the chapter.

4.4 Uses of competence and competitive profile

The competence profile will serve three separate uses for assessment.

- **Assessment of internal strengths and weaknesses** – The competence profile can be used to assess the company's internal resources and to determine the areas in which the company is either very good or very poor. The facts and figures required for the assessment would be obtained from the company's position audit.

- **Assessment of competitiveness** – A part of the appraisal will conduct a competence profile of each of the company's main competitors. Superposition of the company's competence profile with the respective competitive profiles measures the company's competitiveness and determines those areas where the company excels or is deficient.

- **Assessment of external opportunities and threats** – Another part of the appraisal will conduct a competence profile of the company's industry and outside industries. Superposition of these profiles measures the attractiveness, or otherwise, of the company's present industry and other industries. It will also measure the company's 'fit' with its existing industry, and its 'fit' with other industries, thus indicating the chances of a successful entry.

5 Porter's Diamond and the Five Forces model

5.1 Porter's Diamond

Michael Porter, in his book *The Competitive Advantage of Nations*, tries to isolate the national attributes that further competitive advantage in an industry.

His study argues that, for a country's industry to be successful, it needs to have the attributes and relationships shown in the diagram below. He calls this the 'diamond'.

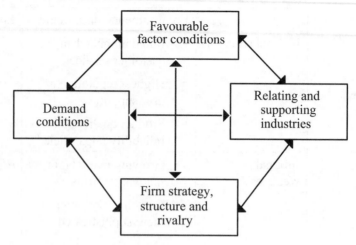

Diagram: Porter's diamond

- **Favourable factor conditions** – factors include the following:
  - physical resources such as land, minerals and weather
  - capital
  - human resources such as skills, motivation, price and industrial relations
  - knowledge that can be used effectively
  - infrastructure.

  Porter also found that countries that had factor disadvantages were forced to innovate to overcome these problems. This innovation has been the basis of competitive advantage, e.g. where nations experienced high energy costs they were forced to develop energy-efficient products and processes that were subsequently demanded worldwide.

- **Demand conditions** – there must be a strong home market demand for the product or service. This determines how industries perceive and respond to buyer needs and creates the pressure to innovate. A compliant domestic market is a disadvantage because it does not force the industry to become innovative and excellent.

- **Relating and supporting industries** – the success of an industry can be due to its suppliers and related industries. Sweden's global superiority in its pulp and paper industries is supported by a network of related industries including packaging, chemicals, wood-processing, conveyor systems and truck manufacture. Many of these supporting industries have also achieved leading global positions.

- **Firm strategy, structure and rivalry** – organisational goals can be determined by ownership structure. Smaller companies may have slightly longer time horizons to operate in because their shares are not traded as much as larger organisations. They might also have different return on capital requirements.

  Porter found that domestic competition was vital as a spur to innovation and also enhanced global competitive advantage. Conversely, where governments have encouraged mergers to reach the critical mass required to be a global player, these national monopolies have not, on the whole, been successful in establishing a global position.

5.2 Porter's five forces model

Porter's five forces model is used to gain insights into the competitiveness of the firm's industry. These forces are illustrated below, and explained in the following subsections.

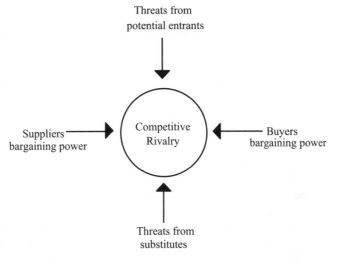

Diagram: Porter's five forces model

It is important to realise in an examination context that the model is concerned with the 'inherent profitability' of an industry (as measured by, say long-term return on investment) and that four of the forces have their effect through intensifying competitive rivalry which in turn impacts on rates of return.

5.3 Threats from potential entrants

New competitors to an industry may make it more competitive in three ways:

- Expanding capacity without necessarily increasing market demand.

- Their need to penetrate the market to achieve critical mass and then build market share, which may include product and marketing innovations.

- Increasing costs as they bid for factors of production.

It is in the interests of existing competitors to deter new entrants. There are seven main barriers to entry.

- Economies of scale.

- Brand (or product) differentiation.

- Capital requirements.

- Switching costs.

- Access to distribution channels.

- Cost disadvantages independent of scale.

- Government regulation (including legal barriers).

Economies of scale

Many industries, such as cement and chemicals, offer increasing returns to scale, and companies benefit by being able to lower unit costs by increasing output volume. Thus potential entrants would be at a considerable cost disadvantage, unless they can immediately set up their operations on a scale large enough to reap similar economies. (This scale is termed the 'critical mass'.) In any case, it might take several years and a heavy investment programme to construct and equip the necessary factories to put them on a competitive footing.

For example, Avon, the cosmetics company, sells part of its line direct to women in their homes, so any company intending to compete on a similar footing would have to:

- recruit and train an efficient sales force skilled in 'party-selling'

- establish warehouses to maintain buffer stocks

- hire a design team to develop a competitive product range

- manufacture and distribute the volume and quality of products required.

Brand (or product) differentiation

Some brands generate a greater consumer loyalty than others and consumers will not be easily lured away by competing products even though they are similar or close substitutes. The cost for a new entrant attempting to penetrate the market in such a situation is likely to be high. The task will involve persuading entrenched consumers to trial their products, perhaps by offering special inducements, such as free samples or gifts. Although the exercise is costly, there is no guarantee of success, particularly as the defending company will combat entry tactics.

Products can be differentiated in terms of: price, quality, brand image, features, distribution, exclusivity, packaging, or value.

For example, Procter & Gamble in the US uses its enormous $500 million media advertising budget to buy and maintain its high market share and deter other companies entering or trying to increase their shares in the markets dominated by P&G products.

Lucas Industries has built up a strong reputation for reliability of supply and quality over the years with the result that almost all British manufactured cars use Lucas lighting. This reputation and market position is sufficient to deter potential competitors.

Capital requirements

This also relates to economies of scale. For example the long-lead, high-cost, high-risk business cycle of the pharmaceutical industry, where the number of successful products reaching the market is relatively small but development costs are between £25m and £50m per product, has deterred all but the largest new companies from entering the market.

Switching costs

These are one-off costs facing a company that switches from one supplier's product to another's. Switching costs may include costs of certification, product redesign, costs and time in assessing a new source, or even the cultural problems of severing a relationship.

For example, In the mid-1970s, FFW-Fokker indicated to British Aerospace (BAe) that it would not tolerate their planned HS-146 aircraft in direct competition against their own existing F28 short-haul jet airliner. Fokker had over 40% of the total cost of both their F-17 and F-28 aircraft supplied by British companies, and indicated that this would be at risk if the HS-146 project continued. BAe correctly considered the threat was not credible since cost shifting (re-design, re-tooling and re-certification for both aircraft using non-British equipment) would be prohibitive to Fokker.

KEY POINT

Products can be differentiated in terms of: price, quality, brand image, features, distribution, exclusivity, packaging, or value.

KEY POINT

Switching costs are one-off costs facing a company that switches from one supplier's product to another's.

Access to distribution channels

One of the biggest dilemmas facing the producer is obtaining shelf or floor space in retail outlets. In order to sell brands the producer must not only persuade the retailer to stock them, but to give them a fair share of shelf/floor space and to feature them periodically. Shelf and floor space is limited (consider here how much high street space an electric dish-washing machine takes to display), and already faced with a bewildering array and assortment of similar products (for example a large Sainsbury store carries some 7,000 products) retail management are not anxious to accept new products, particularly from new entrants lacking a proven track record in the market.

Although BIC, by using its competence in plastics technology, took the initiative by creating the volume market for disposable razors and lighters in the US, it was new to the market and needed to divide its resources between promotion and establishing a national distribution network. BIC did not have the resources to win a battle on two-fronts and leadership went to Gillette.

Cost disadvantages independent of scale

Established companies may have cost advantages not available to potential entrants, no matter what their size and cost levels. Critical factors include: proprietary product technology, favourable locations, learning or experience curve, favourable access to sources of raw materials and government subsidies.

Government regulation (including legal barriers)

Legal restrictions still prevent companies from entering into direct competition with most nationalised industries, while many governments have permitted the establishment of quasi-nationalised bodies controlling marketing operations in milk, eggs, agriculture, etc. Patents and copyright offer inventors some protection against new entrants. Governments also license the right to produce certain categories of products.

Japanese companies use the complexity of the distribution and legal system in Japan to deter potential entrants in the domestic market. Disney spent five years negotiating the licencing agreement for its Tokyo theme Park. Coca-Cola, which now has a 60 percent share of the Japanese soft-drink market, suffered a full decade of red tape, and ROLM, as a small firm, succeeded in Japan but only after senior officers made twenty odd trips, just to conclude the first, tiny sale.

5.4 Threats from substitutes

KEY POINT

Substitutes are alternative products that serve the same purpose, e.g. gas central heating systems in competition with electrical systems.

These are alternative products that serve the same purpose, e.g. gas central heating systems in competition with solid fuel systems. (One of the starkest examples of substitution, and a rapid one at that, was the way in which gas-fired central heating overtook electrical central-heating after the OPEC oil crisis of 1973/74, one result of which was the insolvency of at least one major British company.) The main threat posed by substitutes, though, is that they limit the price that a company can charge for its products. There is also a danger that the threat of a substitute may not be realised until it is too late to arrest their entry. Substitute products that warrant most attention are those that are:

- subject to an environment improving their price-performance trade-off with the industry's product
- produced by industries earning high profits and who have the resources available to bring them rapidly into play.

For example, in 1978 the producers of fibreglass insulation enjoyed unprecedented demand as the result of high energy costs and severe winter weather in the USA. But the industry's ability to raise prices was impeded by the plethora of insulation substitutes, including cellulose, rock wool, and Styrofoam.

5.5 Threats from the bargaining power of buyers

Buyers can reduce profits in an industry by exerting their market power. For example, the concentration of the UK grocery business into a small number of large firms, has allowed those powerful retailers to set high quality targets and low costs. This has dramatically reduced profitability in agricultural markets.

The power used by buyers can have the secondary effect of increasing competitiveness by:

- forcing down prices

- bargaining for higher quality or improved services

- playing competitors against each other

All three of these are at the expense of industry profitability.

Porter purports that the power of the industry's buyer groups depends on the characteristics of its market situation and of the relative importance of its purchases from the industry compared with its overall business. He suggests that buyers are particularly powerful in seven situations, when:

- purchases are large relative to sellers

- purchases represent a significant proportion of the buyers' costs

- purchases are undifferentiated

- buyers earn low profits

- buyers have the potential for backward integration

- the buyer's product is not strongly affected by the quality of the suppliers' product

- the buyer has full information.

KEY POINT

Porter suggests that buyers are powerful in seven situations when: purchases are large relative to sellers, purchases represent a significant proportion of buyers' costs, purchases are undifferentiated, buyers earn low profits, buyers have the potential for backward integration, buyer's product not strongly affected by the quality of the suppliers' product, and buyer has full information.

5.6 Threats from the bargaining power of suppliers

Suppliers can exert bargaining power over companies within an industry in two main ways:

- threatening to raise their prices

- threatening to reduce the quality of their goods and services.

The effect of this power will be to squeeze profitability out of an industry unable to recover cost increases by raising its own prices. This can be seen in the PC business, where software and processor suppliers make great profits, but PC manufacture remains relatively less attractive.

Porter suggests that suppliers are particularly powerful in six situations when:

- there are few suppliers

- there are few substitutes for their products

- the industry supplied is not an important customer

- the supplier's product is an important component to the buyer's business

- the supplier's product is differentiated

- suppliers can integrate forward.

KEY POINT

Porter suggests that suppliers are powerful in six situations when: there are few suppliers, there are few substitutes for their products, the industry supplied is not an important customer, the supplier's product is an important component to the buyer's business, the supplier's product is differentiated, and the supplier can integrate forward.

5.7 Rivalry and competition among competitors

Tactics commonly used to implement competition include product innovations and improvements, price competitions, advertising battles and increased customer services. Rivalry occurs because one or more companies feels threatened or sees a market opportunity to improve its position, although competitive moves by the initiator company usually result in counter-defensive strategies from its competitors. This interactive pattern of offensive and defensive strategies may not leave the initiating company and the industry better off, and on the contrary may leave all the companies in the industry worse off than before.

Porter suggests that there are seven main determinants relating to the strength of internal competition and rivalry within an industry. These are:

- many equally balanced competitors
- slow rate of industrial growth
- lack of differentiation
- capacity can only be increased by large amounts
- high fixed costs in the industry
- there are many diverse competitors
- there are high exit barriers.

5.8 Using Porter's five forces

Inexperienced strategists, and many weak consultants, frequently present a five forces analysis as a series of lists that handle information about the industry well, but don't help to move the strategy forward very much. In this short section, we discuss practical uses of the framework.

Estimating industry attractiveness

The five forces identified by Porter are held to be the ones that determine the level of profits in an industry. For example, in the personal computer business, the power of suppliers (makers of chips and operating systems) is very high, and profits are pulled along the supply chain to that end. In the UK foodstuffs business, the power of buyers – the retailer – is very high, and farm profits have declined as retailers compete with each other on price, forcing down agricultural prices. High profits in an industry will also be lost if cheaper substitutes can be found, or new firms can easily enter the market, increasing competitive pressures and reducing the profitability of existing firms.

After carrying out a five forces analysis, it is possible to judge whether each of the five forces is weak or severe. The more severe the forces, the lower the profits in the industry are likely to be.

Once the severity of the forces is established, it is possible to make inferences about the elements of strategy that are necessary to compete in this business. For example, manufacturers of tin cans are aware that their greatest threat to profitability comes from manufacturers of glass jars (the threat of substitutes), and strategy must be focused on costs to keep under a price that prevents entry (called the limit price in the economics literature). It is common to see firms adopting customer service strategies, which add to cost but not profitability because power of the buyers is weak, or other strategic misalignments. It is important to remember that even when strategies are thought to be intrinsically good – customer service, innovation, management development, excellence, etc – they frequently come at a cost that must be justified in terms of financial results.

Activity 3

How do the five forces help us to understand why European steel companies generally perform poorly?

Feedback to this activity is at the end of the chapter.

6 Data for environmental analysis

6.1 Information as a resource

Organisations are faced with vast amounts of information that they must scan to understand their environment. The main types of information required in making an environmental analysis will cover the following areas.

- **The economic situation** – a multinational company will be concerned about the international situation, while an organisation trading exclusively in one country might be more concerned with the level and timing of domestic development. Items of information relevant to marketing plans might include: changes in the gross domestic product, changes in consumers' income and expenditure, and population growth.

- **Government action** – changes in taxation and subsidies, changes in government spending, import duties, etc.

- **Legal factors** – changes in laws and regulations affecting, for example, competition, patents, sale of goods, pollution, working regulations and industrial standards.

- **Technological factors** – changes in material supply, processing methods and new product development.

The importance of information as a resource cannot be over stressed. As pointed out by Diebold: 'Information, which is in essence the analysis and synthesis of data, will unquestionably be one of the most vital of corporate resources. It will be structured into models for planning and decision-making. It will be integrated into product design and marketing methods. In other words, information will be recognised and treated as an asset.'

6.2 Sources of information

There are many sources of environmental information including:

- economic information from government statistics, trade and banking reports, etc

- market information from specialist libraries, etc.

Economic information is concerned with such factors as gross national product (GNP), investment, expenditure, population, employment, productivity and trade. It provides a company with a picture of past and future trends in the environment and with an indication of the company's position in the economy as a whole.

A great deal of information is freely available in this area from sources such as:

- newspapers and journals providing information ranging from local news in a local paper to issues relating to a particular industry in a trade journal

- government ministries, universities and organisations such as the OECD.

KEY POINT

Economic information is concerned with such factors as gross national product (GNP), investment, expenditure, population, employment, productivity and trade.

Economic forecasts can be bought from various agencies. For example, Predicast provides a continuous review of economic trends, which can be obtained relatively cheaply on a subscription basis.

Market information is information about a company's present or possible future markets. Such information will be both commercial and technical, for example:

- the level of sales of competitors' products recorded by the Business Monitor or Census of Production

- the product range offered by existing or potential competitors

- the number of outlets forming the distribution network for a company's products; the structure of that network by size, location and relation to the end user

- the best overseas markets for a company.

Specialist libraries provide much of this type of information. The Patents Office Library keeps back numbers of nearly all British and many foreign technical journals. The Department of Trade and Industry Expert Intelligence Service has extensive information in its library in the City. The libraries of other ministries contain much valuable information and are very willing to help. The Association of Libraries (Aslib) keeps a record of specialist libraries and can provide the name of a library specialising in, say, the construction industry.

6.3 Information in public and private databases

A **database** is a collection of related information about a subject organised in a useful manner that provides a base or foundation for procedures such as retrieving information, drawing conclusions, and making decisions. In fact, important predecessors of today's sophisticated business database systems were files kept on index cards and stored in filing cabinets. However, using computers for database management is easier than traditional methods.

A database management program allows the computer to sort the records in a few seconds and in several different ways. For example, in a video store's database, you can sort the records by title, category, rating, availability and so on. Furthermore, a database management program can select just those records that meet the criteria you specify in a query. The results of selections or sorts can be displayed on screen or printed in a report.

6.4 The Internet as a source of environmental data

The Internet provides corporate planners with a powerful tool for environmental appraisal. The possibilities are almost without limit:

- **Relations with trading partners** – The use of web-based procurement systems has been exploited by a variety of enterprises who found greater freedom and greater effectiveness over more traditional methods such as electronic data interchange systems. Web-based product catalogues give openness to business transactions. Recently, Japan Airlines published an image of its logo on a cup that was used for in-flight catering systems. The publication was designed to attract potential suppliers who wanted to tender for the supply of cups with the JAL logo.

The accessibility of information creates new horizons for research.

- **Commercial intelligence** – Government agencies now all have websites and information is readily available from a variety of bodies such as Companies House, the Bank of England and internationally recognised credit intelligence agencies such as Dun and Bradstreet. It is possible to search for information that is in the public domain with freedom and flexibility.

    Specialised information is available for a fee. Marketing consultancies offer specialist information that may be strategically sensitive to subscribers over the internet.

- **Specialist on-line databases** – Access is possible to specialist on-line databases. NIMIS Ltd is a specialist company in Newcastle specialising in tools to search internet databases for e-commerce. The University of Bath delivers on-line journals to members of the academic community. The World Conservation Monitoring Centre provides information services on conservation and sustainable use of the world's living resources.

Summary

The key points of this chapter are:

- There are verious methods that can be used to understand the business environment. PEST (or derivatives) is a widely used technique for thinking about events, trends and patterns that will require the business to change its strategy and operations. Porter's 'Diamond' is a model that is used to capture the influence of the home environment on the future of an industry in a global economy. His theory of the competitive advantage of nations takes as its key a 'diamond' of factors that makes some nations (and consequently their industries) more competitive than others.

- Strategic planners are being challenged by the changes in their business environments – internationalism, nationalism, protectionism, environmentalism, recession, inflation, shortages, technological developments, legislation and population shifts. Political, economic, social and cultural, technological, legal and demographic factors are all ingredients in the mix of environmental problems faced by strategic planners.

- The main environmental factors that affect global business strategy are competition, markets, government regulations and technology. These factors are so powerful that it is becoming necessary for organisations to incorporate them into their corporate planning and strategy.

- The objectives of a corporate appraisal are to bring together all the strands of data concerning the company's objectives, present position, extrapolated position, strategic gaps and environmental forecasts, and to profile the company's strengths, weaknesses, opportunities and threats (SWOT analysis). The profile will be conducted for the company's internal, competitive, and industry 'fit' positions. The information provides important, if not vital, information for strategic management, about the company's position, the extent of strategic change required and when, the resources that are available and the direction the organisation ought to be aiming for. By highlighting the company's strengths, weaknesses, opportunities and threats, the profiles produced also provide management with ideas as to how gaps might best be closed.

Having completed your study of this chapter you should have achieved the following learning outcomes:

- evaluate the nature of competitive environments, distinguishing between simple and complicated competitive environments

- distinguish the difference between static and dynamic competitive environments

- evaluate strategies for response to competition

- evaluate the impact and influence of the external environment on an organisation and its strategy.

Self-test questions

1   In the context of systems, define environment. (2.1)

2   What are the three basic forms of environmental influence upon an organisation? (2.2)

3   Specify four types of business environment characterised by change. (2.4)

4   What does PEST stand for? (3.1)

5   What is the trade cycle? (3.3)

6   What aspects of the social framework are relevant to business? (3.4)

7   Define corporate appraisal. (4.1)

8   What is the purpose of a competence profile? (4.2)

9   What does SWOT stand for? (4.3)

10   Draw Porter's diamond and briefly explain each of the elements. (5.1)

11   Summarise Porter's five forces model. (5.2)

12   Which main types of information are required in making an environmental analysis? (6.1)

Practice questions

Question 1: Strengths and Weaknesses

In ascertaining an organisation's strengths and weaknesses, management often concentrate on certain key areas.

Required:

Specify and describe five key areas and explain the way that an assessment of this type may be conducted.

(20 marks)

Question 2: Competitive forces and barriers to entry

Strategic planning is concerned with the task of choosing directions and areas of concentration for an organisation, and the strategic planning process is affected by the nature of the environment.

Required:

(a)   Identify four competitive forces in the environment of a firm and discuss the threat posed to the firm by each of these forces.

(b)   Discuss the nature and effect of significant 'entry barriers' on the formulation of a strategic plan for a business which is already established in the industry.

(25 marks)

For the answers to these questions, see the 'Answers' section at the end of the book.

Feedback to activities

Activity 1

(i)   An example of a simple and dynamic environment is one where the product is only being sold in one market (simple) and where the product is still in the introduction stage and demand might be predicted to increase dramatically (dynamic). Virtual reality games in leisure arcades could fit this description.

(ii) The environment of a group of research scientists working for a pharmaceutical company, funded by an international grant to investigate genetic disorders, might be classified as stable and complex. The stability arises because of the grant which means that they will not be exposed to cuts in funding. The complexity is in the amount of knowledge required which is drawn from different disciplines and is uncertain in its future discoveries.

Activity 2

Looking at the SWOT in order of priority, we see price competition and product innovation rising, but the firm in question has a poor record in innovation and, with its high quality and service expenses, is probably more expensive than the industry average. Sophisticated consumers might not need so much customer service and support, and if innovation is increasing, products may become obsolete before they wear out, reducing the advantage of superior product quality. If nothing is done, the firm will soon be trying to sell inferior products at high prices – a losing scenario in the longer term.

In fact, this is largely what did happen. The firm continued to benchmark against competitors, but did not notice that the critical success factors had changed. It had developed resources and competencies that were not particularly effective in competing in the changed market.

Activity 3

The five forces for steel are adverse, often severely so. There are many companies, often subsidised by national governments, and threat of entry is always high, through subsidised exports or acquisition of foreign steel merchants. The fixed costs in the industry are very high, which puts pressure on prices because individual firms are always tempted to discount to increase contribution, lowering industry prices generally. The number of substitutes is growing for an ever-wider number of applications. Users of steel are generally large companies – auto manufacturers and so on, who have a wide choice and can switch suppliers easily. The merchants themselves are often very large. Consequently, in most years the steel sector performs poorly, doing well only when the world economy is expanding.

Chapter 3

REGULATION IN MAJOR MARKETS

Syllabus content

- Regulation in major markets (WTO, EU, NAFTA, Asia-Pacific).
- Country analysis and political risk.

Contents

1 Introduction

2 Political forces

3 Major markets

4 Barriers to international trade

5 Free trade agreements

6 Global business regulation

1 Introduction

Regulation of business activities has become an increasingly global matter, especially since the 1970s, because of the growth of international trade, because of the emergence of environmental concerns that affect the whole planet, and because of changes in worldwide attitudes and politics that make it desirable to help developing nations rather than exploit them for their resources.

In this chapter we will look at the wide variety of regulatory regimes that organisations have to take into account when formulating their business strategy, and some of the current issues. The subject is vast, and we are really only scratching the surface.

2 Political forces

2.1 Politics

The ways in which government policies might influence future corporate strategy are difficult to forecast. Government's policies in respect to interest rates, exchange rates, taxation levels, incentive schemes, public expenditure levels, consumer and worker protection, restrictive practices, and environment protection will all be ingredients in the political environment facing enterprises.

Porter identifies seven ways in which the government can affect the structure of an industry.

- **Capacity expansion**. The government can take actions to encourage firms or an industry as a whole to increase or cut capacity. Examples include capital allowances to encourage investment in equipment; regional incentives (perhaps funded by the EU) to encourage firms to locate new capacity in a particular area, and incentives to attract investment from overseas firms. The government is also (directly or indirectly) a supplier of infrastructure such as roads and railways, and this may influence expansion in a particular area.

- **Demand**. The government is a major customer of business in all areas of life and can influence demand by buying more or less. It can also influence demand by legislative measures. The tax system for cars is a good example: a change in the tax reliefs available for different engine sizes has a direct effect on the car manufacturers' product and the relative numbers of each type produced. Regulations and controls in an industry will affect the growth and profits of the industry, e.g. minimum product quality standards.

- **Divestment and exit**. A firm may wish to sell off a business to a foreign competitor or close it down, but the government might prevent this action because it is not in the public interest (there could be examples in health, defence, transport, education, agriculture and so on).

- **Emerging industries** may be controlled by the government. For instance the UK government offered only five licences to create networks for third generation (3G) mobile phones.

- **Entry barriers.** Government policy may restrict investment or competition or make it harder by use of quotas and tariffs for overseas firms. This kind of protectionism is generally frowned upon by the World Trade Organisation, but there may be political and economic circumstances in which it becomes necessary.

- **Competition policy**. Governments might devise policies which are deliberately intended to keep an industry fragmented, preventing one or two producers from having too much market share. In the UK, the Monopolies and Mergers Commission regulates the growth of monopolies.

- **New product adoption**. Governments regulate the adoption of new products (new drugs, for instance) in some industries. They may go so far as to ban the use of a new product if it is not considered safe (a new form of transport, say). Policies may influence the rate of adoption of new products: for instance the UK government intends to 'switch off' the analogue television networks sometime between 2006 and 2010, effectively forcing users to buy digital cable or satellite services.

2.2 Planning for political change

The problem facing strategic planners is how to plan for changes in the political environment. As change is not predictable; the planner needs to approach the problem by considering what type of political change could affect the enterprise rather than trying to estimate all the political changes that might occur.

The trend of political actions can be co-related to changes in social behaviour and values, economic activity, and problems arising from the physical infrastructure or environment. Additionally there are a number of indicators of possible, or intended, future government actions and policy. These indicators are obtained from:

- annual conferences of political parties

- public utterances of party leaders and seniors

- international events

- directives from international trading groups (in the case of the UK, the EC directives)

- political commentators and analysts

- international summit meetings

- staged legislation

- efforts of public pressure groups (particularly with regard to local government policy)

- political manifesto.

2.3 Legislation and regulations

This is a complicated area covering companies acts, employment legislation (determining the basic employment rights), health and safety regulations, consumer legislation (credit regulations, etc) and so on. There is an almost endless list of laws, or categories of legislation, that affect business enterprises in domestic, national or international dimensions. The main categories are listed below:

- local by-laws (planning permission, construction of roads, licences, etc)

- labour legislation (safety at work, employee protection, redundancy payments, etc)

- trade union legislation

- consumer protection legislation

- company legislation

- taxation legislation

- anti-trust (monopolies) legislation and rulings

- trade legislation (countries restricted for export, etc)

- business legislation (contract and agency law, etc)

- social legislation (welfare benefits, etc).

The law constitutes a set of environmental factors that are increasingly affecting strategic decisions. Most of the nations of the world are, or are becoming, regulated economies. Government, or self, regulation of business has four principal aims:

- to protect business entities from each other, such as laws putting limits on market dominance

- to protect consumers from business entities, with detailed consumer protection regulations covering packaging, labelling, food hygiene and advertising, and much more

- to protect employees from their employers, with laws that govern the recruitment of staff and health and safety legislation that regulates conditions of work

- to protect the larger interests of society against excessive business behaviour.

Also at the most basic level, perhaps, laws are passed that enable government to levy taxes; whereas company law affects the corporate structure of the business, and prescribes the duties of company directors.

Strategic planners cannot plan intelligently without a good working knowledge of the laws and regulations that affect their own companies and the businesses they operate in. There are special regulatory regimes for particular industries or sectors, e.g. nuclear energy, transport, broadcasting or food. Planners should also know the reasons for the laws, and how they are being interpreted in the courts. They also need to be aware of the many local government by-laws affecting the conduct of their plans. The laws are numerous, most of which you would have studied at your earlier examination stages.

Legislation adapts slowly relative to some other environmental segments, with the exception of company legislation and self-regulation which has seen lots of changes in recent years. In fact, particularly in respect to labour and consumer protection, organisations often pre-empt legislation by providing more than the statutory requirements. However, legislation is becoming more complex, particularly for those companies that trade internationally where the interface, indeed probable conflict, between domestic laws, the host country's laws, and probably also the laws of the trading block of nations the host country belongs to, provides an extremely complicated legal scenario. The legislation associated with the Single European Market gives evidence to this kind of legal complexity.

3 Major markets

3.1 Multinational companies (MNCs)

The market for many goods and services today is international, if not global. Companies therefore develop businesses in several international markets and get involved in overseas ventures. A company may export to one country, license to another, acquire a subsidiary in a third and have a joint-ownership venture in a fourth.

The driving force behind the growth and expansion of MNCs is the belief that vertically integrated companies linked by a global strategic plan should possess a distinct competitive advantage over under-capitalised and technologically-backward local companies in the exploitation of any potentially profitable overseas markets. The reasons why MNCs possess this distinctive advantage are reasonably clear.

- Effectiveness in mobilising, directing and controlling their resources.

- Better opportunities of achieving economies of scale because of their larger production base and market horizons.

- Able to draw on a wealth of corporate experience in strategic planning, forecasting, market research, finance, production and marketing (particularly in the fields of product positioning, pricing, advertising and promotional budgeting, and distribution).

- Ability to keep in close and constant touch with their overseas subsidiaries by the use of high capacity cable, distributed database systems, satellite communications, and efficient airline systems.

Most modern multinational companies (MNC) possess the following characteristics.

- They comprise overseas subsidiaries that are complete industrial and/or commercial organisations covering research and development, manufacturing, selling and after-sales activities.

- There is involvement in numerous countries, which may be at different stages of economic and political development.

- The formulation of a universally accepted and understood corporate policy for the guidance and direction of the overseas subsidiaries in pursuit of declared aims and objectives.

Environmental factors that shape international business strategy can be grouped into four major forces:

- **Competition** – One of the most important characteristics of competition is that it is global. Practically all advanced countries are experiencing competition from abroad. There are few protected industries or regulated monopolies left in the world and even such areas as telecommunications, airlines, and stock market exchanges are becoming privately owned.

  Competition is no longer limited to the more advanced countries of the world and there is a big rise in multinational companies in places such as Brazil, India, Korea and Taiwan. In fact, in many sectors of the world's economy, it is multinational companies from the less developed nations that are dominant. This is particularly so in the areas of agriculture, cut diamonds, textiles, and other low value-added products or commodities. Korea and Taiwan have demonstrated their global competitiveness in products such as consumer electronics.

- **Markets** – One of the characteristics of markets is that customers are becoming global in their orientation. It is not only the industrial and business customers who procure their products or services from global sources, so do the ordinary consumers. Examples of this are consumer electronics, garments, cars, appliances, and even foods and beverages, all of which carry a mixture of domestic and foreign brand names in most countries of the world. The customer, therefore, has expectations of quality, service, and affordability based on world standards. Domestic products such as cars and television sets may not be considered reliable or user friendly once the customer has experienced products from abroad.

- **Regulations and free trade** – There has been a big change over the years in the formation of regional economic alliances such as the European Union (EU) and the freedom of world trade through GATT (General Agreement on Tariffs and Trade) negotiations. Such changes have softened national geographic boundaries for products and services.

  Less developed countries such as India and China have made significant demands upon the multinationals. This has caused a significant change in corporate strategy, structure and even corporate culture. IBM and General Motors, for example, have accepted strategic alliances as the only way of doing business in some countries, despite having strong preferences toward wholly owned subsidiaries.

  Currency exchange rules and regulations and the floating of hard currencies such as the US dollar and the British pound have also had a dramatic impact on the cash flow and pricing decisions by businesses.

  It has become important, therefore, for enterprises to utilise the tools and processes of a political economy, by lobbying through political action committees (PACs), legislative reforms, and government intervention.

- **Technology** – Technology is available worldwide, especially in areas such as electronics and mechanics. Technical barriers across national borders are easily overcome and it is as easy for a less developed country to produce high quality electronic products such as personal computers and television sets as it is for an advanced country.

  Life spans of technologies are also getting shorter and shorter. It is, therefore, becoming necessary to recover capital as soon as 'new technology' is installed. It is less and less desirable to think local first and global second when a business is about to invest in technology as that technology will rapidly become obsolete. Instead, businesses must think globally in relation to product design, manufacturing capacity, and marketing issues.

> **KEY POINT**
>
> It is less and less desirable to think local first and global second when a business is about to invest in technology as that technology will rapidly become obsolete.

3.2 Opportunities of global competition

The opportunities available to an international company arise from different sources, such as the following.

- An inherent national advantage used to gain comparative advantage abroad (e.g. low labour costs in Taiwan and Korea relative to other countries).

- Production economies of scale. In some industries such as steel and car manufacture the minimum efficiency production unit is too great for solely national demand so exporting from a central base will out-compete national producers.

- Operating worldwide may allow necessarily high fixed costs incurred nationally for logistical needs to be recouped, e.g. specialised cargo ships.

- Marketing economies of scale.

- Choices in location. It may be cheaper to produce parts in one country and assemble them in another, and it may be more effective to locate fundamental R&D in a third country. The global company can choose the most advantageous locations for different parts of the business.

- Experience curve advantages. Organisations can gain opportunities from sharing resources and experiences across countries.

- Differentiate with multinational buyers. Where the organisation's customers are multinational, there may be opportunities to organise on a global scale to service them, e.g. consider the trend for accountancy practices to go global to give a better service to their multinational clients.

Activity 1

Describe an organisation or industry that chooses advantageous locations for different parts of its business.

Feedback to this activity is at the end of the chapter.

3.3 Threats to global competition

The scope for global competition is limited by the following factors:

- National tastes and needs can be markedly different, e.g. the German beer trade is strongly regionalised in taste, the opportunities for an imported or licence-manufactured standardised beer being poor.

- Lead times may be critical and only a national company on the spot can provide the service dictated.

- Access to established distribution channels may be blocked.

- Terms of trading may require local ownership or provision of local sales and servicing organisations.

- Government impediments through tariffs, subsidies to national producers, tax regulations, etc.

3.4 The complexity of international operations

KEY POINT

Operational activities conducted on an international scale are far more complex than those confined to the domestic field.

Operational activities conducted on an international scale are far more complex than those confined to the domestic field.

- Communication with subsidiaries is more difficult, documentation procedures tend to lengthen the delivery chain, while the lack of immediate and close contact with overseas customers tends to escalate trivial complaints over such matters as quality and reliability into major issues.

- Where the MNC is a leader in its industry, the problems of the industry tend to hit the MNC more heavily than a smaller company. Industrial problems are often compounded by oil price rises, sluggish development of the home market, industrial disputes, inflation, high interest rates, and world recession.

- Restrictions are imposed by host governments. Whereas the MNC will be principally concerned with prospective return on its capital invested, the host government will be concerned with:

    - number of local people employed, and wage rates paid

    - contribution of the MNC to the local GNP

    - percentage of control exercised by nationals

    - imposition of taxes

    - transfer pricing

    - environmental pollution

    - degree to which the MNC can assist in strengthening the home industrial base.

- The co-ordination and control of activities raises unique problems when dealing with a heterogeneous group of overseas companies operating in countries with a diverse range of cultures and languages at different stages of industrial, commercial and social development, and with no apparent common purchasing behavioural patterns,. There is no folklore to which companies can refer, and central management has to develop its own set of rules, procedures and principles.

- Exchange rate fluctuations, transfer of capital into and out of subsidiaries, and cross border transfer pricing.

- The split between centralised and decentralised control, i.e. the degree of independence to be given to (or taken by) overseas subsidiaries.

- Deployment of limited resources for investment, and the reconciliation of potentially divisive needs and demands of overseas companies and countries.

- Reconciliation of conflicting pressures from overseas markets which are subject to different cultures, political climates, language, geography, time zones, buying behaviour patterns, buying power and susceptibility to advertising and promotion campaigns.

- The growing complexity of the legal environments affecting MNCs. Basically, a government can only effectively legislate for the activities of those of its citizens and companies living or operating within its boundaries. At law, most countries appear to regard MNCs and their overseas affiliates as part of a unitary enterprise, but the plain fact is that national governments accord anti-trust measures and restrictive practices different levels of priority. The regulations of the European Community are a minefield for MNCs.

3.5 Country analysis

Country analysis attempts to answer questions such as the following.

- How has the economic condition of Kenya changed over the last 10 years as measured by macroeconomic indicators – including GDP, inflation, trade balance, exchange rates, etc?

- How many mobile phones were sold in China last year; who were the top competitors in this market; and what were their respective market shares?

- How stable is the government in Venezuela from the perspective of a prospective American investor?

International business is really a collection of domestic industries, where competitive advantage in one country is more or less independent of competition in the others. Therefore many of the activities involved in production, marketing and servicing need to be **tailored** to the particular requirements of the country. This tailoring is critical to competitive advantage.

Strategic planners therefore need a wealth of information about the countries in which they intend to do business.

- Economic conditions and latest indicators: domestic data (GDP, inflation, interest rates, unemployment, etc); forecasts for commodities prices and estimates for manufactured goods, exchange rates and so on.

- Industry reviews: status reports on the condition of an industry in a particular country.

- Distribution, sales and marketing information, for example how consumer markets are segmented, current sales trends, demographic data (population, life expectancy, languages, literacy rates, etc).

- Infrastructure, e.g. the quality of the road infrastructure.

- Banking and financial markets – the credibility of the central banks, for instance, and the availability of sources of finance.

- Local business regulations.

- Human resources: what skills are available?

- Political structure and developments.

- Legislative differences, tax rules.

- The degree of interdependence between the national and global economies and susceptibility to changes in the global economy.

Up to date and accurate information may be relatively easy to collect for developed countries but it is increasingly likely that the planner will want information on emerging markets, especially in Africa, the Middle East, Asia, and Latin America, and this is much harder to find.

Large multinationals may have their own people responsible for country analysis but the majority will also make extensive use of the specialist services of organisations such as LexisNexis and the Economist Intelligence Unit.

3.6 Political risk

A major issue involved in international business is political risk. We examine this under the headings of confiscation political risk, commercial political risk and financial political risk.

Confiscation political risk

A subsidiary in a stable industrialised country may seem free from the risk of confiscation, but as a parent company reviews the list beginning with countries vulnerable to changes of regime, e.g. Chile, or invasion by powerful neighbours, e.g. Lebanon, passing on to countries in which a transition to local ownership is already law, e.g. India, then to countries in which confiscation is a very real possibility, it must be prepared for principled or unprincipled expropriation, nationalisation, or mere interference with its control and management or its ability to operate, and with anything from full to zero compensation.

KEY POINT

The parent company can respond to political risk in part by the way it finances the subsidiary.

The parent company can respond to this risk in part by the way it finances the subsidiary, and sometimes by confiscation insurance. In the UK the Export Credits Guarantee Department (ECGD) operates a confiscation cover scheme for new overseas investments only, and Lloyds offers such a cover for existing and new investments in comprehensive (non-selective) form.

The financing tactics which minimise this risk consist of:

- high gearing

- minimising intra-group sources of finance

- maximising finance from local sources

- subject to the above, avoiding parent group guarantees

- in suitable cases to have the subsidiary partly owned by local shareholders.

The literature lays much stress on the need to value the risk. What is sometimes overlooked is the commercial consequences of confiscation: it may deprive the group of access to a significant share of the world market. The critical issue may be which competitor will gain that share.

Commercial political risk

There are other forms of commercial discrimination against foreign-controlled companies. Protectionist authorities can starve them of orders, give commercial or financial advantages to locally-owned competitors, restrict import licences for imported materials or products, or refuse work permits to expatriate staff.

The financing responses to these risks are much the same as to expropriation above. The selling of equity to local shareholders, by creating a national lobby, may be the most effective way to make the authorities sensitive to the needs of the local foreign investment.

Financial political risk

This risk takes many forms:

- Restricted access to local borrowings. This is sometimes discriminatory against foreign-owned enterprises. Access is often barred or restricted particularly to the cheapest forms of finance from local banks and development funds. Some countries ration all access for foreign investments to local sources of funds, to force the company to import foreign exchange into the country.

- Restrictions on repatriating capital, dividends or other remittances. These can take the form of prohibition or penal taxation.

- Financial penalties on imports from the rest of the group such as heavy interest-free import deposits.

Financing policies to deal with these risks are often difficult. If access is merely barred to the cheaper local funds, the economics of using the more expensive sources of local money must be analysed against the economics and risks of using non-local funds. Where it is not possible to remit dividends, the parent must appraise how fundamental dividends are to its objectives in investing in the company.

Exchange control risk

This risk is not necessarily different from the others, and some specific exchange controls have already been referred to in the above forms of risk. The purest form of exchange control risk is that the group may accumulate surplus cash in the country where the subsidiary operates, either as profits or as amounts owed for imports to the subsidiary, which cannot be remitted out of the country.

However, in financing investments in such countries, it may well pay to have as much local debt as possible, which can often be repaid from such blocked funds if they arise. A low equity also makes it easier to accept restrictions on remittances of capital or profits.

4 Barriers to international trade

4.1 The benefits of international trading

International trade becomes necessary when a nation specialises so that its surpluses can be exchanged for the surpluses of other countries. In theory, free trade between nations is desirable but often, in practice, various forms of protectionism are used.

Specialisation benefits world trade, because it enables different nations, with differing worker skills and resources, to gain the rewards from the division of labour. In theory, nations specialise in the production of goods for which they have a natural advantage. For instance, Saudi Arabia extracts oil, Argentina rears beef and Britain provides financial services. Specialisation usually enables an industry to benefit from large-scale production, thus making the maximum use of resources. Such efficiency has benefits for the trading economies because it should lead to lower prices and better products, and thus improvements in general living standards.

World trade, particularly free trade, should foster competition. A domestic market which is controlled by a monopolist might be subject to a foreign competitor. Alternatively, complacent national consumer goods industries might be revitalised by the entry of foreign firms, e.g. Japanese and American companies. Such competition will usually benefit the consumers through lower prices and greater choice. However, these benefits perhaps need to be considered in relation to the loss of employment in domestic industries.

4.2 The limits to trade

The advantages which can be gained from specialisation and international trade may be limited in practice by many of the following elements:

- **Factor immobility** – Free trade theory assumes that factors are perfectly mobile, thereby enabling resources to be shifted between different sectors of production.

- **Transport costs** – Although the production of certain bulky intermediate goods, such as cement, may be cheaper abroad, the distribution costs are so great that domestic suppliers still have a stronghold over the market. However, transport costs in world trade are generally falling, thereby stimulating trade.

- **The size of the market** – Specialisation and the resultant possible economies of scale are only justified if the production can be sold. The attempts to build a British computer industry between 1975 and 1985 largely foundered because the domestic market was too small at that time to sustain the research needed for competition with international giants, such as the American companies.

- **Trading policies** – There are many restrictions on trade in the real world and these discourage specialisation. Trade may be deliberately limited by a government for political reasons.

4.3 Protectionism

In practice many barriers to free trade exist because governments try to protect home industries against foreign competition. Protectionist measures include the following.

- **Tariffs** or **customs duties**. These are taxes on imported goods. A tariff raises the price of imported goods for domestic consumers (and so makes them less attractive), but leaves the price paid to foreign producers the same, or even lower.

- **Import quotas** restrict the quantity of a product that can be imported. An **embargo** on imports is a total ban, usually imposed on a particular country, for example during a war or if the political regime in that country is regarded as undesirable.

- **Government subsidies** and assistance for exports include export credit guarantees (insurance against bad debts for overseas sales) and government grants.

- Government deterrents (**non-tariff barriers**) against imports may include complicated and time-consuming import regulations and documentation, strict safety standards for imported goods, and so on.

4.4 The arguments for protectionism

Many arguments have been put forward at different times to support import restrictions, but few have any economic logic. Free trade and specialisation, arising from differences in comparative costs, will result in the long-term maximisation of output and economic welfare. Let us examine some of the oft–quoted arguments.

- Keeping money in the country. Mercantilists of the 17th century frequently expressed the view that an excess of exports over imports would make the country rich by, in effect, boosting aggregate demand. Indeed, this was the essence of parts of de Gaulle's economic policy for France in the 1950s. The major flaw in the argument is that a country that exports much and imports little is depriving its population of goods and services, thereby reducing the domestic standard of living.

- Tariffs are not designed to raise revenue, and if they are effective and completely block imports of certain goods then the revenue will be zero. As to the effect of employment: firstly, the imposition of tariffs may lead to a retaliatory tariff war against your exports, reducing demand and employment. Secondly, domestic production of the goods may be so costly compared to the cheaper imports that it absorbs too much of the consumption, depriving other areas and again creating unemployment.

- The most often used 'emotional' argument centres on the desire to protect industry from 'cheap foreign labour'. On this basis it is sometimes proposed that a 'scientific tariff' should be introduced, designed to equalise foreign costs and domestic costs. However, the economic logic of this proposal is very specious. Such a tariff would end all foreign trade completely. Moreover, although foreigners may receive lower wages, it is still possible that output cost per unit is higher than that of the UK because of their lower capital utilisation per worker.

- Strategic industries. Many governments impose trade restrictions because they wish to pursue objectives other than output maximisation. Examples would be the desire to maintain output of the armament and agricultural industries for strategic purposes.

- Another more reasonable argument for interfering with international trade is the infant industry hypothesis. It is suggested that a newly developing industry requires some kind of protection so that it can develop to the point where it can compete. Similarly, a young economy may wish to diversify its activities so that, for example, it can reduce its dependence on a limited number of primary products whose price is likely to fluctuate quite dramatically. The major problem arising from this argument is the determination of exactly when the infant industry or economy has achieved sufficient maturity to be able to compete satisfactorily. It is natural for such industries to suggest constantly that this stage has not yet been reached.

4.5 The arguments against protectionism

- **Inefficiency is encouraged** - If a nation's firms are protected from competition they may settle for their existing market share and profits. Such complacency will discourage innovation and risk-taking. New technology may not be introduced and over-manning may persist. The protected industry may lobby to make temporary help permanent.

- **Resources are misallocated** – By maintaining the existing patterns of trade, resources do not move from declining industries, which are protected, to expanding industries. In addition, protection for one industry (e.g. steel) may adversely affect others (e.g. buyers of steel) because unit costs are raised.

- **The cost of living is raised** – Protection will probably raise prices and so domestic consumers will have to pay higher prices for (the taxed) imported goods or for the (protected) home produced goods. Higher prices reduce the consumer surplus.

- **Welfare gains will be lost** – The welfare gains resulting from specialisation-trade-exchange will be restricted if trade is limited.

- **Retaliation may occur** – Protection by one nation may provoke its trading partners to take similar action and this will reduce the volume of world trade with the attendant consequences outlined above.

5 Free trade agreements

5.1 The World Trade Organisation (WTO)

The WTO, based in Geneva, was formed in 1995 as successor to the General Agreement on Tariffs and Trade (GATT). The GATT was established in 1947 in the wake of the Second World War as an attempt to promote free trade.

Between 1947 and 1994, GATT was the forum for negotiating lower customs duty rates and removing other trade barriers, and it spelt out important rules, particularly non-discrimination. The 'most favoured nation' principle applies, meaning that if a member country offers a reduction in tariffs to another country it must offer the same reduction to all other member countries.

The WTO has 147 members, accounting for over 97% of world trade. Around 30 others are negotiating membership. Russia is the most notable non-member at the time of publication: it has very recently signed a protocol with the EU countries on its terms for entry to the WTO, but has still to reach agreement with some other major players, notably the US, who need to be convinced that it has reformed business practices.

- GATT, as updated in 1995, is the WTO's umbrella agreement for trade in goods. It has annexes dealing with specific sectors such as agriculture and textiles, and with specific issues such as state trading, product standards, subsidies and actions taken against dumping. Average tariffs among industrialised economies have been reduced to around five percent. Average tariffs among developing countries are between 15 and 20 percent.

- The General Agreement on Trade in Services (GATS), also dating from 1995, means that banks, insurance firms, telecommunications companies, tour operators, hotel chains and transport companies that do business abroad now enjoy the same principles of free and fairer trade that originally only applied to trade in goods.

- The WTO's Agreement on Trade-Related Aspects of Intellectual Property Rights (TRIPS) sets rules for trade and investment in ideas and creativity. The rules state how copyrights, patents, trademarks, geographical names used to identify products, industrial designs, integrated circuit layout-designs and undisclosed information such as trade secrets should be protected when trade is involved.

WTO decisions are absolute and every member must abide by its rulings. WTO members are empowered by the organisation to enforce its decisions by imposing trade sanctions against countries that have breached the WTO rules.

5.2 The Doha round

The WTO conducts its business through 'rounds' of trade negotiations, typically taking several years and named after the place at which the negotiations commenced. The latest round began in 2001 in Doha in Qatar, and continued in Cancun in Mexico in 2003.

- A leading goal is to reduce protection of **agriculture**, which remains the most highly subsidised and restricted sector of world trade. Subsidies and tariffs remain very high (tariffs of over 100 percent are common).

KEY POINT

The WTO has 147 members, accounting for over 97% of world trade. GATT, now administered by the WTO, has lowered customs duty rates and removed other trade barriers, and spelt out important rules, particularly non-discrimination (the 'most favoured nation' principle).

- The Doha negotiations have been called 'The Development Round', because the declared political goal is to improve growth in the **developing world**. In addition to agreeing to make further cuts to protection in goods and services, members agreed to work towards a formula which recognised the rights of developing countries with inadequate manufacturing capacity to import generic drugs to deal with public health crises and epidemics.

- Some new issues for the WTO were also put on the table at Doha, in particular **investment, competition policy** and **environment**.

The Doha talks collapsed in 2003 with developing nations blaming richer countries — particularly some EU members such as France and Germany — for failing to address agricultural subsidies. The EU has very recently offered to eliminate its subsidies, although in return it wants the US to make similar moves and for other nations to cut tariffs and increase quotas to provide more access for EU goods.

5.3 The European Union (EU)

The European Union (EU) (formerly the European Community) is one of several international economic associations. It was formed in 1957 by the Treaty of Rome.

The European Union now (since May 2004) has 25 member states and five more are likely to become members by around 2007 or earlier (subject to further political and economic reforms).

The expansion to 25 nations makes the EU the world's biggest trading bloc, with a combined population of 455 million people.

Member States (EU25)

Austria	Italy
Belgium	Latvia (from May 1, 2004)
Cyprus (from May 1, 2004)	Lithuania (from May 1, 2004)
Czech Republic (from May 1, 2004)	Luxembourg
Denmark	Malta (from May 1, 2004)
Estonia (from May 1, 2004)	Poland (from May 1, 2004)
Finland	Portugal
France	Slovakia (from May 1, 2004)
Germany	Slovenia (from May 1, 2004)
Greece	Spain
Hungary (from May 1, 2004)	Sweden
Ireland	The Netherlands
	United Kingdom

Candidates or applications pending

Bulgaria	Romania
Croatia	Turkey
Former Yugoslavian Republic of Macedonia	

The European Union is a 'single market' including a free trade area and a customs union.

- In a free trade area there is no restriction on the movement of goods and services between member countries. In a customs union there are, in addition, common external tariffs applying to imports from non-member countries into any part of the union. This means that the EU promotes free trade among its members but is a protectionist bloc in dealings with the rest of the world. The EU negotiates in WTO discussions as a single body.

- A single market has additional features. As well as free trade there is also complete mobility of the factors of production. For instance a UK citizen is free to work in any other EU country of the European Union, and vice versa.

The ultimate decision-making body of the EU is the Council of Ministers who represent the 'corporate mind' of the member states. However, much of the authority vests with the Commission. Although the prerogative of policy initiation is vested in the Council, most proposals appear to spring from the Commission that also guides the proposals through the tortuous consultative procedures before being presented to the Council in the form of draft regulations and directives for their approval. The Commission ultimately enforces EU law, which becomes part of the domestic law of the member states, and in the event of any clash or conflict, takes precedence over domestic laws.

Key issues for the European Union include CAP, the single European market, the euro, and the Constitution.

5.4   The EU's Common Agricultural Policy (CAP)

Demand for agricultural produce is usually inelastic and farmers lose revenue in years when there is a large harvest. The CAP protects farmers by forcing up prices in the home market.

- A **target price** is set for agricultural prices in the following year.

- A **threshold price** is used to set customs duties on imported foods (so that imports cannot reach the EU market below this price).

- An **intervention price** is the price at which various agencies will buy up surplus stocks of agricultural produce, usually after a large harvest, to prevent the price falling. (The surplus — for example a 'butter mountain' or a 'wine lake' — would be stored, disposed of, or 'dumped' abroad.)

Although some measures have been taken to reform the CAP (and further measures are likely following the enlargement of the EU), it still consumes almost half of the EU budget and perhaps remains the single most contentious EU issue, especially in the context of global free trade, developing nations, and famine in Africa.

5.5   The Single European Market (SEM)

In general terms the SEM reflects the following principles.

- Free movement of goods between member countries, thus making a homogeneous market.

   This involved the following agreements:
   - The different national standards for the quality or safety of products replaced by the establishment of European standards.
   - Use of common European regulations to harmonise laws concerning food in different member countries, e.g. on hygiene, safety and food labelling.
   - The complex and differential regulations concerning pharmaceuticals of member nations simplified by the use of common European licensing rules.

- Free movement of capital between member countries.

- Elimination of differences in national standards for telecommunications equipment in an attempt to foster increased competition within the telecommunications market.

- Liberalisation of transport services, to promote competition between carriers and reduce the practice by which member nations tend to award licences only to their national carriers.

- To reduce the existing tendency for member governments to award contracts to only their own companies, EU measures attempt to ensure free competition for public contracts between companies in the Community.

- Standardisation and tightening up of anti-trust regulations within the EU.

- Removal of barriers that restrict the provision of financial services (such as capital movements, and regulations for banks) across national boundaries within the EU.

- Unrestricted movement of professional people, including lawyers, accountants and teachers between member countries.

5.6 European Monetary Union (EMU)

This is an emotive topic and has strategic implications for any entity doing business in the EU. In October 1997 the then chancellor of the exchequer announced that the UK would not join the EMU starting on 1 January 1999 without holding a referendum on five issues namely:

- sustainable convergence between the economies of UK and EU members

- whether there was flexibility for change

- the effect on investment

- the impact on UK financial services

- the impact on employment.

Since 2002 12 of the member states have exchanged their old currency for the euro. The UK, Sweden and Denmark have not adopted it. The 10 new members typically expect to adopt the euro by 2010.

For the UK to join the EMU would mean exchanging the pound sterling for a new currency called the euro. The UK interest rate would be the same as the common currency areas determined by the European Central Bank (ECB). If the UK does not join then sterling would remain the currency of the UK but businesses would need to be able to handle transactions in the new currency. Even though the UK has opted out of the 'first wave' of countries that opted for the euro, businesses trading with EU entities now have to set up systems to cope with the euro.

Advantages of the euro

- The principal benefit of the euro is the avoidance of currency hedging which is both risky and expensive.

- The euro will reduce transaction costs.

- The euro is likely to act as a catalyst for low inflation.

- There will be greater transparency for customers for price comparisons.

Drawbacks of the euro

- The poor record of the ECB as an economic regulator.

- The stated inflation target of 2% in the EMU can inhibit growth.

- A strong euro can weaken the dollar and this can have an adverse effect on world trade.

5.7 A constitution for Europe?

At the time of publication discussions were about to resume on The Draft Treaty establishing a Constitution for Europe. This was developed, in the face of widespread disaffection with the EU, with the aim of bringing Europe closer to the people — making it more transparent and democratic. Moreover when it became clear that the enlargement of the EU to 25 members would go ahead it was felt that the treaties originally devised for a six-member institution were an inadequate basis on which to run a much larger and more diverse institution.

According to its preface the aims of the Draft Treaty are as follows.

- It proposes a better division of Union and Member State competences

- It recommends a merger of the Treaties and the attribution of legal personality to the Union

- It establishes a simplification of the Union's instruments of action

- It proposes measures to increase the democracy, transparency and efficiency of the European Union, by developing the contribution of national Parliaments to the legitimacy of the European design, by simplifying the decision-making processes, and by making the functioning of the European Institutions more transparent and comprehensible

- It establishes the necessary measures to improve the structure and enhance the role of each of the Union's three institutions, taking account, in particular, of the consequences of enlargement

Many of the details are very controversial and the initial discussions collapsed. A number of countries have declared their intention to put the matter to a referendum. Opponents argue that the constitution would dramatically expand the EU role in setting new rules and regulations for business, while also saddling companies with more human rights obligations. They point out that around four in ten regulations affecting European businesses originate in the EU, and claim that under the EU constitution that figure would double.

Activity 2

Watch the press for further details. There will certainly have been developments in the matter of a constitution for the EU by the time you come to read this.

There is no feedback for this activity.

5.8 The North American Free Trade Agreement (NAFTA)

Canada, the USA and Mexico formed the North American Free Trade Agreement (NAFTA) in 1993. This free trade area covering a population of 360 million was similar in size to the EU before the recent enlargement of the latter.

KEY POINT

NAFTA comprises
Canada, the US and
Mexico. It removes
tariffs and regulations
such as licensing
requirements, enacts
protection for
intellectual property
rights, and institutes the
same requirements for
customs regulations,
documentation, and so
on making it easier and
less expensive for the
countries to trade with
each other.

The objectives of NAFTA are as follows:

- eliminate barriers to trade in, and facilitate the cross-border movement of, goods and services between the territories of the three countries

- promote conditions of fair competition in the free trade area

- increase substantially investment opportunities in the territories of the three countries

- provide adequate and effective protection and enforcement of intellectual property rights in each country's territory

- create effective procedures for the implementation and application of this agreement, for its joint administration and for the resolution of disputes

- establish a framework for further trilateral, regional and multilateral cooperation to expand and enhance the benefits of this Agreement.

The intention was that NAFTA would create hundreds of thousands of new jobs, raise living standards in the US, Mexico and Canada, improve environmental conditions and transform Mexico from a poor developing country into a booming new producer and market.

NAFTA removes tariffs and regulations such as licensing requirements that may hinder businesses trying to enter each other's markets. It enacts protection for intellectual property rights. It institutes the same requirements for customs regulations, documentation, record keeping, and origin verification in all three countries making it easier and less expensive for the countries to trade with each other.

Opinions of NAFTA are very mixed. According to the NAFTA secretariat it has been a great success and three-way trade amongst the countries is now more than double the pre-NAFTA level. The North American Agreement on Environmental Co-operation and the North American Agreement on Labour Co-operation have helped to ensure that the economic integration promoted by NAFTA is accompanied by better environmental performance and efforts to improve working conditions.

NAFTA opponents say that NAFTA has resulted in rock bottom wages, destroyed hundreds of thousands of jobs, undermined democratic control of domestic policy-making and threatened health, environmental and food safety standards.

Despite the opposition there are moves to expand NAFTA and bring in 31 more countries in Latin American and the Caribbean through the proposed Free Trade Area of the Americas (FTAA), and five Central American countries through a Central American Free Trade Agreement (CAFTA).

5.9 Asia-Pacific

KEY POINT

The principal free trade
body in the Asia-Pacific
region is APEC, which
has 21 members and
claims that it accounts
for more than a third of
the world's population
and about 47% of world
trade.

The principal free trade body in the Asia-Pacific region is the Asia-Pacific Economic Co-operation Forum (APEC), based in Singapore.

APEC has 21 members comprising developed, newly industrialising and developing economies. It claims that it accounts for more than a third of the world's population (2.6 billion people), approximately 60% of world GDP and about 47% of world trade (but note that the US is a member: it is never quite clear how much double counting there is in the claims of the various world bodies!).

APEC Members

Australia	New Zealand
Brunei	Papua New Guinea
Canada	Peru
Chile	Philippines
China	Republic of Korea
Chinese Taipei	Russia
Hong Kong	Singapore
Indonesia	Thailand
Japan	United States
Malaysia	Vietnam
Mexico	

Unlike the WTO or other multilateral trade bodies APEC does not require its participants to adhere to treaty obligations. Decisions are reached by consensus and commitments are undertaken on a voluntary basis.

APEC was established in 1989 with the aim of enhancing economic growth and prosperity for the region and to strengthen the Asia-Pacific community. It works to reduce tariffs and other trade barriers across the Asia-Pacific region, to create efficient domestic economies and to increase exports. It also aims to create an environment for the safe and efficient movement of goods, services and people across borders in the region through policy alignment, and economic and technical cooperation.

APEC is founded upon what it calls its 'Three Pillars'.

- **Trade and Investment Liberalisation** reduces and eventually eliminates tariff and non-tariff barriers to trade and investment. Trade and Investment Liberalisation focuses on opening markets to increase trade and investment among economies, resulting in economic growth for APEC Member Economies and increased standard of living for all.

- **Business Facilitation** focuses on reducing the costs of business transactions, improving access to trade information and aligning policy and business strategies to facilitate growth, and free and open trade. Essentially, Business Facilitation helps importers and exporters in Asia Pacific meet and conduct business more efficiently, thus reducing costs of production and leading to increased trade, cheaper goods and services and more employment opportunities due to an expanded economy.

- **Economic and Technical Cooperation** is dedicated to providing training and cooperation to build capacities in all APEC Member Economies to take advantage of global trade and the New Economy. This area builds capacity at the institutional and personal level to assist APEC Member Economies and its people gain the necessary skills to meet their economic potential.

6 Global business regulation

6.1 Actors, mechanisms and principles

KEY POINT

Global business regulation is not a neat and tidy affair. It can be seen as a process in which different types of **actors** use various **mechanisms** to push for or against **principles.**

The previous section may appear to imply that the rules for world business are neatly formulated by a limited number of influential bodies all of whom appear to act in accordance with highly altruistic aims. The reality is of course very far from this.

The key work in the area of business regulation is the very important book by Braithwaite and Drahos, *Global Business Regulation* (2000). They see regulation as a 'process in which different types of **actors** use various **mechanisms** to push for or against **principles**'.

- **Actors** simply means **anyone with an interest** in regulation (i.e. those who argue in favour of it or resist it, not the Tom Cruise type of actor!). Diverse examples of actors are the European Union, the Microsoft Corporation, the International Standards Organisation, the government of an individual country, Greenpeace, an informal group of neighbours who campaign to restrict the speed limit in the street where they live … and so on.

- **Mechanisms** are **tools** that actors use to **achieve their goals**. An obvious example is an economic sanction against those who don't comply: impose fines on those who drive too fast in your street, say. The most common 'mechanism' is **modelling,** which means basing your own rules on rules that have demonstrably worked for others—though your version may have many local changes, necessary for the conditions in which you operate.

- **Principles** are the ideas that are used to justify the supremacy of the actors' **values, goals and desires**. An example of a principle is 'harmonisation': an actor such as a widget manufacturer might push for harmonisation of standards for widgets on a global basis on the perfectly valid ground that it is in everyone's interests to know what they can expect when they buy a widget. But in addition, of course, a common standard helps the widget manufacturer to know how to manufacture widgets that can be sold worldwide.

We will talk about the actors involved in more detail in the next chapter, which deals with stakeholder management. Principles and mechanisms, however, are clearly relevant to an organisation's mission and the formulation of strategy to achieve that mission.

6.2 Principles

These are the grounds upon which arguments are put forward **either in favour** of some sort of regulation **or against** it.

Principles are very often in conflict with other principles. For example mere 'rule compliance' conflicts with 'world's best practice': the former might lie behind a cost-minimisation strategy while the latter would underlie a total quality strategy.

Here are the principles identified by Brathwaite and Drahos.

- **Continuous improvement**: The idea that every year you should do better than the previous year in terms of a regulatory objective such as protecting the environment, even if legal requirements were exceeded in the previous year

- **Harmonisation**: As already mentioned, the idea that everyone should set the same rules.

- **Liberalisation-deregulation**: The idea that the number, stringency or enforcement of rules should be reduced.

- **Lowest-cost location**: Economic activity should be located wherever and under whatever regulatory rules it can be transacted most cheaply. For example it could be argued that NAFTA was a piece of regulation that enabled US firms to relocate their activities to Mexico, where much lower wage rates could be paid.

- **Most favoured Nation**: As we have seen, this is the principle that any regulatory benefit accorded to importers or exporters from one nation should be accorded to importers or exporters from other nations.

- **Mutual recognition**: The argument here is that different levels of government and different governments should recognise one another's rules and allow economic activity to be performed under one another's rules, even if the rules are different.

- **National sovereignty**: This is the principle that the nation-state should be supreme over any other source of power in matters affecting its citizens or territory. For example, following a BSE scare a country may ban imports of another country's beef in defiance of a ruling by a body to which both countries belong.

- **National treatment**: The principle that a state should regulate foreign corporations according to the same rules as national corporations.

- **Reciprocity**: Unlike the most favoured nation idea, the argument is that if one nation grants a regulatory benefit to importers or exporters from a second nation, the second nation should grant the same regulatory benefit to the first nation, *regardless* of the regulatory benefits it accords third nations. The EU works like this, as we have seen.

- **Rule compliance**: The idea is that companies should go as far as the rules require (e.g. in reducing pollution) but no further.

- **Strategic trade**: Designing the content and stringency of regulation to advantage national exporters or importers over foreign exporters or importers.

- **Transparency**: This proposes that 'any person should be able to observe regulatory deliberation or easily discover the outcomes (and their justifications) of the deliberation'. For example, it might be argued that consumers should be able to find out how food standards are set and if the standards for hygiene, say, are lower than they might expect, what the justification for that is.

- **World's best practice**: The principle that economic activity should be conducted under rules that substantially exceed the requirements set by present practice or regulation.

6.3 Mechanisms

Mechanisms are the tools that might be used to get the regulatory outcome that you desire. According to Braithwaite and Drahos these can be summarised as follows.

- **Capacity-building**: This means helping other actors get the technical competence to satisfy standards, where they wish to meet them but lack the capacity to do so.

- **Economic coercion**: The threat, fear or use of economic sanctions.

- **Military coercion**: The threat, fear or use of military force. Libya decommissioning its weapons of mass destruction is an example of a response to a threat. Obviously this is not an option available to businesses, or at least hopefully not, but business objectives might be achieved through the actions of governments.

- **Modelling**: Basing your own rules on rules that have demonstrably worked for others—though your version may have many local changes. This is more than mere imitation; imitation means one actor matching the actions of another, usually close in time.

- **Non-reciprocal coordination**: This occurs when movement toward common rules happens without all parties believing they have a common interest in that movement. One party believes the new rule is in their interest, but this belief is not reciprocated. This underlies the legal battles between Microsoft and Netscape and Sun: the world standardised on Microsoft's versions of technologies invented by the other companies.

- **Reciprocal adjustment**: Parties agree to adjust the rules they follow without coercion, for example all parties agree to drive on the left side of the road to avoid crashes.

- **Rewards**: These are offered to those who comply with a regulation, for example government contracts may only be offered to suppliers who are ISO 9001 certified.

Summary

Key points of this chapter are:

- Regulation in major markets is affected by many different factors including political forces particularly in respect of the actions of government.

- The market for many goods and services is multi-national with large multi-national companies arising to take advantage of this.

- There are various barriers to international trade but also a general movement to develop different free trade areas (e.g. the EU and NAFTA)

- Regulation of global businesses is difficult when most legislation is based on individual countries.

Having completed your study of this chapter you should have achieved the following learning outcomes:

- evaluate the impact of regulatory regimes on strategic planning and implementation

- evaluate the impact and influence of the external environment on an organisation and its strategy.

Self-test questions

1   What according to Porter are seven ways in which the government can affect the structure of an industry? (2.1)

2   List the categories of legislation that affect business. (2.3)

3   Describe the four principal aims of government regulations. (2.3)

4   Why is world trade beneficial? (4.1)

5   Give four examples of protectionist measures. (4.3)

6   What is the 'Doha round' and what matters are under consideration? (5.2)

7 State the principles of the Single European Market. (5.5)

8 What are APEC's three pillars? (5.9)

9 What are actors, principles and mechanisms? (6.1)

Practice questions

Question 1: Electronic equipment

A company manufacturing specialised electronic equipment has so far sold only inside the country where it is established. It has considerable surplus capacity and the chairman has asked you, as his finance director, to prepare a draft memorandum for the board on his proposal to open up export business to a number of countries.

Required:

Prepare this memorandum, setting out the main points that would need to be considered before arriving at a final decision, under the following headings:

(a) export pricing and profitability

(b) credit terms and methods of obtaining payment

(c) risks and methods of reducing them.

Where appropriate, briefly indicate advantages and disadvantages of each point.

(20 marks)

Question 2: Nationalised and semi-state business organisations

The mixed economies of industrialised and less developed countries have large commercial enterprises that are either partly (semi-state) or fully (nationalised) state owned.

Required:

Discuss the policy, planning and operating difficulties that may be faced by nationalised or semi-state business enterprises (in a mixed economy) when they are instructed to act in a more profit-oriented and market-sensitive manner than hitherto.

(25 marks)

For the answers to these questions, see the 'Answers' section at the end of the book.

Feedback to activity

Activity 1

An example of an industry which locates different areas of its business to take advantage of particular skills or low wages is the computer industry. R&D may be concentrated in the US, the microchips and printed circuit boards are constructed in the Pacific Rim, and the machines are assembled in various countries, e.g. the UK.

An example of an organisation is Ford. The components for car manufacture are made in many countries, e.g. gears in Germany; some models are assembled in Spain and others in the UK; and the engine design is undertaken in the US.

Chapter 4

STAKEHOLDERS

Syllabus content

- Interacting with stakeholders and the use of stakeholder mapping.

- Approaches to business-government relations and with civil society (Braithwaite and Drahos).

- Stakeholder management (stakeholders to include government and regulatory agencies, non-governmental organisations and civil society, industry associations, customers and suppliers).

Contents

1   Introduction

2   Stakeholder management

3   Business relations

4   Success for the shareholder

1   Introduction

A stakeholder is anyone who has an interest in a business's strategy or will be affected by its outcome. It is important to understand the values and issues that stakeholders have because they can all have a substantial impact on the overall performance and ultimate success of a company. They need to be measured and managed as a key component of a company's overall management and information systems that lead to overall market and financial success.

In this chapter we will look at stakeholder mapping which analyses stakeholders based on their relative power and level of interest. Then we move on to consider how an organisation can manage its relations with key external stakeholders such as governments and regulators and with pressure groups from civil society. Finally we cover some management accounting, techniques that are relevant in this context, such as shareholder value analysis. Customer and supplier relationships are covered in the next chapter.

2   Stakeholder management

2.1   Introduction

The objectives of an organisation should be derived by balancing the often conflicting claims of the various stakeholders in the organisation.

These stakeholders consist of coalitions of people within the organisation, and external groups.

- Customers and prospective customers

- Managers and employees

- Suppliers and partners

- Capital providers and shareholders

- Governing and regulatory agencies

- The public and influential bodies or people

The organisation has responsibilities to all these groups and should formulate its strategic goals to give each a measure of satisfaction. The difficulty is balancing the conflicting interests and differing degrees of power. For example there might be conflicts of interest between a company's shareholders and its employees. If the strategy of the organisation is to truly reflect the interests of its stakeholders the strategic planner will need to consider, and be influenced by, factors relating to them. These are the:

- composition and significance of each group

- power that each group can exert

- legitimate claims that each group may have on the organisation

- degree to which these claims conflict and significant areas of concern

- extent to which the organisation is satisfying claims

- overall mission of the organisation.

2.2   Stakeholder interest and strategy formulation

The conflict between stakeholder interests is a recurring theme for business planners. It remains a timeless issue and with the globalisation of business it is relevant to the expansionist plans of many multinationals. For example a global business such as BP-Amoco has to consider the social and financial impact of oil and gas exploration. Continued exploration is necessary in order to produce.

How should a business reconcile the expectations of the various stakeholder groups? What might be good for the shareholders could be harmful to the interests of local people or to the environment. Shell Transport and Trading is frequently targeted by pressure groups who allege that they are irresponsible in the way in which they carry out their explorations in areas on the African continent.

Case study

BP–Amoco: The Casper project

In 1884 oil was drilled in the state of Wyoming at what became known as Salt Creek. Standard Oil Company created the refinery using the latest technology to obtain maximum productivity from a barrel of crude oil. The company eventually became known as Amoco Corporation. After 77 years the refinery closed in 1991. The company and the community signed an agreement in 1998 to return the site to productive use in order to benefit the citizens of Casper.

BP and Amoco merged in 1998 and the successor company set up a project with the Wyoming Department of Environmental Quality (WDEQ), several local government agencies and civic leaders in a collaborative process to return the site to productive use. There are plans to convert the former refinery to provide a business park, a golf course and a wildlife sanctuary in a manmade lake. This reuse of land that has been used for some extractive process is known as a 'brownfields' project.

BP's avowed aim is to return the property to the community in a manner that protects human health and the environment.

This case suggests that BP–Amoco have a mechanism to consider the competing claims of stakeholders when making strategic decisions.

How can an organisation ensure that it routinely considers stakeholder interests as a part of strategic planning?

2.3 Stakeholder mapping

Mendelow (1991) has studied the issue of stakeholder interests in a paper on stakeholder mapping. Mendelow suggests a two-way analysis in a type of power interest matrix.

		Level of interest	
		Low	**High**
Power	**Low**	1 Unskilled labour General public Small shareholders	2 Local press and TV Civic leaders Small local suppliers
	High	3 Central government Customers National press	4 Major shareholders Key managers Trade Unions

Table: Mendelow's matrix of stakeholder mapping

The idea of the matrix was to track interested parties and evaluate their viewpoint in the context of some change in business strategy.

(1)	**Low interest – low power**	These could represent the interests of small shareholders, local unskilled labour or the general public.
(2)	**High interest – low power**	This quadrant could represent the views of local businesses.
(3)	**Low interest – high power**	This quadrant could represent central government or the national media.
(4)	**High interest – high power**	This quadrant could represent the unions, key staff and environmentalist groups and institutional shareholders.

Scholes (1998) suggests that this technique can be used in two situations.

- To keep a track of changes in the potential influence of different stakeholder groups. By producing the matrix regularly management can be alerted to when a strategy may need to change to accommodate (or avoid a threat from) particular stakeholders.

- To assess the impact of a particular strategic development on stakeholders. For example managers proposing a branch closure could use mapping to identify where opposition to closure may come from and how it might be managed (e.g. by shifting redundant workers from quadrant 4 to 3 or 2, through generous pay-offs or assistance in finding alternative employment and thus reducing the votes for a strike).

The above matrix analyses stakeholders based on their power and their level of interest. These parameters will now be dealt with in more detail

2.4 Assessing power of stakeholders

Factors that may be associated with a particular group having high power are:

Status of the stakeholders

- their place in the organisational hierarchy

- their relative pay

- their reputation in the firm

- their social standing (e.g. ministers of religion may carry considerable power due to their social status).

Claim on resources

- size of their budget

- number and level of staff employed

- volume of business transacted with them (e.g. suppliers and customers)

- percentage of workers they speak for (e.g. a trade union).

Formal representation in decision-making processes

- level of management where they are represented

- committees they have representation on

- legal rights (e.g. shareholders, planning authorities).

2.5 Assessing the interest of stakeholders

This will typically be more complex than assessing power because it involves two factors.

Where their interests rest

We assume that powerful stakeholders will pursue their self interest. It is important to consider what they wish to achieve.

It is possible to make some generalisations:

- **managers**: want to further the interests of their departments and functions as well as their own pay and careers

- **employees**: require higher pay, job security, good working conditions and some consultation

- **customers**: want fair prices, reliable supply and reassurance about their purchases

- **suppliers**: want fair prices, reliable orders, prompt payment and advance notification of changes

- **local government**: want jobs, contribution to local community life, consultation on expansions.

How interested they are

Not all stakeholders have the time and inclination to follow management's decisions closely.

Again some generalisations are possible about what will generate a relatively high level of interest:

- high personal financial or career investment in what the business does

- absence of alternative (e.g. alternative job, customer, supplier or employer)

- potential to be called to account for failing to monitor (e.g. local councils or government bodies such as regulators)

- high social impact of firm (e.g. well-known, visible product, association with particular issues).

Completing the matrix

The matrix is normally completed with regard to the stakeholder impact of a particular strategy. The purpose is to assess:

- whether stakeholder resistance is likely to inhibit the success of the strategy

- what policies may ease the acceptance of the strategy.

Completing the matrix is a two step process:

- Place the stakeholder in the appropriate quadrant of the matrix.

    Some stakeholders may contain sub-groups with different degrees of interest or power. For example in a branch closure the skilled and unionised workers will have greater power and interest than the casual or temporary staff who may not be unionised.

- Assess their attitude to the strategy.

  a + is used to indicate that the group will support the strategy.

  a - is used to indicate that the group will oppose the strategy.

The matrix could therefore be used to identify the impact of any proposed change on stakeholder groups and how their disparate concerns can be allayed.

2.6 Strategies to deal with stakeholders

Having established the make up of the matrix relating to a given decision as it is at present, the next stage is to establish what the matrix will need to show if the decision is going to be successful.

The key concerns where alignment is poor are:

- the negative attitudes of skilled labour, key managers and national suppliers

- the ambivalent attitude of shareholders and customers

- the potentially negative interventions of national media and central government

- the possible search for power from local council and media

- Scholes (1998) suggests the following strategies to deal with each quadrant: (Note box references are shown in the Mendelow table in section 2.3.).

1. **Box 1 Direction.** This means their lack of interest and power makes them open to influence. They are more likely than others to accept what they are told and follow instructions.

   Management should not reappoint the casual staff but rather provide limited redundancy support. There is no need to tell the small shareholders or customers.

   Box 2 Education/Communication. The positively disposed groups from this quadrant may lobby others to support the strategy. Also if the strategy is presented as rational or inevitable to the dissenters, or a show of consultation gone through, this may stop them joining forces with more powerful dissenters in 3 and 4.

   Management should brief all groups here on the reasonableness of the case for closure and of the provisions being made for the redundant staff. Advance notice will give each more time for adjustment.

   Box 3 Intervention. The key here is to keep the occupants satisfied to avoid them gaining interest and shifting into 4. Usually this is done by reassuring them of the likely outcomes of the strategy well in advance.

   Managers should assure the government and suppliers that the closure will result in a more competitive firm that is able to compete worldwide. A similar message may reassure investors if it is backed up with a reassuring short-term dividend forecast.

   Box 4 Participation. These stakeholders can be major drivers of the change and major opponents of the strategy. Initially there should be education/communication to assure them that the change is necessary, followed by discussion of how to implement it.

Managers should involve the unions in determining the redundancy package or redundancy policy. Key managers should be involved in deciding the basis on which early retirements should be handled and how redeployment or outplacement should be managed. Key shareholders will be consulted throughout to reassure them that costs will not be excessive.

It is clear that communication, and at least the appearance of participation, are regarded as the main tools of stakeholder alignment. However, it should be noted that these approaches cannot overcome a genuine loss to stakeholders. What is more, overuse tends to generate cynicism. For example, a show of participation may be effective once, but if the stakeholders perceive that their involvement was only cosmetic, resistance will be higher on subsequent occasions.

This manner of dealing with unaligned stakeholder interests also assumes that there is a neutral party carrying out the analysis and working for consensus. In fact this is rarely the case, and consensus is frequently no more than the effective imposition of the interests of a dominant stakeholder or coalition, however this may be disguised.

2   Institutional shareholders would be influential in voicing any concerns about a poor environmental track record. The civic leaders would lobby energetically for environmental or social concerns (quadrant 2). Customers may not be sufficiently motivated to protest too strongly (quadrant 3) and the people in quadrant 1 would probably fall into line anyway.

Tony Blair, the current prime minister in the UK, coined the term 'stakeholder society'. Certain companies have unfortunately demonstrated an ambivalent attitude to stakeholders. Barclays Bank plc attracted a good deal of unfavourable comment from customers over its programme of branch closures. The CEO Matt Barratt spoke about the average customer's perception of bank management as 'uncaring' and remote.

2.7   The Clarkson Principles of stakeholder management

The Clarkson Principles, developed in the US by the Clarkson Centre for Business Ethics & Board Effectiveness, grew out of concerns about standards of corporate governance, a topic discussed in much more detail later in this text.

- **Principle 1** : Managers should acknowledge and actively monitor the concerns of all legitimate stakeholders, and should take their interests appropriately into account in decision-making and operations.

- **Principle 2**: Managers should listen to and openly communicate with stakeholders about their respective concerns and contributions, and about the risks that they assume because of their involvement with the corporation.

- **Principle 3**: Managers should adopt processes and modes of behaviour that are sensitive to the concerns and capabilities of each stakeholder constituency.

- **Principle 4**: Managers should recognise the interdependence of efforts and rewards among stakeholders, and should attempt to achieve a fair distribution of the benefits and burdens of corporate activity among them, taking into account their respective risks and vulnerabilities.

- **Principle 5**: Managers should work cooperatively with other entities, both public and private, to insure that risks and harms arising from corporate activities are minimised and, where they cannot be avoided, appropriately compensated.

- **Principle 6**: Managers should avoid altogether activities that might jeopardise inalienable human rights (e.g. the right to life) or give rise to risks which, if clearly understood, would be patently unacceptable to relevant stakeholders.

- **Principle 7**: Managers should acknowledge the potential conflicts between (a) their own role as corporate stakeholders, and (b) their legal and moral responsibilities for the interests of all stakeholders, and should address such conflicts through open communication, appropriate reporting and incentive systems and, where necessary, third party review.

3 Business relations

3.1 Actors

At this point it is worth mentioning Braithwaite and Drahos to consider the full range of 'actors' who may have an influence on the way an organisation conducts its business.

- **Organisations of states**: Organisations formed by groups of states that meet and employ staff to explore common agendas (e.g. the WTO, the EU).

- **States**: Organised political communities with governments and geographical boundaries recognised by international law (e.g. Sweden).

- **Organisations formed by firms** and/or business organisations with common agendas, such as Chambers of Commerce.

- **Corporations**: Organisations formed by actors who invest in them as commercial vehicles (e.g. Ford, British Telecom).

- **Non-Governmental Organisations (NGOs)**: Organisations (excluding business organisations) that explore common agendas. They can be international (e.g. Consumers International) or national (e.g. British Standards Institute).

- **Mass publics**: Large audiences of citizens who express together a common concern about an issue.

- **Knowledge based (epistemic)** communities: These consist of state, business and NGO representatives who meet sporadically and share a common discourse based on shared knowledge – sometimes technical knowledge requiring professional training; CIMA is an example.

The last three groups may be collectively termed **civil society. Civil society** includes, among others, non-government organisations; people's organisations; civic clubs; trade unions; gender, cultural, and religious groups; charities; social and sports clubs; co-operatives; environmental groups; professional associations; academic and policy institutions; consumers/consumer organisations; and the media.

3.2 Business/government relations

Businesses can try to influence government policies in a number of ways.

- By employing lobbyists, who will put their case to ministers and civil servants and try to obtain their support.

- By giving MPs and retired senior civil servants non-executive directorships, in the hope that they will take an interest in legislation that affects the business and will exercise their influence.

- By influencing public opinion, and hence the legislative agenda, using advertising or other means of marketing communications.

Depending on the political regime and the country in question another method may be to make donations to party funds. Obviously this is open to question — it could be seen as a form of bribery.

It is usually in the interest of a government to consult with the business sector when it is forming new policies, both to widen its perspective and so that it can defend its actions politically. In most developed countries there is a strong business lobby consisting of individual companies and business-related organisations.

In the UK, for example, the business lobby consists of protagonists such as the following.

- The Confederation of British Industry (CBI), representing the entire private business sector.

- The Federation of Small Businesses (FSB) and local Chambers of Commerce.

- The Institute of Directors (IOD).

- Several thousand trade associations and employers' organisations, representing particular industries and sectors.

Very large companies are likely to be in frequent contact with government departments and parliament on an individual basis and many have distinct departments for government liaison. Such departments will monitor and advise on political and governmental developments, make regular contacts with politicians and senior civil servants, organise representation and undertake lobbying operations in London, Brussels, Washington, Geneva and so on, often assisted by non-executive directors and consultants.

Activity 1

List the possible ways that government can impact on business both as an aid and as an impediment.

Feedback to this activity is at the end of the chapter.

It may be particularly important to try to influence the drafting process of organisations such as the European Commission and the WTO. As we saw in the last chapter their regulations take priority over national law or more local arrangements and their decisions may be very difficult to change because they are only arrived at after long periods of international negotiation.

- There should be no delay. Firms should monitor the issues that are being dealt with by the governing body and make their views known as early as possible in the process. The governing body will probably publish a 'green paper' discussing proposed changes and inviting comment before issuing a 'white paper' and passing a statute or a treaty or a set of standards.

- Firms should collaborate with others in the same industry and encourage firms in other countries to lobby their own governments. An organisation's opinions will carry more weight if it can show that it is not just self-seeking but that those opinions are shared by others in the industry.

3.3 Civil society and pressure groups

Any group of individuals who share a common view on anything that affects their quality of life can form a pressure group. This is best seen at grass roots level where a group of people in a local community object to a company dumping waste products in an area of natural beauty, or are concerned about the level of heavy traffic using local roads. These people can call themselves a pressure group and petition the relevant parties.

At the other extreme are bodies such as Greenpeace, Friends of the Earth (FoE) and the Campaign for Nuclear Disarmament (CND) who are well-established and tackle issues at a national and international level.

Pressure groups represent the interest of individuals and impact on both government and business. From the viewpoint of their impact on business, pressure groups can be divided roughly into two types: the consumer movement and the environmentalists.

The best known manifestation of the consumer movement in the UK is the Consumers' Association (CA) (founded in 1957) which concentrates on providing researched, comparative information on consumer goods. A European consumer movement was also established in Brussels in 1973. During the 1980s, CA, by demonstrating effective skills in media relations, evolved a powerful established position in UK opinion-forming, and became a strong influence in the UK political and business decision-making mechanisms. CA conducts an energetic and robust programme of political lobbying. Consumer legislation and government policy, both in UK and Europe, over the last 20 years, provide landmarks of the CA's activities.

Environmental groups have also established themselves in a powerful position mainly because of their distinctive and hard-hitting campaign style of highlighting environmental concerns. They have demonstrated their ability to mobilise massive popular support for their campaigns and achieve a level of media coverage which is the envy of public relations experts working in business. For example, the Council for the Protection of Rural England (CPRE) has 44 branches and over 45,000 members, and in 1990 Friends of the Earth (FoE) had a membership in excess of 200,000, with an income of £6.1 million. The CPRE, FoE and other pressure groups such as Greenpeace often combine for research, problem-solving and political lobbying. The impact on business of the activities of pressure groups is considerable. Examples of recent campaigns which may have future impact on business are: the mandatory labelling of electrical appliances; radioactive waste disposal policy; scrapping of the agricultural set-aside scheme; revised planning policy for the extractive industries with a reduction in open-cast mining; and the development of public transport.

The work of pressure groups can affect business organisations both directly and indirectly. The direct form of influence is where the pressure group confronts the organisation itself, the indirect form is where the pressure group influences government policy which, in turn, affects the business. Either way the activities of pressure groups cannot be ignored and do serve a valid purpose in making people and organisations accountable and responsible for their actions.

3.4 Types of pressure group

KEY POINT

Another viewpoint distinguishes three main types of pressure groups: interest groups, promotional groups and political groups.

Another viewpoint distinguishes three main types of pressure groups:

- **Interest groups** – These groups are concerned with social and economic problems. The role of the group is to act as a spokesperson in such matters. Notable examples of interest groups are:

  - Trade unions for electricians, engineers, miners, railway workers, seamen, etc. The combined forces of these unions are known as the Trades Union Congress (TUC).

  - Employers' associations, for example the Confederation of British Industry (CBI).

  - Professional bodies, e.g. the British Medical Association (BMA) and the National Farmers' Union (NFU), accountancy and legal bodies generally.

- **Promotional groups** – These groups tend to specialise in finding solutions to specific problems or strive towards achieving an ultimate target. They can be diverse in their objectives, e.g. charities such as Oxfam, War on Want and the National Society for the Prevention of Cruelty to Children (NSPCC) and environmental protection groups such as Friends of the Earth (FoE) and Greenpeace.

- **Political groups** – Under this heading come the major and minor political parties. A political group will initially seek power and then attempt to realise their political objectives. A good example of a minor political party was the Natural Law Party who, although being spectacularly unsuccessful in the 1992 general election, did at least give themselves a platform to expound their manifesto.

3.5 Pressure groups' influence on government policy

Pressure groups can adopt various methods to attempt to influence policy making. A broad distinction can be made between tactics which try to impact on government directly and those which are more subtle.

Amongst the more subtle methods are the use of the media where the group publicise their views and gather public support. This support builds to a point where government cannot ignore the public movement and so have to consider the issues being raised. This method can be enhanced by public shows of strength such as demonstration marches and public acts, e.g. the Greenham Common camp at the site of nuclear bases.

Pressure groups can try to get their views across in Parliament by gaining the support of an MP. This can be achieved by asking the MP to become the spokesperson of the group or by giving the person a role within the organisation such as president or vice-president. However, there is a potential problem in enlisting the support of an existing MP. Although the MP may be happy to convey the views of the group in Parliament there may come a time when they have to be 'loyal' to their party. The views held by the MP (and hence the group) and the party line may come into conflict which may lead to the MP having to follow the party, lose credibility in the eyes of the group and the public at large, and diminish the case of the group.

A more direct approach is to put forward a member of the group as a prospective MP in a general election in the hope that they will be elected. The Green Party were most active in this approach during the general election of 1992 although ultimately they were unsuccessful in their aims to obtain a seat.

An alternative way of getting the group's views known in Parliament is via a private member's bill. The MP who has launched the bill can be lobbied and the group may try to influence the content of the bill.

In the case of well-established and well-respected groups such as the CBI and the TUC it is not uncommon that the MP approached is a minister or cabinet minister. This then becomes a very powerful vehicle for the group owing to the influence of such a high-ranking MP.

A further form of influence that can be exerted by a group is where government forms a committee to consider a specific area of policy and invites a member of the group to advise or even act on the committee. Clearly, in this situation it is much easier for the views of the group to be reflected in policy especially when the group member on the committee can significantly influence the policy being formulated.

3.6 The impact of pressure groups on business

The majority of the work that pressure groups are involved in will have a direct impact on organisations in the business environment. The groups which have most influence over policies affecting the business world are those which represent workers, the owners of businesses and the ultimate consumers.

Workers' pressure groups

Many workers are members of some form of union. Although locally a union may have influence over management, on a national scale most unions are too small to have any significant impact on central policy-setting. This fact was recognised back in the early nineteenth century, and in 1868 the TUC was formed. The TUC is an association of individual trade unions and is recognised by government as the voice of the workers, today having approximately ten million members. This represents about half of the workforce in the UK and consequently is a powerful body whose views should be respected.

Membership of the TUC is open to a wide range of workers ranging from shipbuilders to the St John Ambulance Association. Its principal objective is to ensure the social and economic conditions of its members are preserved and hopefully improved. The major weakness of the TUC has been the sheer diversity of its membership. It is very difficult for a body of this type to be able to formulate policy objectively and preserve harmony within its ranks when the policy in question affects two different members, one favourably and the other unfavourably.

The TUC is also committed to co-operation with other unions and will negotiate with the appropriate parties to avoid industrial disputes developing. In addition the TUC is represented on a wide range of committees which advise government on policy formulation. However, despite being a potentially influential group it is arguable that the role of the TUC is diminishing rapidly. This can be seen on several levels.

- During the 1980s it was clear that the Conservative government, led by Margaret Thatcher, took far less notice of the unions when forming policy and succeeded in its aims without serious and continual confrontations.

- With unemployment high and membership of the TUC falling the very feature that makes the TUC so impressive, its size, is now declining rapidly.

- The failure of the TUC to influence the government with solutions to the unemployment crisis undermines the credibility of the union in the eyes of its members.

Employers' and trade association pressure groups

Organisations in the business environment are affected by policy imposed on them and on occasions face pressure from the unions of their employees.

Like workers, business organisations can be members of 'unions' known as employers' or trade associations and can be members of the national body, the Confederation of British Industry (CBI).

The CBI was formed in 1965 by amalgamating four existing bodies. The membership today consists of around 12,000 firms and 200 trade and employers' associations. Its function is to act as the spokesperson for British business and it strives to ensure that the business environment enables businesses to prosper. As a result of having this goal the CBI has to act as a pressure group and must negotiate with and influence both the unions and government. Like the TUC, the CBI is represented on various committees and policy-making bodies.

In the current economic climate the role and influence of the CBI is crucial. Government relies on management to carry out policies to ultimately get the British economy going again. The government can only count on the support of the CBI if the CBI are reasonably comfortable with the economic policies adopted by government.

Consumer pressure groups

The ultimate recipient of the output from business is the customer. Customers expect a certain level of quality in products for fair prices. If customers did not have a say then they could be exposed to unscrupulous business practice. The Consumers' Association (which publishes the *Which?* magazine) and the National Federation of Consumer Groups are perhaps the two most effective consumer pressure groups. Consumer pressure groups concern themselves with problems such as:

- reasonable prices in each monopoly-type market

- standard purchasing for products

- clear English in clauses and contracts of sale

- additives in foods

- the safety of products.

Although consumer groups have relatively few members, the results of their findings after testing products for quality, safety and value are widely used and generally well-respected. Consequently government and organisations must respond to the work of these pressure groups or face the backlash of public sympathy.

3.7 Sovereignty of the people

One of the surprising conclusions of the research of Braithwaite and Drahos into global business regulation is that citizen groups and even individual citizens can exert genuine influence over globalisation (and therefore over what businesses can and cannot do). They suggest a number of strategies that members of civil society can employ to force standards to be raised or counter monopolies and so on.

As a business strategist you need to be aware of the methods that your stakeholders might employ. Here are some examples.

- **Exploit strategic trade thinking to divide and conquer business**. Strategic trade, if you recall, means designing the content and stringency of regulation so as to advantage national exporters or importers over foreign exporters or importers. Thus environmentalists concerned about the hole in the ozone layer persuaded the US to pass legislation that favoured US manufacturers of substitutes for CFCs long before there was global agreement elsewhere in the world that CFCs should be banned. As concerns grew over the ozone layer US firms and the US government were able to support the environmentalists — and also corner the market in the manufacture of CFC substitutes.

- **Work directly with a business** to persuade them to be the leader in improving standards: if they are successful the rest of the industry will have to follow, simply in order to remain competitive.

- Target efforts to ensure that rules are not broken at **'gatekeepers'** rather than at the rule-breakers. For example attempts to get states to penalise the **owners** of ships that spilt oil at sea proved fruitless. However, when ship **insurers** and ship **builders** were targeted 98% compliance was obtained. The interesting feature in this success story was that enforcement targeting was shifted from ships, which had an economic interest in cheating, to builders and insurers whose interest, if any, was in more expensive ships.

4 Success for the shareholder

4.1 Pursuit of profit

In this last section we move on to consider what is usually believed to be the overriding mission of a business organisation – that of increasing the wealth of its owners.

Although there have been suggestions that the main objective of a company is simply survival we can surely agree that this is inadequate. Survival is not an end in itself; most organisations would want to reach a certain minimum performance level rather than just 'hanging on', and if this was not attainable the shareholders might not wish for the survival of the company. Shareholders are obviously a major group to be taken into account when setting objectives. If we ask 'why does the company want to survive?' the answer must be to make a profit or to maximise the wealth of investors in the company, i.e. the shareholders.

What about the objective of customer satisfaction? Again, why does the company wish for satisfied customers? – to make a profit.

Thus most commentators conclude that the strategic objective of a company equates with the financial objective determined in financial management theory: the maximisation of shareholder wealth. The objective is quantified by measurement of the dividend yield plus capital growth.

4.2 Measuring shareholder value

Total shareholder return (TSR)

Internal measures of performance such as ROI or residual income (RI) suffer from the drawback that they are subjective and inward looking. How could a divisionalised business explain their performance to the world at large? Certain public companies use measures that 'benchmark' the business as well as the managers who run the business units.

TSR is used to benchmark the company (group) as well as to provide a measure for managerial reward. It is a benchmark worked out by comparing the movement on the company's ordinary shares and dividend record with other comparable companies using the Financial Times stock exchange index of 100 top performing companies (FTSE-100 Index).

The improvement in share price and dividend record is then used to determine the basis of long-term incentives such as share option schemes. The reward of a share option scheme is the ability to sell shares at current market value at some future date (the exercise date) having had the option to acquire them at a price fixed say three years earlier (the grant date).

The measure is used by Peninsular and Oriental Steam Navigation Company (P&O) and is mentioned in their 1998 annual report as an explanation of long-term incentive rewards.

'The plan is based on 4 year performance cycles…During each cycle the performance of executives with group responsibility is measured on the basis of total shareholder return (TSR) which is based on the movement in price of the company's deferred ordinary stock plus dividends, relative to companies in the FTSE-100 index. Performance of companies with primarily divisional performance is measured mainly on the basis of TSR performance but also on divisional performance.

At the conclusion of a performance cycle the value of a participant's reward is calculated. Maximum awards would only be available if the company's TSR performance is within the top 25 companies in the FTSE-100 index. No rewards will be made unless the company's TSR performance is within the equivalent of the top 60 companies in the FTSE-100 Index and the growth in earnings per £1 nominal of deferred stock as defined in the plan exceeds the percentage increase in the index of retail prices by at least 2% per annum during that performance cycle.'

This statement of policy also encapsulates the concept of principal agency theory in that the managers are rewarded on results that reflect the need to balance shareholder reward with manager reward. This acknowledges the concept of the 'optimum sharing rule' that recognises the need to work for the congruence of both business goals and manager goals.

4.3 Shareholder value analysis (SVA)

Rappaport uses another measure called shareholder value analysis. Shareholder value is defined as entity value minus value of debt. Entity value is defined as the present value of free cash flows before interest but after tax and after adding back non-cash items such as depreciation. The internal measure used for divisional evaluation is to try to measure the increase in shareholder value that has been engineered through the new project or acquisition.

The equation used is:

Value of strategy = post strategy value – pre strategy value.

Rappaport tries to measure the increase in value of an entity that results from a strategy and he identifies six key value drivers that affect cash flow generation.

The drivers suggested by Rappaport are:

- sales growth rate

- operating profit margin

- cash tax rate

- fixed capital investment need

- planning horizon

- cost of capital.

4.4 Economic value added®

This measure is similar to residual income and is a proprietary system developed by Stern Stewart and Co that aims to measure economic profit. This can be described as accounting profit after deducting the opportunity cost of group support. If the division were a stand-alone vehicle it would require debt finance for long and short-term purposes as well as equity shareholders to share the risk of the business venture. Many organisations set up divisions and ignore the cost of finance on the grounds that it keeps the accounting uncomplicated.

Summary

Key points of this chapter are:

- Successful management of stakeholder relationships provides a huge opportunity for organisations to differentiate themselves and gain a significant competitive edge.

- The key objective of stakeholder management is to measure the influence of various stakeholders on company performance and on each other and then to manage the linkages between these relationships. Mendelow's theory provides an insight into this area.

- There are various stakeholder relationships that businesses must take account of including pressure groups and government.

- Success in terms of stakeholder management can be measured in various ways including TSR and SVA.

Having completed your study of this chapter you should have achieved the following learning outcomes:

- identify relevant stakeholders in respect of an organisation

- recommend pro-active and reactive approaches to business/government relations and to relations with civil society

- discuss how stakeholder groups work and how they affect the organisation.

Self-test questions

1   List the main stakeholders in a typical organisation. (2.1)

2   Draw a diagram that illustrates the technique of stakeholder mapping. (2.3)

3   What factors may be associated with a particular stakeholder group having high power? (2.4)

4   What are the main tools of stakeholder alignment? (2.6)

5   What do you understand by the term civil society? (3.1)

6   What are workers' pressure groups? (3.6)

7   What sort of problems are consumer pressure groups concerned with? (3.6)

8   What do Braithwaite and Drahos have to say about business relations with civil society? (3.7)

9   What is total shareholder return? (4.2)

10   What drivers affect shareholder value? (4.3)

Practice question

Stakeholders

Stakeholder analysis identifies individuals, groups and organisations who have some kind of interest in the enterprise, and who may exercise some degree of influence over the management of its affairs.

Required:

Describe examples of such stakeholders, and explain how their aims, activities or effects may constrain the exercise of managerial authority and discretion within the enterprise.   **(25 marks)**

For the answer to this question, see the 'Answers' section at the end of the book

Feedback to activity

Activity 1

(a)   An aid to business

- as large buyer

- as sponsor for research and development

- as the champion of free trade (but as protector against unfair trade in certain circumstances)

- as a controller of inflation, and inflationary influences

- by providing help for wealth creation, including skill training

- by providing assistance for the start up of businesses.

(b)   An impediment to business

- as defender of the interest of the consumer

- as the guarantor of health and safety at work

- as the protector of the environment

- as regulator of business practices

- as the protector of minority groupings.

Chapter 5

CUSTOMERS AND SUPPLIERS

Syllabus content

- The customer portfolio: Customer analysis and behaviour, including the marketing audit and customer profitability analysis as well as customer retention and loyalty.

- Negotiating with customers and suppliers and managing these relationships.

- Marketing in a strategic context

Contents

1   Introduction

2   Relationships with suppliers

3   Outsourcing: the risk and benefits

4   The customer portfolio

5   Consumer behaviour

6   Relationship marketing

7   Customer account profitability (CAP)

8   The marketing audit

1 Introduction

Organisations need to buy goods and services before they can engage in any selling so we begin this chapter with two sections on suppliers. Relationships with suppliers used to be characterised by antagonism – getting the lowest price and exploiting bargaining power – but the modern approach is to enter into partnerships with strategically important suppliers.

Outsourcing is one way of obtaining expertise required at a (usually) lower cost than setting up or retaining the function in-house. It is effectively an extension of in-house resources. By outsourcing non-core activities, management can concentrate on bringing future real benefit to their organisation.

The underlying purpose of all strategy is to develop and sell a product more effectively than your competitors. In this chapter we will look at the techniques used to analyse customers and identify market segments in both consumer and industrial markets. We will look at the marketing audit and customer profitability analysis, as well as relationship marketing.

2 Relationships with suppliers

2.1 Supply strategy

In certain types of business purchases make up the major part of the organisation's expenditure. In businesses such as supermarkets and chain stores 'buying' has long been recognised as one of the most important functions of the business. However, in many industries the purchasing function has not, in the past, been subject to the controls that are imposed on other business functions.

A supply strategy is likely to take account of matters such as the following.

- **Sources**. What sources are available and where are they located? Are suppliers' businesses larger or smaller than the buying organisation (this affects bargaining power). Will different suppliers need to be used in different parts of the world?

- **Number of suppliers**. If there is only a single source of supply this may bring the advantage of bulk purchase discounts, but the organisation may prefer to have several or multiple suppliers to avoid the risk of failed deliveries and to prevent a single supplier from getting complacent.

- **Cost, quality and speed of delivery.** These factors are closely interrelated and the strategy will probably need to make compromises to achieve the right balance.

- **Make or buy and outsourcing**. This is a familiar management accounting problem — to make goods/supply services in-house or buy them in? The answer is liable to have a major impact on the organisation as a whole.

2.2 Antagonism

In the past the supply chain was typically defined by antagonistic relationships.

- The purchasing function sought out the lowest-price suppliers, often through a process of tendering, the use of 'power' and the constant switching of supply sources to prevent getting too close to any individual source.

- Supplier contracts featured heavy penalty clauses and were drawn up in a spirit of general mistrust of all external providers.

- The knowledge and skills of the supplier could not be exploited effectively: information was deliberately withheld in case the supplier used it to gain power during price negotiations.

  Hence, no single supplier ever knew enough about the ultimate customer to suggest ways of improving the cost-effectiveness of the trading relationship, for instance buying additional manufacturing capacity or investing in quality improvement activities.

2.3 Partnership

It is now recognised that successful management of suppliers is based upon **collaboration** and offers benefits to an organisation's suppliers as well as to the organisation itself. By working together organisations can make a much better job of satisfying the requirements of their end market, and thus both can increase their market share.

- Organisations seek to enter into **partnerships** with key customers and suppliers so as to better understand how to provide value and customer service.

- Organisations' product design processes include discussions that involve both customers and suppliers. By opening up design departments and supply problems to selected suppliers a synergy results, generating new ideas, solutions, and new innovative products.

- To enhance the nature of collaboration the organisation may reward suppliers with long-term sole sourcing agreements in return for a greater level of support to the business and a commitment to on-going improvements of materials, deliveries and relationships.

This works best if the cultures and objectives of both organisations are aligned.

The ability to strike a long-term partnership with suppliers depends a great deal on how the buying organisation manages its end of the relationship. Organisations should strive for a relationship of mutual trust and respect. Simply paying bills on time can go a long way to fostering good will and can help when the organisation needs a supplier to go an extra mile.

- It is counter-productive to quibble over every bill or to try to get a better price on everything the supplier sells.

- Expectations should be reasonable: for example if the organisation is a new customer it cannot expect that it will immediately get the same kind of attention that a long-standing customer receives. That is a privilege that may have to be earned over time.

The organisation should clearly indicate any special needs it may have. For example, if a certain order needs to be rushed, managers should ask the supplier what delivery options are available based on the specific deadline. Again, the organisation should not expect to get something for nothing – it should anticipate having to pay for both the products and any value-added services received.

An organisation can benefit over time through the open exchange of information with key suppliers. Any strategic information received should be treated confidentially, and the same should be expected of suppliers. For example an organisation may be asked to sign a non-disclosure agreement, and abide by its terms: this is often not so much a matter of trust, but a legal way to ensure that proprietary data stays that way.

2.4 Identifying new suppliers

As we have indicated, building a successful supplier relationship requires the organisation to think about more than just price. The value of a supplier includes how well it is able to serve the organisation's needs and the needs of the organisation's customers. When assessing potential suppliers, therefore, a range factors should be considered, including (in no particular order):

- What does the company charge?

- Does it offer discounts or other incentives?

- Can it deliver the required quality of product or service (for example is it ISO 9001 certified)?

- Is the supplier willing to customise orders or handle other special needs?

- How will it ship its products, and how much will that cost?

- How quickly will orders be delivered?

- Will delivery quantities be accurate?

- How will the supplier handle returns or other problems?

- Is technical support available, if required?

- How will the supplier manage the account? (For example, will a specific person be allocated responsibility for dealing with your orders? What is the general attitude of their personnel towards customer service?)

- Do they have adequate technology? Do they have plans to upgrade their systems that may disrupt supply, or improve it?

2.5 Investigating suppliers

Managers should contact a supplier's current customers and ask for **references**. The supplier should be happy to put a prospective customer in touch with some of its previous clients (if not, what they are trying to hide?). It should be remembered, of course, that they are unlikely to give a dissatisfied customer as a reference.

Questions would include standard concerns such as price and delivery, and managers should also make enquiries about how the supplier handles problems, since even the best relationships have their occasional glitches.

It is common for suppliers to investigate the financial health of their customers, but it pays for an organisation to investigate its major suppliers' **financial condition** too. By getting a credit report on a supplier, the organisation will have a clearer picture of its potential as a long-term strategic partner. For example, a supplier with credit problems may have trouble meeting its obligations, and this can have an impact on its ability to ship orders in a timely manner. This is not a one-off exercise: it should be done at regular intervals, and the more important the supplier the more regularly it should be done.

2.6 Managing the supplier relationship

The organisation should ensure that processes for establishing and managing appropriate supplier relationships are systematically planned, executed, reviewed and improved within the organisation's quality management system. Appropriate levels of senior management time and effort should be invested in managing supplier relationships according to the strategic importance of the IS project to the business.

- For standard, 'commodity' type supplies, all that may be required are good, tight contractual negotiations and a relatively low-level relationship with the supplier.

- For more complex supplies, for example outsourcing arrangements, management should consider the strategic importance of the business area and the cost of failure, and then decide the appropriate investment to make in the relationship with the supplier. For key suppliers it is important to have channels of communication at a number of levels to support the supplier relationship.

In a long-term relationship it is likely that the organisation's business requirements will change, that volumes will grow, that the supplier and purchaser organisations will be restructured, and that budgets and timescales will change. An effective process is required throughout to ensure that the element of surprise is minimised, and that the supplier relationship survives such changes without degenerating into conflict and creating unacceptable additional costs. Problems can be minimised or avoided where the supplier and the purchaser have clearly defined and agreed expectations and good communications channels have been established.

2.7 Problems and warning signs

Management should recognise that problems in supplier relationships can arise because of problems that can be attributed to the purchasing organisation itself: insufficient top management commitment to the relationship; poor communication, leading to poor mutual understanding of, and commitment to delivering, business benefits; lack of end-user involvement in the process; deadlines or budgets that are unrealistic.

Early warning signs that a purchaser and supplier relationship may go off track include:

- Failure to meet the required quantity and quality

- Changes in supplier attitudes or level of support

- Friction or frustration, often evidence of a mismatch of expectations between purchaser and supplier

- An excessive focus on the contract to establish the relationship

- Confrontational attitudes emerging

- Changes in control of the supplier

- Law suits and the like between the supplier and its other customers.

Even if none of these signs are apparent, satisfactory past performance is not necessarily an indication that a supplier will continually perform at an acceptable level. On a periodic basis (depending on the importance of the supplier) a re-assessment should be made.

Organisations should plan for contingencies even if there are no current problems. New avenues of supply should be identified for back-up before there is any possibility that they may be needed.

2.8 Negotiating with suppliers

Objectives

The first step in supplier negotiation is to set negotiation objectives. The key considerations that need to be borne in mind might include price, value-for-money, delivery, payment terms, after-sales service and maintenance arrangements, quality, and so on, as already mentioned.

Before starting to negotiate, managers should draw up a list of the factors that are most important and decide what they are – and are not – prepared to compromise on. For example, if ordering supplies in bulk it might be seen as most important to find a supplier that will offer a discount, but if investing in a complicated piece of computer software the key consideration might be to make sure that training is provided as part of the deal.

Managers should also consider in advance what offer the other party in the negotiations is likely to make and how they will respond to different scenarios.

If the intention is to do more business with the supplier in the future, the aim should be a deal that both parties are happy with. Although getting the best possible deal in the short-term is important, a good relationship in the future may help the organisation to get even cheaper prices or other perks, such as priority delivery. The importance of good will should not be underestimated.

Understand potential suppliers

By conducting some basic research into a potential supplier, managers can work out how valuable their business is to them. The purchaser's bargaining power increases in direct proportion to the supplier's need for the business.

- If the supplier runs a near-monopoly they are likely to have the upper hand because they have enough business already and the purchasing organisation only has a few other places to go to.

- However, if the supplier has a number of competitors - or is a new entrant to a particular market – the purchaser will be in a much stronger position. And, of course, the supplier may already be offering good deals in a bid to increase its market share.

Alternatively, a supplier may need to get rid of old stock or to fill spare production capacity, so it is important to find out as much as possible about the state of the supplier's order book. And in some trades, suppliers put prices up because discounts are commonly given, so it is important to make sure that any concessions the supplier offers are genuine.

If the supplier is a small business and the buying organisation is its main customer, then the buyer's leverage in negotiations may be considerable. But care is needed: if the buyer pushes the supplier too far this may erode goodwill, and that could damage the service provided. There is also the risk that the supplier will drop the very product that the buyer requires, or even go out of business.

It is useful to identify in advance who in the supplier's business is the best person to negotiate with. There is no point trying to squeeze concessions out of a junior member of staff if they do not have the authority to grant them.

Negotiating at the right time can be an important strategic tool. For example, a supplier's sales person may need to meet a monthly sales quota.

Conducting negotiations

Here are some key practical points to remember when conducting negotiations.

- Match the seniority of the supplier's representatives. Do not send a junior account manager to bargain with the managing director, for example.

- At the outset, state the aspects of the deal that are already satisfactory and the points that need further discussion. Ask the supplier to do the same and try to get them to state a starting price. It is probably unwise to indicate that there are things that can be conceded or compromised upon, at least not at the very beginning of the negotiations.

- Make sure both sides are satisfied with what is being negotiated. Get the supplier to restate any discounts offered and payment terms. Keep these key bits of information to hand.

- If possible insist on using your own terms and conditions of purchase.

- Be aware of common negotiating tactics. For example if the other party keeps referring to urgent deadlines or a person they need to confer with they may be playing games in order to get you to concede a point quickly.

- Don't be pressured into agreeing a point you're not happy with. Ask for a break if you need one. Each time a point is agreed, clarify that you've understood it correctly and write it down.

Negotiating on price

Bartering is far more common in business-to-business relationships than it is (in most developed countries) in business-to-consumer relationships. Depending on the relative bargaining power of the participants, price negotiation has something of the street market about it.

The following tips are most appropriate for price negotiations when dealing with commodity suppliers, less so for strategic partnerships.

- The buyer should never accept the first offer and should make a low counter-offer in return. The other party is likely to come back with a revised figure. Always ask what else they can throw in at the given price.

- If the price is suspiciously low the buyers should ask themselves why. Are the goods of sufficiently high quality? Does it really offer value-for-money? What will the after-sales service be like?

- Any ongoing costs (such as repair costs, consumables and other expenses) that may not be included in the asking price should be considered. The buyer may be able to make the asking price look high by exposing these.

- If the current state of the supplier's market means that prices are falling, this should be pointed out.

- If the price includes features that the buyer does not need, the buyer should try to lower it by asking to remove those features from the deal.

- The buyers should use their bargaining power to get a good deal. If they are a big customer of the supplier, they could ask for bulk discounts, for example. There is a limit to this, however: if the price is too low the supplier may have to cut costs elsewhere – meaning customer service will suffer.

Drawing up a contract

When negotiations are concluded the buyer should notify the supplier in writing how they intend to use the supplies and ask for written confirmation that what they are supplying is suitable. A written record should be kept of all assurances given.

A written contract should be drawn up and signed by both parties. From the point of view of the buyer the aim should be to get a contract that protects all the buyer's interests and shifts as much legal responsibility as possible to the supplier.

Typically the contract will include:

*   details of price, payment terms and delivery schedule

*   a clause stating the supplier's right to ownership of the goods until they're fully paid for

*   a clause limiting the seller's liability – taking into account the purchaser's statutory rights

*   penalties for failure to meet delivery times or quality standards, such as a future discount

*   details of what will happen if there are any problems with the goods or services (for example, will the supplier replace individual faulty goods or the whole batch, and within what time period?) and the level of after-sales service that will be provided

*   other terms and conditions as appropriate. Depending on who holds the bargaining power in the negotiations, these may be the buyer's standard terms and conditions or the seller's, or a mixture of the two.

Activity 1

Clearly the issues surrounding negotiations with **customers** are much the same as those identified above, except from the opposite point of view.

Give some examples of how the paragraphs above might need to be modified to produce a guide to negotiating with customers.

Feedback to this activity is at the end of the chapter.

2.9   Sole suppliers

One potential supplier strategy is to appoint one supplier as a sole supplier of a particular product or service. Taking this action will have benefits for both the supplier and the organisation receiving the service. The supplier will obviously work hard to ensure that their customer receives timely and high quality goods or services while the customer will obtain the benefit of the supplier providing a preferential service.

However, cave needs to be taken to ensure that supply of goods or services will continue into the future. The customer would not want to find out that the supplier has gone out of business, meaning that the product/service is unavailable until an alternative supplier can be found. Similarly, the supplier may not want to place too much dependence on their customer in case the customer decides not to continue to purchase from that supplier.

Overall, the best method of managing the relationship is one of a 'partnership' so both parties can trust each other and therefore develop the relationship for their mutual benefit.

2.10 Supply Chain Management (SCM) tools

The idea of Supply Chain Management is not new – it was first mooted by Michael Porter in the 1980s – but the ability to micro-manage it in large organisations has only become a reality thanks to relatively recent developments in information and communications technology.

Supply Chain Management (SCM) is the process of designing, planning and implementing change in the structure and performance of the 'total' material flow in order to generate increased value, lower costs, enhance customer service and to yield a competitive advantage.

SCM software helps to plan and optimise the supply chain as a continuous and seamless activity. SCM products are able to consider demand, capacity and material constraints simultaneously, and to perform real-time adjustments. Changes can be communicated instantaneously to all participants in the supply chain using Internet technology.

To give you a sense of the full capabilities of SCM software here is a list of the modules found in a typical SCM product from PeopleSoft.

Activity-Based Management	e-Procurement	Production Planning
Billing	e-Product Management	Promotions Management
Bills and Routings	e-Supplier Connection	Purchasing
Collaborative Supply Management	Flow Production	Quality
Cost Management	Inventory/Inventory Planning	SCM Portal Pack
Demand Planning	Order Management	Services Procurement
e-Bill Payment	Order Promising	Strategic Sourcing
Engineering	Product Configurator	Supply Chain Warehouse
Enterprise Planning	Production Management	Trading Partner Management

Table: Modules in a typical Supply Chain Management program

Incidentally, there is currently no general agreement as to what comprises SCM software as opposed to SRM (Supplier Relationship Management) software: if you look at the 'SCM' modules above you will spot several that imply long-term relationships, partnerships and collaboration.

Activity 2

One of the main motivations for introducing Supply Chain Management software will be financial. What do you think might be a typical financial impact for an organisation of SCM in terms of revenue and costs?

Feedback to this activity is at the end of the chapter.

2.11 Quality assurance schemes

Under quality assurance schemes quality control standards are agreed between customer and supplier, and checks are made to ensure that they are met. The supplier guarantees the quality of goods supplied and allows the buying organisation's inspectors free access to its production facilities while the items are being manufactured.

KEY POINT

SCM software helps to plan and optimise the supply chain as a continuous and seamless activity. SCM products are able to consider demand, capacity and material constraints simultaneously, and to perform real-time adjustments. Changes can be communicated instantaneously to all participants in the supply chain using Internet technology.

With the prevalence of JIT production, quality is crucial and suppliers' quality assurance schemes are now very widely used, especially in industries where large numbers of high-tech components are needed, such as the aircraft industry and motor manufacturing, but also widely in government purchasing.

The best known scheme entails certification under the ISO 9000 family of quality management standards, covered in much more detail in a later chapter.

3 Outsourcing: risks and benefits

3.1 The benefits of outsourcing

The potential benefits of outsourcing will depend on the extent to which IT services are outsourced. The major advantages are as follows:

- To achieve **savings in costs**. The main perceived benefit of outsourcing is reduced cost. Using external services can be much cheaper than employing in-house IT staff and not using them fully or efficiently.

- To **overcome skills shortages**. The IS/IT function of the organisation may not have all the resources necessary to carry out the full range of IT activities required. In many cases, the IS/IT requirements of the organisation might not justify an in-house IT department, particularly in the areas of systems development. Facilities management specialists will have a larger pool of technical staff than the organisation. This will effectively eliminate the risk of all skills being lost simultaneously.

- **Flexibility**. Using external IT providers allows an organisation to be flexible in its choice of IT services. It can buy in services as and when it needs them.

An argument that has been used in favour of outsourcing (largely by firms of management consultants) is that organisations should focus on their core skills and activities where they have a clear competitive advantage over rival firms, and sub-contract non-core activities. Outsourcing frees up management time, and allows management to concentrate on those areas of the business that are most critical.

Organisations accepting the view, rightly or wrongly, that IS/IT is an non-core activity, have therefore outsourced some or all of their IT operations.

However, there is no accepted consensus on what is a 'core activity'. Different definitions include the following activities:

- activities critical to the performance of the organisation

- activities that create current potential for profits and returns (or non-financial benefits, in the case of public sector organisations)

- activities that will drive the future growth, innovation or rejuvenation of the organisation.

On this basis, IS/IT might be considered a core activity, and if so outsourcing could be a high-risk strategy, because it off-loads a critical aspect of the business to outside organisations.

3.2 The risks, of outsourcing

When an organisation outsources its IT services on a large scale (total outsourcing), the chain of command is effectively broken. The organisation has a contract with the external supplier and therefore has no direct management control. The IS/IT function of the organisation ceases to be a service provider itself and becomes a manager of the service provision contracts. The organisation needs only a core strategy team and a process for monitoring the service supplier's performance.

A further difficulty is that the organisation's goals and objectives will be different from those of the external suppliers providing the outsourced services. For example, the organisation might be interested in ensuring that its IS/IT function remains dynamic, and responds to changes in IT technology and changes in its information systems requirements. The external supplier, on the other hand, might be more interested in stability and minimal change, in order to keep costs under control and avoid the risks that inevitably arise with system changes and upgrades.

Once a company has handed over its computing to another company under a long-term service agreement, it is locked into the arrangement. Should the service of the facilities management provider be unsatisfactory, leading to a cancellation of the contract, the organisation will be faced with the large expense of having to take the work in-house or arrange a new contract with an alternative supplier.

There are a number of other disadvantages with outsourcing. These are:

- dependency on supplier for the quality of service provision. When a company cedes control of IT to a single supplier, it becomes dependent on the quality of the supplier's skills, management, technology and service know-how.

- a risk of loss of confidentiality, particularly if the external supplier performs similar services for rival companies

- difficulties in agreeing and enforcing contract terms

- the length of contract (the risk of being 'locked in')

- lost in-house expertise and IT knowledge

- a loss of competitive advantage (if information systems are a core competence, they must not be outsourced)

- outsourcing might be seen by management as a way of off-loading IS/IT problems onto someone else, rather than as a way of managing them constructively.

Organisations embarking on outsourcing contracts to develop major new systems often find that the actual costs are significantly higher than the expected costs, due to a failure to anticipate the time and the difficulties in writing and testing the system to the client organisation's satisfaction. This is an area where the management accountant should be able to contribute usefully, by applying sensible forecasts and suitable risk analysis to the evaluation of the capital expenditure proposal.

3.3 Management issues with outsourcing

When an organisation decides to enter into an outsourcing arrangement, and having decided which services to outsource, it needs to:

- negotiate a contract with the service provider, and

- when the contract has been agreed, manage the relationship with the service provider.

Contract negotiation

When a contract is negotiated with an external provider of IT services, the ideal outcome is an agreement that benefits both parties and encourages them to develop a constructive relationship throughout the term of the agreement.

Key issues are:

- cost (i.e. the supplier's prices), and

- the level of service obtained in return.

The **service level agreement** with a supplier must specify which of the host organisation's computer systems are covered, and which items of equipment. For example, a maintenance agreement might cover PCs but not printers.

Where the supplier agrees to provide help desk facilities, the agreement has to specify whether the help desk service will be:

- by e-mail only

- by e-mail and telephone only

- by e-mail and telephone, with site visits as required.

The agreement might also specify performance standards that the supplier should meet, such as:

- a minimum percentage of the time that the system must be operating properly and fully functional ('system up-time')

- a minimum response time for requests for service or assistance

- deadlines for the completion of tasks (e.g. payroll processing to be completed by the last Friday in each month, or target dates for the completion of system development projects).

Various contract negotiation issues are set out in the table below.

Problem to negotiate	Contract response
Difficulty of maintaining performance service levels	Include in contract measures on the following and set sliding scale penalties for size and frequency of failing to meet parameters: • availability (uptime percentage) • quality (response time, % of work completed to schedule, time to initiation) • response to requests for new services and capabilities • keeping up-to-date in hardware and software.

Problem to negotiate	Contract response
Inappropriate contract time scale	Make contract term short if major architectural change is expected. Five years is typically long enough to gain benefits without making contract onerous.
Difficulty in protecting software entitlement	Payment must cover where the software is running (make extra licence payment at start and end of outsourcing contract) unless vendor already holds licence.
Loss of copyright on own software run by vendor	Explicit contract clauses must cover: • ownership of software • software security • software confidentiality.
Loss of copyright on software vendor develops as part of outsourcing	Before development, make explicit in the contract the trade-off between value of the product, its exclusivity and cost of development, leading to copyright held by either the outsource client, the outsource vendor or jointly held.
Difficulty of transferring to a new vendor	To avoid becoming dependent on IS elements to which the vendor has exclusive rights, the outsource client should only use: • what they own • what they have rights to • what is publicly available • what is easily replaced.
Client organisation might wish to discontinue the contract before the end of the contract period, because the IT services are no longer required	Contract to include a clause providing for early termination, subject to suitable notice and termination payments.
Difficulty of grouping/separating IS applications or functions	To increase flexibility, split contracts for logically separate services, e.g. data centre management from local equipment support. Closely connected services should be covered in one contract to increase service quality.
Impossibility of regaining original in-house staff	Outsourcing should be viewed as a semi-permanent decision and plans to regain staff should not be relevant. Outsourcing contracts should not prevent re-hiring of staff at contract end.

Problem to negotiate	Contract response
Loss of staff who are familiar with the client organisation's systems	The supplier should agree to create sufficient documentation of the client's systems so that sufficient knowledge is preserved in the event of loss of key personnel.

Unless the contract with the external supplier is properly negotiated, the service provider could be in a powerful bargaining position when the contract period expires. The particular problem for the client is that the supplier is in control of the files and software for the client's systems.

At the end of a service agreement, if the client organisation wishes to switch to a different supplier, or take the IS/IT services back in-house, there could be difficulties in identifying rights and responsibilities.

- If there have been changes to the system software during the period of the agreement with the supplier, who has the rights to the new software, the supplier or the client organisation? Clearly, the client organisation must insist on having rights to use the software for its systems, and to give other external suppliers the rights to use and upgrade the software.

- If the system is moved from one computer system/network to the system/network of a different supplier, there could be problems with the changeover, due to incompatibility between the systems. There is a risk that the 'old' supplier, having been informed that its services will no longer be required, will want to avoid any obligations to ensure a smooth handover to the new supplier. Arrangements for the handover to a new supplier must therefore be written into the original service agreement, so that the obligations are contractual.

Another potential problem is the need to protect the security of the client's data. The contract terms should therefore provide that at the end of the contract period the outsource organisation should hand over data files and backups, and destroy all other files (e.g. out-of-date files and copies). The client organisation might require the right to send in an auditor to check that this has been done.

Managing the relationship

External providers can be considered as partners or as suppliers. How the relationship is perceived will influence the degree of formality in the process of managing outsourcing.

- Where vendors are seen as suppliers, the organisation will use penalty clauses and forced compliance with contracted agreements as the primary management device.

- Where vendors are seen as partners, the primary management devices will be informal communications and negotiated flexibility.

The notion of working 'in partnership', which is encouraged by vendors, is problematic. Firstly, it should be remembered that client organisations and vendors are usually both commercial organisations with separate income statements and balance sheets, and different goals and objectives. Whilst each organisation may wish for an effective and successful partnership, problems arise when the outsourcing company fails to realise the expectations of the client. A common example is the situation whereby the vendor imposes additional fees for work that was not in the original contract.

The client organisation should have a management team with responsibility for the oversight of the contract, to ensure that service levels are met and that any problems are resolved. Outsourcing can be a risky option, and it is essential that the risks should be properly controlled. Equally, the internal controls should be as effective with outsourcing as they would be if the IS/IT function operated in-house.

4 The customer portfolio

4.1 Introduction

Due to the differences that often exist between 'consumer buyers' (those who purchase items for personal consumption), and 'industrial buyers' (those who purchase items on behalf of their organisation), it is traditional to split buyers into these two broad groups for the purpose of analysis.

4.2 Consumer segmentation

There are several different ways of dividing up markets.

- **Psychological** – Consumers can be divided into groups sharing common psychological characteristics. One group may be described as security-oriented, another as ego-centred and so on. These categories are useful in the creation of advertising messages.

  A recent trend is to combine psychological and socio-demographic characteristics so as to give a more complete profile of customer groups. Appropriately called lifestyle segmentation by one of the companies originating the method, this kind of segmentation uses individuals to represent groups that form a significant proportion of the consumer market. These individuals are defined in terms of sex, age, income, job, product preferences, social attitudes, and political views.

- **Purchasing characteristics** – Customers may be segmented by the volume they buy (heavy user, medium user, light user, non user). They may be segmented by the outlet type they use, or by the pack size bought. These variables, and many others, are useful in planning production and distribution and in developing promotion policy.

- **Demographic** – Customers are defined in terms of age, sex, socio-economic class, country of origin, or family status. The most widely used form of demographic segmentation in the UK is the socio-economic classification shown in the table below:

Socio-economic class	Social status	Job descriptions	Approx % of UK population
A	Upper middle class	Higher managerial, administrative and professional	3
B	Middle class	Middle management, administrative and professional	11
C_1	Lower middle class	Supervisory, clerical, junior management, administrative staff	23
C_2	Skilled working class	Skilled manual workers	33
D	Working class	Semi and unskilled manual jobs	22
E	Subsistence	Pensioners, widows, lowest grade workers	8

Table: Demographic segmentation in the United Kingdom

This form of segmentation is particularly useful in advertising. Socio-economic class is closely correlated with press readership and viewing habits, and media planners use this fact to advertise in the most effective way to communicate with their target audience.

Another useful form of demographic segmentation is to divide customers by their position in the family life-cycle.

Life-cycle stage	Characteristics	Examples of products purchased
Bachelor	Financially well off. Fashion opinion leaders. Recreation oriented.	Cars, holidays, basic furniture, kitchen equipment.
Newly married couple	Still financially well off. Very high purchase rate, especially of durables.	Cars, furniture, houses, holidays, refrigerators.
Full nest (i)	Liquid assets low. Home purchasing at peak. Little money saving.	Washers, TVs, baby foods, toys, medicines.
Full nest (ii)	Better off. Some wives work. Some children work part time. Less influenced by advertising.	Larger size grocery packs, foods, cleaning materials, bicycles.
Full nest (iii)	Better off still. Purchasing durables.	New furniture, luxury appliances. Recreational goods.

Life-cycle stage	Characteristics	Examples of products purchased
Empty nest (i)	Satisfied with financial position. Home-ownership at peak.	Travel, luxuries, home improvements.
Empty nest (ii)	Drastic cut in income. Stay at home.	Medicines, health aids.

Table: Demographic segmentation by family life-cycle

- **Geographic** – Markets are frequently split into regions for sales and distribution purposes. Many consumer goods manufacturers break down sales by television advertising regions.

- **Benefit** – Customers have different expectations of a product. Some people buy detergents for whiteness, and are catered for by Daz or Persil. Others want economy, and may buy Surf. Some customers may demand stain removal; one of the biological products is appropriate.

  It can be seen that, within the same product class, different brands offer different perceived benefits. An understanding of customers' benefits sought enables the manufacturer to create a range of products each aimed precisely at a particular benefit.

- **Other classifications of social grades** – Three other well-known market segmentation classifications are (i) 'The National Readership Survey', (ii) Acorn and (iii) Research Bureau Ltd's classification of housewives.

  (i)   The National Readership Survey (UK)

  In the UK, the National Readership Survey's classification of the population is one of the most basic definitions of a target group.

  A – Higher managerial, administrative or professional (3%)

  B – Intermediate managerial, administrative or professional (13%)

  C – Supervisory or clerical, and junior administrative professional (22%)

  D – Skilled manual (31%)

  E – Semi and unskilled manual (19%)

  F – Those at the lowest level of subsistence: pensioners, widows, casual workers, and the unemployed (11%)

  (ii)   ACORN

  ACORN is a 'marketing segmentation system' that classifies consumers by the type of residential area in which they live. There are 11 ACORN neighbourhood groups:

  Group A – agricultural areas; Group B – modern family housing, higher incomes; Group C – older housing of intermediate status; Group D – poor quality older terraced housing; Group E - better-off council estates; Group F – less well-off council estates; Group G – poorest council estates; Group H – multi-racial areas; Group I – high status non-family areas; Group J – affluent suburban housing; Group K – better-off retirement areas.

(iii)   Research Bureau Ltd's classification of housewives

Research Bureau Ltd, a leading British marketing research agency, conducted a study of 3,500 housewives under the age of 45. As a result it classified housewives into the following eight groups.

The young sophisticates (15%)

Extravagant, experimental, non-traditional, young, well educated, affluent, owner occupiers, full-time employed, interested in new products, sociable, and with cultural interests.

Cabbages (12%)

Conservative, less quality conscious, not obsessional, demographically average, more are full-time housewives, middle class, average income, average education, lowest level of interest in new products, very home centred, and partake in little entertaining.

Traditional working class (12%)

Traditional, quality conscious, unexperimental in food, enjoys cooking, middle-aged, less educated, lower incomes, council house tenant, sociable, husband and wife share activities, and keen on betting.

Middle-aged sophisticates (14%)

Experimental, not traditional, less extravagant, middle-aged, well educated, affluent, owner occupiers, full-time housewives, interested in new products, and sociable cultural interests.

Coronation Street housewives (14%)

Quality conscious, conservative, traditional and obsessional, live relatively more in Lancashire and Yorkshire ITV areas, less educated, lower income, lower level of interest in new products, and not sociable.

The self-confident (13%)

Self-confident, quality conscious, not extravagant, young, well educated, owner occupiers and average income.

The homely (10%)

Bargain seekers, not self-confident, house proud, Tyne Tees and Scotland ITV areas, left school at early age, part-time employed, and partake in average level of entertaining.

The penny pinchers (10%)

Self confident, house proud, traditional, not quality conscious, 25–34 years old, part-time employment, less education, average income, betting, saving, husband and wife share activities, and sociable.

4.3   Industrial buyers

In industrial marketing, the buyer is frequently not the customer or the user. For example, a salesperson of grinding wheels may have a company as a customer. The buyer is a member of the purchasing department and the user is a grinding machine operator. As a result there may be major differences between consumer and industrial selling.

Here are the main features of industrial buyers:

(a) **Motivation**

An industrial buyer is motivated to satisfy the needs of the organisation rather than his or her individual needs. Often, purchases are repeat orders when stock of items has fallen below a certain level and thus the buying motive is clear, i.e. avoiding nil stocks. With significant one-off purchases, the motivation will be the achievement of the organisation's goals or targets. Thus a profit target may mean the buyer placing an emphasis on cost minimisation. A growth target expressed in terms of sales motivates a purchase that will promote that goal.

(b) **The influence of the individual or group**

An industrial purchase may be made by an individual or group. The individual or group is buying on behalf of the organisation but the buying decision may be influenced by the behavioural complexion of the individual or group responsible. The behavioural complexion will be influenced by the same influences on consumer buyers already discussed.

KEY POINT

Webster and Wind observe six roles within a DMU: users, influencers, deciders, approvers, buyers and gatekeepers.

Webster and Wind describe the organisational decision-making unit (DMU) as typically consisting of individuals, active both individually and collectively. Within the DMU, there are six roles that can be readily observed.

- **Users of the product** who may have relatively little influence – if the product is to be used by relatively unskilled operatives, or a patient who uses drugs prescribed by a doctor, for example. In other cases, the end user will be paramount in the buying decision.

- **Influencers** who may have an influence on setting the specification for the product, and evaluating alternatives.

- **Deciders** who will actually make the final decision.

- **Approvers** who will give formal authority for a purchase decision.

- **Buyers** who will carry out the negotiations and agree terms.

- **Gatekeepers** who may obstruct a salesperson from influencing the DMU in his or her favour. These would include purchasing agents, diary secretaries and so on.

KEY POINT

Successful industrial selling requires a knowledge of how an organisation makes its decisions.

It should be apparent from this that successful industrial selling requires a knowledge of how an organisation makes its decisions, so that selling techniques can be modified according to the role that each plays.

(c) **General organisational influences**

Personal relationships between the supplier and the buyer will often be very important.

Each organisation will have its own procedures and decision-making processes when purchases are made. Large centrally controlled organisations will often have centralised purchasing through a purchasing department. The purchase decisions will tend to be formal with established purchasing procedures. In small organisations there will not be a purchasing department. Purchasing decisions will tend to be made on a personal basis by persons who have other functions as well in the organisation. Personal relationships between the supplier and the buyer will often be very important.

The salesperson must therefore identify and understand the buyer in the organisation. As the buyer may be a department, the term decision-making unit (DMU) is sometimes used. The DMU is the group of people (there may only be one in the group in some instances) which has some influence on the purchasing process.

(d)   **Reciprocal buying**

A feature in many industrial markets is the purchase of goods by organisation A from organisation B only on condition that organisation B purchases from organisation A.

(e)   **Purchasing procedures**

An industrial buyer appraises a potential purchase in a more formal way than a consumer buyer. Written quotations, written tenders and legal contracts with performance specifications may be involved. The form of payment may be more involved and may include negotiations on credit terms, leasing or barter arrangements.

(f)   **Size of purchases**

Purchases by an industrial buyer will tend to be on a much larger scale.

(g)   **Derived demand**

Demand for industrial products is generally derived from consumer demands. For example, when consumers demand more motorcars, the demand for steel, glass, components and so on will increase in the industrial sector. Industrial strategists have to know what markets the demand for their products is derived from, and monitor this market as well as their own. This may sound obvious advice, but when the firm is selling through intermediaries, or in overseas markets, there may be very little contact with users and end users.

When industrialists predict a downturn in consumer markets, they will often cut back on production in the short run. This, of course, has the effect of lowering demand in the consumer markets through its effect on employment and wages, and is part of the trade cycle process discussed earlier.

Activity 3

Kotler suggests that 'the industrial market consists of all the individuals and organisations that acquire goods and services that enter into the production of other products or services that are sold, rented, or supplied to others.' The industries making up the industrial market are the public sector, banking, insurance, transportation, manufacturing, agriculture, and so on. Consider the industrial market that a brick manufacturer operates in and describe its characteristics.

Feedback to this activity is at the end of the chapter.

4.4 Industrial segmentation

Three of the following types of segmentation are as used in consumer marketing; the other two are different:

- **Geographic** – The basis for sales-force organisation.

- **Purchasing characteristics** – The classification of customer companies by their average order size, the frequency with which they order, etc.

- **Benefit** – Industrial purchasers have different benefit expectations from consumers. They may be oriented towards reliability, durability, versatility, safety, serviceability, or ease of operation. They are always concerned with value for money. Two advertisements illustrate the benefit concept in industrial marketing. Coventry Climax fork-lift trucks were advertised as very durable, and Colt factory air-conditioning systems were promoted as reducing industrial and human relations problems.

- **Company type** – Industrial customers can be segmented according to the type of business they are, i.e. what they offer for sale. The range of products and services used in an industry will not vary too much from one company to another. A manufacturer considering marketing to a particular type of company would be well advised to list all potential customers in that area of business.

- **Company size** – It is frequently useful to analyse marketing opportunities in terms of company size. A company supplying canteen foods would investigate size in terms of numbers of employees. Processed parts suppliers are interested in production rate, and cutting lubricants suppliers would segment by numbers of machine tools.

Activity 4

Give reasons why demographic segmentation, by itself, is not a successful basis for car manufacturers targeting their customers.

Feedback to this activity is at the end of the chapter.

5 Consumer behaviour

5.1 Rational economic behaviour

KEY POINT

A crucial element in the marketing process lies in understanding why a buyer purchases or does not purchase an organisation's goods or services.

A crucial element in the marketing process lies in understanding why a buyer purchases or does not purchase an organisation's goods or services. If the organisation does not understand the process, it will not be able to respond to the customer's needs and wishes.

Traditional views of marketing tend to assume that people purchase according to the value-for-money that they obtain. The customer considers the functional efficiency of the alternative products, and arrives at a decision by comparing this with the price. This set of beliefs is demonstrably inadequate in explaining consumer behaviour. In industrial purchasing, it is somewhat closer to the truth. The organisation places constraints on the freedom of the industrial buyer, causing subordination of the individual's needs and preferences.

5.2 Maslow's need hierarchy

Maslow developed a hierarchy of why people buy what they do and when they do. His 'need hierarchy' is as follows.

- Physiological needs – heat, air, light, etc.

- Safety needs – the need for the familiar, the secure.

- Love needs – the need to be loved by family, friends.

- Esteem needs – the need to be regarded as important, having prestige.

- Self-actualisation needs – the need to initiate, to achieve for oneself.

Products and services could be considered against this hierarchy. For example, insurance and banking are involved with safety needs; cigarettes and alcohol are frequently dependent upon love needs in their promotions; a fast car exploits customers' esteem needs.

Other features that influence the purchasing decision include:

- cognitive dissonance

- personality

- other people.

Cognitive dissonance – Leon Festinger introduced the theory of cognitive dissonance. Dissonance is said to exist when an individual's attitudes and behaviour are inconsistent. One kind of dissonance is the regret that may be felt when a purchaser has bought a product, but subsequently feels that an alternative would have been preferable. In these circumstances, that customer will not repurchase immediately, but will switch brands. It is the job of the marketing team to persuade the potential customer that the product will satisfy his or her needs, and to ensure that the product itself will not induce dissonant attitudes.

Personality and product choice – The personality of individuals is their psychological make-up. It is shown in their beliefs and attitudes, and in their lifestyle. Products, and their brand names, tend to acquire attributes in the mind of the potential customer; indeed, this is one of the primary functions of branding. When considering goods or services for a purchase, customers will invariably select those that have an image consistent with their own personality. Thus, in a public house, the relatively staid middle-aged drinker may prefer mild or ordinary bitter, the young bachelor may choose lager, the sophisticated businessperson could opt for gin and tonic. Personality and value systems are important determinants of choice.

Influence of other people – So far we have considered customers as individuals. This is unrealistic, however, because each customer is a part of larger social groupings. When people make purchase decisions, they reflect the values of their social and cultural environment. In fact, the form of products and services for sale has been determined by that environment. Among the more obvious influences are those of family and of reference groups.

The family is often important in engendering brand purchasing habits in grocery lines, although it also has a far broader influence in forming tastes in its younger members.

Reference groups, which may be school-friends, working colleagues, fellow club members, etc, exert a strong normative influence. That is, they cause members of the group to buy similar things and tend to disapprove of those who behave in too individualistic a manner. It is a bold person who reads the *Sun* in an office of *Financial Times* readers, and groups of teenagers can be seen to dress with almost identical styles.

5.3 Stages in the purchase decision

It is the function of marketing to bring people to the point at which they actually purchase a product. Some potential customers might be completely unaware of a product, others could be vaguely interested in it, whilst the remainder may want to own it. There are several complex models which illustrate the stages through which people pass on their way to a decision, but one of the simplest and easiest to remember is the following:

A – awareness

I – interest

D – desire

A – action

The customer must be made aware of the product, should become interested in it, then desire it, and finally act by purchasing.

6 Relationship marketing

6.1 Concept

The concept of relationship marketing developed in the 1980s. Businesses identified the fickle nature of customers who were ready to break old and established relationships with suppliers in favour of better deals elsewhere. Customer retention became the critical issue, and both businessmen and academics realised that the success of the business could depend on the retention of customer loyalty through trust and familiarity. Customers should not be treated as strangers every time they return for repeat business. An important academic in this field is Professor Adrian Payne of Cranfield Business School who has explored the idea of what is now described as relationship marketing. Customers can be lost by a number of factors:

- unhelpful staff
- poor quality of service
- inappropriate prices
- lack of customer care.

The concept of relationship marketing has been defined as the technique of maintaining and exploiting the firm's customer base as a means of developing new business opportunities. It can be contrasted with transaction marketing, which is concerned with identifying a customer's need for a good or service and seeking ways to satisfy that need. Relationship marketing focuses on customer loyalty and on ways to develop and build on that loyalty.

An eminent research professional in the USA has coined the saying 'A product can be quickly outdated but a brand is timeless'. Brands exist in the consumer's mind. Therefore the consumer is the obvious target for marketing. The term **customer relationship management (CRM)** is now part of the everyday language of marketing and is the value driver of service businesses. Banks, supermarkets and the leisure industry are all learning the benefits of CRM.

The English National Opera is a theatre company based in London. It is using CRM to retain customer loyalty and promote opera as an art form that is not elitist. A customer who pays for tickets with a credit or charge card is entered in the customer database and is thereafter the recipient of mail shots and promotional offers.

Flying Flowers is a public company based in Jersey. It has a small but growing share in the flower delivery business. The company realised that continued profitability depended on customer loyalty and a quality service. The customer base of some three million names was an essential plank to competitiveness. They approached Kainos software who had extensive experience in developing computer systems for call centres. Kainos produced an integrated system to handle the two main strands of the business, namely floristry and plants by post. The user friendly computer interface requires only one day's training to process orders and deal with special marketing promotions or 'upsetting' (e.g. a customer ordering flowers can also obtain garden plants at a discount).

6.2 Transaction marketing contrasted with relationship marketing

Transaction marketing	Relationship marketing
• concentrates on products	• concentrates on retention and loyalty
• little knowledge of customer	• considerable customer commitment
• product quality a key issue	• considerable customer contact
• little effort on customer retention	• emphasis on quality service

Table: Transaction and relationship marketing compared

Supermarkets such as Tesco and Waitrose create mechanisms that promote relationship marketing:

• loyalty cards (Tesco)

• money-off vouchers

• magazines to promote affinity

• newsletters

• retention of customer data in a database

• data mining to identify customer preferences using relational database systems

• automated computer mailing systems.

6.3 Payne's model of customer markets

Payne goes further to postulate what he describes as a six-market model:

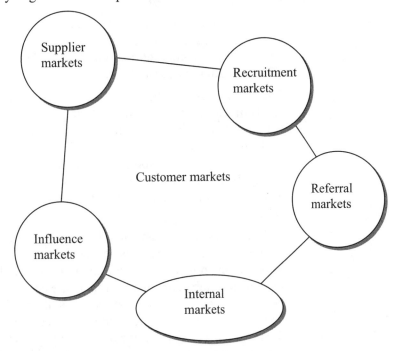

Diagram: Payne's model of customer markets

Payne suggests that there are six possible models in relationship marketing.

- **Customer markets** – The final destination for the product. This ability to reach the customer in a highly competitive environment depends on other parties or relationships.

- **Referral markets** – This is the institution or person who refers the customer to the supplier. A bank refers customers to providers of insurance services. The Automobile Association (AA) refers members to a bank or hire purchase company.

- **Supplier markets** – Partnerships with suppliers have replaced old adversarial relationships. A supermarket sets up a JIT arrangement with a supplier for short-life articles, such as ready-made salads, in order to retain customer interest in an instant healthy food product.

- **Recruitment markets** – A service provider such as PriceWaterhouseCoopers depends on quality staff to deliver quality service. Such an organisation will build up a relationship with careers advisers, professional bodies and others to supply the necessary human resources.

- **Influence markets** – Influence marketing used to be called public relations – a new low fat spread depends upon the sponsorship of a body that promotes healthy eating (Weightwatchers).

- **Internal markets** – This concept is not dissimilar to the concept of internal quality management. Every department has a customer provider relationship with others. The UK corporate lending market recognises that the supplier of banking services (transaction processing) supports the manager of the client account (the relationship manager).

7 Customer account profitability (CAP)

7.1 Problems of measurement

No accountant is under any illusion that the same level of profit is derived from all customers. There are obvious distinguishing features among groups of customers or channels of distribution, and there can also be differences in effective selling prices and variations in the mix of products purchased.

The differences in selling prices may be much less important than the varying levels of customer service that are supplied to each category of customer or market segment. It could be that the lower selling prices charged to one segment of the market are more than justified by cost savings which are generated by the way in which these customers are serviced. Hence these customers may, in reality, be more profitable than those in areas where the higher selling prices achieved are more than offset by the increased costs incurred in achieving the sales.

If the business is to be able to allocate its limited resources most effectively in the future so as to achieve its corporate profit objectives, it must have reliable information on which of its current and potential future customer groupings are its most profitable, and whether there are any existing areas in which the business actually makes a loss, or looks like making one. The senior managers need tailored financial information that helps them to assess the effectiveness of their existing activities in the different market segments. This information would enable sound decisions to be taken with regard to the future allocation of both sales and marketing resources and new product development priorities.

Clearly this financial analysis needs to go beyond a simplistic comparison of the relative gross margins achieved in each market segment but, equally, neatly splitting the existing net profit of the total business exactly across these different areas would provide a very bad basis for future strategic decisions.

7.2 CAP analysis

Many companies refer explicitly to their customers as 'the most important assets which the organisation has', even if they do not feature in the balance sheet. Phrases such as customer orientation and customer focus now proliferate, not only in business strategy books but also in company mission statements and the related business plans.

In recent years there has been a shift towards customer segmentation, with different customer demands in such things as pricing, distribution, sales support and specialised packaging. Without the implementation of sophisticated financial analysis techniques, the company may not be able to decide on the relative costs associated with doing business in these segments. This has led to the development of customer-orientated segment profitability analysis, or customer account profitability (CAP) analysis.

CAP can be defined as 'the total sales revenue generated from a customer or customer group, less all the costs that are incurred in servicing that customer or customer group'.

The essence of CAP is that it focuses on profits generated by customers and does not automatically equate increases in sales revenues with increases in profitability.

7.3 Analysis of customer profitability

If an analysis of customer profitability is provided then marketing decisions are more easily made on such matters as:

- discounts

- special credit terms

- special after-sales servicing

- whether any efforts are required on a sector given its lack of profitability.

The layout of a customer profitability statement can be similar to a product profitability statement:

	Customer Segment A £	Customer Segment B £	Total £
Sales	X	X	X
Variable manufacturing cost	X	X	X
Manufacturing contribution	X	X	X
Variable marketing costs:			
Sales commissions	X	X	X
Selling expenses	X	X	X
Gross contribution	X	X	X
Fixed but direct marketing costs:			
Advertising	X	X	X
Sales salaries	X		X
Telemarketing		X	
Customer net contribution	X	X	X
Indirect marketing costs:			
Corporate advertising			X
Marketing contribution			X
Other fixed costs:			
Administration			X
Net profit			X

Table: Example of a customer profitability statement

7.4 Benefits of CAP

The major benefits that can be obtained from CAP are in the area of strategic planning and decisionmaking. This is because knowledge of the relative profitability of different customer groups can enable a company to focus its resources either on those areas that can generate the most profitable growth for the business or on rationalising areas that are making an unsatisfactory return. It should enable companies to identify unexpected differences in profitability among customer groups and to investigate the reasons for these differences.

In the face of aggressive negotiating by specific customers, the company should be able to quantify the financial impact of any proposed changes and hence argue from a position of relative strength: at least in terms of knowing how much any such changes will cost. For example, consider the situation where one segment or category of customer is considering doing away with the services of field sales support of its suppliers and is trying to negotiate an appropriate discount to reflect the savings to be made to the supplier. From the supplier's point of view, the potential discount should reflect the avoidable cost of the sales force that will obviously be saved if the change is made. However, this cost will not be the same as the historic actual cost which may have been apportioned to this category or segment of customer, as this will include some shared costs, such as sales managers, which will not change if this is the only customer that stops using the support service.

The CAP analysis will reflect the increasing levels of attributable costs as the customer segments are made more general: so that if a change is made to the whole distribution channel, the savings would be much greater. The analysis would also highlight that the potential cost saving may not be equal to the potential incremental cost which would be incurred if a single customer or group of customers wanted to begin using the field sales force service.

7.5 Information for CAP

The above example should have outlined the sort of problems that are likely to be encountered in collecting the information required for a comprehensive system of CAP. Costs must be allocated at varying levels of customer groupings depending on how the cost changes, but more importantly, it may not be relevant to include the actual historic level of cost at all.

The costs required may be hypothetical as in the above illustration of the customers negotiating to stop using the field salesforce. However, the key here is to design a good CAP system that will enable a comparison of relative costs and profitability. Consequently if some customers do not use the field salesforce while other similar ones do, it should be possible to extract the differences in their relative cost levels in respect of the salesforce and hence estimate an approximate avoidable cost involved in ceasing to use it. For this comparison of relative cost levels to generate accurate answers, it is important that each customer analysis is computed on a consistent basis and that there is no attempt to spread the total costs incurred in any area across the customers because, if apportionment is done, the differences will cease to represent the appropriate form of attributable cost which is required.

Some businesses may wish to include some elements of such apportioned costs, particularly if they are likely to have a material impact on the relative levels of customer profit contributions. However it is clear that an even apportionment of such costs will not have any such material impact on relative levels of CAP. Consequently, these shared costs need only be incorporated in the CAP analysis if significantly different levels of cost can genuinely be apportioned to different categories of customers.

8 The marketing audit

8.1 Introduction

The term marketing audit is often used to describe an appraisal of the organisation's marketing activities by examining plans, strategies, objectives, activities and personnel. The desirable features of a good marketing audit are:

- **Independent** – the appraisal is often undertaken by external professionals.

- **Periodic** – marketing is dynamic and the audit needs to be done at regular intervals.

- **Comprehensive** – it must consider all problems and their underlying cause.

- **Systematic** – the audit follows logical series of diagnostic steps.

The advantage of a marketing audit is that it challenges the status quo. People become set in their ways and refuse to change. An audit challenges preconceived assumptions and business practices.

8.2 Checklist for a marketing audit

Kotler et al propose a series of areas for examination and these are given below:

- **Objectives** – Are the organisation's objectives and marketing objectives consistent? Are they compatible with the constraints of the business environment? Have marketing strengths and weaknesses been monitored?

- **Strategy** – Are objectives and strategies compatible? Have the weaknesses of the organisation been evaluated?

- **Environment** – Does the company monitor environmental trends? Are social and psychological factors appraised? How do competitors affect the business? Are there any changes in buyer behaviour that should be monitored?

- **Products** – Are any of the organisation's products obsolete? Should they be phased out? Are new products coming on stream? How good are they?

- **Pricing** – How does the organisation arrive at a selling price? Are prices competitive?

- **Promotion** – How are sales mix decisions made? How are sales staff evaluated?

- **Distribution** – Who decides on the choice of distribution channels? Who decides on distribution policies? Are these policies effective?

- **Market intelligence** – How is market research information communicated and used? How effective are sources of market information?

- **Personnel** – Are they competent and do they understand the product that is being sold?

- **Marketing** – Activities, tasks and controls, i.e. What are the systems of supervision in the marketing department? How are policies evaluated? What reporting systems exist? Are they effective?

Summary

Key points of this chapter are:

- Relationships with suppliers used to be characterised by antagonism – getting the lowest price and exploiting bargaining power –but the modern approach is to enter into partnerships with strategically important suppliers.

- Outsourcing requires constant review and evaluation, and the absence of the in-house facility means managers can concentrate on the core business and treat the outsourced resource as just another service.

- The customer portfolio can be segmented in different ways to assist in the advertising of products. Customers can also be differentiated as personnel and industrial buyers.

- Effective marketing means understanding the relationship with the customer – possibly using some form of CRM system.

- Customer account profitability analysis is used as an important tool to aid marketing decisions and assist in future strategic planning.

- The marketing audit as a means to determining the effectiveness of an organisation's marketing function.

Having completed your study of this chapter you should have achieved the following learning outcome:

- discuss how suppliers and customers influence the strategy process and recommend how to interact with them.

Self-test questions

1   Why might buyers and sellers wish to enter a partnership? (2.3)

2   List a range of factors that should be considered when assessing potential suppliers. (2.4)

3   Why might an organisation outsource some of its activities? (3.1)

4   Distinguish 'consumer buyers' from 'industrial buyers'. (4.1)

5   What are the six roles that may be observed in the organisational DMU? (4.3)

6   What is Maslow's 'need hierarchy'? (5.2)

7   What is relationship marketing? (6.1)

8   Draw Payne's model of customer markets? (6.3)

9   What is customer profitability analysis? (7.1)

10   What are the major benefits of CAP? (7.4)

11   Explain six aspects of a marketing audit. (8.2)

Practice questions

Marketing

Required:

(a)   Distinguish between 'customer' and 'consumer' and indicate the importance to a marketing executive of the distinction   **(7 marks)**

(b)   Explain to what extent, and why, an organisation offering a service (as opposed to a physical product) would require marketing research   **(8 marks)**

(c)   Discuss the idea that 'people don't actually buy what they may appear to be buying – there are deeper reasons involved'.   **(10 marks)**

(Total: 25 marks)

For the answer to this question, see the 'Answers' section at the end of the book.

Feedback to activities

Activity 1

Many of the points will be exactly the same.

The main difference is that the seller will wish to achieve as high a price as possible and will wish to make the potential buyer aware of add-on products and extra services.

Activity 2

Here are some ideas.

- Reduced stock holding costs
- Reduced costs of purchasing
- Less waste because of better understanding of quality standards, fewer errors
- Increased revenue due to higher quality product
- Increased revenue due to better/faster delivery performance
- Increased revenue due to new product ideas and products that more closely match customer needs.

Activity 3

A brick manufacturer's industrial market has characteristics that contrast sharply with consumer markets. These are described below:

(a) **Fewer buyers**

There are fewer buyers in the industrial market than in the consumer market. Although the ultimate users of houses and structures built from using bricks number in the millions, the company's fate critically depends on getting orders from perhaps only a few thousand property developers.

(b) **Large buyers**

Even in popular markets, a few large buyers normally account for most of purchasing. The buyers can thus exert some power over suppliers in terms of price fixing, distribution and product design. These buyers are often geographically concentrated.

(c) **Fluctuating demand**

The demand for industrial goods, such as bricks, tends to be more volatile than the demand for consumer goods and services. A certain change in consumer demand can lead to a much bigger percentage change in demand for the industrial good. Sometimes change in industrial demand can be over twenty times that of the consumer demand change. Economists refer to this as the accelerator principle.

(d) **Derived demand**

The demand for bricks is ultimately derived from the demand for houses and structures built using bricks. If the demand for these declines, so will the demand for bricks decline.

(e)   **Inelastic demand**

The total demand for many industrial goods and services is not much affected by price changes. Property developers are not going to buy many less bricks if the price for bricks rises, unless they can find suitable substitutes such as glass, metal and wood. However, construction companies will use price to decide which suppliers to purchase from, although price levels will have less impact on the quantity purchased.

(f)   **Rational buying**

Industrial goods are usually purchased by professional buyers, who are continually learning new methods of how to make better purchasing decisions. Consumers on the other hand are not so well trained in the art of careful buying.

(g)   **Direct purchasing**

Industrial buyers often buy direct from producers rather than through middlemen.

Activity 4

Reasons include the following:

(a)   A car manufacturer may use buyers' age in developing its target market and then discover that the target should be the psychologically young and not the chronologically young. (The Ford Motor Company used buyers' age in targeting its Mustang car, designing it to appeal to young people who wanted an inexpensive sporty car. Ford found, to its surprise, that the car was being purchased by all age groups.)

(b)   Income is another variable that can be deceptive. One would imagine that a working class family would buy a Ford Focus and the managerial class would buy Ford Scorpions, or BMWs. However, many Focus cars are bought by middle-income people (often as the family's second car) and expensive cars are often bought by working class families (plumbers, carpenters, etc).

(c)   Personal priorities also upset the demographic balance. Middle-income people often feel the need to spend more on clothes, furniture and housing which they could not afford if they purchased a more expensive car.

(d)   The upgrading urge for people trying to relate to a higher social order often leads them to buy expensive cars.

(e)   Some parents although 'well off' pay large fees for the private education of their children and must either make do with a small car, or perhaps no car at all.

Chapter 6

IT AND COMPETITIVE POSITION

Syllabus content

- The impact of IT including electronic commerce on an industry (utilising frameworks such as Porter's Five Forces, the Value Chain) and how organisations can use IT (including the Internet) to enhance competitive position.

- Competing through exploiting information (rather than technology), e.g. use of databases to identify potential customers or market segments, and the management of data (warehousing and mining).

- The relationship between current and predicted strategic importance of IS/IT (the applications portfolio).

- Implications of these interactions for Chartered Management Accountants and the management accounting system.

Contents

1   Introduction

2   IT and competitive advantage

3   Developing strategies

4   McFarlan's strategic grid and the applications portfolio

5   Exploiting information

1 Introduction

IT can be used to enhance competitive position in a number of ways. It can pursue competitive advantage; be used to disturb, enhance or limit competitive forces; be used to enhance a product or service; or be used in the distribution and supply in order to change the basis of competition against rivals.

We discuss McFarlan's grid to indicate how critical information systems and IT are to the success of many companies. The four roles of IT he devised are support, factory, turnaround and strategic. We describe the use of the grid to assess how much an individual organisation depends on its information systems and then show the effect of IT as a catalyst in encouraging or introducing change.

2 IT and competitive advantage

2.1 Introduction

There are many examples where information systems and information technology have given competitive advantage to an organisation. When they are analysed, they can be classified into those instances where IS:

- links the organisation to customers or suppliers

- creates effective integration of the use of information in a value-adding process

- enables the organisation to develop, produce, market and deliver new products and/or services based on information

- gives senior management information to help develop and implement strategy.

However they are categorised, the revolution caused by information technologies has permanently changed:

- distribution channels, e.g. ATMs have changed the way cash is distributed

- production economies and product life cycles, e.g. CAD/CAM and robotics have altered the physical production industries

- value-added services, e.g. information handling related to the acquisition, storage and repackaging of information.

To gain a competitive advantage, an organisation must be able to define when the technology is strategic to its business. They must be able to make a distinction between technology hype, technology capability, useful technology and strategic technology.

- Technology hype is the area of the salesperson's pitch.

- Technology capability represents what technologies can actually do today – the organisation can see these demonstrated.

- Useful technology is the small set out of a larger set of actual capabilities that the organisation would find useful.

- Strategic technology is the area of IS that would lead to the organisation being damaged if it is not adopted.

2.2 IT and the five competitive forces

As we saw in an earlier chapter, Michael Porter identified five forces that determine the extent of competition in an industry.

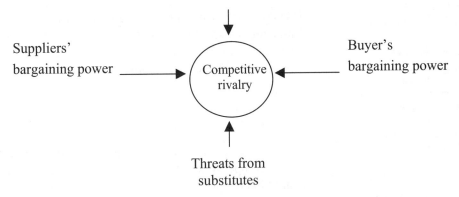

Diagram: Porter's Five Forces model

KEY POINT

Information technology's strategic role can be assessed by its abilities in dealing with the five competitive forces. These forces represent the bargaining power of existing suppliers and buyers (or customers), the threat of substitutes and new entrants and the intensity of existing rivalry. Using this model identifies where IT can be used strategically, e.g. to set up barriers, to enhance a generic strategy.

2.3 Threats from potential entrants

New entrants into a market will bring extra capacity and intensify competition. The strength of the threat from new entrants will depend upon the strength of the barriers to entry and the likely response of existing competition to a new entrant.

IT can have two possible roles to counteract the threat:

(a) **Defensively**, by creating barriers that new entrants to the market find difficult to overcome. IT can increase economies of scale by using computer-controlled production methods, requiring a similar investment in the technology of new entrants.

Another defensive move is to colonise the distribution channels by tying customers and suppliers into the supply chain or the distribution chain. The harder the service is to emulate, the higher the barrier is for new entrants.

(b) **Offensively**, by breaking down the barriers to entry. An example is the use of telephone banking which reduces the need to establish a branch network. Automated teller machines (ATMs) created new distribution channels enabling 'bank branches' to be set up in airports, by out-of-town supermarkets and other areas where there are many potential customers. These machines provided not only expansion of the total market, but also a low-cost method of overcoming the barriers to entry in the areas where the cost of entry was high and space was at a premium.

KEY POINT

The threat from potential entrants depends on the strength of the barriers to entry and the response of existing competition to the new entrant.

2.4 Competitive rivalry

This is rivalry between firms making similar products, or offering the same services, and selling them in the same market. The most intense rivalry is where the business is more mature and the growth has slowed down.

IT can be used to compete. Cost leadership can be exploited by IT, for example, where IT is used to support just-in-time (JIT) systems. Alternatively, IT can be used as a collaborative venture, changing the basis of competition by setting up new communications networks, and forming alliances with complementary organisations for the purpose of information sharing. When Thomson Holidays

KEY POINT

Competitive revalry is between firms making similar products. IT can be used to compete against rivals.

introduced their on-line reservation system into travel agents' offices, they changed the basis of competition, allowing customers to ask about holiday availability and special deals, and book a holiday in one visit to the travel agent.

2.5 Threats from substitutes

This threat is across industries (e.g. rail travel with bus travel and private car) or within an industry (e.g. long life milk as substitute for delivered fresh milk). In many cases information systems themselves are the substitute product. Word processing packages are a substitute for typewriters.

IT-based products can be used to imitate existing goods as in electronic keyboards and organs. In the case of computer games, IT has formed the basis of a new leisure industry.

Computer-aided design and computer-assisted manufacture (CAD/CAM) have helped competitors to bring innovative products to the market more quickly than in the past.

Interactive information systems add value by providing an extra service to an existing product. An example of this is provided by ICI's 'Counsellor', which is an expert system that advises farmers on disease control. It analyses data input by the farmer on areas such as crop varieties grown, soil type and previous history of disease and recommends fungicides or other suitable ICI products to solve the farmer's problems.

2.6 Buyers' bargaining power

The bargaining power of buyers or customers can be based on their size, or the nature of the product that they buy. A powerful customer is one who can, to some extent, dictate the price and quality of what you sell to them. They may be able to do this because they are very large, and buy high volumes, or because they are buying a 'generic' product and can get it elsewhere.

The large supermarket chains exert tremendous buying power on the food and beverage producers. Over 60% of all the soft drinks sold in the UK go through four retail organisations. This means that they can demand huge discounts from manufacturers. On the other hand, the supermarkets are forced to keep their retail prices low because customers are becoming less brand loyal to retailers. They can 'shop around' for the cheapest product because they know that they are buying the same thing from every supermarket.

2.7 Suppliers' bargaining power

The bargaining power of suppliers, and hence their ability to charge higher prices, will be influenced by:

- the degree to which switching costs apply and substitutes are available

- the presence of one or two dominant suppliers controlling prices

- the products offered having a uniqueness of brand, technical performance or design, which is not available elsewhere.

Reducing the suppliers' power to control the supply can erode this power. Where an organisation is dependent on components of a certain standard in a certain time, IT can provide a purchases database which enables easy scanning of prices from a number of suppliers. Suppliers' power can be shared so that the supplier and the organisation both benefit from performance improvements.

The Ford Motor Company set up CAD links with its suppliers with the intention of reducing the costs of design specification and change. The time taken and the error rate was reduced because specifications did not have to be re-keyed into the suppliers' manufacturing tools.

Until the introduction of PCs, most computers used their own software. Generally speaking this meant that you could not run IBM software on ICL mainframes, making a switch in supplier both costly and inconvenient.

Another form of locking customers in is to develop customer information systems, which inform the organisation about the customer's behaviour, purchases and characteristics. This information enables the organisation to target customers in terms of direct marketing and other forms of incentive such as loyalty schemes, where methods of rewarding customer loyalty by giving them 'preferred customer' status are used. If a clothing retailer is launching a new collection it can offer its loyal customers a private viewing. The Habitat retail chain, in common with many others, has special evening showings of their new stock, with added attractions such as drinks and discounts, to which only Habitat card holders are invited.

Most airlines have frequent flyer programmes, and offer deals such as air miles or rewards as incentives.

2.8 Using the five forces model

Porter's model may be used to help clarify the overall business strategy. The model provides a framework to discuss areas where information technology and systems can yield competitive advantage. The advantages may be in defending the organisation against the forces or by attacking and influencing them in its favour.

Management should use the model to determine which of the forces poses a threat to the future success of the organisation. By ranking these threats in terms of intensity and immediacy, the most critical can then be considered in terms of how information technology or systems can be used to gain advantage or avoid disadvantage.

3 Developing strategies

3.1 The strategic options generator

The strategic options generator developed by Wiseman is a checklist that guides the executive through all the parameters that must be considered in seeking strategic opportunities. By promoting a series of thoughts and questions that relate to the strategic thrusts identified in the model, it encourages the search for IS opportunities. Wiseman's strategic options generator is outlined in the following diagram:

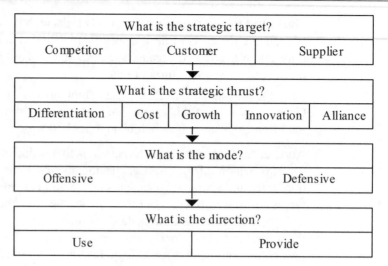

What is the strategic target?		
Competitor	Customer	Supplier

What is the strategic thrust?				
Differentiation	Cost	Growth	Innovation	Alliance

What is the mode?	
Offensive	Defensive

What is the direction?	
Use	Provide

Diagram: The strategic options generator (after Wiseman)

The generator directs its attention towards strategic targets, suppliers, customers and competitors. The strategic thrust is then used to 'hit' them. There are five strategic thrusts that may be used to seek advantage aggressively or defensively to reduce a competitor's advantage:

- differentiation – distinguishing a product from others

- cost – lowering the organisation's cost or causing a competitor's cost to be raised

- innovation – doing something that might change the way that business within the industry is done

- growth – may be by sales or market penetration

- alliance – with another organisation through acquisition or merger or for information sharing.

The direction describes whether the organisation is using the strategy for itself or providing it for the target's use.

3.2 IT as a strategic weapon

Information technology can be used as a strategic weapon in a number of ways.

- It is a potential supplier of competitive advantage to an organisation. We have seen this in travel agents where choosing and reserving a holiday can be done in much less time and more conveniently when the agent is on-line to the suppliers.

- Information technology and systems can be used as a strategic weapon to improve productivity and performance. CAD and CAM are two examples where this might be the case.

- IT can be used in the development of new business. For example, selling the analysis of a large supermarket's sales to market research companies so that they can identify trends in product purchasing.

- Information systems can be used to change the management and organisational structure of the organisation to achieve competitive advantage. Computers with modems enable people to work from home, reducing the cost of travel and office space. Teleconferencing and video conferencing are available to managers, reducing the necessity for them to travel to meetings and making their time more productive.

3.3 Competitive advantage and the value chain

Porter and Miller's article on how information gives you competitive advantage outlines three areas where the 'information revolution' affects the rules of competition:

(a) IT changes industry structure and, in so doing, alters the rules of competition.

(b) IT creates competitive advantage by giving companies new ways to outperform their rivals.

(c) IT spawns new businesses, often from within the organisation's existing operations.

They argue that IT is more than just computers and that the value chain is an important concept linking IT and competitive advantage.

Organisations carry out a range of primary activities and/or support activities, which are concerned with producing the end product or service. All the activities of the value chain have a potential to enhance or impede the organisation's success in adding value to their product or service. The value chain for a company in a particular industry is embedded in a larger stream of activities that we term the 'value system'.

Every value activity has both a physical and an information-processing component. The physical component includes all the tasks required to perform the activity. The information-processing component encompasses the steps required to capture, manipulate and channel the data necessary to perform the activity.

Porter's value chain model, shown in the diagram below, can be used to analyse these activities for the purpose of identifying IT opportunities. It can be used to suggest areas where IT can interpret activities.

KEY POINT

All the activities of the value chain have a potential to enhance or impede the organisation's success in adding value to their product or service.

The value chain

Diagram: The value chain (after Porter and Miller)

The value chain model divides an organisation's activities into nine generic activities: five primary activities and four support activities. The value an organisation creates is measured by the amount that buyers are willing to pay for a product or service. An organisation is profitable if the value it creates exceeds the costs of performing all the activities involved in producing the product or service. To gain competitive advantage an organisation must either perform some or all of the generic activities at a lower cost or perform them in such a way that leads to differentiation, depending on which of the generic strategies is being used in the organisation.

In an exam situation you might be asked to use Porter's value chain analysis to decide how individual activities might be changed to reduce costs of operation or to improve the value of an organisation's products/services.

Only use the diagram if you can show how this would apply in the organisation you are analysing. The first step is to outline the primary activities that may be a source of advantage. Then link these to the support activities, showing how each of them cuts across all of the primary activities.

Firm infrastructure	Planning models					M
Human resource management	Automated employees scheduling					A
Technology dev.	CAD			Electronic market research		R
Procurement	On-line purchasing					G
	Automated warehouse	Flexible manufacturing	Automated order processing	Remote terminals for sales staff	Remote servicing of equip.	I
	Inbound logistics	Operations	Outbound logistics	Marketing and sales	Service	N

Support activities — Primary activities

Diagram: Application of the Value Chain to a typical organisation

In the primary activities of **inbound and outbound logistics**, IT can be used to advantage. Materials planning systems (MRP II) can help capacity and production scheduling. Warehousing can benefit from bar-codes to identify information about stock held.

Physical tasks in the **operations** activities can be automated. Examples are process and machine tool control. Also robots can be used for tasks which are either monotonous or dangerous for people to do, e.g. paint spraying in the manufacture of cars.

Marketing and services activities can be made more effective by databases such as mailing lists or the information provided by EPOS systems.

In the support activities, IT can be used in procurement activities with electronic data interchange (EDI) to link purchasing with sales order systems. CAD and CAM are an important influence on the technology development activities.

Porter and Millar advocate five steps that senior executives may follow to take advantage of opportunities that the information revolution has created. They are as follows:

(i)   Assess information intensity in the value chain of the entire operations.

(ii)   Determine the role of IT in industry structure.

(iii)   Identify and rank the ways in which IT might create competitive advantage.

(iv)   Investigate how IT might spawn new businesses.

(v)   Develop a plan for taking advantage of IT.

3.4 Information intensity matrix

For any organisation it is possible to assess the information content, i.e. the information intensity, of the value chain activities and linkages. Porter and Millar's information intensity matrix considers the role of IT and suggests how it can be exploited for competitive advantage. The matrix evaluates the information intensity of the value chain (how product value is transformed through activities and linkages in the value chain) against that of the product (what the buyer needs to know to obtain the product and to use it to obtain the desired result).

When assessing the degree of information in the product itself, oil, for example, has a low information content and banking has a high information content. The degree of information in the value chain also varies. It is low in the case of a cement manufacturer who makes a simple product in bulk, but high in the case of a complex, sophisticated process such as oil refining.

	Information content of the product	
	Low	**High**
High	Oil refining Legal services	Newspapers Banking Airlines Education
Low	Cement Bricks	Fashion

(Left axis label: **Information intensity of the value chain**)

Diagram: The Information Intensity Matrix (after Porter and Miller)

If the information content of the product is high, information can be used in the product, e.g. Internet sites for newspapers. When the information in the value chain is high, it implies that sophisticated information systems are required to manage the linkages optimally.

The segment where the information content of the product and the value chain information content are high will be represented by banking and financial services. For example, ATMs, credit cards, debit cards and customer databases have all been integrated to give a much more personalised service as well as lowering service costs. There are banks in the UK, e.g. First Direct, that have no branches and retail solely through ATMs and 24-hour telephone phone links.

The segment where the information content of the product and the value chain information content are low contains traditional process-manufactured, widely-available commodity products with several potential producers, such as bricks and cement. The fact that information content is low does not mean that there is no scope for exploiting IT to achieve a business advantage. It is reasonable to assume that most firms in this segment are low-cost producers looking for linkages in the value chain to contribute to overall cost leadership. For example, there could be a niche market for specialist bricks, e.g. in garden design, where expertise is in short supply. Information about their use could provide added value. The production process offers little scope for IT but, since the process is presumably well known and closely controlled, information could be used to provide a safer operation. For example, airline pilots are encouraged to use the autopilot to fly planes because consumption of fuel increases by as much as 30% during a manually-controlled flight.

3.5 Linking IT with the value chain

Information systems can provide linkages within and between value chains. The example outlined in the diagram below shows how an information system could provide a competitive advantage. The aim is to:

- identify customer needs and values in the market, defined either broadly or by market segment

- consider and establish which of the generic strategy routes is most appropriate

- operate this route in such a way that customer needs are being met by a mix of activities which is distinctly different from that of the competitors, and which achieves a coherent set of linkages between the activities

- achieve cost stability or reductions through experience in these crucial activities, especially where they give cost advantages over the competition.

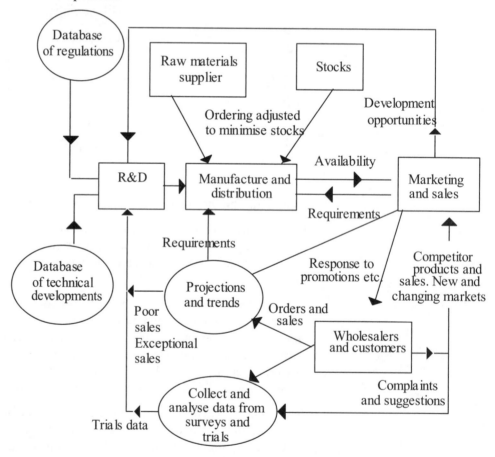

Diagram: Using IT to provide competitive advantage

3.6   The Internet and the value chain

Telecommunications companies can now provide a fully integrated service of traditional telephone, digital cable TV, Internet access and home shopping to most households. The system enables consumers, in both domestic and overseas markets, to order their shopping, browse the Internet, view films on demand and make telephone calls, possibly with integrated video, from their living room. This will have a profound effect on both employment and society.

It will be particularly significant for businesses in the retailing, media and entertainment fields, speeding the development of electronic home shopping and banking, and the 'interactive' communication between a business and its customers. The Internet and electronic commerce technologies will be used to link an enterprise to its customers and to its other external business partners. Many organisations are setting up websites with product or service details for people to access from anywhere in the world. Within the banking and financial industries, EDI and related applications are revolutionising the entire system of moving funds. Supermarkets are delivering shopping ordered over the Internet, selected from a list of more than 20,000 different items. International email systems will enable businesses to communicate cheaply and efficiently around the world. Email also sidesteps busy fax machines and increases the ease of communicating across time zones.

Enterprises will not need to be tied to any particular building or country. People are able to telecommute because communication between computers enables people to work from remote sites. By combining many different businesses via communication links, a virtual company could be created. This will encourage the development of staff working from home and offer the benefit of flexibility. The organisation saves money on office space, and travelling costs might also be reduced if more business can be done with employees using their own telephone connection linked to a computer. It makes part-timers and freelancers easier to use, as they may be happier to work from home.

People can work when they want to, rather than during office hours. There are no routine manual chores of handling and processing data and information. An integrated digital service means that a business's human resources can be used more effectively and efficiently for innovation, planning production, decision making and the servicing of customers' needs.

Developments in 'video conferencing' via personal computers and the telecommunications system, mean that companies can arrange 'electronic meetings' between executives and business partners in different countries. The growing use of video conferencing reduces dramatically the amount of time and money spent by business executives travelling between subsidiary plants and offices located in different countries and continents.

Never before have there been so many options in terms of how, where, when or with whom to work, learn, buy and sell. Teleworking, on-line learning, shopping, banking and even medicine are transcending barriers of organisation, distance and time. Because browsing on the Internet knows no boundaries, it is possible for consumers to buy with confidence after comparing specifications of goods available throughout the world. From the comfort of their living room, people will be able to study, work, organise their finances, do their shopping, browse the holiday destinations and book a holiday, chat on the telephone or send an email and choose from many different channels of television. With connected devices users have access to a huge, up-to-date library of information, help and entertainment, which is on line 24 hours a day.

3.7 Other frameworks to help identify options to use IT strategically

Michael Earl developed a number of frameworks for assessing the strategic implications of IT. These are:

- awareness frameworks

- opportunity frameworks

- positioning frameworks.

Awareness frameworks

These are a series of models which help managers assess the general impact of IT on the organisation. One of the awareness frameworks, the refocus framework, exists to help change 'mind sets' or to challenge assumptions about the use and value of IT, asking questions such as 'Should the organisation use IT to improve access to the market place or use it to improve the organisation's existing operations?'. A building society might question access into European ATMs against improving its existing operations to reduce the time it takes to clear a cheque.

Opportunity frameworks

These are tools designed to analyse whether an organisation has the opportunity of strategic advantage in a particular area. One of these tools, the applications search tool, was used by Ives and Learmouth to develop a customer resource life cycle. This identifies the steps taken by a customer when acquiring a product or service. The phases they identified in the life cycle were:

(a)   requirements – covers what and how much of it?

(b)   acquisition – includes where it is bought, order and payment methods and acceptability testing

(c)   stewardship – covers how it is cared for, repaired or enhanced

(d)   retirement – incorporates the return or disposal of the product or service.

The life cycle is then used to design applications around actual customer behaviour. After studying a customer resource life cycle for kitchen replacements, a kitchen furniture manufacturer might use a CAD package, installed in a portable computer, to help their field sales staff to 'design to fit' the customer's requirements. The software could be used to simulate the look of a new kitchen and several alternatives can be shown to the customer in the comfort of their home.

Positioning frameworks

These help managers to assess the strategic importance of the current situation of IT for their organisation and their industry. This framework is similar to Nolan's stage hypothesis.

4 McFarlan's strategic grid and the applications portfolio

4.1 IT and competitive advantage

Another authority on IT and competitive advantage is McFarlan, who mentions three examples where organisations have gained competitive advantage from IT.

(a)   A major distributor offers its customers the opportunity to enter their orders directly by using an on-line network. The main advantage of the system is to reduce order entry costs, while at the same time allowing customers to be flexible in the time and processing of order submission. Further advantages arise from adding value for customers and increasing sales.

(b)   Similar to the Ford Motor Company, a major aerospace company has requested all its key suppliers to implement CAD to its own CAD installation. This significantly reduces the time and cost of carrying out design changes, parts acquisition and inventory. Such a change would again lead to competitive advantage.

(c)   A national carrier can substantially reduce the competitive position of a regional airline. The national carrier, through access to the reservation levels on every one of the smaller airline's flights, can pinpoint all mutually competitive routes where the regional is doing well and take competitive pricing and service action. The fact that the regional airline is unable to gain access to the data held by the national carrier puts it at a competitive disadvantage.

McFarlan urges companies to address five key questions regarding the impact of technology. He argues that, if the answer to one or more of the questions is yes, the information technology represents a strategic resource that requires attention at the highest level. The questions are:

- Can information technology build barriers to entry?

- Can information technology build on switching costs?

- Can information technology change the basis of competition?

- Can information technology change the balance of power in supplier relationships?

- Can information technology generate new products?

As Porter has identified, **barriers to entry** allow the organisation to hook their customers into using products and services. In the example cited above with the distributor, the company successfully opened up a new electronic channel to its customers which was unrivalled by its competitors.

McFarlan asserts that customer reliance on the supplier's electronic support system, coupled with increased operational dependence and normal human inertia, are likely to reduce the prospects of choosing another supplier. He uses the example of home banking to show that once a customer has learned to use the system, it is likely that the time and cost of selecting and learning another home banking system will be prohibitive. So, the supplier successfully 'hooks' the customer.

Another area that McFarlan uses as an example is cost-based competition. He argues that technology has permitted development of product features that are so different they cause the basis of competition to change radically. The magazine distribution industry was considered to be dominated by cost-based competition. During the 1970s electronic technology was used for cost control in the sorting and distribution processes, allowing companies to be low-cost producers. Later strategies allowed distributors to capitalise on the knowledge that the majority of its customers were small and unsophisticated, and not aware of their profit margins or cost base. One of the big distributors of magazines to news stands and stores decided to utilise its records of weekly shipments and returns from a news stand to provide relevant information of what was being purchased on each news stand. Programs were developed to calculate profit per square foot for every magazine. The information relating to magazine sales from each stand was gathered and the ethnic and economic composition of the locality was taken into consideration. Because of this information, the distributor could forecast how each news-stand could improve its product mix.

McFarlan adds that instead of just distributing magazines, the company had used technology to add a valuable inventory management feature that has permitted it to raise prices substantially and has changed the basis of competition from cost to product differentiation.

4.2 Existing and future systems

Information systems have different degrees of importance for all organisations, although they are critical for some. Many organisations invest large amounts of money in IT, some of it spent unwisely. The importance is not how much is spent but how well the funds are used.

Despite all the expenditure there may be a lag before the new facilities are exploited, the benefits of the expenditure being delayed until the users have caught up with its potential. It is important for organisations to understand whether IT is critical to them or not. If the management can make a case for investing then they should ascertain whether the structure of the organisation can take advantage of the opportunities, decide on an appropriate approach to the management and planning of the information system and then determine the level of expenditure.

The strategic grid from McFarlan and McKenney, 1983, shown below, was devised as a framework for classifying the strategic use of IT (information technology). It arrays an organisation's existing applications against those currently under development.

Diagram: McFarlan's (and McKenney) strategic grid

The strategic grid offers a useful conceptual framework for diagnosing the state of the organisation by looking at the nature of the business, the future plans, and existing and planned computer applications. It reinforces the point that not all firms necessarily use IT strategically. In fact some might not need to employ IT as a strategic device.

Support – where IT has a support role and is also a necessity to the working of the organisation, information systems have little relevance to the organisation's existing or future success. The current information system may include accounting operations and payroll but there are no new developments that can contribute significantly to the competitiveness of the organisation.

There is usually a low level of senior management involvement in this situation because the commitment to information systems planning is low and any development would rely on localised management.

Factory – if information technology has a factory role, the organisation depends heavily on information systems support for smooth operations. Future IT developments are not likely to add to their competitive edge. Some airlines and retailers would come into this category; Earl mentions a steel works with an on-line real time system for controlling production. Even one hour of disruption to these organisations' booking systems or order processing systems could fundamentally damage their competitive performance. McFarlan and McKenney maintain that strategic goal setting and linkage of information systems to the corporate plan are not too important if IT has a factory role.

Turnaround – information technology's turnaround role is where existing IT is not too important, but future development is likely to have a significant impact. In these organisations the applications under development have a high potential to contribute to the organisation's strategic objectives.

The performance of firms in a turnaround situation is often inhibited by lack of support from the information-processing department. There is a need for planning in this cell because the firm cannot maintain control over its rapidly expanding operations without the new computer applications.

Strategic – in some organisations the information technology's strategic role is where existing and future developments are at the heart of the organisation's future success. Banks and insurance companies are typical of this sector. They have applications, which they rely on for the smooth running of their day-to-day activities, and they have future developments, which are vital to their competitive success and are integral to the organisation's strategic objectives. These firms need significant amounts of planning, as the firm would be at a disadvantage if the information processing did not perform well.

In 1991 British Airways spent £150 million on information technology. Although the core of their business activity was transporting people by aeroplane, doing this profitably and maintaining excellence of service was highly dependent on the management of information. To help sell seats one of the largest computers outside the defence industry was used. The BA system could extract data from anywhere in their network in two seconds. The airline could link seat availability to the currency a potential passenger used, limiting the availability for those paying in weaker currencies. It also included sophisticated overbooking management to ensure that the majority of passengers would not be disappointed and, if they were, they would be compensated. The management of BA regarded IT as a key strategic tool for competitive and profitable performance. The airlines continue to spend large amounts on IT.

4.3 Strategic potential for IT

Using IT strategically has enhanced the competitive position of many organisations in a variety of sectors. For example, the financial services sector has witnessed vast changes brought about by new technologies such as the client server architecture, multi-tasking and 4GLs. The strategic potential for information technology can be used in a number of areas, such as the following.

- New business, where information technologies make whole new operations possible. For example point of sale equipment, which includes effective stock and re-ordering facilities.

- Market research information can also be obtained from point of sale equipment.

- Sales – by giving salespeople portable computers they can enter orders directly and receive messages quickly. This can reduce paperwork and speed up delivery.

- Financial management can be improved if a link is set up between the bank and the organisation. This can allow financial information to be obtained quicker.

- Product development such as in-house electronic publishing can help turn out product manuals faster for speedier introductions.

- Training or re-training employees using videodisks allows them to learn at their own speed and cuts training costs.

- Locking in customers by creating exclusive computer communications with customers for order entry and exchange of product and service data. This service can increase the competitive advantage.

4.4 Applications portfolio theory

KEY POINT

The applications portfolio looks at the strategic impact of individual applications within the organisation, and classifies them as if they were products in the BCG matrix.

A development of the strategic grid is the 'applications portfolio' suggested by Peppard. This looks at the strategic impact of individual applications within the organisation, and classifies them as if they were products in the BCG matrix (see diagram).

Strategic importance in the current competitive environment

	Low	High
High	High potential	Strategic
Low	Support	Key operational

(Left axis: Strategic importance in the predicted competitive environment)

Diagram: Peppard's application portfolio

Like McFarlan, Peppard suggests four classifications. This time, an organisation would use the grid to target those applications within its portfolio that have the greatest strategic potential. The four categories are as follows:

- **Support**. These are applications that improve management effectiveness but are not critical to the business. The benefits they deliver are mainly economic. Examples include accounting systems, payroll systems, spreadsheets and legally required systems.

- **Key operational**. These applications are critical to sustain the existing business. Such applications generally support core organisational activities. Examples include inventory control, production control and order management.

- **Strategic**. These applications are critical to future business success (see above for specific examples).

- **High potential**. These applications are innovative, and might be of future strategic potential. Examples might include the use of the Internet, expert systems, or multimedia.

4.5 Forces that drive an organisation round the strategic grid

Companies may be driven from one part of the strategic grid to another depending on the industry sector and the need to stay competitive. Forces that drive an organisation round the strategic grid may be internal or external.

Internal forces will be concerned with matching the potential of information technology to the organisation's operations and strategy, such as a decision to improve productivity.

External forces will be associated with changes in the competitive environment, such as actions of competitors, suppliers or customers.

As a **Support** firm grows it will become increasingly concerned with production and distribution. The need for efficient production, generally using standard IT techniques, will force the company to the **Factory** position. The IT packages, once established, will be fairly static.

If the same firm develops products with high sales potential, and it chooses to market them itself, then it must become more involved with the volatile consumers and in direct conflict with competitors. The environment is likely to change rapidly, and novel IT systems will be required to cope with the situation.

Activity 1

In the past, ShoeMaker's spending on IT has been strictly controlled and used mainly for accounting, processing sales orders and printing invoices. One of its major customers has sent a letter with the following passages in it: 'We have always valued speed and responsiveness, and this has been the main reason behind our sourcing from domestic suppliers of shoes. However, we have recently had offers from suppliers in the Far East offering a wider-ranging flexibility in design with new production technology. Can you offer anything similar?'. One of the suggestions from the customer was that ShoeMaker should automate their sales order processing system to become interlinked with their purchasing systems to increase responsiveness.

(i)   Explain which position on the strategic grid ShoeMaker currently occupies.

(ii)   If the managers decide to introduce new ordering systems and production technology, will their position change?

(iii)   Are there any forces driving it round the grid?

Feedback to this activity is at the end of the chapter.

5   Exploiting information

5.1   Mission critical and analytical systems

Mission critical systems handle the transactions of an organisation. Data is organised to guarantee fast transaction execution. As on-line systems took over, it became obvious that faster transaction execution provided competitive advantage. If you could process an order in minutes rather than hours, you were winning (assuming the competition still took hours).

However, many mission critical systems did not provide much of a query service. Reports would be run overnight or when the system was not busy, because running them reduced the performance of production transactions. Consequently, decision support activity took a back seat.

Systems need analysis to provide accurate feedback, typically through running a system, analysing its behaviour and then feeding back change into the system as a result of the findings. Where analysis is not possible, informed change is unlikely to occur. If we wish to improve the efficiency or effectiveness of operations, we need to find ways to analyse them.

Through decision support software and database engines, the importance of providing good query capabilities has now begun to be recognised.

Decision support systems generally ran on data downloaded to PCs, which allowed managers to launch their own queries on predetermined sets of data. The main limitation was the amount of data, as this had to be managed on a PC. The emergence of the database engine provided computer hardware that was purpose-built to cater for quick answers to queries, even on large amounts of data.

5.2 Computer software

The database and the DBMS allow the manager to interrogate and access a mass of data at will. An enormous range of packages is available to use this data in exploring alternatives and making decisions; for example for:

- modelling and simulation

- spreadsheets

- statistical analysis of all types

- forecasting

- non-linearand linear programming

- regression analysis

- financial modelling

- sensitivity and risk analysis

- expert systems.

Activity 2

Imagine a retail business consisting of multiple locations. What type of questions might the director want answers to?

There is no feedback to this activity.

5.3 Application types

There are two distinct types of computer application.

- **Production applications** – record an organisation's production activity. They generally involve short transactions, most of which add or change information and all of which need a fast response.

- **Query applications** – analyse data to produce useful knowledge. They need to query much of the data created by production applications but they do not change this data. They often need to launch very long and resource-demanding transactions.

Regarding computer usage, these two types are incompatible. Ideally, query applications need their own resources that are properly configured to cope with the workload. This is a major reason for the popularity of the term 'data warehouse', which sums up the following important points.

- The organisation needs a specific hardware resource for their query applications.

- They also need a central database (warehouse) in which to store the data that the query application will use.

Providing access to the right data in the right way is not simple. Improvement to a system is usually incremental; once someone has started examining data, they might need to look at other data, or the same data organised differently. At first, this might seem to be easy but in practice it is not. Designing a data warehouse does not mean dumping lots of data into a database on a regular basis.

5.4 Data warehousing

A data warehouse is a subject-oriented, integrated, time-variant, non-volatile collection of data in support of management's decision-making process.

A data warehouse supports information processing by providing a solid platform of integrated, historical data from which to do analysis. It is a database, data extraction tool, decision support system, or other analysis tool or

procedure that extracts data from the organisation's production database, reformats it and loads it into a database designed for querying with an on-line analytical processing systems (OLAP). OLAP allows users to dynamically extract pertinent summary information.

The conventional data warehousing model is a system in which a large centralised store of consolidated business data is maintained by constant updates from the operational systems (branches/stores). This centralised store is usually a relational database, but often it can be a proprietary multi-dimensional data store, optimised for OLAP queries.

Since operational data is likely to reside in highly heterogeneous systems, e.g. cash register tapes, invoice printing systems and order entry systems, the process of collecting the data needs to be customised and automated. Each store or branch must be responsible for ensuring the timely and accurate delivery of this information. In enterprises where the information is managed centrally, the problem is simpler. But, for very large enterprises, the act of centralising all data in a single data warehouse may not be feasible or may even be logically impossible.

Individual departments may also want autonomy with respect to OLAP. In these cases, smaller data warehouses, called data marts, are often created on a departmental or project basis.

Data warehousing/OLAP even has benefits for organisations that are already using centralised relational database management system technology (RDBMS) to run their operational system – such systems are referred to as on-line transaction processing or OLTP.

- A data warehouse can provide historical information; an operational system typically has only a snapshot view of the business.

- A data warehouse system can be used for extensive querying and reporting without affecting (or being affected by) the operational system.

- OLAP data can be analysed in a detached manner, e.g. on a disconnected notebook PC.

5.5 Differences between databases

There are several other differences between production databases and data warehouse databases.

- A production database is typically associated with a particular application area, e.g. the accounting department has its own database, as does the manufacturing department. The data warehouse database tries to model fragmented data as parts of the entire enterprise so that it focuses on subject areas rather than application areas.

- A production database works best when it is as small as possible, whereas a data warehouse database works best when it has as much data as it can get. The warehouse can also use outside data for its queries.

- You typically want a production database to work as quickly as possible, going as far as to tune the software, de-normalise schemas and reschedule batch jobs. However, speed is not vital for a data warehouse database. The usual pattern is to write a query that extracts a subset (data mart) of the data for a particular area of the business. The initial extraction query is quite slow when it involves a complex query and a large volume of data.

- The goal of a data warehouse system is different from that of a production database system. A production database is used daily and typically has lots of transactions running against it. A warehouse database gets new data less frequently, but in higher volumes. The goal is to find relationships and trends in an organisation's historical data. Typically, a data warehouse user performs more complex queries that tend to involve summaries rather than sets, e.g. 'How many trees did we sell at Christmas?' instead of 'Who bought trees at Christmas?'.

5.6 Data mining

DEFINITION

Data mining is the analysis of data to unearth unsuspected or unknown relationships, patterns and associations.

Data mining is the analysis of data to unearth unsuspected or unknown relationships, patterns and associations.

There are many different definitions of data mining. Almost all of them involve using advanced analytical techniques to discover useful relationships in large databases.

For example, the sales records for a particular brand of tennis racket might, if sufficiently analysed and related to other market data, reveal a seasonal correlation with the purchase of golf equipment by the same people.

The process uses statistical techniques and technologies such as neural networks to discover relationships and then builds models based on them. Data mining results include:

- **Associations** – or when one event can be correlated to another event, e.g. beer purchasers buy peanuts a certain percentage of the time.

- **Sequences** – or one event leading to another later event, e.g. a rug purchase followed by a purchase of curtains.

- **Classification** – or the recognition of patterns and a resulting new organisation of data, e.g. profiles of customers who make purchases.

- **Clustering** – or finding and visualising groups of facts not previously known.

- **Forecasting** – or simply discovering patterns in the data that can lead to predictions about the future.

Some people's definition of data mining is linked with their definition of data warehousing. Data warehouses are for storing data, not turning it into information, whereas data mining turns data into information.

There are two main kinds of models in data mining: predictive and descriptive. Predictive models can be used to forecast explicit values, based on patterns determined from known results. For example, from a database of customers who have already responded to a particular offer, a model can be built that predicts which prospects are likely to respond to the same offer. Descriptive models describe patterns in existing data and are generally used to create meaningful subgroups such as demographic clusters.

5.7 Benefits of data warehousing and data mining

Data warehousing and data mining are only part of the knowledge discovery process. Other steps include identifying the problem to be solved, collecting and preparing the right data, interpreting and deploying models and monitoring the results. The real key however is to have a thorough understanding of the data and the business.

Faster transaction and query execution can provide competitive advantage. A data warehouse is a large database, regularly updated and organised to permit a high level of query activity. Not all organisations will have a need for this; it will depend on the organisation and what it does. With relatively small amounts of data, the specialist data warehouse software and hardware will not be required, as downloading subsets of data from production systems to PCs is a workable solution. However, many organisations need to manage large amounts of data which, when properly analysed, can provide information that leads to competitive advantage.

Large organisations spend immense amounts of money on marketing, but the effectiveness of this is difficult to monitor and is often assumed to be poor. Lord Lever once said that half the company's advertising spend was probably a waste; unfortunately, it was impossible to identify which half. The effectiveness of sales activity is also difficult to assess and might be open to improvement if customer needs and behaviour are understood.

The products or services that a company offers also require analysis. Markets are not static and a change in consumer preferences can be very rapid. Organisations need to be able to respond quickly so they will have to develop new products or services in response. Being able to identify a change in consumer behaviour early is important.

5.8 Problems of establishing a data warehouse

Although the concept of data warehousing appears to offer considerable advantages, especially to organisations with a large number of disparate legacy systems, there may be considerable problems when trying to implement such a system.

The systems used in different departments will often be incompatible, and that is likely to mean that data is in a wide variety of different formats. As noted earlier there are also likely to be inconsistencies between different databases where duplicated items of data should, in theory, be identical, but in practice are not.

The data will either need to be analysed and 'cleansed' before it can be integrated into a warehouse, or else some kind of middleware will be required, probably converting all data to a common format such as XML. This will not be easy, quick or cheap to achieve.

Incompatible systems may also mean that most of the departments will need to be furnished with new hardware and software before they can use the data warehouse. This is likely to be expensive and disruptive to the day-to-day work of each department.

Moreover almost all staff who want to use the new system will need training, both in the use of the data warehouse itself and probably also in the use of new hardware, operating systems and applications software.

Individual departments may use data in widely different ways and require all manner of different reports. It could be very difficult to create a common interface that is capable of delivering information in every format that may be required. Report formats that are only needed in a single department may not be catered for, and this will cause resentment.

Even if the above problems are overcome, scalability is a key issue. As the new system proves its worth, more and more demands will be made of it, so ongoing maintenance, adequate network bandwidth, sufficient storage space, and highly flexible upgrade capability are all essential.

Finally it is worth pointing out that with all data in a single main source it is vital to ensure that effective back-up arrangements are made and strictly adhered to. Depending on how the data warehouse is implemented, loss or serious corruption of data could be disastrous.

Summary

Key points of this chapter are:

- IT can be used to enhance competitive position and gain strategic advantage.

- The use of IT can be assessed using Porter's five forces and value chain.

- Other theories including Strategic Options Generation and the Information Intensity Matrix can be used to help ensure IT is being used effectively within a company.

- McFarlan's grid can be used to show how IT and information systems are critical to an organisation's success.

- IT products such as data mining and data warehousing can be used to enhance the use of information in an organisation.

Having completed your study of this chapter you should have achieved the following learning outcome:

- evaluate the strategic and competitive benefits of IS/IT and advise on the development of appropriate strategies.

Self-test questions

1   How can IT counteract the threat from potential entrants? (2.3)

2   How can IT be used where there is competitive rivalry? (2.4)

3   What can an organisation do to 'lock in' customers? (2.7)

4   How can IT be used as a strategic weapon? (3.2)

5   Draw the value chain. (3.3)

6   Explain the information intensity matrix. (3.4)

7   Draw the information systems strategic grid from McFarlan and McKenney. (4.2)

8   What types of activities are generally included as 'support' in an applications portfolio? (4.4)

9   What are the benefits of data warehousing? (5.4)

10   What is likely to be included in the results of a data mining exercise? (5.6)

Practice question

Competitive edge

Required:

Using examples, show how information technology can be used to give an organisation competitive edge.   **(15 marks)**

For the answer to this question, see the Answers section at the end of the book.

Feedback to activity

Activity 1

(i)   ShoeMaker is currently in the support sector of the McFarlan grid. The commitment to information systems planning is low and IT seems to have below average investment. IT is perceived as having little relevance to the company's existing or future success.

(ii)   If the new ordering system and production technology is introduced, it will be as a result of the customer's suggestion and the fact that it is critical to ShoeMaker's success. The introduction of the changes would place them in a turnaround role. This is where existing IT is not important but future developments are likely to have a significant impact. The role of IT is being enhanced.

(iii)   The forces driving it round seem to be: the competitive environment shaped by the producer from the Far East and the customer's demands; and the management decision to adopt an IT based strategy in response to the threat.

Other frameworks for assessing the strategic options include Earl's awareness framework (for assessing the general impact on an organisation), opportunity frameworks and positioning frameworks, such as McFarlan's grid and Nolan's stage hypothesis. Wiseman also developed an options generator model (see section 2.1), which can be used when assessing the strategic options available.

Chapter 7

THE INTERNET AND ELECTRONIC COMMERCE

Syllabus content

- The impact of IT (including electronic commerce) on an industry (utilising frameworks such as Porter's Five Forces, the Value Chain) and how organisations can use IT (including the Internet) to enhance competitive position.

Contents

1   Introduction

2   The Internet

3   Business on the Internet

4   E-commerce and B2C

1 Introduction

The sheer size and force of the Internet tidal wave of hype, excitement, enthusiasm and acceptance has resulted in the creation of what some might believe to be the biggest business market opportunity since the PC.

The initial assumption was that the Internet presents an environment that can be both seductive and addictive and that all new technology is a 'two edged sword' with the bigger the reward, the bigger the risk.

The power behind the Internet is its ability to deliver information right to the desk. But this power is also being seen as the 'Achilles heel' in the use of the Internet as a business tool.

2 The Internet

2.1 Introduction

The Internet is the global interconnected network of networks. Note that the word is a proper noun (a word like 'Veronica', 'London', etc) and it should **always** be capitalised. There is only one Internet, by definition.

The Internet connects governments, companies, universities and many other networks and users. It is an almost unregulated collection of hardware and software owned by private individuals and organisations.

- Almost all medium to large organisations in the UK and most small businesses have Internet access.

- Almost 60% of the UK population has Internet access in some form (at home or at work). In this respect the UK lags behind the Scandinavian countries, the USA and Hong Kong. The average in developed countries is around 30%. Inevitably third world countries come bottom of the list with less than 1%.

You will probably have experienced the Internet for yourself already, though possibly not for work purposes. We include a few basics only because you might find yourself having to explain them in an exam answer. You are probably well aware of these points already.

- Connection to the Internet is usually made via an **Internet Service Provider (ISP)** such as Freeserve or America Online (AOL) for home users or perhaps Demon or Claranet or UUNet for businesses (there are many others). Users who access the Internet at work may not be aware of the ISP at all.

- Increasingly it is possible to access the Internet via **other devices** such as mobile phones and televisions, but for work purposes it is most likely that people will connect via their desktop computer or laptop.

- Most people use the Internet through interface programs called **browsers** that make it more user-friendly and accessible. But strictly speaking what users usually see when they use a browser is the **World Wide Web (WWW)**, which is **only part** of the Internet.

- As we've seen, another part of the Internet that people are likely to use very often is its **email** services, usually accessed by a program called an 'email client'.

- There are several other ways of using the Internet to connect to computers in other locations, such as **Telnet**. Most users will probably never encounter these other ways unless it happens to be part of their job to do so.

2.2 The elements of the Internet

The Internet refers to the physical aspects of the system, such as the communication lines, computers (often known as 'web servers') and the software required for communication.

The www is menu-driven, following hypertext links between related sources rather than files related to one another by server identification. It allows you to pursue the 'strands' of a web of information distributed across the network. Hypertext is basically text, which can be stored, read, edited and searched. However, over and above these features, it also contains connections to other documents within the text. The connections are known as 'hyperlinks' and users can jump from document to document as they 'surf' the web. By selecting a keyword in one document, they can be transported automatically to another document dealing with the same topic.

Information access and people access is what the Internet is all about. Some people would draw a diagram of a cloud to represent it but in fact, it is a hierarchical assembly of networks; a network of networks. It could be shown diagrammatically as in the diagram below.

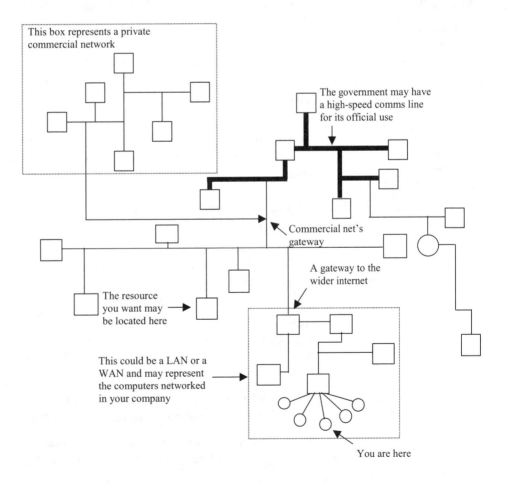

Diagram: Pictorial representation of part of the Internet

The dotted lines correspond to the computers that are networked in a company or university, or gathered together by an Internet connectivity provider. Each square, which represents a computer host, may have files associated with it, software that runs on it and account holders who may have communications privileges.

Some computer networks may not be constantly or continuously connected to the Internet. Instead, they may access the Internet from time-to-time by calling in to a participating host computer.

2.3 Exploring the web

The Internet is a fabulous research tool, and all users require is a web browser. Access to the Internet gives the user the advantage of email, thus enabling messages and documents to be sent around the world to individuals or groups. It also provides access to vast amounts of information. Browsers are software programs used to access the Internet and to search for and view data. The most popular and best known browser, with about 95% of all users, is Microsoft Internet Explorer. (The remaining 5% of users use Mozilla, Netscape Navigator (which is based on Mozilla) or Opera.)

Users move through the web either by typing in web addresses (URLs) directly, or perhaps using search engines such as Google or directories such as Yahoo. Once keywords are entered, the search software will return a list of all websites which refer to those words. Users can read a brief description of the site and choose whether or not to visit it. Hyperlinks can provide links to other pages in the site or to other related sites.

Browsers act as a graphical interface to information available on the Internet. They read and interpret HTML (hypertext markup language) documents and display pages, which may include images, video, sound and hypertext links to other documents.

Web pages may also contain dynamic objects and Java applets for enhanced animation, video, sound and interactivity. Very commonly they include **forms** to allow the user to interact with the web server: entire applications can be built in this way.

2.4 Impact of home use on work

Much or all of the above is probably well-known to you, even if you don't have Internet access at work, and remember that this also applies to the managers and staff described in exam scenarios, who may have been exposed to the Internet for personal/family use – for instance because their children require home access for email and school work.

This is not just a social phenomenon. If an organisation's staff know that it is very easy to do certain things via the Internet at home then they will be frustrated if they cannot do likewise at work.

- Communication between staff may be limited to typed memos, whereas staff will know from their Internet experiences that it is possible to communicate almost instantly across the world via email.

- Staff will also be aware that communication with customers, suppliers, and other third parties could be considerably enhanced using email.

DEFINITION

A web browser is a piece of software that act as a graphical interface to information available on the world wide web. Browsers read and interpret HTML (hypertext markup language) documents and display pages, which may include images, video, sound and hypertext links to other documents. The most popular and best known browser, with about 95% of all users, is Microsoft Internet Explorer.

- Files can also be shared over the Internet almost instantly, either by distributing them as email attachments or by allowing access to shared folders on an Internet or intranet server. The only alternative for an office without such facilities may be to place the files on floppy disks or CD-Rs and to distribute them by post.

- Common formats in use on the Internet such as PDF will have helped staff to appreciate that information can more easily be shared if it is created by a package that is freely available to all. For instance an employee in Office A may not presently be able to view and amend a document created by an employee in Office B because they do not use the same package. If they were to do so, and make the files available for download over the Internet or a WAN it might be possible for staff to work from home, or at least avoid travelling so much between locations.

3 Business on the Internet

3.1 Introduction

DEFINITION

E-commerce is a commercial activity conducted over electronic networks, often the Internet, which leads to the purchase or sale of goods and/or services.

E-commerce is a commercial activity conducted over electronic networks, often the Internet, which leads to the purchase or sale of goods and/or services. The European market for e-commerce is booming and it looks set to become normal practice for organisations that wish to remain competitive.

Many businesses have considered, and are considering, the way in which the Internet might help them to do their business. Others believe that the Internet can, and will, totally transform the business they do. For a rare but increasing number, the Internet is now 'mission-critical' in that without a clear strategy for its use their whole business might reach the point where it is not viable.

3.2 Business applications

There is a whole range of ways in which a business can use the Internet:

- The Internet can be used to extend the organisation's internal network to other organisations and perhaps to employees working from home.

- To retrieve information on products, services, different organisations and interesting topics by using the Internet as a browser and finding the area of interest through a search engine or by knowing the URL.

- To join discussion groups to learn more from others, e.g. if you wanted to find an answer to a problem on a Microsoft product, you could post the question to a newsgroup specialising in that topic and hope that someone would help with the reply. Regularly contributing helpful answers and well-written thoughtful comments will quickly establish some individuals or companies as experts. You can see how this area could also lead to further uses for the Internet. Microsoft staff will also look through the newsgroup questions and answers and, in some instances, will reply to queries themselves. They monitor the replies from individuals with a view to recruitment or using certain groups as their preferred contractors. This is a content-oriented way of advertising a product or of developing name recognition.

- To advertise the organisation and raise awareness among non-customers and potential customers – this treats the Internet like a sophisticated business directory.

- To deliver information to customers and potential customers by means of emailed direct marketing – this uses the Internet as a carrier for email shots as an alternative to conventional mail.

- To advertise products or services and provide detailed information relating to them – this uses the Internet as an electronic on-line catalogue.

- To facilitate the ordering and selling of products – this uses the Internet as an alternative to a human sales force dealing with customers by telephone or face-to-face.

- To deliver the product – if a product consists of data, text, music or video it can be attached to an email. This makes the Internet an alternative to a haulage company or the conventional mail.

- As a telephone, taking advantage of the local telephone rates to communicate internationally.

- Using the same communication channels, individuals can contact each other with email.

3.3 Electronic Data Interchange (EDI)

Electronic Data Interchange (EDI) is the electronic exchange of business documents (purchase orders, invoices, application forms, etc) from one organisation's computer to another organisation's computer in standard data formats.

EDI emerged in the late 1960s when many industry groups realised that processing the large volume of paper documentation accompanying the shipment of goods resulted in significant delays in settlement and product deliveries.

It is currently estimated that around 175,000 companies around the world (consisting primarily of very large public companies and their numerous trading partners) conduct business using EDI. The list of industries in which EDI is actively used includes shipping, retail, grocery, clothing and textiles, financial, health care and many others.

There are three main components of an EDI system (in addition to each organisation's own applications, for instance its own accounting system).

EDI Standards

EDI standards eliminate the need for human intervention in the interpretation of incoming and outgoing data. EDI is based on a set of standard formats that define 'transaction sets' that can be used to send basic business data from one computer to another.

These transaction sets replace paper documents such as purchase orders, invoices, and so on. Standards define the structure, format, and content of EDI documents, including the data fields that may be included in a document, and the sequence and format of fields.

EDI gateway

An EDI gateway reformats outgoing data from an organisation-specific format into an EDI standard format and adds data that enables the EDI message to be routed properly to a trading partner.

A communication network

The main methods of actually communicating the message are through a direct connection, via a Value Added Network Service (VANS) which is not unlike the Internet except that access is restricted to specific organisations, such as travel agents and airlines, or, in more recent years, via the Internet.

EDI has advantages for the organisation ordering goods and for the organisation supplying them.

- The ordering organisation enters the details of the order, perhaps using an on-line catalogue and picking from menu options to save time and avoid errors. The order does not have to be printed out and posted: it is sent via telecommunications and arrives at the supplier's offices almost instantaneously.

- The supplying organisation does not have to transcribe a paper order onto its own computer systems, again saving a large amount of time and eliminating transcription errors. The incoming EDI order automatically updates the stock system and the accounting ledgers.

3.4 EDI on the Internet

Ever since EDI was first introduced, large companies have wanted their smaller suppliers to use EDI. But it was far too expensive.

- Implementing EDI meant purchasing and integrating an unusual combination of software, hardware, and services with an initial cost that could exceed £70,000.

- Transporting data using private or industry-specific Value Added Network Services (VANS) could cost upward of £15,000 per year.

Trading partners of large companies have faced a tough choice until recently: they could either pay the going price of EDI or lose their large company customer.

Web-based EDI services now present the opportunity for everyone to enjoy the undoubted benefits of EDI services.

- EDI on the Internet costs less to buy. Prices range from free to about £350 per month, depending on usage. For instance subscribers to IBM's Web-based service pay as little as £25 per month for a subset of EDI services that once cost between 10 to 100 times as much.

- EDI on the Internet is open and accessible. It is available wherever the Internet is available.

There are, nevertheless, some issues still to be addressed. In particular many companies have substantial investments in their bought-and-paid-for EDI systems and in integrating them with back-end applications. They do not want to retire their systems prematurely, nor do they wish to end up supporting two systems that essentially do the same thing.

3.5 E-procurement or B2B

Many of us have bought a product over the Internet: a book from Amazon, say, or the week's groceries from Tesco.com.

Organisations can do this too, of course: the process is called 'e-procurement' or 'B2B' (business-to-business) and it is now very widely used for non-production purchases such as office supplies.

One-off organisational purchases may be made on-line in exactly the same way as an individual would make them, using an organisational credit card.

If on-line purchases are made regularly it is more likely that the organisation will have an account with the supplier. An authorised and registered user will log in using a password and the organisation will periodically be billed by the supplier. Depending on the status of the buying organisation there may be discounts for volume purchasing or other special offers.

The supplying organisation can set up its website so that it recognises the purchaser once logged in and presents a list of 'favourites' items that the purchaser regularly buys. This saves searching for the items required and also avoids the need to key in name, address and delivery details.

B2B offers similar advantages to EDI in terms of speed and elimination of unnecessary work. It also offers the purchasing organisation much wider choice than it might have had otherwise. In theory, resources can be sourced from suppliers anywhere in the world, perhaps at much lower prices than could be obtained if the organisation only considered local suppliers.

For items where speed or cost of delivery is an issue it may not always be practical to order from a supplier in, say, China, but a London firm, say, may find it gets better value if it orders from a supplier in Manchester rather than the local supplier it had used previously.

As for potential problems for an organisation that allows its purchasing department to use e-procurement, the main issue is control: if anyone can order goods from anywhere there is a major risk that unauthorised purchases will be made. There is also an increased likelihood that purchases will be made from suppliers who cannot deliver the required quality (or cannot deliver at all!). For this reason companies such as Ariba have developed special e-procurement software with built-in tools to control who can place orders at various spending levels, who orders should be placed with and so on.

3.6 Business exchanges

Following on from the success of e-procurement, organisations in many industries are now developing Business Exchanges. Typically an exchange gathers together the major enterprises in a given market sector, e.g. car manufacturing, and creates a market place of sufficient volume to attract increased numbers of suppliers.

All the participants in the formation of the exchange will ask their existing suppliers to join in, thus creating the beginnings of a supplier pool (or **electronic trading room**, to use the terminology of a recent exam question). If each participant adds their own existing suppliers then all participants will immediately be able to enjoy the benefits of increased choice and competition.

A notable example is Covisint, which brings together all the major motor manufacturers – Ford, General Motors, Nissan, Renault and so on.

3.7 Environmental scanning

Many organisations retrieve information on products, services, different organisations and interesting topics by browsing the Internet and finding the area of interest through a search engine or by knowing the URL. A wide variety of information is available from web monitoring activities by accessing sites maintained by competitors, other organisations, governments, universities, individuals or by specialist information-retrieval companies, e.g. Reuters or LexisNexis.

There are also independent companies which monitor web page changes on a daily basis. If an organisation registers with them, they can track any pages that are requested. Most of them boast that their links are verified.

Like any other information source, the information obtained from websites may be subject to errors if it has been entered manually. Another problem with checking for accuracy is that the information may be based on someone's opinion, and that person may or may not be qualified to give an opinion.

If the organisation covers lots of websites, there is a good chance that information they are using will be duplicated over several sites and may have come from different sources. On the assumption that the information was added on the same day for the sites in question, this is one way of checking whether the information is consistent, and probably accurate. For example, if they are using the BBC site, CNN is an alternative that covers the same or similar material each day.

Information sources that are known to have been correct in the past because they have been subsequently verified will be used more confidently than sources that have subsequently been proved wrong. People become experienced at weeding out information that they suspect as being incorrect or comparing it with an independent site that is known to provide more accurate pages.

4 E-commerce (E-business) and B2C

4.1 Introduction

DEFINITION

E-commerce relates to trading on the Internet. B2C specifically refers to the seling of products by businesses to consumers.

When organisations are developing an e-commerce strategy, they should not throw away their traditional business models. Instead, they should look to see where e-commerce provides opportunities to create complementary ways to reach a chosen market. Few e-commerce businesses are self-contained and the need to interact with other types of services, e.g. delivery systems, is an important consideration. If an organisation wants to reach a global audience, then it should be prepared to address markets in the language they understand. Unfortunately, despite claiming to be a world-class attraction, the Millennium Dome's ticket sales site had no plans to offer foreign language versions. Support for multi-languages is a feature of many enterprise-level software vendor sites. In continental Europe, this type of feature is commonplace, with the sites attracting much more traffic than they would if they just kept to their native tongue.

Compelling content that attracts and addresses customer's needs has to be coupled with a solid infrastructure. Users will quickly abandon an e-commerce site if it does not give them exactly what they want – either in terms of service or content – or if it is not open 24 hours a day, every day.

To get started with e-commerce as a buyer, a seller or just a browser, there are many directories of websites, e.g. the Hutchinson directory, the new Riders' Official Internet Yellow Pages and Osborne's Internet Golden Directory.

The Dun & Bradstreet business server (www.dnb.com) has articles on marketing your business globally, strategic business planning, tactical marketing, effective research and a series of tutorials to help the small business owner.

Links to information about thousands of businesses with a presence on the Internet are available from many sites. All that is required is the time to surf and investigate.

4.2 The growth of Internet commerce (e-business)

A truly competitive market place of Internet services, where no single big player or cartel of big players is able to establish dominance, and where start-up entrepreneurs will not be crushed by the giants, would be better for everyone in terms of price and democracy.

At the present time, about 60% of all websites are commercial organisations, although many of them expect little or no direct business to arise from their pages. Those who do tend to use the web as an advertising medium.

The Internet has become the fastest expanding sales channel in history, and e-commerce has become the strategy of note for seeking, capturing and developing customers. Investment in web-based electronic commerce has delivered impressive benefits in terms of market reach, time to market, cost of sales and inventory management. By radically changing the way organisations reach and engage their customers, the Internet has created many new businesses of which Amazon.com and E*Trade are among the best known. These so-called 'dot com' enterprises have changed the economics in business sectors that previously seemed impervious to the Internet phenomenon. Today, there is not an industrial sector that cannot be transformed by the adoption of e-commerce, and entry is so accessible that anyone with a bright idea can make an impression.

4.3 Advantages of e-business

There are a number of significant advantages to both customer and supplier in conducting transactional business over the Internet.

- Access to global marketing capabilities for a single local investment – the Internet generates opportunities for export without local presence and advertising. The websites can be seen by a very large number of people – all potential customers – in many countries, because they have access to the Internet.

- Increased sales revenue.

- Reduced sales and support costs, particularly in administration – it takes less time to reproduce the material, which leads to a reduction in the time taken to market it. The production costs associated with disseminating information on the Internet are significantly lower, and access and printing costs are borne by the potential customer. It is more likely that only people who are interested in the product will access the websites. All visits to the websites, whether they result in sales or not, can be logged and counted. There is less waste compared to sending traditional documents. Potential customers may never read catalogues and brochures, because they are put straight into the wastepaper bin.

- Savings in traditional advertising and mailing costs – when information is maintained on the organisation's websites it can be updated easily, with the latest version becoming immediately available to all Internet customers. Where traditional media, such as brochures and catalogues, is used for disseminating information, the old document becomes obsolete as soon as the new one is released. However this old document may remain in existence instead of being replaced, leading the customer to act upon incorrect information.

- Access to information about products with little or no 'hard sell'.

- Higher customer satisfaction levels due to improved product knowledge.

4.4 Risks

The major risks that concern businesses and customers who are thinking of using the Internet for transactions are as follows:

- the high cost of establishing security and encryption procedures to protect confidential information and customer credit card or bank details from deliberate misuse by third parties

- the lack of a paper-based audit trail for transactions

- the possibility of misuse of customer bank details by an unscrupulous trader.

Although these risks are significant, they are reducing as more companies market e-business software that is specially designed for conducting business on the Internet.

The lack of security on the Internet is generally perceived as the greatest current threat. Security affects companies in two ways:

- the security of information, e.g. the ability of outsiders to hack into a company's system or for a virus to be imported

- the security of sensitive data and transactions over the Internet, which is crucial if it is to become a principal medium for marketing and sales.

4.5 Making the site secure

The threat from hackers and viruses can be combated by a combination of expertise, software tools and procedures, e.g. firewalls and well-policed corporate guidelines.

- A firewall is a security device that effectively isolates the sensitive parts of an organisation's system from those areas available to external users.

- Encryption is the transaction of a message into coded form using a code key that is only known to the sender and recipient of the message.

Ways of passing payment details directly over the Internet are being developed, e.g. through specialised Internet payment systems such as payment service providers (PSPs), or through credit card encryption.

When connected to the Internet, credit card details are entered on the customer's local PC – usually via a browser that has downloaded a web page from a secure environment. Typically a secure server would use SSL (Secure Sockets Layer) which, through the use of digital certificates, provides the transparent authentication of both server and (optionally) client. Basically, SSL scrambles the message and, when the intended recipient receives the message, SSL unscrambles the message. SSL then checks that it came from the correct sender (Server Authentication) and then verifies that it has not been tampered with (Message Integrity).

Giving credit card details via the Internet using security features like SSL is infinitely more secure than giving your credit card number over the telephone for mail order purposes, sending by fax or writing it onto a form which is then dropped into a post box.

For companies that prefer to use a PSP, Netbanx is the UK's largest and has built up a deserved reputation for providing a fast, reliable and secure credit checking and settlement system. It has links to all the major credit card companies and clears transactions in seconds. Cardholder's accounts are directly debited. In use, it is the Internet's equivalent of the swipe machines used by retailers when processing payment by credit or debit card.

DEFINITION

A firewall is a security device that effectively isolates the sensitive parts of an organisation's system from those areas available to external users.

DEFINITION

Encryption is the transaction of a message into coded form using a code key that is only known to the sender and recipient of the message.

The alternative is to have customers either ringing their details through to the business or sending in cheques, neither of which is satisfactory and defeats the object of the exercise.

4.6 What on-line customers want

One of the biggest fears about e-commerce is that it will force businesses to compete purely on price, driving down margins and increasing bankruptcies. Amazon.com, arguably the world's most successful on-line bookshop, welcomes potential customers to its site by offering a discount of up to 40% on the prices of its books.

Massive discounting is certainly viable on-line, supported by savings in property and stockpiling enjoyed by many virtual businesses. Because surfers currently use the medium to shop, low prices appear to be a good strategy for drumming up business. However, the greatest barrier to sales is not high prices but trust. Building trust demands a variety of actions, including speed of delivery, brand identity and reliability of service.

Patrick Lupo, CEO of global courier business DHL International, claims that, for DHL, e-commerce is all about providing customers with better information about their particular needs. Cost is important to DHL customers, many of which are attracted to the dramatically faster Internet service just because time is money. For example, a company can place an order for PCs from Silicon Valley from a terminal in Brussels to be delivered, with all the paperwork, to the company's offices in New Zealand in less than two days. However, DHL's Internet customers are not only attracted by swift delivery times and low cost. Many want precise information on their package's progress, and use the Internet because it enables them to get this data at any point on the package's journey.

Strong branding is a big selling point for companies such as the House of Ireland, a retailer of fine china and glassware from Dublin. They already had a successful US mail order business for products such as Waterford crystal before launching their on-line service. Although the US market forms a solid foundation for their on-line trade, a key part of the company's selling strategy involves diversifying its website content. As well as detailed product descriptions, the company produces Dublin tourist guides and maps to attract casual surf traffic, including people who might be considering a visit to Ireland but did not realise they could buy the souvenirs first.

4.7 What concerns on-line buyers

By far the most popular categories in the on-line shopping world are air travel, books, music and software. This is partly because there can be no mistake about what you are purchasing. The big disadvantage of buying from the web is not knowing exactly what you are getting. Unlike traditional shops, browsing an 'on-line shopping mall' is often an unsatisfactory experience. You are presented with an all-too-brief description of the product and a tiny pixelated gif image. Also, given the slow speed of the web it can take a long time to find anything you would like to buy. If you do buy, the opportunities for misunderstandings and disappointments when you receive the product are huge and returning the item can be an even bigger frustration. With return postage costs (assuming you know where to send the unwanted purchase) and getting the company concerned to give you a refund (assuming you get to speak to a person) it could deter you from buying on-line ever again.

One of the main concerns for on-line buyers is inadequate safety provisions – not just from the ever-present threat of hackers but more mundane, yet just as important, traditional consumer issues. For example, is the company you are buying from reputable? Can you follow the progress of your order? Does it offer privacy and customer service assurances?

There are several useful websites to help allay some of the fears of on-line shoppers:

- The Web Assurance Bureau – www.webassured.com – attempts to provide a service for consumers concerned about the reputations of various e-commerce websites. It includes a best-practice charter which sites promise to uphold. In return, they are allowed to display the WAB logo.

- Participants in the MasterCard Shop Smart scheme – html://globalmastercard.com/shopsmart/shopsmartdetails.html) – again similar to WAB but with the extra weight of MasterCard.

- Storesearch – www.storesearch.com/ - here you can check to see if a store is as safe as it claims; this is another MasterCard initiative.

4.8 Website design

It is still safest to assume that visitors will be new or unsophisticated Internet users, so site designers should ideally design on the assumption that users have never used the Internet before.

The user interface must be designed with great care. The problem, in each case noted below, is anticipating what users might try to do and what will happen in that set of circumstances. Also, of course, solving each of the issues adds to the cost of the design and the time taken to get the site up and running.

- Navigation options need to be as simple and clear as possible. This is much easier said than done. These days good sites tend to offer a combination of menus, text-based links and site maps, to give users as much chance as possible of finding their way about. Template-based design can help to avoid duplication of effort, ensure consistency and avoid problems such as broken links.

- Some items, such as the full text of brochures and the like, can usefully be made available in special formats, such as PDF files for printing out. This may not be understood by inexperienced users so any such items should be explained very clearly and users should be given every assistance in obtaining the required plug-ins. Plain text alternatives that can be viewed in a browser should also be made available.

- A set of Help pages for new users should be provided and should be kept up to date. Plain English and no assumption of computer knowledge is essential so these pages may need to be written by a computer help specialist. A set of FAQs will also be useful: these can be added to over time, as queries arise.

- A contact email link for further support should be provided on every page, as should alternatives to the Internet such as telephone numbers and postal addresses. These additional services will need to be manned and managed, especially if response times are guaranteed.

Any database underlying the website also needs to be carefully engineered to ensure that it is possible to generate the correct results in response to a query. Detailed information about current enquiries and the type of questions asked over the telephone or on retail premises will need to be collected and analysed, and there will need to be a good deal of input into the design process from sales staff.

Search tools on the site also need to be designed with care. Searches that require knowledge of Boolean operators, regular expressions or SQL are rarely appropriate. Enlightened sites generally incorporate features that make such searches as easy as possible to perform, simply by filling in a form that lets the user opt to include or exclude words or phrases, retrieve results by date, select from pre-defined categories, and so on. (Behind the scenes the options chosen may generate a very complex SQL query, but the user does not need to know this at all.)

4.9 Website implementation

The timescale for setting up a site is often fairly short and it would be advisable to bring out a prototype for use by the organisation's staff as soon as possible, so it can at least be fully tested by people who know what results it should give.

Ideally the site should also be tested by a representative sample of users. Finding a representative sample and persuading them to give detailed feedback may be a problem, and there is the danger that problems with the test version will undermine confidence in the final version.

The speed and availability of the site are crucial issues. Above all it must be at least as quick to find the answer to a query over the Internet as it is over the telephone. Some of the potential problems can be taken care of at design stage, for example avoiding large graphics that take a long time to download, but the main problem will be the level of demand for the site.

A suitably powerful Internet server and adequate bandwidth will be needed, and stress testing of the site before it goes live is therefore essential. There are special programs available that can simulate various levels of traffic, or there are companies that will perform stress tests.

Traffic levels will need to be monitored constantly and appropriate actions taken when traffic becomes heavy. As a rule of thumb, simply to provide the same level of service as is currently available by other means (e.g. from a call centre) the number of current users should probably be at least doubled to take account of the fact that visitors are likely to spend more time querying the site and its database than they would if they were talking to a human being.

It must also be borne in mind that any underlying database will need to updated on a regular basis, perhaps daily. This means that there will be periods when the site will not be available at all and that may annoy users who cannot access it during 'normal' hours. It is best to make this clear to users at the outset: for instance the UK Companies House database, which needs a great deal of maintenance, states clearly that it is 'available from Monday to Saturday 7:00am to 12 Midnight'. The further implication of this is that the persons doing the update will need to be paid for working unsocial hours.

4.10 Example of e-business

As an example of B2C e-business we can look at one of the earliest and most successful implementations of this type. Amazon (http://www.amazon.com although there are many regional sites such as www.amazon.co.uk and www.amazon.fr) is a 'virtual bookstore' that was established as a direct result of the growth of the Internet, and is unusual in that it is not a spin-off from a conventional business.

The home page is very user-friendly, and manages to cater for new users and existing customers. There is a direct link to a site-specific search engine (it only searches the amazon website) and a link for new users that takes you straight to the most commonly-asked questions. This 'first-timers' page has information about the service and how to use it but, interestingly enough, gives users two options for security. Users can either order via a 'secure server' which uses encryption technology to apparently guarantee the confidentiality of the system, or can submit an on-line order and confirm it by telephone or fax. It is interesting that in this most mature e-business, customers still believe a fax is more secure than the Internet!

Activity 1

The principles of B2B and B2C are being applied to other business models.

(a)   Briefly explain the likely benefits and drawbacks of what might be called G2C – Government to Citizen.

(b)   Do you think there is any potential for C2C – Consumer to Consumer?

Feedback to this activity is at the end of the chapter.

Summary

Key points of this chapter are:

- The Internet is a world-wide communication and trading medium.

- The Internet provides various business trading systems including EDI and E-procurement.

- The use of E-commerce – trading on the Internet – has now become commonplace and looks set to increase still further in the near future.

Having completed your study of this chapter you should have achieved the following learning outcome:

- evaluate the impact of electronic commerce on the way business is conducted and recommend an appropriate strategy.

Self-test questions

1   Explain hypertext and hyperlinks. (2.2)

2   What does a browser do? (2.3)

3   Define e-commerce. (3.1)

4   Identify three ways that a business can use the Internet. (3.2)

5   Why has conventional EDI not been widely adopted? (3.4)

6   What is a business exchange? (3.6)

7 What are the advantages of e-business? (4.3)

8 What are the main concerns of on-line customers? (4.7)

9 What issues should be considered when implementing a website? (4.9)

Practice question

E-commerce
Required:

Compare and contrast the organisations specified below in terms of:

(a) whether e-commerce should be adopted as part of a business strategy; and

(20 marks)

(b) showing which organisation will benefit more from the use of e-commerce.

(5 marks)

The two types of organisation to be considered in this question are:

- a local independent supplier of garden plants, fences, sheds and other garden accessories selling within 20 kilometres of its main site; and

- an international consultancy supplying financial advice to private individuals and large multinational organisations.

(Total: 25 marks)

For the answer to this question, see the 'Answers' section at the end of the book.

Feedback to activity

Activity 1

(a) **Government to Citizen (G2C)**

G2C offers the promise of transaction-based services for numerous government-related activities such as voting, benefit payments, car road tax renewals, and so on.

The challenge is for the Government to be able to make use of the Internet as a communication medium, whilst adding the unique ability to be able to recognise and transact with each citizen securely.

The scale of this task is huge. It is likely to have to embrace at least interactive TV (iTV) and mobile phones (possibly more so than PCs), and will probably require the use of other enterprises as partners to create the necessary external value chains.

(b) **Consumer to Consumer (C2C)**

Early examples of C2C include the very successful e-Bay site, which allows consumers to sell and buy articles directly to and from other consumers by means of on-line auctions.

A more intriguing guide to the future lies in the WAP mobile phone site somewherenear.com. This site allows consumers in much of the UK to tap in a postcode and ask for a particular commercial heading, such as Clubs, Cinemas, Car parks, or Restaurants.

Not only are the local choices identified, but there are also comments. For example a restaurant may be described as 'good but expensive'. The entries for the local amenities, and the comments, have all been added by consumers for the benefit of other consumers: a true example of the growing strength of consumer power.

Chapter 8

STRATEGIC OPTIONS

Syllabus content

- Forecasting and the various techniques used: trend analysis, system modelling, in-depth consultation with experts (Delphi method).

- Scenario planning and long range planning as tools in strategic decision-making (including gap analysis).

- Strategic options generation (e.g. using Ansoff's product/market matrix and Porter's generic strategies)

- Audit of resources and the analysis of this for use in strategic decision-making.

Contents

1 Introduction

2 Audit of resources and gap analysis

3 Forecasting techniques

4 Scenario planning

5 Ansoff's product/market matrix

6 Porter's generic strategies for competitive advantage

7 Synergy

1 Introduction

In this chapter we will look at the planning gap and the use of scenario planning before moving on to consider the product/market matrix and generic competitive strategies.

As we have already seen, Porter identified the five forces that affect a company's strategic options. A strategy of differentiation of the company's products and services is a competitive response to the pressures exerted by a low-cost competitor. The strategy, if correctly executed, will also protect the company against the five competitive forces in the market and will enable it to remain flexible in both defensive and offensive dimensions. A strategy of market focus will enable a company to concentrate resources and to strengthen both its cost and differentiation positions within the narrow market area.

2 Audit of resources and gap analysis

2.1 Position audit

A position audit is part of the planning process that examines the current state of the entity in respect of:

(a) resources of tangible and intangible assets and finance

(b) products, brands and markets

(c) operating systems such as production and distribution

(d) internal organisation

(e) current results

(f) returns to stockholders.

CIMA: *Official Terminology*

A position audit is an important (some would say essential) part of the strategic planning process. The carrying out of a position audit focuses the attention of those responsible for the formulation of strategic plans upon the question of 'Where are we now?'. In other words it is an examination of the organisation's current situation.

The primary purpose of the position audit is to identify, through systematic analysis and review, the entity's current state and to isolate its strengths and weaknesses. Drucker provides us with a good explanation of the purpose of this analytical approach in his book *Managing for Results*:

> 'The basic business analysis starts with an examination of the business as it is now, the business as it has been bequeathed to us by the decisions, actions and results of the past. We need to see the hard skeleton, the basic stuff that is the economic structure. We need to see the relationship, and inter-relationship of resources and results, of efforts and achievements, of revenues and costs.'

A company's operational environment is composed of those dimensions which directly or indirectly influence corporate success or failure. Most external factors are beyond the control of the company, whereas internal dimensions are generally within its management ambit. The essential purpose of a strategic position audit is to collect and analyse all the relevant and available information about the company and its current operations which will provide strategic planners with information on:

- the competitive strengths and weaknesses of the company's current strategic position

- the consequences of the company continuing its present strategy

- the internal resources that are available for implementing any strategic change that may be required.

Smith (2000) suggests that the position audit can be made memorable by noting all issues that begin with the letter M:

- **Manpower** – The human resources of the firm are an important strategic strength.

- **Money** – The financial resources are obvious indicators of longevity. The key indicators of financial health are important to financial backers.

- **Machinery** – The physical assets are an important source of benefit for the firm.

- **Management** – The skills of the management are an important attribute.

- **Make-up** – The firm's culture and organisation structure are important factors in long-term survival.

- **Markets** – The firm's products and the markets served are important variables in strategic planning.

- **Materials** – The relation that the firm has with its suppliers and the threats from the power of suppliers.

- **Management information** – The quality and timeliness of management information.

2.2 Intangible resources

It is not just the tangible resources that need to be reviewed in the position audit. Intangible resources are just as important and may be divided into four categories:

- **Human resources** – the skills and motivation of the employees.

- **Technological resources** – the knowledge of process and product that the organisation has control of. These are capable of sustaining a competitive advantage if the knowledge is difficult to discover, or protected by patents and so on.

- **Reputation** – the values and trust that stakeholders, particularly customers, build up about a company and its brands.

- **Organisational resources** – some firms manage innovative project management teams very well, others are very good at controlling costs, and some manage information particularly well.

When considering resource use, the following questions need to be addressed:

- **Efficiency** – could the outputs be achieved with fewer or less expensive resources?

- **Effectiveness** – Could the combinations of resources owned be deployed in a more attractive market, or used to compete more effectively in current markets if they were arranged in a different way?

- **Quality** – Having a resource does not in itself confer an advantage. In many cases, the firm could improve itself by reducing its resources, and leasing/factoring expertise from outside.

2.3 Identifying gaps

Before deciding which products and which markets to develop, the organisation should undertake an analysis of its performance in existing products and markets to determine whether there is a gap between its objectives (its desired performance) and its expected performance.

2.4 The concept of gap analysis

Gap analysis is the comparison of an entity's ultimate objective with the sum of projections and already planned projects, and identifying how the consequent gap might be closed.

Having obtained data about its current position and decided its objectives the firm must determine the gap between its predicted and desired performance. The company will already have available various statistics about its past and present performance – sales, profit margin, return on capital employed, turnover ratios, etc – and it can use these to extrapolate from the past and present data to predict what its future position would be if it made no effort to change the situation. The extrapolation would use momentum lines and the method employed is sometimes referred to as status quo forecasting. A momentum line is the conceptual projection of anticipated consequences of pursuing an existing strategy without any major directional changes.

2.5 Strategic gap

A strategic gap is the shortfall between the targeted performance and the projected momentum line at a specific point of time ahead. The concept is useful because it focuses attention on the magnitude of the task facing planners and the time span available to them.

An example of a simple strategic gap is shown below. Although the momentum line can be generated in many ways and from a variety of sources, in this case the profits for the last five years have been plotted and a momentum line derived from the trend. The term simple is used because the gap represents one point of time ahead, and therefore both lines which link the objective and the projected performance at that point in time with the current time are straight lines. For this reason regression formulae can be used to plot the momentum line.

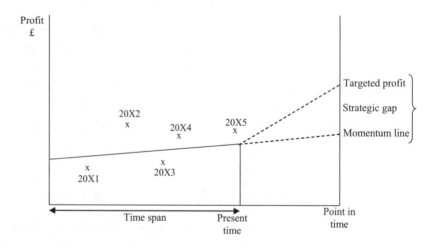

Diagram: A simple strategic gap

2.6 The value of the momentum line

In a business world of rapidly changing customer needs and technology, intense competition, and formidable environmental uncertainty, a large question-mark must be placed firstly on the sense of a company spending time and resources on projecting the momentum line of the existing strategy knowing that there is an odds-on chance that the strategy will be changed or added to anyway, and secondly on the ability of analysts to plot the company's long-term strategic position with any success. What then is the value of attempting to plot the momentum line, which is based on the assumption that the company is going to behave in the future, exactly as it did in the past? In pondering this question some reasons can be found as to why this is indeed a valuable exercise.

- The most important reason is that the whole point of making the forecast is to establish the need for any new strategies. It would destroy the purpose of the momentum line if it included new strategies.

- A forecast that included new activity of which the company has no experience would be more inaccurate than one dealing with only those activities the company has hitherto pursued.

- Any forecast for a company consists of a complex mix of individual assumptions, bias, opinions, separate forecasts and calculations, and it is perhaps sensible to keep this complexity within bounds. Simple momentum lines derived from linear regression remove a lot of the complexity.

- Sometimes a company that is facing threat takes vigorous action to avoid it without first estimating the consequences of not avoiding it. It must sometimes be the case that standing still is preferable to change, for the sake of change, and the momentum line shows what the consequence of a zero change (or 'neutral') strategy might be.

- In order to project the momentum line, analysts have to review the salient features of the company's recent performance. In doing so they may discover, or re-discover, a number of indicators that could have a profound effect on the formulation of future strategy.

- The examination of the company's recent past may place into perspective the size and speed of the changes and associated problems which would help indicate the extent and difficulty of the changes that would be required by the company immediately, or in the medium-term future.

2.7 Forecasting the gap

Clearly, forecasts must be taken far enough ahead to reveal any significant gap, and indeed whether there is a gap on which corrective action needs to be taken now. How far ahead a company must plan for this depends on the lead time for corrective action to take effect, which in turn depends on the nature of the business and on the type of action required. The possible ways of closing a gap are:

- internal efficiency improvement

- expansion within the present industry, which may involve market penetration, product development or market development

- diversification into new fields.

We will examine each of these later in the chapter. The components of the total gap are shown in the diagram below. The tendency will be for the lead time to be longer for diversification than for expansion (which means growth within the existing product-market sphere), and efficiency can usually be improved most quickly of all.

Earnings

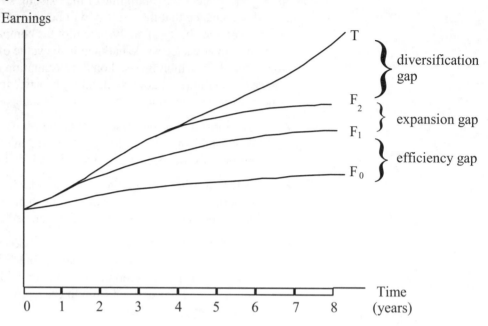

Diagram: Gap analysis – component parts of the total gap

In the diagram showing the gap:

T = target
F_0 = initial forecast
F_1 = forecast adjusted for improvements in internal efficiency
F_2 = forecast adjusted for product-market expansion

Analysis of the gap reveals that in this instance the objectives cannot be achieved beyond year 4 without diversification. This gap is significant if the lead time for diversifying exceeds four years.

2.8 Revision of objectives

The existence of the gap may or may not lead to the revision of objectives. (There are after all two main ways of closing a gap – revising objectives or taking action to improve performance expectations.) Objectives would be revised upwards if the forecasts showed that performance could be expected to exceed objectives: in this case the objectives might also be raised if forecasts showed that the gap was considerably more marked for one objective than for another.

3 Forecasting techniques

3.1 Statistical models

The statistical approach to forecasting is concerned with the projection of time series. Time series analysis involves the identification of short and long-term trends in previous data and the application of these patterns for projections.

A variety of methods is available including:

- moving averages (time series)

- exponential smoothing

- correlation analysis

- sensitivity and key factor analysis

- risk analysis

- multiple regression analysis.

Where there are numerous short and long-term factors at work, forecasting becomes very difficult. If the series of data being analysed is very regular, some simple procedure such as exponential smoothing may be sufficient. On the other hand, more complex patterns may require techniques of regression analysis, risk analysis and multiple regression. By using relatively simple mathematics, it may be possible to calculate to a 'level of confidence' the volume of demand, etc. Trend analysis is a particularly useful tool for companies who have to forecast demand that is influenced by seasonal fluctuations, or where demand is strongly influenced by the business cycle, but in reality many of the techniques are very crude, and cannot predict with adequate certainty.

3.2 Intuitive forecasting methods

All forecasting techniques involve judgement. For example, statistical techniques require judgements about the amount of past data that is relevant, and how this data should be weighted, while causal models involve judgements about what are the critical variables in the situation. Judgements have to be made regarding the reliability of the data, the stability of the relationships between the variables over time, and the accuracy of the predictions. Therefore what distinguishes intuitive techniques is the relative emphasis they place on judgement, and the value of such techniques lies not in their statistical sophistication but in the method of systematising expert knowledge. Intuitive forecasting techniques include the use of think tanks, Delphi methods, scenario planning, brainstorming and derived demand analysis.

Think tank

A think tank comprises a group of experts who are encouraged, in a relatively unstructured atmosphere, to speculate about future developments in particular areas and to identify possible courses of action. The essential features of a think tank are:

- the relative independence of its members, enabling unpopular, unacceptable or novel ideas to be broached

- the relative absence of positional authority in the group, which enables free discussion and argument to take place

- the group nature of the activity that not only makes possible the sharing of knowledge and views, but also encourages a consensus view or preferred scenario.

Think tanks are used by large organisations, including government, and may cross the line between forecasting and planning. However, the organisations that directly employ, or fund them, are careful to emphasise that their think-tank proposals do not necessarily constitute company or government policy.

Think tanks are useful in generating ideas and assessing their feasibility, as well as providing an opportunity to test out reaction to ideas prior to organisational commitment.

The Delphi technique

This is named after the Oracle of Apollo at Delphi, renowned for somewhat ambiguous predictions. The method was pioneered at the Rand Corporation in 1950 to assess the timing and likelihood of new technology, and it since has gained considerable recognition as a valuable planning tool with a great variety of applications.

Delphi seeks to avoid the group pressures to conformity that are inherent in the think tank method. It does this by individually, systematically and sequentially interrogating a panel of experts. Members do not meet, and questioning is conducted by formal questionnaires. Where the experts are speculating about the future, they are asked for subjective probabilities about their predictions. A central authority evaluates the responses and feeds these back to the experts who are then interrogated in a new round of questions

The system is based on the premise that knowledge and ideas possessed by some but not all of the experts can be identified and shared and this forms the basis for subsequent interrogations.

Brainstorming

This is a method of generating ideas. There are different approaches but a popular one is for a number of people (no fewer than six, no more than fifteen) drawn from all levels of management and expertise to meet and propose answers to an initial single question posed by the session leader. Each person proposes something, no matter how absurd. No one is allowed to criticise or ridicule another person's idea. One idea provokes another, and so on. All ideas are listed and none rejected at this initial stage. Rationality is not particularly important, but what is essential is that a wide range of ideas emerges and in the ensuing spoken answers for these to be picked up, developed, combined and reshaped. Only after the session are ideas evaluated and screened against rational criteria for practicability

Brainstorming provides a forum for the interchange of ideas without erecting the normal cultural, behavioural and psychological barriers that so often inhibit the expression of ideas.

Derived demand

Derived demand exists for a commodity, component or good because of its contribution to the manufacture of another product. For example, the demands for the chromium, copper and rubber used in the manufacture of many different products, including cars, are derived demands. The forecasting technique involves analysing some aspects of economic activity so that the level of other aspects can be deduced and projected. The principle is simple, but the practice is complex and costly. Take the example of chrome matched with car manufacture. In order to forecast the demand for cars (thus chrome) the forecaster will be faced with the mammoth task of analysing an enormous number of influences and correlated factors. Due to its cost and complexity the technique has a very restricted use.

3.3 Modelling

A variety of forecasting models might be used by an organisation. One type of model used for both short-term and medium-term forecasting is an econometric model, which examines economic variables and how they are interrelated, using a computer. Econometric models can be used to obtain information about economic developments which might be important for an organisation's future plans, such as the following:

- the likely rate of inflation

- the likely level of interest rates and foreign exchange rates

- expected growth in the economy and consumer demand.

Similar techniques can be used to model the entire system of the organisation, for instance in a 'simulation' model perhaps using random numbers to represent change and uncertainty (the 'Monte Carlo' method). System models can be used to examine specific problems such as inventory management, queuing, or production scheduling and for forecasting problems in general. The difficulty, of course, with something as dynamic as an entire business organisation lies in identifying all the variables and defining how they relate to each other.

A number of software products are available to help with this. Most large accounting packages will include forecasting facilities, and Enterprise Resource Management (ERM) software generally includes facilities to model business processes.

4 Scenario planning

Scenario planning attempts to match specific options with a range of possible future situations (or scenarios). The approach is essentially used as a means of addressing some of the less well structured or uncertain aspects of evaluation. The method of constructing a scenario is described below.

First use the industry scenarios and develop a set of assumptions about the task environment. At 3M, for example, the general manager of each business unit is required annually to describe what his or her industry will look like in 15 years.

Second, for each strategic alternative, develop a set of optimistic, pessimistic, and most likely assumptions about the impact of key variables on the company's future financial statements. Forecast three sets of sales and cost of goods sold figures for at least five years into the future. Look at historical data from past financial statements and make adjustments based on the environmental assumptions listed above. Do the same for other figures that can vary significantly. Plug in expected inventory levels, accounts receivable, accounts payable, R&D expenses, advertising and promotion expenses, capital expenditures and debt payments.

Third, construct detailed proforma financial statements for each of the strategic alternatives. Using a spreadsheet program, list the actual figures from this year's financial statement in the left column. To the right of this column, list the optimistic figures for year one, year two, year three, year four and year five. Go through this same process with the same strategic alternative, but now list the pessimistic figures for the next five years. Do the same with the most likely figures. Once this is done, develop a similar set of optimistic (O), pessimistic (P) and most likely (ML) proforma statements for each second stage alternative.

This process will generate six different proforma scenarios reflecting three different situations (O, P and ML) for two strategic alternatives. Next, calculate financial ratios and common-sized income statements, and balance sheets to accompany the proformas.

The result of this detailed scenario construction should be anticipated net profits, cash flow, and net working capital for each of three versions of the two alternatives for five years into the future.

5 Ansoff's product/market matrix

5.1 The common thread

In his book *Corporate Strategy*, H Igor Ansoff suggests that there is a need for a concept of business which on the one hand will give specific guidance to strategic management and on the other hand will provide room for growth. Corporate objectives that relate to the organisation's mission statement are too broad to be useful as the basis for guidance. After all, there are many ways that a company could achieve, say, a required rate of return on investment. He writes about the need for a common thread which links the company's mission, its history and traditions, its present products and markets and its future products and markets. The thread (or 'components of strategy') comprises four main strands:

- the company's present product market scope
- the growth vector
- the company's competitive advantage
- synergy.

Thus strategy and objectives together specify the extent of growth, the product market area of growth, the directions for growth, the company's distinctive competitive advantages and the corporate targets. Strategy will be planned to achieve (and become) the corporate objectives thus removing the strategic gap.

5.2 Ansoff's components of strategy

Growth in the size of an organisation can be measured in many ways – profit, turnover, earnings per share, manpower, etc – but the real aim of a growth strategy is growth in profits. The pursuit of size or increased turnover is not an end in itself but is only worthwhile if it leads to higher profits. If an organisation has decided that it does need growth in order to achieve its economic objectives, its search for new opportunities must be particularly active (although it would still need new opportunities even if pursuing a non-growth strategy).

Product market scope – This is the product market scope within which the company currently operates. Specifically it is all the products and services of the company and their associated markets.

Growth vector components – 'Vector' in mathematical terms is a line that defines both direction and length. The product market growth vector concerns the possible directions of growth, emanating from the existing product market position, and is usually exemplified in a product market matrix, which we have already looked at previously and which is illustrated again below:

	Existing product	*New product*
Existing market	Internal efficiency and market penetration 1	Product development 2
New market	Market development 3	Diversification 4

The term 'expansion' is often restricted to mean growth by market penetration. However it may be found in many texts to cover vectors 1, 2 and 3 (in which the company remains to some extent, however tenuous, within its present product/market scope), in contrast to 'diversification' that involves the company entering new markets with new product offerings.

- **Competitive advantage** – This is the special characteristic(s) that a company seeks in growth strategy that will enable it to obtain a special sphere of influence or a strong competitive position. Kotler suggests that a company needs to pay attention to its distinctive competence, i.e. 'those resources that the organisation is especially strong in'. The view is that a company will generally find it easier to build on its existing strengths than trying to build from a new position. The company therefore needs to plan strategy that fully utilises areas where it enjoys distinctive advantages, that is 'it can outperform competitors on that dimension'.

- **Synergy** – In the product market growth context the company must essentially have the resources and competence for success in any new venture undertaken – requirements that often limit the company's growth potential.

Our purpose now is to examine each of the quadrants in the product market growth matrix and summarise the possible opportunities they offer, and then to examine competitive advantage.

5.3 Market penetration

This is a strategy by which a company seeks to increase the sales of its present products in its existing markets.

Kotler suggests that market penetration involves aggressive marketing effort, and proposes three main ways a company can penetrate a market. These are:

- The company can try to stimulate customers to increase their current rate of usage. Strategies might include:
  - increasing unit of customer purchase
  - speeding up the rate of product improvement or obsolescence
  - suggesting new uses for the product
  - offering customers price incentives for increased use.

- The company can increase its efforts to attract non-users by using promotional incentives, advertising, pricing up or down, etc.

- The company can increase its efforts to swing competitors' customers by brand differentiation, and stepping up promotion, etc.

Appropriateness of market penetration

Market penetration strategy would be contemplated for the following reasons:

- When the overall market is growing, or can be induced to grow, it may be relatively easy for companies entering the market, or those wishing to gain market share, to do so relatively quickly. (Some companies established in the market may be unable or unwilling to invest resources in an attempt to grow to meet the new demand.) In contrast, market penetration in static, or declining, markets can be much more difficult to achieve.

- Market penetration strategy would be forced on a company that is determined to confine its interests to its existing product/market area but is unwilling to permit a decline in sales even though the overall market is declining.

- If other companies are leaving the market for whatever reasons, penetration could prove easy – although the good sense of the strategy may be in doubt.

- A company that holds a strong market position and is able to use its experience and competence to obtain strong distinctive competitive advantages may find it relatively easy to penetrate the market.

- A market penetration strategy requires a relatively lower level of investment with a corresponding reduction in risk and senior management involvement.

5.4 Product development

KEY POINT

Product development strategy has the aim of a company increasing sales by developing products for its existing market.

This strategy has the aim of a company increasing sales by developing products for its existing market. For our purposes, new-product development is a generic term that incorporates innovative products, and modifications and improvements to existing products. Therefore, product development strategy of the company could:

- develop new product features through attempting to adapt, modify, magnify, minify, substitute, rearrange, reverse or combine existing features

- create different quality versions of the product

- develop additional models and sizes.

Appropriateness of product development strategy

A company might show a preference for product development strategy for the following reasons.

- It holds a high relative share of the market, has a strong brand presence and enjoys distinctive competitive advantages in the market.

- There is growth potential in the market. (You may remember that the Boston Consulting Group, for instance, recommends companies to invest in growth markets.)

- The changing needs of its customers demand new products. Continuous product innovation is often the only way to prevent product obsolescence.

- It needs to react to technological developments.

- The company is particularly strong in R&D.

- The company has a strong organisation structure based on product divisions.

- For offensive or defensive motives, for example responding to competitive innovations in the market.

However, product development strategy does have its downside and there are strong reasons why it might not be appropriate for a company. For example, the process of creating a broad product line is expensive and potentially unprofitable, and it carries considerable investment risk. Empirical research reveals that companies enjoying high market share may benefit in profit terms from relatively high levels of R&D expenditure, while companies in weak market positions with high R&D expenditure fare badly.

Difficulties associated with product development

There are reasons why new product development is becoming increasingly difficult to achieve.

- In some industries there is a shortage of new product ideas.

- Increasing market differentiation causes market segments to narrow with the effect that low volumes reduce profit potential which in turn increases the risk of the investment involved.

- A company typically has to develop many product ideas in order to produce one good one. This makes new product development very costly.

- Even when a product is successful it might still suffer a short life cycle with rivals quick to 'copycat' in the market but with their own innovations and improvements.

- There is a high chance of product failure.

The stages or phases involved in product development

We see from this that developing new products and launching them in the marketplace can be a difficult, costly and potentially damaging venture. However companies are increasingly recognising that the key to their survival and growth lies in the continuous development of new and improved products. Thus the senior managers of a company are in a dilemma; the company must develop new products, yet the odds weigh heavily against their success. An obvious need stands out: the need for an effective new-product development process.

Such a process typically involves the following stages:

- idea generation
- screening ideas
- concept development and testing
- business analysis
- prototype production
- brand naming
- package design
- promotion planning
- pricing
- planning distribution
- test marketing
- product and marketing modification (if required)
- consumer adoption process.

5.5 Market development

In the case of market development, the organisation maintains the security of its present products while venturing into new market areas. Market development can include entering new market segments, exploiting new uses for the product or spreading into new geographical areas. Of course, market development and product development may go hand in hand, since the move into a new market segment may require developments of variants to the existing product range.

Market development strategy has the aim of increasing sales by repositioning present products to new markets.

Kotler suggests that there are two possibilities.

- The company can open additional geographical markets through regional, national or international expansion.

- The company can try to attract other market segments through developing product versions that appeal to these segments, entering new channels of distribution, or advertising in other media.

Example

During 1992 Kellogg undertook a major television and promotion campaign to reposition Kellogg's Cornflakes (traditionally regarded as a breakfast cereal) to provide afternoon and evening meals. In the same way, the malt drink Horlicks had previously repositioned from a once-a-day product ('a night meal') to become a through-the-day 'relaxing drink'.

Appropriateness of market development

Market development strategy would be contemplated for the following reasons:

- The company identifies potential opportunities for market development including the possibilities of repositioning, exploiting new uses for the product or spreading into new geographical areas.

- The company's resources are structured to produce a particular product or product line and it would be very costly to switch technologies.

- The company's distinctive competence lies with the product and it also has strong marketing competence. (Coca-Cola provides a good example of a company that pursues market development strategies, as does the fast food restaurant chain of McDonalds.)

5.6 Diversification

Diversification is a term that is used in different ways. One interpretation is that it is used to identify directions of development that take the organisation away from both its present products and its present markets at the same time. There are two broad types of diversification, related and unrelated diversification:

- **Related diversification** – This is development beyond the present product and market, but still within the broad confines of the 'industry'. Unilever is a diversified organisation with all of its interests in the consumer goods industry. This form of diversification builds on the assets or activities that the organisation has developed in market or product terms. It can take the form of backward, forward or horizontal integration.

    – Backward integration refers to development concerned with the inputs into the organisation, e.g. raw materials, machinery and labour.

    –   Forward integration refers to development into activities that are concerned with the organisation's outputs such as distribution, transport, servicing and repairs.

    –   Horizontal integration refers to development into activities that are competitive with, or directly complementary to, an organisation's present activities. An example of this is a travel agent selling other related products such as travel insurance and currency exchange services.

- **Unrelated diversification** –This is development beyond the present industry into products and/or markets that may bear no clear relationship to their present portfolio. An example of this is an organisation such as Hanson.

Internal or external growth

The forms of diversification that we have just outlined can be achieved through two major alternative ways:

- by internal development, building on existing resources of technical, marketing and managerial skills, and sometimes including a degree of reorganisation

- by buying into new product markets, through licensing agreements, by joint ventures or by merger with or acquisition of another firm.

A merger is the fusion of two or more existing companies, the resultant single company being either one of the existing companies or a completely new company. In the latter case the fusion operations may be referred to as a consolidation. An acquisition is the purchase by one company of a controlling interest in the share capital of another existing company. Although the mechanics of combination will differ, the objectives are likely to be similar in all cases, so that it is convenient to use the term 'acquisition' to cover all types of combination.

It should be noted that acquisitions might be made not only for the aggressive purpose of growth but also for such defensive reasons as the elimination of competition or safeguarding a source of supply. Some acquisitions may be largely opportunistic – for example to obtain the disposal value of surplus assets.

5.7   Kotler's 3-by-3 product market growth matrix

We have examined Ansoff's 2-by-2 product market growth matrix. Kotler expands the original 2-by-2 matrix into a 3-by-3 matrix that includes the 'modified products' and 'geographical markets' options. Similar to Ansoff's model, products relate to columns and markets label the rows. Each of the nine cells relates to a strategy for a particular product market condition. This approach is illustrated in the table shown as follows.

		Products		
		Existing	Modified	New
M A R K E T S	Existing	Strategy : Market penetration	Strategy : Product modification	Strategy : Product innovation
	Geographical	Strategy : Geographical expansion	Strategy : Modification for dispersed markets	Strategy : Geographical modification
	New	Strategy : New markets	Strategy : Modification for new markets	Strategy : Total innovation

Table: Kotler Product-Market growth matrix

(Source: Kotler, P, *Marketing for Non-profit Organisations*, Prentice/Hall, 1982.)

The first cell relates to the strategy of 'market penetration'. This strategy provides the easiest, cheapest and least risky of all the options available and questions whether the company can maintain or expand product sales by deepening penetration into its present markets using its existing products. If further penetration by means of advertising, promotion, price adjustment or expansion of distribution outlets is possible then these options will provide attractive solutions to help solve the strategic problem. If further penetration does not seem hopeful or feasible, then the company will need to look for product market ideas in the other cells.

The 'product modification' cell concentrates attention on whether the company should modify some of its existing products to expand demand. For example, it might be feasible and worthwhile to introduce new product features with the aim of improving product quality. The 'product innovation' cell involves developing new products for existing markets that is one of the strategic options we examined previously.

The 'geographical expansion' cell raises the question as to whether the company should consider offering its existing products in new geographical locations. One idea that might be worth investigating and evaluating would be for the company to consider its export options. The 'modification for dispersed markets' cell suggests that the company might need to modify its existing products and services to meet the specific needs of its new geographically dispersed markets. The 'geographical modification' cell questions whether the company might do best to introduce new products with the aim of attracting new geographical markets.

The 'new markets' cell is ambitious and involves creating new markets for the company's existing products. It might be more appropriate to plan a strategy of 'modification for new markets'. The final strategy, 'total innovation', is the company diversifying into new markets by offering new products.

For our purposes, the first eight cells are referred to as expansion strategy to distinguish them from the final option that represents diversification strategy.

The product/market opportunity matrix approach helps management to identify and consider new and different opportunities in a systematic way. It provides a basis by which opportunities can be identified, evaluated and contrasted, thus providing the planners with important ideas and data for evaluation.

6 Porter's generic strategies for competitive advantage

6.1 Generic strategies for competitive advantage

Competitive advantage is anything that gives one organisation an edge over its rivals in the products it sells or the services it offers.

Porter states that a firm may possess two kinds of competitive advantage: low cost or differentiation. Competitive advantage is a function of either providing comparable buyer value more efficiently than competitors (low cost), or performing activities at comparable cost but in unique ways that create more buyer value than competitors and, hence, command a premium price (differentiation).

It is important to see that competitive advantage is created by superior knowledge, resources or applications of something within the firm itself. Thus Sony's competitive advantage is in developing innovative products that customers want to buy, but the origin of this advantage is in whatever Sony as a company does which results in the company being at the forefront of innovation.

Organisations can choose to apply either of these strategies to a broad market or to a narrow focused market. Porter called these strategies 'generic', and he identified three generic strategies for competitive advantage.

- **Cost leadership** – the lowest cost producer in the industry.

- **Differentiation** – the exploitation of a product or service that is believed to be unique in the industry as a whole.

- **Focus** – a restriction of activities to only a segment of the market by either providing goods or services at a lower cost to that segment or by providing a differentiated product or service for that segment.

6.2 Cost leadership

The first generic strategy is to achieve overall cost leadership in an industry. For companies competing in a 'price-sensitive' market, cost leadership is the strategic imperative of the entire organisation. It is vitally important for these companies to have a thorough comprehension of their costs and cost drivers. They also need to fully understand their targeted customer group's definition of quality, usually denoted in terms of design specifications, contractual requirements, delivery arrangements, and so on. Their essential task is to supply precisely the required quality of goods and services at the lowest possible cost. Of particular importance will be for the company to attain a cost level that is low relative to its competitors.

For companies not competing on price, cost leadership is still vitally important. Companies competing in the industry through product and service differentiation will need to focus on cost effectiveness and quality to maintain or enhance the value perceived by their target customers. Customers will select products and suppliers that provide value that equals or exceeds their actual and perceived cost both at the time of purchase and over the product's life. Price remains a function of value, although not to the same extent as for an undifferentiated market.

Cost leadership must be a goal of every organisation, regardless of their specific market orientation. It enables companies to:

- **Defend market share** – Cost leadership enables the company to defend itself against powerful buyers, because buyers only have power to drive the price down to the level of the next most efficient competitor.

- **Defend supply** – In the same way a low-cost position enables the company to cope with any price increases imposed by powerful suppliers.

- **Build entry barriers** – The factors that lead to a low-cost position, such as scale of economies, the use of advanced manufacturing technologies, quality systems and synergies, provide the company with substantial entry barriers.

- **Weaken threat of substitutes** – The dangers of substitutes are reduced in a low-price market.

- **Defend market share against rivals** – Having a low-cost position yields the company above-average profits in its industry despite strong competitive pressures. Its cost-leadership position also provides the company with a strong defensive position against rivalry from existing or potential competitors.

- **Increase market share** – Cost leadership allows the company to provide its targeted customer group with the best price to quality relationship, by having (i) the resources to vigorously innovate and continuously improve the quality of its products and services, and (ii) the ability to price its products more aggressively than its competitors.

- **Enter new markets** – A cost leadership position enables the company to successfully penetrate new domestic and foreign markets often by brand extension or 'brand stretch' strategy. Its low cost and high-quality position permits it to be selective when targeting markets.

- **Reduce the cost of capital** – The benefits described above allow the company to maintain a strong financial position and to generate superior returns to its shareholders. These in turn reduce the company's costs of capital of both borrowed funds and the cost of raising funds from the equity market.

Achieving a low-cost position thus protects the company against all five of the competitive forces highlighted by Porter. (These were discussed in an earlier chapter.) However attaining a low overall cost position requires sustained commitment throughout the organisation, from senior executives to line employees.

6.3 Differentiation

The second strategy is one of differentiating the company's products or services, in other words creating an offering that is perceived to be unique in the market. It is an obvious defensive competitive response for a company faced by a strong low-cost competitor. The strategy is to gain advantage through differentiating the product from lower priced ones on the basis of some non-price factor such as:

- quality (Marks and Spencer in clothing and other products)

- features (Sony in domestic 'brown furniture' items)

- style (Jaguar in automobiles)

- brand image (Mars in chocolate, drink, and ice-cream)

- dealer network (Caterpillar Tractor in construction equipment)

- customer service (Littlewoods in mail-order shopping)

- technology and performance (IBM in computers of all sizes)

- packaging (After Eight in mint chocolates)

- uniqueness (Coca Cola in taste).

For example, Caterpillar's strategy was to offer a broad product range of high-quality machines at premium prices, using a dedicated dealer network. All parts were standard worldwide. Superior service was an important peg in the strategy. Caterpillar guaranteed 48-hour delivery of parts anywhere in the world and did not charge for the parts if it failed to meet this deadline: '48-hour parts service anywhere in the world – or Cat pays'.

Ideally, the company differentiates along several dimensions. Marks and Spencer, for example, is known for its extensive and localised branch network, for the high quality of its customer services and also for its extremely high-quality durable products linked to the reputation of the St Michael brand.

KEY POINT

A highly differentiated market position will protect the company against the five competitive forces in its industry.

For similar reasons discussed for cost-leadership, a highly differentiated market position will protect the company against the five competitive forces in its industry. Its 'uniqueness', brand loyalty and resulting lower sensitivity to price, will protect it against new entrants, the power of buyers, the power of suppliers, the effects of new substitutes entering the market and rivalry within its markets. However differentiation does have its downside. The customer perception of 'exclusivity' is often incompatible with high market share. Also a lowering of price sensitivity will only be achieved within a price range. Although customers perceive the superiority of the company's offerings they might not be willing to pay prices significantly higher than the industrial average.

6.4 Focus

KEY POINT

The third, and last generic strategy is for the organisation to differentiate its offerings by focusing them on a particular buyer group, market segment or geographical region.

The third, and last generic strategy is for the organisation to differentiate its offerings by focusing them on a particular buyer group, market segment or geographical region. Focus can relate to:

- end-use specialism (Lucas Lighting in automobile electronics)

- customer size specialism

- specific customer specialism (Burton Group with its fashion focus, e.g. Top Shop)

- geographical specialism

- product or product-line specialism (Tie Rack which specialises in one item of clothing)

- product-feature specialism ('Howard Paper' in its narrow range of industrial-grade papers)

- quality-price specialism (Rolls Royce in luxury automobiles)

- service specialism.

For example, Tetra-Pak is the international leader in packaging liquids for human consumption, with worldwide sales of $1.9 billion. It does not sell packaging for non-edible use, e.g. motor oil or washing powder, since its packaging must be clearly identified with liquid foods and drinks only. Involvement with customers is active, not passive. Rather than just leasing machines and selling packaging, Tetra-Pak management will contribute to raising machine efficiency, and feed in market research and creative ideas to help with customers' selling and marketing.

Within its narrow targets the company can attempt to build a low-cost and/or differentiated position. As we have discussed in the context of cost leadership and product differentiation, the focused position will provide the company with protection against each of the five competitive forces.

6.5 Other competitive advantages

We have already seen that companies attempt to achieve competitive advantages through cost leadership, product differentiation and/or market focus. There are other strategies that can also achieve this goal.

- The erection of strong defensive positions or barriers to entry. We already know that barriers to entry may be in the form of low market prices, high levels of advertising investment, technological know-how requirement and so on. Large companies with significant resources may opt to enter markets with high entry requirements in order to build a competitive position over the medium to long term.

- Another game plan that is closely aligned with a strategy of cost leadership is market dominance. Achieving market dominance not only provides the company with a competitive advantage in terms of cost and thus price determination, but also allows it to reduce the adverse influence of its business environment. In other words, to have more control over its environment. Often a market leader provides the force of environment for other companies in its markets.

In situations where demand outweighs capacity, a low-cost position often obtains a very competitive position. However in these markets other companies have more scope to build special spheres of influence or competitive advantage based on their differentiated position. During periods of recession or slump, inefficient companies fall into liquidation and thus leave the market. Their removal frees discrete amounts of the market allowing efficient companies to gain sales volume, often quite considerably. Furthermore, when the market picks up, the number of participants is less, reducing the competition for the market upsurge that ensues.

7 Synergy

7.1 The concept of synergy

Synergy is the advantage to a company gained by having existing resources which are compatible with new products or markets that the company is developing. Synergy has been described as the $2 + 2 = 5$ effect, where a company looks for combined results that reflect a better rate of return than would be achieved by the same resources used independently as separate operations. The combined performance, therefore, is greater than the sum of its parts.

Each product-market makes a contribution to the overall profitability of the company. Each product results in annual sales of £S, with operating costs of £O. To market the product an investment programme of £I is required. The return on investment (ROI) from a product is obtained by dividing the difference between operating revenue and costs in a given period by the investment required to support the venture, i.e.

$$ROI = \frac{S-O}{I}$$

Likewise a similar calculation can be made for all other products. Consequently, if the products are unrelated in any way, by simple addition of the various expressions, the total assessment for the company can be determined, thus:

$$ROI = \frac{(S_1 + S_2 ..... + S_n) - (O_1 + O_2 ..... + O_n)}{(I_1 + I_2 ..... + I_n)}$$

Invariably the economies of scale will apply both in terms of operating costs and investment. In the same way, for a given level of investment a company with a complete product line can usually realise the advantages of higher total revenues and/or lower operating costs than competing independent companies whose product-markets are not as carefully selected. Using symbols this is equivalent to saying that for:

$$S_S = (S_1 + S_2 .... + S_n)$$

we have

$$O_S \leq (O_1 + O_2 .... + O_n)$$

$$I_S \leq (I_1 + I_2 .... + I_n)$$

where subscript S denotes the respective quantities for an integrated company and the right hand side of each equation denotes the sum of the competing independent companies. As a result we see that the potential return on investment for the integrated company is higher than the total return that would be achieved if the same level of sales were produced by the independent companies:

$$ROI_S > ROI_T$$

A similar argument can, of course, be made by keeping the total investment fixed. In which case:

$$S_S \geq (S_1 + S_2 .... + S_n)$$

we have

$$O_S \leq (O_1 + O_2 .... + O_n)$$

$$I_S = (I_1 + I_2 .... + I_n)$$

For a given level of investment a company with an integrated product-market line can usually obtain the advantages of higher sales revenues and/or lower operating costs than its competing independent companies. There are several other combinations of the three main elements comprising the ROI formula that demonstrate the synergy concept. For example, an integrated company could achieve a higher sales revenue than obtained by its competing independent companies, although both its operating costs and investment levels remain the same.

7.2 Categories of synergy

To assist in the quantification of the effects of synergy, it is useful to classify the types of synergy that may exist:

- **Sales synergy** – This is obtained through use of common marketing facilities such as distribution channels, sales staff and administration, and warehousing. Supplying a range of complementary products increases the productivity of the sales force. Shared advertising, sales promotion and corporate image can generate a much higher return for the same unit of outlay. For example, televisions and video recorders are complementary goods that would be advertised jointly. Barclaycard acquired a travel agency in 1988 and advertised the travel agency's services by offering discounts if Barclaycard was used for the purchase of a holiday.

- **Operating synergy** – This synergy arises from the better use of operational facilities and personnel, bulk purchasing, and producing more items with little or no increase in fixed costs. The cost savings associated with experience curves and learning curves may be capable of being transferred from one product to another.

- **Investment synergy** – This results from the joint use of plant, common raw material stocks, and transfer of research and development from one product to another. There is a wider use of a common investment in fixed assets, working capital or research.

- **Management synergy** – This synergy is the advantage gained where management skills and experience concerning current operations are easily transferred to new operations because of the similarity of problems in the two industries. However the opposite may be true. There might be negative synergy at top management level in situations where the problems inherent in new ventures are unrelated to current operations and attempts to solve them in a familiar way lead to incorrect decisions.

Activity 1

Imagine that a manufacturer of cars has to choose between diversifying into (a) motor cycle manufacture or (b) food production. Using the categories of synergy discussed above list the synergies that the manufacturer might have with both choices.

Feedback to this activity is at the end of the chapter.

Summary

Key points of this chapter are:

- A position audit and gap analysis are important in defining the strategic plans for a company.

- Gap analysis involves the identification of different types of gap (e.g. strategic gap) and then taking appropriate action in respect of the gap type.

- Forecasting models include statistical analysis through to the Delphi technique which is based more on subjective data from experts.

- Ansoff and later Kotler provide models to explain the strategic development of an organisation in terms of markets access and suitability of products for each market.

- Porter's theories, including cost leadership, provide the company with the capability to sustain an advantage against all its competitors and to protect its market share and position against the different competitive forces in the market.

- Porter's generic strategy model is the most sophisticated general theory of competitiveness, and can be used to think through strategy issues with great effect, particularly when used in conjunction with the five forces model.

- Synergy is one of the major components of the company's product-market strategy and is concerned with the 'fit' between its different activities.

Having completed your study of this chapter you should have achieved the following learning outcomes:

- evaluate strategic options

- discuss and apply both qualitative and quantitative techniques in the support of the strategic decision-making function.

Self-test questions

1   List the eight Ms on which a postion audit focuses. (2.1)

2   What is gap analysis? (2.4)

3   What is the strategic gap? (2.5)

4   Explain the Delphi technique. (3.2)

5   What is scenario planning? (4)

6   What are Ansoff's four growth vector quadrants? (5.2)

7   List some of the difficulties associated with product development. (5.4)

8   Distinguish related from unrelated diversification. (5.6)

9   What is competitive advantage? (6.1)

10   What are Porter's three generic strategies? (6.1)

11   What does cost leadership enable a company to do? (6.2)

12   What is differentiation? (6.3)

13   What is focus? (6.4)

14   Define synergy. (7.1)

15   Explain the four categories of synergy. (7.2)

Practice question

Leisure and Pleasure

Many boards of directors have been considering for a long time the proposal that 'now is the time to diversify into leisure and pleasure'.

Required:

(a)   Explain such a proposal and the reasons for it.   **(5 marks)**

(b)   Explain the concept of synergy.   **(10 marks)**

(c)   Describe the work which would have to be done before a particular strategy can be put into place to meet that proposal.   **(10 marks)**

(Total: 25 marks)

For the answer to this question, see the 'Answers' section at the end of the book.

Feedback to activity

Activity 1

	Motorcycle manufacture	*Food production*
Sales synergy	Brand stretch Possible price tie-in Image stretch Communications	Nil (possibly negative)
Operating synergy	Commonisation of certain materials Rationalisation of administration	Nil
Investment synergy	R&D stretch Possible rationalisation of capacity	Nil
Management synergy	Quite strong related experience	Weak in the technical aspects

Chapter 9

PRODUCT PORTFOLIO EVALUATION

Syllabus content

- Management of the product portfolio

Contents

1   Introduction

2   Product market portfolio (PMP) and the BCG matrix

3   More complex matrices

4   Product lifecycle

1 Introduction

There are a number of planning tools to assess the position of a company's product within its industry and within its own lifecycle. In this chapter we will look at the Product Market Portfolio (PMP) as developed by the Boston Consulting Group (BCG) to demonstrate this positioning. Other techniques such as the Shell directional policy matrix will also be discussed.

The product lifecycle theory breaks down the life of a product into four or five stages, with the length of each stage varying with the product and state of technology within the organisation. The use of the matrix is explained towards the end of this chapter.

2 Product market portfolio (PMP) and the BCG matrix

2.1 Introduction

Whilst there are companies that produce a single product or service, most organisations are multi-product or consider diversification into other products. Within a multidivisional company, there may be some products at maturity, some at the design stage, and others in decline. Each of these may be in different markets, and different countries. This is a complex planning process, and the product market portfolio (PMP), developed by the Boston Consulting Group, is a technique developed to manage it.

The product market portfolio is a useful tool for strategic planning, in that it allows the planners to select the optimal strategy for individual units whilst aiming for overall corporate objectives. Although the technique was developed to analyse a multi-product situation, it also provides useful information for a one-product organisation (or useful information for a part of the organisation which produces just one product). Indeed, as a first step, the technique requires an assessment of each product of an organisation in isolation from other products.

2.2 The growth-share matrix

This is illustrated by reference to the following simplified example:

Year	Company	Product	Sales £	Sales units	Market growth %
20X8	A	Widgets	500	100	12
20X8	B	Widgets	400	80	12
20X8	C	Widgets	100	10	12
20X9	A	Widgets	750	150	15
20X9	B	Widgets	500	100	15
20X9	C	Widgets	220	22	15

The three key pieces of information displayed in this table are analysed below:

- **Growth rate of market** – It is usually easier to penetrate a growing market than a static or declining market. Equally, existing products will have difficulty in maintaining market share in a static or declining market.

  The market growth rate is plotted, net of inflation, on the vertical axis of the growth-share matrix below. It is plotted on an arithmetic scale.

- **Product's relative market share** – This is the market share relative to the largest competitor. It is found by:

relative market share = unit sales ÷ sales of largest competitor

Applying this to the data above:

Year	Company	Sales units	Relative market share
20X8	B	80	0.80
20X8	C	10	0.10
20X9	A	150	1.50
20X9	B	100	0.67
20X9	C	22	0.15

It is believed that relative market share is a better indicator of relative competitive position than absolute share. For example, a 30% share of a market where the largest competitor has 20% is very different from the same 30% where the largest competitor has 65%.

Relative market share is plotted on the horizontal axis using a log scale in the growth-share matrix below.

- **Money value of product sales** – This is plotted in the display by the relative size of the circle. The results of this analysis for the two years are shown below:

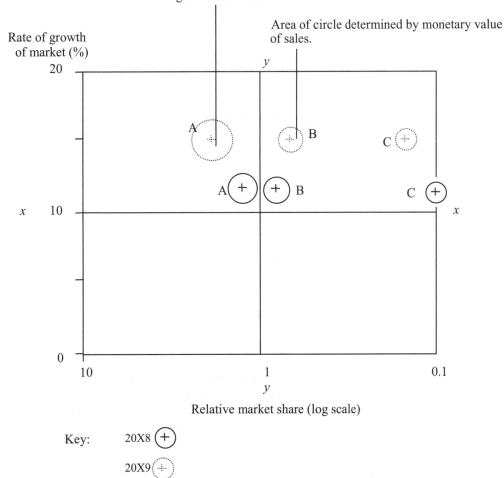

Diagram: The Growth-Share Matrix

2.3 The Boston Consulting Group (BCG) matrix

You will note that the matrix above is divided into four quadrants. These could be defined fairly arbitrarily by setting the growth rate divider at 10%, and the market share divider at 1.0, i.e. joint market leaders. Thus, in terms of market shares, companies to the left are market leaders, and those to the right are market followers. The growth rate divider at 10% is harder to justify. It becomes more acceptable when other products are shown on the matrix that have a range of market growth rates.

The portfolio BCG matrix would be expressed as:

		High	**STAR** Moderate, safe, positive cash flow	**QUESTION MARK/ PROBLEM CHILD** Large negative cash flow
Relative market growth		Low	**CASH COW** Large positive cash flow	**DOG** Modest positive or negative cash flow
			High	Low

Relative market share

Table: The BCG Matrix

The axes are uncalibrated and therefore relative in nature. A market leader is, for example likely to have a high market share. Similarly, market growth is a relative measure. Growth of 8% may seem high in one industry and low in another. The matrix identifies four types of product or service: dogs, cash cows, problem children (question marks) and stars, and suggests appropriate strategies for each.

The **cash cow** has a high relative market share in a low-growth industry and should be generating substantial cash inflows. The period of high growth in the market has ended (the product lifecycle is in the maturity or decline stage), and consequently the market is less attractive to new entrants and existing competitors. Cash cow products tend to generate cash in excess of what is needed to sustain their market positions. An organisation's strategy is oriented towards maintaining the product's strong position in the market.

A **star** product has a high relative market share in a high-growth industry. This type of product may be in a later stage of its product lifecycle. A star may be only cash neutral despite its strong position, as large amounts of cash may need to be spent to defend an organisation's position against competitors. Competitors will be attracted to the market by the high growth rates. Failure to support a star sufficiently strongly may lead to the product losing its leading market share position, slipping eastwards in the matrix and becoming a problem child. A star, however, represents the best future prospects for an organisation. As the growth rate for a star slows, it will drop vertically in the matrix into the cash cow quadrant and its cash characteristics will change. Market share for the star can be maintained or increased through price reductions, product modifications, and/or greater distribution.

A **problem child** or **question mark** is a low market share product in a high-growth industry. Substantial net cash input is required to maintain or increase market share in the face of strong competition. The planner must decide whether to market more intensively or get out of this market. The questions are whether this product can compete successfully with adequate support, and what that support will cost.

The **dog** product has a low relative market share in a low-growth industry. Such a product tends to have a negative cash flow that is likely to continue. It is unlikely that a dog can wrest market share from competitors. Competitors, which have the advantage of having larger market shares, are likely to fiercely resist any attempts to reduce their share of a low growth or static market. An organisation with such a product can attempt to appeal to a specialised market, delete the product or harvest profits by cutting back support services to a minimum.

The logic of the portfolio is that cash cows are the financiers of the other segments. Ideally, some question marks are selected to become stars; this will require demands for capital that will be provided by the cash cows. As a star matures and the market growth slows so it becomes a cash cow for future products. Question marks not selected should be managed to generate cash until they become dogs. Dogs should be harvested or divested from the portfolio.

BCG suggests a company should manage its portfolio of products or business units to maintain this desirable sequence.

Options for the future can be plotted onto a BCG matrix and the long-term rationale of business development can be highlighted by the matrix. Using the original matrix a strategist could address the following issues:

- Which strategies are most suitable to ensure a move from question marks through to stars and eventually to cash cows? In other words, will the strategy move the organisation to a dominant position in its market?

- Will there be sufficient funds from cash cows to provide the necessary investment in stars? Many bankruptcies have occurred because firms have invested heavily in the promotion of products in rapid growth without profitable and well-established products from which it can fund these new ventures.

- Does the portfolio have a balance of activities that matches the range of skills within the organisation? Unless a balance is achieved certain groups are overstretched while others remain underemployed. In general, question marks and stars can be very demanding on the time of management.

- Is the organisation thinking about an acquisition strategy? Firms that embark on acquisition programmes often forget that the most likely targets for acquisition are not the cash cows and stars of the business world but the question marks and dogs. There may be logic in acquiring a question mark for an organisation with the resources to move it towards stardom.

2.4 Strategic movements

A product's place in the matrix is not fixed for ever. The rate of growth of the market should be taken into account in determining strategy. Stars tend to move vertically downwards as the market growth rate slows, to become cash cows. The cash that they generate can be used to turn problem children into stars, and eventually cash cows.

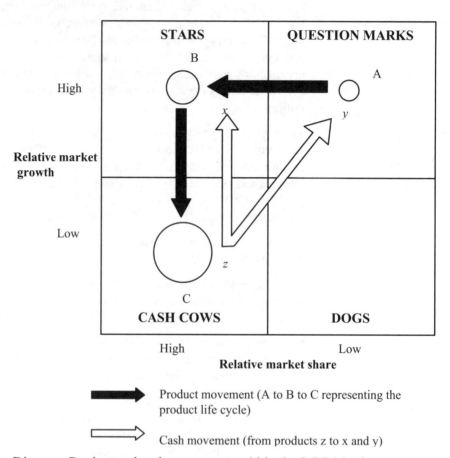

Diagram: Product and cash movements within the BCG Matrix

2.5 Strategic management of the market portfolio

The strategies for the overall portfolio are concerned with balance. Strategies would be to have:

- cash cows of sufficient size and/or number which can support other products in the portfolio

- stars of sufficient size and/or number which will provide sufficient cash generation when the current cash cows can no longer do so

- problem children which have reasonable prospects of becoming future stars

- no dogs, and if there are any, there would need to be good reasons for retaining them.

In deciding which strategy to adopt, numerous factors other than those in the matrix display need to be considered, e.g.:

- risk attached to the strategy

- nature of the products/markets.

Nevertheless, the matrix position provides a good and objective indication of the competitive position of the products.

2.6 Limitations of the BCG matrix

The matrix uses only two measures

The only two measures used in the BCG matrix are growth and market share. These may be too limited as a basis for policy decisions. The Boston Consulting Group has now developed a further matrix to meet this criticism:

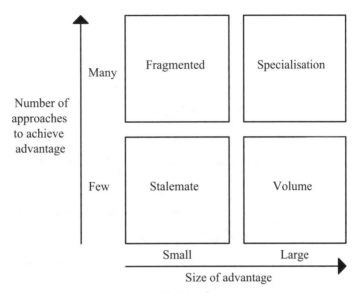

Diagram: Extension to the BCG Matrix

The vertical axis now indicates the number of ways in which a unique advantage may be achieved over competitors, and the horizontal axis is a measure of the size advantage that may be created over competitors.

The new matrix makes the exercise much more a matter of qualitative judgement.

Encourages companies to adopt holding strategies

The strategic principles involved advocate that companies with large market shares in static or low-growth markets (i.e. cash cows) adopt holding or harvesting strategies rather than encouraging them to try to increase the total demand of the markets in which their products are selling. Compliance with these strategic tenets has led to devastating results for some companies.

There are a number of dangers in assuming that a product is a 'cash cow'. (BCG defines a cash cow as a product occupying a strong position in a static or slow growing market.) First management may be tempted to pull back on investment, by treating the product as in 'safe-water', and second make assumptions about future cash flow that may be unrealistic. Radios, for example, form a product line which was treated by a number of manufacturers as a cash cow. Convinced that every product had its 'product lifecycle' they treated the radio as a product that had passed its peak and the radio business as a candidate for cash milking.

Japanese radio manufacturers were not prepared to treat the radio-line in this way and, by creating new markets, expanded the total demand for radios. The result was a flood of innovative products which included: radio-cassette, stereo radio-cassette, ultra-thin radio, 'Walkman with radio', radio-in-pocket with calculator, radio-in-TV and digital clock radio – all successful products.

Yamaha destroyed the dominance of the well-established US musical instrument manufacturers who concentrated on milking their mature products for profit rather than on planning how to defend their market shares.

Implies only those with large market shares should remain

There are many examples of businesses with a low market share continuing to operate profitably. Sometimes this is because the market is not unitary, but fragmented, and the small competitor has found itself a particular market niche; on other occasions large companies may prefer smaller competitors to preserve the impression of competition.

The link between profitability and market share may be weak because:

- low share competitors entering the market late may be on the steepest experience curve

- low share competitors may have some in-built cost advantage

- not all products have costs related to experience

- large competitors may receive more government attention and regulation.

Implies that the most profitable markets are those with high growth

Again this is not always so, due to:

- high entry barriers, especially in high technology industries

- high price competition.

Both of these problems are typified by the microcomputer business. Despite impressive rates of growth, a number of companies have been unable to make profits because of the high levels of initial investment followed by extreme price competition from low-cost late entrants.

The US company Republic Gypsum is a small one-plant manufacturer of wallboards with only a 2% share of the US plasterboard market. It is a lot smaller than the majors with US Gypsum holding 37% and National Gypsum 27%. Republic concentrates on a small geographical niche centred on Oklahoma and North Texas, and meets local prices and absorbs high freight costs by using its own trucking fleet. Its competitors use contract freight carriers at high cost. In 1982 Republic achieved 94% plant utilisation, against 70% for the rest of the industry, and reported a 13.5% operating margin after depreciation, triple that of US Gypsum and almost quadruple that of National Gypsum.

Not all dogs should be condemned

KEY POINT

Dog products are often used not with the primary aim of maximising the profit from the product itself, but to provide economies of scale in manufacturing, marketing and administration to sustain the overall business.

A very large number of small but successful businesses are 'dogs', and according to the BCG concept are ripe for reinvestment or liquidation. However this would not always be the case. Dog products are often used not with the primary aim of maximising the profit from the product itself, but to provide economies of scale in manufacturing, marketing and administration to sustain the overall business. Furthermore the BCG portfolio theory does not seem to take into account the need for competitive strategy. A company might, for example, launch a product to act as a 'second front' to support the thrust of its main offering, although the product, by definition, is a dog.

The Clorox company's purpose of introducing 'Wave' into the US domestic bleach market was to try to deflect Procter & Gamble's attack on the market brand leader, Clorox, by creating a 'second front', rather than to generate substantial profits from Wave.

Despite these criticisms, in certain circumstances the model provides a useful method by which a company can (a) attempt to achieve overall cost leadership in its market(s) through aggressive use of directed efficiency; (b) focus its expenditures and capital investment programmes; and (c) plan for an appropriate balance of resources between conflicting product-market claims. Also the information and analysis required to construct the matrix will provide meaningful indicators. It should, however, not be used in a rigid, stereotype manner. The model ought to be used as a means to an end, not as representing the end objective in itself.

The evidence

Several studies have been carried out into the use of the BCG, and on the whole these would not encourage uncritical use of the model. In particular, the link between quadrant and cash flow is not particularly strong, and there are many exceptions. Fortune once described this model as the worst business model ever devised.

3 More complex matrices

3.1 Shell directional policy matrix

Whereas the BCG matrix seems to imply that all industries can be explained by just two variables, the Shell Matrix (also called the GE Matrix, Nine Cell Matrix and McKinsey Matrix) leaves industry attractiveness and company competitiveness to the analyst. Thus, each company in an industry is likely to prepare different models, depending on their own perceptions and objectives. The matrix uses a number of determinants.

Business sector prospects

- **market** – demographic

- **competition** – number and size of competitors, price competition, barriers to entry, substitutes

- **technology** – sophistication, rate of change, lead time, patents

- **economic** – leverage, capital intensity, margins

- **government** – subsidies/grants, purchases, protection, regulation, taxation

- **geography** – location, markets, communications, environment

- **social** – pressure groups, trade unions, availability of labour.

The business position

- **market** – share, growth, product maturity, product quality, product mix, marketing ability, price strategy, customer loyalty

- **technological** – skills, patent protection, R&D, manufacturing technology

- **production** – costs, capacity utilisation, inventory control, maintenance, extent of vertical integration

- **personnel** – employee quality, top management quality, industrial relations, trade union strength, training, labour costs

- **financial** – resources, capital structure, margins, tax position, financial control, investment intensity.

3.2 The matrix

The result of an analysis may be placed in a matrix as indicated below:

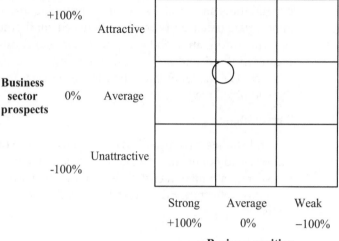

Diagram: The Shell directional policy matrix

In order to interpret the results, the matrix may be divided into nine sectors as below:

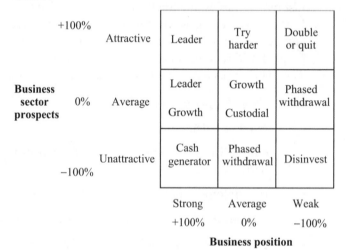

Diagram: Sector names for the Shell policy matrix

These are explained briefly below:

- **Leader** – the most advantageous position, but will require investment to take advantage of the prospects. This is the BCG matrix 'star'.

- **Leader/growth** – leadership in a business sector with more limited prospects implies a cash generator. Midway between BCG matrix 'star' and 'cash cow'.

- **Cash generator** – strong position in unattractive market sector. The BCG matrix 'cash cow'.

- **Try harder** – behind the leader in an attractive business sector. May have zero or negative cash flow. Between BCG matrix 'star' and 'problem child'.

- **Growth/custodial** – no particular advantages in a market with only limited prospects. The BCG matrix 'problem child'.

- **Phased withdrawal** – either a weak business position in an average business sector, or an average business position in an unattractive business sector. However, such businesses may still generate cash surpluses. The policy is to withdraw or harvest. These are between a BCG matrix 'cash cow' and 'problem child'.

- **Double or quit** – a weak position in an attractive business sector. The choice is either to harvest, or invest heavily to improve the position. This is the BCG matrix 'problem child'.

- **Disinvest** – a weak position in an unattractive business sector. The BCG matrix 'dog'.

3.3 Strategic movements

In addition to considering the position on the directional policy matrix in static terms, changes over time need also to be considered.

Ideally, products in the cash generating sectors should be able to finance expenditure on products in the attractive business/weak position sectors, so as to move them to the attractive business/strong position sectors. Later these products move down to become cash generators themselves, and the cycle is completed:

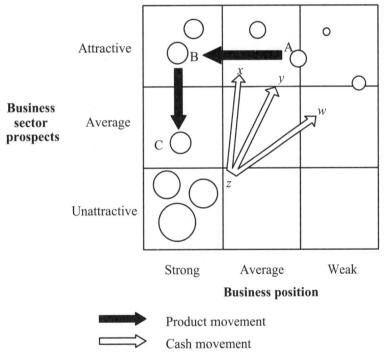

Diagram: Product and cash movements within the Shell policy matrix

The matrices may be drawn up both for one's own company, and for competitors. They may then be used to guide strategic decisions.

The main problem of this approach is the attempt to summarise so many factors in a two-dimensional matrix. This increases subjectivity, and hence reduces the value of the analysis. Also, ultimately a product's position on the matrix is determined by just two nebulous co-ordinates, each summarising a variety of factors.

3.4 The GE/McKinsey directional policy matrix

A more sophisticated directional policy matrix has been developed by General Electric, McKinsey and Shell. As can be seen in the diagram below, the matrix has four dimensions on two axes:

- **Industry attractiveness** – which includes the size, growth, diversity, profitability and competitive structure of the industry, as well as relevant political, economic, social and technological factors.

- **Business or competitive strengths** – another composite dimension including size, growth, share, position, profitability, image, strengths and weaknesses.

- **Size of industry** – size of circle.

- **Share of industry** – segment of circle.

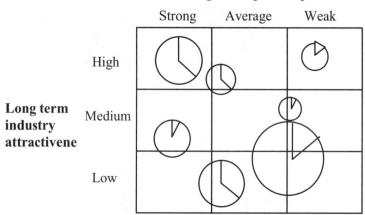

Diagram: GE/McKinsey nine cell business portfolio matrix

Each axis could be defined in terms meaningful to that company. Some illustrations are listed below.

Competitive strengths	Industry attractiveness
Relative market share	Market size, growth, diversity
Distribution/brand strengths	Inflation recovery
Technology strengths	Technology protection
Innovation/management	Socio/political risks
Profit margins relative to competitors	Economies of scale
Ability to compete on price and quality	Seasonality
Knowledge of customer and market	Cyclicality
Calibre of management	Barriers to entry and exit

Products (SBUs)/services are entered onto the policy matrix as circles, with size proportional to turnover. Depending on where a unit is positioned in the matrix, its broad strategic mandate will be to invest/build, hold or harvest. Arrows can be attached to the circles showing the direction in which the strategist wants the product to move. The direction of movement can often be changed by management action, e.g. competitive strength could be increased if resources were directed at technological innovation. The implied strategies may be as shown in the chart below.

Business strength/competitive position

		Strong	Average	Weak
Long term industry attractive-ness	High	– Enhance leadership – Diversify product/ market segments – Re-invest most aggressively in technology, capacity, marketing	– Hold leadership position – Leverage strengths into more attractive segments – Use economics of scale to outspend competition	– Maintain leadership in more attractive segments – Harvest work segments – Shrink product line
	Medium	– Avoid 'me too' strategy – Segment market carefully – Differentiate product, service or business approach – Concentrate on re-investment	– Increase level of segmentation to differentiate strategies between growth and harvest – Avoid perpetrating high shared overheads	– Harvest by pricing up, selling shares and cutting costs aggressively through line pruning
	Low	– Apply high degree of segment focus – Seek advantage, e.g. proprietary technology	– Harvest by sale to larger company in market	– Divest or liquidate

Table: Implied strategies from the GE / McKinsey directional policy matrix

Strengths of this approach

- multiple criteria provide sounder judgement

- relevant to many business situations

- criteria can be tailored to business level or business type

- nine cells is optimal: too few and allocations are restrictive; too many and the diagram becomes confusing.

Weaknesses of this approach

- judgemental – not totally quantitative

- parameter weighting unclear

- needs sophisticated users.

3.5 The Hofer matrix

The Hofer matrix (Hofer and Schendel, *Strategy formulation: analytic concepts*) is an attempt to partially overcome these criticisms by building four dimensions into the matrix:

- competitive position – horizontal axis

- stage of product/market evolution – vertical axis

- size of industry – size of circle

- share of industry – segment of circle.

This is illustrated below with seven examples:

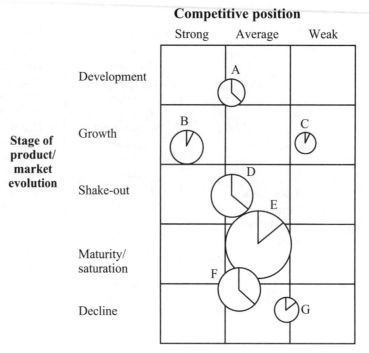

Diagram: The Hofer matrix

This matrix gives a more comprehensive picture, but is more complicated to construct.

4 Product lifecycle

4.1 Introduction

The product lifecycle concept suggests that all products have a similar lifecycle, which affects the current rate of sale and also has significant implications for the strategic options for the future. The theory breaks the economic life of a product into a number of stages (four or five are the most common), as shown below:

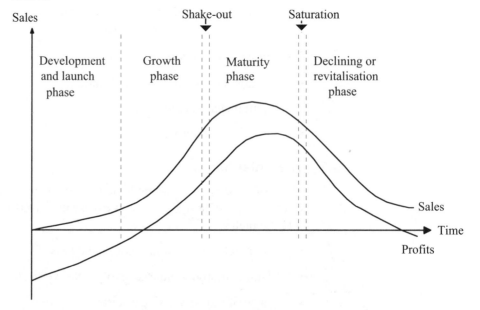

Diagram: The product lifecycle

KAPLAN PUBLISHING

The length of the cycle will vary with the type of product and technology; e.g. long for aircraft, short for fashion garments.

4.2 Lifecycle phases

The characteristics of the various phases are as follows:

- **Development and launch** – The model product is being designed and developed; market research may be undertaken to determine the potential market. The product is launched into the market where it takes time to gain acceptance and thus the initial sales growth is slow. At this stage, losses are made, few companies are in the field and design changes are being made. For this last reason it does not always pay to be an innovator, it may be better to wait until someone else has ironed out all the snags.

- **Growth** – If the product is accepted by the market and becomes more widely known, the growth phase starts and sales begin to take off, prompted by active marketing. The rate of growth and length of the growth phase depends on factors such as novelty value of the product; usefulness of the product; availability of substitutes; rate of growth of consumer incomes and proportion spent on luxuries/necessities; expenditure on advertising, etc.

  The ultimate demand for any product will not be infinite and in time the rate of growth will slow down as all potential customers have entered the market and a normal rate of usage has been established. It is not uncommon for a number of late-entrant organisations to enter the market during the growth phase, where there is a rapid expansion in demand and the consequent opportunity to make a good return for a more limited period.

  When a number of new organisations enter the industry, they will expand the total capacity. If they expect sales to grow rapidly, the increase will probably be substantial, especially if it is combined with the extra production of the existing players. Unfortunately, this extra capacity often occurs just before the rate of market growth starts to slow down, and sales increases will become more difficult to achieve. Many of the organisations will find themselves with spare capacity and there might be a short, sharp shake-out period when several competitors leave the industry or are taken over and capacity is rationalised.

- **Maturity** – Once a more stable position has been established with sales demand relatively balanced by available capacity, the phase is considered mature. Any residual excess capacity will influence the competitive strategies that will be implemented by the organisations left in the industry. Eventually the demand for the product will start to decline because alternative substitute products have been introduced or consumer tastes have changed. With some products, the market may reach saturation point. There is stiff competition among the existing players with profit margins falling. There is a tendency for companies to merge to both achieve cost reduction and put up further barriers to the entry of new companies because they would be too small to compete. Some companies will drop out of the market altogether.

- **Decline or revitalisation** – Sales of the product fall off, and the decline will continue unless the product can be revitalised by new technology, by advertising (likely to be of limited use only), by finding a new use for the product or by some other means. For instance, the introduction of colour television revitalised the television market.

4.3 Implications for strategy

A company is in a weak position if all its products are at the same phase of the lifecycle. If they are all in the growth phase there are problems ahead: if they are all in one of the other phases there are immediate difficulties.

Companies try to overcome this problem by introducing new products that are growing as the old products are declining and by having products with lifecycles of different lengths. This is illustrated below. The example is entirely invented and is not based on actual data.

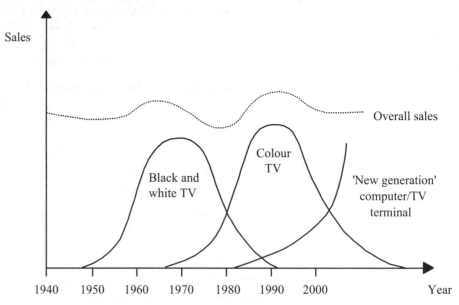

Diagram: Maintain sales in the product lifecycle

In any particular instance the industry analysis will show the company whether it can hope to get the right balance of lifecycle within its own industry or whether it will have to think of diversifying.

4.4 Lifecycle analysis

The product lifecycle concept, commonly known as the S-curve, is valid for most products, markets, economies, industries, technologies, popular movements, fashions and companies. Although the basic concept of the lifecycle is well covered in most study texts which deal with marketing management or new product development policy, and the concept is highly valued as a predictive technique, one has to search quite hard to find an explanation of how the curve is actually projected.

The first task is to project the shape of the S-curve, using historic and forecasting data. The two shapes most widely referred to are the logistic and Gompertz curves; however, as in most concepts there are many variations. Once the basic shape has been projected (in terms of 'relative' duration between development, growth and useful life) the next task is to project the financial parameters. If a cash flow basis is applied, the projection parameters will be:

- maximum net outflow during development

- maximum net outflow immediately prior to take-off

- maximum net positive cash flow at the height of sales volume (after achieving maximum growth)

- maximum net positive cash flow immediately prior to decline

- level of positive net cash flow at the point at which a decision may need to be taken to discontinue the product.

Having established the shape and financial parameters which provide the data required to plot the vertical axis on a graph, the final task is to forecast the duration of each stage required for the horizontal, or time axis. The techniques of intuitive and technological forecasting are available to help project time-spans involved. However, this is an extremely difficult aspect of lifecycle forecasting and, depending upon the shape and time-spans involved, the later parts of the life curve may, perhaps, be calculated in broad terms only.

A product life is influenced by many factors, such as technological innovation, customer behaviour, government fiscal policies (e.g. the incidence and rates of value added tax), the activities of competitors and much more. It is these factors that need to be forecast in order for the lifecycle curve to be projected with any confidence of accuracy.

4.5 Risk and return relationship

KEY POINT

The stages of the lifecycle have different intrinsic levels of risk, and the organisation has little control over the fundamental component of the total risk as it is determined by the external environment.

The various stages of the lifecycle raise a number of important issues with regard to the input of strategic management accounting. The stages of the lifecycle have different intrinsic levels of risk, and the organisation has little control over the fundamental component of the total risk as it is determined by the external environment. As risk and return are positively correlated, i.e. if the risk increases, the potential return must increase to compensate for the increased risk, the organisation should adopt a policy that applies to all levels of investment decision. A guaranteed return would be considered a low-risk investment and, as the risk increases, the return must improve appropriately. Even if there were such a thing as a no-risk investment, an investor will demand a positive return to compensate for the opportunity lost on having the funds available for consumption immediately and for tying their capital up in this project.

The launch period is clearly a time of high business risk as it is quite possible that the product will fail. The risk is still high during the growth phase because the ultimate size of the industry is still unknown and the level of market share that can be gained and retained is also uncertain. During the market maturity phase the risk decreases and the final phase should be regarded as low risk because the organisation knows that the product is dying and its strategy should be tailored accordingly.

If there is an analysis of the developing risk profile it should be compared to the financial risk profiles of various strategic options, making it much easier to select appropriate combinations and to highlight unacceptably high or low total risk combinations. An organisation will normally reject a high product risk project with a high financial risk as being an unacceptable combination and only suitable for organisations with a strong appetite for risk. Financial risk can be analysed by the source of funding used by the organisation. Equity can be regarded as the lowest possible risk type of financing; borrowed money (debt) represents much higher risk. Thus for an organisation to decide to finance with debt the development and launch of a completely new product would represent a high total risk combination.

Looking at the other end of the lifecycle, there are many organisations in a dominant market position with mature products which are holding large positive cash balances. These organisations are obvious acquisition targets. For them to introduce a realistic level of debt can dramatically improve the return to shareholders without increasing the total combined risk to unacceptable levels.

4.6 Industry classification strategies

On a similar theme we can also consider how the characteristics and structure of the main industry classifications affect the strategy selection of an organisation. The classifications include:

- emerging and developing industries

- maturing industries

- declining industries.

Emerging and developing industries

Typically, these industries have been created by technological innovations (computer games) or new consumer needs being defined. In such circumstances there is no accepted strategic pattern, so each participant in the industry can set their own rules. Success in such circumstances depends on understanding the factors in the industry environment and shaping strategies accordingly.

Given the newness of an emerging industry, it is likely to be small in size with uncertain features and lacking any dominant competitor.

Specific characteristics:

- Technology in its infancy. There may be uncertainty regarding design, performance, formulation, production methods, etc.

- Strategic and cost uncertainty. Little information available regarding potential customers, potential competitors, effects of learning curve, critical mass.

- Heavy initial costs. Small production volumes, newness of design, capital set up costs, market research, etc cause heavy initial costs though there may be a steep cost reduction as volume output becomes established and the learning curve declines.

- Embryonic companies often figure as typical participants in an emerging or re-formed industry.

- Sales to customers will be dependent on correct analysis of the first time buyer/early adopter. Initial customers will have to be convinced of the product virtues because there is no inherited knowledge.

- Timescales for planning are short.

- Entry barriers relate more to product knowledge, technology and access to raw materials/markets than capital barriers (e.g. consider video games).

Strategy selection will be constrained by certain factors pertinent to an emerging industry, such as:

- Lack of appeal to the financial market – probably an embryonic company in an unproved market.

- Possible inability to acquire raw materials or install equipment if demand suddenly grows.

- Absence of product standardisation, consistent quality, after-sales image.

- Customers are unprepared and unaware so may be confused and reluctant to commit themselves.

- Customers may believe that later versions will be cheaper and more reliable and so postpone purchase, i.e. unwilling to be the guinea pig.

- Significance of switching costs where the new product/service may require the customer to scrap existing equipment.

In a new industry where the structure is uncertain and there are no competitive rules then there is the widest choice in formulating strategies. General strategies could involve:

- Establishing the industry rules of product quality, method of offering the product to its potential customers, pricing policy.

- Attracting and converting the first time buyer will be the priority of all initial strategies.

- Different phases of strategies may be evolved. To get a foothold, an initial strategy may be actively pursued though it may not be the main strategy or participate in the market segment where the company ultimately aims to concentrate.

- Growth of the company is limited to the growth of the market as a whole. And as the market gets bigger so competitors will probably get bigger and hence change the nature of competition in that industry.

Getting the timing right is important in any strategy but is of paramount importance when deciding to compete in or enter an emerging market. Being the pioneer involves high risk but potentially offers a low entry barrier and a larger market share, if successful.

Maturing industries

An industry that is approaching maturity will experience a slow down in growth and the presence of several major competing companies with established products. The mature stage of the industry will be identified by several factors.

- Increased competition for volume and market share as companies seek to preserve critical mass. (***Note:*** competition in UK between Tesco, Sainsbury, and Asda.)

- Buyers are likely to be repeat/replacement buyers, therefore knowledgeable not only about the product but also about the brands available.

- Buyers may be cynical, actively seeking alternative, more fashionable products.

- There will be a switch towards greater quality, better service standards and, therefore, higher costs.

- There will be a period of dislocation as companies come to terms with the new conditions. Investments in extra production capacity and product research will be phased down but probably not until there is evident over-capacity. Since capacity tends to be added in large chunks, the pressure to preserve the volume of sales is intensified.

- Greater attention is paid to seeking new markets such as exporting, or developing new users for the products. These initiatives will change the cost base upon which the company operates and marginal contribution calculations can become increasingly important.

- Industry profits fall, cash flow reduces and competitors act irrationally in defence of their market share. There is pressure on weaker members to exit the market. Usually those with the smallest market share, who are not dominant in an attractive segment, are under greatest pressure.

- Retailers and dealers finding their margins squeezed look to other products as replacements (for example, consider television retailers in the UK).

It is difficult for a company to identify the early stages of moving into maturity. The tendency is to believe that a temporary stalling of growth has been caused by an adverse environmental factor rather than an inevitable decline. Drucker comments on the difficulty of an organisation having to face up to the fact that its star performer and major profit generator has become a 'yesterday's breadwinner'.

Many constraints on strategy selection stem from management's reluctance to identify the mature phase. Failure to do so can have drastic consequences for even large, well run companies – consider the examples of Volkswagen's persistence with the 'Beetle' that nearly brought VW to its knees, and IBM's commitment to mainframe computers that caused it to record the largest corporate loss in world history.

Other features of companies operating in maturing industries are as follows:

- A key constraint is the company's own perception of themselves as, for example, a belief that they will continue successfully because of quality/service/image advantages. They may be slow to appreciate that the rules of the market are being re-drawn and they are fighting tomorrow's war with yesterday's weapons.

- There will be a temptation to invest heavily to preserve or expand market share. The pitfall is that there is only a limited time span in which to recoup that investment and competitors will be making temporary sacrifices that will further depress margins.

- Falling profits will encourage a company to cut back on marketing, R&D, etc to preserve past profit margins. This may be short-sighted and actually prevent the company holding on to its market share and so speed its exit from the industry.

- As we've seen, Porter stresses that an organisation can achieve competitive advantage through differentiation of product, focusing of market or absolute cost leadership. Where an organisation has successfully achieved competitive advantage through one of these areas, there will be a reluctance to recognise the need to switch into another arena of competitive advantage. Failure to do so can lead a company to edge out of competitive advantage into Porter's 'stuck in the middle' position where it is vulnerable. For example, a company that has successfully pursued product differentiation may react to the maturing of its market by intensifying its differentiation, for instance by developing greater quality differentials, bringing new products into the market and refusing to compete on price. This will be counter productive if the mature market has become price sensitive and subject to over capacity. The company may be better advised to move from differentiation to cost advantage, by cutting prices on its existing range and aiming for volume.

- The presence of an overhang of excess capacity creates pressure to fill it. This desire to fill capacity can become a paranoia in that it is the acid test used for all strategies. However, the correct strategy may be to close down, or switch the use of the excess capacity.

A company can thrive in times of rapid growth despite being unclear in its strategies and not developing a marked competitive strength. Indeed, maturity may force an organisation to confront these shortcomings for the first time. The strategies selected must be consistent in developing a competitive advantage of differentiation, focusing or cost advantage.

- Increased financial awareness and a better understanding of cost structures and cost/volume relationships become paramount. Such information will facilitate correct pricing strategies.

- A mature market may dictate a need to develop and design products for low cost manufacture within strict quality standards. This may involve concentrating on offering a limited range of high quality, good value products rather than seeking to satisfy customer quirks or fashions. The Japanese television receiver industry has successfully followed this strategy.

- It is likely to be easier and more profitable to increase sales of the existing product to existing customers or add-on related products for the existing customer base than battle for new customers. Gerber, the leading baby food supplier in the USA, has added baby clothes and accessories under the slogan 'more bucks per baby'.

- Assets and capacity can be purchased cheaply as distressed companies seek to leave a mature market. An existing company can purchase cheaply and possibly build a low cost position and continue to dominate the market as its majority develops. This strategy will only be successful if there is little opportunity for technological revolution outdating the product.

- There may be more than one optimum cost curve in the mature industry. In addition to the overall cost leadership position based on absolute cost advantage over the whole market, there may be a particular market segment or product type that is based on a different cost equation. This would allow a company to develop cost leadership in that area alone. For example, a company may establish production facilities specifically to satisfy specialist, custom orders at a price that a volume manufacturer cannot match because of disruption to its mass production lines.

Declining industries

A declining industry is one where there is a sustained decline in overall sales. It is characterised by shrinking profit margins, cut backs in R&D and marketing, pruning of production lines, and competitors exiting the industry. The general strategy adopted for such a situation is 'harvest', i.e. stop new investment, maximise return on past investment, maximise cash generation – all aimed at exploiting the product before inevitable divestment. Indeed, the harvest strategy will ensure that divestment is inevitable.

Porter points out that industries differ in the ways in which they decline. Some can offer attractive business opportunities over a sustained period if the correct strategies are adopted. There are many factors involved in classifying or analysing declining industries.

- The falling demand pattern will not be consistent and companies may vary in optimism in forecasting their future position. Where a company has a strong market presence or faces a high exit cost then it is likely to view the future more optimistically and act accordingly.

- As companies adopt harvest strategies or exit the market so they can accelerate the rate of decline in the overall market, although they may be surrendering market share to the survivors. Customers reading the signs of decline will switch to alternatives thus hastening the rate of decline.

- Ready availability of substitutes or changes in fashion will hasten the end of an industry.

- The cause of the decline would provide a basis upon which to select an appropriate strategy. For example, the decline may be caused by technologically superior replacements (e.g. vinyl records replaced by CDs) or demographic changes (e.g. in UK, stagnant birth rate and end of baby boom generation in childhood age) or irreversible shifts in customer needs (e.g. tobacco smoking).

- The presence, nature and size of exit barriers facing a company seeking to leave an industry is perhaps the most influential factor in determining strategy selection and timing.

Exit barriers can arise from:

- Heavy investment in specialised assets. Essentially the choice is sell to a potential competitor or sell as scrap. Neither is appealing.

- Contractual obligations on premises, supplies, labour, after sales provision which can be significant and postpone exit, thereby adding to the excess capacity in the industry.

- Strategic exit barriers that can also arise where a company is vertically integrated and exiting from a particular market may render its end product uncompetitive. Another example could arise if pulling out of one industry is seen to cast doubts on the viability of the whole group.

- Potential artificial exit barriers imposed by legislation or threats from exit barriers nullified by government subsidy (e.g. German coal industry).

- A few participants being left in a declining market, each with substantial investment and resources and a dominant strategic commitment to stay in the industry. In such circumstances, intense, damaging competition prevails as each seeks to obtain volume but none can afford to leave the industry.

There are four main strategic options that can be pursued in a declining industry:

- **Leadership** – the aim is to maintain leadership where the potential exists to reap above-average profits. This basis is used to launch a series of strategies aimed at becoming the sole company or the dominant one of a few companies. Such strategies could involve aggressive marketing to target weaker competitors, purchasing competitor's capacity and generally easing the exit decision for competitors. Clearly this is risky since the industry may not be stable or long-lived enough to enable the investment to be paid back. However it is an option in a slowly declining industry.

- **Niche** – this involves identifying a narrow, attractive segment of the market and investing to build a dominant business position in that specialist area.

- **Harvest** – the aim is to maximise cash flow by curtailing all expenditure, cutting back on maintenance and product support, reducing product range, maybe selling some brands or satellite operations and seeking to push up the price at every opportunity. Essentially a short-term exploitation prior to sale or liquidation. One of the key problems of harvesting is to preserve the motivation and morale of employees, and also to protect the company image in the eyes of customers.

- **Speedy divestment** – once decline is suspected, a company may exit by sale to an existing competitor or a new entrant, or to a management buy-out team. The business would attract a reasonable price as an established concern with previous profit achievements. When decline is established, the opportunity to sell at a reasonable price will disappear.

Summary

In this chapter we have looked at the extent to which different types of strategy may suit an organisation's circumstances in relation to various factors.

Key points of this chapter are:

- The importance of a market-oriented view has led to a relatively new focus in strategic planning methods.

- The best known approach to portfolio analysis was developed by the Boston Consulting Group (BCG), who used a 2×2 matrix to plot the attractiveness of products. Their theory was based on the 'experience curve' and on a product lifecycle view of markets and led to the positioning of products or businesses in one of the four quadrants. Limitations to BCG's portfolio analysis have subsequently been discovered.

- Another approach developed by the Shell Oil Company, and developed further by the McKinsey Consulting Organisation, uses a 3×3 matrix. Essentially the characteristics of the particular product or business sector are compared with its relative attractiveness in the marketplace. Products are plotted according to their attractiveness and strategies are developed on that basis.

- Yet another matrix, developed by Hofer, takes account of a product's competitive position, the stage of its product/market evolution, the size of the industry or market, and its share of the industry or market. Although this matrix provides a more comprehensive picture it is more complicated to construct.

- A product's position within its lifecycle must be clearly understood by management to ensure that new strategies are developed to ensure that the business continues in existence for the foreseeable future. Too many mature products and the company would be a sitting duck, ripe for takeover and further investment; too many new products and the company may go bust through having been unable to recoup large amounts of investment in too short a space of time.

Having completed your study of this chapter you should have achieved the following learning outcomes:

- evaluate the product portfolio of an organisation and recommend appropriate changes to support the organisation's strategic goals

- discuss and apply both qualitative and quantitative techniques in the support of the strategic decision-making function.

Self-test questions

1   What is the product market portfolio? (2.1)

2   What are the four quadrants of the BCG matrix? (2.3)

3   What is a cash cow? What is a problem child? What is a dog? (2.3)

4 What would be good strategies to have in the market portfolio? (2.5)

5 What are the limitations of the BCG matrix? (2.6)

6 Draw an example of the Shell matrix, the GE/McKinsey matrix and the Hofer matrix. (3)

7 What do the circles and segments represent on the GE/McKinsey matrix and the Hofer matrix? (3.4, 3.5)

8 What is the product lifecycle concept? (4.1)

9 What are the phases in the product lifecycle? (4.2)

10 What sort of a position is a company in if all of its products are at the same time phase? (4.3)

11 At what stage would a product be at high business risk? (4.5)

12 In relation to the strategy selection of an organisation, what are the four main industry classifications? (4.6)

Practice questions

Question 1: The product lifecycle

Required:

Explain the product lifecycle concept and why it is important to a company planning for the development of new products. Illustrate your answer with an appropriate diagram and use examples with which you are familiar. **(25 marks)**

Question 2: Megaweb Industries

Megaweb Industries is a large diversified group which operates in several industries including civil engineering, chemicals, commercial heaters and heavy electrical control gear. Each area is organised as a strategic business unit. Corporate management is finalising policy with regard to Heataweb Ltd, its commercial heater division. At present Heataweb produces a range of commercial heaters and heating equipment, but the market is now virtually static, with only a slight growth rate, and its brand, promotional budget and geographical spread are dwarfed by three other competitors, one of which, the market leader, enjoys a market share at least three times as large as Heataweb's. On a Boston Consulting Group's growth-share matrix, this business would be called a dog. Heataweb has two manufacturing sites and Megaweb's corporate management has decided to close one site and concentrate all manufacturing into the other. A decision has not yet been reached on which site to close.

Required:

(a) Discuss the financial criteria for deciding the site closure policy for Heataweb
(10 marks)

(b) List and briefly describe the operational factors which corporate management should consider in deciding which site should be retained **(8 marks)**

(c) Explain what is meant by 'dog' in relation to a growth-share matrix, and describe the main issues to be examined before classifying a product as 'dog', and then formulating strategy appropriate for this category of product.
(7 marks)

(Total: 25 marks)

Question 3: ABC plc

ABC plc has invested £2,000,000 in the acquisition of a wholly owned subsidiary, X Ltd, which makes branded technical products for original equipment manufacturers in the United Kingdom.

The board of ABC plc has been reviewing its medium-term plans for X Ltd, arising from which it forecasts average annual cash flows as follows:

Receipts:

	£000
Profit before tax	520
Add: Depreciation	200
	720

Payments:

Purchase of fixed assets replacements	240
Increase in stocks and debtors, less creditors	80
Taxation	150
Dividend to ABC plc	250
	720

The managing director of X Ltd (an accountant) has confided to you that he considers ABC plc is using his company as a 'cash cow' and he is concerned about the motivational effects of this policy on some of his managers. He had submitted to the board a plan under which, for an investment of £175,000, his company could have marketed products for which it has the necessary technical skills through merchants in Germany. This proposal had been rejected.

Required:

(a)   Explain what you understand by the term 'cash cow'   **(5 marks)**

(b)   Discuss the possible advantages and disadvantages to ABC plc of its financial strategy relating to X Ltd, and the short and long-term risks that might arise from it   **(13 marks)**

(c)   Identify the various financial and strategic considerations that might have influenced the board of ABC plc in rejecting the managing director's proposal.
                                                                                                                    (7 marks)

                                                                                                   (Total: 25 marks)

For the answers to these questions, see the 'Answers' section at the end of the book.

Chapter 10

BENCHMARKING AND VALUE CHAIN ANALYSIS

Syllabus content

- Benchmarking performance with the best organisations.
- Value chain analysis.

Contents

1   Introduction
2   Performance against competitors in practice
3   External data
4   Benchmarking
5   The concept of value
6   Value systems

1 Introduction

This chapter begins by considering how a company can compare its performance with the other companies in its industry. Official statistics, interfirm comparison schemes and analysis by the company's own management and specialists are explained.

The value chain breaks down the firm into its strategically important activities in order to understand the behaviour of costs and the existing or potential sources of differentiation. It reminds us of the systematic nature of business functions and that the overriding goals are to improve margin, generate cash and produce value for stakeholders. Value activities are the technologically and physically distinct activities that an organisation performs.

2 Performance against competitors in practice

2.1 Research into competition

One of the distinguishing features of modern management accounting is the degree to which it concentrates on providing comparative financial information on other businesses. By definition, a competitive advantage can only be created by comparison to competitors and this comparison should be as precise and clearly identified as is practicable. Traditionally, the management accounting systems would include competitive comparisons in the forecasts of market share and pricing levels which can be obtained during the planning period. However, unless the assumptions are made clear, it can be difficult during the monitoring and control process to identify the real reasons for any diversion from the forecast result. For example, if forecast price increases cannot be implemented because competitors do not increase their prices, the planned profitability of the organisation can be seriously affected. In such circumstances, it is vitally important that the managers of the organisation can determine whether competitors are holding down their prices as a short-term marketing tactic to gain market share or whether they have a relative cost advantage which will enable them to maintain the lower price levels over the much longer term. Obviously, the competitive response to these alternative causes of the same market situation should be dramatically different, but the opportunity to identify the correct response will depend on the type and quality of the competitors' financial information.

2.2 Defining the competition

Competitive strategies have to be established at the level where the business sells products or services in distinct markets and against identifiable competitors. If it is not possible to identify the area from which competitors will arise, this normally indicates that the business unit itself has not been properly defined. This is where the concept of the strategic business unit (SBU) can help because each of these units should have a clearly outlined purpose of selling defined products or services to defined markets. The combination of products and markets should distinguish one SBU from another in the organisation. It is important to include other organisations which satisfy similar customer needs, even if in very different ways. This stage should be done from the perspective of the targeted customers by considering which other businesses they would consider as alternative suppliers. For example, cinemas show films to the public and thus compete directly with other cinemas; however, video rental shops also enable people to watch recently released films, as do the satellite-based film channels. Hence these are also competitors which are simply using a different channel of distribution.

2.3 Competitor accounting analysis

We have already seen how difficult it is to gain precise detailed information about competitors from data published at the macroeconomic level or even by specialist firms providing interfirm comparisons.

At the end of the day the company has to provide the data for itself. There are clearly always going to be problems in obtaining good, reliable, meaningful and useful competitor information. It is important to remember that what is needed is relative financial data, i.e. relative to one's own business, not necessarily the absolute figures. The business should have a number of financial experts who totally understand the interactions of volumes, prices and costs. Management accountants are usually acquainted with the internal cost dynamics of their own business, but often have not tried to use their skills in analysing externally-based organisations such as competitors, suppliers and customers.

The objective is to build up, and keep updating, a database of information on each significant competitor. Differences in costs that were considered insignificant last year may now give the competitor a potentially significant and sustainable competitive advantage. Although most of the information is of a financial nature, the competitor analysis should not be regarded as only the responsibility of the management accountant, as detailed knowledge of these relevant differences will be spread throughout the organisation and outside. The management accountants' role is to apply their skills to translating perceived physical or operational differences into an evaluation of the relative financial position of these key competitors.

The potential sources of information are many and varied without resorting to the unethical or illegal methods of industrial espionage, and include the following:

- comparative industry analysis which we have already referred to
- industrial experts and consultants
- published financial statements
- trade associations
- trade and financial media coverage
- competitor press releases
- supplier press releases
- mutual suppliers
- mutual customers
- government statistics
- physical observation
- physical analysis of competitive products
- banks and financial markets
- exhibitions and trade fairs
- own employees
- ex-employees of competitors.

2.4 The limitations of external data

The future size of the market is only based on certain assumptions, which include the relative shares of the market that would be gained both with and without new competitors, and the profit margins that could be earned in the different competitive situations. The entry of a new, and not accounted for, player in the market can upset the best plans because external data may not be available. An example of how this can affect a business is shown by the growth of large out-of-town shopping centres based around a large supermarket. These retailers rapidly identified a new way of attracting customers to their new locations. Discount priced petrol stations were opened, using the logic that customers would have to drive their cars to reach these off-centre locations. Their strategy was not to sell petrol with a small profit margin but to attract customers to their new stores. The original petrol retailers, with their focused business, are now facing competition which is not exclusively driven by the direct financial return which can be made out of selling their mainstream product.

The differences in the asset ownership policies of competitors are difficult to ascertain. The extent to which organisations choose to rent or lease assets rather than purchase them can vary considerably. In order to compare like with like, adjustments must be made to either convert fixed assets that are owned to a rental cost equivalent, or to capitalise rented assets. This might be difficult in the case of plant and machinery, but easier in the case of accommodation, where property values can be estimated from market values.

External data about non-financial indicators is unlikely to be available. It would be very useful to an organisation if it could get hold of information such as: the number of complaints and warranty claims that their competitors had; their non-productive hours; their rework; their machine down time; the repeat business that they were assured of; their delivery to time records; and their quality of product and supplier procedures.

3 External data

3.1 Economic data

External data can come from a number of sources, in particular government publications. Typical data is shown below which will give you an idea of the almost breathtaking diversity and detail of the official statistics. This table is taken from a recent edition of the Monthly Digest of Statistics produced by the Office for National Statistics (www.statistics.gov.uk).

Metals, engineering and vehicles

10.8 Passenger cars[1]

Number

	Total production					Production of export				
	1000 cc and under	Over 1000cc and not over 1600 cc	Over 1600cc and not over 2500²	Over 2500²	Total	1000 cc and under	Over 1000cc and not over 1600 cc	Over 1600cc and not over 2500²	Over 2500²	Total
	GKAB	GKAD	GKAF	GKAH	JCYM	GKAC	GKAE	GKAG	GKAI	JCYL
1997	119894	829079	653147	95881	1698001	85698	432621	357922	75670	961911
1998	112044	814595	720556	101063	1748258	73228	436623	434074	75802	1020727
1999	113204	776111	758478	138830	1785623	76492	439698	509006	113281	1138477
2000	96043	676438	723294	145677	1641452	56556	375528	509591	121315	1062990
2001	93695	632747	634573	131350	1492365	56426	329944	400648	107236	894254
2002	79545	711563	720067	118579	1629744	35866	442975	470285	98168	1047264
2003	23985	760935	739835	142218	1657558	12330	506471	508790	118348	1143769
2002 Nov	3326	62483	61806	11154	138769	585	45206	43034	9920	98745
Dec	1569	49111	39449	7338	97467	1534	34680	28840	6137	71191
2003 Jan	1339	69955	54053	10754	135101	869	43871	32366	8669	85775
Feb	3821	62593	59176	10756	135346	1016	40435	36263	8455	86169
Mar	1495	70053	67813	12517	151878	1216	47033	44165	9950	102354
Apr	1496	64046	67563	11711	144816	972	42896	47393	9510	100771
May	1682	60138	59012	12235	133067	979	42941	43191	10453	97564
Jun	2187	71599	69054	12557	155397	1069	46071	46293	10216	105649
Jul	1914	70985	63818	9575	146292	998	42985	41384	7765	93132
Aug	1639	41615	39549	8573	91375	626	25042	24621	7174	57463
Sep	3286	64634	72295	13330	153545	957	43957	50533	11372	106819
Oct	2348	65713	68789	14956	153370	1429	44957	53262	13538	113762
Nov	1507	60121	66865	14413	142925	1315	45500	51032	12615	110462
Dec	1271	45483	51829	10841	112444	934	38783	38297	8631	83839
2004 Jan					141320					96389

1 Including chassis delivered as such by manufacturers. Taxi-cabs are included. From January 1996, monthly totals are for the calendar month and not for four or five week periods. The monthly aggregates for 1996 are not therefore stricty comparable with those for earlier years.

2 From January 1996, these categories have been amended from Over 1600cc not over 2,800cc and Over 2,800 cc to those shown.

Source: Office of National Statistics

Table: Monthly Digest of Statistics (extract) Passenger car production

3.2 Usefulness of this data

Whilst the data is impressive in its detail (and we have only shown one table: there are, as you may imagine, numerous others) one has to ask whether this sort of data is useful for a company.

Its usefulness is limited because, although detailed, the data is not detailed enough at the operational level to enable a company to compare its performance with other companies. For example, if a company specialised in producing cars over 2500cc for the export market the data would enable it to compare its sales with that of the industry as a whole, but the data does not give any indication about exceptional items or changes in the industry's structure which would be needed to provide useful information. Thus, if a new manufacturer had entered the market in September 2003, this might account for the increase in total market sales and a reduction in existing companies' sales. Without that knowledge, the official data is relatively unhelpful, showing at best a general market trend.

3.3 Macroeconomic statistics

Statistics are also produced by government for all macroeconomic variables, such as:

- inflation

- balance of payments

- terms of trade

- exchange rates

- interest rates – domestic and international

- money supply

- growth of GDP.

Again, these are useful indicators of the country's overall economic position, but are of limited value to an individual company that is trying to assess its performance.

The figures will tell the company if the economy is pulling out of recession, or if factory gate prices or unit labour costs across the whole economy are increasing. But they will not tell the company anything of detail about its own performance compared to those of its immediate competitors in the same industry.

3.4 Interfirm comparison schemes

There are a number of interfirm comparison schemes set up by agencies such as the Centre for Interfirm Comparisons (www.cifc.co.uk), or by various trade associations.

These attempt to produce information about the relative performance of companies that contribute to the scheme.

The difficulties of such schemes are:

- Information supplied by different companies may not be based on the same accounting policies and will have to be adjusted.

- Companies may be reluctant to divulge information that will be used by the competition for reasons of confidentiality.

An interfirm comparison helps to put the company's resources and performance into perspective and reflects the fact that it is the relative position of a company that matters in assessing its capabilities. The performance of different organisations, subsidiaries or investment centres can be compared by calculating suitable financial ratios for each of them to ascertain which are better or worse than the average. Comparative analysis can also be usefully applied to any value activity which underpins the competitive strategy of an organisation, an industry or a nation.

To find out the level of investment in fixed assets of competitors, the business can use physical observation, information from trade press or trade association announcements, supplier press releases as well as their externally published financial statements, to build a clear picture of the relative scale, capacity, age and cost for each competitor. The method of operating these assets, in terms of hours and shift patterns, can be established by observation, discussions with suppliers and customers or by asking existing or ex-employees of the particular competitor. If the method of operating can be ascertained it should enable a combination of internal personnel management and industrial engineering managers to work out the likely relative differences in labour costs. The rates of pay and conditions can generally be found with reference to nationally negotiated agreements, local and national press advertising for employees, trade and employment associations and recruitment consultants. When this cost is used alongside an intelligent assessment of how many employees would be needed by the competitor in each area, given their equipment, etc a good idea of the labour costs can be obtained.

Another difference which should be noted is the nature of the competitors' costs as well as their relative levels. Where a competitor has a lower level of committed fixed costs, e.g. lower fixed labour costs due to a larger proportion of temporary workers, it may be able to respond more quickly to a downturn in demand by rapidly laying off the temporary staff. Equally, in a tight labour market and with rising sales, it may have to increase its pay levels to attract new workers.

In some industries, one part of the competitor analysis is surprisingly direct. Each new competitive product is purchased on a regular basis and then systematically taken apart, so that each component can be identified as well as the processes used to put the parts together. The respective areas of the business will then assess the costs associated with each element so that a complete product cost can be found for the competitive product.

A comparison of similar value activities, e.g. cost structures, between organisations is useful when the strategic context is taken into consideration. For example, a straight comparison of resource deployment between two competitive organisations may reveal quite different situations in the labour cost as a percentage of the total cost. The conclusions drawn from this, however, depend upon circumstances. If the firms are competing largely on the basis of price, then differentials in these costs could be crucial. In contrast, the additional use of labour by one organisation may be an essential support for the special services provided which differentiate that organisation from its competitors.

One danger of interfirm analysis is that the company may overlook the fact that the whole industry is performing badly, and is losing out competitively to other countries with better resources or even other industries which can satisfy customers' needs in different ways. Therefore, if an industry comparison is performed it should make some assessment of how the resources utilisation compares with other countries and industries. This could be done by obtaining a measurement of stock turnover or yield from raw materials.

4 Benchmarking

4.1 Introduction

The shortcomings of traditional interfirm analysis have encouraged many organisations to develop different approaches to their analysis. Benchmarking is a process, developed in America, that allows a company to measure its operation profile against other companies that are considered 'best-in-class'. According to Michael Spendolini, an authority on the subject and the author of *The Benchmarking Book*, benchmarking is defined as:

> 'a continuous, systematic, process for evaluating the products, services, and work processes of organisations that are recognised as representing best practices for the purpose of organisational improvement'.

KEY POINT

One danger of interfirm analysis is that the company may overlook the fact that the whole industry is performing badly, and is losing out competitively to other countries with better resources or even other industries that can satisfy customers' needs in different ways.

KEY POINT

Benchmarking is a process, developed in America, that allows a company to measure its operation profile against other companies that are considered 'best-in-class.'

Case study – Xerox Corporation

Twenty years ago the Xerox Corporation was in deep trouble. The copier manufacturer was operating under the weight of an overgrown and costly bureaucratic structure. It was losing market share. Xerox management called for a formal study to find some solutions to its problems. A team of managers, drawn from several departments, formed to identify standards of measurement in areas such as order fulfilment, distribution, production costs, retail selling prices, and product features. The performance in those areas was then ranked in relation to that of its chief market rivals. The news was not good for Xerox.

However, company executives were impressed with the process that was used to identify the measurement standards, gather the information about other companies, and present the findings in a particularly interesting context. The process became known as benchmarking. Once Xerox applied what it had learned from the benchmarking process to those areas needing improvement, costs were dramatically reduced, customer satisfaction soared to higher levels, and the company once again became a viable competitor.

The news of Xerox's success from its benchmarking study spread, and consequently other companies and industries began to express interest in the process – including the grocery industry. In fact, the benchmarking process is viewed as an important component of the efficient consumer response – or ECR – initiative, which is used to monitor and improve the industry's operating efficiencies. Benchmarking can be particularly helpful in assessing the industry's logistical problems such as inventory management, cost-cutting strategies and customer service.

What's more, benchmarking, some industry observers pointed out, could play an instrumental role in helping the grocery industry in the USA compete against alternative formats such as Wal-Mart Stores and K-Mart, which many view as being years ahead of the grocery industry in areas such as inventory management, distribution, and labour productivity. For the grocery industry, that could entail examining the inventory management, cost-cutting, customer service, and just-in-time delivery strategies of companies that are considered the best in those areas.

4.2 Benchmarking activities

Benchmarking is distinguished by a number of activities: internal, competitive, and process in addition to others. Each is defined by the target or object of the benchmarking activity.

- **Internal benchmarking** assumes there are differences in the work processes of an organisation as a result of geographical differences, local organisational history, customs, differences among business units, and relationships among managers and employees.

  In the wholesale grocery industry in the USA, which has consolidated considerably in the past decade, internal benchmarking is not an uncommon practice. For example, a grocery distributor's sales department in Florida may examine the 'best practices' of the company's customer service department in a recently acquired division in Ohio.

- The objective of **competitive benchmarking**, on the other hand, is for a company to identify specific information about a competitor's products, processes, and business results and then make comparisons to those of its own organisation. Even competitive benchmarking is yielding some seemingly unusual alliances.

For example, some semiconductor manufacturers, including Intel, Motorola, Digital Equipment Corp, and Hewlett-Packard, have agreed to share information in the area of total quality management programmes, even though they are competitors. They are banding together, some experts pointed out, so that the US semiconductor industry can compete more effectively against its Japanese counterpart.

The parallel in the grocery industry is striking. The industry's ECR initiative is a direct response to the competition from alternative formats, and its structure encourages companies to benchmark each other and share information.

- And lastly, **process or activity benchmarking** involves the identification of state-of-the-art products, services, or processes of an organisation that may or may not be a company's direct competitor. The objective of this type of benchmarking is to identify best practices in any type of organisation that has established a reputation for excellence in specific business activities such as manufacturing, marketing, engineering, warehousing, fleet management, or human resources.

A good example of process benchmarking is the experience of Xerox Corp and Bean, the Maine-based catalogue retailer specialising in outdoor clothing. After investigating a host of companies for best practices in the areas of order fulfilment and warehousing, Xerox identified Bean as an industry leader. Xerox managers visited Bean and they began learning about its warehousing and ordering processes. For one thing, Xerox improved order picking as a result of measuring the number of picks per hour at Bean's warehouse.

An increasing number of companies are turning toward process benchmarking because it is non-competitive. Companies not engaged in direct competition are more open, and so the potential for discovering innovative practices is much higher. For example, computer giant Hewlett-Packard was in a quandary as to how to apply computer technology to its packaging and shipping procedures. So they went to Federal Express because they were the best in shipping. The knowledge gained from studying Federal Express's shipping procedures gave Hewlett-Packard the educational tools needed to improve its own material handling operations. When Hewlett-Packard wanted to improve its picking operations, because the process it was using was very time consuming, it benchmarked Certified Grocers of California after one of its material handling suppliers told the managers about Certified Grocers and their use of shipping labels that were integrated with pick lists. So Hewlett-Packard studied their operation, and benefited by increasing its efficiency level as a result of borrowing their ideas.

One of Hewlett-Packard's executives is quoted as saying 'What we did with both Federal Express and Certified Grocers was borrow good ideas we had read or heard about as being the best-in-class from outside our industry in order to improve our efficiencies. That's the whole point of benchmarking'.

Base budget reviews are a similar process to benchmarking, used by many public sector organisations where historically the idea of external benchmarking has been ignored or even resisted. Such reviews are most effective where they are applied to specific services and where four questions are asked:

- Why is this service provided at all?

- Why is it provided in that particular way?

- What are the examples of best practice elsewhere?

- How should the service be reshaped in the light of these comparisons?

4.3 Embarking on benchmarking

When undertaking a benchmark study, success will hinge on the level of commitment from top managers, who must take their blindfolds off and realise that dramatic change needs to be made in certain areas.

Next, companies need to get as specific as possible when identifying areas to benchmark. For example, if a company is interested in studying customer service, it needs to determine what specific area or activity within customer service needs to be examined. Customer service encompasses a broad base of activities, such as order taking, answering inquiries, handling irate customers, issuing credits, or invoicing. Each of these activities is different, each with their own thought processes, techniques, and management controls.

The next step is to establish a work team comprised of strategic, functional, and tactical representatives from all affected areas. For example, if a company needs to reduce the amount of returns coming back to the warehouse, its benchmarking team would likely consist of a customer service representative, a receiving clerk, a loading clerk, and a quality control manager.

The next steps are to determine the issues to be benchmarked, and then determine what company to study. Networking through consultants, trade associations and trade journals can steer companies in the right direction. The vice president of Hershey Chocolate USA noted that his company has engaged in successful benchmarking studies by signing reciprocating agreements with their benchmarking partners. In other words, the companies they studied said they could benchmark them if they could study some of Hershey operations as well.

Once the best practices have been identified, the benchmarking team collects the data, analyses it, then plots its company's performance against the best practices to help them identify improvement opportunities.

The team then determines the level of effort required to re-engineer the best practices to suit its company's unique circumstances. The benefits versus the costs involved with eliminating the gaps between current processes and the best practices are evaluated, and then implementation priorities are established.

One method for an organisation to embark on benchmarking involves the following stages:

1   Obtain senior management approval

2   Identify the processes to be benchmarked. These may be core processes already identified from the organisation's mission statement

3   Investigate the processes and then identify appropriate measures for benchmarking

4   Ensure that the benchmarking information can be obtained from the processes

5   Decide how the processes will be benchmarked e.g. using similar divisions within the organisation or external entities

6   Obtain and analyse the data

7   Draw conclusions from the results of the benchmarking exercise and discuss these results with process management and staff

8   Identify how processes can be improved and implement the necessary changes

9   Monitor the results of changes made to ensure that the benefits of the benchmarking exercise have been achieved.

4.4   Advantages and problems with benchmarking

Advantages of benchmarking include:

- Helps to improve organisational performance by providing positive feedback to the organisation in terms of customer satisfaction and agreement of policies of best practice in different divisions. Benchmarking may also identify areas of wasteage, allowing better control of costs and elimination of un-necessary overheads.

- It will help management understand the procedures and processes within their organisation and identify which processes in particular add value to the organisation. Un-necessary processes can be removed and inefficient processes improved.

- It may help to identify areas where competitive advantage can be obtained or alternatively identify where the organisation is losing competitive advantage.

Despite the benefits, there are some pitfalls. Some companies have been barraged with telephone calls from other companies interested in examining their best practices! As a result, they are starting to close their doors, to the point where they are reluctant to allow companies to come in and speak with them.

There is also the issue of involving and motivating staff. Managers need to be aware that a benchmarking exercise can appear to threaten staff where it appears that benchmarking is designed to identify weaknesses in individual performance rather than how the process itself can be improved. To alleviate this fear, managers need to be involved in the benchmarking exercise and provide reassurance to staff regarding the aims and objectives of benchmarking.

KEY POINT

The more innovative companies are nowadays less concerned with benchmarking numbers (for example, costs or productivity) than they are with focusing on the processes.

Another pitfall is a misunderstanding of what benchmarking involves. Sharing 'war stories' over a sandwich at an industry convention is not what benchmarking is all about. Neither is grabbing an industry report loaded with statistics pertaining to operations and comparing one's own performance standards against those statistics.

In today's environment, the more innovative companies are less concerned with benchmarking numbers (for example, costs or productivity) than they are with focusing on the **processes**. If a company focuses on the processes, the numbers will eventually self correct.

5 The concept of value

5.1 Introduction

The value approach to strategy argues that successful firms are those that create value for an end user above the cost of creating that value. This can be achieved by creating:

- a product or service that is unique and for which customers are prepared to pay a higher price

- equivalent value to competitors, but incurring lower costs in carrying out the necessary activities.

The value that a company creates should be continually assessed from the point of view of the final consumer or user of the product or service. This may be overlooked by organisations that are distanced from their final users by intermediaries such as distributors, leaving them out of touch with the realities of their markets. The consumers' idea of value may change over time, perhaps because competitive offerings giving better value for money become available.

5.2 Value chain

According to Porter, the business of an organisation is best described by way of a value chain in which total revenue minus total costs of all activities undertaken to develop and market a product or service yields value.

All organisations in a particular industry will have a similar value chain that will include activities such as obtaining raw materials, designing products, building manufacturing facilities, developing co-operative agreements, and providing customer service.

An organisation will be profitable as long as total revenues exceed the total costs incurred in creating and delivering the product or service. However, achieving profit does not mean that the firm is successful, as a strategist will want to take into account the return on capital employed and the opportunity cost of investment, as well as the performance of the firm compared to its competitors – a long term view of success as measured by improvements in return on investment is the ultimate test of the success of the firm's strategies. It is therefore necessary that organisations should strive to understand their value chain and also that of their competitors, suppliers, distributors, etc.

The value chain, shown in the diagram below, displays total value and consists of value activities. Value activities are the physically and technologically distinct activities that an organisation performs.

The value chain

Diagram: Porter's value chain

This schematic representation of the value chain clearly shows its constituent parts. The primary activities, in the lower half of the value chain, show in sequence the activities performed by the organisation in converting inputs (of all types) to finished products and the transfer of the product or service to the buyer and any after-sales service. These are grouped into five main areas:

(a)   Inbound logistics are the activities concerned with receiving, storing and handling inputs.

(b)   Operations are concerned with the transformation of the inputs into finished goods or services. The activities include assembly, testing, packing and equipment maintenance.

(c)   Outbound logistics are concerned with the storing, distributing and delivering of the finished goods to the customers.

(d)   Marketing and sales are responsible for communication with the customers, e.g. advertising, pricing and promotion.

(e)   Service covers all of the activities that occur after the point of sale, e.g. installation, repair and maintenance.

Each of these may be a source of advantage. Alongside all of these primary activities are the secondary, or support, activities of procurement, technology, human resource management and corporate infrastructure. Each of these cuts across all of the primary activities, as in the case of procurement where at each stage items are acquired to aid the primary functions. At the inbound logistics stage it may well be raw materials, but at the production stage capital equipment will be acquired, and so on.

This value chain has several important uses in strategic analysis and implementation. Three important ones are listed below.

•   diagnosis of value creating activities

•   identification of cost drivers

•   identification of competitive advantage.

5.3 Diagnosis of value creating activities

Activity Based Management (ABM) is a means of focusing the organisation's competitiveness on efficiency by tightly coupling activities into a well-managed system. Value chain can be used to assist in this, but Porter points out that there are three main differences between ABM and strategic value creation.

- Value chain focuses on effectiveness – selecting what should be done – while ABM aims to improve efficiency.

- Value chain is aimed at securing a competitive advantage in the way that activities fit together.

- Value chain is a means of sustaining that advantage.

As Porter puts it,

'Strategic fit [in the value chain] among many activities is fundamental, not only to creating a competitive advantage but to the sustainability of that advantage'.

It is necessary to consider each of the activities in the value chain in terms of whether or not the firm is the cost leader at it, or the activity adds to differentiation. For example, firms often prefer to run their own transport fleet for deliveries. However, this adds to cost but does not always increase value. It is usually the case that a haulage firm could transport the goods at least as effectively, and would charge less. Porter, using this very example, says that if the transport department cannot compete with other hauliers commercially, it should not be protected internally. If it can, then go into the transport business. Similarly, it is unlikely that the transport fleet adds to differentiation in any meaningful way – unless the ability to run JIT (just-in-time) systems is a threshold competence for example. In short, the transport fleet frequently adds to cost without increasing value – it is a value destroying activity.

The result of managing value creating activities should be a complex system of well-managed activities. Both the competencies and the integration make it difficult for rivals to replicate the system.

5.4 Identifying cost drivers

Whether the firm is trying to compete by differentiation or cost leadership, it is important to keep costs under control. This requires an understanding of where costs are created, and how these might best be minimised. A cost leader, for example, must be excellent at identifying and managing the activities that add most to cost. A differentiator needs to identify cost drivers that do not add to differentiation, and find ways of finding a cost leader to undertake these activities for them whenever possible.

5.5 Value chains and organisational structure

To study the internal structure of the organisation using the value chain, each section must list and harmonise those activities that are strategically significant in adding real value to the product or service. The value chain will differ significantly between organisations, and even between Strategic Business Units (SBUs) within one organisation.

The activities of a cost leader tend to be focused on control. Minimising costs requires excellent monitoring and control systems, and the ability to move swiftly when adverse variances are detected. Quality circles, when operating effectively, can do much to improve operations. Cost leaders tend to be efficient bureaucracies, and the management accountant and process engineer are crucial people.

KEY POINT

Cost leaders tend to be efficient bureaucracies, and the management accountant and process engineer are crucial people.

Differentiators tend to look towards change and service advantages. Consequently, it is more common to see project management and matrix structures, and control systems that are less likely to inhibit innovative and experimental activities. However, it is not the case that differentiators can be lax about cost – there is no point in subsidising inefficiency or wasting money by poor budgeting.

Naturally, these are rather extreme characterisations, and many firms find that they can manage these crucial value-creating activities in different ways. For example, Danny Miller has pointed out that many cost leaders are also differentiated in marketing and brand management without disrupting their structure. However, few cost leaders can carry the informal, flexible structures required for innovation while retaining their cost advantages. One way in which some organisations may be able to combine effective cost control and innovation is via the use of alliances, networks and the creation of virtual organisations – this can be seen as an extension of the outsourcing concept.

This form of strategic architecture may enable an organisation to take advantage of specialist skills and innovation in the possession of others, without the organisation having to commit itself financially to the heavy investment that may ordinarily be required. One industry where these loose structures are widely used to good effect is the pharmaceutical and biotech sector. Pharmaceutical companies, even the large multinationals, will contract out certain aspects of their research and development work to specialist companies which may themselves operate through teams of researchers at a number of remote locations, for example universities, the research company then acting as an agent or facilitator.

This approach, available primarily as a result of developments in information technology, may allow the pharmaceutical companies to obtain access to specialised expertise which is a variable rather than fixed cost – see transaction costs below.

5.6 Identifying sources of competitive advantage

For Porter, sustainable competitive advantage within the value chain lies in the secondary activities. The complex combination of secondary activities and their relationship with the competencies used in the primary activities make the activities of the firm hard to replicate. For example, Sony differentiates on the basis of innovation. It is possible to replicate a Sony product, but replicating the innovation that led to the product is far more difficult.

A second source of sustainable competitive advantage lies in the firm's relationships with other companies. This has already been mentioned in relation to strategic architecture, but the discussion is picked up again in the next section.

6 Value systems

6.1 Systems of value

The company's value chain does not exist in isolation. There will be direct links between the inbound logistics of the firm and the outbound logistics of its suppliers, for example. An understanding of the value system, and how the organisation's value chain fits in to it will therefore aid in the strategic planning process.

The value system

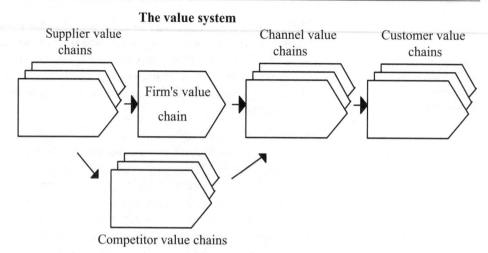

Competitor value chains

Some companies operate in ignorance of the wider value chain – even if they have a successful strategy of being close to the customer. This is a dangerous policy however, because value creation depends upon being part of a successful value creation system, and not merely the prowess of individual performers. There is no point in being an outstanding firm that is locked into an inferior system.

Other firms make a point of active involvement in the wider value creation system – part of what was called the strategic architecture in an earlier chapter. Toyota, for example, actually creates about fifteen per cent of the value added on their vehicles, but they are actively involved in the management of all their component suppliers and similar operations. Consequently, they are able to gain a cost advantage over most of their rivals. If they had chosen to work in a more isolated way, their best efforts would only apply to fifteen per cent of costs, and this would not be enough to deliver a resounding cost advantage no matter how effective they were.

6.2 Transaction costs

Transaction costs are the expenses incurred by allowing some activity to be undertaken outside the organisation. For example, in the case of the transport fleet discussion above, using a haulage firm would require negotiation of contracts and other expenses, that would not have been incurred if the activity had been kept in house. Lewis and Lytton include the following in their costs of using outside suppliers – referred to as outsourcing:

- cost/price of goods and services supplied

- rejects

- invoicing

- supplier selection

- communications

- production delays

- goods inward inspection

- buffer stocks in case supplier fails to deliver on time (also called just in case inventory).

Where the goods or services supplied are commodities, often repeated and unproblematic, transaction costs are relatively low. If there are economies of scale in the activity, an outside supplier is frequently able to reduce costs and pass on enough of these savings to the buyer to overcome the transaction costs.

Value systems arise because transaction costs are relatively low for some activities, such as routine transportation, and an advantage can be gained by outsourcing.

6.3 Outsourcing and strategic architecture

A value system can be advanced to architecture by developing relationships with appropriate suppliers.

The table below outlines some of the key differences between traditional outsourcing and relationship based partnerships.

Contract based outsourcing	Relationship based architecture
• Adversarial negotiation over price • Focus on acceptable quality at lowest price	• Open book accounting • Strategic view of price and quality for end user • Shared strategic purpose • Integrated new product development and process improvement

It is not suggested that the strategic architecture needs to encompass the whole value system, as this would become unnecessarily complex. However, focus on architecture where there is room to develop an integrated, complex competence is likely to lead to a competitive advantage.

Activity 1

Suppose you run a large engineering company. Suggest appropriate forms for the relationships with suppliers of the products below:

1 Bulk paper to be used for boxing your products

2 Complex control systems for your hardware products

3 Finance for a new project

Feedback to this activity is at the end of the chapter.

6.4 Differentiation strategies

KEY POINT

A successful differentiation strategy requires that the product should be made special – almost to the point of uniqueness – in ways that the buyer is prepared to pay a premium for.

A successful differentiation strategy requires that the product should be made special – almost to the point of uniqueness – in ways that the buyer is prepared to pay a premium for. It is worth mentioning that marketers tend to use the term more widely, so that it covers any means to make a product recognisably different from another. Both uses of the term are legitimate, but in this unit we take the strategist's meaning of the term.

A product can be differentiated in an almost unlimited number of ways. Mintzberg has made life simpler by providing a series of categories within which firms can differentiate. The categories are:

- **Design differentiation** – where the product is designed so fundamentally differently that it is almost a separate product category. Sony, for example, has been particularly good at producing products of this kind. Of course, they are frequently easy to copy, and the firm must be ready to follow each success with others.

- **Image differentiation** – where marketing, brand management and the more superficial elements of design make one product stand out. It is worth noting that this is difficult to achieve – and often expensive – but is open to both differentiators and cost leaders.

- **Quality differentiation** – where buyers believe that a product is more reliable, durable or has superior performance. This form of differentiation is difficult to achieve, but is commonly associated with highest profits in an industry

- **Price differentiation** – where a lower price makes the products different from others in the industry. To be successful, this strategy requires that the market is price sensitive and the firm has, or is capable of getting, a cost advantage. Sadly, many firms in the UK opt for this approach without the slightest hope of gaining a cost advantage, and are found to be performing very poorly.

6.5 Further strategic roles of the value system

The value chain, as described here, makes the assumption that the customer's wants are well understood, and the firm is part of a wider value system that delivers value to that customer. Of course, this is a simplifying assumption, and strategists do not really believe that this is the case. The strategist must be aware of developing market trends, and adjust the value system accordingly. Further, there is the possibility of using the value chain to identify new customers and markets that can be satisfied by the same, or a slightly modified, value creation system.

6.6 Identifying new target markets

The value system may develop skills in primary and secondary activities that can be transferred to completely different markets. For example, Lex developed a great reputation for servicing automobiles, but found diversification into related markets difficult. However, they realised that their great success in their main business was largely due to their logistical skills in the movement of spare parts. Consequently, they deployed these skills by diversifying into the distribution of electronic components. Similarly, many manufacturing companies also develop merchandising and distribution skills, and discover that these are both cost drivers and significant sources of differentiation. Consequently, they can factor a whole range of products that can be sold under the brand name competitively. Virgin's skills in marketing and customer service, learned in retail and the airline business, have successfully transferred into the selling of financial services, even though the firm has little expertise in the underlying products.

6.7 New distribution channels and market segments

The value system can also be developed to create opportunities for detecting new market segments within the existing market, and new means of reaching them. In particular, the Internet shows great potential in both these respects, although returns so far have been disappointing.

A typical example of how new distribution and segment strategy can be found is given through the growth of businesses selling wine directly to the consumer. The crucial cost drivers are procurement and outbound logistics in most cases. A large segment of the market enjoys, but does not particularly understand, wine and its peculiar language. Consequently, firms have been able to reduce costs in the value system by omitting established retail outlets, and providing 'tutorial' style clubs and articles to sell their products directly to consumers.

6.8 Sudden environmental shocks

The value chain is set up to optimise the value system given the present environment. As such it is at great risk when the environment changes rapidly. Much can be done by environmental scanning to reduce these risks, but it is important to see that the whole value system must be aware of the changes that are taking place. Firms locked into a good strategic architecture may fare rather better than remote ones

Activity 2

A firm makes automatic filling machines, which are used in the catering industry. It has a large customer base, who are loyal because of good customer service, and a differentiated product based on a patented metal coating process.

A foreign company has attacked the market with lower prices, and ceramic components that equal the performance of the domestic company's machines.

What are the implications for the value system?

Feedback to this activity is at the end of the chapter.

Summary

Key points of this chapter are:

- Interfirm comparisons are difficult to produce because of the difficulties of obtaining reliable data. The firm's own specialists are the best people to produce comparisons because they understand the detail of the business and the competition.

- Many writers have claimed that performance measurement often focuses on the easily quantifiable aspects of performance such as productivity and cost, rather than the other performance criteria such as quality or flexibility which are also critical to the success of the organisation. Competitor accounting requires the input of considerable resources but it can highlight major opportunities for, and threats to, the competitive strategy of the organisation.

- Benchmarking can be used to overcome problems in traditional interfirm analysis by comparing a company to the 'best in class'.

- It is important for companies to create value for customers, shareholders and the future.

- The value chain and the value system can be used to create superior value for buyers and above average profits for the business. The links between value and generic strategy were explored in some detail. The role of strategic architecture as an alternative to a market based value system was considered.

- The value chain can also be helpful in finding new business opportunities and identifying appropriate responses to environmental shocks.

Having completed your study of this chapter you should have achieved the following learning outcomes:

- prepare a benchmarking exercise and evaluate the results

- identify an organisation's value chain.

Self-test questions

1   How may a competitive advantage be created? (2.1)

2   What is an SBU? (2.2)

3   What is competitor accounting analysis? (2.3)

4   List the main sources of information about competitors. (2.3)

5   List five macroeconomic statistics. (3.3)

6   Explain the purpose of an interfirm comparison. (3.4)

7   Explain what benchmarking is. (4.1)

8   Distinguish between internal benchmarking, competitive benchmarking and process benchmarking. (4.2)

9   What are the problems of benchmarking? (4.4)

10   What is a value chain? (5.2)

11   List three uses of the value chain in strategic analysis. (5.2)

12   What are the differences between ABM and strategic value creation? (5.3)

13   What are transaction costs? (6.2)

14   What is a differentiation strategy? (6.4)

Practice question

Interfirm comparison scheme

As the management accountant for a group of four similar companies you have recently introduced an interfirm comparison scheme. A summary of basic information received from each company for the period under review is given below.

Companies	A	B	C	D
	£000	£000	£000	£000
Operating profit	221	209	315	162
Current assets	520	385	525	315
Fixed assets	930	715	975	585
Sales	2,470	1,980	2,925	1,665
Production cost	1,605	1,228	1,784	1,016
Selling cost	370	317	497	300
Administration cost	274	226	329	187

Required:

(a)   Calculate appropriate ratios and tabulate this information for management in such a way as to compare clearly the results achieved by each company with those of the rest of the group.

(10 marks)

(b)   Prepare a short constructive report to the directors of Company A, setting out the possible reasons for the differences in their results as compared with the rest of the group.   **(10 marks)**

(Total: 20 marks)

For the answer to this question, see the 'Answers' section at the end of the book.

Feedback to activities

Activity 1

Since paper is a commodity product in abundant supply, there seems no reason why the open market should not be used.

Control systems are an important part of the value added in a product. If the firm does not have the expertise in house, or cannot gain such expertise through acquisition, close relationships must be developed with the supplier. The relationship should, ideally, go beyond buying, and develop joint development and learning activities.

Opinion differs here. Companies based in the Far East like to develop close relationships with the finance sector. This enables a structured approach and permits higher levels of gearing than would be permitted in the west. In the UK, it is more likely that a venture capitalist would be used. Venture capitalists remain somewhat distant, and like to sell on their investment relatively quickly, ending the relationship with the company.

Activity 2

The company faces some problems, but the situation is not yet critical. It has advantages in service, and a good market position. There are two attacks on the value chain:

Lower prices – is this an entry tactic, or does the foreign firm have lower cost drivers? Are the ceramic parts giving the rival a cost advantage?

Loss of differentiation – the ceramic parts produce equal performance. Can ceramics be developed faster than metal coatings to raise the specifications? Will higher specifications actually add to value?

Depending upon the answers to the questions above, the firm can adjust its value chain, by switching to ceramics, developing metal coatings, reducing costs and so on.

Chapter 11

ACQUISITION AND DIVESTMENT STRATEGIES

Syllabus content

- Acquisition and divestment strategies and their place in the strategic plan

Contents

1   Introduction

2   Strategic choice in organisational growth

3   Development versus growth

4   Acquisitions

5   Joint development

6   Divestment

1 Introduction

Organisations are continually facing challenges to their position. Some are happy with their present position, some are suffering a decline and others are seeking expansion. In this chapter we discuss expansion by the organisation through internal or external growth, including diversification. At the opposite end of the spesctrum we will look at divestment as a means of repositioning the organisation.

2 Strategic options in organisational growth

2.1 Introduction

There are a number of choices management can make in order that an organisation may achieve its stated objectives – firms pursuing virtually the same ends do not have to employ the same change strategies.

Gluck classified the alternatives and identified the following usage frequencies:

- stability

- growth

- retrenchment (defensive)

- combination.

Such strategies can be pursued internally using the company's existing resources and competencies, or external means can be employed such as acquisition, merger or collaborating with other organisations.

2.2 Stability strategies

Although concerned with maintaining the status quo these do not necessarily involve no action although such a course is commonly adopted when the company is doing well and there is no envisaged change in the company's values or its environment.

The consequences of growth are not always seen as beneficial. For example, the owner of a small business may be content to continue at the existing level of operations for a number of reasons:

- If the business is already supporting the owner in a reasonable life-style there may be no motivation to change.

- Growth will probably require finance and the owner may not relish borrowing.

- Growth may mean that the owner is unable to stay close to all aspects of the business, which could reduce personal enjoyment and satisfaction.

- Growth may lead to sacrifice of overall control.

Another 'no-growth' scenario is where future growth is sacrificed for present profits by, for example, reducing expenditure on R&D, maintenance or advertising. This can only be a temporary measure if long-term stagnation is to be avoided. For example, Rolls Royce reduced R&D expenditure by 33% in 1992.

Finally, after a period of rapid growth and even when things are going well, a company may wish to consolidate its position and either temporarily or permanently cease growth activities.

2.3 Greiner's model of organisational growth

The concept of size is problematic and growth can have many characteristics, a number of which are mutually exclusive. In the context of strategic change, growth is normally viewed in terms of output and this is often an attractive option for management. Traditionally literature about organisational growth is written from the stance of an industry leader operating in growth markets. In the case of the public sector it would be a position of expanding budgets. Growth follows the product/market strategies closely, but inevitably the organisation diversifies as growth opportunities dry up.

L E Greiner specifies five aspects of organisational growth.

- Age of the organisation – the older the organisation, the more difficult it is to change.

- Size of the organisation – the larger the organisation, the more complex the change process becomes due to co-ordination and communication issues.

- Stages of evolution – management are stable and only minor change is required. Management are focused on growth.

- Stages of revolution – serious unrest in management due to major turbulence. Management are focused on solving the problems that are hindering growth.

- Growth rate of industry – affects the pace of change, the organisation undertakes.

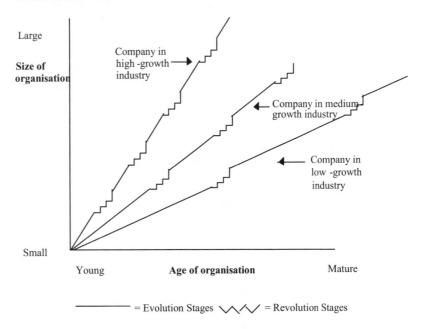

Greiner's model of organisational development

The diagram above illustrates the combined effect of these aspects on organisations. Each dimension influences the other over time; when all five elements begin to interact, a more complete and dynamic picture of organisational growth emerges.

Greiner identifies five phases of growth. Each evolutionary period is characterised by the dominant management style used to achieve growth, while each revolutionary period is characterised by the dominant management problem that must be solved before growth can continue.

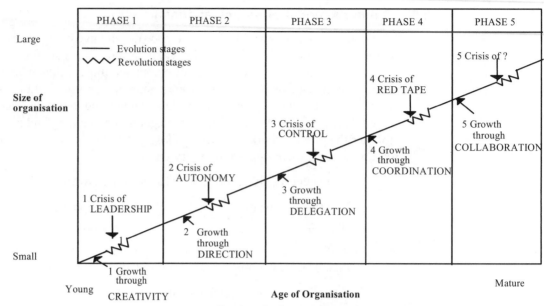

Greiner's five phases of growth

It is important to note that each phase is both an effect of the previous one and a cause for the next phase. For example, the evolutionary management style in phase 3 (above) is 'delegation', which grows out of, and becomes the solution to, demands for greater 'autonomy' in the preceding phase 2 revolution. The style of delegation used in phase 3, however, eventually provokes a major revolutionary crisis that is characterised by attempts to regain control over the diversity created through increased delegation.

- **Phase 1 – Creativity**

  Making and selling, this is the creative stage. Control comes from the feedback gained from customers/clients. As the organisation grows, production becomes more efficient. Management are required to take on additional responsibilities. Unless more sophisticated business techniques can be introduced and maintained, the organisation may stagnate and die. A small firm working informally and collaboratively achieves success through working together. However, as the firm grows, the management cannot manage the complexity in this way, and a crisis of leadership emerges.

- **Phase 2 – Direction**

  The organisation becomes 'structural' with a hierarchy of positions and jobs moving to greater specialism. Accounting systems covering, for example, purchasing are introduced as one standard of working practices. Growth during this phase is usually evolutionary. This phase of growth exposes weaknesses in the functional structure that need to be resolved before the organisation can continue to the next phase. Leadership, professional management and formal systems drive the firm forward. Continued growth makes leadership more remote, and those employees at lower levels feel constrained by top management, leading to a crisis of autonomy.

- **Phase 3 – Delegation**

  Growth is achieved through delegation. The organisation structure moves to becoming decentralised and geographically based. Profit centres may emerge and formal reporting processes are emphasised. Management focus on expansion of the market. The successful firm learns to delegate important activities to middle managers rather than keep top management involved in day-to-day activities. With this delegation of authority comes departmentalisation, in-fighting and increasing remoteness of top management, leading to a crisis of control.

- **Phase 4 – coordination (Watchdog)**

  The organisation structure during this phase moves into product groups with line reporting relationships. Control is exercised through planning. Management reward emphasises profit share and stock options that focus on both short and long-term growth. This phase concentrates on the consolidation of the organisation. Growth continues with co-ordinating and control mechanisms to keep delegated managers to the organisational purpose. Over time, these systems become more complex, and it gets harder to achieve change, or even create value, without creating a crisis of red tape.

- **Phase 5 – collaboration (Participation)**

  Growth is encouraged through participation, and mutual goal setting. Management focus on problem-solving activities that ensure the organisation's survival, but also emphasises innovation to ensure growth and survival. The structure will be team based, with good performance being rewarded through team bonus schemes. Co-ordination mechanisms are replaced by shared values and meanings, and action through teamwork. Greiner does not say that there are no crises that follow this, but they are less well articulated. Teamwork, in particular, may place limits on growth by reducing individual reflection and initiative.

The principal implication of each phase is that management actions are narrowly prescribed if growth is to occur. For example, a company experiencing an autonomy crisis in phase 2 cannot return to directive management for a solution – it must adopt a new style of delegation in order to move ahead.

The implications for management of this model are detailed in the table below, which shows the specific management actions that characterise each growth phase. These actions are also the solutions that ended each preceding revolutionary period.

CATEGORY	PHASE 1	PHASE 2	PHASE 3	PHASE 4	PHASE 5
Management focus	Make and sell	Efficiency of operations	Expansion of market	Consolidation of organisation	Problem solving and innovation
Organisation structure	Informal	Centralised and functional	Decentralised and geographical	Line-staff and product groups	Matrix of teams
Top management style	Individualistic and entrepreneurial	Directive	Delegative	Watchdog	Participative
Control system	Market results	Standards and cost centres	Reports and profit centres	Plans and investment centres	Mutual goal setting
Management reward emphasis	Ownership	Salary and merit increases	Individual bonus	Profit sharing and stock options	Team basis

Greiner: Organisation practices during evolution in the five phases of growth

In summary, organic growth is a relatively safe means of developing the organisation. Its great strength is the ability to develop competencies in prime areas as the firm develops. However, it may be rather slower than other methods available, and is not without the need for disruptive organisational change as the firm gains in size, scope and complexity.

3 Development versus growth

DEFINITION

Organisation development is: 'the formation of new combinations of resources or the formulation of new attainable and visionary objectives'.

Organisation development is: 'the formation of new combinations of resources or the formulation of new attainable and visionary objectives'. Development involves policy decisions that will change objectives, while growth involves technical or administrative improvements that will allow the organisation to achieve its objectives more effectively.

Development is a broader concept, and can happen through innovation and/or acquisition, providing a framework for growth.

Growth occurs during a particular stage of the organisation's development; it is an evolutionary process.

Hicks states:

'Growth asks: how does the organisation get more out of what it now has? Development asks: how does the organisation achieve something different?'.

Development usually changes the organisation fundamentally and can be revolutionary, which results in resistance to the changes.

Growth and development, while separate and distinct concepts, are also interrelated. Development creates the potential for new growth, and as growth reaches its limit, pressures often occur for development. New innovations or markets will lead to development which, if successful, will create the opportunity for growth. This interaction is depicted below:

Relationship of creativity, development and growth (Hicks)

4 Acquisitions

4.1 Growth by acquisition versus internal growth

KEY POINT

Companies make mergers and acquisitions for a variety of reasons including growth, diverisifcation and to decrease costs by obtaining economies of scale.

Companies make mergers or acquisitions as one means of achieving growth, to put up more effective barriers to the entry of new firms by acquisition in their own industry, in order to diversify, to cut costs by economies of scale, to obtain skills, to obtain liquid resources (the acquiring company can defray the purchase price by the issue of additional equity capital, particularly where the price earnings ratio is high), etc. A company might wish to be acquired because the owner wants to retire to obtain additional cash; in order to use the larger company's R&D facilities to assist its expansion; to provide more extensive career opportunities for the owner/directors; etc.

Among factors to be considered when deciding whether to grow internally or make an acquisition are:

- **Timing** – If analysis of the proposed product-market area shows that time is of the essence, acquisition of a company already in the field is indicated as this can generally be achieved much more quickly (except in the case of the relatively small number of industries where the lead time for product development is of the order of weeks or a few months rather than years, or where start-up synergy is large enough to allow a quick start).

- **Start-up cost** – If the cost of entering a new area will be high it might be better to acquire.

- **Synergy** – If the new area has relatively little synergy with the old, acquisition might be better.

- **Structure of the new industry** – If the competitive structure of the new industry would not admit another member, or if barriers to entry are high, acquisition is the only way. If there are no attractive acquisition opportunities in the area, internal growth is the only way.

- **Relative cost and risk** – Acquisition is often more costly than internal development because one has to pay the owners of the acquired company for the risks they have already taken. On the other hand, if the company decides on internal growth it has to bear such risk itself, so that there is a trade-off between cost and risk.

- **Relative price-earnings ratio** – If the price-earnings ratio is significantly higher in the new industry than the present one, acquisition may not be possible because it would cause too great a dilution in earnings per share to the existing shareholders. On the other hand, if the present company has a high price-earnings ratio it can boost earnings per share by issuing its own equity in settlement of the purchase price.

- **Asset valuation** – If the acquiring company believes that the potential acquisition's assets are under-valued it might acquire in order to undertake an **asset stripping** operation, i.e. selling off or using the company's assets rather than operating it as a going concern.

Activity 1

List all the possible motives you can think of for a company attempting to acquire the ownership of some, or all, of another company.

Feedback to this activity is at the end of the chapter.

4.2 Distinction between merger and acquisition

An acquisition involves a company gaining control of another company for its own benefit, possibly against the wishes of the other company (though of course in the case of a public company the shareholders must consent). Usually it is a larger company gaining control of a smaller company.

A merger occurs when a new company is established to take over the assets and trade of two or more companies, with none of the acquired companies having a majority of board members on the board of the new company.

Mergers and acquisitions are often made to achieve diversification but equally a company might choose to merge with or take over another in its own industry. The same considerations apply. The failure rate for mergers and acquisitions shows that there are considerable risks, and the operation should therefore be carefully planned.

4.3 Practical experience of acquisitions

The main conclusions drawn from the practical process – or otherwise – of acquisitions seem to be:

(a) **Plan the acquisition carefully** – This might seem an obvious admonition, but there is considerable evidence that companies do not plan carefully enough before they make an acquisition. Part of the trouble is probably what has been called 'tunnel vision' – once the company has spotted an attractive opportunity it closes its eyes to all others before it has carried out a full evaluation. General guidelines for a company pursuing a strategy of acquisition are:

- Determine the reasons for the acquisition.

- Identify the potential candidate company or companies.

- Investigate candidate(s).

- Evaluate candidate(s).

- Select acquisition target.

- Plan post-acquisition policy:
    - control systems
    - integration
    - legal formalities.

- Set terms of the bid:
    - range of acceptable prices
    - acquisition 'package'.

- Plan the detail of the bid or strike:
    - timing
    - price and package
    - good press
    - smooth transfer of control.

- Make bid.

(b) **Horizontal acquisitions** – Companies buying in their traditional business area are the most successful, and most acquisitions are of this type.

(c) **When diversifying, buy a fairly large market share in the new industry** – Ansoff suggests that one of the criteria on which companies should select the industry into which they will diversify should be the size of the share they would be able to afford in that industry. The exception to the 'buy big' creed would be where the company already owns a fair market share and is doing a 'topping up' operation.

(d) **Don't be over-optimistic** – Many companies think that they can buy a company that is not doing well and 'turn it round'. Experience has shown that this seldom works, and a company should be very sure that there is untapped potential before adopting this strategy. Another interesting observation is that theoretical synergy (especially in production and marketing) is often not realised in practice.

4.4 Selecting the acquisition

There should of course be a thorough analysis of the potential of any company that it is proposed to acquire in order to assess the contribution it could make to the corporate objectives. The analysis will, like the analysis of the firm itself, cover strengths, weaknesses, opportunities and threats, but taking into account the effects of any changes which would be introduced following the takeover. Among points the company must determine are:

- How the proposed acquisition has performed in its industry.

- Whether past performance trends would be likely to continue (here, recent competitive activity must be taken into account).

- How the industry as a whole has performed.

- Whether, if it is an attractive industry, acquisition is indeed preferable to internal growth.

- What resources the parent company would have to commit to the acquisition, over and above the purchase price.

- The fit of the proposed acquisition with the existing business – do they complement each other's strengths and overcome each other's weaknesses?

- How would the combined company stand with regard to anti-monopoly legislation?

If there are rivals in the takeover bid the buying company should assess the consequences of the other company being bought by one of its rivals. If it is a conglomerate acquisition the consequences may be no more serious than the need to continue the search for another candidate; but in a horizontal acquisition the consequences of losing to a competitor could be disastrous. In other words, buying a company might prove to be one of the risks the company cannot afford not to take.

If at all possible, the acquiring company should insist on access to the about-to-be-acquired company to examine production facilities, accounts, management skills, etc. This audit of diligence should be possible in the case of an agreed acquisition and if the request is not granted it could indicate an attempt to hide something.

Activity 2

Write out a detailed checklist of information a company would need about another company that it is targeting for acquisition.

Feedback to this activity is at the end of the chapter.

5 Joint development

5.1 Growth by joint development

Joint development is seen as an attractive way forward for companies that do not have resources or capabilities needed for future expansion. This does not mean that the firms involved will be small. It is common to find large companies undertaking joint development where the costs and risks of a project are high, such as construction and pharmaceuticals.

The term joint development covers a range of possible arrangements including:

- Networks: loose associations of companies that co-operate for mutual advantage. Many biotechnology companies share resources through such arrangements. Of paramount importance is the ability of the network to learn together.

- Licences and franchises: where part of the value creation process is undertaken by other firms under contractual arrangements.

- Joint ventures: where assets are formally integrated and jointly owned.

Activity 3

Indicate the appropriate form for each of the following:

1 Two young entrepreneurs develop a successful format for theme bars, but cannot raise the capital for organic growth.

2 A maritime firm specialising in hull cleaning needs the services of a scaffolding firm.

3 Two pharmaceutical companies are both working on similar drugs, and see the wisdom in co-operating.

Feedback to this activity is at the end of the chapter.

5.2 Principles of effective joint development

Kenichi Ohmae suggests that the following principles are essential for good network management.

- Commitment: particularly between the people concerned. Joint development is about interactions, rather than business plans.

- Time: If you don't have the time or resources to enter a partnership, then don't. It is only one business technique, others may be more appropriate.

- Trust: Behave in a trustworthy fashion and expect nothing less from your partners. Don't get involved with people you don't trust, even if the rewards seem too good to be true.

- Sharing: Both partners must gain from the relationship. Sometimes this means that you have to back off from getting the best advantage that you can, to make sure your partner gets something worthwhile. Both expectations and outcomes must be shared.

- Legal Agreement: A legal process will force you to clarify confusing and difficult details at the outset, rather than halfway through a complex and expensive activity. However, don't rely on the contract to make your partner do something, rely on trust and mutual advantage.

- Flexibility: Products, markets, organisations and aspirations change over time. It is necessary to be sympathetic to changes in a partner, but be willing to end the relationship when it is no longer expedient.

- Socialising: The bond is stronger if made between friends. Mistakes won't immediately lead to mistrust. Partners will frequently respond to a situation in unpredicted ways, due to different cultural, ethnic, religious, social or professional reasons. These are easier to cope with if you know a little of each other's background and preferences.

- Toleration: Don't be jealous if a partner develops satisfactory relations with other firms – even rivals. This is not in itself a problem if there is trust and respect; but beware of hollowing out.

- Planning: Agree on the timescales for particular events and successes, even when these are relatively small.

- Extension: Don't restrict the areas of collaboration unnecessarily. Joint development should lead to joint marketing of what is developed.

- Celebration: Mark the joint successes together.

6 Divestment

KEY POINT

Divestment is the process of disposing of part of an organisation's activities, and usually the assets and personnel that relate to it.

This is the process of disposing of part of an organisation's activities, and usually the assets and personnel that relate to it. One motive for doing so might be simply an opportunistic attempt to make a swift profit. Another reason might be a strategic decision to focus management effort on core activities while disposing of areas that distract from the core activities.

In recent years there have been a number of high-profile demergers of this type (often referred to as 'unbundling'). What was a single entity becomes two or more entities, often with the same owners (shareholders), but typically with separate management teams.

This latter point is well illustrated in the particular type of divestment known as a management buyout. This term describes the case where a strategic business unit (SBU) is sold off, not to another company, but to the existing management team, who become owners as well as managers in the newly hived-off entity. This procedure has many advantages.

- The people most likely to make a success of the business – and hence to agree a high price for purchasing it – are the managers who are already intimately familiar with its products, markets, strengths, weaknesses, etc.

- The investment return demanded by the new owner managers may be less than is required by the head office of a mammoth organisation in which the SBU is just a very small part.

- Managers can put in some of their own capital, but may very likely attract investment also from venture capital providers.

Summary

Key points of this chapter are:

- Mergers, acquisitions and divestments are quite commonplace these days as organisations attempt to reposition themselves within their core markets.

- Griener's model of organisation growth provides one theory of explaining the changes that take place in an organisation as it increases in size.

- Companies may also grow by merger and/or acquisition, with appropriate care being taken in selecting acquisition targets.

- Another alternative method of growth is by joint development.

- Divestments sometimes occur to 'make a quick profit' or as a result of a company buying another company and then divesting itself of the parts it does not really need.

Having completed your study of this chapter you should have achieved the following learning outcome:

- evaluate strategic options.

Self-test questions

1 Why is growth not always beneficial to a company? (2.2)

2 What are Greiner's five aspects of organisational growth? (2.3)

3 What factors should be taken into consideration when deciding whether to grow internally or make an acquisition. (4.1)

4 What is the difference between an acquisition and a merger? (4.2)

5 What sorts of arrangements does the term 'joint development' cover? (5.1)

6 Explain divestment. (6)

Practice question

Constraints to growth

Required:

Discuss the factors which act as constraints to the growth and development of a business enterprise. **(10 marks)**

For the answer to this question, see the 'Answers' section at the end of the book.

Feedback to activities

Activity 1

Among possible aims are to:

(a) General

- obtain joint synergy

- buy management talent

- buy time while the strategy of the acquiring company develops.

(b) Marketing

- preserve the balance of market power

- control spheres of influence of potential competitors

- break into a new market (perhaps export or beachhead)

- take advantage of joint marketing synergies (for example by way of rationalisation of distribution, advertising, sales organisation and sales costs in general)

- reposition markets and products

- obtain the reputation or prestige of the acquired company

- take over 'problem child' products

- obtain a critical mass position.

(c) Manufacturing

- acquire technical know-how

- amalgamate manufacturing facilities to obtain synergies (economies of scale, group technology, shared research, rationalisation of facilities and working capital, and so on)

- extend manufacturing involvement (for example the provision of field maintenance services).

(d) Procurement of supplies

- control spheres of supply influence

- safeguard a source of supply for materials

- obtain operating cost synergies

- share the benefits of the suppliers' profitability.

(e) Financial

- acquire property

- acquire 'cash cow' organisations

- obtain direct access to cash resources

- acquire assets surplus to the needs of the combined businesses and dispose of them for cash

- obtain a bigger asset backing

- improve financial standing (market price and earnings per share)

- speculative gain purposes.

Activity 2

Information checklist

General information

- Name of the company and address of its registered office and principal locations.

- Names of directors and senior managers together with their ages and length of service.

- Main business objectives sub-analysed by product/markets if these are published.

- The general standing and reputation of the company. Facts can be determined by examining product/market growth rates, etc.

- The style of management and the prevailing culture – some hints on these can be obtained from published organisation structures and the stability of tenure of senior executives.

Ownership

- The capital structure and voting rights.

- The disposition of shares including institutional shareholders and whether it is a close company.

- Details of any shares held by trustees.

- Details of any significant disposals of shares by major shareholders or directors.

Financial information for the past few years

- Turnover and profit trends, noting any exceptional items.

- Liquidity trends.

- Capital expenditure on each class of asset.

- Trends in the stock market price and price-earnings ratio.

- Capital expenditure commitments.

- Accounting policies and any audit qualifications.

- Capital gearing including any significant changes.

- Prospects and problems mentioned in the chairman's statements.

Market and product information

- The main fields of activity and approximate market shares.

- Any comments on research and the development or introduction of new products.

- Overseas and any other territorial expansion during recent years.

- Product reputation and the company's reputation for fair dealing.

- The nature and extent of competition.

- Distribution channels.

Management

- The quality of senior and second-tier management.

- The ages, qualifications and, if possible, contractual terms for all key managers (those considered important for the continuance of the company).

Activity 3

1   Franchising should be undertaken quickly. Formats can usually be copied, and the firm is unlikely to have the resources to enforce its distinctiveness legally. With a franchise, the owners of each bar will pay a fee to the entrepreneurs in exchange for fittings, items, training and corporate level advertising.

2   The firm could hire scaffolding firms on an opportunistic basis. However, the specialist nature of the business might mean that there are particular skills that need to be developed, and a simple network arrangement might serve. Indeed, labour in the scaffold company might be trained to carry out some of the low skilled activities in hull cleaning once confidence has been established.

3   The two companies would probably create a joint venture as joint shareholders of a new company. Any discoveries made would be owned by both parties, but losses would not create liability for the parent companies.

Chapter 12

PROCESS INNOVATION AND RE-ENGINEERING

Syllabus content

- The role of IT in innovation and Business Process Re-engineering.

Contents

1 Introduction

2 Innovation in an organisation

3 The role of IT

4 Business process re-engineering

5 Why process innovation and BPR are important

1   Introduction

Although Porter's three generic strategies can indicate the direction an organisation can take, some organisations choose to do different activities, perhaps in different markets, in the hope that this will make their product more attractive.

A successful business must therefore continue to develop its products, markets and manufacturing methods if it is to avoid eventual extinction. This calls for strategic decisions about product-market development and manufacturing, or in the case of service industries, the process of providing the services. Organisations have to innovate to keep up to date with customers, competitors and technologies.

2   Innovation in an organisation

2.1   Introduction

In this section we examine the aspects of the organisation which affect and are affected by information systems. The ideas that academics use when discussing innovation are diverse, which means that there is little agreement on how an organisation should go about the process of innovation. Where there is agreement, it is on the conditions that need to exist within an organisation if innovation is to flourish. We therefore set out those conditions in this section and only refer to the process of innovation to illustrate certain points.

2.2   Innovation and competitive advantage

Innovation is important because it provides the organisation with a distinctive competence. With the ability to maintain such a competence, it might underpin one of the generic strategies and help the organisation's competitive advantage. For example, innovation in production processes might reduce production costs and hence support a cost-leadership strategy. Innovation in products is a source of differentiation, which enables maintenance of this strategy.

Organisations strive for competitive advantage and choose and implement an IS strategy in the hope of valuable gains. Competitive advantage is by definition a relative not an absolute term – ahead of the others, and there are a number of different views about its meaning.

There is the economics of innovation view, where the organisation is able to get a return on its investment that is better than 'normal' in a given industry. Clemons and Kimbrough consider that IS for competitive advantage should reduce costs, add value and entail substantial switching costs for customers and users, and also give enough time for the innovating organisation to reap the benefits before all others imitate.

There is the far less restricted view of competitive advantage where the innovator can conserve the advantage by adding valuable new capabilities to the system. Opportunities exist for a wide range of advantages, including those that can be measured, e.g. market share, number of new customers and return on investment. It may be that an organisation cannot know in advance whether the gain will equal competitive advantage but they can know in advance that the gains will be worthwhile. Strategically important systems exist and, if they are to impact on the competitive position of the organisation, must modify the structure of the industry, improve the competitive position of the organisation or create new business opportunities.

2.3 Process of innovation

Information technology has evolved because of the influences of individuals and groups, and organisational and environmental factors. The elements that influence the rate of change include:

- openness to new ideas

- training and management education

- customer surveys

- monitoring of competitors' activity and performance

- monitoring of own organisation's performance

- valuing of new ideas, innovation and risk-taking.

The diagram below gives an overview of the general phases in the process of innovation.

Diagram: Overview of the innovation process

Some of the terminology used in the process includes:

- Creativity– generation of novel ideas.

- Invention – creation of new and useful products and processes.

- Innovation – commercially successful application of an invention.

- Incremental innovation– small changes built incrementally over time into a competitive advantage.

- Radical innovation – step change which represents a major departure from established method.

- Product innovation– innovation applied to the products or services that the organisation produces or provides.

- Process – innovation applied to the various business processes carried out in the organisation.

- The process of innovation – the phases and stages that an idea needs to go through before it is commercially exploited and as such becomes an innovation.

2.4 Process innovation through multi-disciplinary interactions

In order to be innovative an organisation needs to exploit its creative ideas. There will be certain organisational dimensions which will either support or mitigate against creativity; these include structure, culture, leadership, people and communication.

Structure – can either support or stifle innovation. The two aspects of structure which can stifle creativity are:

(a)　having rigidly established ways of discussing or evaluating ideas

(b)　having structures which are there primarily as career structures – making individuals behave politically will stifle behaviours out of the norm and risk-taking.

To support innovation an organisational structure needs to facilitate creativity, i.e. the structure should be flexible enough to allow it to accept and adapt to changes needed by innovation rather than kill ideas off at an early stage because of the fear of changing the structure.

New ideas need to be exploited in order for innovation to be complete. There exists a continuum for organisation structures which support exploitation of this kind. At one end of the continuum is the organic structure that will adapt to support and exploit new ideas. At the other end of the continuum is the mechanistic structure, which is specifically conceived to support the development and commercialisation of new ideas. The mechanistic structure is more suited to the introduction of new products which do not require fundamental changes to the way the organisation functions. The organic structure will facilitate innovation in the way the organisation carries out its business or even what business it carries out.

Culture – will have several distinctive characteristics. There will be an attitude towards failure which recognises the fact that it will happen more often than success. The organisation will seek to learn from the failure, which will not take the form 'what did we do wrong?' but instead seek to establish a complete understanding of the events with the aim of drawing out positive findings as well as things to avoid. The senior management will have a clear idea of the values which lie at the heart of the organisation's culture. Management will have incorporated these values into the strategy of the organisation and worked hard at developing individuals who share the values. The reward system should not be based exclusively on commercial success, as this will foster risk avoidance and decisions with very short returns on investment. The risky and random nature of decision making in relation to innovation should not be linked to rewards as this may reward a manager for an outcome which occurred largely by chance. Instead the reward system should recognise the way in which decisions are made and projects run.

KEY POINT

Innovation requires
leadership which is both
demanding and tolerant.

Leadership – innovation requires leadership which is both demanding and tolerant. The leader should have a clear idea of what he/she is trying to achieve with their department, business unit or organisation. This needs to be a vision which is appealing to the staff and well communicated to them. If the manager is to conceive a vision, develop it into a strategy, win scarce organisational resources and gain the support of staff, then they will need to be a competent communicator. Innovation takes a long while to see through from inception to

fruition or failure and a manager must be interested in the long-term view of the business unit. The leader should have entrepreneurial abilities and be able to identify opportunities and win the resources necessary to exploit them. It is important that managers should practise what they preach. If a manager is seen to take risks with ideas they can demand the same of their staff.

People – employees will feel that they have an equal ownership in the vision that shapes the strategy. This is because to some extent they will have been involved in the development of the vision by means of open communication with the leader. Innovation will require that the organisation changes – this will be especially felt with innovation in the processes of the business rather than product innovation. Innovation that relates to information systems will predominantly be process innovation. With organisation change there will be upheaval of working relationships, individuals' roles and job content requiring either new staff or highly adaptive individuals. In innovative organisations people work together in teams and, where the success of a project is attributable to a team, then the team is raised up in the same way that an individual might be if he/she were responsible. To be innovative, i.e. create ideas, develop them, and commercially implement them, a team will need a range of skills linked to their personalities.

Communication – ideas need to travel around the organisation. This is because development in one part of the organisation may only be of limited use to that part of the organisation, whereas if it is communicated to other parts of the organisation it may be picked up and developed. This relates to the creative phase of innovation. Also, once a process innovation has been proven, the rest of the organisation needs to be aware of the innovation in order to test it for applicability in the rest of the organisation.

2.5 Protecting innovation in the early phases of evolution

As can be seen in the diagram below, which depicts the process of innovation, the process is complex and consists of more than purchasing equipment and training staff in its use. There will be a period of experimentation that may be quite lengthy, during which time people become accustomed to the new technology and adapt it to the particular organisational setting. The following is a simplification of the process, which illustrates the dangers to the innovation until it is established.

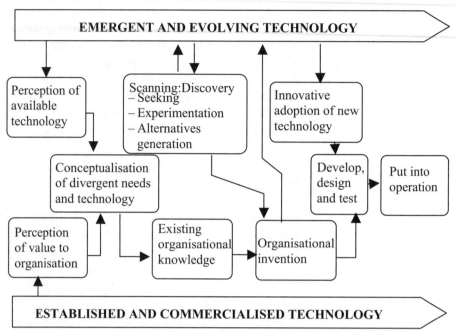

Diagram: Dangers facing new innovation ideas

2.6 The introduction of technologies

McFarlan suggests that there are four stages in the introduction of technologies which affect the planning and managing of the innovation.

(a) The first stage is focused on the technology identification, the initial investment and the development of skills.

(b) The second stage is where the users experiment with the technology and become interested.

(c) The third stage is the rationalisation and management control phase where planning is dominated by short-term efficiency, organisational considerations and cost-effective implementation.

(d) The last stage demonstrates widespread technology transfer and longer term planning in the use of technology.

KEY POINT

The planning approach must evolve along with each new technology and may vary with different innovations.

The outcome of this study is that the planning approach must evolve along with each new technology and may vary with different innovations. An example of this model would be where an organisation had little experience with DBMS (database management systems) and phase two may involve a pilot project to assess the user satisfaction with a new type of database. At another level of familiarity, a different type of user with more experience might be given the latest technology in DBMS to gain renewed interest and identify new 'tricks' or uses for it.

2.7 Process innovation

Thomas Davenport, a leading writer on Process Innovation, suggests the following framework for assessing the priority for investment in competing IT systems.

• Identify processes that are suitable for innovation.

• Identify 'change levers' (enabling or transformation technologies such as the Internet).

- Develop 'process visions'.

- Understand and improve existing processes.

- Design and prototype new processes.

Processes that are suitable for innovation

Basic transaction systems in most organisations are already likely to have been computerised, although often the systems are nothing more than computerised versions of the previous manual system. It will usually be possible to establish closer links between the separate systems such as production, sales and finance.

Change levers

As examples, it is likely that Internet-enabled systems, Enterprise Resource Planning systems and Customer Relationship Management systems will offer considerable benefits to many companies.

Process visions

This stage involves looking at processes as the means of achieving the company's mission. For instance a company may decide that, above all, it wishes to 'stick to the knitting' and not get involved in on-line activities. Nevertheless it is possible that its current products could be improved and better targeted. Perhaps the company has a wealth of historical sales records that could be mined to identify hidden trends and other useful information.

Understand existing processes

This stage would look at the benefits and drawbacks of existing information flows and technologies. Any new process should not prevent the company from carrying out tasks that it can currently do, so long as those tasks add value. There may be some small steps that need to be taken before more radical process redesign is feasible, such as upgrading operating systems or cleansing of existing data stores.

Design and prototype new processes

This stage takes the change levers and uses them to alter the existing processes, for instance using ERP software to integrate production, sales and finance or creating on-line enhancements of existing products.

3 The role of IT

3.1 Introduction

How does a firm take advantage of IT and achieve the highest level of technology and integration? There are two steps to be followed by management:

(a) Look for ways to incorporate technology in a product or service. Does information processing provide an opportunity for a new approach to business? Does the technology make it possible to differentiate a product and services from the competition? Technology can help open new markets or increase market share.

(b) To integrate technology with planning, the firm needs information about likely future technological developments. To conduct a technology assessment, the organisation must invest resources in R&D.

The organisation can develop a distinctive technology to give it a proprietary advantage. Then it protects this lead with barriers such as patents, extraordinary investment, long lead times or rare skills. It can then keep the technology away from its competitors long enough to profit and gain market share. Lotus 123 is an example where Lotus defined the nature of the spreadsheet market long enough to gain a significant advantage for a time.

Alternatively, the organisation can try to be one step ahead of their rivals by continually releasing new and improved technology. For example, banks that were quick off the mark to approve car loans in 24 hours, then bring it down to two hours and recently to instant approval, have won market share and kept ahead of their competitors.

Discontinuity is another way of gaining an advantage. Here an organisation applies technology to produce a quick, decisive shift in the market it serves, e.g. banking on-line has given Egg a considerable advantage over the other banks that are only just beginning to install their systems.

3.2 Technological developments

Established information technologies form part of many work practices. Deficiencies in current working practices reveal opportunities for improvements, and risks from other companies and industries. These deficiencies stimulate searches for technologies that could improve work practices. These new technologies are applied to facilitate new working practices; they initially give the company or industry an advantage. However, the technology is quickly adopted by others and so becomes established technology and working practice.

The stages in development of a technology start much earlier than an identified business need. These early developments enable subsequent developments, which have an application in the work place. It is this later stage of technological development that is influenced by business needs.

Linkage between business and technological developments

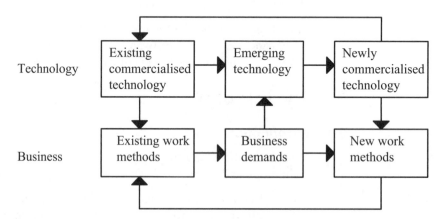

3.3 Waves of technology

In their book *Strategic choices*, Edward Primozic, Kenneth Primozic and Joe Leben have devised a planning methodology which examines the links that organisations have with one another with the objective of creating a strategy which utilises electronic channels.

There are five parts to their methodology:

(a)   To understand the waves of technology which describe the evolution of systems.

(b)   To exploit experience curves.

(c)   To define power relationships.

(d)   To map out the extended enterprise.

(e)   To plan the electronic channels.

These waves describe the evolution of systems, how the technology is used and the importance of IT at each level.

(a)   First wave – covers the DP era with the focus on reducing costs and increasing productivity.

(b)   Second wave – concentrates on making effective use of assets to increase productivity. This stage is seen as saving money by better management of processes.

(c)   Third wave – is concerned with enhancing products and services to gain strategic advantage or create new business.

(d)   Fourth wave – is about changing the structure of the organisation and using the technology to enhance the executive decision making.

(e)   Fifth wave – is about reaching the consumer and restructuring the industry. This stage leads to new marketing, distribution and service strategies.

Primozic is of the opinion that most firms are still only at the top of the second wave and have not started to build information systems that make money because they are concentrating on saving money.

There is a division between the second and third waves with those above two being more involved with organisational effectiveness and those below concentrating on operational control. Crossing the 'line' from wave two to wave three is achieved by market leaders who are concentrating on profitability and remaining competitive.

3.4   Experience curves

Traditionally the concept of an experience curve argued that the cost of using a new technology decreases as the organisation gains more experience with it. The author's idea of experience curves is of a set of curves, rather than one continuous learning curve, each curve representing fundamentally different technologies in areas such as product, manufacturing and support processes. An organisation which identifies a new market, and the technologies to exploit it, shifts to a new experience curve. Unfortunately, management sometimes has such an emotional attachment to the current curve that it fails to see the next one and loses its market share.

To demonstrate the concept, the authors use the shipping industry – shiping is the American term for parcel delivery, not boats – (shown in the diagram below). The trucking industry initially shipped goods from A to B, using either a full, or less than full, truckload. When United Parcel Service (UPS) based its entire business on point to point shipping, a new industry segment – that of package delivery – was initiated. This represented a new experience curve for the shipping industry and UPS became larger than the shipping companies because they served a market with more customers. They then became more experienced, using technology for efficient package sorting at distribution centres to maximise their use of trucks. Because UPS neither guaranteed a delivery time nor tracked packages, Federal Express filled the niches and started yet another industry segment, which included overnight delivery. They became larger than UPS because they served an even larger market.

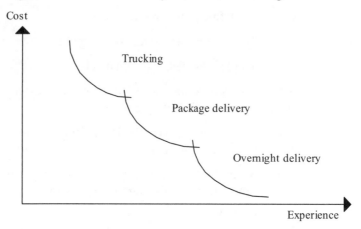

Diagram: The use of experience curves in parcel delivery

3.5 Changing organisational structures

Organisational structure changed in two quite independent ways during the 1980s and 1990s. These two changes are described as:

- downsizing

- business process re-engineering.

Downsizing has probably been carried out as a result of competitive pressures. It is unclear if this approach has yielded results and it is also unclear as to the extent to which the existence of IT has influenced these changes. The role of IT in the case of business process re-engineering is clearer, as certain aspects of these changes are dependent upon information systems, e.g. company wide access to up to date records.

Technology advances so rapidly that today's state of the art purchase is soon tomorrow's dinosaur. However, unlike the dinosaur, PCs can adapt to a changing environment. Without choosing carefully, the organisation can get a PC that is superb today but quite useless tomorrow. The problems that can be encountered if upgrades are not planned are not just expensive but can be insurmountable; if extra speed or functionality is required, the company will have to buy a new PC.

Planning ahead, considering what the current needs are and building in reasonable expectations for the future, will help the company choose a system designed to maximise the potential for upgrades to make sure the purchase won't be obsolete before its time. Expandability is the most important feature to look for when choosing a machine to grow with the organisation's needs.

Over the years there have been numerous articles published in the trade press on the merits of downsizing information systems, but very little on upsizing. Further, there has been virtually nothing on migration, upwards or downwards.

In all cases, where an information system of some kind is already in place, migration is more important than anything else. Otherwise, the business could experience disastrous failures during the changeover period.

One is led to believe that if all the conventional central processing computer systems were replaced by PC local area networks the world would be a better place. All too often an assumption is made that to downsize must be a good thing, though the term is poorly defined and rarely subjected to cost benefit analysis.

Because the cost and resilient advantages of downsizing are so limited, one might ask why companies bother. The answer lies not in downsizing itself, but in a spin-off benefit. When a database system is transferred from one platform to another it will almost always be re-written and ported onto a modern DBMS.

4 Business process re-engineering

4.1 Process innovation and business process re-engineering

DEFINITION

Business process re-engineering is the fundamental re-thinking and rational re-design of the business processes to achieve dramatic improvements in critical contemporary measures of performance, such as cost, quality, service and speed.

Process innovation and business process re-engineering (BPR) are similar concepts that emerged in the early 1990s from the writings of various management gurus. BPR in particular has been interpreted in a wide variety of ways and was much criticised because in some interpretations it took no account of human issues.

- Business process re-engineering is the fundamental re-thinking and rational re-design of the business processes to achieve dramatic improvements in critical contemporary measures of performance, such as cost, quality, service and speed.

- Process innovation emphasises the invention of entirely **new** processes, rather than tweaking existing ones. There is more emphasis on human resource management and the approach may involve rethinking the entire business and its mission rather than focusing on individual processes.

From this point of view process innovation is a more radical approach. It should be noted that there is no general agreement about the precise meanings of the terms or the difference between them.

4.2 Business process re-engineering

Data processing and now information technology and information systems have for a long time been responsible for improving efficiency and cost-effectiveness and providing for information needs. These have contributed to the competitive advantage of many organisations.

The tendency in the past was to simply automate processes that used to be carried out manually. Consequently, there is a legacy of information systems that may be less than effective. Worse still, they may actually be hindering the competitive advantage they once gave the organisation. In order to regain that advantage, rather than improve the current information systems, it may be more effective to change the way that the organisation actually goes about its business and provide a system or systems to support this new approach.

Business process re-engineering was developed because it was discovered that in many companies, while the machinery may be changed, the actual processes of the business remain unchanged. This is the reason why, in many offices, the installation of information technology has not resulted in the scale of increases seen in manufacturing productivity in the 1980s. The aim of the process is to reorganise business around processes rather than around functions or departments.

Business processes evolve over time. The Mead Corporation in America, when re-structuring its management information system, used the analogy of cow paths. When cows cover the distance between the barn to the pasture, they create meandering paths to avoid obstacles and rough terrain. Even after obstacles have been removed, the cows follow the same paths rather than create new, more direct ones. Often, the information organisation does the same thing – paving the organisation's cow paths, simply enhancing the speed of a process without re-thinking the process itself.

Since IT can be used to remove many time and distance barriers associated with business processes, Mead is now using IT to build new information highways rather than simply accelerating the existing processes.

Business process re-engineering (BPR) has been described as 'a new management approach reflecting the practical experiences of managers and providing a source of practical feedback to management science'. It represents a response to:

- failure of business process to meet customers' needs and deliver customer satisfaction

- the challenge of organisational politics

- the yawning gap between strategic intent in the boardroom and the day-to-day practice of the business

- disappointments following the application of information technology to businesses during the 1980s' (Birchall and Lyons in *Creating Tomorrow's Organisation*).

This last point is an important one. There is evidence that many companies have failed to benefit as they had expected from their investment in information technology. Often the reason has been that senior managers have failed to align IT strategy with corporate objectives. BPR is one of a number of techniques that have been advocated to overhaul existing business processes and practices with a view to improving organisational performance.

4.3 The strategic focus of business process re-engineering

Business process re-engineering is usually carried out as part of an overall strategic review of the organisation. Often management want to use the process to achieve a number of objectives in addition to the establishment of user requirements. These include:

- the introduction of Total Quality Management (TQM)

- creating focus within the organisation upon the processes which create value

- identifying internal barriers to serving the customer

- creating a set of benchmarks against which the organisation's processes can be measured against its competitors'.

The strategic focus of business process re-engineering means that the process starts at the top of the organisation. At this level, a strategic planner as opposed to a systems analyst will probably manage the process. This stage can be quite lengthy and it may be some time before the analyst can map the processes, which will define the user requirements but the process will ensure that focus is placed at the output to the customer. This in turn will lead to the introduction of added value activities and the elimination of non-value added activities.

Business process analysis has become a very popular method of producing systems in the late 1980s. This approach is based upon the concept that business processes are the most important activities of the organisation and so information systems should be focused upon supporting these processes. Business processes are the ways in which the organisation carries out its primary and supporting functions.

Primary functions are those by which inputs in the form of materials, know-how, staff's time and other scarce economic resources are transformed into something of value to the customer. Supporting processes are those processes which enable the primary process, examples of which would be the personnel system, the information system and research and development.

These business processes remain fairly constant over time and so the requirements derived from these needs can form the basis of a system which will serve the organisation's needs for some time.

4.4 How BPR works

BPR, as the name suggests, places emphasis on processes as a change mechanism. Consideration of processes may challenge preconceived ideas on the most appropriate structure. It is not confined to manufacturing processes and has been applied to a wide range of administrative and operational activities. Indeed, to overcome the barrier of an inappropriate title, many commentators prefer to use the terms business process re-design, business process re-structure or simply business process improvement.

Process re-design is a way of achieving the simultaneous goals of cost savings, speedier service and improved quality, which are the competitive necessities of the twenty-first century. It is not just re-organisation by another name, since it means re-aligning support services with essential business processes to lead to radical benefits in customer service, product development, production and revenue generation.

In identifying the major processes, there is no consensus over how many there are. Many writers suggest that there are only two – managing the product line and managing the order cycle, while others feel there are three or four core business processes but that some business activities lie outside these. BT (British Telecommunications plc) list five processes:

- manage the business
- manage people and work
- serve the customers
- run the network
- support the business.

The idea is to ask radical questions about why things are done in a particular way, and whether alternative methods could achieve better results. BPR is undertaken to achieve order-of-magnitude improvements over the 'old' form of the organisation. It is **competitive restructuring** that forms the current focus of concern as distinct from simply that of **competitive gain**.

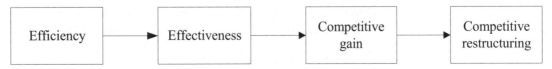

Diagram: The overall objective of BPR is competitive restructuring

4.5 The need for re-design

KEY POINT

At the heart of BPR is the notion of discontinuous thinking, of recognising and breaking out-of-date rules and assumptions that underlie current business operations.

At the heart of BPR is the notion of **discontinuous thinking**, of recognising and breaking out-of-date rules and assumptions that underlie current business operations.

Quality, innovation and service are now more important for survival than cost, growth and control. Processes that suited command and control organisations no longer suit service and quality-driven ones. Earlier assumptions of necessary roles are no longer valid.

When work passes from process to process, delays and errors occur and create further processes to expedite delays and repair the faults. Managers have tried to adapt their processes but usually in ways that just create more problems. For example, if cash flow is poor, debt chasing is stepped up rather than taking steps to avoid marginal accounts. More bureaucracy makes costs rise, which helps give away market share to other, more enterprising, organisations. Dealing with this type of problem is the concern of re-engineering. It is very closely akin to total quality management (TQM) where management seeks to remove the cause of faults instead of merely detecting them when they occur.

One of the themes of organisational restructuring has been to re-organise around the business processes found in organisations, dispensing with some of the functional departments. Most large businesses have traditionally been organised hierarchically. In this form, functions are divided among departments with the communication channels typically going up and down the department with interaction between the departments only occurring at a high level. Where decisions that require consultation between departments are required, the two departments usually refer the matter up the hierarchy to the level where interaction takes place. This is slow and often yields sub-optimal decisions, as the decision takers are usually remote from the point where the problem exists and where the solution will be implemented. The diagram below shows how a problem that concerns making a change to a component affects the production methods and therefore costs and marketability. Referring the problem up the hierarchy increases the number of people involved from three to at least nine.

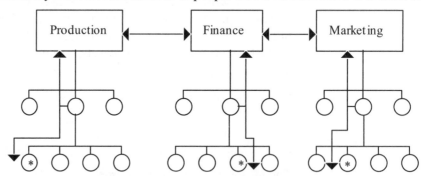

* Managers directly concerned

Diagram: Change in production also affects finance and marketing

New technology and new approaches to organisational design have been combined to produce organisations where the flows of information follow the processes an organisation continually carries out regardless of its structure. Examples of these processes include managing materials chain (production/distribution), conducting market research, conducting sales and marketing, recruiting and developing staff. It can be seen that these processes cut across the traditional functional divisions.

Steve Smith (in *The Quality Revolution,* Management Books, 2000) cites the example of a health insurance company where processing of an application for health insurance used to take 28 days and called for input from seven members of staff. After re-engineering, processing takes only seven days and is completed by a single member of staff. The point is that only 45 minutes of work was needed on each application; the file being in transit previously occupied the rest of the time.

The thrust of BPR is to unpick the old methods and structures that have become inappropriate and replace them with ones that are suitable for the fast-paced, customer-focused business environment that the organisation is competing in. BPR initiatives are undertaken simultaneously to achieve objectives in areas such as cost and service, as shown in the diagram below.

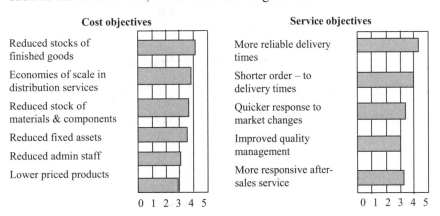

Scale: 1 = not important, 5 = very important

Diagram: Example objectives of a BPR project

4.6 Advantages and disadvantages of BPR

Advantages of BPR include the following.

- BPR revolves around customer needs and helps to give an appropriate focus to the business.

- BPR provides cost advantages that assist the organisation's competitive position.

- BPR encourages a long-term strategic view of operational processes by asking radical questions about how things are done and how processes could be improved.

- BPR helps overcome the short-sighted approaches that sometimes emerge from excessive concentration on functional boundaries. By focusing on entire processes the exercise can streamline activities throughout the organisation.

- BPR can help to reduce organisational complexity by eliminating unnecessary activities.

Criticisms of BPR include the following.

- BPR is sometimes seen (incorrectly) as a means of making small improvements in existing practices. In reality, it is a more radical approach that questions whether existing practices make any sense in their present form.

- BPR is sometimes seen (incorrectly) as a single, once-for-all cost-cutting exercise. In reality, it is not primarily concerned with cost-cutting (though cost reductions often result), and should be regarded as on-going rather than once-for-all. This misconception often creates hostility in the minds of staff who see the exercise as a threat to their security.

- BPR requires a far-reaching and long-term commitment by management and staff. Securing this is not an easy task, and many organisations have rejected the whole idea as not worth the effort.

4.7 The role of information as a resource in organisational re-design

Information systems have played a key role in the above re-organisations. Information and data are captured at source and then stored in a corporate database where they may be used by the entire organisation for various business processes. This is very different from the arrangements that exist in an organisation divided on functional lines. Traditionally a functional department would have held and controlled all of the information it had successfully argued fell within its domain. Typically the information would have been held on manual records or on older computer systems where access to data is restricted. Business process re-engineering depends upon sharing of information and therefore the introduction of information systems where data is accessible to the entire organisation has been a pre-requirement for re-organisation of the kind described.

Activity 1

What does the management accountant contribute to planning a BPR exercise?

Feedback to this activity is at the end of the chapter.

5 Why process innovation and BPR are important

5.1 Continuous change and new opportunities

Changes in information and communications technology have come at an astonishing pace during the late 1990s and the early 2000s, and there is no sign of a slowdown. Each new development offers new opportunities to businesses and it is the businesses that embrace such change that are most likely to survive and thrive.

Managers need to understand the importance of IT to the future of their business.

- Organisations need to invest to maintain their competitive position. If competitors have amended their processes so that they can offer new services such as on-line ordering, then it is imperative to do the same.

- Preferably the organisation should attempt to gain competitive advantage of its own. For example, innovation in products is a source of differentiation, which enables maintenance of this strategy.

- However, innovation must be continuous because it is only a matter of time before competitors catch up with or improve upon another company's innovative ideas.

- Innovation in production processes might reduce production costs and hence support a cost-leadership strategy. Innovation in sales and marketing processes may lead to better decisions about which products to target at which markets.

- Innovative organisations tend to attract and retain higher quality staff, who want to gain experience with the market leader and want the opportunity to contribute to the development of a forward-looking organisation. Or, from the opposite point of view, lack of change tends to demotivate staff, especially if they are aware that other companies have better systems and are able to produce higher quality products and give better service.

Summary

Key points of this chapter are:

- Innovation is being sought more and more with the use of IT. Products have to be innovative and completely up-to-date to ensure advantage over rivals. Creativity leads to innovation that in turn leads to greater market share. Proprietary advantage can be achieved through using technology to develop a distinctive product.

- Business process re-engineering (BPR) was developed to assist companies in changing their methods of working. It had been realised that management had expended effort and money on new technology, but that the underlying processes had not been altered, and that therefore the company still had scope for further improvement. BPR filled this gap and led to companies throwing out old methods of working and streamlining their organisation's processes, thereby achieving further advantage. The secret is to ensure that BPR is not treated as a once-only exercise, but that there is constant review to ensure that processes are at their optimum.

- Process Innovation (PI) refers to the implementation of completely new process, rather than the amendment of existing processes (which is BPR).

- Information Technology (IT) can assist in PI by providing new IT features in products or providing information to assist in planning new products.

Having completed your study of this chapter you should have achieved the following learning outcome:

- evaluate the importance of process innovation and re-engineering.

Self-test questions

1   Why is innovation important for an organisation? (2.2)

2   What is the difference between innovation and invention? (2.3)

3   What are the five waves of technology? (3.3)

4   Define BPR. (4.1)

5 What is the difference between business process re-engineering and business process analysis? (4.3)

6 List the five steps of the business process re-engineering that BT use. (4.4)

7 Describe two advantages of business process re-engineering. (4.6)

8 Why are process innovation and BPR important? (5.1)

Practice question

Pump manufacturer

The Dose Company was established over a century ago and manufactures water pumps of various kinds. Until recently it has been successful, but imports of higher quality pumps at lower prices are now rapidly eroding Dose's market share. The managing director feels helpless in the face of this onslaught from international competitors and is frantically searching for a solution to the problem. In his desperation, he consults a range of management journals and comes across what seems to be a wonder cure by the name of Business process re-engineering (BPR).

According to the article, the use of BPR has already transformed the performance of a significant number of companies in the USA which were mentioned in the article, and is now being widely adopted by European companies. Unfortunately, the remainder of the article, which purports to explain BPR, is full of management jargon and he is left with only a vague idea of how it works.

Required:

(a) Explain the nature of BPR and describe how it might be applied to a manufacturing company like Dose. **(12 marks)**

(b) Describe the major pitfalls for managers attempting to re-engineer their organisations. **(8 marks)**

(Total: 20 marks)

For the answer to this question, see the 'Answers' section at the end of the book.

Feedback to activity

Activity 1

The management accountant contributes to planning a BPR exercise above all by providing the information required to evaluate alternatives. The primary purpose of BPR is to investigate different ways in which defined outcomes can be achieved. The effects of each method on costs and profitability will be a key criterion in determining the best option, and the management accountant is well placed to provide such information.

The management accountant will work closely with operational managers to achieve this. By looking at their existing processes, and helping to formulate alternatives, the management accountant will inform himself or herself in detail about what is involved. The task then is to translate this information into financial form. The methods of reporting on processes may themselves need to be revised as a result: often adoption of BPR has gone hand in hand with a move to activity based costing.

As the term suggests, BPR is concerned with how processes are to work in practice. In implementing a BPR programme, managers will be concerned to have the appropriate information to enable them to manage new processes; management accountants can help by reconsidering the form in which reports are presented. In many cases, the required change will be from an emphasis on transactions processing to an emphasis on decision making and control. Underlying all of this should be a focus on customer needs.

Once the appropriate information has been determined, it is equally important to ensure that it is presented appropriately. If the new emphasis is on support for decision making it is essential that managers can appreciate the information and digest it rapidly. User friendliness is an important criterion, and too much detail is as unhelpful as too little.

Chapter 13

THE ROLE AND RESPONSIBILITIES OF DIRECTORS

Syllabus content

- The role and responsibilities of directors in making strategic decisions (including issues of due diligence, fiduciary responsibilities).

Contents

1   Introduction

2   Who needs strategic decisions?

3   Directors' formal duties

4   Corporate governance

5   Ethical responsibilities

1   Introduction

Strategic decisions involve long-term considerations and frequently affect the entire organisaton, so it is appropriate that they are made at a very senior management level, typically by the Board of Directors. It is in the very nature of strategic decisions that they have a fundamental effect on many of the stakeholders in the organisation and this brings with it significant responsibilities.

We begin this chapter by considering the nature of strategic decisions and the rationale for having a strategy, as opposed to a more opportunistic approach to business. We will look briefly at the formal legal position, but directors' responsibilities are now far more thoroughly defined by the various standards of corporate governance that have emerged in the last decade or so. Finally we will consider the ethical position and corporate culture: directors' responsibilities go beyond the letter of the law and guidelines can be interpreted in various ways.

2   Who needs strategic decisions?

2.1   A reminder

Much earlier in this book we discussed the **characteristics** of the strategic decisions that directors may have to make, but it is worth a reminder in this context.

- Strategic decisions are likely to be affected by the scope of an organisation's activities, because the scope concerns the way the management conceive the organisation's boundaries. It is to do with what they want the organisation to be like and be about.

- Strategy involves the matching of the activities of an organisation to its environment.

- Strategy must also match the activities of an organisation to its resource capability. It is not just about being aware of the environmental threats and opportunities but about matching the organisational resources to these threats and opportunities.

- Strategies need to be considered in terms of the extent to which resources can be obtained, allocated and controlled to develop a strategy for the future.

- Operational decisions will be affected by strategic decisions because they will set off waves of lesser decisions.

- As well as the environmental forces and the resource availability, the strategy of an organisation will be affected by the expectations and values of those who have power within and around the organisation.

- Strategic decisions are apt to affect the long-term direction of the organisation.

What distinguishes strategic management from other aspects of management in an organisation is the complexity. There are three reasons for this:

- it involves a high degree of uncertainty

- it is likely to require an integrated approach to management

- it may involve major change in the organisation.

> **KEY POINT**
>
> Strategy involves the matching of the activities of an organisation to its environment and resource capability.

> **KEY POINT**
>
> Strategic decisions affect the long-term direction of the organisation.

2.2 Freewheeling opportunism

Strategy would seem to be a good and necessary thing then, but there are examples of organisations that have been spectacularly successful because of lucky breaks — just being in the right place at the right time and taking advantage. Arguably, for instance, the success of Microsoft, at least initially, is due solely to an historical accident—a lack of forethought by IBM in the early 1990s that led to Bill Gates' MS-DOS operating system becoming the *de facto* world standard, even though MS-DOS was very far from the best operating system available at the time.

So, do directors have any responsibility for formulating a strategy at all, if they would rather not bother? Opponents of structured long-term strategic planning argue that in instigating explicit long-term strategy, directors may be putting their organisations into what is effectively a strait jacket, resulting in a serious loss of flexibility and making it difficult to exploit opportunities on a more freewheeling basis.

The arguments imply certain weaknesses in the disciplined approach, such as its inflexibility, forecasting inaccuracy, complexity and bureaucratic nature.

The characteristics of **freewheeling opportunism** are as follows.

- It concentrates on finding, evaluating and exploiting new opportunities instead of adhering to the rigidity of a predetermined strategy.

- It is perceived by some to be dynamic, exciting and innovative. Furthermore because of its unstructured approach, strategy arising from it is seen to bear the stamp of influential individuals who are keen on a particular course of action. But this is not necessarily self-seeking: those influential individuals (who may be directors) may honestly consider their strategy to be in the best interests of a company that they care about with a passion, and they may well be right.

- It encourages a non-corporate philosophy, and those who have vested interests will try to exert pressure for the acceptance of their own ideas even if they are incompatible with existing corporate aims. But again, this is not necessarily a bad thing, especially if the organisation has stagnated or become 'too comfortable' in its existing ways.

2.3 The arguments against long-term strategy

- **Setting corporate objectives** – A criticism frequently levelled at the practice of spelling out corporate objectives is that the exercise descends into the formulation of empty platitudes that offer no positive directional indicators for decision making.

  Those executives responsible for decision making need to know not merely the overall direction in which the organisation is supposed to be heading, but also which evaluative standards to apply in order to judge competitive strategies, with the standards expressed in meaningful terms such as market share and sales volume.

  Corporate strategy can be viewed from so many different angles and interests that it may be necessary to apply a whole range of evaluative standards, some of which may be in conflict. For instance, a strengthening of liquid resources may be accompanied by a lower return on capital employed. An individual measure will have to be weighted according to its significance in the problem situation under review, although it is not possible to carry out such evaluation with any sort of mathematical precision.

- **The difficulties of forecasting accurately** – The development of a forecasting capability, and the development of models which relate environmental changes to corporate performance, are significant aspects of strategic planning. While the general level of practice concerning environmental issues is still quite primitive, the state of the art is rapidly advancing.

  There are difficult problems associated with trying to accurately forecast for the long term.

  – The fact that it is a long-term period.

  – The complexity of the environment that needs to be forecast.

  – The rapidity and novelty of environmental change.

  – The interrelationships between the environmental variables involved.

  – The limitations of the data available.

  – The amount and complexity of the calculations involved.

- **Short-term pressures** – The pressures on management are for short-term results whereas strategy is ostensibly concerned with the long term, e.g. 'What should we be doing now to help us reach the position we want to be in, in five years time'. Often it is difficult to motivate managers by setting long-term expectations.

- **Rigidity** – Operational managers are frequently reluctant to specify their planning assumptions because the situations that their plans are designed to meet may change so rapidly that they can be made to look foolish. Even if a plan is reasonably accurate, the situation might change for reasons other than those forecast. Executives are often held prisoners by the rigidity of the planning process, because plans have to be set out in detail long before the period to which they apply.

  The rigidity of the long-term plan, particularly in regard to the rationing and scheduling of resources, may also place the company in a position where it is unable to react to short-term unforeseen opportunities, or serious short-term crisis.

- **Stifling initiative** – If adherence to the strategy becomes all-important, it discounts flair and creativity. Operational managers can generate enthusiasm or dampen down potential trouble spots and quick action may be required to avert trouble or improve a situation by actions outside the strategy. If operational managers then have to defend their actions against criticisms of acting 'outside the plan', irrespective of the resultant benefits, they are likely to become apathetic and indifferent.

- **The cost** – The strategic planning process can be costly, involving the use of specialists, sometimes a specialist department, and taking up management time. The process generates its own bureaucracy and associated paper or electronic data flow. Personal authorities are, to a greater or lesser extent, replaced by written guidelines.

- **Lacks dynamism** – The process might be inhibitive in that it programmes activities and events and removes the excitement and exhilaration of spontaneity and the unexpected.

- **Why start now?** – An attitude particularly shown by managers in small growing companies is that they have managed quite successfully in the past without formalised strategic planning systems. So why start now?

- **Management distrust of techniques** – The strategic planning process involves the use of many management and management accounting techniques, not least forecasting, modelling, cost analysis and operational research. This can produce adverse reactions for two reasons. Firstly, senior management may distrust 'laboratory techniques untested in their ambit of activity', and secondly they may distrust the recommendations of specialists who are 'heavy on academic learning but light on practical experience'.

- **The clash of personal and corporate loyalties** – The adoption of corporate strategy requires a tacit acceptance by everyone that the interests of departments, activities and individuals are subordinate to the corporate interests. Department managers are required to consider the contribution to corporate profits or the reduction in corporate costs of any decision. They should not allow their decisions to be limited by departmental parameters.

  It is only natural that managers should seek personal advancement. As a company is the primary vehicle by which this can be achieved, a cleavage of loyalty may occur. A problem of strategic planning is identifying those areas where there may be a clash of interests and loyalties, and in assessing where an individual has allowed vested interests to dominate decisions.

2.4 The case for long-term strategy

Notwithstanding the points raised above, planning long-term corporate strategy can be justified in the following ways.

- Certain action that is fundamental to the corporate operations is irreversible in the short term at least. It is difficult to imagine managers making decisions that have a degree of permanency without first going through some form of formalised strategic planning.

- The bigger an organisation becomes the bigger are the risks involved in top management decisions. Strategic planning helps to identify these risks and either prevent or mitigate their effects.

- The business environment is dynamic and the rate of change is escalating. Integral to the strategic planning process is environmental appraisal that often uses sophisticated forecasting techniques requiring expert interpretation and evaluation of strategic options.

- Some companies have undoubtedly managed quite successfullyw ithout strategic planning. However it is probable that they could haver performed much better. Even an upward sloping profit line can be criticised if it prevents the occurrence of an even steeper profit line. Strategic planning ensures that performance is targeted rather than merely assessed against loose expectations.

- Corporate planning is concerned with the long term, and the long term is an essential dimension in the overall survival pattern of a company. The planning disciplines concentrate management's attention on long-term matters, but not to the exclusion of short-term considerations. Freewheeling planning is apt to focus only on the short term and there is evidence to suggest that this is perilous.

KEY POINT

Some companies have performed quite successfullyw ithout strategic planning. However, an upward sloping profit line can be criticised if it prevents the occurrence of an even steeper profit line.

- Strategic planning requires the clarification of corporate objectives. The process aids in the formulation of organisational goals and objectives, and the strategy formulation process can be used to evaluate whether or not the tentative objectives established are achievable, given the organisation's resources and the nature of the changes occurring in its environment, and, if not, what other objectives could be achieved.

- The systematic survey of the environment involved in strategic planning can only improve the basis of information on which trends are identified, projections made and evaluative criteria produced.

- Strategic planning quantifies long-term resource problems and produces a basis upon which resources can be planned and rationed between programmes.

- The systematic survey of the corporate environment and of the company's internal strengths and weaknesses acts as 'an early warning system'. The process will, hopefully, identify product/market threats and resource weaknesses in time for the company to bring in preventive or remedial measures.

- Strategic planning helps to integrate long, medium and short-term plans and to harmonise the activities of different departments and functions. The planning process results in people from different functions working together in teams, and the plan itself clarifies the contribution made by the different functions to the achievement of overall objectives.

- The emergent plan should reflect the 'corporate' nature of the company, instead of merely being an aggregation of the plans of individual departments.

- Strategic planning demands a logical, deliberate and analytical approach to decision making. It requires the generation of alternative strategies, and the evaluation of the probable results of their execution.

- The plans formulated can be used as yardsticks against which actual performance can be judged and remedial needs identified.

- The planning process is continuous and not conducted as a 'one-off' ad hoc exercise. This requires the maintenance of an information system that will continuously provide up-to-date data for ongoing decision-making and control purposes.

- The strategy spells out in definite terms the responsibility and authority of each executive and management activity. This tends to boost morale, and produces better results since most groups and individuals perform better if they know what is expected of them and how they contribute to the overall progress of the company.

- Strategic planning, when carried out imaginatively and conducted in the right atmosphere of communication, participation and incentive, helps to develop a climate conducive to creative thinking, initiative and innovation.

3 Directors' formal duties

3.1 Directors and strategy development

There is no comprehensive definition of a company director. Strictly speaking the term director simply means someone who holds that office, having been properly appointed to the Board under the constitution of the company. A director's function is to take part in making decisions by attending meetings of the board of directors.

People who have a job title including the word 'director', such as 'Sales Director' or 'Director of Research' to give them status in the company structure, are **not** really directors, in company law, **unless** they have actually been appointed to the board of directors in the proper legal manner.

That is not to say, of course, that senior managers who are not on the board do not have a very significant part to play in strategy development, simply that the responsibilities that they owe will be owed under a contract of employment.

Typically in a large company in the UK the Board has responsibility for major capital expenditure (e.g. corporate infrastructure such as ICT, and acquisitions and disposals of other businesses), and takes the strategic decisions on overall corporate objectives. It may also have the final say in approving budgets, business plans, etc for strategic business units.

Most executive decisions are taken by tactical and operational managers (employees), who ultimately report to the chief executive officer or managing director.

In some other countries there is a clearer distinction between the functions of senior management and the functions of the directors because there is a two-tier Board, comprising a supervisory board and a management board.

3.2 Executive directors and non-executive directors

Executive directors are the top managers of a business. They have first-hand knowledge and experience of the business and this is vital for planning and decision making and for monitoring and controlling performance.

Non-executive directors have no managerial responsibilities. In terms of decision making they should bring the benefits of their business experience outside the company to the board's thinking and provide a balancing influence when there are potential conflicts of interest between the personal interests of executive directors as managers and the interests of shareholders. In theory non-executives should provide reassurance to shareholders that management is acting in the interests of the company.

3.3 Fiduciary responsibilities

DEFINITION

A **fiduciary relationship** exists where an individual or organisation has an obligation to act on behalf of another person's or organisation's interests in matters which affect the other person or organisation.

The term fiduciary means 'relating to, or founded upon, a trust or confidence'. A fiduciary relationship exists where an individual or organisation has an obligation to act on behalf of another person's or organisation's interests in matters which affect the other person or organisation. A fiduciary is obliged to act in the other person's best interest with total **disregard** for any **personal interests**.

Company directors are said to hold a fiduciary position since they make contracts as agents of the company and have control of its property.

Broadly speaking directors have a fiduciary responsibility to be **honest** and **not seek personal advantage** and they must also show **reasonable competence**.

- **Acting in interests of company**: the directors owe a fiduciary duty to the company to exercise their powers in what they honestly consider to be the interests of the company.

- **Use of powers for proper purpose**: the directors have a fiduciary duty to use the powers given to them by the company's constitution for a proper purpose. The powers are restricted to the purposes for which they were given.

- **Freedom of action**: the directors must retain their freedom of action and not fetter their discretion by agreeing to act or vote as some other person may direct.

- **Conflict of interest**: the directors owe a fiduciary duty to avoid a conflict of duty and personal interest. They must show undivided concern for the company's interests. (For example, there must always be a conflict of interest where a director has an interest, even indirect, in a contract with his company.)

- **Personal advantage**: a director may not obtain any personal advantage from his position of director without the consent of the company for whatever gain or profit he has obtained.

3.4 Duty of care

Directors have a common law **duty of care** to show **reasonable competence**. There are two main points here.

- A director is expected to show the degree of skill which may reasonably be expected from a person of his knowledge and experience. The standard set depends on the person and the situation in each case. For example the standards expected of a managing director of a listed company would be higher than for the MD of a one-man company.

- Directors are required to attend board meetings when they are able but they have no legal duty to concern themselves with the affairs of the company at other times. If a director is also a working executive of the company extra duties are performed as an employee, not as a director.

3.5 Statutory rules

Various statutory rules have been enacted to lay down prohibitions or limits on various **transactions** involving directors.

- Some transactions, such as loans to directors, are prohibited in most cases.

- Other transactions must be approved by shareholders in general meeting.

- There are also transactions such as interests in shares which are not restricted but the details must be disclosed in the annual accounts or directors' report sent to members.

The **duties** imposed on directors are owed primarily to the company as the general body of members (i.e. shareholders). But statute law has modified the rules, for example by:

- requiring the directors to have regard to the **interests of the company's employees** in general as well as the interests of its members

- forbidding (as a criminal offence) **'insider dealing'** in which directors might take unfair advantage of their position for personal gain.

3.6 Due diligence

The term due diligence may be used simply to mean a 'duty of care' as discussed above, but it is most likely to be encountered in the sense of an investigation into the **risks and value of an investment opportunity**.

This may simply mean confirming that the financial and record-keeping aspects of a proposed acquisition are as represented, but more broadly speaking it refers to the complete analysis of a business opportunity to assist in making decisions about it. Examples could be a review of past records, proposed agreements, financing arrangements, employment issues, legal matters, cash flow forecasts — a consideration of practically everything covered in this book, in fact.

Activity 1

Briefly outline the management accounting techniques that might typically be employed as part of a due diligence exercise.

Feedback to this activity is at the end of the chapter.

4 Corporate governance

4.1 Why do we need a code of practice for corporate governance?

It would be naive to expect that directors discharged the duties described above without occasional lapses, and the strict legal position is currently vague, to say the least. (A good deal of new companies legislation is in the pipeline in the UK at the time of publication of this book: watch the press and visit the DTI website for details of developments.)

Directors of public companies have not always considered the interests of shareholders let alone other groups of interested parties. Chairmen of listed companies have embezzled funds and concealed illicit transactions by false accounting. Writers such as John Argenti have written about the harmful effects of the 'despotic chief executive syndrome'. There are still multinational companies whose parent boards are dominated by single powerful personalities.

The best-known example in recent years is the US energy trader Enron which collapsed in 2001. The subsequent investigation found a catalogue of lapses and failures: senior executives who permitted or encouraged misleading accounting treatment; an audit committee that signed off misleading accounts; individuals who were enriched by transactions with the company that employed them; a board that was ineffective in supervising senior managers' actions; and whistleblowers' complaints that were ignored or whitewashed.

It is now very widely accepted that organisations need systems and processes for ensuring proper accountability, probity and openness in the conduct of their business – these systems and processes are known as **corporate governance**.

4.2 Cadbury

Modern developments in the UK concerning the systems by which companies are directed and controlled (i.e. 'corporate governance') began with *The Committee on the Financial Aspects of Corporate Governance* chaired by Sir Adrian Cadbury, which aimed to address the issue of a code of best practice that would be supported by the Stock Exchange as well as the ASB and the Auditing Practices Board (APB).

4.3 The Greenbury Committee

Following the success of the work of the Cadbury committee, in 1995 the Confederation of British Industry (CBI) set up a committee under the chairmanship of Sir Richard Greenbury, chairman of Marks and Spencer, to recommend best practice guidelines for UK company directors' pay. The CBI hoped that the Greenbury committee's work would prevent the government from legislating in what had become a controversial area.

The Greenbury report was duly published in July 1995, containing a code of best practice for determining and accounting for **directors' remuneration**. The report recommends that all UK listed companies should comply with the code and should state this compliance or explain their non-compliance in the annual report.

4.4 The Hampel report

In January 1998 another report on corporate governance was issued, this time from a committee under the chairmanship of Sir Ronnie Hampel. While both the Cadbury and Greenbury reports concentrated on preventing abuses, the Hampel report 'is concerned with the positive contribution which good corporate governance can make'. Throughout, it aims to restrict the regulatory burden facing companies and substitute broad principles where practicable.

Each company's circumstances are different. A 'one-size-fits-all' approach to corporate governance issues is rejected. Instead, each listed company must include in the annual report a narrative explaining how the broad principles of corporate governance have been applied.

The general message of Hampel is that a board must not approach the various corporate governance requirements in a compliance mentality: the so-called 'tick-box' approach. Good corporate governance is not achieved by satisfying a checklist. Directors must **comply with the substance as well as the letter** of all best practice pronouncements.

4.5 The Turnbull report

The Turnbull Committee was set up under the aegis of the Institute of Chartered Accountants in England and Wales (ICAEW) to develop guidance for the accountancy profession in conjunction with representatives of preparers of accounts. The Cadbury committee had identified in its report that an efficient **internal control** system was essential to the efficient management of the company. There was therefore a need for the accountancy profession to develop criteria for the assessment of effectiveness of controls and developing guidance on the form in which directors should report.

For the purposes of this 1999 guidance, internal control in its widest sense is defined as:

'The whole system of controls, financial or otherwise, established in order to provide reasonable assurance of:

- effective and efficient operations

- reliable financial information and reporting

- compliance with laws and regulations'.

Effective and efficient operations addresses the company's basic business objectives including performance and profitability goals, and the safeguarding and efficient use of resources.

Reliable financial information and reporting addresses the maintaining of proper accounting records and the reliability of financial information used within the business for publication to third parties. This includes the protection of records against two main types of fraud, the concealing of theft and the distorting of results.

Compliance with laws and regulations recognises management's responsibility for ensuring that operations are conducted in accordance with legal and regulatory obligations.

Internal controls should also address particular contingencies and commitments which could affect the truth and fairness of financial statements. For example:

- the management and control of foreign currencies, financial futures, commodities, etc

- the management of limited cash resources and controls over cash flow

- companies involved in processes which create risks of environmental pollution and the resultant financial obligations that may arise

- companies vulnerable to the risk of computer breakdown.

4.6 The Combined Code

Hampel envisaged a 'supercode', incorporating the recommendations of Cadbury, Greenbury and Hampel, and endorsed by the Stock Exchange, and the result – the Combined Code – was first published in 1998 with the intention that all listed companies should try to implement the code to the best of their ability.

A revised version was issued in 2003. The new version also incorporates Turnbull's work and work done in the early 2000s – a review of the role and effectiveness of non-executive directors by Derek Higgs and a review of audit committees by a group led by Sir Robert Smith.

> **KEY POINT**
>
> Listed companies are required under the listing agreement, to explain in their annual reports the extent to which they comply or do not comply with the Combined Code.

Listed companies are required under the listing agreement to explain in their annual reports the extent to which they comply or do not comply with the Combined Code. The main provisions of the new code are as follows.

The Board

Every company should be headed by an effective board, which is collectively responsible for the success of the company. There should be a clear division of responsibilities at the head of the company between the running of the board and the executive responsibility for the running of the company's business (i.e. chairman and chief executive). No one individual should have unfettered powers of decision.

The board should include a balance of executive and non-executive directors (and in particular independent non-executive directors) such that no individual or small group of individuals can dominate the board's decision taking.

> **KEY POINT**
>
> The Combined Code covers the make-up and responsibilities of the Board and the need for information and training, remuneration systems, financial reporting, internal control, audit and auditors, and dialogue with shareholders.

There should be a formal, rigorous and transparent procedure for the appointment of new directors to the board. All directors should be submitted for re-election at regular intervals, subject to continued satisfactory performance. The board should ensure planned and progressive refreshing of the board.

The board should be supplied in a timely manner with information in a form and of a quality appropriate to enable it to discharge its duties. All directors should receive induction on joining the board and should regularly update and refresh their skills and knowledge.

The board should undertake a formal and rigorous annual evaluation of its own performance and that of its committees and individual directors.

Remuneration

Levels of remuneration should be sufficient to attract, retain and motivate directors of the quality required to run the company successfully, but a company should avoid paying more than is necessary for this purpose. A significant proportion of executive directors' remuneration should be structured so as to link rewards to corporate and individual performance.

There should be a formal and transparent procedure for developing policy on executive remuneration and for fixing the remuneration packages of individual directors. No director should be involved in deciding his or her own remuneration.

Financial Reporting

The board should present a balanced and understandable assessment of the company's position and prospects.

Internal Control

The board should maintain a sound system of internal control to safeguard shareholders' investment and the company's assets.

Audit Committee and Auditors

The board should establish formal and transparent arrangements for considering how they should apply the financial reporting and internal control principles, and for maintaining an appropriate relationship with the company's auditors.

Dialogue with Institutional Shareholders

There should be a dialogue with shareholders based on the mutual understanding of objectives. The board as a whole has responsibility for ensuring that a satisfactory dialogue with shareholders takes place.

4.7 The Smith guidance on Audit Committees

The July 2003 publication also includes guidance on how to comply with the parts of the Code including the Smith guidance on Audit Committees.

The Committee should include at least three members, all independent non-executive directors. At least one member should have significant, recent and relevant financial experience, and suitable training should be provided for all.

The role of the audit committee can be summarised as follows.

- To monitor the integrity of the financial statements of the company, reviewing significant financial reporting judgements.

- To review the company's internal financial control system and, unless expressly addressed by a separate risk committee or by the board itself, risk management systems.

- To monitor and review the effectiveness of the company's internal audit function.

- To make recommendations to the board in relation to the external auditor's appointment; in the event of the board's rejecting the recommendation, the committee and the board should explain their respective positions in the annual report.

- To monitor and review the external auditor's independence, objectivity and effectiveness, taking into consideration relevant UK professional and regulatory requirements.

- To develop and implement policy on the engagement of the external auditor to supply non-audit services, taking into account relevant ethical guidance regarding the provision of non-audit services by the external audit firm.

In addition the committee should be provided with sufficient resources, its activities should be reported in a separate section of the directors' report (within the annual report) and the chairman of the committee should be present to answer questions at the AGM.

4.8 Higgs suggestions for good practice

Higgs' review focused on the effectiveness of non-executive directors in promoting company performance and on issues of accountability. The recommendations aimed to increase rigour and transparency in the appointment process, to foster meritocracy and to widen the spread of experience in UK boardrooms.

The suggestions in the Combined Code include a number of checklists, for example an induction checklist and a performance evaluation checklist. There is also guidance for various parties involved in corporate governance, as summarised below.

Guidance on the role of the Chairman

The chairman is pivotal in creating the conditions for overall board and individual director effectiveness, both inside and outside the boardroom. Specifically, it is the responsibility of the chairman to:

- run the board and set its agenda

- ensure that the members of the board receive accurate, timely and clear information

- ensure effective communication with shareholders and major investors

- ensure that sufficient time is allowed for discussion of complex or contentious issues

- provide a properly constructed induction programme for new directors and identify and meet the development needs of individual directors

- ensure that the performance of individuals and of the board as a whole and its committees is evaluated at least once a year

- encourage active engagement by all the members of the board.

Guidance on the role of the Non-Executive Director

The role of the non-executive director has the following key elements:

- They should constructively challenge and help develop proposals on strategy.

- They should scrutinise the performance of management and monitor the reporting of performance.

- They should satisfy themselves on the integrity of financial information and that financial controls and systems of risk management are robust and defensible.

- They are responsible for determining appropriate levels of remuneration of executive directors, and have a prime role in their appointment and removal and in succession planning.

- They should be independent in judgement and have an enquiring mind.

- They need to be well-informed about the company and the external environment in which it operates, with a strong command of issues relevant to the business.

- They should ensure that sufficient, accurate, clear and timely information is provided sufficiently in advance of meetings to enable thorough consideration of the issues facing the board.

- They should understand the views of major investors both directly and through the chairman and the senior independent director.

Summary of the principal duties of the Remuneration Committee

The committee should:

- set remuneration for all executive directors, the chairman and the company secretary. The remuneration of non-executive directors shall be a matter for the chairman and executive members of the board. No director or manager should be involved in any decisions as to their own remuneration

- determine targets for any performance-related pay schemes operated by the company

- determine the policy for and scope of pension arrangements for each executive director

- ensure that contractual terms on termination, and any payments made, are fair to the individual and the company, that failure is not rewarded and that the duty to mitigate loss is fully recognised

- determine the total individual remuneration package of each executive director including, where appropriate, bonuses, incentive payments and share options

- agree the policy for authorising claims for expenses from the chief executive and chairman

- ensure that provisions regarding disclosure of remuneration including pensions, as set out in the Directors' Remuneration Report Regulations 2002 and the Combined Code, are fulfilled.

Summary of the principal duties of the Nomination Committee

A nomination committee should lead the process for board appointments and make recommendations to the board. A majority of members of the committee should be independent non-executive directors.

Amongst other matters the committee should:

- evaluate the balance of skills, knowledge and experience on the board and, in the light of this evaluation, prepare a description of the role and capabilities required for a particular appointment

- review annually the time required from a non-executive director. Performance evaluation should be used to assess whether the non-executive director is spending enough time to fulfil their duties

- consider candidates from a wide range of backgrounds and look beyond the 'usual suspects'

- give full consideration to succession planning in the course of its work, taking into account the challenges and opportunities facing the company and what skills and expertise are therefore needed on the board in the future

- make a statement in the annual report about its activities; the process used for appointments and explain if external advice or open advertising has not been used; the membership of the committee, number of committee meetings and attendance over the course of the year.

5 Ethical responsibilities

5.1 Promoting ethical values through the control environment of the business

Guidance for directors of listed companies prepared by the ICAEW identifies the need to promote ethical values despite the need to balance the conflicting interests of the providers of capital, employees, customers, suppliers, regulators and the public at large.

The need to maintain ethical values is complicated by the local conditions and culture which may be different from the culture of the country where the company is based. Each company must work out its own code which is appropriate to its circumstances.

However the following are identified as essential to a good quality of control environment which is necessary if a climate of good ethical conduct is to be fostered.

- Commitment to truth and fair dealing
- Commitment to quality and competence
- Leadership in control by example
- Communication of ethical values
- An appropriate organisation structure
- Independence, integrity and openness at board level
- Appropriate delegation of authority and accountability
- A professional approach to financial reporting.

KEY POINT

If a climate of good ethical conduct is to be fostered directors need to address issues such as: commitment to truth and fair dealing; commitment to quality and competence; leadership by example; communication of ethical values; an appropriate organisation structure; independence, integrity and openness at board level; appropriate delegation of authority and accountability; and a professional approach to financial reporting.

5.2 Moral or immoral organisations

In terms of ethics, organisations will usually be placed somewhere between two extremes: moral and immoral.

Corporate Activity	Immoral Management	Moral Management
Ethical Norm	Actions beyond ethical limits are taken if it will advantage the organisation	Ethical considerations are taken into account, and some options rejected on ethical grounds. An ethical standard might be explicit.
Goals	Profitability, or some other defined success indicator	Profitability within ethical standards and legal framework
Legal Orientation	Legal barriers are no different from any other, and must be overcome when necessary	Letter and spirit of the law are minimum acceptable standards.
Strategy	Exploit all opportunities for corporate gain. Keep ethical costs to legal minimum – or lower if punishment is not severe	Enlightened self-interest. Management confront ethical dilemmas and show leadership in decision taking.

An 'amoral' organisation is something of a compromise – it complies with ethical standards up to a point, but does not actively seek to develop its own ethics in a conscious way.

Here are some examples of the possible impact of corporate culture in cases where the ethical values of management might be questioned.

- In the early 1990s British Airways were adjudged to have been waging a 'dirty tricks' campaign against its competitor Virgin Atlantic. British Airways argued that the 'dirty tricks' (poaching Virgin's customers) were attributable to one or two employees who were over-eager to promote the interests of their employer. However, some observers believed that the real villain of the piece was British Airways' abrasive corporate culture, inspired by the then chairman of BA, Lord King.

- More recently, in 2003 the UK's largest personal injury claims firm, Accident Group, was forced into administration due to 'lower than expected claims success rate'. The 'no win. no fee' company was in the business of persuading members of the public to launch legal claims for personal injury compensation and it had a hard-sell culture — tactics included massive advertising and cold calling, and employees were caught on TV trying to encourage customers to make bogus claims. Again a few individual over-enthusiastic employees were blamed when the company was asked to comment, but in fact many of its staff were **given targets by management** of bringing in four to seven claims a day, and clearly not all of these claims were sustainable when they came to court. (To add insult to injury, when it went into administration the group used text messages to inform many of its 2,500 staff that they were fired!)

Activity 2

In an industry that is noted for dubious behaviour, most of the companies subscribe to an industry code of practice and have ethical guidelines displayed in all company premises. A young manager realises that he cannot meet his performance targets without breaking these guidelines, and seeks help from an older manager. In a formal meeting, he is told that his performance will be judged by the ability to meet his targets within the guidelines, but informally he is told that the performance indicators are more important providing he is not caught. Can the young manager behave ethically?

Feedback to this activity is at the end of the chapter.

There are two basic approaches to the management of ethics in organisations:

- A **compliance-based** approach is designed to ensure that the company and its personnel act within the letter of the law, and that violations are prevented, detected and punished.

- An **integrity-based** approach has a concern for the spirit as well as the letter of the law and combines this with a recognition of managerial responsibility for ethical behaviour.

KEY POINT

Mere compliance does not address the wide range of ethical issues that may arise in business. Integrity-based approaches attempt to define the company's guiding values, aspirations and patterns of thought and conduct with reference to what society considers to be morally acceptable.

Mere compliance does not address the wide range of ethical issues that may arise in business. This approach simply emphasises the threat of detection and punishment and expects that appropriate behaviour will follow. Moreover, it ignores the fact that demonstrably higher ethical standards may be a source of competitive advantage.

Integrity-based approaches attempt to define the company's guiding values, aspirations, and patterns of thought and conduct with reference to what society considers to be morally acceptable. This can help to prevent ethical lapses, and also taps into fundamental human impulses to behave in a moral way.

5.3 Corporate culture and corporate codes

The responsibilities of senior management regarding ethical behaviour might be summarised as follows.

- To determine the organisation's defining values, for example by formulating a Code of Conduct.

- To create an environment that supports ethically-acceptable behaviour.

- To instil a sense of shared accountability amongst employees.

To be effective a code needs to be accompanied by active efforts by senior managers to instil appropriate values, and this may well entail a change of culture. Many organisations now have ethics training programmes for their staff and have set up procedures or even an ethics department for reporting and investigating ethical matters that arise in the company's business.

Many major companies now have a formal Code of Conduct of some kind. For example, Boeing's code is shown below.

Code of Conduct

The Boeing Code of Conduct outlines expected behaviors for all Boeing employees.

Boeing will conduct its business fairly, impartially, in an ethical and proper manner, and in full compliance with all applicable laws and regulations. In conducting its business, integrity must underlie all company relationships, including those with customers, suppliers, communities and among employees. The highest standards of ethical business conduct are required of Boeing employees in the performance of their company responsibilities. Employees will not engage in conduct or activity that may raise questions as to the company's honesty, impartiality, reputation or otherwise cause embarrassment to the company.

Employees will ensure that:

- They do not engage in any activity that might create a conflict of interest for the company or for themselves individually.

- They do not take advantage of their Boeing position to seek personal gain through the inappropriate use of Boeing or non-public information or abuse of their position. This includes not engaging in insider trading.

- They will follow all restrictions on use and disclosure of information. This includes following all requirements for protecting Boeing information and ensuring that non-Boeing proprietary information is used and disclosed only as authorized by the owner of the information or as otherwise permitted by law.

- They observe that fair dealing is the foundation for all of our transactions and interactions.

- They will protect all company, customer and supplier assets and use them only for appropriate company approved activities.

- Without exception, they will comply with all applicable laws, rules and regulations.

- They will promptly report any illegal or unethical conduct to management or other appropriate authorities.

Every employee has the responsibility to ask questions, seek guidance and report suspected violations of this Code of Conduct. Retaliation against employees who come forward to raise genuine concerns will not be tolerated.

Copyright © Boeing

Source: www.boeing.com/companyoffices/aboutus/ethics/code_of_conduct.pdf

Summary

Key points of this chapter are:

- The formal duties of directors include fiduciary duties, a duty of care to the members of a company and statutory duties in terms of complying with the relevant legislation of their particular jurisriction.

- Directors must also comply with the appropriate corporate governance requirements of their country although the UK regulations are used as an example in this manual.

- Finally, directors have a duty to maintain ethical standards which will hopefully be reflected in the overall organisational culture.

Having completed your study of this chapter you should have achieved the following learning outcome:

- discuss the role and responsibilities of directors in the strategy development process.

Self-test questions

1 Why is strategic management different from other aspects of management in an organisation? (2.1)

2 What are the characteristics of freewheeling opportunism? (2.2)

3 Give five arguments against having a long-term strategy and five arguments in favour. (2.3, 2.4)

4 Explain the fiduciary responsibilities of directors, with examples. (3.3)

5 What is corporate governance? (4.1)

6 According to the ICAEW's Guide for directors of listed companies, what is the definition of internal control? (4.5)

7 What provisions are made in the Combined Code regarding the board of directors? (4.6)

8 What is the role of an audit committee? (4.7)

9 What is the role of a non-executive director? (4.8)

10 What issues need to be addressed if an organisation is to foster a climate of good ethical conduct? (5.1)

11 What are the responsibilities of senior management regarding ethical behaviour? (5.3)

Practice question

Responsibility for decisions

(a)   It is felt by the many opponents of strategic planning that in instigating strategy one is putting an organisation into a straitjacket, and that there is a resulting loss of flexibility which renders impossible the exploitation of opportunities on a more freewheeling basis.

Required:

Evaluate this statement.   **(10 marks)**

(b)   A function of non-executive directors is to reduce potential conflicts of interest between management and shareholders.

Required:

Discuss the major potential conflicts of interest that affect non-executive directors.

Note: Do not worry if you find it difficult to answer part b of this question as for this you might need some pre-knowledge of Paper P3 syllabus.

(10 marks)

(Total: 20 marks)

For the answer to this question, see the 'Answers' section at the end of the book.

Feedback to activities

Activity 1

Although the term 'management accounting techniques' could be interpreted very broadly you should have identified the following, at the very least.

(a)   Investment appraisal, both from a financial perspective (e.g. NPV) and considering business issues (SWOT analysis, PEST analysis, and so on).

(b)   Forecasting

(c)   Budgeting and performance measurement

(d)   Shareholder value analysis

Operational and tactical management techniques such as the EOQ model, linear programming and the like should **not** be included in your list.

Activity 2

This is a depressingly common situation. In an immoral company, the guidelines are there to defend senior managers and the company from blame when outsiders discover dubious activities. In truth, there is little that the young manager can do if he believes it is ethical to stick to the guidelines.

Chapter 14

MEASURING PERFORMANCE: FINANCIAL MEASURES

Syllabus content

- Assessing strategic performance (i.e. the use and development of appropriate measures that are sensitive to industry characteristics and environmental factors).

Contents

1   Introduction

2   Creating centres and divisions

3   Divisional assessment

4   Return on investment (ROI)

5   Residual income (RI)

6   Ratio analysis

1 Introduction

Hopefully much of this chapter will be familiar from your earlier studies. The two most common financial measures of assessing an organisation's performance are return on investment (ROI) and residual income (RI). Ratio analysis is useful for identifying trends and for making comparisons with other organisations. The chapter starts with a reminder of the reasons for centralisation and the problems of that organisastional structure.

In the next chapter we will look at control measures that can be used to assess strategic performance from a variety of other perspectives.

2 Creating centres and divisions

2.1 Introduction

In order to approach the difficulties of managing a large organisation a structure based on several autonomous decision-making units is often created. 'Decentralisation', as this is called, could be defined as:

delegating authority to make decisions

or

devolving responsibility for profit.

The second of these two definitions might be called divisionalisation rather than decentralisation, but the distinction is a fine one. Decentralisation can result in the creation of various types of unit. The familiar CIMA definitions are set out below.

DEFINITIONS

A **cost centre** is a production or service location, function, activity or item of equipment for which costs are accumulated.

A **revenue centre** is devoted to raising revenue with no responsibility for costs, e.g. a sales centre. Often used in a not-for-profit organisation.

A **profit centre** is a part of a business accountable for both costs and revenues.

An **investment centre** is a profit centre with additional responsibilities for capital investment and possibly for financing, and whose performance is measured by its return on investment.

- **Cost centre** – a production or service location, function, activity or item of equipment for which costs are accumulated.

  The manager of a segment of a business that is termed a cost centre has responsibility for certain costs, and his performance and that of the business segment will be assessed by the extent to which those costs have been controlled. Typical cost centres might be the various central service departments such as maintenance, research and development or personnel; but the status of these departments can be changed using a transfer pricing policy.

- **Revenue centre** – devoted to raising revenue with no responsibility for costs, e.g. a sales centre. Often used in a not-for-profit organisation.

- **Profit centre** – a part of a business accountable for both costs and revenues.

- **Investment centre** –a profit centre with additional responsibilities for capital investment and possibly for financing, and whose performance is measured by its return on investment.

When talking about a divisionalised or decentralised structure one thinks in terms of an organisation that has been split into investment centres. However, the degree of responsibility for and control over costs, revenues and investments may vary and therefore the validity of certain performance assessment measures may also vary.

2.2 Reasons for decentralising

The benefits of and reasons for decentralising are discussed further below.

- **Size** – the process of decentralisation breaks an organisation up into more manageable units; this enables decision making to proceed quickly and effectively and, in theory, a closer control to be maintained on the day-to-day running of a business's activities.

- **Need for specialists** – as a business grows, the nature of its activities often becomes more complex so that the entrepreneur/chief executive has to rely on experts to run particular segments of the business.

- **Motivation** – if managers are made to feel responsible for a particular part of a business, it is generally found that their efforts within that part of the business are improved and, as a consequence, the business prospers. Some form of incentive may be needed to reinforce this philosophy that has many advocates amongst 'behaviourists' of management accounting.

- **Uncertainty** – with ever-changing market conditions, decisions cannot be preplanned or centrally planned. It is important to have local managers who are closer in touch with each particular part of the business environment to be in a position to respond quickly as problems arise.

- **Geographical** – decentralisation often refers to the delegation of responsibilities at a single location, an office or a factory; however, it is important for a business to get close to markets and to sources of supply and to have a responsible manager in those far-flung locations.

- **Fiscal** – your earlier studies of transfer pricing will have stressed the efforts made by governments to prevent companies taking advantage of local favourable tax regimes. Nevertheless, this still remains a reason for decentralisation and even within the UK there are tax incentives for operating in areas such as Belfast, Scunthorpe or parts of Lanarkshire designated as Enterprise Zones.

- **Training** – it is claimed that a divisional structure can provide a training ground for future members of top management enabling budding chief executives to acquire the required business skills in an environment that provides a stern, but not impossible, test. These managers are given a sense of independence that should allow them to flourish.

- **Releasing top management** – in order to survive and expand time has to be found and efforts made by top management for strategic planning. Delegation of responsibility for mundane matters makes such time available and efforts possible.

2.3 Problems of decentralisation

Whilst it is generally agreed that some degree of decentralisation is essential for the efficient running of a large business, there are some inherent difficulties.

- **Lack of goal congruence** – having set up a number of autonomous divisions run by managers all keen to show themselves as potential main board members, the danger arises that divisional managers will make decisions which, whilst in the best interests of their divisions, are not in the best interest of the company as a whole. This lack of 'goal congruence' leads to 'suboptimal' or 'dysfunctional' decisions, which in part is a result of the inevitable interdependence of divisions. It is often suggested that a necessary condition for successful decentralisation is for:

  - the business to have very separate activities

  - divisions to be independent of each other

–   central management to be able to control divisions to avoid the problems of lack of goal congruence.

However, it is unlikely that these conditions will ever apply since a decentralised structure will either have arisen as a result of splitting up a business that formerly acted as one unit or else by a company taking over businesses with whom it traded.

- **Cost** – the benefits of a large centralised structure result from the possibility of achieving economies of scale. One centralised buying department can achieve more favourable terms and requires fewer staff than if each division has its own buying function. Many examples such as this can be identified indicating that a decentralised organisation may be more costly to operate than a centralised one. Large companies overcome these problems by setting up centralised services, such as accounts departments, but there are problems of controllability and acceptability of these centralised services. One particular example of a cost of decentralisation that has been identified is a loss of 'managerial talent' who might be able to run a division without extending themselves to their full potential.

  There is one company asset that is often put under central control whatever the incentive for decentralisation, and that is cash. Efficient cash management can be achieved much more effectively if all cash balances are centrally controlled. If 'head office' has one single bank account with a nil balance the company will incur no interest charges; but if one division has a balance of £50,000 in hand in one bank and another division has an overdraft of £50,000 in a different bank then there will be a net interest cost.

- **Loss of central control** – with decentralisation top management loses some element of control to managers of independent, autonomous divisions. An effective system of divisional reporting should overcome this problem, but there is always likely to be some decisions made that main board directors feel are inappropriate. An additional problem is the attitudes of senior management and particularly chief executives who set up decentralised structures but then are unwilling to let loose the reins, still wishing to have complete day-to-day control of all aspects of the business.

- **Need for divisional reporting** – whilst an efficient information system is important in any organisation, it is even more important in decentralised firms. In order for effective control of divisions, a suitable reporting system producing the key figures that top management need must be installed, understood and operated conscientiously. The information is needed to help in decisions over divisions and to monitor divisional performance and motivate the staff.

3   Divisional assessment

3.1   Introduction

Having decentralised, it is essential that senior management monitors and controls the performance of the divisions and those with direct responsibility for those divisions. An accounting information system (a management control system) must be in place to allow for divisional assessment. The system used must have a close bearing on divisional goals and must recognise that some costs of a division will be controllable by its managers and some will not.

3.2 Methods

A range of methods is available for assessing divisional performance, the two most common being:

- return on investment (ROI)

- residual income (RI).

These are discussed fully in the next two sections of this chapter. However other methods exist.

- **Variance analysis** – is a standard means of monitoring and controlling performance; care must be taken in identifying the controllability of and responsibility for each variance.

- **Ratio analysis** – there are several profitability and liquidity measures that can be applied to divisional performance reports, as discussed later.

- **Other management ratios** – under this heading would come contribution per key factor and sales per employee or square foot, as well as industry-specific ratios such as transport costs per mile, brewing costs per barrel, overheads per chargeable hour, etc.

- **Other information** – such as staff turnover, market share, new customers gained, innovative products or services developed.

3.3 Points on performance measures

The information system and reports that it produces on divisional performance should follow three simple principles:

- **Timeliness** – any report should be produced sufficiently quickly after the end of an accounting period (week, month, quarter) to allow corrective action to be taken on any unsatisfactory performance. There is a balance to maintain here between the speed with which information is produced, the accuracy of that information and the cost of producing the figures.

- **Goal congruence** – the performance measures used, the assessment criteria, should not encourage divisional managers to make decisions which show their divisions performing well against the criteria set but adopting strategies which are against the well-being of the company as a whole. An example might be a sales department that is judged on total volume of sales made irrespective of the price charged or the credit worthiness of the customers.

- **Controllability** – the important measure of divisional performance will be linked to profit but care has to be taken in deciding how that profit is calculated. Much is written on this aspect of divisional assessment and five factors to consider are:

  - **Definition of controllable or managed cost** – a controllable cost is defined as a cost that can be influenced by its budget holder. It is not always possible to predetermine responsibility, because the reason for deviation from expected performance may only become evident later.

  - **Division or manager** – the measure of profit will depend upon whether it is the performance of the division or its manager that is being assessed as discussed below.

- **Short-term v long-term** – few costs are controllable in the short term and it is only in the longer term that action can be taken to control most costs. For instance, if the rent on premises is deemed to be too high, moving an office or a factory cannot happen at a week's notice. This means that short-term performance reports should concentrate on those costs controllable in the short term.

- **Absorption v marginal format** – it is often suggested that a marginal costing format for profit statements and performance reports is more appropriate for management purposes. In divisional assessment there is an argument in favour of a marginal format to assess divisional managers since many fixed costs with which a division may be charged are unlikely to be under the control of the manager. However some fixed costs will be controllable at divisional level. It is suggested that a use of absorption costing information may, on the one hand, be demotivating (in view of uncontrollable costs it contains); on the other hand, it might encourage divisional managers (and therefore senior management) to question the wisdom of using certain central services whose costs are apportioned out to divisions.

- **Interdependence** – whilst it is a desirable aim in a divisionalised organisation that the actions of one division cannot affect the performance of another, in most cases it is unrealistic. When assessing divisional performance, care has to be taken in deciding the true cause of any adverse performance by a division.

3.4 Divisional v managerial performance

The main board of a decentralised company will wish to assess two aspects of performance:

- the personal performance of the divisional manager

- the economic performance of the manager's division.

The type of measures used and the way in which they are evaluated will vary according to who or what is being assessed.

It is quite possible that the best manager within an organisation produces the worst divisional profit; because that manager is operating in the toughest or newest market, but is still doing well under the circumstances. By the same token good divisional performance might not indicate a well-run division and a competent manager, but rather a controllable business environment. This raises the issue of performance targets. An organisation will compare the performance of divisions and set targets for managers, but this will have to be done with caution. Targets set should take into account:

- the difficulty of the economic environment in which a division is operating

- the motivational value of tough or lenient targets for the divisional manager concerned.

Added to the difficulty or leniency of targets, the question must be asked of profit-based measures, 'which profit to use?' To answer this question the proforma below shows a profit and loss account (section of a performance report) for a division.

	£000	£000
Outside sales		X
Internal transfers		$\underline{X}$
		X
Variable cost of goods sold and transferred	(X)	
Other variable divisional costs	$\underline{(X)}$	
		$\underline{(X)}$
Contribution		$\underline{X}$
Depreciation on controllable fixed assets	(X)	
Other controllable fixed costs	$\underline{(X)}$	
		$\underline{(X)}$
Controllable operating profit (1)		X
Interest on controllable investment		$\underline{(X)}$
Controllable residual income before tax (2)		X
Non-controllable divisional fixed costs	(X)	
Apportioned head office costs	(X)	
Interest on non-controllable investment	$\underline{(X)}$	
		$\underline{(X)}$
Net residual income before tax (3)		$\underline{X}$

Table: Example of a performance report for a division

The features of this statement are:

- **Absence of tax charges** – it is generally felt that the tax charge of a company cannot be controlled at divisional level and therefore any profit-based measures should be pre-tax.

- **Inclusion of interest charges** – this is a contentious issue and is discussed further when explaining the two main measures ROI and RI.

- **Which profit?** – a divisional manager's performance should be assessed by reference to figures (1) or (2) whereas the division, which received the benefits from head office costs and other non-controllable elements even if the manager cannot influence them, should be assessed by reference to figure (3).

4 Return on investment (ROI)

4.1 Introduction

Return on investment (ROI), or return on capital employed, is calculated for an investment centre for a particular period as follows:

$$\text{ROI} = \frac{\text{Earnings before interest and tax}}{\text{Capital employed}} \times 100$$

KEY POINT

The Return On Investment should show the return on capital employed for a division. It includes profits from all projects and controllable costs for that division for a specific year.

If assessing the performance of a manager the earnings figure should be controllable operating profit, and capital employed should be controllable investment. When assessing a division's performance costs and assets that are not controllable at divisional level could be included, although all interest costs are usually excluded. This is very similar to the return on capital employed (ROCE) traditionally used to analyse capital investment projects; the only difference is that here the profits from all projects for a single year are compared to the book value of all investments, whereas in investment appraisal the profits of a single investment project over the several years of that investment's life are compared to the book value of that one single investment.

The return on investment is widely used by external analysts of company performance when the primary ratio is broken down into its two secondary ratios.

$$\text{ROI} = \frac{\text{Earnings}}{\text{Capital employed}} \times 100 = \frac{\text{Sales}}{\text{Capital employed}} \times \frac{\text{Earnings}}{\text{Sales}} \times 100$$

On the right, the first term is the asset turnover ratio and the second is the net profit percentage. These are discussed later in the chapter.

4.2 Advantages of ROI

Just as the IRR suffers from comparison with the NPV, so the return on investment is regarded as inferior to the residual income; nevertheless it is widely used and has several good features.

- As a relative measure it enables comparisons to be made with divisions or companies of different sizes. It could be argued that it is particularly appropriate for profit centres rather than investment centres since the former are not in a position to increase overall profit by undertaking further capital investments.

- It is used externally and is well understood by users of accounts.

- The primary ratio splits down into secondary ratios for more detailed analysis as mentioned above and discussed further later.

- ROI forces managers to make good use of existing capital resources and focuses attention on them, particularly when funds for further investment are limited.

- The nature of the measure is such that it can clearly be improved not just by increasing profit but also by reducing capital employed; it therefore encourages reduction in the level of assets such as obsolete equipment and excessive working capital.

4.3 Disadvantages of ROI

The disadvantages fall into two categories: those that are problems common to both ROI and RI; and those that are specific to ROI.

Specific disadvantages

- **Disincentive to invest** – a divisional manager will not wish to make an investment that provides an adequate return as far as the overall company is concerned if it reduces the division's current ROI. By the same token existing assets may be sold if, by doing so, ROI is improved even though those assets are generating a reasonable profit.

- **ROI improves with age** – on the other side of the coin most conventional depreciation methods will result in ROI improving with the age of an asset, being unsatisfactory initially then improving as the net book value of assets improves. This might encourage divisions hanging on to old assets and again deter them from investing in new ones. Alternatively a division may try to improve its ROI still further by leasing its assets. It is suggested that gross book value or even replacement cost should be used when evaluating performance. Also complex depreciation calculations are recommended by academics to overcome some of these difficulties.

- **Corporate objectives** of maximising total shareholders' wealth or the total profit of the company are not achieved by making decisions on the basis of ROI. In this way, as a relative measure, it can be compared to the internal rate of return whose use is also dysfunctional.

General problems

Whether it be ROI or RI that are used, there are certain problems common to both measures.

- **Calculation of profit** – apart from issues such as its controllability mentioned earlier there is some scope, even within the strictures of a group accounting policy, for some variation in treatment of depreciation. Also the need to increase profit may lead to cutting down on discretionary costs such as training, advertising and maintenance which, whilst improving short-term profit figures, will jeopardise the long-term future of a business. Standards for these should be set and monitored.

- **Asset measurement** – again group policies should ensure a consistent treatment, but comparison is difficult when some divisions buy and some lease assets. Thought has to be given to the treatment of permanent bank overdrafts; are these current liabilities or a source of finance?

- **Conflict with investment decisions** – the performance of a division will be influenced by investment decisions that it makes; however those decisions should be made on the basis of NPV calculations, whereas the subsequent performance of the division is assessed by a different criterion. Clearly there is likely to be a problem when a long-term investment decision is accepted, but the short-term effect on profit is detrimental. Again academics recommend changing depreciation methods so that the ROI or RI calculation is consistent with DCF calculations. A more realistic approach, where the actual cash flows associated with an investment that has been made can be identified, suggests that the performance of a division should be carried out by comparing those actual cash flows with the budgeted figures used when the initial investment decision was made.

Activity 1

The Arcadia division of Botten Ltd currently has an investment base of £2.4m and annual profits of £0.48m. It is considering the following three investments, funds for which will be supplied by the company.

Project	A	B	C
Initial outlay (£000)	1,400	600	400
Annual earnings (£000)	350	200	88

You are required to find the current ROI of the Arcadia division, the ROI of each investment and the ROI of Arcadia with each of the three additional investments added to current earnings in turn.

Feedback to this activity is at the end of the chapter.

Activity 2

McKinnon Ltd sets up a new division in Blair Atholl investing £800,000 in fixed assets with an anticipated useful life of 10 years and no scrap value. Annual profits before depreciation are expected to be a steady £200,000.

You are required to calculate the division's ROI for its first three years by expressing annual (post depreciation) profits as a percentage of the book value of assets at the start of each year.

Feedback to this activity is at the end of the chapter.

5 Residual income (RI)

5.1 Introduction

In view of the disadvantages of ROI, particularly its tendency to induce under-investment, most management authors recommend that the performance of investment centres is assessed by calculating an absolute measure of profitability – residual income – as follows:

RI = Controllable profit – Imputed interest charge on controllable divisional investment

The two figures shown in the earlier profit and loss account were residual income figures; one (with controllable profit and controllable investment) being used to assess a manager's performance, the other (with all costs included) being used to assess the performance of the division. The rate at which interest is charged on assets is open to debate; various possibilities exist:

- **Group cost of capital** – commonly used although it reflects the risk of the group as a whole and not the individual divisions.

- **Current group ROI** – again the specific circumstances of the division are overlooked.

- **Different rates** – either of the above might be starting points for an interest rate but it is then adjusted for the specific circumstances of the group: the business environment, the type of investments being made and the motivational requirements for the divisional manager. It may be necessary to use different interest rates for different types of asset.

5.2 Advantages of RI

Residual income overcomes many of the disadvantages of ROI, specifically:

- It reduces the problem of under investing or failing to accept projects with ROIs greater than the group target but less than the division's current ROI.

- As a consequence it is more consistent with the objective of maximising the total profitability of the group.

- It is possible to use different rates of interest for different types of asset.

- The cost of financing a division is brought home to divisional managers.

Despite these advantages (and there are few significant disadvantages that are specific to RI apart from the difficulty of comparison with different sized enterprises), it is not as widely used as ROI. In one of the more recent surveys on the subject, albeit with transatlantic origins, the methods used amongst a sample of 459 companies were:

	%
ROI only	65
Both ROI and RI	28
RI only	2
Other criteria	4
No response	1
	100

Activity 3

Division Z has the following financial performance:

Operating profit	£40,000
Operating assets	£150,000
Cost of borrowing	10%

Would the division wish to accept a new possible investment costing £10,000 which would earn profit of £2,000 pa if the evaluation was on the basis of

(a)   ROI

(b)   Residual income?

Feedback to this activity is at the end of the chapter.

6   Ratio analysis

6.1   Introduction

KEY POINT

Ratio analysis can be used as a method of assessing divisional performance. Various ratios can be calculated and compared using a ratio pyramid.

One important means of assessing performance both of companies by outside observers and of divisions by senior management is by the use of assorted accounting ratios. The reason for this is the difficulty of getting a true picture of performance by just using one figure. The starting point for ratio analysis is the primary ratio ROI which then splits down into the asset turnover ratio and net profit percentage. The first of these, asset turnover, then leads on to various liquidity ratios whilst the net profit percentage can be investigated further by calculating additional profitability measures.

The whole process is best shown as a ratio pyramid or ratio tree.

6.2   Ratio pyramid

The initial split of ROI into secondary ratios has been mentioned before.

$$\text{ROI}^{(1)} = \frac{\text{Profit}}{\text{Capital employed}} \times 100$$

$$\text{Net profit \%age}^{(2)} = \frac{\text{Profit}}{\text{Turnover}} \times 100 \qquad \text{Asset turnover}^{(3)} = \frac{\text{Turnover}}{\text{Capital employed}}$$

They are linked since (1) = (2) × (3).

After this there is no clear relationship, although net profit percentage can be investigated by finding:

$$\text{Gross profit percentage} = \frac{\text{Gross profit}}{\text{Turnover}} \times 100$$

and

$$\text{Operating ratios} = \frac{\text{Various expenses}}{\text{Turnover}} \times 100$$

Asset turnover can be investigated by finding:

$$\frac{\text{Turnover}}{\text{Fixed assets}} \quad \text{and} \quad \frac{\text{Turnover}}{\text{Net current assets}}$$

The first pair of ratios (or group of ratios) would require careful study if the net profit percentage indicated problems over profitability to determine whether this was due to an unduly low margin or poor control of overheads. The second pair of ratios would indicate whether sufficient sales were being generated and whether working capital was being sufficiently well controlled. If a problem was detected in this last area then various liquidity ratios would be found:

$$\text{Current ratio} = \frac{\text{current assets}}{\text{current liabilities}}$$

$$\begin{array}{l}\text{Quick ratio} \\ \text{(Acid test ratio)}\end{array} = \frac{\text{quick assets (CA's} - \text{stock)}}{\text{current liabilities}}$$

$$\text{Debtors period} = \frac{\text{debtors}}{\text{daily credit sales}}$$

$$\text{Stock period} = \frac{\text{stock}}{\text{daily cost of sales}}$$

$$\text{Creditors period} = \frac{\text{creditors}}{\text{daily credit purchases}}$$

These ratios could be found using year-end figures or average figures. In some divisionalised companies some of these liquidity ratios are less important since the assets are managed centrally. Comparison would be made with group standards, other divisions, other periods and other firms in the same business.

Example

The example which follows shows an evaluation of the production, commercial and financial management of a company using key ratios.

The following information relates to a company manufacturing consumable goods.

	Actual		Budget
	20X5/6	20X6/7	20X7/8
	£000	£000	£000
Sales	215	236	276
Less: Production costs:			
Material	79	82	96
Labour – direct	34	33	37
Labour – indirect	35	39	44
Other costs	26	29	36
	174	183	213
Administration	21	26	33
Selling	6	7	7
Distribution	3	3	4
	204	219	257
Net profit before tax	11	17	19

Balance sheet (at year end)

Fixed assets at cost	120	155	175
Less: Depreciation	(65)	(65)	(80)
	55	90	95
Stocks and work-in-progress	55	62	68
Debtors	35	32	34
Bank	4	4	3
	94	98	105
Less: Current liabilities	(17)	(13)	(15)
	77	85	90
	132	175	185

	Actual		*Budget*
	20X5/6	*20X6/7*	*20X7/8*
Number of people employed:			
Average during year:			
Direct	43	41	47
Works indirect	31	35	40
Administration	30	37	36
Sales	6	7	7
	110	120	130
Floor space occupied (square feet)	30,000	30,000	32,000

Give your interpretation of the production, commercial and financial management of the company over the period shown illustrating your conclusion with selected key ratios through the period.

Solution

Evaluation of performance

			Budget
	20X5/6	*20X6/7*	*20X7/8*
Profitability			
Profit: Capital employed	8.3%	9.7%	10.3%
Profit: Sales	5.1%	7.2%	6.9%
Sales: Capital employed	1.63 times	1.35 times	1.49 times
Production costs			
% of works cost	%	%	%
Materials	45.4	44.9	45.0
Direct labour	19.5	18.0	17.4
Indirect labour	20.1	21.3	20.7
Other costs	15.0	15.8	16.9
	100.0	100.0	100.0
Labour			
Indirect/Direct			
Monetary values (£)	1.03	1.18	1.19
Numbers	0.72	0.85	0.85
£ per employee per annum:			
Direct	£791	£804	£787
Indirect	£1,129	£1,114	£1,100
Profit:			
Per direct worker	£256	£415	£404
Per indirect worker	£354	£485	£475
Sales			
Selling costs/Sales	2.8%	3.0%	2.5%
Sales per sales employee	£35,833	£33,714	£39,429
Profit per sales employee	£1,833	£2,428	£2,714

Financial control

Stock period			
Stock and WIP: Production cost	115 days	124 days	117 days
Debtors period			
Debtors: Sales	59 days	49 days	45 days
Creditors period			
Current liabilities: Materials	78 days	58 days	57 days
Current ratio			
Current assets/Current liabilities	5.5	7.5	7.0
Acid test			
(Debtors + Bank)/Current liabilities	2.3	2.8	2.5

Interpretation

- **Profitability** – The profit increase from £11,000 to £17,000 represented an increase of more than 50% from a sales volume increase of only 10%. The ROCE improved whilst sales as a percentage of capital employed declined, indicating increased efficiency but lower utilisation. This has been recognised in the higher sales to capital employed set for the next budget. Although budgeted sales are much higher for 20X7/8 the target profit to sales figure is reduced suggesting effort to increase volume at the expense of price.

- **Production** – Material content as a proportion of total cost remains constant whilst direct labour is declining. Other costs have shown an increase in proportion suggesting a change in production methods. This is supported by the increased ratio and cost of indirect compared with direct employees. Profit per worker of both categories has risen whilst earnings have remained constant suggesting improved productivity as a result of plant and methods rather than labour. Selling costs to sales did not change significantly, the addition to staff being represented by higher volume of turnover. Since no increase is planned in staff numbers to achieve the substantially higher sales budgeted for 20X7/8 there is still some capacity available in the existing sales force.

- **Balance sheet** – Plant has increased this year and a further increase is planned for the coming year. The higher stock relates to the increased turnover budgeted but maintenance of the debtors figure suggests a quicker turnover confirmed by the debtors turnover rate. All working capital ratios are better than standard supporting interpretation of effective financial control. The current year indicates investment in new equipment reflected in higher productivity from labour. The budget forecasts the intention to continue this trend through the next period.

Comprehensive example

The following example requires a use of both the major performance assessment measures, ROI and RI, as well as the assorted accounting ratios just discussed.

Babble plc has decentralised its operations into autonomous product divisions. All divisional managers are responsible for all aspects of the operations of their divisions, including revenue, expenditure, the financing and acquisition of assets, and general cash management. Head office, nevertheless, reserves the right to make such charges on a division as it deems necessary.

The performance of divisions and of divisional managers is measured on the basis of their return on investment (ROI) before taxation.

Division X was set up in 20X0 and is managed by Mr Mouth. It is required to produce a rate of return of 20% per annum. Division Y has been in existence for 20 years and is managed by Mr Blab. Because it sells a much older product and is in a less risky line of business, the required rate of return is 16% only. The company's average cost of capital on the same basis is 18%.

Both Mr Mouth and Mr Blab were appointed on 1 January 20X1 on four-year service contracts. As these contracts will shortly be due for renewal, the performance of these two managers over their first three years of employment is to be evaluated in order to determine the need for revision of the remuneration clauses in their contracts.

The financial results for the two divisions for the years 20X1 – 20X3 are given below.

	Division X (£000)			Division Y (£000)		
	20X1	20X2	20X3	20X1	20X2	20X3
Estimated industry sales	10,000	15,000	17,000	31,000	34,000	42,000
Division sales	1,100	1,700	3,350	3,300	3,500	3,600
Direct labour	165	240	430	730	720	790
Direct materials	110	160	320	370	480	510
Plant, equipment depreciation	50	68	97	6	6	7
Plant leases	22	41	54	–	–	13
Factory rent	–	–	–	20	20	20
Maintenance and repairs	35	38	52	115	130	142
Energy costs	50	79	112	70	80	81
Indirect production overheads	100	142	205	377	369	372
Research and development	63	67	89	15	10	12
Advertising, sales promotion	78	81	147	193	211	215
Other committed costs	178	231	349	699	714	620
Other managed costs	104	113	315	330	310	298
Head office allocated costs	110	340	840	330	350	360
Total costs	1,065	1,600	3,010	3,255	3,400	3,440
Net profit	35	100	340	45	100	160
Assets employed:						
Fixed (net book value)	500	700	900	50	45	47
Current	500	500	800	450	465	433
	1,000	1,200	1,700	500	510	480
Liabilities:						
Long-term loans	90	460	560	–	–	–
Current	35	70	170	50	60	80
	125	530	730	50	60	80
Return on net investment	4%	15%	35%	10%	22%	40%

You are required to compare the performance of the two divisions, stating which manager and which division appears to have achieved the better performance and calculating those financial ratios which you feel will be of assistance.

Solution

On the face of it both divisions have performed extremely well and one would be inclined to congratulate the managers of both division X and division Y. They have both shown significant increases in profit and in return on net investment and their ROI figures exceed their respective targets of 20% and 16%.

However, it is possible to manipulate ROI figures by 'window dressing', by cutting down on discretionary costs or, most deviously, by aiming to reduce the capital employed figure rather than increase profit. This practice can be circumvented by assessing divisions using residual income (RI) rather than return on investment (ROI). These are calculated below with two adjustments made; long-term loans are excluded from liabilities in order to get a correct figure for capital employed; also head office costs are excluded, the resultant figures give a better measure of the performance of Messr's Blab & Mouth. These profits will be used for all subsequent calculations.

	Division X (£000)			Division Y (£000)		
	20X1	20X2	20X3	20X1	20X2	20X3
Assets	1,000	1,200	1,700	500	510	480
Current liabilities	(35)	(70)	(170)	(50)	(60)	(80)
Capital employed	965	1,130	1,530	450	450	400
Net profit	35	100	340	45	100	160
Head office costs	110	340	840	330	350	360
Controllable profit	145	440	1,180	375	450	520
Interest (@20% or 16%)	(193)	(226)	(306)	(72)	(72)	(64)
Residual income	(48)	214	874	303	378	456

This shows that although in relative terms Y has done better than X, in absolute terms X has performed better – Mr Mouth can be said to have contributed more to Babble plc's profit. This appears to reflect X's investment programme which has produced the rewards of high profits, whereas Y has made little or no investment over the period and the ROI is no doubt benefiting from the effects of decreasing net book values of assets. This effect is amplified by the fact that Y appears to be renting premises whereas, presumably, X has bought its factory.

Other useful figures to calculate are:

Net profit percentage

	X	Y
20X1	$\dfrac{145}{1,100} \times 100 = 13.2\%$	$\dfrac{375}{3,300} \times 100 = 11.4\%$
20X2	$\dfrac{440}{1,700} \times 100 = 25.9\%$	$\dfrac{450}{3,500} \times 100 = 12.9\%$
20X3	$\dfrac{1,180}{3,350} \times 100 = 35.2\%$	$\dfrac{520}{3,600} \times 100 = 14.4\%$

Both divisions have been showing increased profits, although the growth of division X is considerably greater than that of Y. Since X is a new division it has the greater scope for growth; however, since it also has the greater scope for making a complete disaster of its new function, Mr Mouth deserves credit.

Sales growth

	X	Y
20X1/X2	$\left(\dfrac{1,700}{1,100} - 1\right) \times 100 = 54.5\%$	$\left(\dfrac{3,500}{3,300} - 1\right) \times 100 = 6.1\%$
20X2/X3	$\left(\dfrac{3,350}{1,700} - 1\right) \times 100 = 97.1\%$	$\left(\dfrac{3,600}{3,500} - 1\right) \times 100 = 2.9\%$

Again X is seen to perform well with significant growth in its new area. When this is matched with the increasing net profit percentage the eight-fold increase in profit is explained. The increase in the profit percentage may, in part, be attributable to this growth as fixed costs are more easily recovered at higher sales levels. Division Y is still growing but the falling growth rate should be investigated to see if it is due to the end of several product cycles, a fall in the overall market or inefficiency.

Market shares

	X	Y
20X1	$\dfrac{1,100}{10,000} \times 100 = 11.0\%$	$\dfrac{3,300}{31,000} \times 100 = 10.6\%$
20X2	$\dfrac{1,700}{15,000} \times 100 = 11.3\%$	$\dfrac{3,500}{34,000} \times 100 = 10.3\%$
20X3	$\dfrac{3,350}{17,000} \times 100 = 19.7\%$	$\dfrac{3,600}{42,000} \times 100 = 8.6\%$

This shows that, as hoped from a new division, X's market share is growing; Y's share on the other hand is falling which must reflect badly on Mr Blab.

Other useful ratios that could be found would be:

- **Asset turnover** – to see if assets are being utilised efficiently.

- **Gross profit percentage** – to compare margins from year to year.

- **Revised ROI figures** – based on controllable profit.

It is difficult to compare the first two of these ratios for the two divisions since they are operating in different markets and may be involved in very dissimilar businesses. Seeing how each division's figures changed from year to year might prove instructive.

Other figures that could help would be individual costs as a percentage of sales; such figures as discretionary costs:

- maintenance and repairs

- research and development

- advertising, sales promotion.

These would indicate the extent to which each manager is looking for long-term, sustainable growth in profits. There is the danger that, in view of the imminent review of their contracts, the divisional managers may be trying to produce impressive short-term results at the expense of future profits.

Division X seems to have been successfully launched by Mr Mouth whereas Mr Blab's slowly falling market share gives cause for concern.

Summary

Key points of this chapter are:

- Decentralisation is the process of devolving the authority to make decisions; the divisions thus created are most likely to be investment centres or at least profit centres although they may only be cost centres.

- A cost centre is a location or function for which costs may be ascertained; a profit centre is a segment of a business where costs are incurred and revenue received, and performance is evaluated by reference to profit; an investment centre is one in which the manager has control over profit and also over investment decisions.

- The reasons for decentralisation include: size, need for specialists, motivation, uncertainty, fiscal, geographical, training and releasing top management.

- The problems of decentralisation include: lack of goal congruence, cost and loss of central control.

- The most common methods of assessing divisional performance involve the use of return on investment (ROI) and/or residual income (RI); however, other methods include: variance analysis, ratio analysis and other management information and ratios.

$$\text{ROI} \quad = \quad \frac{\text{Controllable divisional profit}}{\text{Controllable divisional investment}} \times 100$$

$$\text{RI} \quad = \quad \text{Controllable divisional profit} \quad - \quad \text{Imputed interest cost on controllable divisional investment}$$

- Both measures suffer from: difficulty in defining which profit to use, asset measurement, and conflict with investment decisions. ROI is often criticised for its disincentive to divisions to invest, the fact that it improves with the age of an asset and that corporate objectives are not achieved by acting on the basis of ROI information.

- The primary ratio, ROI, can be split into two secondary ratios: asset turnover and net profit percentage. The first leads on to various liquidity ratios, the second to other measures of profitability.

Having completed your study of this chapter you should have achieved the following learning outcomes:

- evaluate and recommend appropriate control measures

- identify problems in performance measurement and recommend solutions.

Self-test questions

1   What is an investment centre? (2.1)

2   What are the problems of decentralising? (2.3)

3   What are the advantages of ROI as a means of divisional appraisal? (4.2)

4   How do you calculate residual income? (5.1)

5   Name four liquidity ratios. (6.2)

Practice questions

Question 1: Theta Ltd

Theta Ltd compares the performance of its subsidiaries by return on investment (ROI) using the following formula:

Profit: Depreciation is calculated on a straight-line basis.

Losses on sale of assets are charged against profit in the year of the sale.

Capital employed: Net current assets, at the average value throughout the year.

Fixed assets, at original cost less accumulated depreciation as at the end of the year.

Theta Ltd, whose cost of capital is 14% per annum, is considering acquiring Alpha Ltd whose performance has been calculated on a similar basis to that shown above except that fixed assets are valued at original cost.

During the past year, apart from normal trading, Alpha Ltd was involved in the following separate transactions:

(A) It bought equipment on 1 November 20X4 (the start of its financial year) at a cost of £120,000. Resulting savings were £35,000 for the year; these are expected to continue at that level throughout the 6 years' expected life of the asset after which it will have no scrap value.

(B) On 1 November 20X4 it sold a piece of equipment that had cost £200,000 when bought exactly 3 years earlier. The expected life was 4 years, with no scrap value. This equipment had been making a contribution to profit of £30,000 per annum before depreciation and realised £20,000 on sale.

(C) It negotiated a bank overdraft of £20,000 for the year to take advantage of quick payment discounts offered by creditors; this reduced costs by £4,000 per annum.

(D) To improve liquidity, it reduced stocks by an average of £25,000 throughout the year. This resulted in reduced sales with a reduction of £6,000 per annum contribution.

The financial position of Alpha Ltd for the year from 1 November 20X4 to 31 October 20X5, excluding the outcomes of transactions (A) to (D) above, was:

	£000
Profit for the year	225
Fixed assets:	
Original cost	1,000
Accumulated depreciation	475
Net current assets (average for the year)	250

Required:

(a) Calculate the ROI of Alpha Ltd using its present basis of calculation:

    (i) if none of the transactions (A) to (D) had taken place

    (ii) if transaction (A) had taken place but not (B), (C) or (D)

    (iii) if transaction (B) had taken place but not (A), (C) or (D)

    (iv) if transaction (C) had taken place but not (A), (B) or (D)

    (v) if transaction (D) had taken place but not (A), (B) or (C)

(b) Calculate the ROI as in (a)(i) to (a)(v) above using Theta Ltd's basis of calculation

(c) Explain briefly whether there would have been any lack of goal congruence as between Theta Ltd and the management of Alpha Ltd (assuming that Alpha Ltd had been acquired by Theta Ltd on 1 November 20X4 and that Theta Ltd's basis of calculation was used) in respect of:

(i) transaction (A)

(ii) transaction (B).

Taxation is to be ignored. **(25 marks)**

Question 2: Hawlit Ltd

Hawlit Ltd, a transport company, is planning its future investment strategy. Hawlit's best projections of profit outcome are dependent upon the cost of diesel fuel.

Annual investment level (£000)	Annual net income at following costs per gallon:				
	£1.20 (£000)	£1.25 (£000)	£1.30 (£000)	£1.40 (£000)	£1.50 (£000)
350	55	52	46	40	30
400	60	58	52	46	35
450	68	63	55	47	35
500	72	68	58	49	34
550	74	67	56	43	30
600	75	64	53	40	25
Estimated probability of outcome	0.1	0.1	0.4	0.3	0.1

The company's minimum required rate of return is 10% pa.

Required:

(a) Compute, for each level of investment, the return on investment (ROI) and the residual income

(10 marks)

(b) Calculate the optimal investment level, stating your reasons **(3 marks)**

(c) Evaluate the merits of residual income and return on investment as measures of performance. **(12 marks)**

(Total: 25 marks)

For the answers to these questions, see the 'Answers' section at the end of the book.

Feedback to activities

Activity 1

$$\text{Return on investment, ROI} = \frac{\text{Earnings}}{\text{Capital investment}} \times 100$$

(a) Current position

$$\text{ROI} = \frac{480}{2,400} \times 100 = 20\%$$

(b) Additional investments

$$\text{A: ROI} = \frac{350}{1,400} \times 100 = 25\%$$

$$\text{B: ROI} = \frac{200}{600} \times 100 = 33^{1}/_{3}\%$$

$$\text{C: ROI} = \frac{88}{400} \times 100 = 22\%$$

(c) Potential position

$$\text{Arcadia + A:} \quad \text{ROI} = \frac{830}{3,800} \times 100 = 21.8\%$$

$$\text{Arcadia + B:} \quad \text{ROI} = \frac{680}{3,000} \times 100 = 22.7\%$$

$$\text{Arcadia + C:} \quad \text{ROI} = \frac{568}{2,800} \times 100 = 20.3\%$$

Note: although all three projects have returns that are greater than the current 20%, once project B is accepted the ROI rises to 22.7% making C look less attractive. It would be worth Arcadia's while accepting projects A and B, if this were possible since this would raise its ROI to: 1,030 ÷ 4,400 = 23.4%.

Activity 2

$$\text{ROI} = \frac{\text{Earnings before interest and tax (but after depreciation)}}{\text{Capital employed (book value at start of year)}} \times 100$$

Year	Opening book value of assets £000	Annual depreciation £000	Closing book value of assets £000	Pre-dep'n profits £000	Post-dep'n profits £000	ROI %
1	800	80	720	200	120	$\frac{120}{800} = 15\%$
2	720	80	640	200	120	$\frac{120}{720} = 17\%$
3	640	80	560	200	120	$\frac{120}{640} = 19\%$

Note: ROI increases, despite no increase in annual profits, merely as a result of the book value of assets falling. It would be more appropriate to use the average book value of assets, although the use of opening book values is common.

Activity 3

(a)   Current ROI = $\dfrac{£40,000}{£150,000}$ = 26.7%

If the investment is accepted, revised ROI

$= \dfrac{£42,000}{£160,000}$ = 26.3%

i.e. REJECT the project

(b)   Current RI = £40,000 − (10% × £150,000) = £25,000

Revised RI = £42,000 − (10% × £160,000) = £26,000

i.e. ACCEPT the project.

Note: here is a classic example of ROI giving the wrong conclusion in that a project that was worthwhile as far as the company was concerned is rejected since it reduces the division's current ROI.

Chapter 15

NON-FINANCIAL AND MULTIDIMENSIONAL PERFORMANCE MEASURES

Syllabus content

- Non-financial measures and their interaction with financial ones. (Note: candidates will be expected to use both qualitative and quantitative techniques.)

- Multidimensional models of performance (e.g. the balanced scorecard, the results and determinants framework, the performance pyramid).

- Critical success factors: links to performance indicators and corporate strategy, and their use as a basis for defining an organisation's information needs.

Contents

1   Introduction

2   Critical success factors (CSFs)

3   The balanced scorecard and the performance pyramid

4   Results and determinants

5   Not-for-profit organisations (NFPOs)

6   The nature of value for money (VFM)

1 Introduction

Critical success factors (CSFs) are the limited number of areas in which results, if they are satisfactory, will ensure successful competitive performance for the business. Sources include the industry that the business is in and the environment.

Newer approaches also consider how non-financial measures can be used in conjunction with other types of measure. We concentrate on the balanced scorecard, the performance pyramid, and the results and determinants framework (originally developed in the context of service industries).

Not-for-profit organisations use a range of both financial and non-financial measures of performance, particularly as 'making a profit' is not a consideration for them. Value for Money (VFM) is generally taken to mean the pursuit of economy, efficiency and effectiveness. It is a particularly important measure in the not-for-profit sector, but it has much relevance for all organisations.

2 Critical success factors (CSFs)

2.1 Introduction

Critical success factors (CSFs) are the limited number of areas in which results, if they are satisfactory, will ensure successful competitive performance for the business. They are the vital areas where 'things must go right' for the business to flourish.

They were developed by John Rockart at the Sloan School of Management at MIT, as an attempt to identify the real information needs of management, mainly chief executives.

There must be a clear and shared understanding of what the critical success factors of the business are, and a recognition throughout all levels of the organisation of what the overall business objectives are, and how each unit or department can contribute to satisfying these objectives. The management process itself must be integrated in the sense of sharing a common purpose and approach.

Generally, the corporate objectives are defined, e.g. increase profits, develop new products or diversify. Once they have been stated, the managers involved in strategy formulation will identify the critical success factors whose success is necessary for the organisation to flourish.

2.2 Source of CSFs

The source of critical success factors can be wide ranging. It is useful to categorise the sources to understand the nature of CSFs. Rockart claims that there are four sources for them:

(a) **the industry that the business is in** – each has CSFs that are relevant to any company within it. For example, the car industry must have as one of its CSFs 'compliance with pollution requirements regarding car exhaust gases'.

(b) **the company itself and its situation within the industry** – e.g. its competitive strategy and its geographic location. CSFs could be to develop new products, create new markets or to support the field sales force. Actions taken by a few large dominant companies in an industry will provide one or more CSFs for small companies in that industry.

(c) **the environment** – e.g. the economy, the political factors and consumer trends in the country or countries that the organisation operates in. An example used by Rockart is that, before 1973, virtually no chief executive in the USA would have stated 'energy supply availability' as a critical success factor. However, following the oil embargo many executives monitored this factor closely.

(d) **temporal organisational factors** – are areas of company activity that are unusually causing concern because they are unacceptable and need attention. Cases of too little or too much inventory might classify as a CSF for a short time during recession.

Rockart identified two types of CSF:

(a) monitoring – keeping abreast of ongoing operations

(b) building – tracking progress of the 'programmes for change' initiated by the executive.

Chief executives have both monitoring and building responsibilities and CSFs will reflect this. The CSFs will vary with the level in the hierarchy; the higher up the management triangle the more likely it is that CSFs will be of the building variety. For example, 'decentralise the organisation' and other programmes for change concerned with tracking the progress are building CSFs. 'Expand foreign sales' is a monitoring CSF that requires keeping abreast of the ongoing sales operations.

There may be more than one source of information that can be used. It will be up to the managers concerned to decide what information is required, how much of it, the frequency of collection and the level of aggregation.

Examples of information that can be used to monitor some of the CSFs of a garden furniture manufacturer include:

CSF	Information needs
Achieve quoted delivery dates	Production schedules Inventory levels
Performance to budget on major jobs	Job cost budgeted/achieved
Market success	Change in market share
Image in financial market	P/E ratio
Morale of employees	Turnover, absenteeism, sickness Informal communication

2.3 Critical success factors and performance indicators

All CSFs should have known and reliable performance measures. These are used to monitor the actual success of each factor and will require information to be supplied in a form that the executives and managers can use. We have already discussed the fact that not all the information needed will be available from existing or new information systems. If this is the case, new ways of acquiring the information will need to be evaluated.

The organisation will identify its CSFs by first determining its goals and objectives.

DEFINITION

Goals are long run attributes an organisation seeks to satisfy its mission.

DEFINITION

Objectives are time-assigned targets derived from the goals, and are set in advance of strategy.

- Goals are long-run, open-ended attributes or ends a person or organisation seeks and are sufficient for the satisfaction of the organisation's mission

- Objectives are time-assigned targets derived from the goals, and are set in advance of strategy.

Goals represent the aspiration of the organisation; the direction in which it will focus its effort. Objectives are measurable targets that an organisation sets to meet its goals. Each set of objectives will support one goal. There may be many or few objectives supporting one goal.

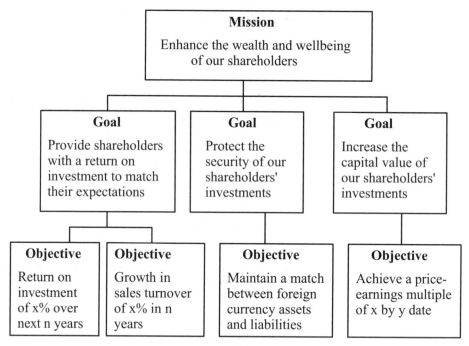

The goals, objectives, CSFs and information needs need to be aggregated to eliminate overlap and check that there are no obvious omissions. Once the objectives are identified, they can be used to determine which factors are critical for accomplishing the objective. Not all objectives are equally important. Management need to obtain a relative ranking to assign priorities; this can be carried out using techniques such as incidence scoring or pairwise comparison.

To feed back the results and obtain a consensus, all the managers involved in the strategy formulation should meet and confirm the understanding of the business strategy and its information needs to support that strategy. Any conflict between management and departments must be resolved.

The performance measure for the CSF is a characteristic of its associated objective. Knowing the units of measurement for each objective makes it easy to identify the information required.

KEY POINT

After the critical factors have been determined, two or three prime measures for each factor are found.

After the critical factors have been determined, two or three prime measures for each factor are found. Some measures use hard, factual data and these are the easiest to identify. Other measures are 'softer', such as opinions, perceptions and hunches and take more analysis to uncover their appropriate source.

One of the major problems with strategy implementation in many organisations is a failure to translate declarations of strategic purpose into a practical statement of those factors which are critical to achieving the targets, and the key tasks which will ensure success.

These issues can be addressed systematically:

- The critical success factors for the specific strategy must be agreed and scrutinised to make sure that all the factors are genuinely necessary and the list is sufficient to underpin success.

- The key tasks which are essential to the delivery of each critical success factor must be identified. These may relate to the organisation's value activities, identified in the value chain, and include improvements in support activities or changes in linkages within the value system. For example, an office supplies company with a critical success factor of customer care would underpin the CSF through the three key tasks of responding to enquiries, supplying accurate information and an efficient and quick breakdown and maintenance service. These tasks are dependent on the office supplies company's infrastructure, particularly the database of customer installations.

- Allocate management responsibility for the key tasks identified. For the office supplies company, the area which could go wrong is the maintenance of the customer database. The responsibility for this is assigned to the maintenance department but there should be linkages established with both the sales and the software department to ensure accurate information.

Activity 1

Draw Porter's value chain, identifying the areas that show where the key tasks, underpinning the critical success factor of customer care, will appear on it.

Feedback to this activity is at the end of the chapter.

2.4 CSF analysis

Analysing the CSFs allows managers to articulate their needs in terms of the information that is absolutely critical to them. The process can be illustrated as follows:

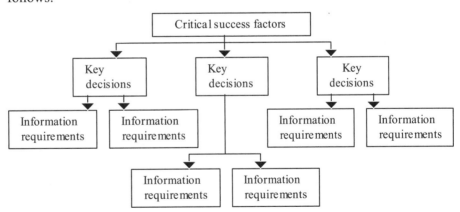

Diagram: Identification of information requirements using CSF analysis

The relationship between the critical success factors, key decisions and information requirements is a process whereby the identification of the CSFs will allow the manager to identify the key decisions related to those CSFs and then the key decisions will give a bridge into the information requirements. The point is to structure and highlight the link between what must be done and why it is needed, either to support a key decision or because it forms a key performance indicator or because it would be a measure of situational control or situational effectiveness.

CSFs provide a way of achieving a clear definition of the information that is needed, limiting the costly collection of more data than is necessary. For example, the parts department of a large organisation may have a business strategy where the CSF is to minimise the length of time a part is kept in stock. One of the key decisions related to that CSF might be to decide what quantities must be ordered. The information requirements may be the order demand.

Meeting the CSF ensures that the investment in stock is kept low and that parts are distributed quickly. IS supplies support for this, e.g. a key report would compare part purchasing with part demand patterns to help managers anticipate order demand without overstocking, whilst at the same time help avoid shortages.

The lower down in the management structure one goes, the more difficult it becomes to express only a few things that must go right, especially for those management layers that focus on gathering and filtering data for other parts of the organisation. It could be that they have no CSFs and nothing they do is critical.

2.5 Using Anthony's levels of management

As we have already discovered, the type of decision making varies depending on the levels of management.

The following tables outline the key decisions that must be taken in order to manage the particular CSF and the IS activity necessary for its support, i.e. the information requirements, for three levels of management – strategic, tactical and operational management in a manufacturing organisation.

Strategic – the top management level is associated with long term planning that is unstructured and difficult to measure. The decisions are high risk and have a major impact on the organisation.

Decision making		Information requirements	
CSF examples	**Key decisions**	**Type of IS**	**Examples**
Attain profits New products Market share Customer services Quality control Cost control	Investment needs Profit targets What to make How to sell Sales targets Location of new factory Physical requirements R&D investment	Simulation models Private viewdata Public viewdata Graphical EIS Information retrieval Operational summaries and trends	Profit forecasts Economic trends Industry trends Sales analysis SBU performance Market research Cost centre analysis Demographic survey

Tactical – this management level, e.g. SBU manager, is focused on control and probably has short-term (budget year), medium risk planning that is structured. The characteristics at this level are performance monitoring, setting rules and motivating.

Decision making		Information requirements	
CSF example	Key decision	Type of IS	Examples
Effective management and control of: • Money • People • Machines • Resources • Stock	Set standards Monitoring and action on variances Order levels and quantities Select best option for identified need Overtime introduction Specify training	Budgets Modelling Performance and exception reporting Quantitative techniques Office automation Report generators	Sales analysis Summary totals Variance reports Cash flow forecast Personnel records Management reports (for editing)

Operational – this management level, e.g. supervisory, is focused on routine day-to-day control, low risk planning that is highly structured.

Decision-making		Information requirements	
CSF example	Key decision	Type of IS	Examples
Meet targets Follow procedures Attain standards	Schedule production Requisition materials Buy stock Re-order stock Price an order Allow credit	Transaction processing Database to support enquiries e.g. • Production control • Purchase ledger • Sales ledger • Order processing	Stock list Picking list Invoices Production order Completion dates Outstanding debts

2.6 Critical set analysis

The critical set analysis is a variant of CSF analysis. It includes the analysis of the critical assumptions made as well as the critical success factors and key decisions. This approach is very much about business alignment and ensuring that the IS vision aligns with senior management's vision.

The critical sets model outlines a three-stage process to identify the IS strategy:

(a) understanding the organisation using the five forces model and value chains

(b) identifying information needs using critical sets and high level data modelling

(c) segmenting/ranking the IS/IT opportunities. This is done by analysing the critical/key assumptions by their degree of stability and their importance to the business strategy, and the scope there is for IS/IT to enhance the decision-making process.

3 The balanced scorecard and the performance pyramid

3.1 The balanced scorecard

The concept of the balanced scorecard is based on the idea that no single measure can be used to control performance. Measures such as return on investment (ROI), net profit and earnings per share (EPS) are often criticised as being short-termist and ignoring vital factors that are significant in the long term purely because they cannot be measured by some objective basis such as money value.

The term 'balanced scorecard' is credited to Kaplan (*Relevance Lost*) and Norton of the Nolan Norton Consultancy. It has become a tool for performance measurement in many businesses in the UK and North America.

The approach uses the analogy of flying an aircraft. In order to keep an aircraft safely airborne, the pilot uses a number of control devices such as rudder, airspeed measurement, visual checks and radar in order to avoid hazards such as mid-air collisions or losing ability to fly at all. The balanced scorecard therefore uses a number of perspectives in order to achieve long-term control and direction of the business.

The four quadrants

The concept of the balanced scorecard can be illustrated in a diagram.

FINANCIAL PERSPECTIVES What do our shareholders expect from us?		CUSTOMER PERSPECTIVES What do our customers expect from us?
	VISION	
INTERNAL PROCESS PERSPECTIVES How can we improve our internal processes?		INNOVATION PERSPECTIVES How do we benefit from change?

Each quadrant represents a feature of business performance.

The corporate vision of a business looks at features of performance dispassionately in order to establish indicators of performance that show that we are meeting the expectations of shareholders, customers, employees and trading partners.

Financial perspectives

Typical measures of performance are:

- ROI %
- contribution/sales %
- net profit growth
- improvement in cash flow.

Customer perspectives

Typical measures of performance are:

- increase in customer base

- increase in units sold

- increase in significant customer activity

- reduction in warranty claims

- reduction in complaints and rejections.

Internal process perspective

Typical measures of performance are:

- meeting internal project deadlines

- starting projects on time

- reduction in errors or process failures.

Innovation perspective

Typical measures of performance are:

- new money saving ideas

- registration of trade marks and/or patents

- reduction in waste or scrap by new processes

- reducing machine down time by re-engineering.

How does the balanced scorecard work?

KEY POINT

The idea behind the balanced scorecard is to arrive at a single score or number that is made up of a number of individual scores for each measure or key performance indicator.

The idea behind the balanced scorecard is to arrive at a single score or number that is made up of a number of individual scores for each measure or key performance indicator. In order to smooth out or 'normalise' the process, each score is multiplied by a weight or constant in order to assign a degree of importance to the measure. This is not a novel concept and is used by people such as internal auditors who try to measure relative risk. Like all such measures, experience of the users and a consensus view on the relative importance of the various measures is critical to the process. It is unlikely that any organisation applying the balanced scorecard will get it right first time. It will be an adaptive process of learning before the technique is fully fledged. The most obvious problem is the difficulty of measuring qualitative criteria. A measure like ROI may be flawed but it can be measured from historic money value data. It is a 'hard' measure because it is measurable in quantitative terms. A measure such as improving customer care is a 'soft measure' in that there is no objective formula that you can apply (unlike ROI). Consequently there must be a consensus view among the users on which measurers when taken together indicate that customer care has improved in the year 20X4 over the year 20X3.

Example

Assigning scores to financial perspectives
31 March 20X4

KPI	Score	Weight	Normalised score
ROI 25%	8	30%	2.4
Contribution margin 48%	10	40%	4.0
Earnings per share 75p	10	20%	2.0
Sales growth +12%	8	10%	0.8
Total			**9.2**

This score would have to be compared with an equivalent for the same time period in order to provide a meaningful frame of reference. The score will not mean very much unless it is viewed against the other three perspectives. This balanced view would allow managers to study cause and effect and consider how to change in order to improve the strategic direction of the business.

3.2 The performance pyramid

The Performance Pyramid is a multidimensional model developed by Coopers and Lybrand (now called PriceWaterhouseCoopers) in their consultancy practice to help organisations improve their information provision.

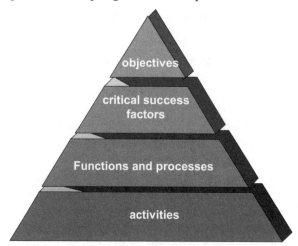

Diagram: The Performance Pyramid

Critical success factors (CSFs) relate to how objectives can be attained.

Functions and processes refer to KPIs that help to measure the achievement of CSFs.

Activities refer to the day-to-day functions that drive the organisation and the need to do these with excellence.

This model is similar in concept to the balanced scorecard in that it aims to overcome the drawbacks of traditional financial based reporting and provide a balanced view of the factors that create sustainable competitive advantage in a dynamic organisation.

The apex defines the **objectives** for the organisation:

- improve shareholder wealth

- improve ROI

- improve EPS

- improve market position

- develop innovation

- identify environmental issues

- objectives for good corporate citizenship.

The whole of this appraisal process demonstrates a commitment to strategic business information.

4 Results and determinants

4.1 Performance evaluation in service industries

In many developed countries service businesses now account for a significantly larger proportion of the economy than manufacturing. The measurement and appreciation of service businesses cover both financial and non-financial issues in seeking ways to inform management on how best to plan control and make decisions in order to achieve corporate goals. The importance of this topic was recognised in the early 1990s by the research report sponsored by CIMA written by Fitzgerald, Silvestro et al.

4.2 Key differences in measurement of services

There are four key differences between manufactured products and service products.

- **Intangibility** – The purchase of a motorcar is tangible; it is an object that can be touched. The outputs of a service provider may be performances rather than objects. When travelling by air one is influenced by many intangible factors, such as the helpfulness of the cabin crew, as well as more tangible and hence measurable aspects of the package: the arrival of your luggage with you. Customers are therefore buying a complex bundle of tangible goods and intangible services: this makes the service process difficult to control as it is hard to know what the customer values in the process. Consider the use of management consultants. The service is intangible; it can only be experienced when it is delivered.

- **Heterogeneity** – Service outputs are heterogeneous. The standard of performance may vary, especially where there is a high labour content. It is hard to ensure consistent quality from the same employee from day to day, and harder still to get comparability between employees, yet this will crucially affect what the customer receives.

- **Simultaneity of production and consumption** – The production and consumption of many services are simultaneous, for example having a meal or taking advice from your solicitor. Most services therefore cannot be counted, measured, inspected, tested or verified in advance of sale for subsequent delivery to the customer. Unlike a motorcar that delivers its potential over its useful life a service is immediate.

- **Perishability** – Services are perishable; that is, they cannot be stored. Perishability thus removes the inventory buffer frequently used by manufacturing organisations to cope with fluctuations in demand. Therefore scheduling operations and controlling quality are key management problems in services, which are made more difficult by the presence of the customer in the service process. Although the simultaneity of production and consumption enables cross-selling and the collection of feedback from customers in real time, an unfavourable impression of the service process may erode a customer's satisfaction with the service product: which of us has not fumed at slow, thoughtless service in an otherwise excellent restaurant or despaired at the time spent queuing at a supermarket checkout?

4.3 The need for a range of performance measures

Organisational control is the process of ensuring that an organisation is pursuing actions and strategies that will enable it to achieve its goals. The four unique characteristics of services cause problems in this area. The measurement and evaluation of performance are fundamental to control. We should recall the concept of 'contingency theory' that postulates that systems of control should vary according to a wide range of variables in which the chosen strategy should largely determine what is relevant. Information, both financial and non-financial, should include feed forward control via plans, budgets, standards and targets, and feedback control by analysis of significant variances and the use of a range of performance measures, both competitor-based and customer-focused. To be of use, feedback control must drive managers to take appropriate action to ensure that the direction of the enterprise is orientated towards the goals identified through the framework of planning and control.

Furthermore, the information supplied should be targeted to the needs of the various levels of management; strategic, tactical and operational. What is needed is information for diagnosis, control and performance measurement.

4.4 Results and determinants

The CIMA identifies six generic performance dimensions:

- competitive performance
- financial performance
- quality of service
- flexibility
- resource utilisation
- innovation.

This can be displayed in a matrix as shown below:

	Dimensions of performance	Measures
R		
E	Competitive performance	Market share
S		Sales growth
U		Customer base
L		
T	Financial performance	Profitability
S		Liquidity
		Capital structure
		Market ratios

D	Quality of service	Reliability
E		Responsiveness
T		Aesthetics
E		Tidiness
R		Communication
M		Competence
I		
N	Flexibility	Volume flexibility
A		Delivery speed
N		Specification of service
T		
S	Resource utilisation	Productivity
		Efficiency
	Innovation	Ability to innovate
		Performance of the innovations

4.5 Designing performance measures

We need to consider performance measures which will be relevant to service industries who strive to achieve competitive advantage. Examples of three typical service types are:

- professional services, e.g. a management consultancy

- service shops, e.g. a bank or a retailer

- mass services, e.g. a monopolistic postal entity like the Royal Mail in the UK.

The control of operations and the implementation of strategy can be delegated and understood, using a simple input-process-output model.

4.6 Competitive performance

A suggested framework for building and routinely monitoring competitive advantage is that proposed by Day and Wensley. They argue that companies may build and maintain a competitive advantage in two ways:

- by focusing on the needs of customers

- by making comparisons with significant competitors.

Ideally they should do both. A conclusion from Day and Wensley's work is that customers may be consulted when trying to measure the results of competitive success, but what determines those results largely depends on comparisons with competitors. Consequently, relevant measures of competitive and financial performance will embrace both competitor-based and customer-focused approaches.

4.7 Financial performance

Conventional financial analysis distinguishes four types of ratio: profitability, liquidity, capital structure and market ratios. Analysis of a company's performance using accounting ratios involves comparisons with past trends and/or competitors' ratios. As is well known, such time-series and cross-sectional analyses are problematical. Typical ratios could be:

- turnover per product group

- turnover per 'principal' in say a management consultancy

- % staff costs to turnover

- % space costs to turnover

- % training costs to turnover

- % net profit

- current ratio

- quick asset ratio

- % market share

- % market share increase year by year.

The 'untraceability' of common costs to product outputs and the high level of stepped fixed costs will also make the use of financial ratios problematical.

Example 1: service shop – Barclays Bank plc

Barclays Bank has segmented its business between corporate and retail customers. The bank has over 350 products and services, most of which are variants on borrowing or lending, whose profitability is tied to inter-bank borrowing and lending rates as affected by transactions with the Bank of England and government economic policy. Individual retail customers can consume a mix of these services – albeit in most cases a limited sample of the total range – via several possible service delivery processes: by post, telephone, automatic teller machines (ATMs), cashiers or the branch manager. Whilst the gross margins of individual services are known, no attempt is made to trace costs, even labour costs, to them.

Example 2: service shop – commonwealth Hotels

Each hotel (an SBU) had a general manager and a number of responsibility centres: rooms, food, bar, reception (including telephones) and marketing. Individual customers could consume any mix of these services. Here gross margins (after deducting all direct costs) were known, but indirect costs were not allocated to the responsibility centres. As a result the information was there to undertake marginal cost pricing to maximise the use of fixed capacity, and the management team was rewarded by a bonus system related to the hotel's total profit.

In this case costs were used to plan and control the SBU via responsibility centres which, in Porter's terms, constituted its 'value chain' via which the hotel added value to its services. This contrasts with the situation at Barclays, where costs were not broken down in the branch along the value chain for planning and control purposes, nor did they separate the assets and costs of the SBUs. In such service shop businesses, however, it is often not apparent how the attributes that are important to the customer are influenced by activities in the value chain. In securing a competitive advantage companies would not just look at their competitors but also use performance measures at the SBU level that are 'customer-focused'. Examples would include customer satisfaction questionnaires, estimates of customer loyalty, relative share of end-user segments, etc. Commonwealth Hotels successfully use such measures with competitor comparisons.

KEY POINT

Performance measures at the SBU level that are customer-focused include: customer satisfaction questionnaires, estimates of customer loyalty, and relative share of end-user segments.

4.8 Key points

Measures of competitive and financial performance should include both competitor-based and customer-focused measures.

There are no good reasons why the use of measures of competitive performance should vary across the three generic service types. This is also true of three of the four traditional financial performance ratios: liquidity, capital structure and market ratios.

The make-up of the fourth financial performance ratio – profitability – will vary across the three service types because of their different cost structures. Cost traceability affects the extent to which costs can be used to plan, control and make decisions in organisations, and cost collection should be done in three ways to match our input-process-output model: to inputs, to outputs and to the functional activities of the firm. Professional services have high cost traceability; mass services have low cost traceability.

Only professional services appear to use costs routinely for pricing decisions. This is a function of the culture of the service sector in that the customer pays for service on the basis of time and responsibility. An organisation with a large and complex infrastructure will 'load' its charging rates accordingly and customers pay or go elsewhere where the structure may be different (and the quality of service also). A feature of competitive strategy in such a sector is the willingness to 'low-ball' the opposition by tendering at levels designed to undercut competitors.

4.9 Quality of service

Introduction using BAA plc

BAA uses regular customer surveys for measuring customer perceptions of a wide variety of service quality attributes, including, for example, the cleanliness of its facilities, the helpfulness of its staff and the ease of finding one's way around the airport. Public correspondence is also analysed in detail, and comment cards are available in the terminals so that passengers can comment voluntarily on service levels received. Duty terminal managers also sample the services and goods offered by outlets in the terminals, assessing them from a customer perspective. They check the cleanliness and condition of service facilities and complete detailed checklists that are submitted daily to senior terminal managers. The company has also a wealth of internal monitoring systems that record equipment faults and failures, and report equipment and staff availability. These systems are supported by the terminal managers who circulate the terminals on a full-time basis, helping customers as necessary, reporting any equipment faults observed and making routine assessments of the level of service provided by BAA and its concessionaires.

4.10 Examples of service quality measures and mechanisms at BAA plc

QUALITY	MEASURES	MECHANISMS
Access	Walking distance/ease of finding way around	Surveys operational data
Aesthetics	Staff appearance/airport Appearance, quality of catering	Surveys inspection
Availability	Equipment availability	Internal fault monitors
Cleanliness	Environment and equipment	Surveys/inspection
Comfort	Crowdedness	Surveys/inspection
Communication	Information clarity/clarity of labelling and pricing	Surveys/inspection
Competence	Staff efficiency	Management inspection
Courtesy	Courtesy of staff	Surveys/inspection
Friendliness	Staff attitude	Surveys/inspection
Reliability	Equipment faults	Surveys/inspection
Responsiveness	Staff responsiveness	Surveys/inspection
Security	Efficiency of security checks/ number of urgent safety reports	Survey/internal data

Table: Examples of quality measure and mechanisms

Internal quality measurement

Inspection and monitoring of the inputs to the service process is important for all organisations. The quality of the solicitors in a practice or the number and grades of staff available in a consultancy organisation are crucial to the provision of service quality. Multibroadcast measures the number of shop refits per month, and BAA monitor the availability and condition of equipment and facilities.

Many service companies use internal mechanisms to measure service quality during the process of service delivery. Multibroadcast uses managers to formally inspect the premises, goods and service provided by the staff using detailed checklists covering, for example, the correct pricing of items, correct layout of displays and attitude of staff to the customers. BAA have advanced systems to monitor equipment faults and the terminal managers are expected to report any problems they see.

The quality of the service may be measured after the event, which is by measuring the results by outputs of the service. For example, Multibroadcast measures the number of service calls they have to make for each of their products, in order to assess product reliability.

4.11 Key points

- Providing high level of service quality may be a source of competitive advantage.

- Achieving high service quality means ensuring all the factors of the service package meet customer requirements.

- There are 12 factors of service quality: reliability, responsiveness, aesthetics/appearance, cleanliness/tidiness, comfort, friendliness, communication, courtesy, competence, access, availability, and security.

- The relative importance of the factors will vary from company to company and between customers.

- Service quality can be measured using external customer satisfaction measures and internal organisational quality systems at different stages of the service process.

- Both internal and external measures of the service quality factors are required to facilitate target setting, the tracking of the costs of changing quality targets and the linking of pay to quality performance.

- Quality control systems vary between professional, service shop and mass service organisations.

> **KEY POINT**
>
> There are twelve factors of service quality: reliability, responsiveness, aesthetics/appearance, cleanliness/tidiness, comfort, friendliness, communication, courtesy, competence, access, availability, and security.

4.12 Resource utilisation

The matching of inputs to outputs is often difficult in a service organisation due to the factors of heterogeneity and simultaneity of service and consumption. However many large organisations collect data for feedback and control on the issue of resource utilisation, either maximising outputs or minimising inputs for a given level of outputs.

For example a bank would use the volume of transactions processed as a measure of output; a hotel would use the room occupancy rate; and a consultancy would use the number of chargeable hours per man per year as a basis of output measurement.

> **KEY POINT**
>
> The matching of inputs to outputs is often difficult in a service organisation due to the factors of heterogeneity and simultaneity of service and consumption. However many large organisations collect data for feedback and control on the issue of resource utilisation, either maximising outputs or minimising inputs for a given level of outputs.

Example 1 – Performance indicators of a clearing bank

- budgeted costs per balance v actual costs
- average debit balances per employee
- average credit balances per employee
- number of transactions processed/man hours worked.

Example 2 – International firm of auditors

- chargeable hours
- non-chargeable hours
- ratio of chargeable/non-chargeable time
- budgetary excesses (excess time to complete from agreed budget)
- ratio of manpower cost to fee charged (the rule of thumb in the business is that the multiple should be 3; recovery of staff cost plus overhead assumed to be 100% of staff cost plus profit).

4.13 Innovation

The service qualities of intangibility, heterogeneity, simultaneity, etc all combine to make the measurement of innovation difficult. Voss and De Bretan suggest the following:

Financial issues

- Does the service achieve high profitability?

- Are costs lowered?

- Are operating efficiencies achieved?

Competitiveness issues

- Is the product exceeding expectations of market share?

- Is the product having a strong impact on brand image?

- Does the provider experience considerable competitive advantage?

Quality issues

- Service outcome superior to competitors?

- Unique benefits perceived as superior?

- Greater reliability?

- More user friendly.

A good example of innovation that aims to deliver all the above and more besides is in the IT solutions developed by the clearing banks. The reduction in headcount has resulted in lower operating costs to the firm. The improvement in technology in providing information to users on cleared funds in their account, as well as the automation at branch level of front office procedures, has meant tighter credit control from the point of view of the bank and greater flexibility for the (good) customer.

4.14 Manufacturing industries

Although we have described the results and determinants framework in the servce context in which it was originally developed, you will probably appreciate that it might be used equally well to control manufacturing businesses. The principal difference is that it will be easier to measure certain things.

5 Not-for-profit organisations (NFPOs)

5.1 Introduction

DEFINITION

A **not-for-profit organisation** (NFPO) can be any organisation that delivers products or services to client groups irrespective of their ability to pay for the goods or services delivered. For example, a charity delivers services to people according to the charity's aims and constitution.

A **not-for-profit organisation** (NFPO) can be any organisation that delivers products or services to client groups irrespective of their ability to pay for the goods or services.

Much of the public sector falls into the NFPO category. A local authority supplies services to many at no cost to the consumer. The street lighting is paid for out of revenue but it is provided to all in the community. The streets are kept clear of rubbish irrespective of which person is enjoying the aesthetic experience of a litter-free pavement. In this section we discuss the control issues that affect such organisations especially those in the public sector.

The lack of a profit motive, the absence of financial measures to evaluate performance, and the concept of entity makes it difficult to use conventional financial evaluation. NFPOs have multiple objectives that cannot always be measured in money terms. It would be possible to measure the cost of food supplied to the needy but is it possible to establish that all the aims of a charity have been met? It is possible to measure the sums disbursed by a government department precisely. But the issue of whether the money was well spent raises the question of a value for money exercise.

5.2 Cash limited control

The commonest way of controlling the activities of an NFPO is via the supply and disposition of cash. If a charity has no cash it cannot make grants. If a public sector body is allowed £1m to spend on a programme such as providing a day centre for the aged and that money is spent then the supply of service stops. It is not uncommon to find a patient receiving NHS treatment but the budget for that specialism is now spent and no more care is forthcoming. In some cases cash limited control can be alleviated when spending on one project is below limit and the 'free amount' is allocated to another programme. This is called virement; some bodies permit it and others do not.

5.3 Contracting out

The technical term is compulsory competitive tendering and refers to the ethic that no service should be offered at a subsidy by an NFPO. If a service is to be offered it must compete with a private sector contractor. It is thus becoming more and more common to find NFPOs using private contractors for the supply of services.

This activity of market testing is compulsory and is a feature of public sector life in a market economy.

In the UK the Department of the Environment requires all local authorities that offer services through special bodies called Direct Service Organisations (DSO) to report their results and compute a figure of ROI that must be above a minimum rate of 5%. Failure to meet the target can lead to the DSO being dissolved.

This practice of contracting out is part of the concept of the 'internal market' that is a feature of all public sector operations. Providers of service win their contracts from consumers by bidding against other providers. In the UK the oldest public sector audit body is the District Audit service. It tenders for work from the purchaser of audit, that is the Audit Commission, and competes with selected high profile private sector firms. The police may be used by the prison service for escort duty or the contract may go to a private contractor.

Contracting out is part of the framework to ensure that public sector services are delivered with due regard for value for money.

5.4 Executive Agencies

The development of the Executive Agency is part of the process of introducing market disciplines into the sphere of central government that of course does not recognise the concept of profit.

In the 1980s the government came up with a new concept to make the provision of certain designated services more efficient and free of direct ministerial control. The 'Next Steps' programme and subsequent initiatives up to the present day have led to the creation of 'Executive Agencies' which deliver special services to Government or to the citizen, while the policy-making aspects of government remain with the relevant ministry.

Four examples of Executive Agencies are:

AGENCY	SERVICE PROVIDED	MINISTRY
Driving Standards	Driving tests	Transport
JobCentre Plus	Benefits and labour exchanges	Work and Pensions
Companies House	Administration of Company Law	Trade and Industry
Highways	Road building	Transport

5.5 Framework of control

- The executive functions of government, as distinct from policy advice, are carried out by units referred to as agencies. They are controlled by a chief executive working under the relevant minister who sets policy-making objectives and who agrees the supply of resources from the Treasury.

- The staff are supposed to be properly trained and prepared to deliver services 'inside and outside' central government.

- Clear objectives are set and adequate resources are allocated to enable objectives to be achieved either via annual cash limits or by treating the organisation as a trading fund.

- Chief executives have a maximum freedom of action to utilise their resources within the civil service framework while preserving the essential ethic of the civil service.

- There are agreed performance targets, both financial and non financial to judge the success in meeting the aims of the agency.

5.6 Summary

In effect these proposals treat the specialised services of government as 'profit centres' and attempt to introduce a profit responsible culture into what was, in the past, a not-for-profit environment. Certain bodies now trade through an internal market to exchange services for value. For example, the toxicologists in the Home Office regard the police as their client who in turn are charged for services rendered at a commercial rate. The supplier's business manager is evaluated on his capacity to at least break even in any one fiscal period. There are clearly a number of practical difficulties that will be experienced in such matters as setting transfer prices for the services rendered.

Executive Agencies are required to prepare an annual report and publish accounts that are audited by the National Audit Office. The NAO audits all central government departments, and as executive agencies are under ultimate ministerial control they are 'clients' of the NAO. The accounts identify the relevant financial and non-financial indicators of performance to demonstrate whether the agency has met the criteria for value for money, i.e. the three Es of economy, efficiency and effectiveness. As clients of the NAO the agency also falls within the ambit of control, criticism and even censure from Parliament through the medium of the Public Accounts Committee.

6 The nature of value for money (VFM)

6.1 What is value for money (VFM)?

Value for money is a notoriously elusive concept and yet it is assumed that everyone recognises it when they see it. If a random sample of one hundred people were asked what they understood by the term, there would almost certainly be as many different answers as there were people asked. The term is frequently bandied about but is rarely defined.

VFM can simply be described as 'getting the best possible combination of services from the least resources', i.e. to maximise the benefits available at the lowest cost to the taxpayer. It is generally taken to mean the pursuit of economy, efficiency and effectiveness.

6.2 Why the concern?

It was not until the early 1970s that concern was regularly expressed about VFM, but since that time the feeling has intensified, and it is now an issue of major importance. It is difficult to point to a particular happening that explains the increased concern but four events of the decade coincided:

(a)   In 1974, local government, health and water authorities re-organised.

(b)   Partly as a result of (a), public sector expenditure increased at a rate never seen before.

(c)   Several experts recommended the adoption of management techniques that had hitherto been considered inappropriate to the public sector.

(d)   A Conservative administration came to power in 1979 with a set of policies totally different from those of the previous government.

During the decade it was frequently claimed that the public sector did not give value for money, that it was over-staffed and inefficient, and that expenditure ought to be drastically cut. On the other hand, some felt that officials of the public sector provided an excellent service and that criticisms were based on political ideology rather than quality of provision. What became apparent was the difficulty in substantiating any argument with hard and fast and meaningful facts. There was no suitable parallel upon which comparisons could be made. We have already covered the efforts made to promote more efficient forms of financial management and control; efforts have also been made to establish criteria that can be used to measure a wide variety of inputs and outputs.

6.3 Inputs and outputs

Inputs and outputs can best be described in diagrammatic form:

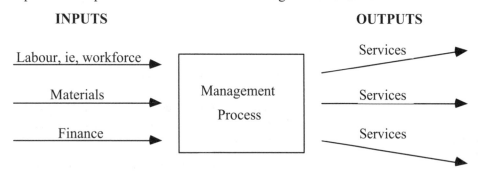

Diagram: Typical inputs to and outputs from a management process

DEFINITION

Economy – The terms and conditions under which the authority acquires human and material resources. An economical operation acquires resources of the appropriate quality and provides a service to the appropriate standard at the lowest cost.

Effectiveness – This is the extent to which a programme achieves its established goals or other intended effects.

Efficiency – This is the relationship between goods or services produced and resources used to produce them. An efficient operation produces the maximum output for any given set of resource inputs; or, it has minimum inputs for any given quantity and quality of services provided.
(The Chartered Institute of Public Finance and Accountancy (CIPFA))

The resources available to public sector organisations are organised by management in such a way as to provide services/facilities for the public.

'Economy' is a measure of inputs to achieve a certain service.

'Effectiveness' is a measure of outputs, i.e. services and facilities.

'Efficiency' is the optimum of economy and effectiveness, i.e. the measure of outputs over inputs.

The terms economy, effectiveness and efficiency are the fundamental prerequisites of achieving VFM. Their importance cannot be emphasised enough, so much so that external auditors in some parts of the public sector, i.e. local government, are now charged with the responsibility of ensuring that bodies have made adequate arrangements for securing economy, effectiveness and efficiency in the use of public funds.

6.4 Market forces and the profit motive

The idea of measuring performance in any organisation is sound. Unless a retrospective look is taken there is a danger that a business will stumble on as before, possibly failing to adapt to changing circumstances. It is necessary to question past performance.

- Has the organisation fulfilled its objectives?
- Has management organised resources satisfactorily?
- Are the customers/clients content with the produce and service?
- Are staff sufficiently motivated and happy at work?

Or more to the point, is profit being maximised or costs minimised? Are resources being managed in the best way possible?

Whether the organisation is Marks and Spencer plc, British Telecom plc, the Department of Health, or any other body, these are important questions that must be answered.

If the organisation forms part of the private sector there are two factors that largely determine whether or not it is being managed efficiently:

- Is it selling its produce?
- Is it making a profit?

The interaction of supply and demand will occur in the marketplace, and if products/services are of a suitable quality and price they will be purchased by consumers. Market competition will weed out those firms whose product is not in demand and the product will either have to be modified in line with consumer tastes, or die. Competition ensures that organisations are geared to meet the needs of consumers.

If demand for a product exists, sales revenue will be attracted. It is the task of management to ensure that the total expenses incurred in running the business are less than total revenues. A firm cannot survive in the long run without making profits. This causes a detailed analysis of expenses and revenues in an effort to maximise profit.

The two measures outlined above are largely inappropriate to the public sector. Only in a few isolated areas, i.e. some nationalised industries and certain spheres of activity in local government, can market forces and the profit motive be used as indicators of performance. It should be said, however, that the two factors are equally applicable in the public sector. Services and facilities must be provided to meet the needs of consumers (whether market forces are apparent or not), and costs must be minimised (whether or not profit can be calculated).

If private sector measures are not available to the public sector then different criteria must be used.

6.5 Input and output measures

The criteria chosen will vary from organisation to organisation. A relevant set of statistics in one department might be much less appropriate in another. Each service/department has to be considered in its own right and suitable indicators selected accordingly.

The expectations of politicians/management must ultimately be translated into the identification of targets and subsequently into standard costs or times or performance norms. This becomes one type of yardstick against which performance is measured. Common ratios include the following:

$$\frac{\text{Standard input}}{\text{Actual input}} \times 100 \qquad \text{(a measure of economy)}$$

e.g. $\dfrac{\text{Standard cost of materials used £725}}{\text{Actual cost of materials used £730}} \times 100 = \text{approximately 99\%}$
economical

$$\frac{\text{Actual output}}{\text{Standard output}} \times 100 \qquad \text{(a measure of effectiveness)}$$

e.g. $\dfrac{340 \text{ dustbins emptied per hour per team}}{360 \text{ dustbins standard per hour per team}} \times 100 = \text{approximately 95\%}$
effective

Actual output/Actual input

compared to standard output/ standard input

(a measure of efficiency)

e.g.   £7,250/1,440 home help hours
= £5.10 approximate average cost per hour

£7,000/1,440 home help hours
= £5 average cost per hour.

The methods are easily understood but care must be taken in setting 'standards' which are realistic and acceptable to all. Failure to construct standards that are seen as attainable will lead to bad feeling and demotivation of staff. Additionally, there is the ongoing problem of making allowance for the less quantifiable factors, e.g. it will take much longer to collect refuse from a house whose garden path is 25 metres in length than a property whose path is only 5 metres long.

6.6 Comparative analysis

The ratios and other cost information calculated are useful as they give management an indication of how well resources are being used. This allows the organisation to look at its performance but a clearer picture can be derived if the data is compared with some other factor. There are numerous types of gauge that can be used. Hatry et al (1979) suggested a general approach to performance measurement involving:

- comparisons over time
- measures compared between geographical areas of institutions

- comparison of actual performance with 'standards', particularly in relation to standardised procedures

- comparison of actual performance with performance targeted at the beginning of the year

- comparisons with similar private sector activities

- inter-department/authority comparisons.

Comparisons give an indication of how economically inputs are managed. If a particular service in one area is provided at an average cost of £240 per 1,000 population it is reasonable to think that similar areas should provide at a comparable cost. Those areas whose costs vary wildly must look at themselves and investigate the reasons.

6.7 Problems in assessing VFM

Unfortunately, the evaluation of VFM is not as clear-cut as it first appears. Allowances must be made for the unique problems faced by each locality and extreme care exercised before categorical judgements are made. The following examples illustrate this.

Two small Department of Employment area offices handle a similar number of claims each week. One office costs £240,000 per annum to run, the other costs £175,000. It would be tempting to assume that the low cost office is comparatively more efficient; and it may well be. But there could be many more social costs incurred at the 'more efficient' office, which are not broadcast:

	£240,000 office	£175,000 office
Claimants' average waiting time before being attended to	15 minutes	70 minutes
Mistakes made in calculating benefits	12 per 1,000	55 per 1,000
Staff morale	high	low

There are two towns of similar size, each has a public library. The total number of books in one library totals 18,000, in the other there are 30,000. It is assumed that the library with more books provides better for public needs, as the variety of titles on offer is greater, and this could be the case. But are the titles spread evenly over different sections or are the majority concentrated under a few headings? Do readers tend to favour a certain type of book? If so, are their needs being catered for? Is the library quiet to work in, or is the noise level intolerably high? Are the staff helpful?

6.8 Limitations

It cannot be disputed that comparative analysis, when based on relevant criteria, is a worthwhile exercise. On several occasions the comparisons have led to investigations that have resulted in cost reductions. It must be understood, however, that the usefulness of comparative analysis has two severe limitations as described below.

- Each locality is unique and will face problems different from those elsewhere. (This should not be overemphasised as failure to achieve economy might be inequitably explained.)

- The difficulty in measuring the quality of service provided. For example, two similar authorities provide home help services. The time spent by home help workers on each case per week averages to approximately one hour in one authority and one and a half hours in the other. The immediate impression drawn from the figures is that the area receiving the greater time per case is more effective. However, the quality of help has not been measured and it is possible that the authority giving one hour per case has specially trained its workers so that the time spent in the home is high-quality support. The other authority may not have undertaken a suitable programme of training, thus failing to provide a high standard of service.

6.9 Reducing the barriers to valid assessment of VFM

What can be done to alleviate the drawbacks of comparative analysis? There is no easy solution but some or all of the following would be beneficial.

- A clear statement of policies should be made by each organisation.

- The policies must be translated into more detailed objectives.

- Working plans/programmes/targets should be formulated and communicated to all units and sections for implementation (hopefully this will ensure that all staff 'pull in the same direction').

- A review of performance and policies should be undertaken to identify areas for improvement and to minimise waste. Policies would be amended where necessary and the process continued in an ongoing cycle.

- The carefully directed use of:

  - audit

  - staff appraisal

  - performance review

  - various studies, e.g. organisation and methods, work study, cost benefit analysis

  - a suitably rewarded scheme where staff are encouraged to suggest improvements.

- The sensitive interpretation of a few key statistics, e.g. the number and type of complaints received, the trend of staff absence over a number of years or the percentage of telephone calls answered within thirty seconds.

There is undoubtedly a need to assess performance in the public sector. The current generation of public sector employees have been indoctrinated into a VFM way of thinking. The situation is still not ideal but much progress has been made since the concern for openness and VFM became widespread.

The rather crude performance indicators of previous years have been defined and now help to create an overall if fragmented picture of each organisation. This is normally publicised in an annual report that is available to all. Allowances must be made, however, as the large majority of indicators do not quantify quality, and misinterpretation could lead to false conclusions being drawn.

Activity 2

Summarise the concept of VFM.

Feedback to this activity is at the end of the chapter.

Summary

Key points of this chapter are:

- Critical success factors (CSFs) are used as a means of driving the information needs of an organisation. All CSFs should have recognisable and reliable performance measures to ensure that each factor's success is monitored. CSFs can only be identified after the organisation has identified its goals and objectives.

- Multiple measures of performance such as the balanced scorecard and the performance pyramid recognise that no single measure can be used to control performance.

- Control and measurement of performance is more difficult in not for profit organisations, although measure such as cash limited control provide some assistance in this area.

- Value For Money can be used to 'get the best possible combination of services from the least resources' and uses the three 'Es' (Economcy, Efficiency and Effectivneness) as performance measures.

Having completed your study of this chapter you should have achieved the following learning outcomes:

- evaluate and recommend appropriate control measures

- prepare and evaluate multidimensional models of performance measurement.

Self-test questions

1   How would you describe a CSF? (2.1)

2   Identify Rockart's four sources of CSFs. (2.2)

3   Give examples of hard and soft prime measures for critical factors. (2.3)

4   What is the balanced scorecard? (3.1)

5   What are the four quadrants of the balanced scorecard? (3.1)

6   What are the objectives of the organisation according to the PriceWaterhouseCoopers pyramid? (3.2)

7   What are the four key differences between manufactured products and service products? (4.2)

8   What are CIMA's six generic performance dimensions? (4.4)

9   Name six measures of quality. (4.10)

10   What is the commonest way of controlling the activities of an NFPO? (5.2)

11   What is contracting out? (5.3)

12   What is the benefit of an executive agency? (5.4)

13   What is VFM? (6.1)

14 Explain the three 'Es'. (6.3)

15 What are the limitations of VFM? (6.8)

Practice question

Lindleys Bank

Lindleys plc ('the bank') is a United Kingdom clearing bank. It has 2,000 retail branches. It categorises its business as retail and corporate. Each category currently accounts for half of the bank's turnover.

The bank defines retail business as 'banking for customers in their own right and small businesses where lending would not exceed £1,000,000 in any one year'.

Corporate business is defined as '... where lending would exceed £1,000,000 in any one year'. Corporate lending includes international lending.

Traditionally, corporate lending has been the most profitable business, yielding 70 per cent of profit before taxation. Corporate lending has been carried out by six regional offices and a department at head office in London. The London office is also responsible for international lending. There are 200 staff employed in corporate lending.

Retail banking has operated in the following way.

The number of retail and small business customers at each branch has ranged from 1,000 to 10,000, although 5,000 is typical. The bank has employed the following mission statement for its retail banking: 'Our mission is to deliver a high-quality service to customers based on our managers' personal knowledge of customers' affairs'.

The bank recognised that retail banking was relatively unprofitable. It was willing to operate a policy of cross-subsidisation between corporate and retail, as it hoped that some retail customers would become corporate customers. It saw its branch managers as assisting in this process because of their financing expertise and deep knowledge of their customers.

The bank has operated each branch as a cost centre. Managers have been provided with a three-monthly expenditure report which compared committed expenditure to budgeted expenditure. The bank had not operated an accrual accounting system as regards branch expenditures for these three-monthly reports. However, year-end adjustments reconciled committed, actual and budgeted expenditures. These accounting operations were carried out by management accounting staff based at head office.

The managers' remit was to operate within their expenditure budgets. In addition to this, they were set targets, for example number of new accounts opened, amount of holiday insurance sold, level of bad debts.

The managers were not consulted about the size of their budgets or their targets. These were imposed by head office.

Proposals for change

The bank is reappraising its corporate posture. Its corporate lending has declined in profitability because of problems with third-world debt and movements in foreign exchange rates. The bank has also become concerned about the attitudes which it believes have become dominant in retail banking. Most of its managers have found their targets relatively easy to achieve. They have been criticised for a lack of entrepreneurial awareness and for being too inward-looking. The managers have retorted that 'as soon as a customer gets to be interesting we lose them to corporate, so why bother?'. Because of these factors the bank has decided upon the following changes.

- Retail banking must in future earn 50% of the bank's profit before taxation.

- There will be a programme of branch rationalisation in which half the branches will close.

- New 'superbranches' will be established. These will be at the centre of a network of 6–8 existing branches. The superbranch will contain the manager, who will make all the major decisions for the network of branches. He will be assisted in this by two assistant managers, who will probably be drawn from the existing managers in the network.

- Each superbranch will be designated as an investment centre and must earn a return of 15%. No target has been set for residual income, although the bank intends to set such targets after it has gained some experience of the operations of the superbranches. (Residual income should be taken as pre-tax profits less an imputed interest charge for net assets.)

- Each superbranch has been given an expenditure budget which equates to that of the cumulative total spent by its network branches in the previous year. No extra funds have been allocated for the establishment of the superbranches. The manager of the superbranch has discretion as to where the superbranch will be located. This could be inside an existing branch or in new premises.

- The manager of the superbranch will be responsible for the design and operation of all of the information systems of the network. These will be capable of being interrogated by head office, which will continue to draw up the statutory accounts.

- The manager of the superbranch has discretion as to the number of employees working in the network. If there are to be any redundancies, head office will negotiate nationally to determine the terms for redundant staff. The superbranch will be charged with the costs, if any, of redundancies in its network.

The managing director of the bank has described the new philosophy for retail banking thus: 'We are operating in a very competitive environment and in order to survive, we must change. We must never forget that we are a profit-seeking organisation. Retail banking has been subsidised in the past and has become inefficient. Our proposals will enable us to deliver an efficient, low-cost service. However, I am afraid the days of the bank manager being a personal friend and adviser are over'.

Required:

(a) Discuss the advantages and disadvantages of the proposal to make superbranches investment centres.

(b) Describe the reports you believe will be necessary for the manager of a superbranch to manage successfully. Your answer should include the reasons for your suggestions.

(c) Identify, and describe, three qualitative performance indicators you consider would be of assistance to a superbranch manager. **(25 marks)**

For the answer to this question, see the 'Answers' section at the end of the book.

Feedback to activities

Activity 1

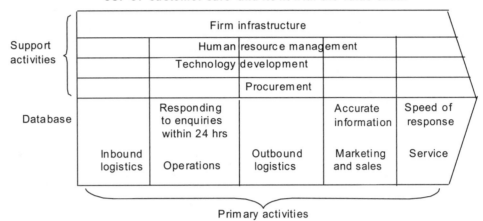

CSF of 'customer care' and its fit with the value chain

Activity 2

VFM is an elusive concept but is generally taken to mean the pursuit of economy, efficiency and effectiveness, i.e. getting the best possible combination of services from the least resources.

Chapter 16

BUSINESS UNIT PERFORMANCE

Syllabus content

- Business unit performance and appraisal, including transfer pricing, reward systems and incentives, and agency theory. (Note: Details of agency theory will not be tested.)

Contents

1   Introduction

2   International operations

3   Transfer pricing

4   Simple market-based transfer prices

5   Further considerations of transfer pricing

6   International transfer pricing

7   Rewards, incentives and agency theory

1 Introduction

Significant business organisations conduct business on a global basis. Companies such as Ford, General Motors and Nestlé are household names across the globe. They are multinational companies. Ford is essentially an American company with its corporate headquarters in Michigan in the USA. Nestlé is a Swiss-based corporation but has no cultural or national links with that country which itself is a confederation. Nestlé can be described as a global company for that reason.

The management of global or multinational companies is affected by various problems such as national culture, the drive to satisfy shareholders' expectations, and government constraints such as foreign exchange controls or taxation policy. Multinational companies may also manipulate the results of their overseas ventures to exploit taxation loopholes or to repatriate funds to benefit the parent company.

Alongside all of this are the problems of monitoring the performance and interaction of both strategic business units and of managers. A manager's remuneration may be based on performance and therefore it is crucial that the measurement is fair and the targets reasonable.

2 International operations

2.1 Definitions

- **International trading** occurs where one company located in its 'home' country trades with other non-associated people and companies in other countries.

- A **multinational company** (MNC) is defined as one that generates at least 25% of its sales from activities in countries other than its own. It generally operates through overseas subsidiaries and divisions and will have a 'head office' located in one country with which it will probably have strong cultural or national links.

  The United Nations describes what we have just defined as multinational companies as 'transnational companies' to illustrate more clearly their developing nature. There is some merit in this nomenclature and it may become the norm. Indeed one could go further and consider the concept of a 'global' company.

- A **global company** has no cultural or national links with any one country. Its capital is raised internationally, the head office is based in the most tax efficient and loosely regulated country, the operational headquarters is located in the most effective centre, subsidiaries are established worldwide and the personnel are international in character and multilingual.

2.2 The role of MNCs

The activities of MNCs are of major importance because of their size and the increasingly preponderant part they play in the world economy. The very largest MNCs have revenues greater than the GNP of all except the top 15 or so national economies. Their significance is increasing all the time since they are growing (looking at the totality) at a rate some three or four times the rate of the world economy.

2.3 Internal factors that encourage and discourage multinational trading

The factors which play a part in an MNC's operations and may affect its success can be conveniently divided into two classes: those that are internal to the firm and may be described as ownership specific, and those that are external to the firm.

- **Process specialisation** – This is of two kinds. In the first place the move to standardisation of products, both in terms of adhering to internationally accepted standards and in methods of production, has made it possible and often desirable to locate stages of production in different countries – perhaps labour intensive activities in low wage areas and final assembly in the ultimate market. Secondly, it refers to the particular features of the firm that make it distinctive and confer on it a measure of competitive advantage, often referred to as 'know how' and embracing patents, trade marks and managerial skills.

- **Product specialisation** – In spite of the move to standardisation mentioned above, the vagaries of human taste are such that most markets exhibit different characteristics. Identifying these and matching products to them can be a potent factor in success; equally the failure to do so can be disastrous. In the simplest case consumers occasionally gain the impression (sometimes justified) that goods made for export are of a higher quality than those foisted onto the home market. But the process goes much further than that. For example, one well-known beverage sold internationally is called the same everywhere and looks the same but is in fact produced in forty different varieties.

- **Research and development** – The larger the part R&D plays in a company's activities the more sense it makes to spread the cost by operating internationally. Drugs companies are a good example. The largest have annual R&D budgets of more than half a billion pounds. Few, if any, national markets can support outlays of that kind. Logically there is no reason why R&D should not be regarded in the same light as process specialisation and after a hesitant start this is gradually becoming the case. It is becoming quite usual for R&D to be located wherever there is a natural affinity in terms of expertise, educational skills and university liaison to the desired activities.

- **Vertical and horizontal integration** – Due to the large size of many MNCs, scope to integrate their activities often exists. Vertical integration occurs when a company gains control of its suppliers or raw materials (backward vertical integration) and/or its distribution networks (forward vertical integration). The classic example is an oil company that finds and controls the producing wells, refines the product and organises the distribution through its own outlets. A tobacco company, on the other hand, tends to buy in its supplies, perhaps because of the complexity of blending, and cannot control the distribution because of the proliferation of brands. It therefore expands horizontally by setting up factories wherever deemed suitable.

- **Transfer pricing** – This is an important technique that can offer major financial advantages to an MNC (although not always to any particular host country). It permits an MNC to minimise its tax liabilities by maximising profits as far as possible in the country with the most favourable tax regime. Essentially this is achieved by selling products between component parts of the group at artificial prices so that higher costs are incurred where taxes are high and lower costs where taxes are lower.

It is worth noting that there has been a swing away from expansion into less developed countries and more emphasis placed on expansion into developed countries.

- International trade has greatly expanded in the last half century and adversarial competition has increased very considerably. In the light of this new threat there is an incentive for a company to meet its competitors head-on in their own marketplace.

- Also, the fast pace of technological change has created opportunities for new products to be introduced continually even in developed nations.

- Further, the development of international capital markets has made it easier for MNCs to mobilise funds for their expansion.

- Finally, some projects are now of such enormous cost that they are best undertaken by international co-operation and they are generally of such a nature that they can only be undertaken in the developed nations.

3 Transfer pricing

3.1 Introduction

Large diversified groups will be split into numerous smaller profit centres, each preparing accounts for its own sphere of activities and paying tax on its profits. Multinational groups are likely to own individual companies established in different countries throughout the world; transfer pricing is the process of deciding on appropriate prices for the goods and services sold intra-group.

This section begins by summarising the theory of transfer pricing in a one-country context, then expands to consider the setting of transfer prices between parts of a group located in different countries. You can appreciate that international transfer pricing requires a consideration of multiple currency effects and multiple tax regimes.

3.2 The need for a transfer pricing policy

One condition for successful decentralisation is that the various divisions should be more or less independent of each other. However, in practice, this is unlikely to be the case and a certain amount of inter-divisional trading will take place. A transfer pricing policy is needed if goods or services are passed between divisions.

It might appear that the credit to the supplying division is merely offset by an equal debit to the receiving division and that therefore, as far as the whole organisation is concerned, it has a net zero effect. This is true in terms of the physical application of a transfer pricing system once it has been decided upon and implemented. However, there are important behavioural and organisational elements associated with transfer pricing and the choice of which method to adopt. The transfer price does affect the profit of each division separately and, therefore, can affect the level of motivation of each divisional manager.

3.3 Criteria for judging a transfer pricing policy

Adopting a transfer pricing policy will result in:

- total corporate profit being divided up between divisional profit centres; it may result in a cost centre being converted into a profit centre (e.g. if centralised services charge other divisions for the work that they do)

- information becoming available for divisional decision making (particularly over whether or not to accept an internal transfer and the level of activity required)

- information being made available to help assess the performance of divisions and divisional managers (for instance allowing the performance of former cost centres to be compared with outside, specialist, profit-making firms in the same field).

The rules for the operation of a transfer pricing policy are the same as for any policy in a decentralised organisation. A system should be reasonably easy to operate and understand as well as being flexible in terms of a changing organisational structure. In addition, there are four specific criteria that a good transfer pricing policy should meet:

- it should provide motivation for divisional managers

- it should allow divisional autonomy and independence to be maintained

- it should allow divisional performance to be assessed objectively

- it should ensure that divisional managers make decisions that are in the best interests of the divisions and also of the company as a whole.

This final feature is usually referred to as goal congruence and is perhaps the most important of the four.

3.4 Methods of setting transfer prices

In the first in its series of Management Accounting Guidelines, the CIMA put forward three main types of transfer price:

- cost-based prices

- market-based prices

- negotiated prices.

The first of these uses a cost-plus approach to transfer pricing, the second uses intermediate market price and the third could be regarded as a particular form of bargaining. Each method will be discussed in turn. However, there are several variations on these that are of greater or lesser importance:

- **Using marginal cost and marginal revenue data** – much loved by academics and often tested in exams but rarely used in practice due to the lack of information; this will be explained later.

- **Using dual prices** – the use of two prices to encourage or discourage a transfer, possibly by ensuring that each division makes a satisfactory profit from a desirable transfer (it can overcome some of the problems that may arise from the previous – MC & MR – method).

- **Incorporating opportunity costs** – this method, discussed briefly later, may simply provide support for cost-based or market-based methods under the relevant circumstances; however the term could also encompass the use of output from linear programming formulations to help arrive at transfer prices when divisions have limited production capacity.

4 Simple market-based transfer prices

4.1 Introduction

Where the product (or service) that is subject to internal transfer could be sold to other outside organisations by the supplying division and, similarly, where the product could be purchased from other outside organisations by the receiving division, a competitive market exists and a market price will have been established under normal supply and demand conditions. Such a market price would be a very suitable basis on which to make inter-divisional transfers; it would be easy to operate provided the source of the market price was clearly stated.

It would allow each division to remain autonomous, so that the profit of the division would not be affected by any decision to buy/sell externally or to trade internally. The resultant profits would be determined in an objective way. In most situations the use of a market price as a transfer price will not lead to any divergence between divisional and company goals. However, there is a particular problem when there is spare capacity; this is dealt with in the next section.

Market prices are sometimes adjusted downwards for use as transfer prices, to recognise the benefits or savings from internal trading. Such a reduction might relate to:

- lower packaging and advertising costs for goods sold internally in comparison with outside sales

- the benefits derived from purchases and sales in large volumes (where bulk discounts might be expected)

- the advantages of having an exclusive supplies contract.

An adjusted market price should encourage internal trading because it should lead to higher divisional profits than buying or selling in the open market.

4.2 Problems with market-based transfer prices

Before adopting a market-based transfer pricing policy, the inherent dangers must be recognised and, where possible, steps taken to overcome these problems.

- There may be no intermediate market price. The product or service might not be readily available on the open market (an example might be a partly completed car being transferred from one division to another).

- The market price might not be independent. This would occur if the transferring division were in the position of a monopolist both within the company and in the outside market.

- Difficulty in agreeing a source of market prices. Debates will occur over the size, quality, timing and location of internal transfers compared with a range of published prices.

- The need to adjust prices for different volumes. Prices quoted may well not relate to the levels of transfers that are likely to take place; in the same way, the extent of reductions due to saved selling costs will be difficult to estimate.

- Published prices may be fictitious. This is a variation on the previous problem but is typified by those products for which it is customary for a seller to publish a price then the buyer to negotiate a lower figure.

In a situation where there is spare capacity in the supplying division, the use of a market-based transfer price will not ensure that the divisional managers will be motivated individually to take independent action that is in the best interests of the whole company. This is because the manager of a receiving division may see his divisional profits fall as a result of a move to utilise spare capacity, even though it would benefit the overall profits of the company. A comprehensive example follows to illustrate this situation, and it will be referred to again in a later section.

Example

Kwaree Ltd, producing a range of minerals, is organised into two trading groups – one group handles wholesale business and the other deals with sales to retailers.

One of its products is a moulding clay. The wholesale group extracts the clay and sells it to external wholesale customers as well as to the retail group. The production capacity is 2,000 tonnes per month, but at present sales are limited to 1,000 tonnes wholesale and 600 tonnes retail.

The transfer price agreed is £180 per tonne, in line with the existing external wholesale trade price.

The retail group produces 100 bags of refined clay from each tonne of moulding clay that it sells at £4 per bag. It would sell a further 40,000 bags if the retail trade price were reduced to £3.20 per bag.

Other data relevant to the operation are:

	Wholesale group	Retail group
Variable cost per tonne	£70	£60
Fixed cost per month	£100,000	£40,000

You are required to prepare estimated profit statements for the current month for each group and for Kwaree Ltd as a whole when producing at:

(a) 80% capacity
(b) 100% capacity, utilising the extra sales to supply the retail trade.

Solution

(a)   **Wholesale group at 80% capacity**

Estimated profit statement for the current month

Transfer price: £180 per tonne

Wholesale group operating at 80% capacity.

	Wholesale group £000	Retail group £000	Kwaree Ltd £000
Sales outside the company:			
1,000 tonnes @ £180/tonne	180		180
60,000 bags @ £4/bag		240	240
Internal transfer of 600 tonnes	108	(108)	Nil
Less: Costs:			
Variable:			
1,600 tonnes @ £70/tonne	(112)		(112)
600 tonnes @ £60/tonne		(36)	(36)
Fixed:	(100)	(40)	(140)
Profit	76	56	132

(b)   Wholesale group at 100% capacity

Estimated profit statement for the current month

Transfer price: £180 per tonne

Wholesale group operating at 100% capacity.

	Wholesale group £000	Retail group £000	Kwaree Ltd £000
Sales outside the company:			
1,000 tonnes @ £180/tonne	180		180
100,000 bags @ £3.20/bag		320	320
Internal transfer of 1,000 tonnes	180	(180)	Nil
Less: Costs:			
Variable:			
2,000 tonnes @ £70/tonne	(140)		(140)
1,000 tonnes @ £60/tonne		(60)	(60)
Fixed:	(100)	(40)	(140)
Profit	120	40	160

If it is assumed that the group (divisional) managers of Kwaree Ltd are being measured in terms of the profitability of their divisions, then the effect on divisional profits of utilising the spare capacity in the wholesale group can be summarised as follows:

	Profits in Wholesale group £000	Profits in Retail group £000	Profits in Kwaree Ltd £000
80% capacity	76	56	132
100% capacity	120	40	160
Increase/(decrease)	44	(16)	28

As a result of utilising spare capacity the profits of Kwaree would increase by £28,000. However, the wholesale group profits would increase by £44,000, whereas the manager of the retail group would see his division's profits fall by £16,000.

This fall is caused by the reduction in the selling price per bag of the moulding clay, affecting all the sales of the retail group and not only the additional sales. The manager of the retail group, acting independently, is unlikely to accept a decision to increase his production and sales if, as a result, the profit on which he is assessed is likely to decline. The action that he sees to be most beneficial for the retail group, for which he is responsible, is not the action that is in the best interests of the whole company. This is an example of sub-optimisation. Ideally the transfer price should be such that the profits of the wholesale and retail groups and the company would all increase as a result of moving from the 80% to 100% capacity. Transfer price bases that would give rise to this situation are identified in the next section.

Where the goods produced by the supplying division are only transferred internally to the receiving division, so that there is no existing market price, it may be possible to establish the identity of a substitute product that is freely available and does have a market price that could be used as the basis for the transfer price. The problems are associated with determining whether the other product is a valid substitute and, if so, what is the appropriate market price.

4.3 Optimal transfer price – net marginal revenue

A transfer price must be adopted which will encourage the higher level of transfer to take place – since Kwaree Ltd then makes an additional £28,000 profit. At the moment it will not occur since the retail group can see its profits fall. The only way to encourage the retail group to increase its purchases from the wholesale group is to reduce the transfer price. Marginal cost and marginal revenue considerations will be used (strictly incremental costs and revenues).

As a result of increasing output:

	£000
Retail group's revenue increases by (320 – 240)	80
Retail group's own variable costs rise by (60 – 36)	24
'Net marginal revenue' (£'000)	56

This must be compared with the cost that the wholesale group charges for these extra 400 tonnes. This cost is currently (400 × £180) = £72,000; hence the fall in retail profit by £16,000.

The transfer cost of these 400 tonnes must fall to no more than £56,000 or (£56,000 ÷ 400) £140 per tonne.

If the wholesale group is considered the transfer price must be at least £70 per tonne (its own variable production cost per tonne). Although this range of £70 – £140 per tonne has been calculated by reference to the incremental sales (of 400 tonnes) the transfer price will apply to all transfers. As a consequence some care must be taken over where in the range (£70 – £140) the final price is set, since the two groups must make enough contribution to cover their fixed costs. A transfer price at the top end of the range will prove more equitable, such as £135 per tonne.

4.4 Demonstration of goal congruence

If a transfer price of £135 per tonne is adopted, both divisions will see their profits increased by increasing output, and this is in the best interests of the company as a whole. Goal congruence is achieved. The two profit statements, at 80% and 100% capacity, with a transfer price of £135 are shown below.

(a) **80% capacity, transfer price £135**

	Wholesale group £000	*Retail group* £000	*Kwaree Ltd* £000
Outside sales			
1,000 @ £180	180	–	180
60,000 @ £4	–	240	240
Internal transfer			
600 @ £135	81	(81)	–
Variable costs			
1,600 @ £70	(112)		(112)
600 @ £60		(36)	(36)
Fixed costs	(100)	(40)	(140)
Profit	49	83	132

(b)   **100% capacity, transfer price £135**

	Wholesale group £000	Retail group £000	Kwaree Ltd £000
Outside sales			
1,000 @ £180	180	–	180
100,000 @ £3.20	–	320	320
Internal transfer			
1,000 @ £135	135	(135)	–
Variable costs			
2,000 @ £70	(140)	–	(140)
1,000 @ £60	–	(60)	(60)
Fixed costs	(100)	(40)	(140)
Profit	75	85	160

(c)   **Benefits from increasing output**

	Wholesale group £000	Retail group £000	Kwaree Ltd £000
	26	2	28

Whilst noting the fact that this new transfer price 'works', a few points are worth making.

- If this problem were observed by top management and the transfer pricing policy changed as a result, the manager of the wholesale division would need to be reassured that his performance would be compared with earlier periods under the revised transfer price and he would not be penalised for the reduced profit that came from the change.

- The wholesale group can see two markets, external and internal, in which different prices prevail. The reason why the two prices are permitted is because wholesale sales cannot be increased at present. The manager of the wholesale group would wish to make initial sales outside then transfer the balance internally; however this makes no difference to overall sales and profit.

5   Further considerations of transfer pricing

5.1   Negotiated prices

In any practical application of transfer pricing there is usually going to be some element of negotiation between the two divisional managers involved. Such negotiation may be loosely based on a market price or on costs, because it is difficult to negotiate in a complete vacuum. Empirical evidence has suggested that, where divisional managers are left to negotiate freely, market prices and costs do figure in the exercise. However, in addition, the strengths and weaknesses of individual managers in a bargaining situation will play a role.

The problem with negotiated prices is when the two divisional managers cannot agree: they then have to seek a decision from higher central management on what transfer price to charge. This conflicts with one of the main criteria set out for transfer prices, i.e. that the divisions should remain as autonomous decision-making units. Management theory suggests that decisions should always be made at the lowest appropriate level in an organisation structure.

CIMA's Management Accounting Guideline recommends the following four principles.

- Prices of all transfers in and out of a profit centre should be determined by negotiation between buyers and sellers.

- Negotiators should have access to full data on alternative sources and markets and to public and private information about market prices.

- Buyers and sellers should be completely free to deal outside the company.

- Negotiators should be fully informed on the significance of the transaction in relation to the profitability of the company as a whole.

If these principles are followed goal congruence should be achieved.

5.2 A general rule for transfer pricing

The following general rule has been put forward for setting transfer prices.

Transfer price per unit = Standard variable cost in the producing division plus the opportunity cost to the company as a whole of supplying the unit internally.

KEY POINT

Transfer price per unit = Standard variable cost in the producing division plus the opportunity cost to the company as a whole of supplying the unit internally.

The opportunity cost will be either the contribution forgone by selling one unit internally rather than externally, or the contribution forgone by not using the same facilities in the producing division for their next best alternative use.

The application of this general rule means that the transfer price equals:

- the standard variable cost of the producing division, if there is no outside market for the units manufactured and no alternative use for the facilities in that division

- the market price, if there is an outside market for the units manufactured in the producing division and no alternative more profitable use for the facilities in that division.

6 International transfer pricing

6.1 Introduction

The additional factors that need to be considered in international transfer pricing are:

- Currency risk management, which is covered in the Paper P3, but note that the following decisions should be made:

  – In which currency should the transfers be denominated? Possibilities include the supplier's currency, the receiver's currency or the parent company's currency.

  – In which currency should the supplier's invoice be settled, i.e. which currency should be used for the intra-group transfer?

- Cash funds management, which refers to the decision as to where and in which currency should cash balances be held. Some governments place restrictions on dividend payments by subsidiaries to foreign parents. It would be tempting in such a situation to sell goods intra-group to such a subsidiary at an artificially high transfer price to shift the subsidiary cash to the parent without a dividend being paid. Such a tactic is not possible where foreign governments require transfer prices to be set on an arm's length basis.

- The use of tax havens as part of the tax management of transfer pricing, which is looked at in the next section.

6.2 Transfer pricing and tax authorities

One common approach to setting international transfer prices adopted by multinational companies is to seek to minimise the group's overall total tax liability. The objective is to set transfer prices in order to report low profits in countries with high tax rates and high profits in countries with low tax rates.

This objective is frustrated in many countries whose governments require that transfer prices are set on an arm's length basis, i.e. using the prevailing market price. The principle is still useful however as a broad objective and particularly valuable when transferring goods for which no external market price exists or when operating in countries without an arm's length transfer price requirement.

If transfer prices are set on the basis of minimising tax, this can have consequences for the whole company. The three principles for a good transfer pricing system are:

- maintain divisional autonomy
- assess divisional performance objectively
- ensure goal congruence.

Clearly autonomy will be compromised if the parent company fixes transfer prices throughout the group to minimise total tax. This can have adverse motivational consequences. In extreme cases the diminished autonomy can even have adverse tax consequences, since the division could be taxed as a foreign branch rather than a subsidiary. So the objectives of reducing a group's total tax bill can even result in the group paying a higher tax bill than if the group were left alone!

6.3 The use of tax havens

Usually a country is offering low tax rates in an effort to attract foreign investment to create jobs for its workforce. A tax haven will be most attractive with the following criteria:

- low rate of corporation tax
- low withholding tax on dividends paid to overseas holding companies
- comprehensive tax treaties with other countries
- stable economy with low political risk
- lack of exchange controls
- good communications with the rest of the world
- developed legal framework so that rights can be safeguarded.

7 Rewards, incentives and agency theory

7.1 Rewards and incentives

A performance measurement and reward system influences the implementation of strategy and the behaviour of personnel, so it is important that the system is designed to foster behaviour that will encourage the strategy objectives. When designing the measurement and reward system, management must balance the short-term and long-term perspectives. A high growth strategy for an SBU could be measured on the basis of market share and on the development of an asset, e.g. service or quality performance. Cash flow and return on assets might be used exclusively to evaluate a low growth SBU.

For most monitoring systems of the strategic process, there is little relationship between the achievement of strategic objectives and the reward system. Unless great care is taken with the setting of the objectives, the organisation could have many problems.

7.2 Problems

Suppose, for example, that a multinational company paid its senior divisional managers substantial salary increases based on the division's achievement against short-term financial performance targets. These targets were expressed as a return on total assets (ROTA) percentage and this was calculated as profits divided by gross assets:

$$\text{Return on total assets (ROTA)} = \frac{\text{Profit before interest and taxes and depreciation}}{\text{Gross fixed assets} + \text{total current assets}}$$

Given huge incentives to beat these targets, it should have come as no surprise that the managers concentrated on keeping gross assets to a minimum. Initially all fixed assets were changed to leased assets and the group changed the rules to include leased assets as part of the denominator – adding to the effective costs of the asset by capitalising the lease. Then, the outstanding debtors were factored so that they were taken off the balance sheet and, again, the rules were changed to accommodate factored debtors. As a consequence, the division introduced settlement discounts directly to its customers, which encouraged them to pay early. The level of settlement discount bore no resemblance to the prevailing interest rates, but were set with reference to the divisional targets for ROTA, which were much higher.

One division even introduced a scheme whereby it sold all its stocks of raw materials and finished goods over its balance sheet date (sell at two minutes to midnight and buy back at two minutes after midnight). Since the division used overdraft financing, the funds notionally received from the sale reduced a current liability on the balance sheet, but the sale of inventories removed a major asset and hence increased the all-important ROTA percentage.

7.3 Principal and agency theory

In both decentralised and functionally organised businesses there is a need to motivate employees to strive for the good of the group. In decentralised organisations the manager of the strategic business unit (SBU) is given considerable autonomy to enable him to achieve the goal of the employing undertaking. As recent press coverage indicates, the employer is prepared to enter into substantial and complex reward schemes for key executives that are intended to secure their commitment to the goal or mission.

The concept of principal and agency theory (PAT) is based on the idea that the management of the group act for the shareholders who seek to either maximise their wealth or have a satisficing objective within certain environmental constraints. The group chief executive officer (CEO) is therefore cast in the role of a principal who hires the manager of the SBU to act as an agent to secure the fulfilment of certain tasks for a given reward. The theory behind this is that both parties are not altruistic; the agent strives for the goal because of self-interest. The principal is also prepared to pay substantially for the expertise of the manager to ensure a similar self interest.

In the parlance of this subject the success of the theory depends on a key variable (the 'optimal sharing rule') and the negotiation of a particular hazard that is referred to as the 'moral hazard'. Both these are dealt with below.

7.4 The optimal sharing rule

The idea behind an optimal sharing rule is to secure the maximum reward for both parties by means of an incentive scheme that will allow the agent freedom of action. For practical and also cultural reasons it may not be possible to monitor the performance of the agent too closely. A manager responsible for the profit of a division will expect a 'hands-off' style of management. However, through greed and other motivational factors the manager will wish to perform, or even out-perform, the target or benchmark set for him. This is achieved by a mechanism that is styled the 'incentive-compatible scheme'.

The advantage of an incentive-compatible scheme is that it lessens the principal's exposure to risk. If the SBU does well the manager prospers. If it does badly the manager does not prosper. Otley quotes the experience of International Harvester, whose CEO agreed to accept minimal rewards if he failed to outperform competitors.

The problem is that such a concept requires a method of performance evaluation that separates the performance of the manager from the performance of the division. The manager's performance is not observable; it can only be measured through a measure of profit. What PAT needs is an 'observable and well-defined surrogate of managerial performance' (D Ashton).

The implementation of any employment contract therefore depends on some unambiguous set of rules to define a contract that is legally enforceable.

If the manager feels that the method of evaluation is either illogical or biased, de-motivation may be the result. Many reward systems are designed to improve profits of the employer and wealth for the manager, therefore the evaluation process must be seen as acceptable and fair to both parties.

Clearly the manager can only be called to account if he is capable of influencing the outcomes of the division. As divisions bear allocations of head office costs, various arbitrary measures must be used so that the data is refined by filtering out those elements that are relevant to the performance of the investment from those that relate to the performance of the manager.

For example managers of profit centres will be evaluated using different data from managers of investment centres. As the latter are capable of influencing decisions on capital expenditure they will clearly bear the costs of depreciation charges as this would be regarded as a controllable cost.

For most managers, net profit would be an unacceptable measure due to the subjectivity of policies used to measure profit. Managers should therefore be evaluated on the basis of controllable operating profit.

The strategic business unit, however, must be evaluated on the basis of whatever is relevant to the success or failure of the unit/division, whether or not it is within the control of the individual unit. The crucial issue is the economic performance of the division.

7.5 Practical difficulties with measurement

- **Controllable cost** – The calculation of controllable profit depends upon the calculation of controllable and uncontrollable expenses. These are often difficult to distinguish in practice. The division may or may not be free to shop around for the goods or services used. Central computer costs are a good example of practical difficulty. The division may be obliged to use the central service but may have some discretion on the quantity of service used. On the other hand personnel department costs may be an example where the division has no choice over the quantity or price of the service offered.

- **Controllable investment** – The controllable investment consists of all the assets less liabilities that can be influenced by the manager. Assets managed by head office should not be included in the calculation. For example cash and debtors may be administered centrally and should be excluded from the calculation. Liabilities within the control of the division must be deducted from the asset base. In any event the choice of asset base must be unbiased and any performance measure must encourage the manager to act in the best interests of the group.

  The use of measures such as ROI is complicated by the various inconsistencies of traditional accounting measurement. If fixed assets are revalued upwards this will dilute ROI. A long-lived asset that is written down may produce a distorted ROI that does not accord with the reality of managerial performance.

  Similar inconsistencies arise in the use of RI because of the problems of using historic cost as the basis of measurement.

7.6 Devising a scheme

The examiner has indicated that complex mathematics will not be required in describing the ideal scheme for implementing PAT. However you should be aware of the existence of complex models which attempt to model the behaviour of principal and agent in the language of microeconomics and with the use of calculus to compute the results.

In a nutshell any scheme should concentrate on the following issues or postulates:

- The larger the fund of profits the greater the agent's share of it.

- The agent is essentially work shy or exhibits a disutility of effort. If the agent were paid a guaranteed salary he would exhibit maximum disutility of effort and would collect his salary for zero commitment. Therefore the best contract is one that rewards the agent for his effort.

The rewards should reflect the 'market rate' for the job or the agent will take no further part in the performance of the contract. This need to secure commitment must be balanced by the principal's need to maximise his own wealth in the process.

7.7 Net loss to principal: the concept of 'moral hazard'

In the literature on this subject, the subject of moral hazard refers to the problem that the principal is almost inevitably going to incur a 'loss' in economic terms as he is unable to distinguish between the genuine uncertainties of the business environment and the variances caused by the agent's behaviour. Poor profits may arise as a result of uncontrollable factors or as a result of agent incompetence. Conversely, good results can be caused by environmental cycles or through the skill of the agent. It is argued that moral hazard is a short-term phenomenon. It would be difficult to claim that poor performance was the result of uncontrollable factors in the environment and hide his incompetence or lack of drive indefinitely. Multi-period contracts may supply the answer to the problem of moral hazard.

Good accounting information that allows insightful monitoring of agent performance is the key to a successful implementation of any incentive-compatible contract.

The development of evaluation schemes is often based on relative as opposed to absolute measures. For example, a sales manager should not be evaluated on an absolute sales target as that can be manipulated by problems such as slack. An alternative would be to consider achievement in terms of relative market share as a better indication of performance.

7.8 Weaknesses of principal and agency theory

The concept of modelling employee behaviour on the basis of economic theory may appeal to those who distrust the behavioural approach to management accounting problems. However, regardless of the mathematics of agency theory there are a number of assumptions that are inherently simplistic in the view of employee behaviour.

- The principal is risk neutral and the agent risk averse.

  This may not necessarily be reasonable; there are many managers who relish work and who are genuinely motivated by the risks and rewards of business.

- The agent is a rational being who seeks to maximise his wealth (utility) by trading off the utility from earnings against the disutility of having to work for those earnings.

  This may appeal to a car assembly worker on a piecework rate but may not appeal to a complex social animal who works hard to improve his own track record and marketability in case he has to take himself off elsewhere.

- The optimal contract is one that cannot be improved on by principal or agent.

  This assumes an almost superhuman insight into the behaviour of the agent in the areas of risk, reward, money and attitude to work.

- The choice of contract is determined by some competitive market for agents in that the agent has the choice of going elsewhere in return for some financial reward.

  This may not always be clear-cut in practice.

- Finally, it is not always reasonable to analyse a single contract between agent and principal. Reward schemes are complex and hierarchical. This tends to reduce the reasonableness of the assumption of risk neutrality.

Summary

Key points of this chapter are:

- Multi-national corporations (MNCs) are very large companies, some with overall turnover in excess of all but the largest national economies.

- Transfer prices have to be set where goods are transferred internally within a company.

- Setting transfer prices can be difficult as the 'wrong' transfer price can result in sub-optimal decision making within the company.

- One method of setting the 'correct' transfer price is to set the transfer price per unit to equal the standard variable cost in the production division plus the opportunity cost to the company of supplying the unit internally.

- International transfer prices are difficult to set due to issues including different taxation rates in different countries and currency risk management.

- Principal and agency theory can assist with the setting of appropriate reward systems in a company.

Having completed your study of this chapter you should have achieved the following learning outcomes:

- evaluate and recommend appropriate control measures

- identify problems in performance measurement and recommend solutions.

Self-test questions

1   What is an MNC? (2.1)

2   What is process specialisation? (2.3)

3   What is transfer pricing? (3.1)

4   List four criteria that a transfer pricing policy should meet. (3.3)

5   What are the three main types of transfer price? (3.4)

6   What are the problems associated with market-based transfer prices? (4.2)

7   What is an optimal transfer price? (4.3)

8   What is goal congruence in terms of transfer pricing? (4.4)

9   What problems are associated with negotiated prices? (5.1)

10   What are the additional factors that need to be considered in setting a transfer pricing policy for an international organisation? (6.1)

11   What are the criteria that make a tax haven attractive? (6.3)

12   What is the agency theory? (7.3)

13   In the context of a company, who is the principal? (7.3)

14   Describe the optimal sharing rule. (7.4)

15   What is the concept of 'moral hazard'? (7.7)

Practice question

Transfer pricing

Chambers plc produces motor components and a vehicle called the Rambler. The company is split into three operating divisions - Engines, Transmissions and Assembly. The Rambler is produced in the Assembly division. Each Rambler incorporates an engine produced in the Engines division and a transmission system produced in the Transmissions division.

Each operating division is both a profit and an investment centre, with the performance of divisional managers assessed on return on capital employed (ROCE) achieved. In addition to their salary, each manager is paid a bonus each year linked to ROCE achieved in the current year. Chambers plc is financed by various means and has an average cost of capital of 7% per annum.

Relevant details concerning the three operating divisions in the coming year are as follows.

Engines division

- The variable cost of engine production is £600 per unit.

- Annual demand from outside customers for engines varies with price: it is 5,000 units at unit price £1,000 and changes by 5 units with each £1 change in unit price.

- Fixed costs are £5,000,000 per year, and capital employed is £5,200,000.

Transmissions division

- The variable cost of transmission unit production is £350 per unit.

- Annual demand from outside customers for transmission units varies with price: it is 2,500 units at unit price £1,200 and changes by 5 units with each £2 change in unit price.

- Fixed costs are £5,200,000 per year, and capital employed is £8,100,000.

Assembly division

- The variable cost (excluding transfer charges) of Rambler production is £1,500 per unit.

- Annual demand for Ramblers varies with price: it is 4,000 units at a unit price of £6,000 and changes by 2 units with each £1 change in unit price.

- Fixed costs are £5,800,000 per year, and capital employed is £10,200,000.

There are no capacity constraints in any of the divisions.

Chambers plc's transfer pricing policy is that goods transferred between divisions should be at the price charged to outside customers for the relevant units. In setting selling prices to outside customers, the Engines and Transmissions divisions must ignore the effect of transfers to the Assembly division. The manager of the Assembly division treats transfer prices for units received as variable costs.

An investment in new equipment (having a life of 5 years and a residual value of nil) is being considered by the management of the Transmissions division. The equipment would cost £850,000 and would reduce the variable cost per transmission unit by £30.

'An effective transfer pricing system in the context of a divisional organisation has to satisfy several basic criteria. The problem is that nobody has yet invented a system of transfer pricing that is capable of doing this with perfection.'

Required:

Having regard to the above statement:

(a)   list and briefly explain the criteria an effective system of transfer pricing has to satisfy

(7 marks)

(b)   discuss how far the system used by Chambers plc meets the criteria you have identified in your answer to (a); and advise Chambers plc on how it might modify its transfer pricing system in order to make it more effective   **(9 marks)**

(c)   explain the features of transfer pricing systems based on

(i)   marginal cost

(ii)   opportunity cost

(iii)   cost plus

and explain whether each of these systems meets the criteria you have identified in your answer to requirement (a).   **(9 marks)**

(Total: 25 marks)

For the answer to this question, see the 'Answers' section at the end of the book

Chapter 17

LEAN SYSTEMS, R&D, AND PRODUCT AND PROCESS DEVELOPMENT

Syllabus content

- The implementation of lean systems across an organisation.
- The role of research and development in an organisation, particularly the need to integrate product and process development.

Contents

1   Introduction

2   Lean systems

3   Just-in-time (JIT) and ERP

4   Total quality management (TQM)

5   Research and development

6   Quality management systems

1 Introduction

The business environment continues to change rapidly. Organisations are faced with fiercer competition, increasing customer expectations and the opening of new markets. This chapter considers various tools used by management in the modern business environment to give their organisations the leading edge.

2 Lean systems

2.1 Elimination of waste

'Lean' means using less human effort, lower capital investment, less floor space, fewer materials and less time in production or service delivery. In other words, it means operating with only the essential resources, preserving the good and eliminating the 'fat'. Lean systems also have a customer-oriented focus. Items are manufactured or services performed to meet specific customer orders.

Lean systems originated in a manufacturing context in Japan. A systematic approach is taken to identifying and eliminating waste in production or service performance. Waste is any activity that either:

- does not add value for the customer, or

- costs more than the value it creates.

Lean systems are closely associated with total quality management. Two essential aspects are:

- achieving a flow of production in response to customer demand, and

- a continuous search for small improvements in methods, processes and products. This should be ingrained into the culture of everyone in the organisation. Continuous improvement in Japanese is called 'kaizen'.

The lean approach calls for an attack on waste, and eliminating waste wherever it is found. There are several categories of waste.

- Waste from *over-production*, i.e. producing more than customers have ordered. If customer demand fails to materialise, the excess production has to be discarded, or sold off at a heavily-discounted price.

- Waste from *part-finished work-in-process*. Work-in-process builds up when there is a long lead time in production and delays between one stage in processing and the next. Work in process has a cost, but adds no value.

- Waste from *transporting materials* from one location to another. Any form of motion is waste, whether it involves the movement of people, information, materials, part-finished items or finished goods. Reducing movement is one of the benefits of work cell production.

- Waste in *production process procedures and methods*. Activities within manufacturing operations that do not add value should be eliminated.

- Waste from *time spent idle waiting for machines* to complete a process. The aim should be to maximise the use of the worker, not the machine.

- Waste from the manufacture of *defective items*. If defective items are spotted before they leave the factory, they must be either scrapped or re-worked. If they are not discovered until after they have been delivered to the customer, costs will arise from handling the complaint and having to take back and replace the item. Even more significantly, poor-quality output risks the loss of customer goodwill.

2.2 Continuous improvement

Continuous improvement, or kaizen, is an integral part of the lean systems approach.

- The organisation should always seek perfection. Perfection is never achieved, so there must always be some scope for improving on current methods and procedures. Improvements should be sought all the time.

- The search for perfection should involve all employees, and be part of the culture of the organisation.

- Improvements will be small and numerous rather than occasional and far-reaching.

The continuous improvement philosophy contrasts sharply with the concept underlying business process re-engineering (BPR). BPR is concerned with making far-reaching one-off changes to improve operations or processes.

3 Just-In-Time (JIT) and ERP

3.1 Introduction

Just-in-time is a system whose objective is to produce or to procure products or components as they are required by a customer or for use, rather than for stock. A just-in-time system is a 'pull' system, which responds to demand, in contrast to a 'push' system, in which stocks act as buffers between the different elements of the system, such as purchasing, production and sales. (CIMA, *Official Terminology,* 2000)

This system has gained considerable popularity in both the United States and Europe. It has a wide ranging impact upon many of the traditional organisational functions.

The production of components only when they are needed and in the quantity that is needed shortens lead times and virtually eliminates work in progress and finished goods inventories.

- **Conventional production** provides monthly production schedules to every process including the final assembly line. The preceding process supplies the parts to the subsequent process (**push through system**) that is unable to respond quickly. Each process must adjust their schedule simultaneously requiring back-up inventory between processes.

- **JIT** does not provide simultaneous schedules to every process, only for the final assembly line. Goods are built for the customer, not for stock. The system works on a **pull through basis**, drawing components through the system. It can respond quickly drawing parts as required. As soon as items are completed in one process, so the next process produces to replace.

3.2 Impact on purchasing and production

Just-in-time production is a production system that is driven by demand for finished products whereby each component on a production line is produced only when needed for the next stage. (CIMA, *Official Terminology,* 2000)

Just-in-time purchasing is a purchasing system in which material purchases are contracted so that the receipt and usage of material, to the maximum extent possible, coincide. (CIMA, *Official Terminology,* 2000)

DEFINITION

Just-in-time – a system whose objective is to produce or to procure products or components as they are required by a customer or for use, rather than for stock. A just-in-time system is a 'pull' system, which responds to demand, in contrast to a 'push' system, in which stocks act as buffers between the different elements of the system, such as purchasing, production and sales. *(CIMA Official Terminology)*

DEFINITION

Just-in-time production – a production system that is driven by demand for finished products whereby each component on a production line is produced only when needed for the next stage. *(CIMA Official Terminology)*

DEFINITION

Just-in-time purchasing – a purchasing system in which material purchases are contracted so that the receipt and usage of material, to the maximum extent possible, coincide.

- **Suppliers** – Under JIT, a buyer can **reduce the number of their suppliers.** GM reduced their suppliers by 50%. Warner-Lambert has replaced its costly batch production by a JIT based controlled process. Suppliers are also chosen because of close proximity to the plant. Long-term contracts and single sourcing is advocated to strengthen buyer-supplier relationships and tends to result in a higher quality product. Inventory problems are shifted back onto suppliers, with deliveries being made as required.

- **JIT delivery and transportation** – The spread of JIT in the production process inevitably impinges upon those in delivery and transportation. This emphasises to the student who may feel that JIT is too production orientated that it can turn up in the service sector. Ryder has established distribution centres close to its manufacturing plants. These are not warehouses, but rather extensions of the production process. As soon as an order to move material or to call off material is received, the truck moves and delivers. This means smaller more productive loads, more frequently.

  The use of JIT puts new demands on the schedules of the hauliers. Tighter schedules are required, with penalties for non-delivery. The haulier is regarded as almost a partner to the manufacturer.

  Does the haulier benefit from JIT? Tom Peters describes Union Pacific, a JIT haulier. As a result of moving to the JIT philosophy, traffic volume is up 18%, revenue 25%, productivity per employee nearly doubled, failure costs reduced to 15% of gross revenue, a saving of $750 million, and locomotive downtime reduced from 13% to 8%, a further saving of $150 million. More important, Union Pacific is now regarded by its parent company as an 'invest and grow' division.

- **Impact on cost systems** –The traditional short-term approach of the cost accountant is seen as an obstacle to the implementation of JIT. Costing systems need to be simpler and more flexible. However, before making any changes, a thorough review of the costing systems is required.

- **Inventory valuation** – The inevitable reduction in inventory levels will reduce the time taken to count inventory and the clerical cost. As for valuing inventory, Hewlett-Packard no longer adds conversion costs to inventory, but treats them as period costs.

3.3 Enterprise resource planning (ERP)

In the 1960s the focus of manufacturing systems embraced 'traditional' stock control concepts such as the EOQ. In the 1970s the focus changed to manufacturing resource planning (MRP I), enabling sub-assemblies and components to be planned for on a timely basis. In the 1980s this concept evolved into MRP II, extending MRP I first to planning and distribution management. In the 1990s MRP II was further extended into areas such as finance, human resources, project management, etc, and the concept of enterprise resource planning (ERP) was born since it encompassed all the activities carried on within both manufacturing and service enterprises.

ERP is multi-module application software that help an organisation to manage and streamline the important components of its business, including product planning, procuring parts, maintaining inventories, dealing with suppliers, providing customer service and tracking orders. It can also include modules to manage the finance and human resources responsibilities of a business.

ERP therefore attempts to provide a **total integrated solution** to integrate the suppliers and customers into the manufacturing environment of the organisation.

Traditional application packages within a business (e.g. payroll or purchasing) operate independently of each other within the boundaries of their function. The power of an ERP system is that it brings all these packages together so that the data can be used by multiple users and for multiple purposes. Initially the high cost of software and hardware meant that only the largest companies could consider adopting an ERP approach. However, the advent of cheap powerful PCs and developments in database management systems and middleware have enabled an increasing number of companies to adopt ERP. The different geographical locations can be linked using Electronic Data Interchange (EDI) or the Internet.

While MRP systems were originally designed for manufacturing companies only, ERP can be implemented in **any type of business organisation**. Benefits are not typically enjoyed immediately, but most companies who have chosen the ERP route believe that the integration of all their activities is a necessary step towards the world class excellence that they are seeking.

4 Total quality management (TQM)

4.1 Introduction

TQM is 'an integrated and comprehensive system of planning and controlling all business functions so that products or services are produced which meet or exceed customer expectations.' (CIMA *Official Terminology* 2002) Again, its origin lies primarily in Japanese organisations. It is a philosophy of business behaviour, embracing principles such as employee involvement, continuous improvement at all levels and customer focus, as well as being a collection of related techniques aimed at improving quality such as full documentation of activities, clear goal-setting and performance measurement from the customer perspective.

The basic principle of TQM is that costs of prevention (getting things right first time) are less than the costs of correction.

This contrasts with the 'traditional' UK approach that less than 100% quality is acceptable as the costs of improvement from say 90% to 100% outweigh the benefits. Thus in an analysis of quality related costs there may be a trade-off between a lowering of failure at the expense of increased prevention and appraisal costs.

Which view is correct is a matter of debate but the advocates of TQM would argue that in addition to the cost analysis above the impact of less than 100% quality in terms of lost potential for future sales also has to be taken into account.

It is apparent from the rather lengthy definition that TQM goes beyond the isolated notions of statistical quality control into the whole operating process. This means designing in quality manufacturing procedures possibly through the use of CAD/CAM, training all personnel involved with the product/service, continually maintaining equipment to ensure that standards remain up to specification and working with suppliers to eliminate defects. The latter may well involve the use of JIT. It is worth adding that TQM is expected to cross all the company's functional activities, even the accounting function.

4.2 Quality chains

The philosophy of TQM is based on the idea of a series of **quality chains** that may be broken at any point by one person or service not meeting the requirements of the customer.

The key to TQM is for everyone in the organisation to have well-defined customers – an extension of the word, beyond the customers of the company, to anyone to whom an individual provides a service. Thus the 'paint shop' staff would be customers of the 'assembly shop' staff who would themselves be the customers of the 'machine shop' staff.

The idea is that the supplier-customer relationships would form a chain extending from the company's original suppliers through to its ultimate consumers. Areas of responsibility would need to be identified and a manager allocated to each, and then the customer/supplier chain established.

True to the principle outlined above the quality requirements of each 'customer' within the chain would be assessed, and meeting these would then become the responsibility of the 'suppliers' who form the preceding link in the chain.

4.3 Characteristics of TQM companies

Thackray writing in *Management Accounting* (November 1990) indicated the following features of companies that follow TQM:

- Absolute commitment by the chief executive and all senior managers to doing what is needed to change the culture.
- People are not afraid to try new things.
- Communication is excellent and multi-way.
- There is a real commitment to continuous improvement in all processes.
- Attention is focused first on the process and second on the results to encourage employees to look for potential improvements.
- There is an absence of strict control systems.

4.4 Analysis and restructuring of resources

In many businesses, employees' time is used up in **discretionary activities** such as checking, chasing and other tasks related to product failures. Some/most of this time may be capable of being redeployed into the two other categories of work:

- core activities
- support activities.

Core activities add direct value to the business. They use the specific skills of the particular employees being examined and are the reason for their employment. Support activities are those activities that clearly support core activities and are thus necessary to allow core activities to add value. The importance of this analysis can be seen in a quote from a US Chief Executive some years ago: 'The only things you really need to run a business are materials, machines, workers and salesmen. Nobody else is justified unless he's helping the worker produce more product or the salesman sell more product.'

Analysis of employees' time will provide a clearer view of the costs of poor quality and whether efforts in other departments could reduce the amount of time spent by a department further down the product chain on discretionary activities.

For example, suppose there are seven processes from purchasing of raw materials through various stages of production to delivery of the product to the customer. If each process is 90% effective then there will be only a 48% success rate at the end of the seventh stage (90% × 90% × 90%, etc). What happens in practice however may be that personnel employed in stage 4 of the process spend a lot of their time on discretionary activities trying to remedy the effect of defects at earlier stages. It is suggested that it would be more sensible for departments in the earlier stages to **get things right the first time**.

An example quoted in a CIMA *Management Accounting* article is of an office equipment supplier that analysed employees' time into core, support and discretionary activities. It was found that half of the salesmen's face-to-face selling time with customers consisted of listening to their complaints about poor customer service.

4.5 Quality circles

Quality circles consist of about 10 employees possessing relevant levels of skill, ranging from the shop floor through to management. They meet regularly to discuss the major aspect of quality but other areas such as safety and productivity will also be dealt with.

The main aim is to be able to offer management:

- ideas connected with improvements and recommendations
- possible solutions and suggestions
- organising the implementation of the first two.

The development of quality circles allows the process of decision making to start at shop floor level, with the ordinary worker encouraged to comment, and make suggestions, as well as being allowed to put them into practice. Circle members experience the responsibility for ensuring quality, and have the power to exercise verbal complaint. Quality circles may be applied at any level of organisational activity, being used to cover all aspects, and could conceivably involve all employees.

Jaguar has effectively used this system resulting in the involvement of 10% of the workforce. A notable point here is that in one decade the number of quality inspectors required has been roughly halved. Clearly, quality circles are a practical means of gaining employee participation; they are not mainly for reducing costs although this aspect will be a major topic for discussion. Other benefits are increased awareness of shop-floor problems, members gaining confidence over problem solving, etc, greater output, improved quality and shop-floor participation.

Equally, putting this system into practice can prove difficult. The well established system of hierarchical management is difficult to penetrate, and to some organisations it would present extreme changes. Some systems may not be able to accommodate such change, e.g. the armed forces or police force where a powerful hierarchy has developed.

DEFINITION

Quality control is the process of:

- establishing standards of quality for a product or service

- establishing procedures or production methods that ought to ensure that these required standards of quality are met in a suitably high proportion of cases

- monitoring actual quality

- taking control action when actual quality falls below standard.

4.6 Quality control

Quality control is the title given to the more traditional view of quality. It is the process of:

- establishing standards of quality for a product or service

- establishing procedures or production methods that ought to ensure that these required standards of quality are met in a suitably high proportion of cases

- monitoring actual quality

- taking control action when actual quality falls below standard.

The contrast with TQM is that less than 100% quality may be regarded as acceptable. Eradicating the costs of failure of a product should be weighed against higher prevention costs for example. Charts such as **statistical control charts** are often used to monitor quality in such instances especially in terms of the physical dimensions of the component parts of a product or the strength of a product.

4.7 Measurement of quality

Many companies in industrialised countries are adopting quality improvement as a primary corporate objective. As a management accountant this will impinge upon you in two ways. First, the implementation of TQM on all the company's functional activities. Secondly, and perhaps more important, where quality priorities are tied to enhancing the value of products/services that an entity provides to its customers. This covers a wide range of criteria. Measures that might be used to control and improve quality of performance include:

- proportion of deliveries made on time

- number of sub-standard products

- the amount of reworks

- frequency and length of machine breakdowns

- the launch time of new products

- number and gravity of customer complaints.

4.8 Quality related costs

CIMA *Official Terminology* defines and analyses the types of cost related to quality. A report, *The effectiveness of the corporate overhead in British business* (Develin & Partners 1989), estimated that the average cost of waste and mistakes in the UK at that time represented 20 per cent of controllable corporate overhead.

Cost of quality is defined as the difference between the actual cost of producing, selling and supporting products or services and the equivalent costs if there were no failures during production or usage. (*CIMA Official Terminology* 2000)

The cost of quality can be analysed into:

- **Cost of conformance** – The cost of achieving specified quality standards.

  - **Cost of prevention** – The costs incurred prior to or during production in order to prevent substandard or defective products or services from being produced.

  - **Cost of appraisal** – Costs incurred in order to ensure that outputs produced meet required quality standards.

- **Cost of non-conformance** – The cost of failure to deliver the required standard of quality.

  - **Cost of internal failure** – The costs arising from inadequate quality that are identified before the transfer of ownership from supplier to purchaser.

  - **Cost of external failure** –The cost arising from inadequate quality discovered after the transfer of ownership from supplier to purchaser.

4.9 Classification of quality costs

From the CIMA definitions quoted above, we can analyse and illustrate the different costs of quality.

(a) Costs of non-conformance can be sub-divided under two headings:

- **Internal failure costs** – Failure costs discovered **before** the product is delivered to customers. Examples include:

  - rework or rectification costs

  - net cost of scrap

  - disposal of defective products

  - downtime or idle time due to quality problems.

- **External failure costs** – Failure costs discovered **after** the product is delivered to the customer. Examples include:

  - complaint investigation and processing

  - warranty claims

  - cost of lost sales

  - product recalls.

The inclusion of **cost of lost sales** emphasises another important feature of TQM, that it crosses the traditional functions within an organisation. Marketing and sales have to be concerned about the quality of the product they are presenting.

Product recalls do little for the image of the product/service. While it does show concern for quality and safety, it emphasises that a procedure failed somewhere and was not detected until too late.

KEY POINT

Costs of conformance
are costs required to
prevent the production
of poor quality goods in
the first place.

(b)   **Costs of conformance** are also subdivided:

- **Appraisal costs** – Costs of monitoring and inspecting products in terms of specified standards before the products are released to customers. This is very much the traditional view of quality control. Examples might be:

    –   the capital cost of measurement equipment

    –   inspection and testing

    –   product quality audits

    –   process control monitoring

    –   test equipment expense.

- **Prevention costs** – Investments in machinery, technology, education and training programmes designed to reduce the number of defective products during production. Examples are:

    –   customer surveys

    –   research of customer needs

    –   field trials

    –   quality education and training programmes

    –   supplier reviews

    –   investment in improved production equipment

    –   quality engineering

    –   quality circles.

In western industrialised countries, products have always been considered defective if they do not conform to internally set and agreed specifications and standards. Today, however, a customer has a higher expectation of the product he is buying and his standards may be higher than that of the manufacturer. The customer of the future will expect a longer guarantee for his durable product, possibly even over life. Thus prevention will be about making design standards that conform to the expectations of customers in the form of 'super-prevention costs'.

5 Research and development

5.1 Introduction

Any strategy built around lean systems thinking presupposes that the company has the ability to improve existing products and systems, to introduce new ones, to innovate, and to adapt, and this probably means that it needs an active research and development department.

Diagram: The effect of R&D on product development

The firm will hope, as a result of research and development, to come up with completely new products or with better products that may be one of three basic types:

- an improved product, which is based on and is not very different from an existing product but which is clearly superior

- a competitive product, which is similar to existing products but which offers some advantages and some disadvantages compared with existing products

- a breakthrough product, which offers a dramatic improvement over an existing product (usually as a result of new technology) in terms of much lower price, or much better performance, or both.

5.2 Choice of research and development strategies

There are several different research and development strategies a firm could pursue.

- The R&D department responds to the needs specified by the marketing department or the production department. The production department needs a new process – the R&D department designs one. The marketing department thinks there is a need for a product with certain characteristics aimed at this market and employing that technology – the R&D department produces one. In this case there is very little innovation and the R&D department is largely an extension of the marketing department. In advising the R&D department, the marketing department will be taking account of latent demand (where there is an identified group of customers who have expressed a desire for a product to fill a particular need for which no present product exists) or incipient demand (where the customers have not yet themselves identified a need, but trends point to the emergence of a need in the future). These are contrasted with established demand, which is known to exist because products are available for a specific need, and have been bought.

- At the other extreme, the R&D department engages in pure research; that is, it examines new technology generally without any particular purpose in view, in the hope that something useful will emerge. This implies that the company will employ highly qualified academics to conduct its research and that large sums of money will be spent – possibly for little commercial return. Probably few companies today are prepared to do this, even when they are doing well. Besides, there are other ways of keeping abreast of developments in pure research – the company can, for instance, buy knowledge from the universities.

- In between these two extremes comes applied research. The basic pure research has been done, the characteristics of the new technology are known, and it is the job of the R&D department to see how this knowledge can be applied to the company's advantage. Again, it is not certain that anything positive will emerge, but there is less uncertainty than in pure research. As the result of applied research, the development part of the R&D department might pursue ideas for product development or for product or process application (i.e. finding new uses for existing products or processes). Applied research can of course lead to diversification as well as to product development for existing markets.

5.3 Structure of the research and development organisation

In deciding the size and aims of the R&D department, the company must take into account the following.

- Its R&D competence. Ability of staff, experience, its record of success in development of new products and in new applications, etc.

- Minimum effective size. It is no good pretending to engage in R&D if in reality the firm is not prepared to commit enough resources to make the research worthwhile. The minimum effective size will differ from industry to industry but ought to be considered before any resources are committed.

- Competitive activity. It is not worthwhile developing a new product if a larger competitor is likely to do something similar (better?) at the same time. This means that a company should know its competitors' research competence as well as its own, and try to concentrate on areas where it is strong and they are weak.

- Whether it wants to be/needs to be/has the ability to be an innovator. This is largely a question of available resources (money, people and facilities). It is no good researching an idea if there is not enough money to finance the development right up to the stage when the idea becomes a marketable product, or if production facilities cannot be expanded in time to manufacture the new product in sufficient quantities to be economic.

KEY POINT

There have been some notable successes by companies coming second into a new field.

There have been some notable successes by companies coming second into a new field. They let someone else develop the product, test the market and discover the snags; then when it looks as though sales are beginning to 'take off' they enter the arena with a slightly better product. (This still means having an active R&D department, keeping abreast of what the first company is up to and having one's own product ready at just the right time.) They avoid some of the research expenditure and most of the initial 'teething troubles', and they end up with more up-to-date equipment than the company who began earlier, and can therefore manufacture more economically and continue for longer. They both overtake the innovator and have a head start on those who attempt to enter the field at a later stage.

Such an approach is, of course, not without its own risks – the company has to have very good intelligence about its competitors' activities and has to pick just the right moment to enter the fray. It also has to negotiate patent laws carefully. Nevertheless the risks are less than for innovation.

KEY POINT

A company need not always adopt the same research strategy – it might be an innovator in one field, a 'copier' in another, and do no development work at all in another field.

A company need not always adopt the same research strategy – it might be an innovator in one field, a 'copier' in another, and do no development work at all in another field. One possibility that should not be forgotten is the use of licence arrangements. For instance, Fiat cars are made under licence in Poland – this provides the Polish company with a ready-made product. There is also the possibility of an acquisition of or merger with another company already engaged in a different field.

5.4 The role of innovation in strategy

The importance of innovation in strategy is one of the most hotly disputed questions in the subject. In many cases, the most innovative companies in an industry consistently fail to be among the most profitable. This creates a divergence of opinion over the role of innovation-based strategy.

KEY POINT

It is innovation that frequently undermines the basis of competition in existing markets, and creates new markets that may supersede old ones.

A company that chooses not to be innovative is still influenced by the effect of innovation. It is innovation that frequently undermines the basis of competition in existing markets, and creates new markets that may supersede old ones. Firms must learn to innovate with greater commercial effectiveness than is the case at present, or learn to replicate innovations more quickly than they would choose to as the rate of innovation is often too quick for a balanced assessment of it to be carried out in a sensible time period.

Richard Lynch identifies three distinctive roles for innovation within a business level strategy:

- achieving new growth through entry into new products and markets
- retaining competitive advantage by strengthening the product offering
- achieving competitive advantage through jumping ahead of existing rivals.

6 Quality management systems

6.1 Introduction

There is no one best approach to implementing lean systems across all organisations. In this section we are going to look at the approach advocated by the ISO 9000 family of standards on quality management systems — not because they are specifically mentioned in your syllabus, and certainly not so that you can learn them off by heart, but because the latest versions, published in 2000, encompass much modern thinking about the issues and best practice. At a more pragmatic level, for very many organisations it is either highly desirable to achieve quality certification or even a requirement for doing business.

The term 'ISO 9000' refers to a family of quality management standards. In the UK ISO 9000 is more properly referred to as BS EN ISO 9000, the BS indicating that it is endorsed by the British Standard Institution (BSI), and the EN indicating that it is endorsed by the Comité Européen de Normalisation (CEN).

Quality management standards began in the UK with BS 5750 in 1979. This was reissued in 1994, in slightly modified form, as BS EN ISO 9000 which had three parts: ISO 9001, ISO 9002 and 9003. The 1994 version has now been entirely superseded by the 2000 version. The numbers 9002 and 9003 are no longer used.

6.2 The ISO 9000 family

The ISO 9000 family includes four principal standards.

- **ISO 9000:2000**. *Quality management systems. Fundamentals and vocabulary*. This describes basic concepts and specifies the terminology for quality management systems.

- **ISO 9001:2000**. *Quality management systems. Requirements*. This specifies the requirements for a quality management system where an organisation needs to demonstrate its ability to provide products that fulfil customer and applicable regulatory requirements and aim to enhance customer satisfaction.

  If an organisation wishes to obtain independent **certification** of its quality system it will be audited and assessed according to the requirements set out here.

- **ISO 9004:2000**. *Quality management systems. Guidelines for performance improvements*. This is a more detailed version of ISO 9001:2000: it includes all the key sections of ISO 9001:2000 and adds further notes explaining the requirements in more detail and giving examples. It is used for guidance purposes, not for certification.

- **ISO 9011:2002**. *Guidelines for Quality and/or Environmental Management Systems Auditing*. This provides guidance on auditing quality and environmental management systems.

There are also a number of subsidiary standards on more specialist topics such as requirements for measuring equipment, requirements specific to automotive suppliers, and so on.

6.3 Certification under ISO 9001

Organisations may decide that they need to develop a quality management system that meets the ISO 9000 family of standards for a variety of reasons.

- because they feel the need to control or improve the quality of their products

- to reduce costs, or become more competitive

- because customers expect them to do so

- because they want to supply products to a government body that refuses to do business with organisations unless their quality management systems are independently verified.

In the last two examples it is clearly helpful to be able to produce proof of compliance with the standards and this is available in the form of a certificate.

To become certified the organisation has to develop a quality management system that meets the requirements specified by ISO 9001:2000. (Note that ISO 9000 and ISO 9004 are guidelines, not requirements.)

Once the quality system has been fully developed and implemented, the organisation must ask an independent Registrar to audit it. Registrars are organisations who are accredited to issue ISO 9001 certificates by the relevant national body, e.g. the United Kingdom Accreditation Service (UKAS). After the audit, all being well, the Registrar will issue an official certificate and potential customers will accept this as proof of compliance with ISO 9001.

6.4 Key concepts and outline

Customer focus

The starting point for quality is in the wants and needs of customers and this is very much recognised in the ISO 9000:2000 family. ISO 9000 states from the outset that the purpose of a quality management system is to assist organisations to enhance customer satisfaction.

This means finding out and understanding customer needs, and then at least meeting those needs and, preferably, exceeding expectations.

Continuous improvement

The standards also recognise that in the modern world, with its ever-increasing competitive pressures and technological advances, customers' needs and expectations will constantly change. Great emphasis is therefore placed on continuous improvement of products and processes.

This means that the organisation should engage in a constant cycle of analysing the existing situation to identify areas for improvement, seeking possible solutions, and then measuring results once the chosen solutions have been implemented to ensure that things really have improved.

Top management leadership and involvement

Quality management systems should be initiated and championed by the most senior management in the organisation. They should promote the quality objectives to ensure that all staff are aware of them and are involved in implementing them. They should ensure that any resources that are needed are available and they should keep the quality management system under constant review.

A process approach

The ISO 9000 family take the view that if an organisation is to operate effectively it needs to identify and manage a large number of linked activities. Work activities (processes) use resources and transform them into outputs. The output from one process often forms the input into another.

This 'process approach' is seen as the best way of achieving control over the linkage between individual processes and ensuring that they combine and interact effectively.

Products and product realisation

The ISO 9000 family use the term 'product' in a very broad sense: a product is simply the 'result of a process'. There are 4 generic product categories.

– Services (for example a restaurant)

– Software (for example a dictionary, or a computer program)

– Hardware (for example a mechanical part)

– Processed materials (for example lubricant)

Many products are actually a combination of one or more categories. A car, for instance, is a combination of all four things.

Product realisation is another important term, as we shall see later. This refers to the interconnected processes that are used to bring products into being. A product starts out as an idea which is then realised by following a set of product realisation processes.

Outline

ISO 9001:2000 has three introductory sections covering matters such as the above and then sets out its requirements under five main headings.

- Quality management system

- Management responsibility

- Resource management

- Product realisation

- Measurement, analysis and improvement

6.5 Quality management system

General requirements

An organisation should identify and describe the processes that it wants to make up its quality system, and then use and manage those processes. The performance of the system should be monitored and improved where necessary.

Documentation requirements

Quality system documents consist of a quality manual, forms and checklists, external documents such as government regulations or customer specifications, and records such as accounting records, timesheets, production schedules, correspondence – anything, in fact, that provides evidence of the processes being carried out.

In a modern organisation it is unlikely that quality 'documents' will be printed, paper documents. The organisation's intranet is the ideal home for such documentation.

In a complex organisation the quality manual may be a very large and detailed document. It defines the scope of the quality system, documents all of its processes and describes how they interact.

Note that the manual should explain how processes interact. This is a crucial point. Although staff may not need to know in detail how every other part of the organisation does its work, they must always remember that what they do has an impact on other parts of the organisation.

6.6 Management responsibility

The initiative to implement a quality management system needs to come from the very top of the organisation and be communicated to everyone within the organisation. A positive attitude towards quality management needs to be so deeply ingrained that it is an expectation: something so fundamental that staff would never even consider approaching their work in any other way.

Management commitment

Top management should be heavily involved in the quality management system and give it their unqualified support. ISO 9001 stipulates that such managers should be involved in formulating quality policy and objectives (see below), should actively promote the importance of quality throughout the organisation and should periodically perform quality management reviews and provide whatever resources are needed for maintenance of the system and further improvement.

Customer focus

Customer focus is about identifying customer requirements, meeting those requirements and enhancing customer satisfaction.

ISO 9001 says that top management should approach their own work with these aims in mind and they should expect everyone in their organisation to do likewise.

Quality policy

ISO 9001 says that management should devise a quality policy and ensure that it is appropriate to their organisation's purpose. It should emphasise the need to meet quality requirements and make a commitment to continuous improvement. It should facilitate the development of quality objectives (see below). It should be communicated and understood throughout the organisation and it should be reviewed regularly to ensure that it is still suitable.

Planning

ISO 9001 requires management to ensure that appropriate and measurable objectives are set for all functional areas and at all organisational levels. It is top management's responsibility to plan a quality management system such as that described in ISO 9001 and make sure that it continues to work effectively and is improved where possible.

Responsibility, authority and communication

Management should define, clarify and communicate responsibilities and authorities for people whose work affects quality. They should appoint a person to oversee the quality management system, report on the status of the system and support its improvement, and they should ensure that internal communication processes are established and that communication occurs throughout the organisation.

Management review

The quality management system should be kept under review. In most organisations this is probably done via a monthly or quarterly meeting of directors and other managers at which performance to date is discussed, and ideas for improvements are presented and approved. The meeting or other review process is likely to have a regular agenda of matters to discuss, or 'inputs'. Outputs from the review process should be decisions and actions that will improve the quality system, improve products so that they better meet customer requirements, and obtain whatever resources will be needed to achieve this.

6.7 Resource management

Quality resources

To meet the requirements of this section of ISO 9001 the organisation must be able to show that it has identified and provided the resources needed to implement, maintain and improve the quality system and to enhance customer satisfaction.

This means people, the place where they work and the things that they work with.

Human resources

Everybody in the organisation may affect quality in some way, but some people's work will have a more direct impact than others. An organisation's staff should have the right experience, education, training and skills to do the job that they do.

The organisation should define acceptable levels of competence for each job, and maintain records of competence (typically this would be part of an individual's personnel record).

The organisation needs to be able to show that it takes measures to identify individuals' training needs and then delivers training programmes to meet those needs.

The organisation also needs to evaluate the effectiveness of training. For example, if people continue to miss deadlines after going on a time management course, perhaps there is another reason for the problem such as insufficient knowledge of the system, or perhaps something not related to training at all.

Infrastructure

Infrastructure consists of buildings, workspace and associated utilities, hardware/equipment, software (this means reference books as well as computer programs) and support services (for instance the internal telephone system, the fleet of delivery vehicles). ISO 9001 requires organisations to identify, provide and maintain infrastructure needs.

Work environment

This requirement says that the organisation should identify and manage work environment factors needed to ensure that products meet quality requirements. There is some overlap with infrastructure here: for instance the lighting, temperature and décor might be considered part of the environment as well as part of the infrastructure.

Some aspects of the work environment are merely practical: for example people whose work needs quiet concentration should not be expected to work in areas that have constantly ringing telephones or machinery noise.

Some aspects are social, psychological and cultural: auditors might be able to observe whether staff willingly co-operate with their colleagues, and can ask them, say, if they feel that they are given enough freedom, or a host of other questions. Of course, there are no right answers that apply to all organisations: different environments suit different companies.

6.8 Product realisation

A product starts out as an idea which is then made real by following a set of product 'realisation' processes.

Because of the huge variety of possible products and methods of realising them the ISO allows organisations to ignore or exclude any requirement in the product realisation section if they cannot apply it because of the nature of the organisation or the nature of the product.

Planning of product realisation

This is a general requirement to plan and develop product realisation processes in the light of the organisation's quality objectives and its customers' requirements. Planning will include devising product realisation documents and record-keeping systems, and methods to control quality during product realisation.

Customer-related processes

Requirements related to the product need to be considered from three points of view: the customer, any relevant external body, and the organisation itself. External bodies may set legal requirements or industry standards that the product has to meet. The organisation's own requirements cannot be ignored. For instance, although the customer may not care if a product bears a company logo and contact details, it is likely to be a very good idea for the producing organisation's marketing purposes. Perhaps the most important organisational requirement is cost: the organisation may be able to produce what a customer wants, but not at a profit. As a one-off this may be a worthwhile gesture of goodwill, but the company will soon be bankrupt if it ignores the organisational requirement to cover its costs. Whenever an organisation commits itself to providing a product it should be sure that the customer's requirements are fully defined and understood and that the organisation has the ability to meet those requirements. Requirements will, of course, change from time to time and appropriate records should be kept of new instructions, negotiations, and contract changes.

The organisation should establish effective communications with the customer to ensure that product information is available and there are suitable channels for enquiries, feedback and complaints.

For a typical modern organisation this means (at the very least) that there should be customer service staff answering telephones, sending out product information on request and dealing with written correspondence. In addition a website is now almost obligatory: this can show product information in detail, provide e-mail links for enquiries and allow customers to view the current status of their orders.

Design and development

ISO 9001 has seven requirements under this heading. Remember that we are talking about product realisation – taking an initial idea and turning it into something that the customer wants – and that a 'product' need not be a physical product.

- Design and development planning
- Design and development inputs
- Design and development outputs
- Design and development review
- Design and development verification
- Design and development validation
- Control of development changes

Purchasing

ISO 9001 says that organisations should establish criteria for selecting, evaluating and re-evaluating suppliers and purchased products and services. One way of doing this, of course, is to insist that the suppliers themselves are certified under ISO 9001.

Documentation should clearly describe the products or services being purchased and include details of whatever specifications are appropriate: size, colour, format, length and so on. If this information is spelled out in detail it is easier for purchasing staff to buy the right items and easier for suppliers to supply them.

The organisation should also have systems to verify purchased products before they use them.

Production and service provision

This section deals with the actual production processes.

The organisation should carry out production and service processes under 'controlled' conditions. Here are some examples of controls.

- Information that describes the product should be available.
- Work instructions should set out how the product is made.
- Any equipment used should be suitable for the job.
- Monitoring and measuring devices should be available and properly used.
- Authorisation to release the product for despatch.
- Controls over product delivery and post-delivery activities.

Control of monitoring and measuring devices

This requirement is about monitoring and measuring of product realisation processes as opposed to monitoring and measuring of the quality management system as a whole, which is dealt with in the final section of ISO 9001.

Practically all physical products need to conform to size, shape, weight or volume requirements. If an organisation claims to produce 2cm tap washers those washers should measure 2cm, otherwise they will not fit into the taps they are intended for.

This requirement says that organisations should identify the monitoring and measuring that needs to be done; select devices (weights, meters, computer software and so on) that meet those monitoring and measuring needs; and protect them from unauthorised adjustment, damage or deterioration. Equipment should regularly be 'calibrated', which means that its operation should be checked against a standard measure.

6.9 Measurement, analysis and improvement

In broad terms the final section of ISO 9001 is about 'remedial processes'. The requirements are intended to ensure that the organisation makes the effort to find out whether it is conforming to its quality objectives and takes appropriate action if not.

Monitoring and measurement

Organisations are firstly required to identify ways to monitor and measure customer satisfaction—and then actually do so and use the customer satisfaction information.

Third party registrars will conduct an independent 'external' audit of the entire quality management system, but one of the things they will be looking for is evidence that the organisation carries out its own regular 'internal' audits and that any problems discovered during audits are solved.

The organisation should use suitable methods to monitor and measure its processes and take action when the processes fail to achieve planned results. Obviously the way in which this is applied will vary enormously, depending on the process in question and what its planned result is.

Even if the organisation has decided to ignore or exclude the detailed product monitoring and measurement requirements under the product realisation section because they are inappropriate, it is still required to make some effort to verify that product characteristics are being met and it should keep a record of product monitoring and measuring activities.

Control of non-conforming products

A non-conforming product is any product that the organisation produces that does not conform to the customer's expectations for some reason: it is the wrong size or shape; it is delivered late; it breaks after the first use and so on.

- Take measures to prevent the delivery of non-conforming products. Ideally this means developing a quality management system that is so good that non-conforming products can never be delivered. Failing that, it means taking positive action to test products before sending them out.

- Eliminate or correct product non-conformities. Records should be kept describing product non-conformities and the actions taken to deal with them.

If the organisation does ever deliver non-conforming products the system should control subsequent events. In other words there should be an effective system for dealing with refunds or replacements or repairs, with minimum fuss for the disappointed customer.

The organisation should decide how non-conforming products should be identified and how they should be handled.

Analysis of data

This requirement simply emphasises the need to determine, collect and analyse the information needed to evaluate and improve the organisation's quality system. Specifically it mentions information about customers, suppliers, products and processes.

Improvement

If an effective quality management system is in place there will always be room for improvement. Organisations should use the information they glean from audits, management reviews, corrective and preventive actions and so on to generate improvements.

Summary

Key points of this chapter are:

- Lean systems are used to try and eliminate waste in a company and provide a basis for continuous improvement (Kaizen)

- Other methods of minimising costs in inventory systems include Just-In-Time and Enterprise Resource Planning.

- The concept of Total Quality Management (TQM) – that is managing quality at each stage in the production process – has been developed to assist in monitoring the different costs of quality.

- Research and development is used to enhance product quality although being first with a new product does not necessarily mean that product is the 'best'.

- Quality management systems include the ISO 9000 and 9001 series with many companies choosing to implement these systems as a method of providing external recognition of maintaining product quality.

Having completed your study of this chapter you should have achieved the following learning outcomes:

- evaluate and recommend appropriate control measures

- identify problems in performance measurement and recommend solutions.

Self-test questions

1   What does the term lean systems mean? (2.1)

2   Give examples of waste in production. (2.1)

3   Explain the term 'kaizen'. (2.2)

4   Explain how just-in-time parameters affect suppliers, delivery and transportation and cost systems. (3.2)

5   What are discretionary activities, core activities and support activities? (4.4)

6   Give two examples of each of the following quality costs: internal failure, external failure, appraisal, prevention. (4.9)

7   What types of products could an organisation hope to derive from R&D? (5.1)

8   What types of R&D strategies might a firm pursue? (5.2)

9   What factors should a firm take into account in deciding the size and aims of its R&D facility? (5.3)

10   What roles might innovation play within a business level strategy? (5.4)

11   What is a product, in the view of the ISO 9000 standards? (6.4)

12   The ISO 9001 requirements are organised under five main headings. What are they? (6.4)

13   How can an organisation meet the resource management requirements of ISO 9001? (6.7)

14   What is a non-conforming product and what should be done about it? (6.9)

Practice question

Limitation of traditional management accounting

The modern manufacturing environment is characterised by more flexibility, a readiness to meet customers' requirements, smaller batches, continuous improvements and an emphasis on quality. In such circumstances, traditional management accounting performance measures are, at best, irrelevant and, at worst, misleading.

Required:

(a)   Discuss the above statement, providing specific examples to support or refute the views expressed   **(10 marks)**

(b)   Explain in what ways management accountants can adapt the services they provide to the new environment.   **(7 marks)**

(Total: 17 marks)

For the answer to this question, see the 'Answers' section at the end of the book.

Chapter 18

KNOWLEDGE MANAGEMENT

Syllabus content

- The concept of knowledge management and its role as a key element in an organisation's success.

Contents

1 Introduction

2 Knowledge building

3 Knowledge management

4 Learning

5 The learning organisation

6 Channels of communication

7 Appropriate systems

1 Introduction

According to the management gurus, we now live in a knowledge society. Yet evidence suggests that we have not begun to use our knowledge effectively in business, let alone in society at large.

Though information technologies can offer ever-expanding possibilities to collect, process and distribute information, turning that information into useful knowledge, and then that knowledge into value, is a more subtle art in which technology only plays a supporting role.

2 Knowledge building

2.1 Introduction

In *Images of Organisations*, Gareth Morgan identifies eight ways of looking at organisations. One of these ways is to view the organisation as a human brain. This metaphor could lead us to think that:

- organisations are networks of information flows rather like a telecommunications network

- organisations can learn and new expertise can be developed

- organisations are stocks of knowledge.

Any organisation contains expertise accumulated from experience. This ties in with the notion of synergy. Knowledge exists in teams and ways of working as well as in individuals.

Much attention has been focused on new product and process developments to sustain competitive advantage. Organisations have been advised to invest heavily in technology, take advantage of cheap overseas labour, revise employment contracts to favour short-term arrangements, and to downsize or rightsize their organisational structures to enhance efficiency. However, the link between theory and practice in managing knowledge for competitive advantage has not been fully exploited. In particular, managers need to consider how organisations learn and how knowledge and experience can be exploited for competitive advantage.

2.2 Knowledge creating

Tom Peters has stated that one of the keys to organisational success is constant innovation (continuous improvement). Innovation can occur in a variety of areas, e.g. new product or production technology. Where quality, technology and variety are all becoming widely available at relatively low cost, the only sustainable competitive advantage that a company can create may be the ability to learn faster than its rivals and to anticipate changes in the business environment. Peters argues that 'successful companies are those that consistently create new knowledge, disseminate it widely throughout the organisation and quickly embody it in new technologies and products. These activities define the knowledge creating company, whose sole business is continuous innovation'.

Creating new knowledge depends on tapping the highly subjective insights, intuitions and hunches and making those insights available for testing and use by the company as a whole. This implies that:

- no one individual or group of individuals can, even in principle, be the source of all knowledge about an organisation's activities

- there must be a way whereby all individuals can communicate their insights to other members of the organisation, so that these insights flow into a pool of knowledge from which the whole organisation can draw.

There are two types of knowledge:

- **Explicit** – this is formal and standardised and can be easily shared and communicated. For example, knowing the basics of how to drive a car is explicit. You could explain it to someone else.

- **Tacit** – is personal and rooted in a specific context. Once you learn how to drive a car and have been doing it for some time, you develop certain techniques (and bad habits) and driving becomes second nature. However, this phase is more difficult   to articulate.

KEY POINT

Explicit knowledge is formal and standardised and will normally be written down.

Tacit knowledge is peronsal and not normally written; it resides in a person's head.

Using these two types of knowledge, we can see that there could be four ways of acquiring or creating knowledge:

(a)   **Explicit to explicit** – is the standard way that management information is created and amalgamated, e.g. monthly sales figures.

(b)   **Tacit to tacit** – the data capture skills, e.g. keying in the invoice details from different suppliers, can be transferred to a trainee whilst sitting next to someone who has been doing it for a while.

(c)   **Tacit to explicit** – this is where the knowledge can be articulated to another person and understanding takes place.

(d)   **Explicit to tacit** – individuals take in the knowledge and it becomes a part of their expertise, i.e. internalised. Experience and learning enables individuals to make connections between events and to increase their knowledge and understanding of certain situations.

To ensure that the interchanges between individual tacit and shared explicit knowledge take place, tacit knowledge has to be tapped and articulated.

When an organisation needs to find out how to do something, e.g. how to make a bread-making machine, they can visit a baker and watch the way he or she kneads and rolls the dough and then incorporate this knowledge into the machine specification. This is a form of benchmarking.

To obtain cost-reducing ideas, Xerox attempted to identify organisations in other industries that were particularly good in functional areas similar to themselves. One of their models for the warehouse operations was LL Bean, a sportswear retailer and mail order house. They were chosen because they dealt with products that were diverse in shape, size and weight. Altogether Xerox made six warehouse benchmark studies, which helped it improve its annual productivity gains in the logistics and distribution area. Company-wide efforts of this type meant that Xerox overcame a cost gap with respect to Japanese manufacturers.

Companies not engaged in direct competition are more open, and so there is more chance of discovering innovative practices. For example, Hewlett-Packard wanted to apply computer technology to its packaging and shipping procedures, so they went to Federal Express because they were the best in shipping. The knowledge gained from studying Federal Express's shipping procedures gave them the educational tools needed to improve their own material handling operations.

2.3 Knowledge building

Deciding what data to select and how to form it in order to produce information requires some prior knowledge or understanding of the nature of the problem to be solved. This means that there is a relationship between knowledge, data and information. Knowledge of a particular kind of situation will guide the search for data and the filtering of unwanted data. Knowledge will also influence how the data is transformed into information. The information produced in this process will have an effect on knowledge, which will then affect further selection and filtering of data.

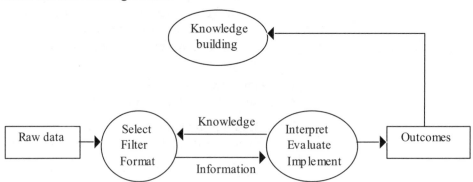

Diagram: How raw data is used to build knowledge

2.4 Knowledge acquisition

In the process of a person gaining knowledge in a particular domain they become more effective at problem solving in that domain and they also become more efficient in use of information in that decision-making context. This means that a given quantity of information supplied to an 'expert' has greater value than the same quantity supplied to a non-expert. Expertise is gained by building general knowledge of a field, and this is distinct from gathering information for solving a particular problem. Therefore information of a general nature which is collected by individuals has a value because it increases the value of specific information which is later used by that same individual to solve problems.

3 Knowledge management

3.1 Introduction

Mayo defines knowledge management as the management of the information, knowledge and experience available to an organisation – its creation, capture, storage, availability and utilisation – in order that organisational activities build on what is already known and extend it further.

Knowledge management is a relatively new approach to business in which an organisation consciously and comprehensively gathers, organises, shares and analyses its knowledge to further its aims.

The capture of knowledge that is generated by learning is one of the key factors that is driving the interest of knowledge management.

A number of organisations are appointing managers as learning officers or knowledge officers and installing networked software to accentuate the process.

3.2 Assessing its worth

As early as the 1960s some American companies were already trying to put a value on their knowledge holders, calculating the worth of staff qualifications, training and experience. In technology-intensive industries such as pharmaceuticals and electronics, investment in recruitment and training were regarded as capital rather than current items. These ideas never spread far, owing to the practical difficulties of measurement and the subjective judgements involved. Since then, however, IT has transformed the way we handle data and more effective human resources management has brought greater precision to the assessment process.

Unfortunately, conventional balance sheets reveal less and less about the real strength and value of a company, as the service and knowledge sectors continue to grow. When IBM bought the software firm Lotus, which had a book value of around $500 million, it actually paid $3.5 billion – the additional $3 billion representing Lotus's intellectual assets.

To be of any interest to managers and shareholders alike, intellectual capital should not be measured in terms of past performance but should be identified in ways that reassure stakeholders of the sustainability of future performance.

3.3 Where the knowledge resides

Knowledge-based companies will vary from industry to industry but there are some broad common principles about where knowledge resides and how to capture its value. The intellectual capital can be divided between:

- **human capital** which comprises:

    human resources – the knowledge, skills and experience possessed by employees can be easily overlooked in times of crisis, just when it is most needed; this knowledge is vital to all service companies

- **structural capital**, which is in turn divided into:

    – innovation capital – intellectual property

    – customer capital – address lists and client records

    – organisational capital – e.g. systems for processing policies and claims.

Examples of structural capital are:

Patents and technical knowledge – e.g. these resources are often bigger than expected and rarely fully utilised.

Marketing and sales knowledge – i.e. precise knowledge of how, where and when to sell and who may buy becomes critical in attacking new market niches and international opportunities.

Operations knowledge – i.e. better access to operational knowledge distributed widely throughout the organisation can speed processes, reduce duplication and reveal new competitive opportunities. However, staff must be integrated and taught to co-operate and communicate.

IT knowledge – i.e. competitiveness demands that organisations use all available techniques to exploit their knowledge and stay ahead.

The relative importance of each category varies according to the nature of the business. For pharmaceutical companies, intellectual property such as patents and clinical test data are the lifeblood of the business. For computer or chemical companies, technology is important, but so is the knowledge of applying it to suit customers' individual needs. For food and drinks companies or retailers, the crucial knowledge is of consumers' purchasing habits and ways of influencing them.

Knowledge management is most likely to yield dividends when applied to patents and technology and companies have been searching for ways of making the best use of their R&D operations. But the pace and cost of technological change keeps rising, while physical assets are declining as a source of competitive advantage. A further complicating matter is the growing pressure from tax authorities to state the value of technology transferred to overseas subsidiaries and that of resulting royalties.

3.4 Launching a knowledge management campaign

Until recently it was believed that few enterprises actually had a comprehensive knowledge management practice in operation. Instead, they were focusing on current processes and striving to bring them together.

A knowledge management campaign might take the form shown in the diagram below:

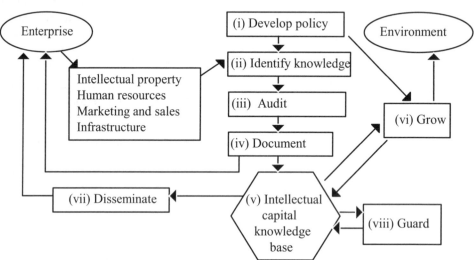

Diagram: A knowledge management campaign

(i)   Develop and determine a policy for owning, growing and sharing knowledge within the organisation.

(ii)   Identify critical knowledge functions within each department.

(iii) Audit knowledge to determine its type, location, longevity and whether it is explicit or tacit.

(iv)   Document knowledge in a medium that best suits the purpose for which it will be used.

(v)   Store it in a repository where it can be easily updated and retrieved.

(vi)   Determine ways in which it can be grown and tracked.

(vii) Decide how the knowledge will be disseminated inside the organisation and possibly outside.

(viii) Ensure this valuable organisational asset is kept secure.

A variety of methods can be used to facilitate sharing of knowledge:

- more regular meetings and/or conferencing in various forms

- e-mail links between locations via the Internet, or a private network

- a bulletin board and shared data stores on an intranet

- groupware.

The last three of these topics are dealt with in more detail later in this chapter.

3.5 Problems in implementing a knowledge sharing system

It is not always necessary to invest in expensive technology to address problems in information sharing: often the problem will arise because of **organisational** matters such as an inappropriate organisation structure. The solution may be simply to expand the size of a department or merge departments or relocate departments or individuals, so that those who need to share knowledge are actually in the same physical place.

There may be some **technological barriers** to overcome, such as the need to roll out a suitable modern network across an organisation, if one is not in place already.

There will be situations in which problems arise because of incompatible systems and working methods in different parts of the organisation. The least disruptive solution may appear to be finding out what systems are in use throughout the company and to rolling out the **most common** technologies across all offices. This may not be ideal, however, because it is **driven by the technology** rather than by the current and future needs of the business.

It is inevitable that some data will have to be transferred into a new common format and this can lead to errors, omissions and inconsistencies if not done with great care.

It may be that not all information actually needs to be shared, or at least not in the short-term. Managers will need to make a decision about this and draw up a timetable for the changeover.

In certain systems it is possible that older information will not be held in digital form at all, or not in a format that can easily be converted into a suitable modern equivalent. Examples include architect's drawings, medical notes written by hand and so on.

A decision is needed about how to archive this material. Will individual older systems be maintained and thoroughly indexed, or will it be accepted that such material has to be recreated from paper records on an ad hoc basis, if it is ever needed? Will archives be held locally or centrally?

Above all there are **social barriers** to information sharing. For some staff the notion of making their information available to other staff in other offices may be difficult. They will have their own established and familiar methods of organising their information and may even refuse to change their current practices to fall in line with a centrally imposed system.

At the very least there is likely to be some demotivation amongst staff. Some may resent having to give up a system that they know and like and learn a new one, especially if they are not given adequate training and adequate time to adapt.

Beyond this there may be political issues and inter-office rivalries: information is power and some staff may fear that their own status within the organisation will be impaired if they have to share the source of their power with others.

4 Learning

4.1 Process

DEFINITION

Learning is the process of acquiring knowledge through experience which leads to a change in behaviour.

Learning is the process of acquiring knowledge through experience which leads to a change in behaviour.

Learning might be the acquisition of a new skill, new knowledge, a modified attitude or a combination of all three.

We refer to the process of how we come to know things at all as learning. After that comes the organisation in our minds of our ideas and thoughts which constitutes memory. We refer to this result as knowledge. Learning is the result of experience. People use the knowledge of the results of past behaviour to change, modify and improve their behaviour in future. Learning cannot take place without appropriate feedback. The experience may be planned, as in studying this book, or it may be accidental, e.g. learning from one's mistakes. However, learning cannot be seen; it can only be inferred by observing changes in behaviour.

4.2 Learning cycles

Experiential learning theorists Kolb, Rubin and McIntyre see learning as a continuous cyclical process with four stages:

(a)   Experience – either planned or accidental.

Reflective observation – which is looking back at the experience and introspectively reviewing the general issues raised.

(c)   Abstract conceptualisation – seen as generalising from reflection and developing hypotheses based on experience and knowledge.

(d)   Active experimentation – which is consciously trying out hypotheses in other situations.

The learning cycle is shown in the diagram below.

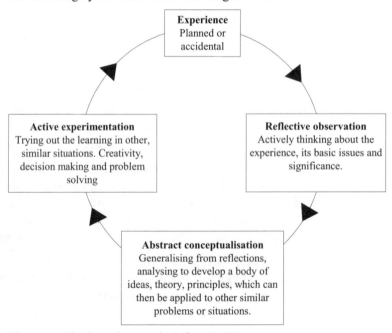

Diagram: The learning cycle (after Kolb)

According to Kolb, learning occurs through the grasping of experience and the transformation of it. This method proposes putting the learner in an active problem-solving role and using a form of self-learning which encourages him or her to be committed to the chosen learning objectives.

(You must be careful when answering questions in an exam to stress the aspect of 'experience' because behaviour can also change in ways which are not classed as learning, e.g. behaviour changes due to alcohol, drugs, ageing and fatigue!)

The transformation of the impact of experience on the senses, through internal reflection, allows the emergence of ideas that can be extended into the external world through new actions. Unless the process can be completed in full, learning does not occur and individuals may not begin the journey to qualitatively finer and higher forms of awareness, which may be called development.

Organisational development is an approach which allows an organisation to adapt to its environment by continuously learning about itself and its environment, and to identify viable ways of carrying out the necessary adaptations.

4.3 Learning in the workplace

When people refer to learning lessons they are normally referring to experiences they have had outside formal education. Learning frequently occurs when an individual has to deal with a situation new to them. Learning is about developing new skills, competencies and attitudes to meet new situations.

Courses and teachers can help, but most valuable learning occurs outside this context. The individuals and organisations that do this best seem to be the ones that also do best in life. It is possible to learn how learning happens and this will help the process of future learning.

The basic process is simple. All learning begins when we ask ourselves a question. This may be a simple question of a factual nature such as: 'how much of product X did we sell last year?' or a question about process such as: 'how can I arrange for my results to be available three days earlier each month?' or it could be a question about purpose: 'what is the main aim of this organisation?'.

These questions may come about because we considered a particular situation and doing so has raised questions. Alternatively it may have come about because a situation has forced the question upon us.

Whatever the source of the question, the situation will demand an answer. Then the answer needs to be tested out in practice. If it works then something has been learned. If it does not then the process starts again with the question.

4.4 Learning curve

The ability of employees to learn is more important to organisations that are preoccupied with controlled performance; needing to know what the staff must do, how they are to do it and how well they are expected to perform. In these organisations the induction of new recruits, job training, reward systems and performance evaluation have all been influenced by learning theories.

Changes in workplace behaviour and comparison of individuals can be quantified using a 'learning curve'. A fictitious curve for learning from a study guide such as this one is shown below:

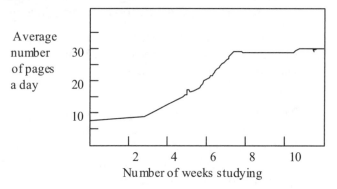

Diagram: Effect of the learning curve on reading ability

The shape of the curve depends on the type of work, the task and the individual learner. Experience has shown that learning does not take place at a steady rate.

Initially progress may be slow with sudden improvement followed by further progress for some time. There will be a final levelling off when, without enormous effort, little further progress will be achieved.

When you have finished reading this study guide you will expect to have learned something. The test is whether or not you will be able to do things that you could not do before you read the book.

5 The learning organisation

5.1 Introduction

Organisational learning is the process by which an organisation, like an individual, adapts its behaviour on the basis of experience. For example, when new employees join the firm the formal induction procedures are based on previous understanding. The individuals will also be given additional information, usually orally by their supervisor, colleagues and subordinates, representing more recent learning that may become part of the formal knowledge of the firm.

A learning organisation is an organisation skilled at creating, acquiring and transferring knowledge and at modifying its behaviour to reflect new knowledge and insights. It is an organisation that facilitates the learning of all its members and continuously transforms itself. The concept of organisational learning is difficult to define since it embodies intangible processes of knowledge and skills generation and shared insights, experiences and memory.

Learning organisations encourage questions and explicitly recognise mistakes as part of the learning process. They encourage testing and experimentation. Because they want to find new answers they recognise that failed answers are as important as successful ones.

5.2 Designing the learning organisation

The aim is to design an organisation which is capable of adapting, changing, developing and transforming itself in response to the needs, wishes and aspirations of people, inside and outside. These organisations will be able to achieve their objectives without predatory takeovers, mergers or divestments.

KEY POINT

A learning organisation is an organisation skilled at creating, acquiring and transferring knowledge and at modifying its behaviour to reflect new knowledge and insights. It is an organisation that facilitates the learning of all its members and continuously transforms itself.

They will be able to avoid the large-scale restructuring that is now commonplace in industry.

Actions that are carried out therefore have two purposes:

- to resolve the immediate problem
- to learn from the process.

Pedler, Burgoyne and Boydell believe that the current state of an organisation is due to three forces:

(i)   the idea behind it

(ii)   the phase of its development

(iii)   the era it is in.

Although these three perspectives are in principle independent, in practice they may be linked. If an organisation is going through a development phase that integrates its activities, employees and ideas, this is when the organisation starts to take a 'learning approach' to change.

Self-development and action-learning are also part of the foundation of the learning organisation; as the organisation learns from the actions that it carries out so does the individual.

5.3   The learning organisation profile

Pedler et al have identified 11 characteristics of the learning company – see the diagram below.

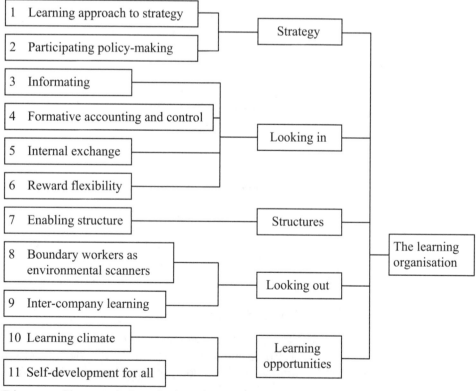

Diagram: Characteristics of a learning company (after Pedler et al)

For the learning organisation to become a reality there must be constant energy flows and connections between the individual and collective levels.

- **Strategy** – the process of strategy formulation is designed with learning in mind and incorporates experimentation and feedback. All members of the organisation are encouraged, and given the opportunity to contribute to policy-making as part of the learning process. Knowledge is now often the main determinant of strategic success.

- **Looking in** – information is a resource to be exploited by all members of the organisation, not a 'power tool'. reserved for a chosen few. Accounting systems are designed in such a way that members of the organisation can learn how the cash resource is used. Members of the organisation are encouraged to see internal users of their outputs as 'customers' and they are also encouraged to see the diversity of rewards they enjoy (not just cash). There is an openness about why some people are paid more than others.

  Internal benchmarks are ways of encouraging one internal unit to learn from another. They assume there are differences in the work processes of an organisation as a result of geographical differences, local organisational history, customs, differences among business units, and relationships among managers and employees.

- **Structures** – everything from the office layout to the managerial hierarchy is regarded as temporary arrangements that can be altered in response to changing conditions. Communication channels encourage the dissemination of knowledge throughout the organisation.

- **Looking out** – members of the organisation who have contacts outside the organisation – salesmen, customer service staff, purchasing staff, etc – should impart the knowledge they derive from such contacts to improve the organisation's knowledge base. A common example of inter-company learning is benchmarking, where one company studies a particular system or process within another company with a view to improving its own performance.

  Process or activity benchmarks involve the identification of state-of-the-art products, services, or processes of an organisation that may or may not be a company's direct competitor. The objective of this type of benchmarking is to identify best practices in any type of organisation that has established a reputation for excellence in specific business activities such as manufacturing, marketing, engineering, warehousing, fleet management, or human resources.

- **Learning opportunities** – management must foster a climate in which workers understand that part of their task is to improve their own knowledge and to share knowledge with other members of the organisation. A priority for management should be the provision of opportunities for structured learning – courses, seminars, etc.

5.4 Role of management

The role of management in a learning organisation is to encourage continuous learning and acquisition of new knowledge and skills and to transform these into actual behaviour, products and processes within the organisation.

In his book, *The Fifth Discipline – The Art and Practice of the Learning Organisation*, Peter Senge outlines five disciplines that individuals and groups should be encouraged to learn to create a learning organisation.

(a)   **Systems thinking** – is the ability to see particular problems as part of a wider whole and to devise appropriate solutions to them.

(b)   **Personal learning and growth** – individuals should be encouraged to acquire skills and knowledge.

(c)   **Mental models** – are deeply ingrained assumptions that determine what people think, e.g. a marketing group may think that price is more important than quality. Learning organisations can use a number of group techniques to make these models explicit and to challenge them.

(d)   A **shared vision** that does not filter knowledge which undermines learning.

(e)   **Team learning** – teams must be trained to learn because there are factors in group dynamics that impede learning.

The responsibility of management is to create a learning climate and to encourage continuous learning and knowledge around the organisation. For example, those who are involved in supporting the operational workforce must appreciate that these people have the greatest knowledge of the inefficiencies and efficiencies of the process. Soliciting their expertise, and allowing them to take some operational decisions by bringing the organisation's resources to bear on problems identified by them, could lead to innovation and a sustainable competitive advantage.

Individuals within an organisation gain unique information about both the organisation and their functions in it, and they can derive power from this information ownership. For example, a production manager may know what mix of personalities can be problematic if put together on a shift and he or she can perform more effectively than one who does not have the information. Unfortunately, in some situations, sharing the information with others would erode their source of power.

5.5   Working with diversity

KEY POINT

How an organisation manages to work with diversity is one of the keys to learning and productivity.

Diversity is one of the most vital aspects of the learning organisation. How an organisation manages to work with diversity is one of the keys to learning and productivity. Organisations usually try to ignore or suppress diversity, as acknowledging it can lead to a loss of control.

The learning organisation approach takes the stance that learning begins in differences. Pressure groups, interest groups and other stakeholders may have different concerns and the organisation needs to identify where the key differences are. Each organisation has to decide what level of diversity and difference it is ready to deal with and what its potential for learning and development is. In this way pressure groups are valued for their diversity and the possible new ideas they may generate.

The learning approach stresses that an organisation will only be successful in the long term by striving to delight customers and by meeting the requirements of other stakeholders. The overall purpose is to take charge of the process of continuously improving the relationship between the organisation and its members.

6 Channels of communication

6.1 Introduction

One of the functions in a learning organisation is to create processes to move knowledge around the organisation.

Communication in business can be defined as the transmission of information so that it is received, understood and leads to action.

This definition enables us to understand some of the key aspects of business communication:

(a)   Information, and not data, should be communicated. Information is active, relevant and prompts action; data, on the other hand, is passive, may be historical or irrelevant and does not lead to action.

Information can be classified as 'hard' or 'soft'. Hard information includes documents, reports and facts, whereas soft information covers less tangible information such as feelings, points of view, morale and body language.

(b)   Clearly, if information has not been received or is not understood by the receiver, then communication has not taken place.

(c)   The communication should lead to action. This action may take the form of a positive decision or may be a change in attitude. If the communication does not lead to any action then, probably, it ought not to have taken place.

For information to have value, it must lead to a decision to take action which results in reducing costs, eliminating losses, increasing sales, better use of resources, prevention of fraud or providing management with the means to choose between alternative courses of action.

6.2 Formal and informal communication systems

In organisations, formal communication channels are normally established as part of the organisation's structure. Workflow is an important factor that shapes the formal pathway or channel for the sending and receiving of communications. Communication flow may be downwards, from superior to subordinate; upwards from subordinate to superior; or lateral between equals.

Downward communication provides a basis for giving specific job instructions, policy decisions, guidance and resolution of queries. Such information can help clarify operational goals, provide a sense of direction and give subordinates data related to their performance. It also helps link levels of the hierarchy by providing a basis for co-ordinated activity. Too much emphasis on downward communication can create problems. People will become reluctant to come forward with their suggestions and problems and may be averse to taking on new responsibilities. There is also a risk of management getting out of touch with their subordinates. For these reasons it is important to stress upward communication.

Upward communication provides management with feedback from employees on results achieved and problems encountered. It creates a channel from which management can gauge organisational climate and deal with problem areas, such as grievances or low productivity, before they become major issues.

DEFINITION

Communication in business can be defined as the transmission of information so that it is received, understood and leads to action.

KEY POINT

Hard information includes documents, reports and facts, whereas soft information covers less tangible information such as feelings, points of view, morale and body language.

The typical hierarchical organisation structure formally recognises only vertical (i.e. upward and downward) communication. Yet as organisations become larger, more complex and subject to environmental changes, the need for horizontal or lateral communication becomes increasingly apparent. In particular, lateral communication is essential in the corporate planning process if efforts are to be successfully co-ordinated in order to achieve organisational objectives.

While the organisational structure will have a designed, formal communications network, it is inevitable and not necessarily bad that in almost all organisations there will be a number of informal communication channels, e.g. **grapevine**, rumour and gossip. The channels are described as informal because they are not consciously structured by management into a fixed pattern.

Davis has defined the grapevine as 'the network of social relations that arises spontaneously as people associate with one another. It is an expression of people's natural motivation to communicate'.

6.3 Communication methods

Information will often be gathered by one group and used by another, as can be shown when we categorise information into:

- control information which is gathered in the process of running the daily operations of the organisation, e.g. invoicing

- tactical information, which is produced by combining data gathered as part of the control of operations, e.g. production requirements: generally the users of this information will only be involved in the design process which dictates what is gathered

- strategic information which is a combination of information from internal and external sources. The consumers of this kind of information will have had some involvement in the data collection.

Organisations can restrict access to information on the basis of either 'the need to know' or on the security threat posed by the disclosure of any particular piece of information.

There are so many different methods of communicating this information, and choosing the right one is important. For example, a job vacancy might be communicated in a national or local newspaper, the organisation's in-house magazine, job centres or school careers offices.

Depending on the purpose and content, information can be formally communicated in writing or figures. Informally it can be communicated verbally (by telephone or word of mouth) or by e-mail systems.

7 Appropriate systems

7.1 Networks

Since the early 1980s when the first computers began arriving on desktops, the prices have tumbled and each new generation of microprocessors puts more raw computing power into the hands of the user. PCs already undertake much of the work that was previously done by huge mainframe computers. This migration of data processing power out of the computer room and onto the desktop has become known as 'downsizing' or 'rightsizing'. The benefits include cost savings, improving company flexibility and responsiveness, and empowering users. Another key feature of the developing technology has been the move away from using PCs as stand-alone units; most organisations hook their PCs and other computers together in local area networks (LANs), enabling them to share data and peripherals such as printers.

Networks, which can be built from scratch or formed by linking an organisation's existing computers and peripherals, have other advantages. They are flexible and can be adapted quickly, enabling a company to respond to changing circumstances or opportunities rapidly. They can bind together previously disparate departmental systems and provide every user with access to the organisation's information.

LANs may be grouped together into 'work groups' which, in addition to sharing information and software facilities such as electronic mail, can run software such as groupware and/or an intranet (see below). LANs themselves are also being interconnected using sophisticated new hardware to create wide area networks (WANs), sometimes called enterprise networks.

The demand from end users is for network systems that link together all their information resources, regardless of the types of machine and technology or their geographical location. They want to squeeze more productivity out of their IT investment by hooking together desktop PCs, high-power workstations, departmental mini-computers and corporate mainframes, and have them work in seamless harmony. Some analysts believe that many of the remaining distinctions between LANs and WANs will evaporate as network users demand ever greater network capacity or 'bandwidth', to 100 Mbps and beyond. This increase in bandwidth is needed to accommodate new forms of data and information such as multimedia and desktop video conferencing, which are likely to be distributed over the corporate computer networks of the future.

7.2 Groupware

DEFINITION

Groupware is a generic term for software that helps work groups to collaborate on projects.

Groupware is a generic term for software that helps work groups to collaborate on projects.

The best-known general purpose groupware product is Lotus Notes, although the various packages within Microsoft Office could also be considered to be a form of groupware when used on a networked system in conjunction with Microsoft Exchange Server software.

A groupware system might have the following features for individual time management. (What we are describing is based on Microsoft Outlook.)

- A **scheduler** or **calendar** allowing users to timetable their activities for the day and plan meetings with others. It will also be able to generate reminders, for example when a deadline is approaching, or if it is somebody's birthday.

- An **address book**.

- **'To do'** lists.

- A **journal**. This can automatically record interactions with people involved in a project, such as e-mail messages and record and time actions such as creating and working on files. The journal will keep track of all of this and is useful both as a record of work done and as a quick way of finding relevant files and messages without having to remember where each one is saved.

- A **jotter** for jotting down notes as quick reminders of questions, ideas, and so on.

The advantage is that all this information is available at the touch of a button, rather than relying on post-it notes, memo pads, hard copy out-of-date address books, and company telephone directories.

When groupware is used **collaboratively** across a network it becomes even more useful, especially when the project team members are widely dispersed. A typical system will have the following features.

- **Workflow management**. The overall project manager can define the workflow for a project to ensure that work is automatically routed between the project participants so that when one task is finished the results are sent on to the person responsible for the next stage.

- **Task assignment**. A 'task request' can be sent to someone else working on the project or a group of others. They can accept or decline the task or reassign it to someone else. When the task is accepted, the groupware will keep a record of what progress is being made. This simply reflects the way work is organised in any office, but when a project involves people who may be on the road or in a different country in a different time-zone, the advantages are clear.

- **Messaging**. In other words e-mail facilities for exchanging messages with others involved in the project. A message may be sent on a round trip to individuals, who can add their own comments before passing it on to the next person, or it can be sent to everyone involved at once.

- **Group scheduling**, to keep track of the activities of others involved in the project. For instance networked groupware may be capable of checking the calendars of people needed to take part in a videoconference and automatically working out when they will be available, what the most convenient venues are in each country, what other resources will be required and so on.

- **'Public' folders** to store files and share them with others involved in the project throughout the organisation.

- **Delegate access**, so that a team member can allow an assistant or substitute to look at their groupware folders and send messages, read, modify, or create new documents in public and private folders on their behalf, for instance if they are on holiday or sick.

- **'Voting' facilities**, which may be used to canvass team members' opinion on some aspect of the project.

7.3 Intranet

An intranet is a private network that is contained within an organisation. It may consist of many interlinked local area networks and also use leased lines in the wide area network. Typically, an intranet includes connections through one or more gateway computers to the outside Internet.

The main objective of an intranet is to make information flow more freely by sharing company information and computing resources among employees. This means making it more widely available to those who need to have the rights to it, and less widely available to those who do not. As part of an overall communications strategy, an intranet offers tremendous potential for growth. With control of content, real improvements can be made to the quality and availability of corporate data. Similarly, it is far easier to monitor and manage sensitive data in a secure way. Wider access to more electronic server-held information means the elimination of unnecessary paperwork and more opportunities to improve direct and effective interaction between people who really should know about each other. An intranet can also be used to facilitate working in groups and for teleconferences.

KEY POINT

When groupware is used collaboratively across a network it becomes exceptionally useful, especially when the project team members are widely dispersed. A typical system will have features such as workflow management, task assignment, messaging, group scheduling, public folders, delegate access and voting facilities.

KEY POINT

An **intranet** is a private network that is contained within an organisation.

Broadly speaking, an intranet operates within seven general areas of corporate information management.

(a)   At the simple physical level, it holds the file directories and allows resource sharing like any other network, e.g. printer.

(b)   Moving up a level, it is a publishing resource, enabling messages, detailed information and maps to be displayed and disseminated to as many or as few people as need to see it.

(c)   Because it is based on Internet technologies, there is extensive connectivity across multiple platforms enabling the implementation of comprehensive messaging systems.

(d)   Similarly, an intranet gives instant access to established tools for the management of information and a wider range of approaches to security and firewalls for dealing with external information.

(e)   The attributes of an intranet make it a powerful tool for information management at both a general, strategic level and a far more micro, departmental and individual level. As a publishing resource, for example, the intranet confers considerable power on individuals to create their own content. It also imposes a responsibility for the management of that content – often a far more pressing issue.

(f)   The intranet drives the formation of group or team working cultures and enables such teams to define themselves by creating their own pages and information.

(g)   The result is employee empowerment, although it only works when it is managed and directed within the context of a more coherent corporate strategy.

Simple applications include the publishing of corporate information and employee handbooks. For larger companies, bureaucratic procedures around form-filling (requests for stationery, invitations to tender, expense claims) can also be automated, simultaneously eliminating the hassle of paper forms whilst also converting data into digital format straight away. All internal communications, routine data completion tasks, presentation and reports can be made available and held on a central resource that is accessible by any target group. There are occasions when e-mail can lead to better provision of information. For example, when an individual employee is privy to information that could benefit the whole company, communicating this information to everyone concerned could lead to cost savings within the company. Answers to questions and solutions to problems can be found quicker if an e-mail can be targeted to hundreds of people.

The brain of an intranet is, like any other network, the server. This is a large central machine that holds an organisation's data and receives, processes and replies to user queries. What sets it apart form the standard network server is the type of additional software it holds – normally broken down into three key technologies.

•   At the user end is the browser, a software program that connects desktop machines to the server and allows users to view data held there, and navigate around other data and servers.

•   Residing on the server is a type of software dealing with hypertext transfer protocol (HTTP), the protocol that retrieves whatever information is requested by the browser. It manages the links between related data and displays it within the user's browser.

- The third key technology is Hypertext Mark-up Language (HTML). This allows complex data to be structured and held in a format that HTTP can recognise and work with. Put more simply, HTML is the data format that allows the creation of links between data items throughout the world wide web.

7.4 Extranet

An extranet is a private, secure extension of the enterprise via the corporate intranet. It allows the organisation to share part of its business information or operations with suppliers, customers, and other business partners using the Internet. For example, an organisation could connect its browser based purchase order system to the product catalogue database on a supplier's intranet.

Organisations can use an extranet to:

- exchange large volumes of data using Electronic Data Interchange (EDI)

- share product catalogues exclusively with wholesalers or those 'in the trade'

- collaborate with other organisations on joint development efforts

- jointly develop and use training programmes with other companies

- provide or access services provided by one company to a group of other companies, such as on-line banking applications managed by one company on behalf of affiliated banks

- share news of common interest exclusively with partner companies.

Issues in implementing an extranet

An extranet is likely to **relieve the burden** upon the owner's staff of dealing with enquiries from suppliers, customers, and other business partners, assuming the on-line version of the data is easy enough to use and provides information in the form required by callers.

Not all callers will have Internet access, of course, so it will still be necessary to provide a telephone option, though there is probably a good case for making this available only during normal working hours. An extranet may also need to be off-line for short periods to allow for **updating and maintenance** of the on-line database, but downtime can probably be kept to a minimum – say one hour in every 24.

It is possible that the extranet could generate **new income** if it is run on a subscription basis.

Demand for information should be carefully considered. An extranet will need to be able to cope with a good deal **more traffic** than would be anticipated on the basis of current enquiries by other means, since enquirers are likely to spend more time searching for peripheral information that they might not ask for on the telephone, and there will be sundry casual visitors who might not have considered bothering the business with a telephone call but will feel perfectly free to explore its databases on-line.

Assuming the database that underlies an extranet already exists and will continue to be maintained whatever the case, it should be cheaper to provide the extranet than to have staff deal with calls, but a **suitable interface** will have to be devised and it must be easy enough for a **non-expert** to use. This may not be easy to achieve and it is liable to require some kind of support service. Call centre staff may find that, although they are no longer answering the telephone, they are now offering a computer helpline service rather than focusing on matters that are really important to the business.

Care is also needed where databases contain **sensitive personal data**. This ought not to be made available to the general public without the individual's permission, both from a general ethical point of view and more particularly from the point of view of data protection legislation.

Copyright will also have to be carefully considered. In making material available over an extranet a business is allowing free access to (and so potential abuse of) its own copyright material and could be breaching the rights of others if material is also collected from other sources.

Summary

Key points of this chapter are:

- Knowledge management is important in determining the future success of an organisation.

- Creating new knowledge to achieve success leads to innovative new products and methods of working.

- The value of knowledge is difficult to assess in many organisations, with many having tried in the past to place a monetary value on their employees' qualifications. Where the knowledge leads to a tangible product, then a patent may be sought whose value can be measured, otherwise it is an almost impossible task.

- Learning organisations have specific skills in acquiring and transferring knowledge as well as adopting new and revised methods of obtaining knowledge where necessary.

- Formal and information communication channels are used to transfer knowledge.

- IT systems including groupware, intranets and extranets assist in the transfer of knowledge.

Having completed your study of this chapter you should have achieved the following learning outcomes:

- evaluate and advise managers on the development of strategies for knowledge management, IM, IS and IT that support the organisation's strategic requirements

- identify and evaluate IS/IT systems appropriate to the organisation's strategic requirements, and recommend changes where necessary.

Self-test questions

1   Briefly describe four ways of acquiring knowledge. (2.2)

2   What are the stages in the process of knowledge building? (2.3)

3   Explain intellectual capital. (3.3)

4   Define the learning process. (4.1)

5   Draw the Kolb learning cycle. (4.2)

6   What factors affect the shape of the learning curve? (4.4)

7   What are the attributes of a learning organisation? (5.1)

8   List five levels of a learning company. (5.3)

9   What are the benefits of upward communication? (6.2)

10   What are the features of groupware? (7.2)

Practice question

Organisational learning

JUS is a recently-formed organisation arising out of a joint venture between a Japanese company (J) and a United States company (US). The objective of the joint venture is to set up and run a production plant, which manufactures state-of-the-art high-speed gas ovens. These ovens incorporate the latest technology and the inventors claim that they reduce cooking time by half.

The market for ovens is a very competitive one in which product innovation as well as price and quality play a major role in the battle for market share.

The production plant is to be based on the European site of one of the US company's former automobile production plants. While the building is available, new structures in terms of production lines, staff relationships, accounting systems, etc. will all have to be estasblished and maintained.

The management of JUS now need to integrate the J and US sections of the new company so all staff from managers to production workers are familiar with the company's aims and are prepared to work towards producing high quality products.

The team member responsible for human resource management has been asked to prepare a detailed Human Resource (HR) Plan for consideration at the next meeting of the new management team.

Required:

(a)   List and briefly explain the key features of organisational learning.   **(6 marks)**

(b)   Describe how JUS can go about developing itself as a learning organisation.

(8 marks)

(Total: 14 marks)

For the answer to this question, see the 'Answers' section at the end of the book.

Chapter 19

INFORMATION STRATEGY AND IMPLEMENTATION

Syllabus content

- The purpose and contents of IM, IS and IT strategies, and the need for strategy complementary to the corporate and individual business strategies.

- Project management: monitoring the implementation of plans.

Contents

1 Introduction

2 The evolving role of ICT

3 Information strategy

4 IS, IM and IT strategies

5 Project management

1 Introduction

Traditionally, information systems planning was primarily technical, focusing on the hardware and software. However, with the advent of strategic systems, planning required linkages with the business planning process and the managers have had to learn that the uses of computers can have a significant effect on their organisation's competitive position.

Any one of several methodologies may be adopted when developing the strategy. The methodology described here can be broken down into six activities: initiation; clarifying business strategy; modelling the business; reviewing current information systems; building the information system architecture; and developing the strategy. We will also look at an approach that distinguishes between information systems (IS), information management (IM) and information technology (IT) strategies.

Finally we will look at the various issues surrounding project monitoring and management: the problems that can arise and the tools that can be used. This part of the chapter may apply to any kind of project undertaken to implement a strategy, not just an IT project.

2 The evolving role of ICT

2.1 Nolan's stage hypothesis

A useful starting point for thinking about the use of information and related technology in organisations is the stage hypothesis developed by Nolan in the late 1970s. They found that data processing (DP) expenditure followed an S-curve of increasing costs, expenditure being gradual at first but increasing dramatically before adopting a more gradual slope again. This curve also represented a path of organisational learning about information technology and its uses within the corporation.

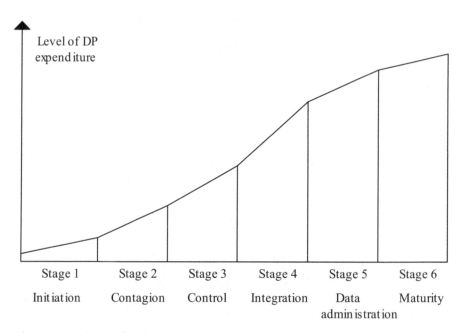

Diagram: Nolan's six stage hypothesis of IT expenditure

(a) Initiation stage – automation of clerical operations. Typically the more technically-minded employees use technology because they are keen, rather than use it for cost effectiveness.

(b) Contagion stage – rapid growth as users become more familiar with applications and demand more, and where the wider benefits of technology are perceived by more staff.

(c) Control stage – planning and methodologies are introduced in order to assert control over developments, and investment in technology is taking place in a planned manner. Controls may be introduced by setting up steering committees and project management teams.

(d) Integration stage – the integration of the various computing functions within the organisation and there is user involvement in the development stage of information technology.

(e) Data administration stage – emphasis is placed on information requirements rather than just processing requirements and there is sufficient information available to support the appointment of staff to manage it.

(f) Maturity stage – the IS/IT planning is brought into line with the business planning and development. The data resources are flexible and the information flows mirror the real-world requirements of the firm. The firm will be using a variety of applications to support their information needs.

2.2 Uses of the model

Despite some criticism over the years (along the lines that the model is too simplistic, or that it inhibits strategic use of information), it is generally accepted that a model of the evolving role of information and communications technology (ICT) in an organisation is of value and that Nolan's model is a good starting point.

Uses for Nolan's stage hypothesis include:

(a) being able to classify organisations into the stage they are presently at, thereby being able to predict their future reactions to technology

(b) being able to identify how the organisation passed through the earlier stages and the problems they specifically encountered

(c) understanding the current status of the organisation in terms of technology and being able to produce strategic plans that are not too ambitious for the stage they have reached

(d) being able to develop plans that will avoid the pitfalls of the later stages in the hypothesis.

Activity 1

Identify a type of organisation for each of the stages outlined by Nolan.

Feedback to this activity is at the end of the chapter.

3 Information strategy

3.1 The need for planning

As we saw in the last chapter, information usage needs effective strategic planning as much as, or even more than, other functional areas do. Information systems without planning may mean financial losses and additional hidden, and often greater, costs such as lowered staff morale, missed opportunities, continuous management fire-fighting and customer dissatisfaction. Planning helps an organisation identify its information needs and find new opportunities for using that information. It also defines the activities required to implement the chosen strategy.

3.2 Consistency with corporate strategy

The organisation's information strategy must be consistent with:

- the corporate strategy

- the management view of the role of information in the organisation

- the stage of maturity of use and management of information.

As you know, identifying an organisation's overall goals and objectives should lead to an overall corporate strategy. This strategy then feeds down, through divisional or business unit strategies, into a number of functional strategies. One of these is the IS strategy, which feeds into a number of sub-strategies, e.g. the technology strategy and the communications strategy.

Like any planning, strategic planning of information usage is not a one-off activity. Ideally, it would be a continuous cycle synchronised with or, even better, embedded into the cycle of the corporate planning.

There are common circumstances that require frequent revision to reflect technology changes. These include the following.

- **Major organisational changes** (e.g. new ownership, new management, rationalisation programmes, restructuring exercises) will mean that the 'new' business will require different things from its information. If this is so, the primary objective of the information strategy will be the definition of the new role for information systems.

- **External competitive opportunities and threats** – the symptoms of this kind of change are the emergence of new markets and/or products that may be created by information systems or the competitive need for major cost factor changes and improved performance. The emphasis of the objectives is to exploit information strengths and the weaknesses of competitors by being entrepreneurial and developing new attitudes, skills and uses of information and technology.

- **Evolutionary change** – probably the most frequent reason for re-assessing the information strategy. The most obvious symptom of this is the changing views on the required level of control over IS, or its budget allocation and/or the degree of dissatisfaction expressed by everyone. Unfortunately, moving from one stage to another generates fears and anxieties. Under these circumstances, the IS objectives will be to get and keep senior management commitment and to demonstrate managed evolution.

3.3 Developing the strategy

When developing an information strategy the following aspects should be taken into consideration:

(a) What are the **key business areas** that could benefit most from new investment in information systems, what form should the investment take, how should the project be managed, and how can such strategically important units be encouraged to use new technology effectively?

(b) How much would the system **cost** in terms of: software; hardware; management commitment and time; education and training; conversion; documentation; operational manning; and maintenance? The importance of lifetime application costs must be stressed. Most companies try to assess how much it will cost them to install a new system, but all too few measure the costs and benefits after implementation. Yet this is the area of greatest potential loss.

(c) What criteria for **performance** should be set for information systems? The quality of an application should be measured in two ways: the technical standard it achieves and the degree to which it meets the perceived and often changing needs of the user.

(d) What are the implications for the existing **work force**; have they the requisite skills; can they be trained to use the systems; will there be any redundancies?

3.4 Information systems planning projects

The six stages of an information systems planning project will normally include the following:

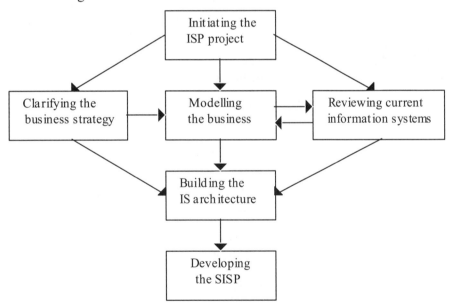

Diagram: Stages of an Information Systems Planning Project

3.5 Initiating a project

This stage includes understanding the scope of the new project, the approach to be adopted and how it is going to be organised, resourced and managed. At this stage it is important to identify and document the scope, goals and objectives of the project.

In determining the scope, the project manager should ascertain whether there are any previous or current planning activities. It is obviously unwise to duplicate effort or produce conflicting plans.

The sequence in which projects are carried out may also impact on the strategic advantage gained. For example, spending money on a new system for a business which fell into the dog category in the BCG matrix would not be sensible when the continuing profitability of the organisation would presumably depend on those business units in the star or problem child categories.

3.6 Clarifying the business strategy

The purpose of this stage is to develop an IS strategy which is aligned to the business strategy, in a way that can give the greatest benefit. Developing a picture of the organisation using a SWOT analysis can give valuable insight into the business. The range of models which can contribute to this process include Porter's five forces, the generic strategies and the value chain and value system.

3.7 Modelling the business

Models provide a means for the project team to develop, confirm and present their understanding of the business in a form that is verifiable by the business users and the business management. The four areas that can be modelled successfully are the strategy, functions and processes, data, and structure and hierarchy.

(a) The strategy of a business can be modelled with goals and their dependent objectives.

(b) Functions and processes can be modelled by considering the functions that support the business, e.g. finance, personnel and marketing, and then breaking down the main business activities (or processes) which form part of those functions.

(c) The data can be modelled using a variety of modelling techniques, such as dataflow diagrams, entity relationship models, entity life histories, Unified Modeling Language (all beyond the scope of this syllabus).

(d) The structure and hierarchy of the organisation can be modelled in an organisation chart.

3.8 Reviewing current information systems

Unless the business is a start-up it is probable that the organisation will have some IT facilities already in place and these must be recognised as a major building block for the future information systems. The review must take into account the views of the people in IT areas who support and keep the system running and maintained and also the business users who have to operate the applications.

KEY POINT

Existing systems may
be analysed using
Earl's grid comparing
business value and
technical quality.

Information system use

Michael Earl has devised an audit grid to analyse an organisation's information
system use:

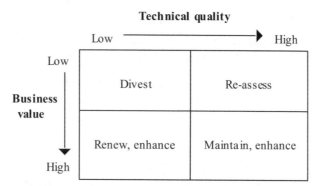

Diagram: Earl's Audit Grid of information systems

- A system of low quality and little business value should be divested.

- A system with high business value and low quality should be enhanced
  because the low quality aspects might make it a risk, or might damage the
  business if it failed.

- A system of high quality and low business use should be re-assessed. If
  the users had complained about user-friendliness, modifications to this
  aspect of the system might increase its business value.

- A system of both high quality and high business value must be
  maintained and possibly enhanced as newer features are introduced.

During the review, it is important to distinguish between investment in the
application and investment in the means of delivery, so that the review covers
the current and planned information systems and also the technology, the
management organisation and the control of information systems.

One of the activities in the review is documenting resources. These resources
can be divided into the following categories:

(a) **Information and communications technology**: a complete inventory of
the technology resources should include the technical details, the costs of
maintenance, upgrades and financial commitment.

(b) **The information systems infrastructure** review document should cover
the personnel, their function and skills, the space they occupy and the
facilities they use. The costs, financial commitment, revenues and
expenditure, where appropriate, form a part of the review. Models that
can help with this review are: Nolan's six stages of growth; McFarlan's
phases of technology assimilation and also his strategic grid; and
Primozic's waves of innovation, all covered earlier.

(c) **The applications and data collections** review document identifies all of
the major applications as well as any enhancements to them. The data
collections are the physical groupings of data maintained by the
organisation, e.g. computer-based files and databases.

Liaison between IT managers and users

Because the existing portfolio of IT applications will influence future policy, there should be an evaluation of the efficiency of current systems. The types of question that managers need to ask are about the satisfaction of the users and the reliability of the system.

The evaluation is a bottom-up exercise, depending vitally on the contribution of the users. The benefits of the exercise are:

(a)   users may suggest evolutionary add-ons to systems

(b)   users and systems specialists can indicate the technical quality of the current system in terms of its reliability, ease of maintenance and cost efficiency

(c)   users can rate a system on: its business impact (how would we manage without it?); its ease of use and user-friendliness; and the frequency of its use, giving an indication of its importance and value.

3.9   Building the information systems architecture

Before the strategy can be prepared, it is necessary to describe the 'vision'. This vision encompasses the data collections, the applications, a description of the technology and the management and organisation required to deliver and to support them. This is generally called the **architecture** and is a framework which drives, shapes and controls the information systems requirements. It not only defines the vision for the future but it must identify the costs and risks associated with that vision.

The architecture must cover the new opportunities yielded by the IT, which may offer competitive advantage or create new strategic options. These opportunities may be enhanced use of an existing IS or a completely new IS which supports an entirely different approach to some business problem or strategy.

There are four interdependent components to the architecture, as shown in the diagram below:

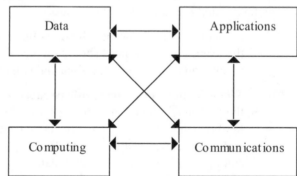

Diagram: Components of Information Systems architecture

Each of the architectures will comprise the same components – parameters, principles, schema and assessment.

* The **parameters** are concerned with the essential needs, constraints and preferences that each element should attempt to satisfy. They are assumptions, which are made so that alternative architectures may be evaluated.

* The **principles** are the policies that guide decision making during the development of the architecture. They are concrete, practical statements of how each technological element is to be delivered.

- The **schema** describes the architecture, its requirements and how it will work. Schemas are sometimes called models or blueprints; they may be the visual, logical state of the frame as it exists now or an agreed detailed model of what is being pursued.

- The plans may include project plans or performance goals plus time-phased actions that will move the framework to the next state of evolution.

Computing architecture

This refers to the information processing hardware and its associated operating systems software. This architecture describes the platform and facilities needed to realise the IS vision of the organisation. It will include:

- the type of processing architecture, e.g. client server, etc

- the processor configuration: hardware, software, development tools, etc

- the communications network: LAN and WAN

- the facilities needed to support both the hardware and the staff.

The type of hardware, its capacity and location are influenced by the application needs and the requirement to share data. Information systems management and organisation will be influenced by the location of the hardware and the type of data communications required, and vice versa.

Communications architecture

This describes the infrastructure required for the application, data and technology architectures. It includes an identification of:

- the staff and skills required to support the development, operation and maintenance of the future information system

- management practices, e.g. reporting structures, data administration, back-up, recovery, security, quality assurance, change control and training

- organisation design, e.g. resource placement, staffing levels, charging structures and the outside services required.

It also refers to telecommunications networks and their associated devices for inter-linking. The topology of a communications network is influenced by applications needs, data transmission requirements and information processing geography, as well as by its own capabilities.

Data architecture

This relates to the data assets of the organisation and the requirements of use, control and storage. The schema for the data architecture should include descriptions of the data collections required to support the application architecture. The costs and benefits, return on investment and payback period of the proposed architecture should be analysed and estimated.

Applications architecture

This covers the main application systems of the organisation, their functions and relationships, as well as the development methods. The activities associated with drawing up the schema for the applications architecture will include identifying the information systems and their applications, and also describing, classifying and assigning priorities to each application. For example, cash management, accounts receivable and general ledger applications may form part of the financial information management system.

Applying the parameters and development principles a decision must be taken on which application or applications to develop or redevelop. The development decision should include whether to build or to buy, or whether re-engineering is appropriate for existing applications. Alternative application architectures can be considered and selection will be based on a cost-benefit analysis.

Because the four elements of the IT architecture are interdependent, each influences and is influenced by the other elements. For example, the structure of a communications network is influenced by applications needs, data transmission requirements, information-processing geography and by its own capabilities.

The type of hardware, its capacity and location are influenced by the application needs and the requirement to share data. The IS management and organisation will be influenced by the location of the hardware and the type of data communications required, and vice versa.

Each of the components of the IS architecture, whilst being interdependent on the others, is also an architecture in its own right.

3.10 Developing the strategic information systems plan (SISP)

The final plan is inevitably a set of compromises between development and maintenance, risks and returns, infrastructure and applications and long-term and short-term benefits.

There are typically three sections to the plan: architecture migration strategy, schedule, and maintenance and evolution of the SISP

- **Architecture migration strategy** – this describes how the move from the current position to the vision that is defined in the architectures should be implemented. It shows the phases for implementation, along with an assessment of time, organisational impact, risks, resources, costs and benefits. It also defines the dependency between phases.

- **Schedule** – each architecture migration phase is reviewed and divided into manageable projects. The projects are then reviewed alongside the application portfolio and the priorities and dependencies are determined.

- **Maintenance and evolution of the plan** – the plan will need to be monitored and updated like all plans. Similarly the architectures will also need to be revised as the migration moves forward. The roles and responsibilities for the maintenance of both the plan and the architectures will need to be decided and the procedures to accomplish this maintenance should also be considered. Major reviews of the plan should be defined and the policies concerning them established.

Activity 2

Backwater is a company with an established base of IT applications. The finance department has a fully computerised accounting system. The marketing department has a customer-modelling package and the production department does not see the need for technology.

The Finance Director is in charge of IT and he is proposing a 12% increase in IT expenditure to upgrade systems in the relevant departments, based on last year.

Comment on the situation at Backwater.

Feedback to this activity is at the end of the chapter.

4 IS, IM and IT strategies

4.1 Introduction

It is pretty clear that the thing called IT (or often, these days, ICT – information and communications technology) is concerned with technology. However, in current usage there is not really any agreement over what is 'Information Systems (IS)' strategy as opposed to 'Information Management (IM)' strategy … or 'Knowledge Management (KM)' strategy, or whatever the latest buzz words happen to be when you come to read this.

In some views IT strategy is regarded as the link between IS and IM, but this is putting the cart before the horse in our opinion and is out of touch with modern thinking: the technology is simply the resource used by the manager.

In spite of the above, in many organisations technology has, until relatively recently (that is until the early to mid 1990s), been allowed to dictate information strategy as a whole. Because the initial investment in computers was such a large expense and the possibilities were not well understood by senior managers, organisations simply equipped themselves with the best they could afford and were then limited in what they could do with their information by the capabilities of the technology they had locked themselves into, and the imagination, or lack thereof, of technology suppliers.

Clearly business goals should come first and managers should be able to choose what resources they use to achieve those goals, but this has only really become possible in the last four to five years thanks to rapidly falling costs of hardware, the rise and rise of the Internet and associated technologies and long-overdue co-operation between hardware and software suppliers to develop open standards.

4.2 Earl's strategic framework

In the late 1980s Michael Earl developed a strategic framework that differentiates between these three interrelated types of strategy formation.

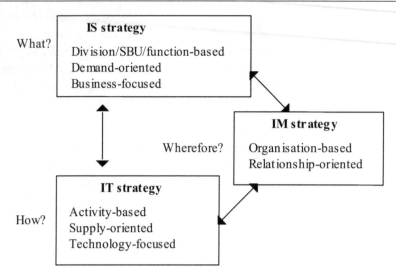

Diagram: Earls strategic framework for IS, IT and IM strategy

- **Information Systems (IS) strategy** – is considered to be long-term in orientation.

  The term Information Systems (IS) refers to the interconnected organisational activities that gather and process data and provide information. Some of these activities may be carried out by technology, but many may be human processes achieved by human interactions. Key questions relate to what an organisation should plan to achieve by its investment in information systems. The strategy is business-led and demand-oriented and is either supporting existing business strategies or developing new strategic choices.

  A strategy for information systems is concerned with identifying what information is needed by the organisation to enable it to achieve its business objectives. This includes considering the information needed at strategic, tactical and operational levels and the ways in which those levels of information should interconnect and interact.

  Because the term 'systems' is often associated with tangible things (a central heating system, the Underground system, etc) it might better to refer to this part of the chain simply as 'Information Strategy'.

- **Information Management (IM) strategy** is distinguished from the IS and the IT strategies because it is involved in the 'wherefores'. It is described as organisation-based, relationships-orientated and management-focused.

  Information management is a highly complex activity, concerned with identifying the sources of the information that is needed, collecting that information in appropriate formats, storing information, facilitating existing methods of using information and identifying new ways of using it, and ensuring that information can be accessed by all who need it (but only by those people).

  Information Technology (IT) strategy – is concerned with how IS strategies will be implemented. IT strategy is described as activity-based, supply-oriented and technology-focused.

Information Technology (IT) refers to the resources used to manage information: basically hardware and software used for everyday data processing, communication, office automation and production automation: IT describes any 'kit' concerned with the capture, storage, transmission, presentation or interpretation (e.g. by a robot) of information.

4.3 IS strategy

Irrespective of organisational structure, market and product grouping and nature of the business, an effective IS strategy may be formed with the key objectives of using the information resource and, more ambitiously, generating new businesses.

The strength of this type of strategy rests on it being demand-oriented where the managers of the divisions, business units or departments communicate their needs to the wider organisation.

IS strategies must be business-driven and capable of delivering tangible benefits, e.g. increased productivity, enhanced profits and perhaps a reduction in the workforce.

Earl asserts that IS strategies are intended to be directional and not detailed in scope and content. He also notes that a single IS strategy formulation model does not exist and that attempts to impose one should be avoided. He outlines some problems with IS planning:

(a)   Many organisations have failed to develop adequate business plans – this confuses decision makers about the nature and scope of the IS plan.

(b)   Many organisations fail to agree on priorities and may inhibit rather than support technical change.

(c)   Traditional IS plans are not appropriate to guide contemporary IS strategy making. New technologies confuse managers since they demand new performance measurement criteria. Also, new jargon, e.g. TQM, MRPII, JIT, together with new technologies in the form of client server, multi-tasking and multimedia, do not translate into traditional IS planning terminology.

(d)   The rapid rate of technical change can overwhelm IS planners, especially when it is aggravated by IT skills shortages that exist in most companies.

(e)   Traditional organisational structures that divide business functions are not suitable for the new 'process orientated' environment. New developments in client server technologies have the capability to integrate business functions. This results in a blurring of the divisions found in the old functional-based organisation structure and demands a different way of conceptualising organisations and their associated business processes.

(f)   Although IS strategies may help to locate where competitive advantage may be gained, it still relies on management's ability to pinpoint where process improvements and innovations can be made and to develop and apply technologies accordingly.

4.4 IM strategy

The burgeoning financial investment in IT throughout the 1980s provided the impetus for organisations to seek more effective financial control over the range of IT activities.

Because IM is concerned with the 'wherefores', in this context IS and IT strategies can only be implemented if they are managed. It is described as organisation-based, relationships-oriented and management-focused.

Earl outlines the four tasks of information management:

- **Planning** – involves the integration of IS and IT strategies with other decision-making processes.

- **Organisation** – involves issues of decentralisation and centralisation of the IT function, the formation of steering committees, management education and training, reporting procedures and the responsibilities of IT managers.

- **Control** – issues relate to the relationship between IT and finance. Key management activities are performance measurement and investment appraisal of IT.

- **Technology** – is related to priorities of the IT strategy, e.g. the design and development of methodologies for IT, security practices and data management techniques.

Earl gives several reasons that underpin the formation of the IM strategy.

- Information and technology need to be managed as efficiently and effectively as other resources.

- The organisational, business and management impact of ICT requires these resources to be managed as an integral part of the organisation.

- The information function is too important to be managed without some formalisation when the business strategies are increasingly dependent on or created by ICT.

- In the past, lack of management support and involvement has impeded the successful exploitation of ICT.

- As ICT becomes part of business and organisational life and pervasive in use, many shareholders/stakeholders are involved so management needs to take strategic views.

4.5 IT strategy

IT strategy is about the delivery of workable solutions to business problems – the practical application of IT to the organisation. In his discussion Earl identifies the same four interdependent components to the architecture that we discussed in a previous section:

- computing architecture

- communications architecture

- data architecture

- applications architecture.

Because the four elements of the IT architecture are interdependent, each influences and is influenced by the other elements. For example, the structure of a communications network is influenced by applications needs, data transmission requirements, information-processing geography and by its own capabilities.

Earl writes that the architecture is a framework for making technological decisions and therefore must help firms to determine how the various elements or pieces of the IT jigsaw fits together.

The task of creating architectures is very difficult and Earl gives four reasons for undertaking the activity:

(a)   As technology becomes more embedded in the operations and sector infrastructure, the need for systems and technology integration increases. Architecture provides a framework for and a mechanism to consider and design necessary interfaces, compatibility and integration.

(b)   Architecture provides a framework for resolving and reviewing technology choices over time.

(c)   Architecture provides a structure for implementing the IS needs of the organisation.

(d)   As the relationship between business strategy and capability and information strategy and capability become closer, a technological model of the organisation is required.

5   Project management

5.1   Introduction

Any project, whether it is the development of an information systems solution or the construction of a major capital asset, must be planned, implemented and controlled effectively.

A successful project will require that an effective solution be delivered to the standards required and within the established time and cost constraints. Organisations frequently succeed in achieving only a proportion of these objectives satisfactorily; the result may be that the required standards are met, but costs exceed those budgeted and delivery is much later than planned.

Management of, and participation in, projects is one of the core skills of the chartered management accountant. It is also one of the skills most in demand in the modern business environment.

5.2   Project objectives

The objectives of a project must be clearly understood at the outset. Objectives often take three forms, and project management is often a delicate balancing act, as the various objectives normally conflict with one another.

KEY POINT

The three dimensions of project management are cost, scope and time. These objectives will normally conflict with one another.

The three dimensions of project management objectives are as follows:

- **Cost.** There are two main aspects to cost that must be considered for any project. In almost all cases there is a budget available for project completion, and the project manager should not exceed the budget without authorisation. This may be very difficult to achieve as often the budget is set without a clear idea of exactly what is going to be involved in the project. It is not uncommon, as a project manager, to be put in the position of having to make a project solution 'fit' the budget available.

The second aspect to cost is the need, in most projects, to prove that the benefits of the project exceed the costs. This is a major problem because often the costs are all financial or can be stated in financial terms (e.g. the time taken by staff) but the benefits are difficult or impossible to quantify.

- **Scope.** Once again, there are two aspects to the scope dimension of a project. Firstly, there are a certain series of tasks or activities to be performed in reaching the project solution. It is important for the project manager to ensure that all the work required is completed.

  Secondly, each task will have an expected quality level associated with it. It is also important that the tasks are performed well, and that the sponsor's quality expectations are met.

- **Time**. There are two aspects to the time dimension of a project. Firstly, there is often an overall time constraint on a project (sometimes called a deadline) by which time the project must be completed. This may be due to an internal business constraint such as a financial reporting deadline, or an external commercial constraint such as a promise made to a customer.

  Secondly, there may be a 'time budget' for the project. This is often expressed in terms of resource availability and measured in hours or days. This may be due to a resource shortage within the organisation or a constraint placed on a supplier if the project is outsourced to a specialist contractor.

It is essential not only that all the objectives are achieved to the greatest possible extent, but also that a balance is maintained between them. There are a number of conflicts between the various objectives, as we shall see later.

5.3 Conflicting objectives

As mentioned above, the different objectives of a project normally conflict with one another. This can be seen clearly if we look at scope compared with time or cost. It obviously takes longer and costs more to carry out more tasks or increase the quality level. However, there may also be a conflict between cost and time. In order to reduce the labour cost of a project, it may be possible to avoid overtime working, or only use staff when they are surplus to requirements or under-utilised. This would inevitably increase the time taken to complete the project.

There are two approaches to the management of conflicting objectives that a project manager might take:

- It is always necessary to **compromise** between conflicting objectives, and to recognise that it is impossible to achieve a perfect solution. The project manager must manage the expectations of the users and sponsor in this respect.

- If two objectives conflict, but one of them is directly related to a **CSF** of the project, then that objective will be given priority.

5.4 Implementation problems

It will be useful to examine the problems that may arise when implementing any kind of plan.

- **Unrealistic deadlines** – The deadline may be accepted at too early a stage in the planning process, based on when the users believe they need the solution. It may be too early to appreciate the realism or otherwise of the timescale.

- **Planning** – If the project is not planned sufficiently well, then problems will inevitably ensue.

- **The project manager** – In many cases the project manager will be technically skilled, but may be lacking in management skills. This may be brought about by the career path that staff often follow. A project presents various conflicts for the project manager and, without the appropriate skills, problems may occur. The project manager experiences pressures from different sources.

  - The **project sponsor** requires that the project be delivered within budget, on time and to agreed specification.

  - The **users** require that the solution meets their needs – though they may not know exactly what they are. The users are expecting the project to be completed on time, within budget, and capable of doing all that is required of it. Their input is crucial, but they may not be in a position to give up the time to make a contribution.

  - The work of the **project team** members and **subcontractors** needs planning and supervising by the project manager.

  As you might imagine, a very specific management style will need to be adopted to ensure the success of the project.

- **Control** – Another cause of potential problems is inadequate, or non-existent, control mechanisms.

- **Modifying the specifications** – As the solution is being developed, sponsors frequently modify their original specification. This may be due in part to the sponsors discovering, once the project is underway, more precisely what they require and because of insufficient time spent with the sponsor or users in the early stages of the project. These late modifications can have disastrous effects on the project in terms of timing, actual costs, staffing, etc.

- **Inadequate scheduling and resourcing** – This again is a question of planning. The project must be planned in such a way that if one stage must be completed before another can commence, these constraints are built into the schedule.

5.5 Resource allocation

It is important to allocate resources accurately. Take the example of human resources. People are a resource that is usually limited. The number of individuals available to do a job at a specific time with a particular skill mix will be predetermined in many cases (offices, factories, etc).

In most projects it is necessary to avoid sharp fluctuations in labour levels. This is partly for economic reasons – it is expensive to recruit and train staff – but also for social reasons – it is not desirable to hire personnel, lay them off, hire them again, etc. An efficient use of human resources is to aim for a smooth build-up followed by a tapering off, which can often be achieved by rescheduling.

The same principle can also be applied to other resources.

5.6 Project management tools

Since the earliest developments of project management as a discipline, a number of 'tools' have been developed to improve the effectiveness of the project management process. These should all be familiar from your earlier studies, so we will only cover them in outline.

Projects are most likely to be managed using some kind of project management software. Remember also the value of groupware, described in the previous chapter.

5.7 Project initiation document

The project initiation document (PID) is a formal document listing the goals, constraints and success criteria for the project – the rules of the game.

The PID, once written, is subject to negotiation and modification by the various stakeholders of the project. Once they formally agree its content, it becomes the document that is referred to in the case of any disagreement later as to precisely what the project was intended to achieve.

5.8 Critical path analysis

The most commonly used technique for managing projects is critical path analysis (CPA), sometimes called network analysis.

A project can be defined as being a series of activities designed to achieve a specific objective, and which has a definite beginning and a definite end point. For critical path analysis to be of use, the project must be capable of being split into a number of discrete activities, which relate together in a logical and well-defined manner.

Critical path analysis involves the breaking down of a project into its constituent activities, and the presentation of these activities in diagrammatic form.

The critical path through a network is the chain of activities whose times determine the overall duration of the project. Activities on the critical path are known as critical activities, and any increase in the duration of a critical activity will result in an increase in the project duration.

5.9 Gantt charts

The ideal project-reporting system is a mixture of graphics and tables. One form of graphical presentation that is commonly used as a part of network analysis is the Gantt chart.

A Gantt chart is a kind of horizontal bar chart where the length of the bar represents the duration of the activity. When a Gantt chart is used to help in the control of a project, two bars are used to represent each activity – one the planned duration and the other the actual duration.

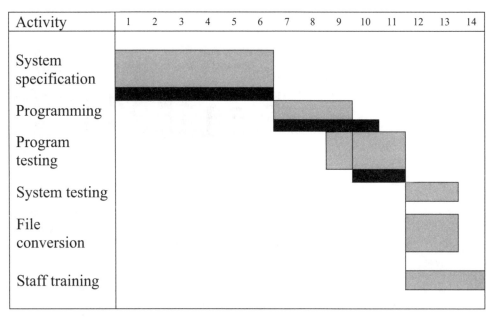

Activity	1	2	3	4	5	6	7	8	9	10	11	12	13	14
System specification														
Programming														
Program testing														
System testing														
File conversion														
Staff training														

▨	Planned duration
▮	Actual duration

Diagram: Example of a GANTT chart

In the example shown above, the programming took longer than expected, but extra resources were put into program testing to enable the project to be put back onto course.

5.10 Resource histogram

A resource histogram is simply a stacked bar chart showing the number and mix of staff over the duration of the project. It is used to plan and control the human resource requirements of the project.

5.11 Budgeting and cost control

It is very common for a project budget to be constructed as shown below. The use of a spreadsheet package for project budgeting makes variance analysis and financial control much easier.

Month	1	2	3	4	5	6	7	8	9	10	11	Total
Salaries	420	285	662	850	122	453	411	502	850	421	409	5385
Materials	0	125	0	0	1000	250	400	325	100	125	800	3125
Overheads	180	55	320	123	249	402	111	122	451	123	201	2337
Sub-con.	0	200	200	200	200	0	0	560	560	250	0	2170
Total	600	665	1182	1173	1571	1105	922	1509	1961	919	1410	13017

Such a budget can, of course, be shown as a histogram for immediate visual impact, as shown below.

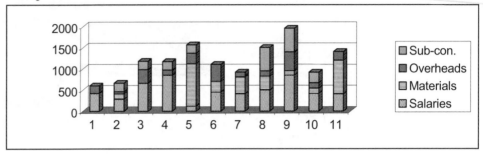

Diagram: Example of a budget histogram

You have learned about **cost control** in considerable detail in your studies for other papers, but you may be expected to draw on this knowledge as part of a question for this paper. Here are reminders of some key points that you might mention.

- There should be a central management group responsible for the overall budget for the project.

- The overall budget should be broken down into budgets for each specific activity, and these specific activity budgets should also be prepared in detail.

- Project managers for each specific activity should receive financial training, if necessary, with a particular emphasis on what they must do to manage their budget.

- The budgets for each project manager should be prepared in detail.

- Project managers will be expected to manage these budgets. Any divergence between actual spending and the sub-project budget can then be identified early, and acted on.

- Budget reports from the project managers to the budget committee should be at least monthly, and possibly more frequent at critical stages of the project development. Variances between budgeted costs and actual costs should be explained and justified. Exception reporting can be used to highlight significant differences between budget and actual costs.

- Major items of expenditure should be kept under constant review.

- As the project progresses, the budget committee needs to monitor the expected costs to complete the project. In other words, there should be forward-looking assessments of the expected final cost, for continual comparison with the budget.

- The management information system for budgeting and budgetary control must be sufficient to support the requirements for cost control. It is therefore essential that data about costs should be accurate and gathered as quickly as possible. The IT systems for costing and budgeting must therefore be suitably designed and in place.

- The recording of cost data should be consistent, so that it can be properly integrated for reporting to management. Common reporting systems and cost terminology should be used, so that managers can discuss budgets and costs with a shared understanding of what the information means and signifies.

5.12 Progress report

A periodic progress report should be sent from the project manager to the project sponsor or steering committee, often on a monthly basis.

A typical progress report will contain the following sections:

- A report identifier – the project name, report sequence number and date.

- A short review of progress since the last report.

- Problems encountered and actions taken or planned.

- Revised plans for cost and time, together with details of any agreed variations to scope.

- A SWOT analysis.

The progress report will often be used as the basis of discussion at a meeting between the project manager and the project sponsor or steering committee.

Summary

Key points of this chapter are:

- The main aim of an information strategy is to complement the organisation's strategy. Strategic management should ensure that information strategy is considered at the earliest possible stage to ensure that the organisation's objectives are achievable.

- Nolan's stage hypothesis might help us to identify where the organisation is now and where it is likely to be going in terms of information strategy.

- Information strategy development may use any of the familiar strategy tools covered elsewhere in this book such as SWOT analysis, Porter's five forces and the value chain.

- A formal methodology for strategy development might be broken down into six activities: initiation; clarifying business strategy; modelling the business; reviewing current information systems; building the information systems architecture; and developing the strategy.

- Earl's strategic framework incorporating IS, IM, and IT and the IS audit grid may help an organisation to sort its priorities according to its needs.

- Successful implementation of information strategies, calls for strong project management skills. Various techniques including Critical Path Analysis and GANTT charts can be used to help control IS projects.

Having completed your study of this chapter you should have achieved the following learning outcomes:

- evaluate and advise managers on the development of strategies for IM, IS and IT that support the organisation's strategic requirements

- identify and evaluate IS/IT systems appropriate to the organisation's strategic requirements, and recommend changes where necessary.

Self-test questions

1 What is the difference between the integration stage, the data administration stage and the maturity stage in Nolan's stage hypothesis? (2.1)

2 What common circumstances may require a revision to information strategy? (3.2)

3 What are the six stages of a typical information systems planning project? (3.4)

4 Draw a grid that could be used to analyse information system use. (3.8)

5 Why should IT managers consult users when considering systems development? (3.8)

6 What is the difference between data architecture and applications architecture? (3.9)

7 What problems may be encountered during IS planning, according to Earl? (4.3)

8 What underpins the formation of information management strategy? (4.4)

9 Project management has three dimensions – cost, scope and time – and each dimension has two aspects. What are these? (5.2)

10 What points would you mention if asked about how the costs of a project can be controlled? (5.11)

Practice question

KJ plc

KJ plc supplies office and stationery products by mail order to a wide range of companies and individuals. Customers telephone or fax their orders to KJ plc's sales department which takes the order details, checks the stock in real-time to ensure that the order can be fulfilled and then transfers the order to a central warehouse for packing the stock ready to deliver to the customer. All orders received before 5.00 pm are delivered on the next working day.

Because KJ plc is in a service industry, it has always tried to maintain a good standard of customer service. On the whole, this objective has been met. A recent survey of 100 customers, which asked them to rank the importance of various aspects of the business, produced the information shown in Table 2.

Existing computer systems

KJ plc's Transaction Processing System provides a vast amount of information, which is used by managers at all levels in the organisation. Very few complaints have been received concerning the information that is normally supplied. The DP department has therefore concentrated on maintaining the system and fine-tuning this to requests of employees, where the Managing Director would allow this. Significant change was not allowed because of the authoritarian approach of the MD.

IT strategy

The main objectives of the IT strategy have been to:

(a) ensure goal congruence between the different sections of the company (such as sales, warehouse despatch and stock control) so that they are all working together to provide good customer service,

(b) ensure that good service has been provided to customers, *from the point of view of the customer,* and

(c) maintain an acceptable Transaction Processing System.

This strategy has been successfully implemented in recent years. However, there is now evidence of potential problems: a meeting of managers has revealed that some managers are uncomfortable with the MD's authoritarian style of management, and the latest customer survey indicates revised customer priorities.

Management structure

The MD takes most tactical and strategic decisions. This limits the decision-making ability of managers and has resulted in a fairly high staff turnover in middle management positions.

Middle management now consists of two distinct groups: a minority of long-serving managers who are satisfied that the MD should continue to make most of the strategic/tactical decisions, and a majority who have been recently appointed and would like to take a more active role in decision making. The concerns of the majority were expressed to the MD in a recent meeting. One manager from this group resigned following the lack of any definite action plan from the MD. Also, as a result of this meeting, some long-serving managers have been expressing dissatisfaction with the amount of control exercised by the MD.

The MD has finally recognised the need to enhance the decision-making opportunities of his managers, although he does not know how to implement an acceptable solution.

Systems change information

Because the computer systems are now approximately 5 years old and maintenance and other costs are increasing, the board of KJ plc has decided to replace the Transaction Processing System. Two alternative systems are currently under review, details of which are given in Table 1 below. The company could pay for either alternative by outright cash purchase or an operating lease agreement.

Table 1

	Alternative One	Alternative Two
Supplier	KJ plc's current supplier (well-established but not industry-standard)	Y plc, an established supplier specialising in IBM-compatible equipment.
System structure	Centralised, with one large mainframe computer being maintained by a specialist department. All staff would have access to a common database, which would keep information concerning all of the company's activities. The MD would retain control of major decisions regarding the computer system.	De-centralised, with each department maintaining its own computer systems and making its own decisions regarding the use of those systems. Managers would be given responsibility to make the tactical and operational decisions necessary to run their own departments and computer systems. Essential information, e.g. store transactions, would still be shared, but via an internal Intranet system, not by all individuals having access to a shared database.
New features	Delivery times decreased to allow same-day deliveries in major cities for orders placed before 11.00 am. A fully integrated system will mean that stock-outs can be rectified within 24 hours, not 72 which is the fastest time under the existing system.	Email for all employees and Internet access for some employees. Ease of upgrade due to purchase of industry-standard equipment. Customer orders will be taken by telephone, fax, email or Internet, with the company's own branded products being offered as a first choice in all ordering methods. Speed of delivery is likely to be adversely affected because of the increased time required to transfer information between the company's new computer systems.

| Information to be provided | The same as KJ plc's existing system with the addition of a strategic planning module for use by the MD. Historical data from the old system would not be transferred, although access to this would continue to be available up to six months after the system changeover. | A full range of strategic to operational information to meet all managers' information needs, including some powerful database query tools designed for analysis of old databases. Key historical information would be available on the new system if managers can afford to make the transfer from their own department budgets. |

Table 2

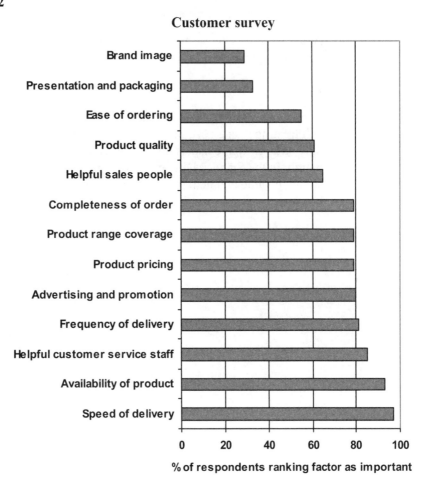

Customer survey

% of respondents ranking factor as important

Required:

(a) Compare the two new systems to show whether either of them would provide an acceptable basis for the three key areas of IT strategy for KJ plc. **(22 marks)**

(b) Explain to what extent KJ plc's current system meets the information requirements of managers in the company, and whether you consider Alternatives One and Two would provide any improvement in the information provided. **(14 marks)**

(Total: 36 marks)

For the answer to this question, see the 'Answers' section at the end of the book.

Feedback to activities

Activity 1

In the early 2000s most organisations are between stages 3 and 6. Substantial new businesses may well skip the first two or three stages.

(i)   Initiation stage – a very small start-up business.

(ii)   Contagion stage – a start-up business that has begun to show some growth and employ more people.

(iii) Control stage – local government.

(iv)   Integration stage – most medium to large commercial enterprises.

(v)   Data administration stage – banks and insurance companies.

(vi)   Maturity stage – airlines, large retailers such as Tesco, Internet-based companies such as Amazon, some publishers.

Activity 2

There is no strategy for information technology at Backwater. The Finance Director is still treating it as a cost, rather than a way of achieving competitive advantage. The only strategy that exists is directed to enhancing its existing base, which seems to be mainly in the Finance Director's domain, rather than areas where it may prove to be of strategic value and help the company gain strategic advantage.

Chapter 20

CHANGE MANAGEMENT

Syllabus content

- Change management in a strategic context.

Contents

1   Introduction

2   Basic features of organisational change

3   Effect on the individual

4   The change process

5   Strategy review and strategic issue management

1   Introduction

The modern business environment is characterised above all by rapid change and businesses must respond in order to remain competitive. Change can be difficult to initiate unless the organisation is facing a threat which all parties recognise and which makes them agree that changes are needed for the survival of the organisation. Overcoming the resistance to change in situations other than those of immediate threat can involve considerable time and effort.

2   Basic features of organisational change

2.1   The need to change

Buchanan and Huczyknski claim there are four basic features of organisational change. These are listed below.

Triggers

Change is initiated by some kind of disorganising pressure or trigger arising either within or outside the organisation. Changes may thus be triggered by the discovery that one of the company's machines is old or beyond repair, or by changes in legislation that affect the ways in which employees have to be treated.

Interdependencies

The various facets of an organisation are interdependent. Change in one aspect of an organisation creates pressure for adjustments in other aspects. The introduction of word processing in the typing pool may require authors to alter the style in which they write and present reports and letters for typing.

Conflict and frustrations

The technical and economic objectives of managers may often conflict with the needs and aspirations of employees and this leads to conflicts that in turn create pressures for and resistance to change. The new machine that management want to buy may lead to demands for a new payment system from the people who will have to operate it.

Time lags

Change rarely takes place smoothly. Instead it happens in an 'untidy' way. Some parts of the organisation change more rapidly than others. People and groups may need time to 'catch up' with everyone else. The maintenance staff may still be learning new skills months after that new machine has been installed.

Whether a change does or does not take place within an organisation is dependent on the relative strength of the various positive and negative feedback loops affecting the situation. Positive feedback invokes change whereas negative feedback leads to stable and consistent behaviour.

2.2   Reasons for organisational change

Internal triggers for change are those factors that can cause organisational disequilibrium and include:

- questioning authority and intra-organisational conflicts

- adverse organisational climate

KEY POINT

A change trigger is an event which leads to change taking place.

KEY POINT

Change in one aspect of an organisation creates pressure for adjustments in other aspects.

KEY POINT

Change rarely takes place smoothly.

KEY POINT

Positive feedback invokes change whereas negative feedback leads to stable and consistent behaviour.

- poor performance – unstable labour relations, low output and high costs

- presence of entrepreneurs and other innovators

- changes in or reordering of organisational goals

- favourable changes experienced in the past.

These internal triggers may, or may not, be related to external forces operating within the organisation's environment which, according to Martino, revolve around:

- changes in knowledge both technical and social

- economic opportunities

- distribution of political power

- demographic make-up of the population

- ecological considerations

- ideological and culture factors.

2.3 Attitudes to change and the future

There are varying attitudes to change as Robertson's classification shows.

- **Inactivists** could be focused on:

    - **Business as usual** – such people seek stability and survival within the organisation and include those conservative satisficers who make up the establishment at large. They work very hard to keep still – a process termed 'dynamic conservatism'. Their efforts appeal to placid and pragmatic people including both moderate reformers and those content with the present situation.

      This attitude attracts defeatists, cynics and the worldly wise

    - **Disaster** – appeals to calm and thoughtful people although it can attract pessimists, preachers and doomsters.

- **Reactivists** – would be interested in totalitarian conservation and would include all those reactionaries who prefer a previous state to the one they are in. Such people:

    - feel there is more to lose from disorder than dictatorship

    - are of an authoritarian, dominating temperament

    - take a low view of other people

    - think they belong to a governing class.

- **Proactivists** – These liberal optimisers are interested in much more than mere survival and they are generally means orientated. Their approaches appeal to optimistic, energetic, ambitious, competitive people for whom material growth is more important than personal and social growth. Such persons are often male, toy loving and over intellectual.

- **Interactivists** must be interested in a sane, humane, ecological future and as radical idealisers they want to control their own destiny. Optimistic, participating, reflective people are attracted to such an attitude together with a number of cranks.

2.4 Strategies for managing change

The five strategies for managing change are:

- participation
- education – communication
- power/coercion
- manipulation
- negotiation.

Participation

This approach aims to involve employees, usually by allowing some input into decision making. This could easily result in employees enjoying raised levels of autonomy, by allowing them to design their own jobs, pay structures, etc.

Employees are more likely to support changes made and give positive commitment as they 'own' the change. Another advantage of participation is the improved utilisation of employee expertise.

Studies undertaken by Coch and French from America and Pirelli UK demonstrate the effectiveness of this strategy. Coch and French, in their book *Overcoming Resistance to Change*, suggest involving the people affected as early as possible, as deeply as possible.

The possible disadvantages include:

- **The time element** – The process can be lengthy due to the number of people involved in the decision-making process.

- **The loyalty element** – There is a need for a strong trusting relationship to exist between management and workforce.

- **The resistance element** – Management may suffer from restricted movement as the amount and direction of change acceptable to employees will have some influence.

Education and communication

Usually used as a background factor to reinforce another approach. This strategy relies upon the hopeful belief that communication about the benefits of change to employees will result in their acceptance of the need to exercise the changes necessary. The obvious advantage is that any changes could be initiated easily. However, employees may not agree about the benefits of proposed changes as being in their best interests. Also, the process of education and persuasion can be lengthy to initiate and exercise unless there is a firm mutual trust. Without this they are not likely to succeed.

Power/coercion

This strategy involves the compulsory approach by management to implement change. This method finds its roots from the formal authority that management possess together with legislative support. When there is a state of high unemployment, management enjoys greater power and is therefore able to use this strategy with more success.

The advantages of this method are:

- Changes can be made with speed.

- Adhering to management's requirements is easy when opposition is weak from the work force.

The disadvantages are:

- The lack of commitment of the workforce and determination to reverse policy when times change.

- Poor support resulting in weak motivation, low morale and performance.

Future implications also need to be considered. For example, when employees enjoy a stronger position, i.e. union representation, they are less likely to cooperate due to their experiences of past management treatment.

Manipulation

A manipulative strategy has many of the advantages and disadvantages of the power strategy. It can therefore be viewed as part of a power strategy.

Negotiation

This particular strategy is often practised in unionised companies. Simply, the process of negotiation is exercised, enabling several parties with opposing interests to bargain. This bargaining leads to a situation of compromise and agreement.

Branching from this are two strategies:

- Each party involved seeks to negotiate for itself, at the cost of the other parties involved.

- Each party aims to find an agreement with aspects advantageous to all concerned.

The advantage of negotiation strategy is that it offers the company the opportunity to note possible conflict and allows it to be dealt with in an orderly fashion. This hopefully prevents such problems as industrial action. Also, when an agreement has been made, the outcome can be to encourage commitment, preserve morale and maintain output.

The main disadvantage is that this approach may be time consuming, and should opposition be strong enough the management might choose to adopt a power strategy instead.

2.5 A model for cultural change

Andrew Mayo describes a simple model of cultural change illustrated by the diagram below.

A model of cultural change

Each circle must be in place or change will not be effective, Mayo argues.

Top management vision and determination – senior management must share and own the end goals so that they visibly drive and articulate the changes needed. Employees tend to follow the lead of senior management.

Education and communication – in order to change the way people think in an organisation, educational programmes are required; first for management and then for all staff. In this way employees are encouraged to think through the implication of the desired culture change for themselves and work out what they must do to help achieve it.

British Airways invested in education programmes in order to achieve cultural change, first through a programme entitled 'putting people first' and then 'managing people first'.

There is no easy method or choice when handling change. Much will depend upon the nature of relationships between the workforce and management, market conditions, the amount of power parties involved possess, as well as the degree of change proposed. The culture of the organisation will have a significant influence upon the approach used.

2.6 Targets for organisational change

Many managers focus their change efforts at a specific level within the organisation, such as the level of the:

- **Individual** – in the belief that organisational behaviour is determined by the characteristics of its members.

    The aim is to improve individual skill levels, attitudes and motivation. Techniques employed include:

    – education and training

    – management development.

- **Organisation structure and systems** – claiming that organisational behaviour is determined by the characteristics of the organisational situation in which people work.

    The aim is to direct member's behaviour to organisational goals and techniques involving structural and procedural modifications such as:

    – divisionalisation

    – matrices

    – size

    – job redesign

    – reward systems

    – management by objectives (MBO).

- **Organisational climate and interpersonal style** – such managers believe that organisational behaviour is determined by emotional and social processes that characterise the relations among members.

    Their aims are to create a system with a wide climate of high interpersonal trust and openness and a reduction in the dysfunctional consequences of excessive social conflict and competitiveness. The principal technique is organisation development.

KEY POINT

There is no easy method or choice when handling change. Much will depend upon the nature of relationships between the workforce and management, market conditions, the amount of power parties involved possess, as well as the degree of change proposed. The culture of the organisation will have a significant influence upon the approach used.

Obviously no one level should be focused on exclusively and a balance of approaches should be the aim.

Activity 1

What behaviour problems are likely to arise from changes imposed by a parent company upon a company it has recently taken over?

Feedback to this activity is at the end of the chapter.

3 Effect on the individual

3.1 Change, work and self-identity

We need to consider the general issue of changes at work on the individual. Rapid and major changes can easily undermine a self-identity that has been built up over time in reasonably stable conditions. For example, technological innovations can make a person's skills no longer relevant; re-organisation can reduce status and prestige; entering new markets can devalue experience of the traditional markets. The threat to self-identity is one of the main factors leading to resistance to change.

3.2 The fears and worries

The fears and worries of the individual facing change has been the subject of considerable study. It is possible to classify them in terms of job factors, personal factors and social factors.

Job factors

- fear of technological unemployment
- fear of changes in working conditions
- fear of demotion and reduced pay
- fear of increased effort and less bonus.

Personal factors

- resentment of the implied criticism that present methods are inadequate
- resentment of the implied criticism that present performance is inadequate
- fear that skill and ability are no longer needed
- fear of increased boredom and monotony and a decreased sense of personal worth
- inconvenience of having to unlearn present methods
- inconvenience of having to learn new methods
- fear that harder work will be required
- fear and uncertainty of the unknown.

Social factors

- dislike of having to make new social adjustments
- dislike of need to break present social ties
- fear that the new social situation will bring less satisfaction

- dislike of outside interference and control

- dislike of those initiating change

- resentment over lack of consultation and participation in the change

- perception that the change will help the organisation at the expense of the individual, the work group or society.

It is clear from the above list that change can provoke severe psychological difficulties for the individual experiencing it. It is no less a problem for the manager who has to plan for, organise and control change in the organisation. Indeed, the threats and challenges of change are accelerating in business.

3.3 Resistance to change

Resistance to change often manifests itself in one form (the symptoms) but the actual cause may initially be hidden. It can take many forms and range along a continuum from open debate through to covert sabotage. In practice most resistance is encountered somewhere in the middle of the continuum. Some examples include:

- **Change avoidance**. In this situation individuals do not openly question the change. They simply avoid implementing the change and carry on as they did before.

- **Starve the change**. In this situation a manager who is responsible for helping the process of change by allocating people and resources always has a good excuse for not allocating the resources when they are needed and so the change is starved of the resources it needs to succeed.

- **Subtle sabotage**. A manager may sabotage the change by allocating the wrong resources to the project. This normally takes the form of putting junior or inexperienced staff into the project team.

- **Over complication**. A manager may bring the progress of the change to a halt by identifying lots of problems and raising the apparent complexity of the situation by suggesting interrelationships between problems.

A combination of the above often manifests itself in the form of a committee. When faced with a request to change something a manager may say it's worth looking at but because of its complexity a committee should be formed to investigate. The manager then puts inappropriate staff members on the committee and does not allocate them sufficient time away from their normal duties to be able to progress the matter. When the committee does report, the manager raises yet more questions. This continues until the committee gets fed up and slowly lets the matter drop.

3.4 Root causes of resistance

The form of the resistance is quite separate from the cause of the resistance. The basic cause of the resistance can be:

- **Pure self-interest**. The individual will actually lose something by the change going ahead and, acting on self interest, resists the change.

- **Misunderstanding**. Individuals are resisting the change because they do not understand it. Their misunderstanding may make them think they will lose (pure self-interest) or it may make them think the change is wrong for the organisation (different views of the situation).

- **Different views of the situation**. Here the person resists because they have a different view ofthe situation, which leads them to believe that the organisation will suffer if the change is implemented.

- **Fear of change**. Some people thrive on change, others fear it.

When attempting to understand the factors causing resistance the system itself should be examined to establish to what extent the design of the system is causing resistance. Another cause of resistance is the interaction between people and the system.

The following are some examples of explanations of resistance to the introduction of information systems. Each example examines the resistance from the people, system and interactions perspectives.

Resistance caused by people factors	Resistance caused by system factors	Resistance caused by interactions between people and the system
Example 1		
The users want a system that meets all of their requirements – some of which do not justify the cost of development.	The system does not meet some of the needs that it should do.	The users are unaware of the work involved in producing some of the features they require. The systems designers have not understood the relevance of some of the features that the users are demanding.
Example 2		
The users are currently engaged in a political battle of no relation to the system.	The system has sparked the political struggle by changing power relationships.	The introduction of the system has initiated the political conflict by redistributing information power.
Example 3		
The users do not have the intellectual capacity to recognise the benefits of the system.	The system is too complicated and also difficult to learn.	The system is incorrect for these kinds of users.
Example 4		
The users are set in their ways and do not want to make the effort required to change.	The system will require considerable effort to implement and does not bring many benefits.	The system brings significant benefits to certain user classes but causes other groups to lose something they value.
Example 5		
Users resist the use of the system on the basis of the false excuse that the system is unsuitable.	The system is unsuitable.	The users' needs have not been fully addressed nor have the users fully understood the features that the system does have.

3.5 Approaches to overcoming resistance

As already mentioned, the most effective method of overcoming resistance to change is to avoid resistance occurring in the first instance. This is most effectively done by gaining user participation at a very early stage. Management often feels that they should not discuss plans for changes until they have made all of the decisions and worked through all of the details. This comes from the feeling that many managers have that because they are managers they should have all of the answers. Announcing an information systems project without knowing its precise structure and scope would for some managers be an admission of not knowing all of the answers. However in practice it has been shown to be counter-productive to formulate too much detail before introducing the ideas and plans to those affected by them because this can damage the chances of gaining effective participation. Gaining and maintaining full participation is the primary strategy to minimise resistance.

4 The change process

4.1 Framework for the management of change

The idea of change that is planned assumes that the management can identify gaps between current conditions and desired conditions on the following dimensions:

- How can this organisation be more effective?

- Can we operate more efficiently?

- How can we make it a more satisfying place of work?

Whenever the organisation can identify differences between where it currently is and where it would like to be on any of the dimensions, it can pursue planned change or improve the organisation.

Systems would be implemented to identify and diagnose particular problems within these general areas, e.g. poor morale, inefficient computer programs, lack of quality control or inadequate downward communication. Depending on the problem, a suitable change effort can be designed.

If the process of planned change is to become part of the culture of the organisation, provisions must be made for introspection and self-criticism on a routine basis. It should also be followed up as a natural part of the managerial style.

4.2 Why change is a challenge to management

For managers the management of change is about maintaining a dynamic equilibrium. By diagnosing events and situations and making adjustments which are appropriate for coping with current conditions, the management would ensure that:

- there is enough stability to achieve current goals

- there is continuity to allow orderly change in either ends or means

- the organisation is adaptable and can react to external opportunities and demands as well as changing internal conditions

- there is enough innovativeness for the organisation to be proactive and initiate change when conditions are right.

The managerial role involves coping with accelerating change in both the external environment and the internal subsystems that affect the managerial process.

Accelerating change can lead to increasing complexity, making the job of the manager increasingly difficult. They need a tolerance for ambiguity and an ability to diagnose situations and identify opportunities and problems.

As decision-makers, managers are the ultimate change agents, whether they are centrally involved or merely guiding and co-ordinating activities. Change can stem from adjustments in managerial behaviour, e.g. leadership style, approach to planning and controlling or degree of participation in decision making. When the focus is more technical, structural or psychosocial, managers may respond to suggestions from others or actively instigate changes.

There are external or internal consultants that facilitate organisational change. Specialists in economic and marketing research, industrial relations and organisational development are all examples of change agents.

4.3 Alternative models of change management

Lewin's 3-step model of change

This model is based on the effectiveness of using group norms and consensus decision making to change individual and organisational behaviour.

Lewin's research programmes included Weight Watchers and the effect of group discussion and commitment in changing eating habits. The key findings were that behaviour change is more likely to occur and persist when commitment is on a group basis, rather than an individual one.

KEY POINT

According to Lewin change is a three-step process: unfreeze, change, refreeze.

The process of change, shown in the diagram below, includes unfreezing habits or standard operating procedures, changing to new patterns and refreezing to ensure lasting effects.

Existing behaviour

New behaviour

Unfreeze

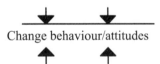
Change behaviour/attitudes

Refreeze

Diagram: Lewin's three step model of change

The process of change comprises three stages:

(a) **Unfreezing** - create the initial motivation to change by convincing staff of the undesirability of the present situation.

(b) **The change process itself** - mainly concerned with identifying what the new behaviour or norm should be. This stage will often involve new information being communicated and new attitudes, culture and concepts being adopted.

(c) **Refreezing or stabilising the change** - implying reinforcement of the new pattern of work or behaviour by rewards (praise, etc). Develop the belief that the changed situation satisfies organisational and personal values.

Analysis of failed attempts to carry out organisational change can be traced back to failure to address issues that arose in one of the three phases above. All stages of the change process need to be properly managed starting with the unfreezing stage. It is important that at this stage the roots of resistance to the change are identified.

4.4 Leavitt

Approaches to change that succeeded in one organisation were not necessarily successful in another. Leavitt suggests that the chosen approach to change in a particular organisation reflects the underlying beliefs within that organisation.

KEY POINT

Leavitt viewed any organisation as having four interacting variables - tasks, structure, technology and people - each of them giving rise to different approaches to change.

Leavitt viewed any organisation as having four interacting variables, each of them giving rise to different approaches to change.

- **Tasks** – approaches to change will be largely technical, that is seeking to improve the quality of decisions. The task approach will be interrelated to the other three approaches.

- **Structure** – the traditional performance approach is of ensuring proper division of labour, levels of authority and responsibility, defining chain of command and span of control. Another approach is the creation of project centres and localising of decision making creating a high level of local autonomy. The communication channels and flows may also need to be changed. Repetitious, predictable work may succeed with a highly centralised communication structure, whereas for novel, loosely structured tasks, a more open multi-channel communication network may seem more appropriate.

- **Technology** – An early example of a change approach to this category includes method study approaches where an outsider views the work pattern and suggests changes in a technological approach (Taylor). Updating and replacement of equipment is a natural example of an external approach. The essence is that the approach occurs outside the work group itself.

- **People** – Group working, attitude training, changes in styles of management are examples of the people approach.

Implementing change through power politics

If transformational change is required in an organisation, it is likely that there will be a need for the reconfiguration of power structures

Any manager of change needs to consider how it might be implemented from a political perspective. For example, a critical report by an outside change agency such as market research findings on customer perceptions of service may be 'rubbished' by the board because it threatens their authority and power.

There is often a need to plan changes within this political context. The political mechanisms include the following.

- **The control and manipulation of organisational resources.** Acquiring, withdrawing or allocating additional resources, or being identified with important areas of resource or expertise, can be an important tool in overcoming resistance or persuading others to accept change. Being able to manipulate the information opposing the changes can also be important.

- **Association with powerful groups or elites** can help build a power base. This may be useful for the change agent who does not have a strong personal power base to work from. Association with a change agent who is seen as successful or who is respected can also help a manager overcome resistance to change.

- **Handling the subsystem effectively** can achieve acceptance of change throughout the organisation. Building up alliances and a network of contacts and sympathisers may help win over powerful groups.

- **Symbolic devices** that may take different forms. To build power the manager may become involved in committees that reinforce and preserve the change model. Symbolic activity can be used for consolidating change by positive reinforcement towards those who most accept change. These rewards include new structures, titles and office allocation.

4.5   Warren G Bennis

KEY POINT

Bennis identifies five avenues of change: dissent and conflict; trust and truth; cliques and cabals; external events; and culture or paradigm shift.

Bennis is an influential American author on leadership and change. He focuses on the need to inspire change rather than merely imposing it.

He identifies five 'avenues of change'.

- Dissent and conflict. Top management impose change by means of their position power, the result being rancour amongst those affected.

- Trust and truth. Management must gain trust, express their vision clearly, and persuade others to follow.

- Cliques and cabals. Cliques have power, money and resources. Cabals have ambition, drive and energy. 'Unless the cliques can co-opt the cabals, revolution is inevitable.'

- External events. Forces of society can impose change, e.g. by new government regulation or through overseas competition.

- Culture or paradigm shift. Changing the corporate culture is the most important avenue of change.

Bennis also provides advice on avoiding disaster during change.

- Recruit with scrupulous honesty.

- Guard against the crazies. (Innovation may attract people who will distort its ideas.)

- Build support among like-minded people.

- Plan for change from a solid conceptual base.

- Don't settle for rhetorical change.

- Don't allow those who are opposed to change to appropriate basic issues.

- Know the territory.

- Appreciate environmental factors.

- Avoid future shock.

- Remember that change is most successful when those who are affected are involved in the planning.

5   Strategy review and strategic issue management

5.1   The importance of reviewing progress

The success of any change should be reviewed to make sure that it meets the objectives that it was supposed to achieve.

By building into the change process a means of reviewing its progress, the organisation is making strategic change more coherent, which in itself is a way of making the change a success. Being coherent across all aspects of the organisation means that:

- there is a consistency between the intended strategy, the stated strategic objectives, their expression in operational terms, the behaviour of executives in reinforcing the strategy and a means of assessing performance and progress

- the direction of strategic change is consistent with what is happening in the environment and with what is understood in the organisation

- the strategy is feasible in terms of the required resources, the structuring of the organisation and the changes that need to occur in organisational culture and operational routines

- the strategic direction is clearly related to achieving competitive advantage or excellent performance, and internally it is understood how this is happening.

The key issue is finding an appropriate means of reviewing the progress and success of any strategic change and identifying strategic issues as they arise.

Performance measures for strategic change are not easy and, more often, financial results are relied upon. In their book *Strategic control: milestones for long-term performance*, Gould and Quinn suggest that most companies take a pride in fostering a performance-driven culture that emphasises profitability as the key goal for business management, but too much emphasis on budgetary control and short-term profit can disguise strategic problems from senior managers.

5.2 A framework for strategy review

The introduction of a strategic control system to monitor the organisation's strategic position has advantages that include:

- planning realism

- encouraging higher performance standards

- motivation

- ability to intervene when the activity is not going to plan.

Gould and Quinn identify a formal and an informal system of strategic control.

The formal process begins with a strategy review where the organisation's key success factors are outlined. A cost leadership strategy would identify cost measures, which are one of the easiest to monitor. Milestones of performance are then identified, both of a quantitative and a qualitative nature. These milestones are short-term steps towards long-term goals and act as a way of pulling the organisation towards its goals. Milestones are the means to monitor both the actions, such as the launching of a new product, and the results, e.g. the success of the launch. The areas that milestones cover include:

- market share

- quality measurement

- innovation

- customer satisfaction.

When setting target achievement levels the targets must be reasonably precise, suggesting strategies and tactics. Competitive benchmarks are targets that are set relative to the competition. It may be difficult to obtain data about the competitor, but a relative advantage is important in competitive terms.

Informal systems of strategic control exist where the organisation does not define explicit strategic objectives or milestones that are regularly and formally monitored as part of the management control system. The argument in favour of informality mainly concentrates on aspects such as flexibility and openness of communication. However, these systems do not always work because they enable managers to ignore important strategic issues.

5.3 The importance of strategic issue management

Gould and Quinn suggest the characteristics of strategic control systems can be measured on two axes.

- The formality of the process.

- The milestones that are identified for performance.

Whilst there may be no optimum degree of formality of the process and no optimum number of milestones identified for performance, the following guidelines are recommended.

- If there are important linkages among businesses, the formality of the process should be low, to avoid co-operation being undermined.

- If there is a lot of diversity, it is doubtful whether any strategic control system is appropriate, especially where the critical success factors for each business are different. Formal processes may not find the right objectives while informal ones may confuse the issue.

- Where an organisation's strategic stance depends on decisions which can, if they go wrong, destroy the company as a whole (e.g. launching a new technology), then there is a need for strategic control systems which have a large number of performance criteria so that emerging problems in any area will be easily detected. Where there is high environmental uncertainty, a strategic control process monitors some of the background assumptions.

- Fashion-goods manufacturers, and other industries which are prone to many changes, must respond to relatively high levels of environmental turbulence and must be able to react quickly. Where changes are rapid, a system of low formality and few measures may be appropriate, merely because the control processes must allow *ad hoc* decisions to be taken.

For businesses with few sources of competitive advantage, control can easily focus on the key factors, where market share or quality is the source of success. Where there are many sources of advantage and success covers a wide area, e.g. market share, sales mix, pricing policy and distribution, there is the danger that control can be misdirected because it focuses on inappropriate objectives and carries a high cost because measurement of performance is difficult.

Summary

Key points of this chapter are:

- Change takes place in response to a change trigger.

- Within an organisation, there are various attitudes to change including Inactivitists and Reactivists.

- Organisations need a strategy for managing change.

- Change may have a negative effect on an individual so organisations must manage change carefully.

- Lewin's three step model of change attempts to explain change in terms of amending the behaviour of individuals.

- Having implemented some form of change, a review should take place to ensure that the objectives for that change have been achieved.

Having completed your study of this chapter you should have achieved the following learning outcome:

- discuss the role of change management in a strategic context.

Self-test questions

1 What are the four basic features of organisational change? (2.1)

2 What is a reactivist? (2.3)

3 What are the five strategies for managing change? (2.4)

4 Describe Mayo's model of cultural change. (2.5)

5 What fears and worries may individuals have with regard to organisational change? (3.2)

6 What are the root causes of resistance to change? (3.4)

7 What is Lewin's 3-step model of change? (4.3)

8 Identify four political mechanisms that a manager may need to consider when planning change. (4.4)

9 In the context of change, what is a milestone? Give examples. (5.2)

10 What kind of strategic control system is appropriate in an industry where changes are very rapid? (5.3)

Practice question

Managing change

Required:

Explain four strategies for managing change, giving the advantages and disadvantages of each. **(20 marks)**

For the answer to this question, see the 'Answers' section at the end of the book.

Feedback to activity

Activity 1

In the event of a takeover or merger, behavioural problems will arise out of fear of change and there will be resistance to it. They will manifest themselves as follows:

(a) **A conflict of loyalties** – Many people who were loyal to the old firm or organisation will find it difficult to adjust to the new arrangement. This will manifest in an inability to integrate, to accept changes in work patterns and new managers. This in turn will lead to poor performance, possibly even outright opposition or even a possible attempt to undermine the new manager's authority.

(b) **Fear** – This will arise initially from the changes at higher levels. Suspicion of changes will cause doubts and uncertainty.

The fear will develop if the merger leads to redundancies. This will especially hit higher levels of management since there will be no requirement for two chief accountants or two marketing directors.

(c) **Loss of status** – The loss of status can cause serious problems even where jobs and autonomy remain. For example, the chief accountant of the firm which is taken over may remain as divisional controller but report only functionally to a general manager, having another chief accountant senior to him. The job remains unchanged but the man may well grieve over lost status, especially if any privileges are removed. The situation may be further aggravated by the fact that an internal struggle may take place, possibly arising from the downgraded accountant being technically superior to his new function head.

Chapter 21

ANSWERS TO PRACTICE QUESTIONS

Chapter 1

Corporate mission and strategies

(a) REPORT

To: The Managing Director

From: The Management Accountant

Subject: Corporate mission statements

The meaning of corporate mission

The corporate mission embodies the overall purposes of an organisation. A corporate mission statement is formulated to express the company's philosophy and should answer fundamental questions such as: Why does the company exist? Who will be served by and benefit from the company? What products or services will be provided? The majority of mission statements are presented using general, rather than detailed, concepts.

Corporate mission and strategic planning

In order to prepare an effective strategic plan, the management must first address the organisation's mission. There is a certain amount of controversy regarding the point in the planning process at which the mission statement is best formulated. One view is that the mission statement is of such a fundamental nature that the strategic plan cannot be prepared without reference to it. Another view, expressed by Argenti, is diametrically opposed. He postulates that the mission statement is the end result of the strategic-planning process. These opinions demonstrate how difficult it can be to differentiate between an organisation's mission and its objectives. The mission is a wide-ranging statement that presents the organisation's raison d'être in terms of its ability to satisfy some of society's needs whilst its objectives are the company's broad goals.

Areas to be covered

The mission statement is likely to be formulated by the company's board of directors. Although it will not be quantitative in nature it will usually highlight several areas:

- the kinds of products and services the company aims to provide

- the customers to be served

- the markets in which the company anticipates operating

- an overview of the company philosophy and the broad expression of its policies

- the company's attitude towards matters encompassing social obligations

- the manner in which management wishes the firm to be perceived by the public.

Benefits from developing a mission statement

The usefulness of a mission statement may be summarised as follows.

- All staff will gain an understanding of the firm's purpose and philosophy.

- Expectations and attitudes within the firm will be expressed in terms of a long-range vision.

- The organisation will benefit from a unanimity of purpose that should result in decisions advantageous to the purposes of the company.

- The boundaries within which the company operates will be clearly laid down. This will assist in developing co-ordinated plans.

- An unambiguous statement regarding the overall direction of the company should lead to enhanced allocation of resources.

Conclusion

The company would gain several benefits from the formulation of a mission statement. It would greatly assist the decision-makers and those responsible for implementing the firm's policies. The mission statement also has an important role to play in helping management focus on fundamental issues in terms of strategic planning and will ensure that strategic plans do not conflict with the basic purpose of the organisation.

(b) **Strategies**

(i) An intended strategy is a plan. Those intended strategies that actually get implemented are deliberate strategies. The deliberate strategies and the emergent strategies, or patterns of behaviour, together form the realised strategies. A realised strategy is what actually happens.

(ii) The rational model of strategy management, i.e. the management of deliberate strategies, has three elements.

- Strategic analysis - what is the organisation's strategic position?

- Strategic choice

- Strategic implementation - planning how the chosen strategy will be implemented.

Strategic analysis is concerned with understanding the strategic position of the organisation. It deals with the following:

- The environmental and competitive factors surrounding the organisation, which offer both opportunities and threats. The environmental factors include the political, economic, social and technological issues that affect the organisation.

- The resources of the organisation, i.e. its strengths and weaknesses.

- The stakeholders' expectations.

Strategic choice is based on strategic analysis. Briefly, it involves the following:

- strategic options generation - a variety of alternatives are considered

- strategic options evaluation - each option is then examined on its merits

- strategy selection.

The implementation of the strategy has to be planned. This is the conversion of the strategy into detailed specification as to how the activities should be carried out.

Others will specify targets which managers are expected to reach on their own initiative.

The concept of emergent strategies holds that a strategy can develop from patterns of behaviour, or from consistency in the types of decisions it makes. Emergent strategies are not thought out before being realised. They are a reaction to circumstances.

(iii) Strategic decisions deal with the long term, the organisation's overall relationship with the environment and the shape of the business and its activities. Operating or non-strategic decisions do not.

Chapter 2

Question 1: Strengths and Weaknesses

When conducting a survey of the strengths and weaknesses of an organisation, invariably there is a tendency for management to concentrate on certain aspects of the operation. This is not to say, however, that the extent of the survey will be identical in each area on every occasion. Neither does it imply that other areas of investigation should automatically be eliminated. A strengths and weaknesses appraisal is part of the work of a position audit.

(a) **Financial resources** – As with internal appraisal, this consists of constructing a series of accounting ratios to measure profitability, growth and liquidity, and then comparing them with earlier results and also with results of other firms in similar circumstances. Such an exercise will indicate the firm's strengths and weaknesses both in terms of former occasions and current competitiveness.

(b) **Profitability** – This involves a series of analyses each with the aim of identifying the organisation's operational position. For example, it might include an analysis of sales and profit involving sales mix, pricing strategy, discount facilities, and an assessment of the returns on total assets employed. Costs obviously have important implications for profitability and therefore, determination of operational costs and internal efficiency is also required.

(c) **Effectiveness of functional departments within the organisation** – This is normally done by defining the specialist knowledge available, specialist activities undertaken, and the significant factors on which the company depends, including the areas of vulnerability.

During the exercise these issues will be raised in connection with all the functional activities; in addition, it is necessary to ascertain specific details for each function. For example, the plant utilisation rate, the proportion of bad debts, the extent of production delays due to failure of supplies, etc.

(d)　**Product range** – Often companies have an extensive product range that needs frequent reviewing to ensure that it is well balanced and relevant to current market needs. This involves the determination of the profit contribution of each product in relationship to the resources it utilises. It is also necessary to pay particular attention to market trends to ascertain whether, in the product mix, certain products need upgrading whilst others require phasing out. In addition, there is the need to establish the position regarding the introduction of new products, both in terms of frequency and timing, to ensure the company's competitive position is maintained. All these various activities add up to an extensive marketing research assignment.

(e)　**Human resources of the organisation** – Any such appraisal must ensure that personnel are suitably motivated and adequate facilities are available for appropriate staff development. One technique that many companies have adopted in one form or another is management by objectives (MBO). This includes establishing key tasks for a job and agreed performance standards, and providing suitable encouragement for such standards to be achieved, and is followed by a subsequent stage in which a review is conducted involving the managers and their superiors to compare actual performance against the standards agreed. It also provides, from time to time, an assessment of the potential of each manager.

Whatever form of management style the organisation uses, it is essential that a thorough assessment of the human resources of the organisation is carried out. The main purpose of this should be to ensure that the manpower resources of the company match both the current technical and social skills requirements, and also those that it is anticipated will be required in the future.

In addition, it is necessary to ensure that the organisational structure is the most suitable for present day needs. With rapid technological, economic, political and sociological changes, an organisation can rapidly become out of date. Conducting frequent organisational appraisals should avoid this happening.

Therefore, it can be seen that an appraisal of the firm's strengths and weaknesses is a considerable task with a notable contribution required from the accountant. The exercise involves considerable analysis and invariably leads to certain criticisms of the existing arrangements. Such criticisms, even if only implied, may not always be readily acceptable but must be carried out, and carried out authentically, if the company is to obtain the maximum benefit from an appraisal of its strengths and weaknesses.

Question 2: Competitive forces and barriers to entry

(a)　**Competitive forces**

(i)　**Threats from substitutes**

These are alternative products that serve the same purpose, e.g. gas central heating system in competition with electrical systems. The main threat posed by substitutes is that they limit the price that a company can charge for its products. There is also a danger that the threat of a substitute may not be realised until it is too late to arrest its entry. Substitute products that warrant most attention are those that are subject to an environment improving their price-performance tradeoff with the industry's product, or are produced by industries earning high profits and who have the resources available to bring them rapidly into play.

(ii)   **Threats from the power of buyers**

Porter suggests that buyers are particularly powerful in seven situations. These are:

–   purchasers are large relative to sellers

–   purchase price represents a significant proportion of the buyer's costs

–   purchases are undifferentiated

–   buyers earn low profits

–   buyers have the potential for backward integration

–   the buyer's product is not strongly affected by the quality of the supplier's product

–   the buyer has full information.

The threat is that buyers compete with the suppliers by forcing down prices, bargaining for higher quality or more services, and playing competitors against each other - all at the expense of the profitability of the supplier group.

(iii)   **Threats from the power of suppliers**

Porter suggests that suppliers are particularly powerful in six situations. These exist where:

–   there are few suppliers

–   there are few substitutes for their products

–   the industry supplied is not an important customer

–   the supplier's product is an important component of the buyer's business

–   the supplier's product is differentiated

–   suppliers can integrate forward.

In these situations suppliers can squeeze profitability out of an industry by raising prices or reducing the quality of purchased goods and services. Participants in the industry often have limited freedom to raise their own prices or take other actions to recover the cost increases which are contributing to an erosion of their profitability.

(iv)   **Rivalry and competition among competitors**

Porter suggests that there are seven main determinants relating to the strength of internal competition and rivalry within an industry. Competitive forces will be strong where the following exist:

–   many equally balanced competitors

–   a slow rate of industrial growth

–   a lack of differentiation

–   a capacity that can only be increased by large amounts

–   high fixed costs in the industry

–   many diverse competitors

–   high exit barriers.

Rivalry takes the form of jockeying for position, with companies using tactics such as price reductions, advertising campaigns, and increased customer service and guarantees. Moves and countermoves of this type usually leaves the industry worse off than before.

(b)   The extent of threat of entry will be influenced by **barriers to entry**, the **extent of competition** within the industry and the **difficulty of leaving** the industry. Factors include:

Economies of scale

Many industries, such as cement and chemicals, offer increasing returns in manufacture, and companies benefit by being able to lower unit costs by increasing output volume. Thus potential entrants would be at a considerable cost disadvantage, unless they can immediately set up their operations on a scale large enough to reap similar economies. (This scale is termed the 'critical mass'.) In any case, it might take several years and a heavy investment programme to construct and equip the necessary factories to put them on a competitive footing.

Brand differentiation

Some brands generate a greater consumer loyalty than others and consumers will not be easily lured away by competing products even though they are similar or close substitutes. The cost for a new entrant attempting to penetrate the market in such a situation is likely to be high. The task will involve persuading entrenched consumers to trial their products, perhaps by offering special inducements, such as free samples or gifts. Although the exercise is costly, there is no guarantee of success, particularly as the defending company will combat entry tactics.

Products can be differentiated in terms of: **price, quality, brand image, features, distribution, exclusivity, packaging, value.**

Capital requirements

This also relates to economies of scale. For example the long-lead, high-cost, high-risk business cycle of the pharmaceutical industry, where the number of successful products reaching the market is relatively small but development costs are between £25m to £50m per product, has deterred all but the largest new companies from entering the market. In fact with the exception of Janssen and Syntax no totally new company to this market has succeeded, from start up, in becoming medium-sized in the last thirty years.

Access to distribution channels

One of the biggest dilemmas facing the producer is obtaining shelf or floor space in retail outlets. In order to sell his brands the producer must not only persuade the retailer to stock them, but to give them a fair share of shelf/floor space and to feature them periodically. Shelf and floor space is limited (consider here how much 'high street' space an electronic dish-washing machine takes to display), and already faced with a bewildering array and assortment of similar products (for example a large Sainsbury store carries some 7,000 products) retail managements are not over anxious to accept new products, particularly from new entrants lacking a proven track record in the market.

Government regulation

Legal restrictions prevent companies from entering into direct competition with most nationalised industries, while the government has permitted the establishment of quasi-nationalised bodies controlling marketing operations in milk, eggs, agriculture. Patents and copyright offer inventors some protection against new entrants. The government also licences the right to produce certain categories of products.

The existence of significant entry barriers will make it difficult for new competitors to gain a foothold in the market, and this gives some advantages to the firms already operating in it. However, although entry barriers will discourage new entrants to the market, the same barriers will result in firms being faced with 'exit penalties' and they will thus need to be committed to investments involved. This is likely to result in a very competitive market, particularly as the market matures.

These factors will influence the preparation of a strategic plan.

Chapter 3

Question 1: Electronic equipment

COMPANY MEMORANDUM

Date: 19 November 20X5

From: Finance director

To: Chairman

Subject: Initiation of export trade

The following memorandum sets out the main points requiring consideration before a final decision is taken on whether or not to embark upon export trade.

(a)   **Export pricing and profitability**

 (i)   A starting point would be to consider the market situation for products of the sort we produce, in the various countries where we might consider initiating this export trade. Assuming that demand exists for this type of product, we must ascertain the current prices and quality of competing products in these countries. Provided that these foreign markets are effectively segmented from our existing home market (i.e. our domestic customers cannot economically switch their purchases of our products to these new overseas markets), we may be able to set a lower price (as compared with our domestic price) for our output. Provided that the marginal costs of manufacture and sale are covered, the profits of the company would be increased as our surplus production capacity is available to meet the export demand. This may give us the ability to compete effectively on a price basis. Alternatively, we may be able to charge prices that exceed our domestic prices if local competition is such that this strategy would be successful. I suggest that potential markets be ranked in terms of their potential contribution to company profits (marginal revenue less incremental production and selling costs) and, assuming other factors to be similar, exploited in order of the size of their potential contribution to company profits.

(ii)   A study should be made of the additional costs that might be necessary to achieve export sales in the potential overseas markets, such as:

- transport, insurance and storage up to the point of sale

- customs duties

- additional documentation and certification of documents to satisfy import and possibly exchange control formalities

- insurance against the special risks of export trade (see (c) below)

- new staff requirements for translation of correspondence, quotations, invoices and publicity materials

- other advertising and promotion costs in the new market, especially on launching the product

- cost of establishing a physical presence in the new market such as agent's commission, warehousing and display facilities (see below).

(b)   **Credit terms and methods of obtaining payment**

(i)   **Assessment of credit worthiness**

- Potential customers' accounting reports may be informative for analytical purposes.

- Bank references may be available.

- Consular staff and the Export Credits Guarantee Department may be of assistance.

- Contacts with other United Kingdom companies who trade with our potential overseas customers may also provide useful information.

(ii)   **Methods of payment**

- Collection of money may be facilitated by:

  - using and discounting bills of exchange (forfeiting)

  - using letters of credit under which collection can be made from a bank in our country upon presentation of the shipping documents. We may wish the letters of credit to be made irrevocable and to ensure that they are 'confirmed' by a bank.

  The costs of the above would have to be considered in our pricing policy.

- Pre-payment or part-payment for our goods at the time of ordering may be possible if our products have clear advantages over those of our competitors.

(c)   **Risks and methods of reducing them**

The major risks of the export business include:

- insolvency of customer

- customer's failure to pay within a reasonable time

- customer's failure to take up goods ordered and sent to him.

It is difficult to make an overall recommendation at present due to lack of input from the Board. When these factors have been discussed at Board level then an overall strategy for the company in respect of exporting can be decided.

Question 2: Nationalised and semi-state business organisations

(a) **Nationalised enterprises and commercial viability**

Examples of such enterprises include London Underground, postal services, and the British Broadcasting Corporation (BBC). Whilst there are a number of reasons why the state should be so actively involved in such industries, there has emerged during the past few years a strong school of thought that state enterprises are not capable of operating as efficiently as similar types of organisation within the private sector. This approach has found its fullest expression in the UK where a significant proportion of the nationalised industries have now been returned to private ownership.

A number of difficulties may face nationalised or semi-state enterprises which have, for whatever reason, to operate in a more profit-oriented and market-sensitive manner than hitherto. These will be examined under three headings, as follows:

- policy difficulties
- planning difficulties
- operating difficulties.

(b) **Policy difficulties**

Whilst public statements may have been made about the need 'to break even' or 'to improve the return on taxpayers' money', etc, decision-makers in state commercial enterprises may have difficulty in discerning whether in reality commercial criteria are actually uppermost in the minds of those government and civil service policy-makers who exercise influence over their policy formulation. This difficulty arises from the problem of the clarity and priorities of government policy towards nationalised or semi-state enterprises. Are these priorities clearly and consistently formulated and expressed? Is the government prepared to accept their implications? For instance, has the choice been made between continuing subsidies or accepting plant closure and the run down of communities formerly dependent upon them? Does the withdrawal of subsidy mean changes in (or the abandonment of) policies of regional intervention and development?

The need for public accountability may provide another problem. Expectations of a high and continuing degree of public accountability could place a nationalised enterprise at a competitive disadvantage because it could hinder the development of an entrepreneurial market-oriented approach to business, whilst encouraging the retention of bureaucratic attitudes not suited to market conditions.

Finally, the organisation culture may be wholly inappropriate to the change in circumstances. The enterprise may have what CB Handy describes as a role culture. Role cultures are slow to perceive the need for change. Such organisations were 'used to operating in a sellers' market ... or ... with the state as their only customer'.

Government approval of top management changes may be needed. Can the government actually appoint the kind of person with the aggression and market-oriented experience needed to 'turn the business round'? Will the candidates have to be politically acceptable? Can the government actually deliver the guarantees of autonomy they are likely to demand as a condition of taking on the job?

(c)   **Planning difficulties**

The management of a nationalised enterprise may face a problem in planning capital investment, since there is a risk that investment decisions may be manipulated by governments in accordance with political events or election horizons.

Where capital investment decisions are subject to government sanction, commercial planning can also be affected by unevenness in government planning. This can lead to cyclical variations in business planning which are not related to market circumstances.

Finally, there may be difficulties in managing enterprise adaptation to changing markets and technology. So many compromises may be forced upon the organisation (for instance to protect employment and manning levels), as to restrict the effectiveness of the organisation in the marketplace, and perhaps make it dependent on government generated and financed orders. This may then herald a difficult period of adjustment and re-orientation in the face of harsh and unfamiliar commercial pressures.

(d)   **Operating difficulties**

Nationalised or semi-state enterprises may face a whole range of difficulties which may inhibit the search for greater market sensitivity and profit performance. These could include:

*   State-imposed restrictions on freedom to charge market or fully commercial rates for the product or service. Such restrictions have in the past, in the UK, been imposed on railway passenger prices, coal supplies for electricity generation, postal services, etc. Evidently, such restrictions will have an eventual effect on performance indicators for turnover and profitability.

*   The state may insist on the continuing of loss-making activities, such as uneconomic railway routes. This obligation may or may not be matched by the provision of proportionate subsidies, and profit-making activities may be expected to subsidise those that make losses.

*   The enterprise may remain under an obligation to purchase home-produced raw materials, supplies or components, to protect those who provide them. These products may not be price competitive, thus placing the manufacture at a cost disadvantage in home markets.

*   The government may attempt to persuade the enterprise to maintain existing work practices or manning levels, so as to maintain employment. Such pressure will hamper the search for improved productivity and cost savings which may be essential to commercial competitiveness.

*   Remuneration policy may make it difficult to reward and retain senior and middle levels of management. It may prove difficult to attract the desired calibre of applicant, who knows that better remuneration (salary, car, expenses, perks, etc) is available in the private sector.

*   Finally, management that has been accustomed to production orientation (for instance in supplying guaranteed government orders) may take a considerable time to adjust to the level of market orientation that is characteristic of much of the private manufacturing and service sector.

Chapter 4

Stakeholders

Note: you should be able to identify the three main types of stakeholder and give examples of each.

Analysing the stakeholder and the possible restraints on managerial authority

The types of stakeholder can be roughly categorised into three areas. They are as follows:

(1)   The stakeholder involved within the enterprise.

(2)   The stakeholder who is immediately external.

(3)   Any other externally involved stakeholder.

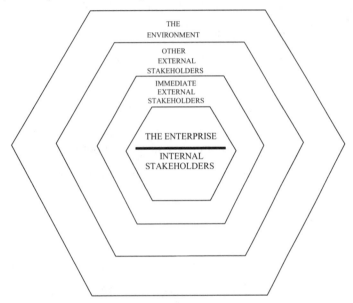

The figure above shows the three categories within the environment context. It is axiomatic to the analysis that, depending on such factors as circumstances or events which may occur concerning the enterprise, people, teams or organisations may be seen to have an interest of some nature with a resulting level of influence over business matters.

Therefore, it is important to study stakeholder analysis, with aims, objectives, actions, etc of the aforementioned all affecting the managerial situation.

Category 1

Those involved from within or internal stakeholders, can include employees up to members of top-level management teams, e.g. the chairman. Either type is able to influence the management process.

Category 2

The external stakeholder with immediate connections. This involves a wide range of connection such as financial investors, individual or groups, banks, etc. Secondly, suppliers or distributors or those involved in between. Thirdly, customers or consumer representatives and fourthly, employer organisations or trade unions.

Category 3

This includes any other externally involved stakeholders. For example, professional bodies, pressure groups or those with a special interest, the community on a broader basis with which the business operates may be involved, and finally local and central government representatives with legislative or regulative influences.

Stakeholders, enterprise and relative links

The stakeholder experiences different levels of influence over management, also the level they are able to apply force within the hierarchy varies. Both depend upon the following two variables:

(a)   The relationship between the enterprise and stakeholder. Characterised by an enterprise relationship or response to stakeholders, either may:

- wish to hold a dominant role

- engineer a reactive strategy

- use a proactive strategy

- wish to seek equality within the relationship

- adopt a defensive attitude or approach.

The nature of the relationship will depend upon the attitudes, philosophies, strengths and relative powers of both sides.

(b)   Effecting or operating the relationship. Signified by an enterprise response, the basis being any of the following:

- communication and consideration of the stakeholder's advice, etc

- command

- participation and acceptance of the stakeholder's advice

- diplomatic bargaining between both parties

- a democratic system for the stakeholder

- to surrender upon occasion to the stakeholder albeit technically, and exercise planned withdrawal to create a better position of negotiation.

Restraints on the managerial process of authority and discretion

The stakeholder is able to exercise at any level influential constraints on the management. The following situations could occur:

(a)   At a tactical level stakeholder influences could include the following:

- Employees – stakeholders affecting work groups, units, works production, etc.

- The arrangements by which suppliers operate could impose restrictions on output, finance, etc.

- The customer is able to affect management's freedom to plan and organise finance by their demands. Distributor and customer demands concerning advertising, product development and efficient manufacture systems are also to be considered.

- Developing a professional approach towards attitudes and activities affecting planning and functioning successfully within the organisation.

- The relationship that the management and employees experience. Workforce attitudes towards such aspects as pay rates, operational systems, the nature of supervision practised, etc are important. The power of the workforce should not be ignored by management, and the strength of unions allows such aspects as collective bargaining, negotiations, procedures and agreements to be a joint management-union situation thereby restricting authority.

(b)   The strategic level must also be considered. Many business aspects are decided upon by the chairman and board of directors. Aims, objectives and strategies all have to be considered by top level management who must respond to the needs of investors and financial sources as well as distributors and customers. Management discretion is restrained by meeting legislative or statutory requirements protecting the shareholders, e.g. financial, such as interest rewards.

It is also possible for two opposing pressures to develop. Firstly operating a serviceable strategy of management control and finance. Secondly, recognising strategies geared to market sensitivity. Any concept developed can penetrate throughout the business.

Other external influences may run concurrently applying pressure upon the thinking character and culture of the organisation causing necessary change and adaptation. For example, the need to produce more 'acceptable' products for an ever-changing society.

Chapter 5

Marketing

(a)   Irrespective of the customer or consumer role as such, executives in marketing are directly involved in the processes of customers buying and consuming the products of their organisation which are being put on to the market. Any buying decision involves:

- the influences which affect the decision to buy

- the buying decision itself

- the act of buying (by the customer)

- the consumption of the goods/services (by the consumer).

The customer role is the purchasing role, and the user role is the consumer role. On many occasions, someone buys something to be used by someone else (as in the case of, say, a birthday present).

In industrial markets (where the customers themselves are organisations) the person actually buying is the purchasing manager (or whoever has this role) and sometimes the individual could be a relatively junior member of the hierarchy. But the actual consumers (users) may well be occupying different grades in that hierarchy. In the consumer markets (where the buyers are individual persons, not organisations) the purchase of some products may be differentiated. In the case of, say, washing-up liquid, the person who does the washing-up is likely to be the buyer.

A clear instance of the importance of the distinction being discussed here lies in the purchase of, say, a tin of meat from the corner shop. The customer may well be the user (or only one of the users) whereas the shop may have obtained the tin through a wholesale unit (so the shop is a customer here but not, obviously, the consumer). The middleman may have a similar relationship in relation to the producers of the tin of meat. This means that there have been three steps in this buying-selling process – and in two of these the customer is not the consumer.

The point is that the marketing executive has to deal with markets and demand. To be effective, the executive has to be able to identify each specific need/demand. It is not sufficient to look only at the actual buying role. The market must be segmented.

(b)   The concept of marketing relates to the organisational awareness that it is necessary to know every factor of the organisational activity that is concerned with customer attitude to the current/future output of the enterprise. Marketing is an entity that is incorporated in the activity which creates viability of production, and which includes the selling activity.

Service-producing organisations need to consider specific marketing attributes in particular, and these are:

- Opportunity analysis must be carried out carefully – the 'target markets' need to be assessed and market segments determined. This enables needs of different customer groupings to be considered and suitable services generated for each.

- The service offered will have the elements of:

    –   the offering itself

    –   the terms of sale (contract)

    –   the manner in which the service is to be distributed

    –   the communication with the market and potential customers.

However, in marketing a service it must be realised that there is no way in which the service can be stored and warehoused:

- it is produced and consumed at once

- services cannot be generated and held back for future sales.

Services are also directly linked to human beings and offered (sold) directly by the person providing the service. There is therefore no 'middleman'.

The many different types of service-providing organisation (churches, circuses, car hire firms, theatres, cinemas, TV companies, governments and so on) all require the marketing approach.

(c)   People don't just buy transport when they buy a car, and they don't only want confectionery when they purchase a box of luxury chocolates. A motorcar is more than basic transport: it has a certain performance, and a particular style. It is associated with a specific level of comfort, of safety, of economy, and may have individual product features such as a fifth door or a built-in roof rack.

Most importantly, however, it satisfies a psychological need in the purchaser. A powerful sports car endows its owner with feelings of power, individuality, and perhaps aggressive masculinity.

A Rolls Royce owner acquires social prestige, and the vehicle is a sure sign of status, competence, success and superiority. The Citroen 2CV, while cheap, was an unusual car. Its owner identified with a group of fellow owners who perceived themselves as socially superior to the owners of some more expensive cars.

After Eight mints are promoted, presented and packaged in a way which guarantees that they are regarded by the consumer as an 'up-market' product – that is, one which is associated with a highly placed socio-economic group.

All products can be analysed in the same way. Every piece of goods has its place, not just in the retail store, but also especially in the system of psychological needs and attitudes of every potential customer.

Chapter 6

Competitive edge

The strategic and competitive value of information technology has advanced in recent years to be a critical factor in systems planning issues. The high capital expenditure that new systems command, together with the greatly-enhanced information-processing capacity provided by technological developments, has meant that organisations are reviewing in detail the positive commercial advantage that can accrue from an imaginative application of information technology to their activities as a whole.

Much depends on the organisation's perception of the future strategic and competitive value of its information systems and on the role of the current information systems. If management simply see the function of information systems as the provision of support for other production or managerial structures, then the strategic and competitive value of future systems will not be regarded as particularly important.

Alternatively, information systems might by viewed as a means to 'factory' produce its information to enable the organisation to produce its goods or services efficiently. The systems might be felt to be vital in providing a competitive edge in existing products or markets, and to make new kinds of products possible.

Michael Porter emphasises that tomorrow's successful organisation will be a collection of skills and capabilities, which are ready to pounce on any market opportunity. Possessing competitive edge means having those factors which lead customers to consistently prefer your products. He has suggested three overall competitive strategies that an organisation can implement.

(a) Overall cost leadership

This means becoming the most efficient producer. The objective to achieve overall cost leadership in the market is generally held by organisations in very competitive price-sensitive markets, where any means of reducing costs, or maintaining margins on lower prices, can lead to price reductions in goods and services offered to clients or customers. Information systems can reduce staff time spent on clerical work, allowing more to be spent on business development. Information technology can help not only by mechanising production systems but also by making the planning of production more efficient and using effective accounting control systems, e.g. activity based costing (ABC). Cost containment measures can include detailed control of stock levels, and an information system might allow a company to tie up its purchasing services directly with its suppliers by the use of computerised just in time (JIT) systems, reducing stock-holding costs and delays in processing orders.

(b)   Product differentiation

This means having unique products or varying them in such a way that they appear to be different from those offered by competitors. IT can help in the design of products, e.g. computer-aided design. Information systems can enhance an organisation's ability to compete by providing it with up-to-the-minute information as to customer needs and in tailoring their products or services to a customer's specific requirements. IS can also be used to compare customer purchases of the organisation's goods with those of other suppliers, allowing an organisation to differentiate its products on factors other than price.

(c)   Market niche

A niche market is a relatively small section of the overall market where customer needs are not fully satisfied. Information technology may be used to identify or exploit such a market niche by the analysis of market research data and other sales statistics. An example of the competitive value of information technology is the introduction of automated teller machines.

Additional to the provision of competitive advantage in the market place, internal changes in an organisation's structure can enhance its competitive edge, by encouraging more effective use of its human and material resources. Sometimes changes can be radical, e.g. a distribution organisation may get rid of one of its warehouses and employ a more efficient computerised distribution system.

Information systems might be used to foster innovation, by encouraging a free flow of ideas in a large organisation. A computer conferencing system, where individuals communicate their ideas with relative informality, is an example of such a system.

Chapter 7

E-commerce

(a)   We can compare and contrast the two types of organisation from six different perspectives:

- Overall business strategy
- Objectives of the organisation
- Expertise available
- Customers
- Competition, and
- Legal issues

Overall business strategy – here assumes that an organisation has its product range, market segment, competitors and customer base already defined, and that e-commerce will support the strategy of the organisation.

Product range – from financial advice being provided to a wide range of garden products being supplied, the ranges of both organisations are quite diverse.

E-commerce may be beneficial to both types of organisation. Websites can be maintained to show the full product or service range. For the international consultancy supplying financial advice, it would help them to avoid sending printed financial information which would quickly become out-of-date. For the supplier of garden plants and accessories, the website would allow them to show the types and prices of goods they supply and the geographical area they deal with.

Although the website may be expensive to maintain, there appears to be no reason why product information and sales cannot be carried out on the Internet. Because the garden centre limits its sales to within 20 km of its main site, it is probably not the most efficient way of promoting its products.

Market segment – both organisations appear to have a clearly defined market segment. They know what goods they want to sell and where these will be sold. The profit margins associated with each organisation are very different. Selling products or services with higher margins to the organisation, e.g. financial advice, may be more attractive to newer forms of commerce simply because more profit can be made per unit of sales than for low value products. Because of the lower margins on its products, the garden centre will have to sell garden accessories, etc to make the same profit, compared to the multinational organisation selling, say, one pension scheme. The market segment of the international organisation may, therefore, be more suited to e-commerce.

Competitors – the competitors for the international organisation will also be large organisations whereas the garden centre's competitors are likely to be locally based.

Establishing an Internet site with e-commerce may not be beneficial to the garden centre because there is no real value over competitors and customers may not expect to use this purchase medium. However, provision of a website if only to provide information to customers, is likely to be expected for an international consultancy. A website will have to be established simply to remain competitive.

Customer base – the local customers can visit the different garden centres easily and compare prices and product quality. It is much more difficult for an international consultancy to reach all of their potential customers.

Customers of the financial consultancy will expect them to have a website and use e-commerce and, because the products being sold are not tangible, there is no need for customers to actually visit a supplier to see the goods. As the customers of the garden centre will not expect to use the Internet for their gardening requirements, it appears that e-commerce is more likely to support the strategy of the financial advice organisation than the garden centre.

Objectives of the organisation – the business strategy of each organisation will normally define the short and long-term goals/objectives of that organisation. Typical objectives will include profit maximisation and growth. Other objectives may be employee satisfaction or environmental impact.

For the international organisation, achieving profit maximisation and growth will mean utilising sales opportunities where the net revenue from those sales is positive (over a number of years). If organisations providing financial advice use 'increase in profit' and 'absolute growth' as performance indicators, and if e-commerce is shown to increase sales and profit, then this selling medium will be adopted.

The other objectives of employee satisfaction and environmental impact may have less effect on determining whether the international organisation uses e-commerce. If e-commerce is chosen the organisation will be required to ensure proper employee welfare under the Health and Safety at Work Act. There may be a slightly positive environmental impact if sending documents electronically decreases the amount of paper used in the organisation.

Although the smaller garden centre will still require sufficient profit and growth, absolute growth and profit may be less important. As long as an adequate return on capital is achieved, other objectives, such as customer and employee satisfaction, may be more important. So, unless e-commerce can be used to provide an adequate profit, or increase customer satisfaction, it is unlikely to be part of the overall strategy of the garden centre.

Expertise available – one of the main supports of the strategy for any organisation is having appropriate staff to implement and maintain that strategy.

A large international organisation is more likely to have the resources to set-up a website and to start using e-commerce. The main reasons for this are that the cost of setting up an Internet site can be offset against a larger sales volume and that administrative staff costs become a smaller proportion of total costs. A large organisation can, therefore, afford the expert staff needed to establish and maintain the site, even if revenue does not immediately cover costs.

A smaller organisation will find the expense of setting up and maintaining a website more difficult to meet, due to smaller sales volume and the difficulty of attracting expert staff to a small organisation with potentially lower salaries and fewer staff benefits. Alternatively, an agency could be employed, although this would raise the issue of ensuring that the agency produces exactly what the client requires.

Customers – the buying habits of customers will probably have an effect on whether e-commerce becomes part of the business strategy of an organisation. Situations where customers normally use the Internet, or expect information on a particular product or service to be available, will prompt an organisation to make e-commerce available. Large multinational organisations will definitely expect to find out information on suppliers from the Internet. Private individuals who want to purchase financial services are likely to be in higher income brackets and will probably have Internet access at home or work. They will also expect a well-known, well-established and trustworthy provider of financial advice to have a website. They may also require detailed information on the organisation and products that can be easily provided on a web site. Use of e-commerce appears appropriate for a provider of financial advice and this will become part of the business strategy.

Although purchasers of garden products will be representative of most social groups, most people will want to see what is being purchased and choose from a selection. Providing an Internet site for this type of customer will be less important, although a website may be useful if it provides an overview of product availability and illustrations that may entice customers to visit the garden centre. However, e-commerce aspects of the site will be restricted where customers want to see what is being purchased or where they live more than 20 km away from the garden centre.

Competition – the garden products' supplier is selling a generic type of product where specialist selling skills and customer contact are not likely to be important to the customer. There are probably many competitors in the surrounding area, given the relatively low value of the product and relatively large size of garden furniture, etc. Large, bulky and low value products tend to have a limited geographical market. Additional sales potential is limited due to the small area they can sell into. E-commerce may have very little effect on any garden centre. There is no need to establish a site simply to remain competitive and the costs of setting up e-commerce may outweigh the benefits.

Multinational, international and domestic competitors in the financial advice market, on the other hand, may have a website and use e-commerce. It will, therefore, be appropriate for the large international organisation to establish and maintain a website just to remain competitive. As already noted, the selling of financial advice may be appropriate via e-commerce because the product is not tangible. However, by its nature, the selling of financial services will involve direct contact with the customer, either to determine accurately the customer's requirements, or because customers expect this method of selling rather than having to visit a more impersonal website, and this may limit the extent to which e-commerce can be used by the organisation.

Legal issues – if e-commerce is adopted as part of the strategy of an organisation, then its implementation, and hence achievement of business strategy, may be limited because of legal issues. At the very least, the organisation will need to ensure that no national laws are broken and that the products or services they are selling are not banned from being sold in certain countries. The international availability of any website means that an organisation must know whether any countries are barred from purchasing.

Because the supplier of garden products will only be selling to customers in a small geographical area, if e-commerce is adopted by this organisation there will only be the requirement to meet the law of the country it is operating in. Sales to other countries can be banned, although it is unlikely that people in other countries would purchase bulky goods of low value anyway, due to high transportation costs.

In contrast, the supplier of financial advice will be selling products and services to a diverse market where there are different laws and different personal requirements

(b)   In summary, an international supplier of financial services to private individuals and large multinationals is more likely to benefit from e-commerce because:

- its potential market is wide and not limited by the difficulty in delivering large and bulky items

- it is selling to higher income groups and companies which are likely to have Internet access

- its IT strategy, aligned with its overall business strategy of increasing growth and profit, is directed to finding new sources of sales

- sales could fall if e-commerce is not made available because customers can access competitors' web sites easily.

Alternatively, the garden centre has some persuasive reasons for not investing in e-commerce such as:

- too small to warrant setting up and maintaining a costly web site

- insufficient resources in terms of skilled staff

- lack of appropriate business objectives (profit or growth) to require e-commerce to be part of the business strategy.

In summary, the local garden centre may have different goals that are not met by the Internet, but a large international organisation is likely to see the Internet and e-commerce as a means of achieving faster growth and profit and being part of their overall strategy.

Chapter 8

Leisure and Pleasure

(a) 'Diversification' means a departure from the company's existing products and markets into new fields. The company considering 'leisure and pleasure' might have a number of possible areas in mind: sports equipment, provision of sports facilities, entertainment, gambling, hobbies such as gardening, photography, etc.

The reason for considering a move in this direction is the current (and forecast) social and economic situation. People today have far more leisure time than, say, 30 years ago. At the same time they earn more in real terms and therefore spend a smaller proportion of their income on necessities, leaving more for enjoyment of their leisure time. In addition, saving is not considered the virtue it used to be: indeed many people see little point in saving at all when inflation is eroding the real value of their savings. They prefer to spend their money on current pleasure, believing that the welfare state will take care of them in their retirement or in any unforeseen emergency.

(b) Synergy may be one of the major components of the firm's product-market strategy. It is concerned with the desired characteristics of fit between the firm and its product-market entries. The measurement of synergy is similar in many respects to the 'evaluation of strengths and weaknesses'. In synergy, joint effects are measured between two product-markets, which contribute to the decision whether to make a new entry. In strength and weakness evaluation, the firm's competences are related to some desired performance level, i.e. a contribution to the decision to exploit certain strengths or remedy certain deficiencies within the firm.

Synergy is the effect that can produce a combined return on the firm's resources greater than the sum of its parts and it may be classified into several types:

- **Sales synergy** – applicable when products use common marketing resources, e.g. distribution channels, warehousing, sales administration, advertising, sales promotion, etc. All of these can contribute to the multiple returns for the same unit of outlay.

- **Operating synergy** – results from increased utilisation of resources, more efficient recovery of overheads, bulk purchases, etc.

- **Investment synergy** – can result from the joint use of plant, common raw material inventories, transfer of R&D from one product to another.

- **Management synergy** – may arise from past experience gained in a similar situation.

  The strength of this synergy will result from the particular circumstances to the extent that if past experience is applied in the wrong concept, negative synergy may result. (Incorrect applications may cause negative synergy in the other classifications also, in which case the operating of two independent units may prove more beneficial.)

It is always necessary to distinguish between potential and actual synergy. To what extent the potential of the joint effects materialises depends upon the success achieved in integrating the two operations. In addition it is necessary to distinguish between positive and negative synergy that will result from the starting up in new product-market areas, and the operating synergy, if the new entry involves a going concern. Synergy effects may be symmetrical, both firms, in the case of diversification, enjoying benefits.

Obviously it is desirable to measure the effects of synergy in terms of increased sales revenue, decreased operating costs and decreased investment requirements, all of which have to be related to time, i.e. the rate of change.

However, it is often found difficult to quantify and combine the respective effects, a problem which occurs in many other parts of the strategic decision process. The normal procedure is to determine a separate measure for each important effect, which will be determined by the particular circumstances of each individual situation, and then apply these measures jointly to provide an overall evaluation of the project.

Therefore, the application of synergy can be seen as an important component of any corporate planning programme but its relevance and application must be studied fully in the light of individual circumstances to ensure maximum benefits are derived from its use.

(c) Before putting into effect a particular strategy a company should undertake a thorough appraisal of the 'leisure and pleasure' market to identify more precisely possible areas of opportunity. This would involve an examination of current products and facilities, and very likely market research to discover what the public want.

Having identified 'gaps' in the range of products and facilities on offer, the company must assess its own capability to fill them. This involves assessing its own skills and resources, including an assessment of whether any of the prospective opportunities have any synergy with the existing operations. (If potential synergy can be realised, it might be possible to gain a competitive edge.)

The company might find that the barriers to entry into the leisure and pleasure business are too large to be overcome by a new entrant to the field. If this is so it need not abandon the proposed strategy, but could look for a company to acquire or with which to merge.

Before implementing any particular strategy there must be a thorough assessment of the potential of the chosen area in terms of likely revenue and costs, hence profit and return on capital; nature of the competition; risk attached to the diversification; likely duration of the leisure and pleasure boom; etc. The company must assess not only the new field but also its overall position taking into account the combined potential of its existing and proposed fields. Will there still be a gap in its strategy leaving it exposed to threats? Will its objectives be capable of achievement?

Is there any area other than 'leisure and pleasure' that would provide a better 'fit' with existing operations and build more on the company's strengths? (A proposed strategy should never be considered in isolation but as one of a number the company might pursue – otherwise no comparative measure is available and the company might overlook important factors.) The further away the diversification is from the firm's existing operations, the greater will be the risks involved, and the company must beware of making too abrupt a change in direction, even into an area which appears at first sight to have exciting prospects, without a thorough assessment of the implications.

Chapter 9

Question 1: The product lifecycle

Many products pass through a number of stages in their history until they eventually decline in the face of outside competition or a change in consumer tastes. As illustrated below, it is very important to consider carefully when to start developing new products in order to achieve a steady rate of growth in both turnover and profits for the whole company.

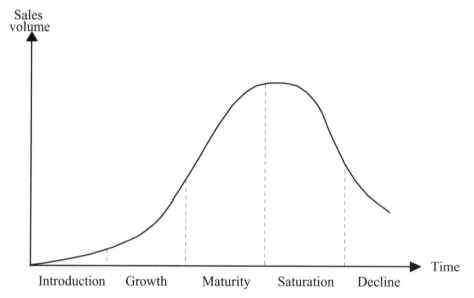

It should be noted that periods are only shown in the diagram as being of equal size for convenience. For example, product development may take three years but the product may be in decline for four years after market introduction. If this were the case, the product development of the second product would need to be started before market introduction of the first.

Some products have much longer life cycles than others – basic foodstuffs have much longer lives than more fashionable products such as clothes, although perhaps the days of the white loaf are numbered. The time required to develop a product also varies tremendously - forty years so far have been spent developing the fast breeder nuclear reactor and it is still not commercially viable. Conversely, it now takes about 4 years to develop a new car although the Mini took 15 years.

It should also be realised that within an industry different products will have reached different stages which might not be typical of the industry as a whole. It is commonly believed that the electrical domestic appliance market has reached the maturity stage. However, although refrigerators are already in 90% of homes, microwave ovens have less than 15% ownership and it is consequently hardly surprising that the Japanese have decided to focus on this segment in order to enter the industry globally.

Marketing activities will change as a product passes through its life-cycle. For example, strategic issues at the development stage of a grocery product would be concerned with such questions as 'What business are we in?' whilst marketing research would be concerned with new product testing. Marketing mix considerations would be at the planning stage although sales training would be taking place.

During the market introduction of the product the overall strategic decision would be whether to continue or to cancel. Marketing research would be directed at customer and consumer reactions which could lead to modifications to the product or to the pricing policy which could initially have been based on skimming or a penetration price. Promotion would be concentrating on the 'creation of demand' while the sales force would be dealing with unforeseen problems and gaining new distribution outlets.

In the growth stage the company can take risks with over-capacity and even with quality in order to establish a market position – profit margins will permit production inefficiencies. Strategic issues would include how to deal with private brands and marketing research would be focusing on brand share information. Price falls are likely and new variants would be introduced as a result of new product development. Promotion would be building up brand loyalty as the sales force battled for shelf space. Distribution would have to cope with the surge of demand as new outlets stocked up.

During maturity and saturation, efficient use of plant and close attention to production costs become much more important. Strategy will be concerned with the introduction of new products and the relation of these to existing products. Marketing research will be looking for signs of market saturation and stagnation. Price will remain steady if no private brands exist; otherwise it will fall, particularly as large outlets pressure for special terms. 'Below the line' promotional expenditure will rise if private brands exist.

The decline stage will raise the question 'Do we wish to remain in business?' and how much will depend on the forecasts provided by marketing research. Prices would continue to fall and there would be greater promotional expenditure in an attempt to maintain sales.

It can therefore be seen that the product life cycle concept is not only a useful tool for analysing demand but is also valuable in managing the marketing mix during the introduction of a product and throughout its life cycle.

Question 2: Megaweb Industries

(a) **Financial criteria** that should be used to decide the site closure policy for Heataweb will include the following:

  (i) **Rental costs** – These vary quite considerably between different locations. Consideration should be given as to which location is cheaper. Contractual conditions for renting or leasing should also be evaluated and compared.

  (ii) **Rateable value** – Rates can be a major cost. Consideration should be given as to which of the two locations is cheapest. Local grants, etc would need to be taken into account.

(iii) **Labour costs** – Labour costs may be relevant. The North/South divide, a popular catchphrase used by the media, does represent a considerable difference in labour costs. Heataweb would be advised to consider and compare for each location:

- differentiation in local pay rates

- the extent of competition for local labour

- the quality of labour available

- the scarcity of labour.

(iv) **Site valuation** – A number of questions will be pressing:

- Which site has the largest resale value?

- Does the company own one site and rent/lease the other?

The questions will provide important answers if the company is considering liquidating its investment held in property, or in comparing long-term operating costs.

(v) **Cost of moving key personnel** – It is assumed that although with the rationalisation envisaged there will be staff surplus (leading to redundancy), key personnel will move from the closing site to the one remaining. The cost of compensating staff for the disruption and inconvenience caused would need to be costed.

(vi) **Cost of transporting products to the other market** – The cost of transporting products to the market area of the closed site will need to be evaluated. For example, it may be advisable for Heataweb to close the site with the smallest market size (growth trends taken into account).

(vii) **Productivity** – The level of productivity, taking into account labour relations, union militancy, etc compared between the two sites would be a further financial factor to be considered. Labour flexibility, versatility, training levels, etc are also relevant factors.

(viii) **Level of technology** – The level and quality of technology (newness, etc) and the costs of increasing the level of technology in one site to meet the combined output of both would need to be costed.

(ix) **Level of specific (attributable) fixed cost** – Both sites would need to be compared in terms of the level of fixed cost specific to each that would be avoided if the site were closed. There might well be a significant difference between the two.

(x) **Contribution analysis** – It can be expected that the level of all costs will differ between sites, variable as well as fixed. A contribution analysis taking into account sales and variable costs, including additional costs arising from the need of extra transport to the market, will provide useful data about the financial worth of each site.

(b) **Operational factors** that Heataweb's corporate management should consider in deciding which site should be retained are enumerated below:

(i) **Labour factors** – Questions will include:

- Is one location more attractive to work and live near?

- Unemployment levels?

- Productivity levels?

- Skill levels?

- Labour problems?

- Industrial relations and organisational climate?

(ii) **Level and quality of plant and technology**

(iii) **Expansion possibilities** – Does either site present problems in terms of factory expansion? Local planning regulations and local government policy will need to be considered.

(iv) **Premises** – Which site has the superior premises in terms of carrying out the work required? Also local services, proximity to supply, energy supplies, etc will need to be considered.

(v) **Effect of move on customers** – Will the company lose customers because of the move? Also because of increased transport costs? Comparisons should be made between the two sites.

(vi) **Opposition to the move (internal)** – To what extent, and in what ways, will the move be resisted by managers and employees within each site?

(vii) **Opposition to the move (external)** – To what extent, and in what form will the move be resisted by pressure groups, etc? Such pressure and resistance will mostly be centred on the site gaining the additional work.

(viii) **Proximity to market** – Considerations here will take into account the nearness of the market and the quality of communication links including motorways and rail links.

(ix) **Production systems** – Systems are extremely important and should be considered when the value of a production unit is evaluated. The quality of production planning, material control, quality control, performance control and budgetary control systems should be included within this analysis.

(x) **Preferences of senior management** – Decision makers are often influenced by a number of factors that have indirect influence on operational performance. Costs of housing, local amenities and natural aspects of each site are likely to be considered in the final analysis.

(c) A dog is part of the terminology used in the work of the Boston Consulting Group (BCG) that has come to be widely recognised in business and national economic strategy. The BCG theory can in part be explained by displaying a growth-share matrix, as shown below:

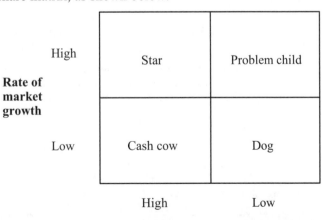

As can be seen products will fall into one of four categories – cash cow, star, problem child and dog.

The cash characteristics of each quadrant in the matrix are illustrated in the diagram below:

	High	Low
High	Cash in balance 0	Cash users –
Low	Cash generators +	Cash in balance or loss –

Dog products are illustrated in the bottom right quadrant as having low relative market shares in low growth markets. The situation may have been caused by high inflation rates, slumping market growth rates or a rapid shift in patterns of consumption. It is probable that a 'dog product' faces poor future prospects with estimates of low profits or losses.

A relatively recent update in the BCG theory has suggested that there are two main categories of Dog:

(i) **Cash Dog** – In some markets it is extremely difficult for a product to increase its relative market share, and anyway there may be no conclusive advantages to leadership, or large growths in market share. The product may be earning a net cash inflow although not to the same levels as cash cows. The product may have developed a niche in the market. In this case it may be wise to continue marketing this product.

(ii) **Genuine Dogs** – Due perhaps to slumping growth rates, high inflation rates and rapidly changing patterns of consumption, genuine dogs have very weak competitive positions, and adverse cash balances with very little prospect of becoming profitable. For such products liquidation, either immediate or gradual, is likely to be the appropriate strategy.

Question 3: ABC plc

(a) **Cash cow products**

A cash cow is part of the terminology used in the work of the Boston Consulting Group (BCG) that has come to be widely recognised in business and national economic strategy. The BCG theory can in part be explained by displaying a growth-share matrix, as shown below:

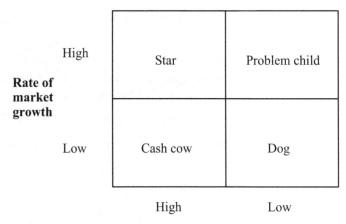

	High	Low
High	Star	Problem child
Low	Cash cow	Dog

Rate of market growth (vertical axis)

Relative market share

As can be seen, products are classified in four categories – cash cow, star, problem child and dog. The cash flow characteristics of each quadrant in the matrix are illustrated in the diagram below:

	High	Low
High	Cash in balance 0	Cash users –
Low	Cash generators +	Cash in balance or loss –

High   Low

'Cash cow' products are illustrated in the bottom left quadrant in the matrix as having high relative market shares in low growth markets. These products should generate large amounts of net cash inflow. This net inflow is used to pay dividends, pay overheads, provide debt capacity, and perhaps most importantly provide funds for other parts of the company's product portfolio. The rationale behind the cash cows concept is that they represent high volume, low investment cost output which the matrix also recognises to be key to strategy in situations of high competitive advantage and few competitive weapons (e.g. a bulk steel manufacturer). The strategy of 'milking' a product with minimum investment in areas such as research and marketing underlies the concept of cash cow.

The 'Cortina' range provided the Ford company with a cash cow product through the 1970s. It was a mature product holding a strong market share in a relatively static market. Likewise sports education and sports facility services provided cash cow products for the YMCA movement during the 1960s.

Without cash cows an organisation would require continuous subsidy.

(b)   **Advantages to ABC plc of its financial strategy**

A number of factors need to be considered before the advantages accruing to ABC plc can be assessed with confidence. Whether its financial strategy with regard to its acquisition is suitable will depend upon numerous factors concerning X Ltd, including:

- overall composition of the firm's product-market portfolio

- position of any particular product in the matrix

- corporate resources

- nature of the company's markets

- strengths and characteristics of competing firms

- likely strategic responses and actions of competitors.

For example a cash cow strategy is usually an appropriate holding strategy when the product and its market have reached the mature stage and it is considered desirable to maintain the status quo. By holding a high relative market share cash cow products should have acquired greater experience than their rivals and thus the firm should enjoy cost and profitability advantages. X Ltd might also be operating at an optimal level: optimal in the sense that the cost or the risk attendant upon increasing market share would be greater than the likely benefits, while any decline in market share would reduce profitability.

The main advantages to ABC plc of using X Ltd as a cash cow may therefore include the following:

(i)   An assumption that X Ltd will be a regular net provider of finance for a number of years.

(ii)   The relatively little management time or involvement required from ABC plc in the affairs of X Ltd.

(iii) An assumption that new investment in X Ltd (with related investment risk) will be minimised.

(iv)   Corporate integration with the use of centralised reporting and control systems should be accomplished relatively easily.

Disadvantages and risks to ABC plc

(i)   Competitors of X Ltd holding lower market shares may attempt to build market shares through innovation, promotion, market creation, and so on, to the detriment of the company. In the business of 'branded technical products' it is certain that X Ltd cannot be complacent about its position, and will need to maintain its competitiveness through aggressiveness in product and service innovation, cost cutting, improving distribution methods and market targeting. It will need to 'keep ahead of the posse' and this may require considerable investment. This investment may include projects designed to fill all or some related product niches, and/or to defend its present position through aggressive advertising or price cutting.

(ii)   The group strategy may prohibit X Ltd from exploiting new profitable opportunities.

(iii) The management of X Ltd may be demotivated and become apathetic, and may indeed try to restrict the flow of cash to prolong the life of their company.

    (iv)   Branded technical products for original equipment manufacturers are governed by very strict technical standards requiring a high level of quality. A lack of investment in quality maintenance could lead to an eventual loss of business. Also, original equipment manufacturers will wish to ensure a continuing supply source, and perceiving that X Ltd has no long-term future, they may well seek out alternative suppliers.

(c)   **Considerations that might have influenced the decision of the board of ABC plc**

ABC plc may have rejected X Ltd's managing director's proposal for one or more of the following reasons:

    (i)   ABC plc may see no long-term future for X Ltd. It may have been a purchase to acquire short-term benefits.

    (ii)   The proposal does not 'fit' the group's long-term plans.

    (iii)   X Ltd is a manufacturer of original equipment for sale in the UK, but this proposal includes a number of changes:

- the company to sell in Germany where, presumably, it has little market experience

- the company to distribute its products through merchants, rather than by a direct selling (or 'zero-channel') strategy.

The board of ABC may consider that the management of X Ltd does not have the necessary skills involved to manage such changes in its business.

    (iv)   The projected return on the investment required may not reach the group's hurdle rate.

    (v)   ABC plc may want the £250,000 dividend from X Ltd, which perhaps would not be available if the company had to use internal funds to finance the project.

Chapter 10

Interfirm comparison scheme

(a)   **ABCD Group – comparative ratios**

	A	B	C	D	B, C & D average
	%	%	%	%	%
Return on capital employed (operating profit:gross assets)	15.2	19.0	21.0	18.0	19.3
Profit:sales	8.9	10.6	10.8	9.7	10.4
Sales:capital employed (times)	1.7	1.8	2.0	1.9	1.9
	%	%	%	%	%
Costs:sales					
Production	65.0	62.0	61.0	61.0	61.3
Selling	15.0	16.0	17.0	18.0	17.0
Administration	11.1	11.4	11.2	11.3	11.3
Total	91.1	89.4	89.2	90.3	89.6

	£	£	£	£	£
Assets per £ of sales					
Current	0.21	0.19	0.18	0.19	0.19
Fixed	0.38	0.36	0.33	0.35	0.35
Total	0.59	0.55	0.51	0.54	0.54

Note: not all these ratios need have been computed. The key ratios are ROCE and a profit to sales percentage. They are shown at the top of the report to emphasise their importance. The next 'box' of ratios give more detailed information on profitability. The last 'box' shows a breakdown of assets employed in the business. Without further information as to the make up of the fixed and current assets, the last group is not very helpful.

(b)

Report

To: Directors, A Limited

From: Group Management Accountant

Subject: Comparative ratios: year ended 31.3.20X6

The attached statement shows how the results of the companies in the group compare, and I should draw your attention to the differences between your company and the rest of the group. Whilst I recognise that each company operates in slightly different circumstances, this analysis does at least provide an indication as to possible areas of improvement.

Your return on capital employed is 4.1% below the average for the rest of the group, and this is due to both low sales turnover in relation to capital employed and to low profit margins. I suggest the following areas of investigation.

Sales turnover

Your selling costs as a percentage of sales are low by comparison with the rest of the group and may be an indication that increased marketing effort is needed. Increased turnover would lead to better utilisation of assets.

Capital employed

Whilst your investment in fixed assets cannot be reduced unless surplus assets can be disposed of, it might be possible to reduce the level of current assets by careful control of stock levels and by tightening debt collection procedures.

Profit margins

The margin between selling price and production cost is comparatively small and indicates that either production economies should be sought or that selling prices may need to be increased or both (although the effect on sales volume would have to be carefully considered before taking any decision on increasing selling prices). It is possible that your higher production costs are unavoidable owing to the specialised nature of your work: if so, this should preferably be reflected in selling prices. As regards the more standard areas of your operations, it might be useful for you to consult the management of the company. It may be that if increased marketing is successful, economies of scale will operate to reduce production costs, but this does not mean that further economies of scale should not be sought.

Chapter 11

Constraints to growth

The constraining factors that apply to the growth and development of a business enterprise may be expressed as internal and external, as discussed below.

(a) **Internal constraints**

    (i) **Availability of capital**

        Indeed, the characteristic of under-capitalisation is a common reason for the failure of smaller business enterprises. However, capital investment cannot be carried out unless capital is available to the firm and, therefore, this is a major constraint.

    (ii) **Scale diseconomies**

        Diseconomies of scale – especially in relation to organisational growth and ensuing difficulties in controlling a diversity of activities – are regarded as inhibiting further development. A business enterprise may, for instance, be able to raise the level of its turnover yet expansion may also be restricted due to the problems of control and extra administration. Increased turnover, therefore, may well result in diminished profitability.

    (iii) **Resource availability**

        As well as capital availability (a major point), it may be that the organisation has the opportunity to grow and develop, but lacks space, machine capacity, human resources (skills) and materials. A shortage of, say, human skills can seriously restrict any idea of growth and development.

(b) **External constraints**

    (i) **Product constraints**

        The product marketed by the enterprise may not be up-to-date or attractive to potential customers; hence opportunities to expand are denied unless and until the product is upgraded or a substitute evolved.

    (ii) **Market size**

        It may be that the size of the market is in itself restricted, or may contract because of economic conditions (e.g. recession).

    (iii) **Competition**

        Where there are a number of competitors in a given market, the market share of one of them may only be increased by causing a contraction of the share of one (or more) of the others. It is possible that excessive competition will result in an increase in turnover but, because of price competition, profits are reduced.

Chapter 12

Pump manufacturer

(a)   Business Process Re-engineering (BPR) is one of a number of techniques that have been advanced to overhaul existing business processes and practices with a view to improving organisational performance. It is an approach where management ask radical questions about why things are done in a particular way, and ask whether alternative methods could achieve better results. The aim is to reinvigorate a staid management structure and culture, and end up with a company better able to serve customers' wants at lower cost.

It seems as though the structural and cultural emphasis of the Dose Company has remained static over its whole existence. They probably exist in isolation from their suppliers and customers, with each department handling different functions with no idea of their place in the value chain. Re-engineers are not constrained by existing methods, people or departments. They ask 'why' and 'what if' questions about everything that happens in the organisation and then begin to explore better ways of doing it. They start from the future and work backwards.

The first step for the management of Dose is to look at the customer interface and improve sensitivity to the customer needs. Unless Dose is providing the best quality at the best price, it will face extinction.

To achieve this it needs to address the primary processes and:

(i)   re-develop the demand process of customer links, marketing and service

(ii)   re-develop the product – looking at innovation in design

(iii)   ensure that quality is built into the product from inception and not merely inspected afterwards

(iv)   re-design the order fulfilment process – investigate the acquisition of resources, reduce development and production costs and reduce the lead time between product inception and commercial sale and delivery.

The secondary processes that may need re-engineering include the support services of administration, finance and personnel management.

After BPR the company should see itself as part of a longer value chain and organise along activity streams (or processes) running through the business. In this respect, there is a similarity to other management theories. Value Chain Analysis looks at the physically and technologically distinct activities that an organisation performs and looks for the sources of advantage that can be obtained from each stage. Activity Based Management also discards the old departmental approach of R&D, Finance, Marketing, Personnel, Purchasing, Production and Sales, and re-organises these activities along tightly-linked systems running through the business.

As Dose is a manufacturing company, its managing director will be able to find numerous examples of similar businesses that have tried BPR. Some have succeeded in adding profits by improving the processes and the efficiency of activity flows in the business. Others have failed at huge cost because it was either too late when they applied the re-engineering or the reforms were not suitable for the culture and structure of the company.

Dose, like other manufacturing companies, needs to examine radical change ideas as they come up, but healthy scepticism is also wise. Although outdated management techniques and manufacturing methods are a significant reason why new competitors are taking market share from established industrial groups, other reasons are also important. Manufacturers need to look at their fundamental cost structure (labour rates, automation, capital costs) and at their responsiveness and innovation in design, delivery, service, etc.

Dose needs to appreciate the lessons learned by others over the last few years, and if the BPR path is chosen it needs to be done with commitment and leadership from the top. The managing director should not rely too heavily on expensive and temporary external consultants. Top management need to understand the likely impact and thorough analysis of what the business is about with no preconceptions. Once plans for change are decided, management must ensure they implement the appropriate changes fully and carefully, guiding through any cultural change needed to match structural ones.

(b) In attempting BPR, managers might encounter the following major pitfalls:

(i) There are many consultants advertising their services as BPR experts. Companies could be tempted to pay exorbitant fees and have somebody else implement the re-engineering. However, successful BPR depends on a hands-on approach with management's personal commitment, communal ownership and shared learning.

(ii) BPR is sometimes regarded as a means of making small improvements to existing practices. In reality, it is a radical approach that questions whether existing practices make any sense in their present form.

(iii) As the managing director at Dose found out, BPR is seen as a fashionable cure-all where the advantages are widely written about, but the explanation of how to do it is surrounded by management jargon.

(iv) Enthusiasm for BPR may encourage management to throw out much that is good within the organisation without achieving the potential gains of BPR.

(v) During the re-processing programme, managers may be distracted from changes in their markets, changes in technology, and the more routine, gradual advances their competitors might be making in the secondary processes areas, e.g. human resource management.

(vi) Any new ideas or methods will challenge traditional power hierarchies and this will leave some employees – even managers – feeling threatened. Radical change makes staff feel as if they have not been doing their job well previously. It also exposes management to resistance and high stress in a climate of uncertainty. The disruption costs can be very high.

(vii) It is tempting for management to use BPR as a cover for something much more familiar such as cost-cutting. Re-engineering may have the intention of lowering costs, but the benefits come through a much bigger re-working than a mere trimming exercise. It is very difficult to re-engineer properly. With so many other calls on organisational effort, and the high risk inherent in a BPR type of strategy, the company often makes a mess of re-engineering.

Chapter 13

Responsibility for decisions

(a)   Strategic planning, if implemented properly, will have implemented the strategy which is best suited to the objectives of the organisation in the light of its own strengths and weaknesses and the environmental threats and opportunities. It must therefore have considered the alternative strategies available and hopefully developed reserve contingency strategies.

Planning may provide a straitjacket in situations where the constant process of monitoring and review is missed. The planning process should provide a mechanism for identifying opportunities at an early stage and should revise strategy to exploit them, if this is appropriate. The implementation of strategy is not the end of the planning process, but merely part of a continuing cycle. To treat the strategy as sacrosanct is to deny the underlying philosophy of planning as a mechanism of change.

The defence of strategy above leads on to questioning of the merits of freewheeling opportunism. This approach has several drawbacks including:

(i)   The loss of a corporate approach - instead ideas will be pursued by executives with a vested interest even if it is inconsistent with the existing system and strategy.

(ii)   The dominance of short-term profitability at the expense of social responsibility and the ethos of the organisation. Entrepreneurial decision making of this nature may actually harm long-term profitability.

(iii)   The less structured approach of opportunism may allow a more rapid response to opportunities but may also result in a less ordered response to threats, i.e. crisis management.

Strategic planning provides a framework for developing projects within an overall corporate framework with managers working towards an agreed goal. Planning facilitates a detailed and logical consideration of alternatives in the light of internal and external environments, including the consideration of contingencies. As such it allows considerable flexibility.

(b)   **Non-executive directors and conflicts of interest**

Without controls, executive directors are in a postion to neglect their fiduciary duties and manage the business with too much regard for their own interests.

The major areas of conflict, all of which are addressed in the latest version of the Combined Code, are as follows.

(i)   **Remuneration**. Directors may be inclined to reward themselves excessively via both salary and bonuses if they are allowed to decide such matters for themselves. The Combined Code says that no director or manager should be involved in any decisions as to their own remuneration.

(ii)   **Nominations to the board**. Executive directors would typically prefer to appoint people who share their own views about the management of the business or can be manipulated. The Combined Code says that a nomination committee should lead the process for board appointments and make recommendations to the board, and that a majority of members of the committee should be independent non-executive directors.

(iii) **Audit**. The danger here is that executive directors could appoint 'friendly' auditors, who will turn a blind eye to misuse of company assets for the directors' benefit or to misreporting of the company's financial postion. The Combined Code says that an audit committee should include at least three members, and all should be independent non-executive directors.

(iv) In many areas of **board level decision making** executive directors may be incilined to make decisions that enhance their own position and may not be in the best interests of the company. Examples could range from major investment in an executive director's 'pet' project to rejecting a takeover bid, irrespective of its merit, simply to preserve their own jobs. Non-executive directors will not have these personal issues and can take a more objective view. The Combined Code says that the board should include a **balance** of executive and non-executive directors (and in particular independent non-executive directors) such that no individual or small group of individuals can dominate the board's decision taking.

Chapter 14

Question 1: Theta Ltd

(a) **ROI using Alpha's basis**

		£000
(i)	Profit	<u>225</u>
	Capital employed:	
	Fixed assets (at cost)	1,000
	Net current assets	<u>250</u>
		<u>1,250</u>

$$\text{ROI} = \frac{225}{1,250} \times 100 = 18.0\%$$

(ii)	Profit	225
	Add: Savings less depreciation	
	$(35,000 - \frac{120,000}{6})$	<u>15</u>
		<u>240</u>
	Capital employed:	
	Fixed assets (at cost)	1,000
	Add: Purchases (at cost)	<u>120</u>
		1,120
	Net current assets	<u>250</u>
		<u>1,370</u>

$$\text{ROI} = \frac{240}{1,370} \times 100 = 17.52\%$$

(iii)	Profit as stated	225
	Less: Contribution lost	<u>30</u>
		195
	Add: Depreciation not charged	<u>20</u>
		<u>215</u>

Capital employed:		
Fixed assets (at cost)		1,000
Less: Disposals (at cost)		200
		800
Net current assets		250
		1,050

$$\text{ROI} = \frac{215}{1,050} \times 100 = 20.48\%$$

Note: As the net current assets are average for the year the inflow of £20,000 realised for sale of asset has not been included. Similarly in (ii) above it is assumed that the machine was purchased out of additional funds and not from existing cash resources (a common assumption in this style of question).

		£000
(iv)	Profit	225
	Add: Reduction in cost	4
		229
	Capital employed:	
	Fixed assets (at cost)	1,000
	Net current assets	250
		1,250

$$\text{ROI} = \frac{229}{1,250} \times 100 = 18.3\%$$

Note: the reduction in creditors is offset by bank overdraft therefore no change in 'net' current assets. Overdraft interest ignored.

		£000
(v)	Profit	225
	Less: Lost contribution	6
		219
	Capital employed:	
	Fixed assets	1,000
	Net current assets	
	(£250,000 – £25,000)	225
		1,225

$$\text{ROI} = \frac{219}{1,225} \times 100 = 17.9\%$$

(b)   ROI using Theta's basis

All profit figures are as computed in part (a). Capital employed must be recomputed on basis of original cost less depreciation for fixed assets.

		£000
(i)	Profit	225
	Capital employed:	
	Fixed assets (£1,000,000 – £475,000)	525
	Net current assets	250
		775

$$\text{ROI} = \frac{225}{775} \times 100 = 29.03\%$$

(ii)	Profit		$\underline{240}$
	Capital employed:		
	Existing fixed assets		525
	Addition (£120,000 − £20,000)		$\underline{100}$
			625
	Net current assets		$\underline{250}$
			$\underline{875}$

$$\text{ROI} = \frac{240}{875} \times 100 = 27.42\%$$

(iii)	Profit			$\underline{215}$
	Capital employed:			
	Existing fixed assets			525
	Net sales at book value:	£000		
	Original cost	200		
	Accumulated depreciation	200	$\underline{}$	
			525	
	Net current assets		$\underline{250}$	
			$\underline{775}$	

$$\text{ROI} = \frac{215}{775} \times 100 = 27.74\%$$

£'000

(iv)	Profit	$\underline{229}$
	Capital employed:	
	Fixed assets	525
	Net current assets	$\underline{250}$
		$\underline{775}$

$$\text{ROI} = \frac{229}{775} \times 100 = 29.54\%$$

(v)	Profit	$\underline{219}$
	Capital employed:	
	Fixed assets	525
	Net current assets	$\underline{225}$
		$\underline{750}$

$$\text{ROI} = \frac{219}{750} \times 100 = 29.2\%$$

Summary

	(a) %	(b) %
(i)	18.0	29.0
(ii)	17.5	27.4
(iii)	20.5	27.7
(iv)	18.3	29.5
(v)	17.9	29.2

(c) **Goal congruence**

Goal congruence is the state that exists in a control system that leads individuals or groups to take actions that are both in their self-interest and also in the best interest of the entity. *(CIMA Terminology)*

(i) **Transaction A**

Theta uses ROCE for assessing performance of subsidiaries. The implementation of transaction A reduced this ratio from 29.0% to 27.4% and from this point of view was incorrect.

Alpha uses the same ratio but a different base. Even here, however, there is a deterioration from 18.0% to 17.5%.

In answering parts (a) and (b) the cost of capital of 14% has not been utilised. From a decision-making point of view it may be informative to discount the annual cash flows of £35,000 in order to see how it relates to capital cost.

(ii) **Transaction B**

The calculation for this transaction indicates that from the view of Theta there is a decline from 29.0% to 27.7%, whilst from the view of Alpha there is a rise from 18.0% to 20.5%. The movements are opposite, indicative of a lack of goal congruence. Without computation, it seems questionable whether selling for £20,000 a machine that is producing annual cash flows of £30,000 is good management.

Question 2: Hawlit Ltd

(a) **ROI and residual income**

		Annual and expected net income at the following annual investment levels										
		£0.35m		£0.40m		£0.45m		£0.50m		£0.55m		£0.60m	
Price/ gallon £	Prob	£000	EV £000	£000	EV £000	£000	EV £000	£000	EV £000	£000	EV £000	£000	EV £000
1.20	0.1	55	5.5	60	6.0	68	6.8	72	7.2	74	7.4	75	7.5
1.25	0.1	52	5.2	58	5.8	63	6.3	68	6.8	67	6.7	64	6.4
1.30	0.4	46	18.4	52	20.8	55	22.0	58	23.2	56	22.4	53	21.2
1.40	0.3	40	12.0	46	13.8	47	14.1	49	14.7	43	12.9	40	12.0
1.50	0.1	30	3.0	35	3.5	35	3.5	34	3.4	30	3.0	25	2.5
	1.0		44.1		49.9		52.7		55.3		52.4		49.6

Annual investment level £000	Expected annual net income £000	Minimum required return on investment (10% pa) £000	Residual income £000	ROI %
350	44.1	35.0	9.1	12.6
400	49.9	40.0	9.9	12.5
450	52.7	45.0	7.7	11.7
500	55.3	50.0	5.3	11.1
550	52.4	55.0	(2.6)	9.5
600	49.6	60.0	(10.4)	8.3

Notes: (1) Residual income = expected annual net income less minimum required return on investment.

(2) ROI = expected annual net income as a percentage of investment.

(b) **Optimal investment level**

On the basis of giving the highest level of residual income (£9,900) an investment level of £400,000 pa is the optimum.

The annual investment levels given are in steps of £50,000 and, in stating an optimum, any levels between these steps have not been considered. Further information would be required to determine a more 'precise' optimal level.

Residual income is chosen as the basis for determining the optimal level as it takes account of the absolute surplus of income after deducting the minimum required return on the investment. The maximisation of profit is assumed to be a major objective of the company, that is the maximisation of an absolute sum.

(c) **Residual income and return on investment (ROI) as measures of performance**

Residual income and return on investment are just two approaches to the measurement of performance. The problem of measuring performance is considerably magnified in a company that has an organisation structure in which different segments or parts have been clearly defined. The management in each section should have clearly specified responsibilities and, therefore, there is a need to be able to assess segment performance.

Traditionally ROI has been considered the best measure of performance. It is an all-embracing ratio that relates net income to the level of investment. It is generally easily understood by all levels of management. It can be used as a basis for comparison with investment opportunities both inside and outside the company.

As the key ratio in a company it can be sub-divided into a series of secondary ratios as part of an analysis. The first stage in such a breakdown can be illustrated:

$$\text{ROI} = \frac{\text{Net income}}{\text{Investment}}$$

$$= \frac{\text{Net income}}{\text{Sales}} \times \frac{\text{Sales}}{\text{Investment}}$$

Such a sub-analysis assists management in making appropriate decisions and assessing their effect on ROI, which may well be the subject of a target or objective.

The use of ROI as a measure of performance focuses the attention of management on the key factors of net income and the level of investment. A profit maximisation objective for the company is assumed.

Briefly, the problems or limitations of ROI are very much associated with the measurement of net income and investment. The value that has to be placed on fixed assets is a particular problem; if valid comparisons are to be made, should it be based on historical cost, depreciated book value or on replacement cost? Furthermore, in a divisional organisation structure the apportionment of costs and assets between the different parts of the organisation has to be considered. This applies where there are shared facilities.

In a divisional structure, each segment will have a different ROI that will not necessarily tally with the overall company ROI. Where a division has an ROI in excess of the company's, the manager will not be motivated to accept a project that gives a lower ROI than his division currently attains although that return is above the company's ROI target. If the project was accepted the divisional manager would see his measure of performance fall, yet it would be in the best interests of the company as a whole to accept the project. (It was because of this type of conflict that the General Electric Company in the USA introduced the concept of residual income in the 1950s.)

ROI is a relative measure of performance (net income being related to investment), whereas residual income is an absolute measure, being the net income less the minimum required return on the investment. It is the return over and above the minimum required. A comparison can be made between the IRR and NPV approaches in capital budgeting, which are relative and absolute measures of projects respectively, and ROI and residual income in performance measurement.

The conflict, already mentioned, where the divisional and the overall company ROI do not tally can be overcome if a residual income approach is adopted rather than a ROI one. A project yielding at least the overall company's ROI will increase the division's residual income.

ROI, as a measure of performance, is widely used in practice. It relates net income and investment in an easily understood concept. The bases of measuring cost and investment need to be considered and consistently applied where ROI is used for comparison purposes. In a divisional organisation structure particularly, the residual income approach overcomes a lot of the conflict that can arise between divisional goals and overall company goals.

Chapter 15

Lindleys Bank

(a)   Changing the superbranches to investment centres will focus attention both on the profitability and the capital employed in each superbranch. This contrasts with the previous situation, in which the branches were treated as cost centres. The new approach to performance measurement means that the management of each unit will be able to take decisions which commit resources, knowing that the performance of the unit will be measured in terms of profitability.

Managers will have a greater degree of freedom and authority to undertake projects that are expected to meet the organisation's performance criteria. This autonomy is likely to increase the motivation and experience of the managers, as it will be possible to operate with a degree of independence. This may mean a change in attitudes of managers, from being mainly concerned with cost control to becoming revenue generators. A staffing implication of this is whether the existing managers will have the necessary skills and outlook to adapt to the new way of thinking. It will also enable the senior management to compare the performance of each superbranch and this may encourage improved performance through generating inter-branch competition. In the longer term it may be possible to 'float off' parts of the bank into specialist sections.

A possible disadvantage of using profitability to measure performance is that the managers may concentrate on activities which will show improved performance only in the short run. This will mean that the targets for the current year may be achieved at the expense of the longer-term growth and progress of the organisation. An example of this problem is the reduction in advertising expenditure in order to improve the profit in a particular accounting period. However, this will have a detrimental effect on future business. In addition, concentrating only on projects which do not use large amounts of capital may result in the rejection of capital-intensive projects, because they do not meet the immediate criterion of profitability targets.

Another possible problem area is the lack of experience in using profitability as a measure of performance. Inappropriate targets may be set and this may affect the managers' motivation and behaviour.

(b) To assess the performance of each branch, reports will be required by the branch managers, the superbranch managers and the senior management of Lindleys plc. To supply the relevant information, regular and frequent reports will be required.

Although it is possible that residual income will eventually be used, it is proposed initially to introduce return on capital employed. With either of these performance measures, the managers should be provided with regular reports to provide information about the profit generated by each branch, the amount invested by each branch and details of other important factors. These might include the number of new accounts opened. The reports should provide information to both the superbranch managers and the senior management within the bank. This will enable appropriate action to be taken and allow for comparison of the performance of the different superbranches.

The annual budget should include details of the expected revenue from the different activities of the bank and a forecast of the total expenses. The staff costs will represent a high proportion of the total costs and so details of both staffing numbers and costs will need to be made explicit in the report.

The monthly reports will contain details of the revenues, expenses and staffing for the current month and also for the year to date. Finally, both the profit of the superbranch and the return on investment will be shown, to ensure that each manager is aware of the performance of each superbranch.

Details of the level of sales of holiday insurance and similar financial products will be needed regularly, possibly weekly. However, as a high proportion of the expenses of each branch will be relatively fixed, a monthly report is likely to be adequate for the purpose of controlling these expenses. Since travel costs, advertising and entertainment are likely to be substantial, the management will need to monitor the monthly details of these expenses.

Non-financial measures, such as details of new accounts opened, existing accounts closed and complaints about the service offered in a branch, will need to be presented to the management regularly. It is possible that bi-monthly reports will be sufficient to monitor these aspects of the performance of each branch.

Finally, the managers will need ad hoc reports to provide information about the profitability of different categories of customer, services or products offered by the bank.

(c)   There are a number of non-financial areas which should be monitored continuously by the managers of the superbranches. These include the qualitative performance indicators for:

- staffing levels

- the number of new customer accounts opened

- the quality of service offered to customers, especially in comparison with the service provided by the bank's competitors.

Since the number of staff employed is a major expense of a bank, it is essential that this is monitored. However, length of service, experience, and training are qualitative indicators that should be available to the management in respect of individual staff members. In particular, the level of staff competence in information technology is an area which should be monitored, as the retail bank's operations use computers extensively.

In order to monitor the bank's growth, details should be provided of the number of new customers. This information, if provided on a regular basis, will reflect the growth of the business. Details of the different types of customer will be an important aspect in monitoring the success of the activities to attract new customers, and also in assessing the needs of the public.

As the bank aims to offer an 'efficient, but low-cost service' it is vital that the management is aware of the customers' opinions regarding the quality of service offered to them. This information may be difficult to measure accurately, but some possible qualitative measures are queuing and waiting times in branches, the number of mistakes in customers' accounts and the number of complaints lodged by the public. In addition, regular surveys could be organised to measure the reactions of the bank's customers. A matter that should be of major concern to the management of the bank is the nature and frequency of complaints that are received from the public. This information should be recorded to indicate the areas which need to be improved. This type of indicator will be crucial in a period of cost-cutting to ensure that the customers are not dissatisfied with the changes.

Another area which should be considered by the management of each superbranch is the activities of competitors. Within the bank it will be possible to compare the performance of each superbranch. This information will be relatively easy to obtain. However, it will be necessary to take into account differences between superbranches in terms of the profile of their customers and the nature of their services. Although the performance of other banks is difficult to measure, appropriate measures should be devised in order to assess the relative performance of Lindleys plc.

This qualitative information will be important in the planning and management of both the individual branches and the superbranch. In fact, qualitative data will provide information regarding the staff, the growth of the business and the levels of customer satisfaction. This is essential information for monitoring performance and for developing strategic plans.

Chapter 16

Transfer pricing

(a) An effective system of transfer pricing has to:

(i) be clear and well understood

(ii) provide motivation for divisional managers to act in the best interests of the organisation as a whole, which is usually assumed to be to maximise shareholder wealth (i.e. goal congruence)

(iii) allow divisional autonomy and independence to be maintained

(iv) ensure that resources are used where they are most productive

(v) allow divisional performance to be assessed objectively and ensure that any savings made from trading internally are shared fairly between the divisions.

(b) Chambers uses a market-based transfer price system which is clear and probably well understood by the divisional managers.

Given certain reservations, the market price system should ensure that resources are used well and that managers act in the best interests of the organisation whilst preserving their autonomy.

However, it does not seem from the information provided that any savings from trading internally are being treated fairly. For example, when Engines or Transmissions 'sell' to Assembly they do not incur such costs as marketing, distribution or debtor management. Such savings should be shared out so that all divisions are motivated to trade internally if it reduces the costs of the organisation as a whole.

Any modifications made to the current system must ensure that divisional managers are motivated to achieve the aims of the overall organisation. For example, one possible modification would be to use a dual pricing system so that the Assembly division can buy at marginal cost to the making divisions, but the Engines and Transmissions divisions maintain their motivation by recording such sales at market price. This would encourage all divisions to trade internally and to set optimum prices for goods sold externally, without distorting performance appraisal.

(c) (i) A transfer pricing system based on marginal cost values items transferred internally at their marginal cost, i.e. the addition to total cost that their production caused. Such a system provides the manager of the Assembly division with the most meaningful cost information as far as decision making in his own division is concerned. Any such decisions will be in the best interests of the Assembly division and Chambers as a whole.

The problems with setting the transfer price at marginal cost come if Engines and Transmissions do not have spare capacity. They will prefer to sell their products to external customers, and thus make a profit, than transfer them to the Assembly division at marginal cost, even though that is in the interests of the organisation as a whole.

(ii)   A transfer pricing system based on opportunity cost considers the alternatives to supplying the Assembly division. The transfer price set is the price forgone by not selling the engines and transmissions for their best possible external price. Such a system ensures autonomy and optimal decision making, but with constantly fluctuating or difficult to ascertain opportunity costs it is very difficult to implement or for managers to understand.

(iii)   A transfer pricing system based on cost plus (either full or marginal cost) works by adding a mark-up to cost to set the transfer price. This ensures that the selling division makes a profit and thus is motivated to sell internally as long as the mark-up is greater than it could achieve externally. But of course, if this makes the cost to the Assembly division greater than buying from an external supplier, the Assembly division will buy from outside with no regard to whether this is best for the organisation as a whole. The opposite problems arise if the mark-up is less than the selling divisions could achieve externally. It is unlikely that such a system would produce the optimal transfer price for Chambers.

Chapter 17

Limitation of traditional management accounting

(a)   The traditional management accounting techniques for performance measurement are based around budgetary control and standard costing and the associated variances. The budgets are normally prepared annually and the standards are applied to all products of a particular type.

The move towards more flexibility, a readiness to meet customer requirements, smaller batches and continuous improvements results in a wider range of products or 'jobs' geared to customers' specifications with an associated variation in cost, making it difficult to apply a single standard cost. If a single standard were used in this context to calculate variances, these variances would be partly attributable to changes in product specification.

The effect of advanced manufacturing technology is that a greater emphasis is placed on machines and much less emphasis on direct labour. This has two major implications. Firstly the traditional direct labour efficiency variance is of limited use and secondly the method for calculation of unit cost needs to be amended.

The increased emphasis on quality contradicts assumptions made by traditional management accounting, which assumes that products should be made as reliable as is 'cost-effective'. This has been shown to be a short-sighted approach. In the long run, an emphasis on total quality, not only of products but of services to customers and services within the organisation, not only increases sales but enormously reduces many costs associated with reworking and correcting errors.

Overall the traditional performance measures may, therefore, be misleading in the new manufacturing environment.

(b)   Activity-based costing is being introduced in order to identify more accurately the activities or 'cost drivers' which are causing costs to be incurred. The advantage of this technique is that not only can standard costs be adapted more quickly to custom-made products or batches made to customers' specifications, but also they can be quickly updated for changes in methods of manufacture.

If management accountants are to produce meaningful performance reports in the future, they should be concerned not only with comparing results against budgets but also against alternative methods of working. For example, they should be comparing the costs of traditional stock-holding policies against new techniques such as 'just-in-time'.

They should also be concerned with non-financial measures of performance, particularly those associated with quality, such as statistical control charts and reject rates.

Ultimately, management accountants are judged by the usefulness of the information that is given to management. They should be aiming to 'own' the information system of a company so that they can present integrated reports involving financial and non-financial factors. In order to do this, they must become very familiar with their firm's technical operations.

Chapter 18

Organisational learning

(a) Organisational learning is the process by which an organisation, like an individual, adapts its behaviour based on experience. For example, when new employees join the firm the formal induction procedures will incorporate previous understanding. Their supervisor, colleagues and subordinates will also give them additional information. This will represent more recent learning, which may become part of the formal knowledge of the firm.

The key features of this type of learning are where the organisation:

(i) encourages continuous learning and knowledge generation at all levels

(ii) can transform knowledge into actual behaviour

(iii) encourages questions and explicitly recognises mistakes as part of the learning process. It tries to resolve any immediate problems and learns from the process

(iv) practises self-development and action-learning. As the organisation learns from its actions, so does the individual

(v) recognises that failed answers are as important as successful ones, because they want to find new answers

(vi) has the processes to move the information/knowledge around

(vii) encourages testing and experimentation.

(b) The aim is to design an organisation which is capable of adapting, changing, developing and transforming itself in response to the needs, wishes and aspirations of people, inside and outside.

The role of management in a learning organisation is to encourage continuous learning and acquisition of new knowledge and skills and to transform these into actual behaviour, products and processes within the organisation. If JUS wants to develop itself as a learning organisation, the following approach should be adopted by management.

(i) The process of strategy formulation should be designed with learning in mind, and should incorporate experimentation and feedback.

(ii)   All members of the organisation should be encouraged, and given the opportunity, to contribute to policy making as part of the learning process.

(iii) Information should be seen as a resource to be exploited by all members of the organisation, not as a 'power tool' reserved for a chosen few.

(iv)   Accounting systems should be designed in such a way that members of the organisation can learn how the cash resource is used.

(v)   Employees should be encouraged to see internal users of their outputs as 'customers'.

(vi)   Employees should be encouraged to see the diversity of rewards they enjoy (not just cash), and there should be openness about why some people are paid more than others.

(vii) The structures of the organisation – everything from office layout to managerial hierarchy – should be regarded as temporary arrangements, which can be altered in response to changing conditions.

(viii) Employees who have contacts outside the organisation – salesmen, customer service staff, purchasing staff, etc – should impart the knowledge they determine from such contacts to improve the organisation's knowledge base.

(ix)   Management must foster a climate in which workers understand that part of their task is to improve their own knowledge, and to share knowledge with other members of the organisation.

(x)   A priority for management should be the provision of opportunities for structured learning – courses, seminars, etc.

Chapter 19

KJ plc

(a)   A strategy is a general statement of long-term objectives and goals and the ways by which these will be achieved, i.e. the necessary level of operational support. The main objectives of the IT strategy have been to:

(i)   ensure goal congruence between the different sections so that they are all working together to provide good customer service

(ii)   provide good customer service (from the point of view of the customer)

(iii) maintain an acceptable Transaction Processing System (TPS).

Alternative One

Goal congruence

The system structure and the information to be provided sounds similar to the existing transaction processing system. The main difference is the addition of a strategic planning module. Although its use would be for the MD, there is no reason why other managers could not use the facility in time. The large, centralised computer will provide efficient and economic operation, and the common database will ensure that this system would support goal congruence between the different sections, because everyone would be working from the same information.

To evaluate any system there must be an analysis of both the current and expected future size of KJ plc's business. This analysis must include the number of transactions that the system needs to process. Provided the centralised database is large enough, it could provide a suitably congruent solution and any future organisation changes could be accommodated within such a structure if required. However, organisational changes may detract from the level of congruence that this alternative could support.

One of the disadvantages with this alternative is that it does not enhance the decision-making opportunities of the managers or facilitate change to the management structure, although the MD has recognised that this is an important issue. In the long term, overall goal congruence would be achieved, but the MD would retain control of the decisions regarding the computer system and individual departmental development might be limited. This system offers no impetus to change the management structure and if it is selected other organisational development techniques would need to be employed.

The other disadvantage is that there is no provision to transfer the historical data from the old system to the new system. Employees would have access to it up to six months after the system changeover, but this might cause problems with goal congruence and affect the service offered to customers.

Customer service

This system offers improvement to the two top-ranking factors in the customer survey – speed of delivery and availability of product. The promises on same-day delivery in major cities for orders placed before 11.00 am will make a valuable contribution towards customer satisfaction and support the IT strategy based on meeting customer needs. Because the system is fully integrated, stock-outs can be rectified in half the time. As well as ensuring a better service to customers, these new features could also be a source of competitive advantage for KJ plc.

The lack of historical data from the old system might be a disadvantage. Although it would be available for up to six months after the systems changeover, this is insufficient to enable some analyses to be performed effectively, e.g. full trend analysis and monitoring of sales demand. This could have an effect on future business planning and the further development of the IT strategy, especially if middle managers take a more active role in decision making in the future.

The maintenance of an acceptable TPS

KJ plc's current supplier would supply this system. We could assume that the supplier knows KJ plc's business and has provided support for the existing TPS over the last five years. The DP department would probably have formed a relationship with the suppliers, and know who to contact when there are problems. This can be an important advantage to the DP department and the other departments in KJ plc because the business knowledge would tend to minimise the disruption caused by undergoing a systems changeover. It would also be a relief to the employees in the DP department as this system needs to be maintained by a specialist department so there would be little disruption to their employment contracts.

Because the suppliers are well established, it means that other organisations with similar TPS to KJ plc may be available in the locality to co-operate in a mutual aid contingency plan to provide hardware back-up in a crisis situation.

The downside to the system is that it is not industry-standard. This could cause problems for KJ plc in respect of future upgrade capability. They could find themselves in a similar position to the current one, but in less than five years. Technology moves on quickly and there is a better chance of upgrades being available for standard hardware and software than bespoke systems. There is also a risk that continued support might not be available from the current supplier.

Alternative Two

Goal congruence

A de-centralised system with no centralised database will not support goal congruence as well as a centralised system. However, it will improve the motivation of the recently appointed middle managers because this type of system will facilitate delegation to departmental managers. It will probably alienate the long-serving managers who are happy with the status quo. Because each department would be responsible for maintaining its own computer systems and making its own decisions on the use of those systems, it is unlikely that department managers would be working together to provide good customer service. The potential for sub-optimisation is high because individual managers would have responsibility to make tactical and operational decisions for their own departments. This would force them to focus on their own goals and objectives rather than the overall strategic corporate objectives.

The current system allows employees in the sales department to take the order details, check the stock in real-time to ensure the order can be fulfilled and then to transfer the order to a central warehouse for delivery to the customer. This alternative system would require the information to be transferred and updated without having one comprehensive view; it would break down the processing into separate 'compartments'. Each department would have its own version of the data and there might be delays in updating, accessing and communicating information across departments. Because the speed of delivery of the goods is likely to be adversely affected by this system, the staff are going to blame other departments for causing these delays and it is not going to aid goal congruence. All departments will not be working together to provide good customer service.

Customer service

The extra facilities of email and Internet over fax and telephone give this system a big advantage. Most modern companies use email, and the Internet is becoming more popular as companies use it as a marketing tool. The ability to use a wide variety of communication media, together with the focus on KJ plc's own branded products, would facilitate organisational improvements, which may give KJ plc a competitive advantage over their competitors. However, these extra facilities would not be addressing the customer requirements outlined in the survey. Ease of ordering and brand image are not very highly rated in the list of desirable attributes.

There will be a full range of operational through to strategic information provided by this system. The powerful database query tools will allow full trend analyses to be carried out with key historical information being available to the new system if managers can afford to make the transfer from their own budgets. The ability to draw up these reports could improve customer service by producing individual customer demand profiles, which would help in avoiding stock-outs and would minimise manufacturing delivery lead times.

Although this system offers several new facilities, it does little to improve on the current response time when accessing certain databases. Customer service staff would be unable to be very helpful if the system response time was so slow that both staff and customers became frustrated. As this factor is ranked third most important characteristic of the customer survey, it must be taken into consideration.

Acceptable TPS

A de-centralised system is a more modern approach than the existing centralised computer system. The advantages are those associated with client/server developments. The processing is distributed across a network of servers to PC-based desktop clients. To evaluate this system there must be an analysis of the speed of access on the internal Intranet system. Estimates should be made using the current number of transactions and the expected future transactions that the system will encounter. If extremely high volumes were involved, the Intranet may not be able to cope and a large centralised facility might provide better response times. This would have a major impact on the customer service staff and affect the customers.

The supplier for this system will provide industry-standard equipment that is IBM compatible. Because many organisations have IBM systems, future compatibility, maintenance and upgrades are more assured. Even if their supplier goes out of business, KJ plc will have the ability to purchase the equipment, network and database management software from leading companies that specialise in these areas. IBM compatible equipment would also make it easier to find an organisation in the locality to co-operate in a mutual aid contingency plan, providing hardware back-up in a crisis. These advantages would make it easier to maintain the strategy of an acceptable TPS.

A disadvantage with this system is that the DP department would have to change. Each department would have the responsibility of maintaining their own system and the managers may not choose to use staff from the existing DP department because they may not be experienced enough in the new system maintenance. This could cause problems during the system changeover and may affect the service given to customers.

Conclusion

Alternative One shows marked improvements over the existing system. There is ample support for goal congruence, and improvements to facilities concerning customer service. However, maintenance of an acceptable TPS may cause problems in the future because of the future upgrade limitations, but the future of the DP department looks assured if this alternative is adopted. This system would achieve the objectives of the IT strategy to provide good customer service, but it would not address the management structure or motivational problems. Enhancing the decision-making opportunities of the elite group of managers would need further organisational development.

Alternative Two addresses the motivational aspects of the majority of the managers and would provide some improvements to customer service, but not in the high priority ranking factors outlined in the customer survey. The benefits of future upgrades and use of modern standardised components are also advantages of this option. This system represents a possible acceptable basis for the customer service and maintenance of the TPS objectives of the IT strategy, but it would not address the goal congruence objectives. It might provide other organisational advantages concerning the morale and motivation of most of the managers, but it would leave the future of the DP department needing further organisation.

There is a difficult choice for KJ plc because both systems would provide an acceptable basis for some of the three key areas of the IT strategy. The company could focus on the internal improvements offered by Alternative Two or could concentrate on providing better customer benefits offered by Alternative One.

(b)   Transaction processing systems provide the raw material, which is often used more extensively by management information systems, databases or decision support systems. The TPS might be used to produce management information such as reports on cumulative sales figures to date, total amounts owed to suppliers or owed by debtors, total stock turnover to date and value of current stock in hand. However, the main purpose of the TPS is operational, as an integral part of day-to-day operations.

The current TPS allows for the continual receiving and rapid processing of data which validates and updates the files with every transaction. There do not seem to be any problems with response times from the system. The reason it is being replaced is because of the increased maintenance and other costs due to the system's age. It provides a vast amount of information, which is used by managers at all levels in the organisation. There are very few complaints concerning the amount or the quality of information that is normally supplied.

The TPS currently supports the three main areas of the IT strategy but the ability to bring about change has been restricted because only the MD authorises changes to the system. The scenario does not mention whether the current system could support enhanced decision making by middle managers, only that the MD does not know how to implement an acceptable solution.

If Alternative One were adopted, there would be additional benefits to customer service and customer satisfaction would increase. However, unless this brought about more business, it is doubtful whether the information emanating from the system would show this improvement.

All staff would have access to the centralised database. In the future, managers might be given the authority to make more decisions and this type of system would facilitate control. Unfortunately, the current situation would prevail in the short term and the managers would be in no position to influence matters. Because historical data would only be available six months after changeover, this could create problems at KJ plc. Full trend analyses would not be possible and managers would find it difficult to produce some reports, e.g. stock levels in relation to sales and purchases. There could also be lost opportunities in recognising the potential of new products.

The strategic planning module that comes as an extra with this system would allow the MD to use the information from the TPS in a different way. He would be able to consider a number of alternatives and evaluate them under a variety of potential conditions. However, unless he shares this facility with the managers and gives them the opportunity to exercise some control over their departments, they would probably be indifferent to the information provided by the new system.

The information to be provided by Alternative Two includes a full range of strategic to operational information, with database query tools to access as much information as KJ plc want from the TPS. The system offered by Alternative Two will only satisfy low-level customer requirements in the short term, but could bring about a significant change to the marketing and sales procedures with the introduction of email and the Internet facilities. These facilities will make more information about KJ plc and its products available on the Internet for customers and potential customers. They can also be used to obtain environmental information to help in the decision-making process.

The Intranet can be used for information that ranges from the financial data that management needs, to the scheduling of workgroups within certain departments, down to the latest changes to the staff handbook. The database query tools will enable specific items of information to be obtained from the TPS. This should improve the motivation of managers, because they will be taking more control of their departments and the decision-making process. Managers should also be able to develop the system and produce reports tailored to their departmental needs and information to suit their requirements, provided that the query system uses a structured query language that is fairly simple to master. Motivating the managers and supporting organisational change could bring about significant cultural and attitude improvements, allowing an information infrastructure to be developed. Communications and information flow could be improved and put into practice by a well-motivated workforce. As the control over departmental systems is localised, then potentially each department can maximise the use of its systems to provide the information required by managers.

Chapter 20

Managing change

(a) **Participation**

This approach seeks to involve employees in the decision-making process. There are cases where this has been extended to the designing of own jobs, payment systems, etc. This has proved successful, as the American Coch and French study of Harwood Manufacturing and the UK experience of Pirelli would suggest. The advantage of this method is that it enhances commitment to change, since the employees have developed their own change. In addition, the wider range of input into the change process will bring in an equally wide range of knowledge and experience.

However, there are a number of significant disadvantages. First of all, there must be the culture and climate to permit participation in change. RC Townsend boasted how change worked in Avis with the same people. However, the type of person who would work for a car-rental firm is likely to be different from, and probably more adaptable than, someone who is in a very highly programmed job with little scope for creativity. The cynic would view the Pirelli example in terms of what were the implications upon the shop floor.

Secondly, the greater number of people in the decision-making process can give rise to an extremely protracted decision-making process. Also, as is evidenced from the Japanese ringi approach, no one is responsible and hence accountable for the decision.

Thirdly, there is a need for a high degree of trust between the management and work people. Again, there may not be the culture and tradition of this, with the result that the invitation to participate will be treated with considerable suspicion.

Fourthly, participation must be honest. Pseudo-participation is always exposed for the sham that it is, and only serves to exacerbate the problem. This can easily happen since, with the wide variety of people being involved, there is a high risk that plans for change degenerate into a talking shop.

(b) **Education**

There is a mistaken view that if people are better educated and trained, then they will be receptive to change. While better education and training may make changes easier, and create an environment where people are prepared to participate in the change process, it will also raise the expectation of the individual. This could mean an increased turnover as people become more marketable, or an exacerbated hostility derived from frustration where enhanced expectations have not been met.

(c) **Communication**

This assumes that if the plans for change are effectively communicated, then people will understand the need for change and accept the changes. This would lay the foundations for change to be implemented fairly easily and painlessly.

Sadly, the communication of the plans for change is subject to misinterpretation and, if the wrong medium is selected, manipulation into disinformation by self-seeking interests. In addition, communication can be a two-edged sword. People may learn of the need for change and morale may drop, exacerbating the current situation. Similarly, the more marketable people may move, and this will also create a situation where change is needed, but the best people to implement it have left.

(d) **Power**

This is where management exerts what is perceived as its 'right to manage' and imposes change unilaterally. Management has the formal authority to do this within the parameters of appropriate legislation, and the de facto situation in relation to the labour market. In periods of high unemployment, management may elect to take this option, knowing that if employees do not like the situation, then they should look very carefully at the alternatives. It is argued that this draconian method is a viable option only in times of high unemployment, but it could be argued that in times of full employment those who are not prepared to go along with the changes can be eased out less painfully.

Such a strategy has the obvious advantage of being easy and quick to implement, especially if the workforce is in a weak and demoralised position. However, there are two significant potential disadvantages. First, in the short term, there is the obvious problem identified by Etzioni that such a coercive strategy will fail to gain the wholehearted support of the workforce, with the result that the desired levels of motivation, morale and output will not be achieved. Secondly, in the long term the company may be building up further problems for itself. Unions have long memories, and a coerced, demoralised workforce provides a fertile area in which confrontation and antagonism will develop. As a result, when the time becomes ripe for a more co-operative approach, the management is unlikely to find the unions and the employees very helpful, or predisposed to comply with managerial wishes.

(e) **Manipulation**

This can be very similar to the power strategy. It is ostensibly less coercive. A management team may use the media of pseudo-participation and pseudo-effective communication to persuade the workforce about the need for change. Ideally it will be done through a mass meeting, similar to union meetings outside the factory gate. Agreement comes from position power and an unwillingness to step out of line. The benefits are the same as from the power strategy, as are the considerable disadvantages.

(f) **Negotiation**

This moves along the spectrum from autocratic styles to a more consultative approach, usually through the media of the unions. The objective is an acceptable compromise solution. Two possibilities exist. First, that one side wins and one loses. Compromises are often unsuccessful, so this approach may be the best way. Secondly is the possibility to work towards a compromise. This option may not exist or it may be very unpalatable. The obvious example is where rationalisation is required. The unions may resist the closures, but the future of the whole company or even the industry may be at stake. This may mean that the path towards a compromise is really not available. It also means that one party to the negotiations is fighting with a considerable handicap.

The obvious advantage of negotiation is that it recognises potential conflict and seeks a solution without running the risk of creating damaging industrial disputes. It has the further advantage that the resultant agreement will produce a commitment to the changes and maintain the morale of the workforce and the output that management requires. However, it can be a protracted process, and if it goes on too long, patience may be lost on both sides. It also depends upon the level of confidence that exists in the union and the negotiating team. If there is a feeling that the unions have sold the employees out, if they could have got a better deal, and if they feel they have been the victims of cynical manipulation, then the whole process will fail.

Note: Change is going to be a function of contingency management. There is no one simple answer, and most strategies will have to be a combination of the examples cited above. Six examples have been included, although the question only required four.

Index

A

Acquisition, 177, 240

Activity Based Management (ABM), 226

Activity benchmarking, 221

Adaptive strategy, 12

Agency theory, 353

AIDA, 113

Analysis software, 140

Analytical systems, 139

Ansoff's product/market matrix, 172

Antagonism, 92

Anthony's levels of management, 316

APEC, 67

Applications, 140

Applications architecture, 416

Applications portfolio theory, 138

Applied research, 372

Appraisal, 369

Architecture, 229

Asia-Pacific Economic Co-operation Forum (APEC), 67

Assessing strategic performance, 289

Attitudes to change, 435

Audit committees, 280

Audit of resources, 164

Awareness frameworks, 134

B

Backward integration, 176

Balanced scorecard, 318

Barriers to entry, 125, 135

Base budget reviews, 222

Benchmarking, 213, 219

Benefits of outsourcing IT/IS, 100

Boston Consulting Group (BCG) matrix, 188, 190

BPR - advantages and disadvantages, 263

Brainstorming, 170

Braithwaite and Drahos, 68, 80

Branding, 158

Browser, 150

Buchanan and Huczyknski, 434

Budget, 425

Business exchanges, 154

Business modelling, 412

Business process re-engineering (BPR), 259

Business relations, 80

Business strategy, 1

Business unit performance, 341

Business use of the Internet, 151

Business-to-business (B2B), 153

Business-to-consumer (B2C), 155

Buyers, 42

Buyers' bargaining power, 126

C

Cash cow, 190

Central American Free Trade Agreement (CAFTA), 67

Centre for Interfirm Comparisons, 218

Change, 443

Change levers, 255

Change management, 433, 442

Change process, 442

Channels of communication, 398

Civil society, 80, 82

Clarkson principles, 79

Cognitive dissonance, 112

Combined Code, 279

Commercial political risk, 58

Common Agricultural Policy (CAP), 64

Communication, 398, 436

Communications architecture, 415

Comparative analysis, 333

Competition and rivalry, 43

Competition, 53

Competitive advantage, 124, 129, 134, 173

Competitive advantage, 206, 214, 227

Competitive advantage, 37

Competitive benchmarking, 221

Competitive environments, 26

Competitive forces, 37

Competitive performance, 323

Competitive rivalry, 125

Competitors, 214

Complex environment, 27

Compulsory competitive tendering, 329

Computing architecture, 415

Confiscation political risk, 57

Conflict and frustrations, 434

Conflicting objectives, 422

Conformance, 369

Consultation with experts, 169

Consumer behaviour, 111

Consumer pressure groups, 85

Consumer protection, 51

Consumer segmentation, 105

Consumer to Consumer (C2C), 161

Consumers' Association, 85

Continuous change, 264

Continuous improvement, 363, 375

Contract negotiation, 102

Contracts, 98

Control, 420

Core activities, 366

Corporate codes, 285

Corporate culture, 285

Corporate governance, 277

Corporate governance, 79

Corporate objectives, 13

Corporate objectives, 271

Cost centre, 290

Cost control, 426

Cost drivers, 226

Cost leadership, 179

Cost of quality, 369

Country analysis, 56

Covisint, 154

Creativity, 238

Critical Path Analysis (CPA), 424

Critical success factors (CSFs), 312

Cultural change, 437

Culture, 252

Customer account profitability (CAP), 116

Customer portfolio, 105

Customer Relationship Management (CRM), 114

Customer-related processes, 379

D

Data architecture, 415

Data for environmental analysis, 44

Data mining, 142

Data warehousing, 141

Davenport, T, 254

Deadlines, 423

Decentralisation, 290

Decision-making unit (DMU), 109

Declining industry, 207

Delegation, 238

Deliberate strategies, 12

Delphi technique., 170

Demographics, 105

Derivatives of PEST, 35

Derived demand, 110, 170

Design and development, 380

Design differentiation, 229

Development, 240

Differentiation, 180

Differentiation, 229

Direction, 238

Directors, 269

Directors' duties, 275

Discontinuous thinking, 262

Discretionary activities, 366

Distribution channel, 41, 230

Diversification, 176

Diversity, 397

Divestment, 209, 245

Divisional assessment, 292

Domain, 26

Downsizing, 399

Drucker P, 5, 19, 164

Duty of care, 276

Dynamic environment, 28

E

Earl, M, 413, 417

E-business, 156

E-business - advantages, 156

E-business - risks, 157

E-commerce strategy, 155

E-commerce, 151

Econometric model, 171

Economic data, 216

Economic environment, 30

Economies of scale, 39

Economy, 332

Education, 436

Effectiveness, 332

Efficiency, 332

Electronic Data Interchange (EDI), 152

Electronic trading room, 154

Emergent strategies, 13

Emerging and developing industries, 204

Employers' pressure groups, 85

Encryption, 157

Enron, 277

Enterprise Resource Management (ERM), 171, 364

Entrepreneurial strategy, 11

Environment, 7, 26

Environmental scanning, 154

Environmental shocks, 231

E-procurement, 153

Ethical responsibilities, 283

EU, 63

EU constitution, 66

Euro, 65

European Union (EU), 63

Exchange control risk, 59

Executive agencies, 329

Executive directors, 275

Exit barriers, 208

Experience curves, 257

Explicit knowledge, 387

External data, 216

External failure, 369

Extranet, 402

F

Factory role, 137

Fear of change, 439

Festinger L, 112

Fiduciary responsibilities, 275

Financial performance, 323

Financial political risk, 58

Firewall, 157

Five forces, 39, 125

Focus, 181

Forecasting, 14, 272

Forecasting models, 171

Forecasting techniques, 169

Forecasting the gap, 167

Formal communication systems, 398

Forward integration, 177

Free trade agreements, 62

Free Trade Area of the Americas (FTAA), 67

Freewheeling opportunism, 271

G

Gantt Charts, 424

Gap analysis, 164, 166

GATS, 62

GATT, 62

GE Matrix, 195

General Agreement on Tariffs and Trade (GATT), 62

General Agreement on Trade in Services (GATS), 62

Generic strategies, 178

Global business regulation, 68

Global company, 342

Global competition, 54, 55

Gluck, 236

Goal congruence, 291

Goal congruence, 349

Goals, 2, 3

Gould and Quinn, 446

Government policy, 83

KAPLAN PUBLISHING

Government to Consumer (G2C), 161

Government, 81

Grapevine, 399

Greenbury Report, 278

Greiner, 237

Groupware, 400

Growth, 240

Growth-share matrix, 188

H

Hampel Report, 278

Hard information, 398

Harvest, 208

Heterogeneity, 321

Hierarchy of objectives, 3

Higgs, 281

Hofer and Schendel, 7

Hofer matrix, 199

Holding strategies, 193

Home use of the Internet, 150

Horizontal acquisitions, 242

Horizontal integration, 177

Horizontal integration, 343

Human resources, 378

Hypertext transfer protocol (HTTP), 402

I

Identifying the gap, 166

Image differentiation, 229

Immoral organisations, 283

Implementation problems, 423

Importance, 264

Imposed strategies, 13

Inactivists, 435

Inbound logistics, 225

Incentives, 352

Incipient demand, 372

Incrementalism, 16

Industrial buyers, 108

Industrial segmentation, 111

Industry analysis, 30

Industry attractiveness, 43

Industry classification strategies, 204

Industry-specific ratios, 293

Informal communication systems, 398

Information intensity matrix, 131

Information Management (IM) strategy, 418, 420

Information sources, 44

Information strategy, 410

Information Systems (IS) strategy, 418

Information systems planning projects, 411

Information Technology (IT) strategy, 418, 420

Infrastructure, 378

Initiative, 15

Innovation, 250, 253, 327, 373

Intangibility, 321

Interactivists, 435

Interdependencies, 434

Interest groups, 83

Interest of stakeholders, 77

Interfirm comparison schemes, 218

Internal benchmarking, 220

Internal failure, 369

Internal market, 330

International operations, 55

International trade, 59

International transfer pricing, 351

Internet research, 150

Internet Service Provider (ISP), 148

Internet strategy, 151, 155

Internet, 45, 148, 401

Intuitive methods, 169

Investment centre, 290

ISO 9000, 100, 374

IT – role in process innovation, 255

J

Johnson and Scholes, 6, 8, 20

Joint development, 243

Just-in-time (JIT), 363

K

Kaizen, 363

Kaplan, 318

Knowledge acquisition, 388

Knowledge building, 386, 388

Knowledge creating, 386

Knowledge management, 388

Knowledge sharing - problems, 391

Kolb, 392

Kotler, 119

Kotler, 176

Kotler's 3-by-3 product market growth matrix, 177

L

Labour, 51

Latent demand, 372

Leadership, 208, 253

Lean systems, 362

Learning curve, 393

Learning cycles, 392

Learning in the workplace, 393

Learning organisation, 394

Learning, 392

Leavitt, 444

Lewin's 3-step model of change, 443

Life-cycle analysis, 202

Life-cycle phases, 201

Lindblom, 16

Local area networks (LANs), 399

Logical incrementalism, 16

Long-term strategy, 273

M

Macro environment, 26

Macroeconomic statistics, 218

Major markets, 53

Management accounting techniques, 15

Management buyout, 245

Management commitment, 377

Management responsibility, 377

Management review, 378

Managerial performance, 294

Manipulation, 437

Market development, 176

Market penetration strategy, 173

Market penetration, 173

Market segments, 230

Market-based transfer prices, 346

Marketing and sales, 225

Marketing audit, 118

Markets, 54

Maslow's need hierarchy, 112

Maturing industries, 205

Mayo, A, 437

McFarlan, 134, 254, 413

McFarlan's strategic grid, 136

McKinsey matrix, 195

Measuring devices, 381

Mechanisms, 69, 70

Mendelow's matrix, 75

Merger, 177, 241

Mintzberg, 7, 8, 11, 18

Mission critical systems, 139

Mission statement, 3

Mission, 3

Modelling, 171

Monetary union, 65

Moral hazard, 356

Moral organisations, 283

Morgan, G, 386

Muddling through, 16

Multidimensional models of
performance, 318

Multinational companies (MNCs),
53, 342

N

NAFTA, 66

National Audit Office, 330

Negotiated prices, 350

Negotiating with customers and
suppliers, 96

Negotiation, 97, 437

Negotiations with suppliers, 97

Networks, 399

New opportunities, 264

Niche, 208

Nine cell matrix, 195

Nolan's stage hypothesis, 408

Non-conformance, 369

Nonconforming products, 381

Non-executive directors, 275

Non-Executive Directors, 281

Non-financial measures, 311

North American Free Trade
Agreement (NAFTA), 66

Not-for-profit organisations, 328

O

Objectives, 2, 3

Office for National Statistics, 216

Ohmae, Kenichi, 244

On-line analytical processing
systems (OLAP), 141

Operational management, 317

Operational planning, 10

Operational plans, 3

Operations, 225

Opportunities, 37

Opportunity frameworks, 134

Optimal sharing rule, 354

Optimal transfer price, 349

Organisation development, 240

Organisation, 2

Organisation, 420

Organisational barriers, 391

Organisational change, 434, 438

Organisational growth, 236, 237

organisational growth, 237

Organisational structures, 258

Outbound logistics, 225

Outsourcing IT/IS, 100

Outsourcing, 229

Overcoming resistance, 442

P

Participation, 239

Participation, 436, 442

partnership with suppliers, 93

Payne, 113

Payne's model of customer
markets, 115

Pedler et al, 395

People, 253

People, 444

Peppard, 138

Performance evaluation in service
industries, 321

Performance pyramid, 320

Perishability, 322

PEST analysis, 30

PESTEL, 25

PESTLE, 30, 35

Peters, Tom, 386

Planning, 10, 420

Political environment, 30

Political forces, 50

Political groups, 83

Political mechanisms, 444

Political risk, 57

Porter, 37, 39, 42, 50, 125, 206,
207, 224, 226, 227, 412

Porter and Millar, 129, 131

Porter's Five Forces model, 125

Porter's generic strategies, 178

Porter's diamond, 37

Porter's five forces model, 39

Position audit, 164

Positioning frameworks, 134

Potential entrants, 125

Potential entrants, 39

Power and coercion, 436

Power of stakeholders, 76

Power of suppliers, 42

Power politics, 444

Pressure groups, 82, 83

Prevention, 369

Price differentiation, 230

Primary activities, 129

Principal and Agency Theory
(PAT), 353

Principles, 69

Problem child, 191

problems with outsourcing, 101

Process approach, 375

Process benchmarking, 221

Process innovation, 249, 254

Process of innovation, 251

Process specialisation, 343

Process visions, 255

Product development, 174

Product life-cycle, 200

Product Market Portfolio (PMP),
188

Product portfolio, 187

Product realisation, 375, 379

Product/market matrix, 172

Production applications, 140

Product-Market Growth Matrix,
177

Products, 375

Profit centre, 290

Profit, 86

Progress report, 427

Project budget, 425

Project initiation document (PID), 424

Project management tools, 424

Project management, 421

Project manager, 423

Project objectives, 421

Project sponsor, 423

Promotional groups, 83

Protectionism, 60

Purchases, 92

Q

Quality assurance schemes, 99

Quality chains, 365

Quality circles, 367

Quality control, 368

Quality differentiation, 230

Quality management standards, 374

Quality management systems, 374, 376

Quality of service, 325

Quality related costs, 368

Query applications, 140

Question mark, 191

Quinn, 16, 17

R

Rappaport, 87

Ratio analysis, 299

Reactivists, 435

Regulation, 41

Regulations, 54

Related diversification, 176

Relationship marketing, 113

Remedial processes, 381

Research, 150

Research and development, 343, 371

Residual income (RI), 298

Resistance to change, 440

Resource allocation, 423

Resource histogram, 425

Resource management, 378

Resource utilisation, 327

Results and determinants, 321, 322

Return on investment (ROI), 295

Revenue centre, 290

Rewards, 352

Rigidity, 14, 272

Risk and return relationship, 203

Risks of outsourcing IT/IS, 101

Rockart, J, 312

Role and responsibilities of directors, 269

S

Scenario planning, 171

Scholes, 76

S-curve, 202

Segmentation, 105

Senge, P, 397

Service, 225

Shareholder value, 87

Shareholder value analysis, 87

Shareholder wealth, 86

Shell directional policy matrix, 195

Short-term pressures, 14, 272

Simple environment, 27

Simultaneity of production and consumption, 321

Single European Market (SEM), 64

Social barriers, 391

Social environment, 33

Sociocultural environment, 33, 34

Soft information, 398

Sole suppliers, 98

Sovereignty, 86

Specialisation, 59

Stability strategies, 236

Stakeholder management, 74

Stakeholder mapping, 75

Stakeholders, 16, 74

Static environment, 28

Status-quo forecasting, 166

Stifling initiative, 272

Strategic architecture, 227, 229

Strategic business unit (SBU), 27, 245

Strategic decisions, 19

Strategic decisions, 270

Strategic gap, 166

Strategic information systems plan (SISP), 416

Strategic issue management, 445

Strategic management of the market portfolio, 192

Strategic management, 316

Strategic movements, 197

Strategic options generator, 127

Strategic options, 236

Strategic planning, 10

Strategic potential, 137

Strategic role, 137

Strategies for managing change, 436

Strategy review, 445

Strategy, 3, 6

Structure, 252, 444

Substitutes, 41, 126

Supplier Relationship Management (SRM) software, 99

Supplier relationships, 92

Supplier/customer relationships, 19

Suppliers, 42

Suppliers' bargaining power, 126

Supply Chain Management (SCM), 99

Supply strategy, 92

Support activities, 129, 366

Support role, 136

Switching costs, 40

SWOT analysis, 35, 412

Synergy, 173, 182

System modelling, 171

Systems of value, 227

T

Tacit knowledge, 387

Tactical management, 316

Tactical planning, 10

Tactics, 3

Target markets, 230

Tasks, 444

Tax haven, 352

Taxation, 52

Technological barriers, 391

Technological environment, 34

Technology, 54, 420, 444

Telnet, 149

Think tank, 169

Threats from substitutes, 41, 126

Threats, 37

Top management involvement, 375

Total Quality Management (TQM), 260

Total quality management (TQM), 365

Trade association pressure groups, 85

Trade cycle, 30

Trade union, 51

Trade, 52

Trade-Related Aspects of Intellectual Property Rights (TRIPS), 62

Traffic levels, 160

Transaction costs, 228

Transfer pricing, 344

Trend analysis, 169

Triggers, 434

Turnaround role, 137

Turnbull Committee, 278

U

Unified Modeling Language, 412

Unrelated diversification, 177

V

Value, 224

Value Added Network Service (VANS), 153

Value chain, 129, 224, 225, 412

Value for money(VFM), 331

Value systems, 227

Vertical integration, 343

W

Waste, 362

Watchdog, 239

Waves of innovation, 413

Waves of technology, 256

Web browser, 150

Website design, 159

Website implementation, 160

Website security, 157

Webster and Wind, 109

Wide area networks (WANs), 400

Wiseman, 127

Workers' pressure groups, 84

World Trade Organisation (WTO), 62

World trade, 59

WTO, 62

X

Xerox Corporation, 220

PUBLISHING
FOULKS LYNCH

STUDY TEXT REVIEW FORM
Paper P6

Thank you for choosing a Kaplan Publishing Foulks Lynch CIMA Study Text. As we are constantly striving to improve our products, we would be grateful if you could provide us with feedback about how useful you found this Study Text.

Name: ....

Address: ....

....

Email: ....

Why did you decide to purchase this Study Text?

Have used them in the past ☐

Recommended by lecturer ☐

Recommended by friend ☐

Saw advertising ☐

Other (please specify) ☐

Which other Kaplan Publishing Foulks Lynch products have you used?

Exam Kit ☐

Distance Learning Course ☐

Pocket Notes ☐

How do you study?

At a college ☐

On a distance learning course ☐

Home study ☐

Other ☐

Please specify..

Overall opinion of this Study Text

	Excellent	*Adequate*	*Poor*
Introductory pages	☐	☐	☐
Syllabus coverage	☐	☐	☐
Clarity of explanations	☐	☐	☐
Clarity of definitions and key points	☐	☐	☐
Diagrams	☐	☐	☐
Practice/exam-type questions	☐	☐	☐
Self-test questions	☐	☐	☐
Layout	☐	☐	☐
Index	☐	☐	☐

If you have further comments/suggestions or have spotted any errors, please write them on the next page.

Please return this form to: Mirjana Jeremic, Editor, Freepost RRAT-HLYC-5KXA, FTC Foulks Lynch, Unit 2 The Business Centre, Molly Millars Lane, Wokingham, RG41 2QZ

Other comments/suggestions and errors

....
....
....
....
....
....
....
....
....
....
....
....
....
....
....
....
....
....
....
....
....
....
....
....
....
....
....
....
....
....
....
....
....

Other comments/suggestions and errors ....
....

KAPLAN

PUBLISHING
FOULKS LYNCH

CIMA Publications

Student Order Form

Please send your completed order form by post to:
Leeds NDL, West Gate, 6 Grace Street, Leeds LS1 2RP
Tel (UK): 0845 678 0022

Tel (International): + 44 (0) 113 200 6360

Fax: +44 (0) 113 243 0133

Order online: www.kaplanfoulkslynch.com
Email: cimaflexiblelearning@ftckaplan.com

Examination date: Nov 06 ☐

		Study Text £28.00 each	Exam Kits £15.00 each	Pocket Notes £10.00 each	Practice 4 Success CDs 100Qs £10.00 300Qs £25.00		Course in a Box (Text, Kit, P/Notes, Tests, CD, Folder) £150.00 each	Total Value
		Quantity	Quantity	Quantity	100Q	300Q	Quantity	
Professional level								
Paper P1	Management Accounting Performance Evaluation	☐	☐	☐	☐	☐	☐	
Paper P2	Management Accounting Decision Making	☐	☐	☐	☐	☐	☐	
Paper P3	Management Accounting Risk and Control Strategy	☐	☐	☐	-	-	☐	
Paper P4	Organisational Management & Information Systems	☐	☐	☐	☐	☐	☐	
Paper P5	Integrated Management	☐	☐	☐	☐	☐	☐	
Paper P6	Management Accounting Business Strategy	☐	☐	☐	-	-	☐	
Paper P7	Financial Accounting and Tax Principles	☐	☐	☐	☐	☐	☐	
Paper P8	Financial Analysis	☐	☐	☐	☐	☐	☐	
Paper P9	Management Accounting Financial Strategy	☐	☐	☐	-	-	☐	
TOPCIMA								
Test of Professional Competence in Management Accounting Study Text		£28.00 ☐		The Knowledge			£28.00 ☐	

SUB TOTAL	£
PLUS DELIVERY CHARGE (see chart below)	£
TOTAL	£

Cardholder Details

Name on card: ....

Address:
....
....
....

Telephone:
....

Delivery address (if different from above – a signature will be required)

Name:
....

Address:
....
....
....

Telephone: ....

Payment

1 I enclose Cheque/Postal Order/Bankers Draft for £......................................

  Please make cheques payable to '**Kaplan Publishing Foulks Lynch**'.

2 Charge MasterCard/Visa/Switch/Delta no:

Valid from: | | | | Expiry date: | | | |

Issue no:
(Switch only) ☐   Security Code: ☐

Signature: ....   Date: ....

POSTAGE	Text Books	Pocket Notes	Course in a Box
UK	£5 for one book + £2 for each extra	£2 for one book + £1 for each extra	£6 for one package + £4 for each extra
Europe	£7 for one book + £4 for each extra	£3 for one book + £2 for each extra	£12 for one package + £8 for each extra
Rest of World	£22 for one book + £8 for each extra	£8 for one book + £5 for each extra	£30 for one package + £20 for each extra

Please note that all prices on this form are subject to change.

CIMA Publications

College & Bookshop Order Form

Please send your completed order form by post to:
Kaplan Publishing Foulks Lynch,
Unit 2 The Business Centre,
Molly Millars Lane, Wokingham RG41 2QZ
or by fax to 0118 979 7455

**For all queries relating to this order please call
0118 912 3000 or e-mail
info@kaplanfoulkslynch.com**

ACCOUNT:

Examination Date: Nov 06 ☐

		Study Text £28.00 each	Exam Kits £15.00 each	Pocket Notes £10.00 each	Practice 4 Success CDs 100Qs £10.00 300Qs £25.00		Course in a Box (Text, Kit, P/Notes, Study Notes, Tests, CD, Folder) £150.00 each	Total Value
		Quantity	Quantity	Quantity	100Q	300Q	Quantity	
Certificate (Current syllabus only)								
Paper C1	Management Accounting Fundamentals	☐	☐	☐	☐	☐	☐	
Paper C2	Financial Accounting Fundamentals	☐	☐	☐	☐	☐	☐	
Paper C3	Business Mathematics	☐	☐	☐	☐	☐	☐	
Paper C4	Economics for Business	☐	☐	☐	☐	☐	☐	
Paper C5	Business Law	☐	☐	☐	☐	☐	☐	
Professional								
Paper P1	Management Accounting Performance Evaluation	☐	☐	☐	☐	☐	☐	
Paper P2	Management Accounting Decision Making	☐	☐	☐	☐	☐	☐	
Paper P3	Management Accounting Risk and Control Strategy	☐	☐	☐	-	-	☐	
Paper P4	Organisational Management & Information Systems	☐	☐	☐	☐	☐	☐	
Paper P5	Integrated Management	☐	☐	☐	☐	☐	☐	
Paper P6	Management Accounting Business Strategy	☐	☐	☐	-	-	☐	
Paper P7	Financial Accounting and Tax Principles	☐	☐	☐	☐	☐	☐	
Paper P8	Financial Analysis	☐	☐	☐	☐	☐	☐	
Paper P9	Management Accounting Financial Strategy	☐	☐	☐	-	-	☐	

TOPCIMA

Test of Professional Competence in Management Accounting Study Text	£28.00 ☐	The Knowledge	£28.00 ☐	

SUB TOTAL	£	
LESS _____ % DISCOUNT	£	
TOTAL	£	

Account details

Contact name: ....

Address: ....

....

....

Telephone:..

Delivery address (if different to above)

Name: ....

Address: ....

....

....

Telephone: ....

Payment

1 Please invoice account ....

under Purchase Order Reference ....

2 I enclose Cheque/Postal Order/Bankers Draft for £...................................

(Please make cheques payable to '**Kaplan Publishing Foulks Lynch**')

3 Charge MasterCard/Visa/Switch/Delta no:

Valid from: ☐☐☐☐   Expiry date: ☐☐☐☐

Issue no:
(Switch only) ☐   Security Code: ☐

Signature: .... Date: ....

Please note that all prices on this order form are subject to change